Constructivist Instruction

Constructivist Instruction: Success or Failure? brings together leading thinkers from both sides of the hotly debated controversy about constructivist approaches to instruction. Although constructivist theories and practice now dominate the fields of the learning sciences, instructional technology, curriculum and teaching, and educational psychology, they have also been the subject of sharp criticism regarding sparse research support and adverse research findings. This volume presents

- the evidence for and against constructivism;
- the challenges from information-processing theorists; and
- commentaries from leading researchers in areas such as text comprehension, technology, as well as math and science education, who discuss the constructivist framework from their perspectives.

Chapters present detailed views from both sides of the controversy. A distinctive feature of the book is the dialogue built into it between the different positions. Each chapter concludes with discussions in which authors with opposing views raise questions about the chapter, followed by the author(s)' responses to those questions; for some chapters there are several cycles of questions and answers. These discussions, and concluding chapters by the editors, clarify, and occasionally narrow the differences between positions and identify needed research.

Sigmund Tobias is Distinguished Research Scientist, Institute for Urban and Minority Education, Teachers College, Columbia University.

Thomas M. Duffy is the Barbara Jacobs Chair of Education and Technology at Indiana University, Bloomington, where he was founding director of the Center for Research on Learning and Technology.

D1158801

Constructivist Instruction
Success or Failure?

Edited by

Sigmund Tobias

Institute for Urban and Minority Education, Teachers College, Columbia University

Thomas M. Duffy

School of Education, Indiana University

Routledge
Taylor & Francis Group

NEW YORK AND LONDON

First published 2009
by Routledge
270 Madison Ave, New York, NY 10016

Simultaneously published in the UK
by Routledge
2 Park Square, Milton Park, Abingdon, Oxon OX14 4RN

Routledge is an imprint of the Taylor & Francis Group, an informa business

© 2009 Taylor & Francis

Typeset in Minion by Wearset Ltd, Boldon, Tyne and Wear
Printed and bound in the United States of America on acid-free paper by
Edwards Brothers, Inc.

Library of Congress Cataloging-in-Publication Data
Constructivist instruction : success or failure? / [edited by]
Sigmund Tobias, Thomas M. Duffy.
p. cm.
1. Constructivism (Education) 2. Instructional systems. I. Tobias,
Sigmund. II. Duffy, Thomas M.
LB1590.3.C6785 2009
370.15'2–dc22   2009005021

ISBN10: 0-415-99423-3 (hbk)
ISBN10: 0-415-99424-1 (pbk)
ISBN10: 0-203-87884-1 (ebk)

ISBN13: 978-0-415-99423-1 (hbk)
ISBN13: 978-0-415-99424-8 (pbk)
ISBN13: 978-0-203-87884-2 (ebk)

For Lora and Cindy

Contents

Foreword   x

ROBERT J. STERNBERG

Preface   xii

PART I
Introduction   1

1 **The Success or Failure of Constructivist Instruction:**
   An Introduction   3
   SIGMUND TOBIAS AND THOMAS M. DUFFY

PART II
The Evidence for Constructivism   11

2 **Reconciling a Human Cognitive Architecture**   13
   DAVID JONASSEN

3 **Constructivism in an Age of Non-Constructivist**
   Assessments   34
   DANIEL L. SCHWARTZ, ROBB LINDGREN, AND SARAH LEWIS

4 **Taking Guided Learning Theory to School: Reconciling the**
   Cognitive, Motivational, and Social Contexts of Instruction   62
   PHILLIP HERMAN AND LOUIS M. GOMEZ

5 **Beyond More Versus Less: A Reframing of the Debate on**
   Instructional Guidance   82
   ALYSSA FRIEND WISE AND KEVIN O'NEILL

6 Constructivism: When It's the Wrong Idea and When It's
    the Only Idea   106
    RAND J. SPIRO AND MICHAEL DESCHRYVER

PART III
Challenges to the Constructivist View   125

7 What Human Cognitive Architecture Tells Us About
    Constructivism   127
    JOHN SWELLER

8 Epistemology or Pedagogy, That Is the Question   144
    PAUL A. KIRSCHNER

9 How Much and What Type of Guidance is Optimal for Learning
    from Instruction?   158
    RICHARD E. CLARK

10 Constructivism as a Theory of Learning Versus Constructivism
    as a Prescription for Instruction   184
    RICHARD E. MAYER

11 The Empirical Support for Direct Instruction   201
    BARAK ROSENSHINE

PART IV
An Examination of Specific Learning and Motivational Issues   221

12 Learning and Constructivism   223
    WALTER KINTSCH

13 From Behaviorism to Constructivism: A Philosophical Journey
    from Drill and Practice to Situated Learning   242
    J. D. FLETCHER

14 What's Worth Knowing in Mathematics?   264
    MELISSA SOMMERFELD GRESALFI AND FRANK LESTER

15 "To Every Thing There is a Season, and a Time to Every Purpose
    Under the Heavens": What about Direct Instruction?   291
    DAVID KLAHR

16 Beyond the Fringe: Building and Evaluating Scientific
    Knowledge Systems   311
    RICHARD A. DUSCHL AND RAVIT GOLAN DUNCAN

PART V
Summing Up   333

17 An Eclectic Appraisal of the Success or Failure of
    Constructivist Instruction   335
    SIGMUND TOBIAS

18 Building Lines of Communication and a Research Agenda   351
    THOMAS M. DUFFY

    Index   368

Foreword

Robert J. Sternberg Tufts University

When I was in elementary school during the 1950s, there was clearly no debate about constructivism in my school: We were taught on a continual basis with didactic, expository instruction. I can remember few projects or opportunities for discovery learning. I think the term had not yet entered the vocabulary, although John Dewey's work had been around for some time. I did not learn particularly well through this method of teaching, and elementary school is something of a blank to me today, perhaps because so many years have passed. But all those facts they taught us have gone like the wind from my head: I think I needed more discovery learning!

By the time I was in secondary school in the 1960s, the new wave had come. Discovery learning was definitely in. We had SMSG math, PSSC physics, BSCS biology, and CHEM Study chemistry. The heavy emphasis was on discovery learning. Students were expected, in large part, to construct their own learning. I don't remember much from those days either! In tenth grade, while I was studying BSCS blue-book biology, I suggested to my biology teacher that I do a study comparing learning in BSCS students with that of students who were studying from the book *Modern Biology*, which was actually the old-fashioned biology. I said to her that I thought those students were learning more than we were. She did not take well to this suggestion, but she did allow me to do the study, in collaboration with the teacher of the other class. Each group took its own test as well as the test of the other group. The results were clear: The *Modern Biology* students did as well as the BSCS biology students on the BSCS exam, but the *Modern Biology* students did better on their own test. So the didactic, expository-instructional approach seemed to produce better results. I did not learn much in those years. I think I needed more expository learning!

I learned something important that the theorists of the 1960s seemed to ignore: To think critically, you need first to have content about which to think. Content in the absence of thinking is inert and meaningless; but thinking in the absence of content is vacuous.

Thank you for the opportunity to report on my biology experiment from 1966 when I was aged 16, as I never got to write it up and never got publication credit before now! That said, I am trying to make a serious point: As most of the authors in this book recognize, the question is not whether expository or discovery learning is better; I think we left that question behind some time ago. The current question is under what circumstances, and for whom, is one kind of instruction superior to the other. That is the question most of the authors in this book address.

The issue is particularly highlighted in the case of science instruction, to which the chapters in this book pay special attention. You cannot think like a scientist if you have nothing to think with. Moreover, discovery learning can be a clunky and confusing way of learning the basic content of a discipline. But you cannot learn to be a scientist if you absorb a knowledge base without learning to think scientifically. And when we talk about scientific thinking, we are talking about scientific thinking as it is really done, not the textbook, idealized "scientific method" that is often taught to students but that few if any scientists actually use.

The extremes are not useful, I believe. Those of us who have taught graduate students in the sciences have all, I suspect, encountered students who do excellently in tests and in courses but who seem to have developed little skill in thinking scientifically with regard to theoretical and experimental development and analysis. But we also get students who, lacking the basic facts, want to be creative but are unable to go beyond past ideas because they do not even know what the past ideas are.

It is important to remember that just teaching the facts—even at the elementary college level—is not all that helpful. I studied introductory psychology in 1968. If one looks at an introductory psychology text today, there will be very little overlap with my introductory text of 1968. That is a good thing, I suppose, since I received a C in the introductory psychology course! The content of science courses changes as science changes. But if one goes through introductory psychology without learning the basics of how the brain works, of how people convince or fail to convince others of their beliefs, and of some of the ways in which people can behave abnormally, it is not clear one can say that one has truly learned "introductory psychology."

This book does a superb job of representing alternative points of view regarding constructivism in learning. The chapters, taken together, represent a balanced approach to the issue of constructivism. For the most part, the book achieves balance not only between, but within chapters. I learned a great deal in reading this book; you will too. Whether you learn from the book actively or passively, in a more direct or more discovery-based fashion, you will learn a lot from reading the book!

Preface

This book was stimulated by a debate held at the 2007 annual convention of the American Educational Research Association. It is interesting to note that many well-known scholars declined to participate in the live debate, whereas virtually everyone we contacted agreed to contribute a chapter to this volume. The difference is especially remarkable because something like a debate also appears in this book. After completing their chapters, authors on both sides of the controversy regarding the success or failure of constructivist instruction agreed to respond to questions from two scholars on the other side of the issue, and in some cases there were several cycles of questions and answers. Perhaps the ability to consider issues raised in these exchanges at greater leisure than is possible in a live debate contributed to the greater readiness to participate.

In order to complete the book in a timely manner, we had to impose strict and relatively rapid time lines on chapter authors. The time lines became even more stringent for the dialog portion of the book so that questioners would have the opportunity to respond to the initial answers of authors. We want to thank all of the chapter authors for generally abiding by these guidelines so that the book could be produced while the issue was still actively discussed by the educational researchers and practitioners to whom this book is directed. We trust that chapter authors can now appreciate the need for the many reminders they received from us regarding the various deadlines. We hope they are as pleased with the results of all our efforts as we are.

We are grateful to Naomi Silverman for her help and encouragement in all phases of the book's preparation. She made herself available on weekends and even while on vacation to answer the many questions that arose in the preparation of this volume. This book could not have been completed as smoothly without her assistance. We also thank Thea Freygang for her help in assembling the manuscript. Finally, the preparation of this book was supported in part by funding to the first author from the United States Army Research Institute, Fort Benning through an Inter Personnel Agreement.

Part I

Introduction

1 The Success or Failure of Constructivist Instruction

An Introduction

Sigmund Tobias Institute for Urban and Minority Education,
Teachers College, Columbia University
Thomas M. Duffy School of Education, Indiana University

The design of effective learning environments is taking on increasing importance with the growing dissatisfaction with our education systems at both the pre-K–12 and the post-secondary levels. There have been wide fluctuations in strategies at both levels, but over the past two decades arguably the dominant approaches to the design of instruction have been driven by the conceptual frameworks and theories called "constructivism." The purpose of this book is to discuss the present status of constructivism, applied to teaching and the development of instructional materials.

Of course constructivism is not a new view. Von Glasersfeld (1989) attributes the first constructivist theory to an Italian philosopher, Giambattista Vico, in the early 18th century. As described by von Glasersfeld, "one of Vico's basic ideas was that epistemic agents can know nothing but the cognitive structures they themselves have put together ... 'to know' means *to know how to make*" (1989, p. 123). The foundation for the current resurgence in interest, as reflected in the chapters in this volume, can be traced to the work of Vygotsky (1978), Dewey (1929), Piaget (1952), and Bruner (1966). But the more immediate stimulus for the growth of constructivist theory and its application to instruction can arguably be linked to three more recent articles. Brown, Collins, and Duguid (1989) argued that knowledge is situated in the activity of the learner and is a product of that activity and the context and culture in which it occurs. This situativity view is one of the defining characteristics of the constructivist framework. It contrasts to the then prevailing information-processing view of learning as processing information composed of concepts, procedures, and facts. While context was of little importance in the traditional view (Chanquoy, Tricot, & Sweller, 2007), the constructivist saw the context, including the goals of the learner, as integral to the understanding that developed.

Resnick (1987), in her AERA presidential address, examined the situativity view from the perspective of informal learning out of school. Specifically, she contrasted learning in everyday activities to the design of learning in school and explored how those two contexts or situations affected what is learned. She noted four contrasts with learning out of school typically involving: socially shared activities rather than individual learning; direct engagement rather than decontextualized symbolic thinking; the use of cognitive tools (e.g., the roofer using a pitch calculator) rather than unaided thought; and, learning situation-specific skills rather than general skills.

Lave and Wenger (1991) extended the situativity framework to a more ethnographic analysis of learning in communities. Their study of communities of practice demonstrated the role of situated learning through apprenticeship and, most importantly, the development of identity as one participates in a community of practice.

Duffy and Jonassen (1992) speculated that the interest in constructivism arising from this work stemmed in large part from the impact of the information age on instructional requirements. "Traditional models of learning and instruction emphasized forms of mastering the information in a content domain…. However, it is simply no longer possible (there is too much) or even reasonable (it changes too rapidly) to master most content domains" (1992, p. ix). Thus, from this perspective, the interest was not so much in learning's theoretical base but in the need for a new approach to meet new learning demands.

Duffy and Jonassen (1992) sought to identify the implications of the constructivist views of learning for the design of instruction by engaging constructivist and traditional instructional designers in a conversation about instructional design. The goal was to find common threads to form the basis for an instructional theory based on constructivism and the development of principles for the design of instruction.

In the 17 years since the Duffy and Jonassen (1992) book was published, there has been little progress in developing the instructional theory or identifying those design principles tied to constructivism. The lack of an emerging instructional theory parallels the lack of refinement of constructivist theory. Indeed, to us it would appear that constructivism remains more of a philosophical framework than a theory that either allows us to precisely describe instruction or prescribe design strategies.

Of course, there are numerous instructional models proposed based on the constructivist framework. But there are seldom efforts to look across models to define common principles or to refine the model and its theoretical underpinnings in ways that can be tested. A notable effort to identify design principles has been supported by the National Science Foundation and spearheaded by the Israeli Institute of Technology (Kali, in press; http://design-principles.org). This database defines design features primarily for the use of technology. The features are linked to principles that, in turn, are hierarchically linked. Thus the database provides potential. However, it does not provide or attempt to induce a theoretical framework in which the consistency of principles and features can be assessed. Nor does it seem to have generated the research base that would help provide stronger instructional guidance on the use and limitations of the principles and features.

The lack of a well-specified instructional theory or articulation of learning principles may also be seen in the discussions of scaffolding, i.e., providing guidance in instruction. It was introduced by Wood, Bruner, and Ross (1976) and referred to creating a "highly constrained situation" (Pea, 2004). This is interesting since Bruner also introduced discovery learning, which has been interpreted as providing minimal guidance in learning (Kirschner, Sweller, & Clark, 2006). Scaffolding differs from the broader use of guidance in two ways (see Pea, 2004). First, guidance is provided only when learners are unable to proceed. That is, it scaffolds or helps learners move beyond what they can do without assistance. Second, guidance is gradually withdrawn or faded as the learner develops competence. Perhaps the idea of providing guidance only as needed may be the basis for the misinterpretation that constructivists do not provide guidance.

While scaffolding is central to the design of constructivist learning environments, constructivists have been slow to formulate testable principles—or even specific guidance—for the use of scaffolding. In discussing the papers in a special issue on scaffolding in *The Journal of the Learning Sciences*, Pea (2004) noted that:

> A theory of scaffolding should successfully predict for any given learner and any given task what forms of support provided by what agent(s) and designed artifacts would suffice for enabling that learner to perform at a desirable level of proficiency on that task, which is known to be unachievable without such scaffolding.
>
> (2004, p. 443)

> [T]he instructional designer does not have at hand any rules for making decisions about what kinds of scaffolds ... to provide in what kind of adaptively relevant sequencing for advancing a learner's capabilities.
>
> (2004, p. 445)

In view of this lack of specificity, and with the popularity of constructivism in education, it is not surprising that the instructional models derived from the constructivist framework have been challenged. Most recently, Kirschner et al. (2006) argued that constructivist-based instructional approaches could not be effective given our knowledge of human cognitive architecture. Their contention about cognitive architecture is based on the widely accepted information-processing model that defines a limited-capacity working memory as the gateway to storage in long-term memory. From this information-processing perspective, they maintain that learners, especially novices, are unable to effectively process information due to the limits of working memory, hence learning suffers. According to Kirschner et al., minimally guided instruction overtaxes working memory. They review research which, they argue, demonstrates the failure of constructivist paradigms they considered to be paradigms where there is minimal guidance for the learner.

The publication of the Kirschner et al. (2006) article was followed by a set of papers defending the constructivist position (Schmidt, Loyens, van Gog, & Paas, 2007; Hmelo-Silver, Duncan, & Chinn, 2007; Kuhn, 2007) and a rejoinder to those by Sweller, Kirschner, and Clark (2007). The original article also stimulated a debate, organized and chaired by the first author of this chapter, held at the

2007 conference of the American Educational Research Association (Debate, 2007) regarding the paper's main assertion that all constructivist approaches failed. However, they viewed instruction based on constructivism as offering minimal guidance for learning, a view hotly contest in the chapters in this book. All the participants in the debate (Kirschner, Rosenshine, Jonassen, and Spiro) have written chapters for this volume in addition to many other scholars.

This book was stimulated by the debate, and asks both supporters and opponents of constructivist instruction to present their views in the kind of detail possible in a book chapter where evidence supporting or refuting constructivist claims may be presented and discussed. Therefore we have sought to promote a discussion between the researchers to try to clarify the different perspectives and seek common ground—or at least an agreement on strategies for evaluating the implications of the constructivist perspective for teaching. In the first section of the book we have asked constructivists to provide their instructional theory and its links to constructivism, as well as to describe the research that supports that approach to instruction. In the second section we asked those who question the constructivist-based instructional theory to critique it and present their alternative view along with the research evidence to support it. Finally, we asked both constructivists and those holding alternative views to examine the research in specific domains with the goal of evaluating support for constructivism. These domains are reading comprehension, mathematics, science, and use of technology.

One major problem in chapters written by supporters and opponents of a position is that they too often talk past one another. In the case of instruction informed by constructivism there are different assumptions about what constitutes evidence, what is meant by "guidance," the learning outcomes sought, etc. We have tried to promote discussion that will help to resolve, or at least clarify these issues and perhaps establish common ground by promoting discussion between authors. We have asked those generally considered constructivist to ask questions of the authors of at least two chapters representing the opposing view and then offered them a chance to react to the responses they received. Similarly, we asked those who question the constructivist view to ask questions of at least two authors of "constructivist" chapters and react to the responses. This dialog is inserted following the chapter of the author(s) being questioned.

Relationships of Chapters

In the section of the book devoted to chapters by constructivists, Jonassen (Chapter 2) provides a general overview of the constructivist position and takes issue with Kirschner et al.'s (2006) definition of learning as a change in long-term memory and describes several other ways of examining cognitive architecture. He maintains that what is really important is the kind of learning that is stored in long-term memory. Jonassen then proposes a number of different kinds of learning. He also suggests that unitary definitions of learning ignore such concepts as the bio-chemical basis of learning, and conceptual change, among others.

Schwartz, Lindgren, and Lewis (Chapter 3) suggest that constructivist instruction may not be ideal for all purposes. They contend that constructivist teaching may be superior for situations in which current learning is a preparation for future learning, rather than for sequential problem solving. Schwartz et al. maintain, and point to some supporting research, that knowledge building after instruction ends is critically important for individuals after they leave school, and the superiority of constructivist instruction becomes most apparent at that time. If the objective of instruction is for immediate problem solving they suggest that constructivist instruction may be less ideal.

Herman and Gomez (Chapter 4) maintain that critics of constructivist instruction ignore such critical components of the instructional process as motivation, the social context of the classroom, and other aspects of the dynamics of instruction. They then discuss their work on supporting students' reading in science and describe tools developed to guide students' reading in that domain.

Wise and O'Neill (Chapter 5) argue that experimental "high versus low guidance" studies cannot provide a valid basis for making inferences about the fundamental merits of constructivist teaching. Reviewing some of the literature, with a special focus on worked examples, they argue that the quantity of guidance is just one dimension along which guidance can be usefully characterized. They suggest that the context and timing in which guidance is delivered are two additional concerns that have to be considered. They then suggest research about the optimal quantity, context, and timing of guidance in ill-defined problem domains.

Spiro and DeSchryver (Chapter 6), like other constructivist authors, contend that constructivist approaches to instruction may not be ideal for all instructional purposes. They maintain that constructivist instruction will lead to superior results in ill-structured domains such as medical diagnoses, whereas explicit instructional approaches may be superior in well-structured domains such as mathematics, for example. Spiro suggests that cognitive flexibility theory leads to the best approaches for teaching in ill-structured domains.

Sweller (Chapter 7) kicks off the section of the book devoted to chapters by advocates of explicit instruction. He argues from an evolutionary perspective that constructivists advocating discovery, problem-based, or inquiry learning among other constructivist approaches, appear to assume that evolutionary secondary knowledge, such as intentional school learning, can occur as easily as evolutionary primary knowledge, such as learning to speak, listen, or use means–end analysis when students are left to their own devices to acquire the knowledge. Reading, writing, and other evolutionary secondary subjects taught in school, Sweller argues, have evolved relatively recently, and therefore—unlike speaking—have to be taught explicitly. He argues that it seems likely that we have evolved to imitate others, hence withholding information in the constructivist approaches discussed above runs counter to such evolutionary principles.

Kirschner (Chapter 8) suggests that constructivists tend to assume that pedagogy and epistemology are similar. He points out that children differ from adult experts in many ways, hence teaching science by requiring students to act as scientists can hardly succeed. Kirschner argues that children do not have many of the cognitive abilities of adult experts, such as their content knowledge, their conditionalized knowledge, i.e., understanding the limiting conditions about when to apply a procedure, or their ability to retrieve knowledge rapidly. All of these, he maintains, are required if children are to learn science by acting like scientists.

Clark (Chapter 9) notes that different researchers frequently give guidance and instructional support varying operational and lexical definitions. He questions the practice of constructivists who withhold available answers so that students can arrive at them by themselves. Clark indicates that guidance should provide accurate and complete demonstrations of how and when a task should be performed. Further, when transfer to a new situation is required, guidance must provide the practice and declarative knowledge permitting learners to function in that situation. Clark maintains that guidance should involve application of procedures with immediate corrective feedback.

Mayer (Chapter 10) differentiates, as do several other authors, between constructivism as a theory of learning and as prescriptive theory of instruction. He also suggests that there is a difference between behavioral activity, which he maintains does little to advance learning, and cognitive activity which is vital for learning. Mayer suggests that in discovery learning constructivists tend to confuse the two, leading to considerable confusion since the behavioral activity seen in discovery learning does little to promote learning.

Rosenshine (Chapter 11) reviews classical findings developed by process–product studies of students' learning from classroom instruction. That research is composed of both experimental and correlational work, and has largely been ignored with the advent of constructivist approaches. Rosenshine suggests that those findings are as valid now as they were over 50 years ago, and indicates that many of the results are consonant with Kirschner et al.'s (2006) expectations in terms of cognitive architecture and the limitations of working memory.

Kintsch (Chapter 12) begins the section of the volume prepared by scholars concerned with content and application areas. He points out that there is confusion between the commonly accepted notion that all knowledge is constructed by the individual, and the constructivist approaches to instruction, such as discovery, problem-based, and other instructional approaches. Kintsch then discusses the construction of knowledge evident in reading comprehension where capable readers combine their prior knowledge and the information from the text to form a situation model needed to lead to deep comprehension of the text.

Fletcher (Chapter 13) overviews the philosophical and psychological roots of both constructivist and, to a smaller degree, explicit instruction. He then relates this background to a number of issues of importance for learning and instruction. Fletcher reminds readers that even though drill and practice have been ridiculed as "drill and kill," there is empirical evidence indicating that such practice is helpful to students, that they have positive attitudes toward it, and that it is cost effective. He also points out that simulations, which were developed to deal with practical training problems that were entirely independent of the situative movement, are nevertheless excellent implementations of situated learning.

Gresalfi and Lester (Chapter 14) write from the perspective of mathematics education. They oppose many of the assertions in the Kirschner et al. (2006) chapter beginning with defining learning as a change in long-term memory. Instead, they assert that a constructivist approach sees learning as a change in social activity that integrates what is known with how one came to know it, and emphasizes understanding of math and when to apply that understanding. Further, they maintain that the contrast between constructivist and explicit instruction is not in the amount of guidance but in the type of guidance offered. The approach Gresalfi and Lester advocate offers guidance in the form of teacher questions, probes, and offering explanations that are appropriate to the understanding of students at that point.

Klahr (Chapter 15) describes his research on the control of variables strategy which teaches students to design unconfounded experiments so that the causal variable can be unambiguously determined. Amusingly enough, he notes that his research has been called "direct instruction" by some critics and labeled "guided inquiry" by others, which emphasizes the need to clearly describe the procedures used in research. Klahr's findings have shown clear superiority for a condition similar to direct instruction, compared to conditions similar to discovery learning. He concludes that research on cognitive processes should be taught, with the emphasis that the processes students are learning about are the same ones they use in their learning of science and other school subjects.

Duschl and Duncan (Chapter 16) oppose Kirschner et al.'s (2006) position regarding science education. For them science education is not only knowing "what" is known, but also knowing "how" and "why" it is known. They recommend aligning learning of science with the way scientists "do science." Duschl and Duncan deplore Kirschner et al.'s argument that students lack the cognitive abilities to learn science as a "deficit" model. They see no age-related stages of development preventing students from learning science, and point to supporting research about the cognitive abilities of children. Rather than seeing science learning as accumulating knowledge in long-term memory, they see it as facilitating conceptual change and reorganization in memory. They feel that when science content becomes very abstract or complex, careful curriculum design and instructional support by teachers can help students learn to reason effectively about abstract scientific concepts, represent data patterns, develop and revise explanations, and argue about their conceptual constructions.

Tobias (Chapter 17) appraises the issues in the book from an eclectic perspective. He urges both critics and supporters of constructivist instruction to support their views of differences between the two positions with research results rather than stirring rhetoric. Tobias examines the recent history of paradigms in psychology and discusses the reasons paradigm shifts occur. He then examines the controversy about constructivist instruction from the perspective of a number of questions, such as motivation, structure of the subject matter, guidance and instruction support, and time needed for learning, among others. At each step specific suggestions for needed research are made.

Finally, Duffy (Chapter 18), in his reflection on the chapters, notes the failure to communicate with the direct-instruction researchers ignoring the extensive guidance provided in the constructivist environments while the constructivists seem to ignore the role of information processing in general and memory limitations in particular in the learning process. Duffy also argues that the focus on the amount and type of guidance provided to learners as discussed in many of the chapters is a distraction from the key difference impacting the instructional practice: the focus by constructivists on the goals of the learner as the driver for learning.

References

Brown, J. S., Collins, A., & Duguid, P. (1989). Situated cognition and the culture of learning. *Educational Researcher, 18*(1), 32–42.

Bruner, J. (1966). *Toward a theory of instruction.* Cambridge, MA: Harvard University Press.

Chanquoy, L., Tricot, A., & Sweller, J. (2007). *La charge cognitive.* Paris: Armand Colin.

Debate. (2007). Debate: Constructivism, discovery, problem based, experiential, and inquiry based teaching: Success or failure? *The World of Educational Quality* (Program for the *AERA 2007 Annual Meeting*, pp. 218–219). Washington, DC: American Educational Research Association.

Dewey, J. (1929). *My pedagogical creed.* Washington, DC: Progressive Education Association.

Duffy, T. M., & Jonassen, D. (Eds.). (1992). *Constructivism and the technology of instruction: A conversation.* Englewood, NJ: Lawrence Erlbaum Associates.

Hmelo-Silver, C., Duncan, R., & Chinn, C. (2007). Scaffolding and achievement in problem-based and inquiry learning: A response to Kirschner, Sweller, and Clark (2006). *Educational Psychologist, 42,* 99–108.

Kali, Y. (in press). The Design Principles Database as means for promoting design-based research. In A. E. Kelly, R. A. Lesh, & J. Y. Baek (Eds.), *Handbook of innovative design research in science, technology, engineering, mathematics (stem) education.* Mahwah, NJ: Lawrence Erlbaum Associates.

Kirschner, P. A., Sweller, J., & Clark, R. (2006). Why minimal guidance during instruction does not work: An analysis of the failure of constructivist, discovery, problem-based, experiential and inquiry-based teaching. *Educational Psychologist, 41,* 75–86.

Kuhn, D. (2007). Is direct instruction the answer to the right question? *Educational Psychologist, 42,* 109–114.

Lave, J., & Wenger, E. (1991). *Situated learning: Legitimate peripheral participation.* Cambridge: Cambridge University Press.

Pea, R. (2004). The social and technological dimensions of scaffolding and related theoretical concepts for learning, education, and human activity. *The Journal of the Learning Sciences, 13*(3), 423–445.

Piaget, J. (1952). *The origins of intelligence in children* (M. Cook, Trans.). New York: International Universities Press.

Resnick, L. (1987). Learning in school and out. *Educational Researcher, 16*(9), 13–20.

Schmidt, H., Loyens, S., van Gog, T., & Paas, F. (2007). Problem-based learning is compatible with human cognitive architecture: Commentary on Kirschner, Sweller, and Clark (2006). *Educational Psychologist, 42,* 91–108.

Sweller, J., Kirschner, P. A., & Clark, R. E. (2007). Why minimally guided teaching techniques do not work: A reply to commentaries. *Educational Psychologist, 42,* 115–121.

Von Glasersfeld, E. (1989). Cognition, construction of knowledge, and teaching. *Synthese, 80,* 121–140.

Vygotsky, L. S. (1978). *Mind in society: The development of higher mental processes* (M. Cole, V. John-Steiner, S. Scribner, & E. Souberman, Eds.). Cambridge, MA: Harvard University Press.

Wood, D., Bruner, J., & Ross, G. (1976). The role of tutoring in problem solving. *Journal of Child Psychology and Psychiatry and Allied Disciplines, 17,* 89–100.

Part II
The Evidence for Constructivism

2 Reconciling a Human Cognitive Architecture

David Jonassen University of Missouri

Toward a Human Cognitive Architecture

This book evolved from the debate instigated by Kirschner, Sweller, and Clark (2006), where they set out to theoretically support the superiority of direct instruction over "minimally guided instruction" by describing a human cognitive architecture. Articulating a human cognitive architecture is a very important goal in the evolution of a science of learning, and I support the collaborative articulation and construction of such an architecture. I believe that the architecture that Kirschner et al. (2006) articulate is too focused in its theoretical orientation, does not account for considerable contemporary research in psychology, and therefore cannot adequately account for many or most cognitive activities. Their architecture is based entirely on changes (without regard to their nature) in long-term memory. Kirschner et al. (2006) claim "minimally guided instruction appears to proceed with no references to the characteristics of working memory, long-term memory or the intricate relation between them" (p. 76). My concern is that their cognitive architecture focuses only on working memory and long-term memory, ignoring all other cognitive constructs. A cognitive architecture must account for the context, the learner, and the processes of cognition (social and cognitive) in order to explain or predict cognitive activities. At the risk of being dismissed as a relativist, I support those claims in this chapter in an attempt to contribute alternate perspectives to a human cognitive architecture.

Kirschner et al. (2006) claim that "long-term memory is now viewed as the central, dominant structure of human cognition" (p. 76); however, they make no attempt to articulate what is stored in long-term memory, how it gets there, or what learners do with it, except to retrieve it. Although few educators or psychologists would ever deny the essential role of long-term memory in learning (there are some who would), decades of learning research has examined many facets of cognition that affect and are affected by long-term memory. A human cognition architecture cannot be adequately defined by the stuff of long-term memory. Difference in long-term memory cannot "fully explain problem-solving skills." The ability to solve problems clearly relies on the contents of long-term memory but is not sufficient to explain learning or problem solving. Solving a problem is not merely a process of retrieving a solution from long-term memory. Long-term memory is not the only component or mechanism of cognition.

Several cognitive researchers have attempted to synthesize models or architectures of cognition. Jenkins (1979) conceived of a tetrahedral model of learning that considers the nature of the learner, the material to be learned, the type of task to be accomplished, the products (i.e., recognition or recall) of learning, and the setting or context in which material is learned (including orienting activities, instructions, and strategies used). More recently, Alexander, Schallert, and Reynolds (2008) presented a topography (that is, an architecture) of learning that describes learning in terms of what is being learned, where it is being learned, who is learning, and when learning is occurring. While structurally similar to Jenkins' tetrahedron, their architecture attempts to synthesize contemporary research and theory into a model of learning. Their assumption, like mine, is that learning is complex and multidimensional and cannot be understood from a single perspective.

In order to articulate a human cognitive architecture, numerous questions remain. In this chapter, I explore three: how do humans learn, what is learned, and how do humans reason with what they know? These are essential components, it seems to me, in any architecture of human cognition.

How Do Humans Learn?

Theories of learning abound, both grand theories such as cognitive psychology and more specific theories such as subsumption theory (Ausubel, 1968). Each theory provides an alternative conception of how humans learn that we must reconcile in order to construct our own interpretation of the world (Spiro & Jehng, 1990). Despite the inconsistencies in how theories explain learning and their differential effectiveness in predicting learning outcomes, students of learning too often assume absolutist or dualist conceptions of theories (Jonassen, 2008). If it is in the textbook, it must be true. Learning researchers generate or appropriate theories that explain their own conceptions of the learning or predict their preferred hypotheses. This chapter is dedicated to the notion that, like Alexander et al. (2008), a human cognitive architecture is multidimensional, that is, it must include multiple theoretical perspectives in order to explain the complexities of human learning. The how of learning cannot be comprehended through a single theoretical lens.

Learning is the Processing, Storage, and Retrieval of Information

Kirschner et al. (2006) embed their human cognitive architecture in an information-processing model where humans take in information through sensory memory, hold it briefly in short-term memory until they can find a place to store it permanently in long-term memory. They base their human cognitive architecture exclusively on an information-processing conception of learning. "If nothing has changed in long-term memory, nothing has been learned" (p. 77). In order to explain their conception of learning, they invoke one of several early information-processing models of human memory (Atkinson & Shiffrin, 1968) as the basis for their architecture. That conception of learning influences their conceptions of knowledge, which in turn influences their beliefs about the essential nature of formal, direct instruction and the need to reduce cognitive load. When faced with a task, information from long-term memory is shifted into working memory where it is used to perform some task (e.g., probed recall). Because the capacity of working memory is limited, they promote instruction that reduces requirements on working memory. While their research has shown consistent effects (Atkinson, Derry, Renkl, & Wortham, 2000) on a limited number of tasks, many other tasks do not affect working memory or any of the other mechanisms of cognition in the same ways. However, because most formal educational institutions measure knowledge in terms of what students are able to recall from long-term memory when given an examination, learning has been institutionalized as a process of knowledge acquisition, a filling up of long-term memory. What other theories explain the "how" of learning in ways that should be accommodated in an architecture of cognition?

Learning is Biochemical Activity in the Brain

Cognitive neuroscientists examine learning on the biochemical level. In order to store information in long-term memory, the hippocampus must release a neurotransmitter that facilitates the transmission of minute electrical pulses through synaptic connections between neurons in the brain. Neuroscientific research has demonstrated that patterns of behavior and cognitive activity are associated with patterns of neuronal connections. Using fMRI, EEG, PET, and SPECT technologies, cognitive neuroscientists are able to demonstrate various kinds of cognitive attention, decision-making, metacognitive control, and memory (Gazzaniga, 2004). Arguably, neurons represent the most fundamental cognitive architecture. To what degree should neurological conceptions of cognition be included in a cognitive architecture?

Learning is a Relatively Permanent Change in Behavior or Behavioral Dispositions

Behavioral psychologists of the late 19th and early 20th centuries (Thorndike, 1927; Watson, 1928) believed that learning is evidenced by behavioral dispositions. When exposed to certain stimuli, people respond in predictable ways if they are reinforced for their performance. Even complex behaviors, such as language learning, have been described (albeit unsuccessfully) as behavioral tendencies (Skinner, 1957). Behavioral psychologists focused their research on describing laws of human behavior without positing mental activity. Because objectivist theories of learning examine the interaction of knowledge, behavior, and learning (Jonassen, 2003) and because knowledge (though not for neuroscientists) must be inferred from behavior, how can we articulate an architecture of cognition without explicating learning behaviors?

Ontogenesis of Knowledge Construction

Jean Piaget considered himself a genetic epistemologist. He studied the genesis (genetics) of knowledge construction (Piaget, 1970). The ways in which we construct knowledge affects the way we understand. His genetic epistemology also explained that humans develop cognitively through four primary stages of development (sensorimotor, preoperational, concrete operational, and formal operational). The ways that people construct knowledge and represent it in long-term memory changes with age and intellectual development. Shouldn't an architecture of cognition accommodate these developmental changes?

Learning is Conceptual Change

Learning is a process of making sense out of domain concepts in such a way that they develop coherent conceptual structures. In order to make meaning, humans naturally organize and reorganize their naive models of the world in light of new experiences. The more coherent their theories of the world, the better are their conceptual structures. Conceptual change theorists (Limón & Mason, 2002; Schnotz, Vosniadou, & Carretero, 1999; Sinatra & Pintrich, 2003) examine changes in personal theories and conceptual frameworks. Because their research shows significant changes to learners' conceptual frameworks over time, an architecture of cognition must be able to accommodate and explain the structural changes to knowledge that is stored in long-term memory.

Learning is Problem Solving

My own research over the past decade has focused on the pre-eminence of problem solving in learning (Jonassen, 1997, 2000, 2004). While I do not claim that all learning is problem solving, I believe that problem solving is ubiquitous, especially in everyday learning contexts, as reflected in Karl Popper's *All Life is Problem Solving* (1999).

My problem-solving architecture diverges from traditional approaches (Bransford & Stein, 1984). Rather than conceiving of problem solving as a uniform activity (frame the problem, search for solutions, evaluate solutions, implement, evaluate), there exist many different kinds of problems that are distinguished by their structuredness, complexity, dynamicity as well as the discipline and context in which the problem occurs (Jonassen, 2007). I agree with Kirschner et al. (2006) that most forms of problem solving, especially everyday and professional problems, do make heavy demands on working memory. However, I cannot accept their claim that cognitive load does not contribute to the accumulation of knowledge in long-term memory. While research by Sweller and colleagues (e.g., Cooper & Sweller, 1987; Sweller & Cooper, 1985) has shown that extrinsic cognitive load can impede recall and rule-using imitation in math problems, in my years of work in medical and engineering education, the problems that engineers and physicians remember the best are those on which they have expended the greatest cognitive effort, the ones that were complex and ambiguous, and the ones that had the heaviest germane cognitive load (Jonassen, Strobel, & Lee, 2006). That is, problem solving entails a lot more cognitive activity than searching long-term memory for solutions. Problem solving should be accommodated by an architecture of cognition.

Learning is Social Negotiation

While Kirschner et al. (2006) assume that learning is an individual process of knowledge acquisition, a host of contemporary researchers assume that learning is seldom accomplished individually. Rather, humans naturally tend to share their meaning and co-construct reality in communities of practice (Lave & Wenger, 1991) or communities of learners (Scardamalia & Bereiter, 1991). Humans are social creatures who rely on feedback from fellow humans to determine their own identity and the viability of their personal beliefs (Suls & Wills, 1991). Social constructivists believe that knowledge is distributed among a community rather than sequestered in the minds of individuals. Shouldn't an architecture of cognition accommodate the vast number of social roles in knowledge building?

Learning is Activity

Activity theorists (Leont'ev, 1972) claim that conscious learning and activity (performance) are interactive and interdependent (we cannot act without thinking or think without acting; they are the same). Activity and consciousness are the central mechanisms of learning. Human activity cannot be understood without considering the intentions of activity, the object that is being acted on, the rules of the community in which the activity is taking place, and the division of labors between the many persons who are also responsible for the activity (Engeström, 1987). Activity theory provides perhaps the broadest theoretical brush for describing learning, and appears to be the antithesis of the conception held by Kirschner et al. (2006). What parts of activity theory are appropriate for inclusion in an architecture of cognition?

Learning is Tuning Perceptions to Environmental Affordances

Ecological psychologists (Gibson, 1979) believe that learning results from the reciprocal perception of affordances from the environment and actions on the environment. That is, different environments afford different kinds of thinking and acting. As learners, we become tuned to what the environment affords us and so we act on the environment in some way. The changes in our abilities to perceive and act on an environment provide evidence of learning. In ecological psychology, the role of perception is paramount in learning, and the role of memory is ignored. The primary cognitive component in perception is pattern recognition. Given the obvious role of cognition in perception (Arnheim, 1969), shouldn't perception be an important component of a cognitive architecture?

What Do Humans Learn?

Alexander et al. (2008) attempted to describe "the what of learning" in terms of different levels of complexity. They argued that learners acquire/construct scientific (defined) concepts, spontaneous concepts, acquired habits (explained by behaviorist theories), and inborn reflexes (similar to direct perceptions in ecological psychology). In this section I examine the "what" of learning in terms of knowledge types. Long-term memory is not a monolithic structure, where information, like in a computer, is assigned a specific memory location containing zeros and ones. Rather, long-term memory is replete with schemas, schemata, stories (experiences), procedures, behavioral sequences, patterns, and many other structures. An architecture of cognition must assume an underlying morphology that articulates the structures of what is known. While learning is undoubtedly associated with changes in long-term memory, Kirschner et al. (2006) make no attempt to describe those changes structurally. Even early schema theorists described information processing as accretion, restructuring, and tuning (Rumelhart & Norman, 1978), with cognitive structures resulting (Preece, 1976). Information coming into long-term memory is reorganized according to the kind of information it is in order to make it retrievable and useful. Paivio (1986) spent an entire career distinguishing between verbal and visual memory stores. Piaget proposed three types of knowledge: physical, logical mathematical, and social knowledge. That is, a human cognitive architecture must accommodate the complexity of human learning by affording multiple kinds of cognitive structures representing multiple kinds of knowledge.

I claim that a human cognitive architecture must be multifaceted and multidimensional, able to accommodate multiple knowledge types that are differentially constructed based on different types of interactions with the environment. Second, different learning outcomes, especially more complex and ill-structured kinds of problem solving, call on different knowledge types which are accessed by working memory in different ways. As evidence supporting the claim, research has shown that experts are better problem solvers than novices because they construct richer, more integrated mental representations of problems than do novices (Chi, Feltovich, & Glaser, 1981; Chi & Bassock, 1991; de Jong & Ferguson-Hessler, 1991; Larkin, 1983). Experts are better able to classify problem types (Chi et al., 1981; Chi & Bassock, 1991) because their representations integrate domain knowledge with problem types, that is, they construct multidimensional problem schemas. Additional research shows that the conceptual frameworks that experts and novices use to comprehend processes are described by different ontologies (Chi, 1992, 2005; Chi & Roscoe, 2002; Slotta & Chi, 2006). Novices are unable to explain concepts such as heat, light, electrical current, and mechanical forces because they are committed to a single materially based knowledge structure. We know that long-term memory holds different types of knowledge, but we do not know how different knowledge types are structured and represented in long-term memory.

In the following sections, I describe three general kinds of knowledge (the what of learning)—ontological, epistemological, and phenomenological—that subsume many more specific types of knowledge that humans use to function. These knowledge types must be accommodated by a human cognitive architecture.

Ontological (Domain) Knowledge Types

Ontological (not to be confused with the idea of ontological frameworks described earlier) knowledge types are those that are meant to describe or convey what exists. Ontology is the branch of philosophy that studies the nature of reality and existence by describing the basic entities and types of entities within its framework. Ontology describes the kinds and structures of the objects, properties, and relations in every area of reality (Floridi, 2003). There are at least three kinds of ontological knowledge that have been extensively described in the literature: declarative, structural, and conceptual knowledge. These are the kinds of knowledge that are most often associated with learning in formal learning contexts. They are also the kinds of knowledge for which worked examples and reduced cognitive load have been most effective.

Declarative Knowledge

Declarative knowledge is static knowledge about facts, concepts, and principles, what Ryle (1949) called "knowing that" something exists. Declarative knowledge is expressed in declarative sentences or propositions. Because declarative is not necessarily applied in performing some skill or task, it often becomes inert (Whitehead, 1929). Knowledge becomes inert because learners do not connect ideas that they are learning to the world around them (Perkins, 1999). Declarative knowledge is the coin of the realm for most formal education. Students are assessed on how many ideas they recall after they were taught. Most textbooks, curricula, and syllabi are organized by hierarchical lists of topics and propositions that are learned declaratively. Declarative knowledge is the most commonly tested stuff of long-term memory.

Structural Knowledge

Structural knowledge mediates the translation of declarative into more meaningful kinds of declarative knowledge or other forms of knowledge (Jonassen, Beissner, & Yacci, 1993). Structural knowledge is the knowledge of how concepts within a domain are interrelated (Diekhoff, 1983). Those interrelationships are the propositions that are formed by combining concepts or schemas. For example, birds have wings is a proposition taking one argument, while relationships (birds use wings to fly) is a proposition taking two or more arguments. Structural knowledge is the explicit awareness and understanding of those interrelationships and the ability to explicate those relationships.

Structural knowledge is also known as cognitive structure, the organization of relationships among concepts in long-term memory (Shavelson, 1972). Cognitive structure evolves from the ascription of attributes (any objective or subjective feature) to objects in the world, which enables the definition of structural relations among concepts. The way that individuals organize and represent constructs, that is, their cognitive structure, determines how they interact with the environment. Structural knowledge is morphological by nature and is essential in defining an architecture of human cognition. Unfortunately it is not assessed consistently enough.

Conceptual Knowledge

Conceptual knowledge implies higher levels of integration of declarative knowledge. Conceptual knowledge is the integrated storage of meaningful dimensions in a given domain of knowledge (Tennyson & Cocchiarella, 1986). It is more than the storage of declarative knowledge; it is the understanding of a concept's operational structure within itself and between associated concepts. Changes in conceptual knowledge are referred to as conceptual change (Limón & Mason, 2002; Schnotz et al., 1999; Sinatra & Pintrich, 2003). Conceptual change is a process of reorganizing personal conceptual models. From an early age, humans naturally build simplified and intuitive personal theories to explain their world. Through experience and reflection, they reorganize and add complexity to their theories or conceptual models. The cognitive process of adapting and restructuring those models is conceptual change. Because conceptual knowledge is the basis for conceptual change, it must be integrated into any architecture of human cognition.

Epistemological Knowledge Types

The most commonly described knowledge types include declarative and procedural. As just described, declarative knowledge is an ontological knowledge type which conveys the attributes and structures of objects. Procedural knowledge, on the other hand, is an epistemological kind of knowledge that describes how declarative knowledge types are used. While ontological knowledge types are used to describe content or domain knowledge, epistemological knowledge types are used to describe task-related procedural knowledge (de Jong & Ferguson-Hessler, 1996). There are different kinds of epistemological knowledge because different classification schemes exist for different types of tasks (Gott, 1989). That is, knowledge acquired while learning to solve physics problems is different from that acquired while learning to write a summary paper. Alexander, Schallert, and Hare (1991) referred to task knowledge as understanding the cognitive demands of a task or knowledge-in-use (de Jong & Ferguson-Hessler, 1996). At least three kinds of epistemological knowledge exist: procedural, situational, and strategic. These knowledge types result from action and application of declarative knowledge. While they are not as easy to identify and articulate, they are essential cognitive components.

Procedural Knowledge

Procedural knowledge is the knowledge required to perform a task; knowledge that can be applied directly and is represented most often as production rules (Anderson, 1996). That is, knowing how to perform a surgical procedure is different from knowing the parts of the body being surgically altered or the steps in the procedure declaratively. Because it is a different kind of knowledge, it may not be as easily articulated as declarative knowledge but is just as important to a human cognitive architecture. There are so many things that we know how to do without being able to describe what or why we are doing it.

Situational Knowledge

One of the task-dependent knowledge types described by de Jong and Ferguson-Hessler (1996) is situational knowledge, that is, knowledge about situations as they usually appear. They focused their typology development on problem solving. For example, knowing that a rougher surface means more frictional force that can work against motion is required for predicting the outcome of some motion. Schank and Abelson (1977) referred to this kind of knowledge as scripts. Scripts consist of knowledge about problem types, context, and solution processes. Because experts' scripts are better developed, they are more easily able to recognize problem types and execute solution processes with less cognitive effort. In order to do so safely, a pilot landing a plane in Denver engages different situational knowledge than landing a plane in New York. Because this knowledge is normally associated with practice and its resulting phenomenological (experiential) knowledge (described next), it is integral to a human cognitive architecture.

Strategic Knowledge

Strategic knowledge consists of knowledge of learning strategies and activities to invoke in order to perform a task. As such, strategies aid in the regulation, execution, and evaluation of a task (Alexander & Judy, 1988, p. 376). Strategic knowledge (also known as conditional knowledge) is the understanding of when and where to access facts and to apply procedural knowledge, a form of metacognitive knowledge. While metacognitive knowledge is widely acknowledged in the literature, its place in a human cognitive architecture is unclear.

Phenomenological Knowledge Types

Because humans are able to acquire/construct a great deal of ontological and epistemological knowledge, their role in a human cognitive architecture is obvious. Ironically, however, the most natural form of meaning making results in phenomenological knowledge. Phenomenology describes the knowledge of which we are introspectively aware, that we perceive through our experiences, realizing that our perceptions are often incongruent with objects in the world.

According to phenomenologists, we can only know the world as we consciously experience it, not as it really is. We bracket aspects of reality to enable us to capture the *essence* of phenomena (Jonassen, 1984) because we cannot attend to all aspects of reality simultaneously. Phenomenological knowledge types represent our perceptions of our experiences. As such, they are less constrained by formal syntaxes or structures. The medium through which phenomenological knowledge is conveyed, if it can be, is a story (Jonassen & Hernandez-Serrano, 2002). Stories are the most natural form of sense making. Humans appear to have an innate ability and predisposition to organize and represent their experiences in the form of stories because stories require less cognitive effort than exposition owing to the narrative form of framing experience (Bruner, 1990). There are at least four kinds of phenomenological knowledge, including tacit, compiled, sociocultural, and experiential knowledge. Again, there are conceivably many other kinds of phenomenological knowledge.

Tacit (Implicit) Knowledge

Most kinds of phenomenological knowledge are tacit. Tacit knowledge is not readily available to consciousness. Tacit knowledge is that which we know but cannot tell, which is similar to Kant's notion of pure knowledge, that which cannot be known but only inferred (Jonassen, 1984). We have all experienced some of our own behaviors, unable to explain what we did or why we did it. Implicit learning results in tacit knowledge that is abstract and representative of the structure of the environment; they are independent of conscious efforts to learn and their functional, controlling properties operate largely outside of awareness; and tacit knowledge can be used to solve problems and make decisions (Reber, 1989). How to integrate tacit knowledge into a human cognitive architecture is very problematic.

Sociocultural Knowledge

Sociocultural knowledge comprises the world view, belief systems, attitudes, and socially shared knowledge among a culture of people. It represents a pervasive filter through which all human experiences and understandings must pass (Alexander et al., 1991). If directly addressed, sociocultural knowledge becomes explicit; however, more often it functions in a less conscious way to affect individuals' perceptions and understanding of different experiences. Differences in communication styles among different cultures provide direct evidence of varying sociocultural knowledge. This is perhaps the most problematic kind of knowledge to a cognitive architecture that is individually based and therefore begs the question about the distribution of cognition among people. Knowledge in the head is often contrasted with knowledge in the world (Jonassen & Henning, 1999).

Experiential (Episodic) Knowledge

Much of what we have learned from life is conveyed to others in the form of stories. When faced with similar circumstances, we recall stories of our experiences or someone else's. The reasons for recalling this experiential knowledge (knowledge of episodes) is to help us solve problems, design things, plan for activities or events, diagnose situations, explain phenomena, justify beliefs or argue for or against ideas, classify and interpret new phenomena, or predict effects (Kolodner, 1992). Given a new situation, we remember previous problem situations that were similar to the current one and use them to help solve the current problem. The previous cases suggest means for solving the new case. If old cases are not directly applicable, we adapt our experiential knowledge to meet the new situation. Experiential or episodic knowledge is a dynamic form of memory that changes over time as we integrate new experiences with those we already know (Schank, 1982). Schank (1999) has argued that human intelligence is nothing more than an internal library of indexed stories. Given the number of theories and knowledge types that I have identified, it would be hard to justify that. However, stories are the most memorable form of knowledge and therefore deserve an important place in any human cognitive architecture.

Summary

Are all kinds of knowledge (ontological, epistemological, and phenomenological) found in long-term memory? If so, are they stored the same way, and do they each entail cognitive load in the same way? I doubt it. Phenomenological knowledge types tend to be more compiled, more easily fired when needed, and more resistant to forgetting. Shouldn't an architecture of cognition accommodate all ways of knowing and all types of knowledge in memory?

How Do Humans Think About What They Know?

The dimension of learning that seems to be missing from all of the architectures and topographies is how the various kinds of knowledge in long-term memory are used. While long-term memory contains sophisticated scripts (Schank & Abelson, 1977) and process schemas, meaningful learning requires original manipulations of knowledge in long-term memory, that is, transfer. Earlier, I showed that multiple knowledge types exist. How are those types of knowledge used? How are they functionally related? How do learners reason with the knowledge they have?

Although numerous forms of reasoning have been researched, including deductive, inductive, adductive, and argumentative, my research in problem solving over the past decade has isolated the two most basic forms of reasoning in problem solving and perhaps in most other tasks as well: analogical and causal reasoning.

Analogical reasoning is most commonly thought of in terms of the mapping of a source concept onto a target concept in order to explain the target in terms the learner already understands (e.g., a cell is like a city/factory/house) (Glynn, 1996). Analogies can also be used to compare relationships among concepts (predicates taking two or more arguments; e.g., syllogisms). Analogies are also used to compare problems, cases, or experiences. When faced with a new problem, case-based reasoning (Kolodner, 1992) predicts that the problem solver first attempts to retrieve the most similar experience from memory and apply it to the new problem. If the solution suggested from the previous case does not work, then the old case must be revised (Jonassen & Hernandez-Serrano, 2002). When either solution is confirmed, the learned case is retained for later use.

Analogical reasoning may also be used to help learners to induce schemas through analogical encoding. Analogical encoding is the process of mapping structural properties between multiple analogues. Rather than attempting to induce and transfer a schema based on a single example as is required by worked examples, research has shown that comprehension, schema inducement, and long-term transfer across contexts can be greatly facilitated by analogical encoding, comparison of two analogues for structural alignment (Gentner, Lowenstein, & Thompson, 2003; Gentner & Markman, 1997; Loewenstein, Thompson, & Gentner, 2003). When learners directly compare two examples, they can identify structural similarities. If presented with just one example, students are far more likely to recall problems that have similar surface features. Analogical encoding fosters learning because analogies promote attention to commonalities, including common principles and schemas (Gick & Holyoak, 1983).

Causal reasoning represents one of the most basic and important cognitive processes that underpin all higher-order activities, such as conceptual understanding and problem solving (Carey, 2002). Hume called causality the "cement of the universe" (Hume, 1739/2000). Causal reasoning is required for making predictions, drawing implications and inferences, and explaining phenomena in any domain. Causal propositions may be described quantitatively in terms of direction, valency, probability, and duration and also qualitatively in terms of mechanisms such as casual process, causal force, and necessity/sufficiency (Jonassen & Ionas, 2008). Solving any problem requires comprehension of the causal propositions that describe the problem.

Implications of a Human Cognitive Architecture

Among the most troubling of claims by Kirschner et al. (2006) is that filling up long-term memory "provides us with the ultimate justification for instruction" (p. 77). Although the most common purpose of formal education is to fill up long-term memory, so many of the kinds of learning and kinds of knowledge associated with that learning result from informal circumstances, because learning is inevitable, essential, and ubiquitous (Alexander et al., 2008). They go on to claim that learning can be resisted and is often disadvantageous. That is, so much of what we learn emerges from everyday, non-school activity and is therefore not the result of direct instruction. If the architecture of long-term memory is replete with emergent, socioculturally mediated knowledge, how can it provide the "ultimate justification for instruction"? The reality is that humans have been learning for thousands of years without the benefit of formal instruction. One of the most sophisticated and complex examples of learning, language acquisition, occurs without formal instruction. Many kinds of phenomenological knowledge cannot even be expressed, let alone taught.

An architecture of human cognition must provide more descriptive goals than changes to long-term memory. No one doubts that long-term memory changes, but how and with what, and for what purpose? What kinds of knowledge are necessary for solving different kinds of everyday problems? How are those types of knowledge altered in long-term memory when used to analogically compare problems or make inferences and predictions? The primary question is how many of those knowledge types can be acquired through direct instruction, and how many must be constructed based on personal elaborations and experience? Wisdom cannot be told (Bransford, Franks, Vye, & Sherwood, 1989).

An architecture of human cognition must be able to account for all types of learning, not just that resulting from direct instruction. Many types of problem solving (e.g., design, policy analysis, strategic performance) cannot be effectively taught via direct instruction because they call on different types of knowledge (epistemological and phenomenological) in order to solve. These kinds of problems implicitly demand high levels of germane and intrinsic cognitive load. And while direct instruction in the form of worked examples (the dominant mode of instruction in the sciences) may facilitate some forms of ontological and epistemological knowledge construction, they actually result in misconceptions and inadequate conceptual models (Jonassen, Cho, & Wexler, under review; Mazur, 1997) when learning physics. Students learn to get the correct answer by applying equations, but they fail to construct conceptual understanding of the principles of physics. An architecture of cognition must encompass all kinds of knowledge for different purposes.

Question: Sweller. *Your chapter is primarily concerned with asking and providing answers to two important questions: How do humans learn and what do humans learn? The answers provided consist of an immense list of possibilities. In fact, I feel the list is not long enough: to be complete it needs to be effectively infinite. It is always possible to devise new categories of knowledge because we can always argue that anything we know or could potentially know belongs to a discrete category learned in a particular way under particular circumstances. To be viable, we need distinctions and categories that have instructional implications and instructional implications are completely missing from the analysis. Thus, my question is: Is there a body of literature consisting of multiple, randomized, controlled experimental studies indicating the instructional importance of any of the categories identified? What evidence is there that, for example, some categories of knowledge identified in the chapter should be taught using explicit, direct instruction but others should be taught using discovery learning/constructivist teaching techniques?*

Reply: Jonassen. The goal of experimental research is to generate universal principles. Assuming that, there is not a body of randomized controlled experiments focusing on any type of learning, except possibly for declarative knowledge (recall). Although there is a lot of empirical research on procedural knowledge, the procedural learning outcomes are not consistent enough to render universal instructional principles. Concept learning, feedback, practice, and a few pre-instructional strategies are the only instructional concepts that have what any empirical researcher would call an adequate body of research to justify solid instructional principles. I do not include worked examples in that lot because they have only been applied to a narrow band of learning outcomes. I am sure that you will disagree with that assessment.

Despite the goal of experimental research to engender universal principles, learning is not a universal process. The very best results from a experimental research study that I ever performed was in ninth grade. I showed how a plant hormone called gibberellic acid in ascending concentrations in light and no-light conditions affected bean-seed germination, for which I won the Indiana state science contest. Since then, I have conducted many randomized experiments with human learning and never have approximated the quality of the data that I found then. Why? Because humans have emotions, motivations, beliefs, moods, a host of individual differences, all of which are confounds to the experimental study of human learning. The point of my chapter is that learning is a far more complex process than we will ever be able to fully articulate. However, we cannot ignore types of learning or prevent their presence in an architecture of human cognition simply because we are unable to conduct randomized field trials on them. Werner von Heisenberg would argue that randomized experiments are impossible to perform without significantly affecting the nature of the learning. Unfortunately, as experimental researchers, we will never know how learning is affected.

Question: Sweller. *You state,*

> *The ability to solve problems clearly relies on the contents of long-term memory but is not sufficient to explain learning or problem solving. Solving a problem is not merely a process of retrieving a solution from long-term memory. Long-term memory is not the only component or mechanism of cognition.*

By omission, it seems to be implied that working-memory limitations are not critical for problem solving. Is that a valid interpretation of the above passage? If it is not valid, what are the instructional implications of a limited working memory when dealing with novel information?

Reply: Jonassen. All of the research on cognitive load that I have read focuses on well-structured (primarily mathematics) problems. But the kinds of problems that I am more concerned with are the ill-structured, interdisciplinary problems without known solution methods or accepted answers and often requiring immense cognitive load. Many are so complex that the problem elements cannot be simultaneously retrieved into working memory. They represent what it means to be a citizen, a professional, or even a knowledgeable person. Intelligence, for me, has little to do with what you know and more to do with how you can construct meaningful models of the world and apply what you know. I believe that we need to engage students in complex, ill-structured problem solving, a process that will heap germane cognitive load on the learners. There are many kinds of learning that cannot be made easier. We can make transmissible knowledge easier to learn using worked examples or other multimedia devices, but should we?

Reaction to Jonassen's reply: Sweller. *I asked whether there was any evidence from randomized controlled experiments indicating that the cognitive distinctions you make have instructional implications. The answer presented is unambiguously "no," an answer I agree with. You go on to suggest that lack of evidence from randomized, controlled experiments is unimportant because such experiments are themselves unimportant or perhaps impossible, based on atomic physics. We'll have to agree to disagree on that but there are serious consequences of this position.*

Is there any technique that could be used to provide evidence that constructivist teaching is a relatively poor method of teaching? When I hypothesize that studying worked examples is superior to problem solving, and test the hypothesis by comparing the consequences of studying worked examples or solving problems, it is at least possible to obtain results contrary to my hypothesis. Techniques that could in principle prove negative for constructivist teaching seems to have been ruled out as illegitimate.

My second question concerned the role of working memory in problem solving. The last paragraph of your reply is concerned with issues of cognitive load saying that cognitive-load theory is concerned with well-structured problems and that it is ill-structured problems that impose the heaviest cognitive load. First, does that mean that constructivist teaching does not apply to well-structured problems and that they are best handled with explicit instruction (as indicated by Spiro, for example)? If so, we have another point of agreement. Note, nevertheless, that the distinction between well-structured and ill-structured problems is probably unsustainable and as a consequence, cognitive-load effects are just as obtainable using ill-structured as well-structured problems—for detailed references, see my response to Spiro's questions.

Response to Sweller: Jonassen. I certainly did not aver nor mean to imply that randomized, controlled experiments were "unimportant because such experiments are themselves unimportant or perhaps impossible, based on atomic physics." I alluded to Heisenberg's uncertainty principle, which is actually based on sub-atomic physics. I continue to conduct experimental research along with various forms of qualitative inquiry. What I have learned from my experimental studies is that experiments are capable of revealing changes in behavior; however, those results must always be interpreted, a process that necessarily interjects subjectivity into the findings. In order to uncover the complexities of learning, we must use a variety of lenses and tools. I have also learned that randomized experiments are very difficult to conduct in any authentic learning context. Research results are clouded by confounds that compromise the integrity of the research. If we want to exercise the kinds of control that are demanded of experimental research, we resort to generalizing laboratory results into the classroom, a specu-lative venture at the very least. In summary, there is no holy grail, no single theory or research method that is able to explicate learning. Rather than asserting theoretical or methodological superiority, we should collaboratively address the unsolved mysteries of learning.

Question: Mayer. *If I understand correctly, your main point is not that Kirschner et al. are incorrect in their description of how learning works, but rather they are incomplete. You also seem to attribute to Kirschner et al. the idea that "learning has been institutionalized as a process of knowledge acquisition, a filling-up of long-term memory." However, let's suppose for the moment that we can agree that learning is a multifaceted process of knowledge construction, in which learning depends on appropriate cognitive processing during learning and that the outcome of learning is a change in the learner's knowledge (including facts, concepts, procedures, strategies, and beliefs)? Do you agree with this view of how learning works?*

Reply: Jonassen. I absolutely agree that learning depends on appropriate cogni-tive processing during learning and that the outcome of learning is a change in the learner's knowledge. However, I would add that learning in different contexts also depends on appropriate social interactions, observations, participation in a community, and several other processes. Being an applied cognitive psychologist, my primary focus has always been on the cognitive processes, although I accept the essentiality of other processes. That is why all of my research now focuses on examining the cognitive requirements for solving different kinds of problems. Yes, appropriate cognitive processing is integral to most forms of learning, but it is not enough to accept a change in knowledge as the arbiter of learning, just the same as "a change in behavior" doomed the behaviorists when we began looking under the hood. We need to articulate the kinds of knowledge that are con-structed as well as the quality of that knowledge. The conceptual change research provides valuable insights into how to examine conceptual frameworks for the quality of the learner's knowledge. I have never subscribed to the postmodern notion that all knowledge is acceptable and fundamentally equal, especially when I choose a doctor to provide medical service. Some people do have more viable knowledge than others.

Second, as researchers we must be able to articulate different cognitive out-comes that discriminate the various ways in which people know and think. From an empirical perspective, that means measuring multiple kinds of knowledge during our investigations. I encourage my students to include multiple measures in the hope of finding discontinuities in main effects and interactions among the main variables. When interventions or emergent processes results in some kinds of knowledge gains but not others, we get a window inside the mind where we can see how certain actions affect different kinds of cognitions and others do not.

Third, learning, especially in classrooms and in the wild, is a complex, sto-chastic process. We delude ourselves into thinking that we can control meaning-making processes. If we are unable to articulate many kinds of learning nor means for assessing it, how can we ever pretend to predict the effects of every kind of intervention? Some kinds of learning (tacit knowledge, for instance) cannot be known in any external way.

Question: Mayer. *Educational research is often criticized as being low in quality, such as not having testable theories, not using scientifically rigorous research methods, and not basing arguments on valid research evidence. Do you think it is appropriate to ask, "What works in helping students to learn?". If so, please provide examples of high-quality research studies comparing the effectiveness of inquiry methods and direct instruction in promoting meaningful learning. I could not find any such evidence in your chapter.*

Reply: Jonassen. Yes, absolutely it is appropriate to ask what works in helping students to learn. If it is not, we had all better begin searching for new jobs. But here is where the schism begins. We each make different assumptions about what learning is. We invoke different theory bases to explain and predict what kind of learning may occur. I am not able to identify "high-quality research studies comparing the effectiveness of inquiry methods and direct instruction" because it probably does not exist and cannot exist. Researchers examining the effectiveness of direct instruction begin with fundamentally different assumptions, evoke significantly different theory bases, and use different research methods than researchers examining informal or inquiry learning. Therefore the questions they ask, the learning outcomes they seek and the research tools and methods they use are also quite different. We cannot compare apples with oranges. Each relies on intellectual biases that would leave the other at a disadvantage were we to compare results.

All of the above said, learning research is not a contest; it is a quest. That is why we should stop polemicizing the discussion and work together to identify where and when those theories, outcomes, and methods may intersect or at least contribute to each other. Direct instruction is not better than inquiry instruction. Nor is inquiry learning better than direct instruction. That is a dualistic discussion that is epistemically naive. We need to hold ourselves to a higher standard.

Reaction to Jonassen's reply: Mayer. *It is clear that we both share a commitment to "work together" to address the basic issues in our field, such as understanding how people learn and how to help people learn. First, we share a fundamental commitment to a scientific approach in which our arguments are based on evidence rather than on doctrine. I am delighted to see that we can agree that it is reasonable to ask, "What works in helping students to learn?". I also agree with your reasonable assertion that learning is a complex process, so our challenge is to work hard to collect appropriate evidence. Second, concerning dependent measures, we agree that an important task is to measure the kind and quality of knowledge that is learned by people under different instructional methods, that is, we agree on measuring "multiple kinds of knowledge." Third, concerning independent variables, we appear to have an impasse when you say that it is impossible to conduct high-quality research* *studies comparing the effectiveness of inquiry methods and direct instruction. However, if I interpret your answer correctly, it does appear that we can compare different instructional methods as long as we can agree on a legitimate set of dependent measures—that is, if we can agree on the desired learning outcomes. For example, let's say we can agree that an important goal is to help students become proficient mathematical problem solvers and we can develop some corresponding dependent measures. Then, it would be possible to compare the effectiveness of inquiry and direct instructional methods on multiple measures. If instead we say that it is not possible to test the effectiveness of inquiry methods (as compared to other methods) because real life is just too messy, then we have no scientific justification for using them. In short, let's agree that we can make progress in our field to the extent that we are able to base instructional practice and educational theory on scientific evidence rather than on "isms" and the opinions of experts.*

References

Alexander, P. A., & Judy, J. E. (1988). The interaction of domain-specific and strategies knowledge in academic performance. *Review of Educational Research, 58*(4), 375–404.

Alexander, P. A., Schallert, D. L., & Hare, V. C. (1991). Coming to terms: How researchers in learning and literacy talk about knowledge. *Review of Educational Research, 61*, 315–343.

Alexander, P. A., Schallert, D. L., & Reynolds, R. (2008, March). *What is learning anyway? A topographical perspective considered.* Paper presented at the annual meeting of the American Educational Research Association, New York.

Anderson, J. R. (1996). *The architecture of cognition.* Cambridge, MA: Harvard University Press.

Arnheim, R. (1969). *Visual thinking.* Berkeley, CA: University of California Press.

Atkinson, R., Derry, S. J., Renkl, A., & Wortham, D. (2000). Learning from examples: Instructional principles from the worked examples research. *Review of Educational Research, 70*, 181–215.

Atkinson, R., & Shiffrin, R. (1968). Human memory: A proposed system and its control processes. In K. Spence & J. Spence (Eds.), *The psychology of learning and motivation* (Vol. 2, pp. 89–195). New York: Academic Press.

Ausubel, D. P. (1968). *Educational psychology: A cognitive view.* New York: Holt, Rinehart & Winston.

Bransford, J. D., Franks, J. J., Vye, N. J., & Sherwood, R. D. (1989). New approaches to instruction: Because wisdom can't be told. In S. Vosniadou & A. Ortony (Eds.), *Similarity and analogical reasoning* (pp. 470–497). New York: Cambridge University Press.

Bransford, J. D., & Stein, B. S. (1984). *The ideal problem solver: A guide for improving thinking, learning, and creativity.* New York: W. H. Freeman.

Bruner, J. (1990). *Acts of meaning.* Cambridge, MA: Harvard University Press.

Carey, S. (2002). The origin of concepts: Continuing the conversation. In N. L. Stein, P. J. Bauer, & M. Rabinowitz (Eds.), *Representation, memory, and development: Essays in honor of Jean Mandler* (pp. 43–52). Mahwah, NJ: Lawrence Erlbaum Associates Publishers.

Chi, M. T. H. (1992). Conceptual change within and across ontological categories: Examples from learning and discovery in science. In R. N. Giere (Ed.), *Minnesota studies in the philosophy of science, vol. xv: Cognitive models of science* (pp. 129–186). Minneapolis, MN: University of Minnesota Press.

Chi, M. T. H. (2005). Commonsense conceptions of emergent processes: Why some misconceptions are robust. *Journal of the Learning Sciences, 14*(2), 161–199.

Chi, M. T. H., & Bassock, M. (1991). Learning from examples vs. self-explanations. In L. B. Resnick (Ed.), *Knowing, learning, and instruction: Essays in honor of Robert Glaser* (pp. 251–282). Hillsdale, NJ: Lawrence Erlbaum Associates.

Chi, M. T. H., Feltovich, P. J., & Glaser, R. (1981). Categorization and representation of physics problems by experts and novices. *Cognitive Science, 5*, 121–152.

Chi, M. T. H., & Roscoe, R. D. (2002). The processes and challenges of conceptual change. In M. Limón & L. Mason (Eds.), *Reconsidering conceptual change: Issues in theory and practice* (pp. 3–27). Dordrecht: Kluwer Academic Publishers.

Cooper, G., & Sweller, J. (1987). Effects of schema acquisition and rule automation on mathematical problem solving. *Journal of Educational Psychology, 79*, 347–362.

de Jong, T., & Ferguson-Hessler, M. G. M. (1991). Knowledge of problem situations in physics: A comparison of good and poor novice problem solvers. *Learning and Instruction, 1*, 289–302.

de Jong, T., and Ferguson-Hessler, M. G. (1996). Types and quality of knowledge. *Educational Psychologist, 31*, 105–113.

Diekhoff, G. M. (1983). Relationship judgments in the evaluation of structural understanding. *Journal of Educational Psychology, 75*, 227–233.

Engeström, Y. (1987). *Learning by expanding: An activity theoretical approach to developmental research.* Helsinki, Finland: Orienta-Konsultit Oy.

Floridi, L. (Ed.). (2003). *Blackwell guide to the philosophy of computing and information.* Oxford: Blackwell, 155–166.

Gazzaniga, M. S. (2004). *The cognitive neurosciences* (Vol. 3). Cambridge, MA: MIT Press.

Gentner, D., Lowenstein, J., & Thompson, L. (2003). Learning and transfer: A general role for analogical encoding. *Journal of Educational Psychology, 95*(2), 393–405.

Gentner, D., & Markman, A. B. (1997). Structure mapping in analogy and similarity. *American Psychologist, 52*(1), 45–56.

Gibson, J. J. (1979). *An ecological approach to visual perception.* Hillsdale, NJ: Lawrence Erlbaum Associates.

Gick, M. L., & Holyoak, K. J. (1983). Schema induction and analogical transfer. *Cognitive Psychology, 15*, 1–38.

Glynn, S. M. (1996). Teaching with analogies: Building on the science textbook. *The Reading Teacher, 49*, 490–492.

Gott, S. P. (1989). Apprenticeship instruction for real world tasks: The coordination of procedures, metal models, and strategies. In E. Z. Rothkopf (Ed.), *Review of research in education* (pp. 97–169). Washington, DC: American Educational Research Association.

Hume, D. (1739/2000). *A treatise of human nature.* Oxford: Oxford University Press.

Jenkins, J. J. (1979). Four points to remember: A tetrahedral model of memory experiments. In L. S. Cermak & E. I. M. Craik (Eds.), *Levels of processing in human memory* (pp. 429–446). Hillsdale, NJ: Erlbaum.

Jonassen, D. H. (1984). The mediation of experience and educational technology: A philosophical analysis. *Educational Communications and Technology Journal, 32*(3), 153–167.

Jonassen, D. H. (1997). Instructional design model for well-structured and ill-structured problem-solving learning outcomes. *Educational Technology: Research and Development, 45*(1), 65–95.

Jonassen, D. H. (2000). Toward a design theory of problem solving. *Educational Technology: Research & Development, 48*(4), 63–85.

Jonassen, D. H. (2003). The vain quest for a unified theory of learning? *Educational Technology, 43*(4), 5–8.

Jonassen, D. H. (2004). *Learning to solve problems: An instructional design guide.* San Francisco, CA: Pfeiffer/Jossey-Bass.

Jonassen, D. H. (Ed.). (2007). *Learning to solve complex, scientific problems.* Mahwah, NJ: Lawrence Erlbaum Associates.

Jonassen, D. H. (2008). It's just a theory. *Educational Technology, 48*(6), 45–48.

Jonassen, D. H., Beissner, K., & Yacci, M. (1993). *Structural knowledge,* Hillsdale, NJ: Lawrence Erlbaum Associates.

Jonassen, D. H., Cho, Y. H., & Wexler, C. (under review). Facilitating schema induction during problem solving through analogical encoding. *American Journal of Physics.*

Jonassen, D. H., & Henning, P. (1999). Mental models: Knowledge in the head and knowledge in the world. *Educational Technology, 39*(3), 37–42.

Jonassen, D. H., & Hernandez-Serrano, J. (2002). Case-based reasoning and instructional design: Using stories to support problem solving. *Educational Technology: Research and Development, 50*(2), 65–77.

Jonassen, D. H., & Ionas, I. G. (2008). Designing effective supports for reasoning causally. *Educational Technology: Research & Development, 56*(3), 287–308.

Jonassen, D. H., Strobel, J., & Lee, C. B. (2006). Everyday problem solving in engineering: Lessons for engineering educators. *Journal of Engineering Education, 95*(2), 1–14.

Kirschner, P. A., Sweller, J., & Clark, R. E. (2006). Why minimal guidance during instruction does not work: An analysis of the failure of constructivist, discovery, problem-based, experiential, and inquiry-based teaching. *Educational Psychologist, 41*(2), 75–86.

Kolodner, J. (1992). An introduction to case-based reasoning. *Artificial Intelligence Review, 6*(1), 3–34.

Larkin, J. H. (1983). The role of problem representation in physics. In D. Gentner & A. L. Stevens (Eds.), *Mental models* (pp. 75–98). Hillsdale, NJ: Lawrence Erlbaum Associates.

Lave, J., & Wenger, E. (1991). *Situated learning: Legitimate peripheral participation.* New York: Cambridge University Press.

Leont'ev, A. (1972). The problem of activity in psychology. *Voprosy filosofii, 9,* 95–108.

Limón, M., & Mason, L. (2002). *Reconsidering conceptual change: Issues in theory and practice.* Amsterdam: Kluwer.

Loewenstein, J., Thompson, L., & Gentner, D. (2003). Analogical learning in negotiation teams: Comparing cases promotes learning and transfer. *Academy of Management Learning and Education, 2*(2), 119–127.

Mazur, E. (1997). *Peer instruction.* Upper Saddle River, NJ: Prentice-Hall.

Paivio, A. (1986). *Mental representations: A dual-coding approach.* New York: Oxford University Press.

Perkins, D. N. (1999). The many faces of constructivism. *Educational Leadership, 57*(3), 6–11.

Piaget, J. (1970). *Genetic epistemology.* New York: Columbia University Press.

Popper, K. R. (1999). *All life is problem solving.* New York: Routledge.

Preece, P. F. W. (1976). Mapping cognitive structure: A comparison of methods. *Journal of Educational Psychology, 68,* 1–8.

Reber, A. S. (1989). Implicit learning and tacit knowledge. *Journal of Experimental Psychology – General, 118,* 219–235.

Rumelhart, D. E., & Norman, D. A. (1978). Accretion, tuning and restructuring: Three modes of learning. In J. W. Cotton & R. Klatzky (Eds.), *Semantic factors in cognition* (pp. 37–53). Hillsdale, NJ: Lawrence Erlbaum Associates.

Ryle, G. (1949). *The concept of mind.* New York: Barnes & Noble.

Scardamalia, M., & Bereiter, C. (1991). Higher levels of agency for children in knowledge building; A challenge for the design of knowledge media. *Journal of the Learning Sciences, 1*(1), 37–68.

Schank, R. C. (1982). *Dynamic memory: A theory of learning in people and computers.* Cambridge: Cambridge University Press.

Schank, R. C. (1999). *Dynamic memory revisited.* Cambridge: Cambridge University Press.

Schank, R. C., & Abelson, R. (1977). *Scripts, plans, goals and understanding.* Hillsdale, NJ: Lawrence Erlbaum Associates.

Schnotz, W., Vosniadou, S., & Carretero, M. (1999). *New perspectives in conceptual change.* Amsterdam: Pergamon.

Shavelson, R. J. (1972). Some aspects of the correspondence between content structure and cognitive structure in physics instruction. *Journal of Educational Psychology, 63,* 225–234.

Sinatra, G. M., & Pintrich, P. R. (2003). *Intentional conceptual change.* Mahwah, NJ: Lawrence Erlbaum Associates.

Skinner, B. F. (1957). *Verbal behavior.* New York: Appleton-Century-Crofts.

Slotta, J. D., & Chi, M. T. H. (2006). Helping students to understand challenging topics in science through ontology training. *Cognition and Instruction, 24*(2), 261–289.

Spiro, R. J., & Jehng, J. C. (1990). Cognitive flexibility and hypertext: Theory and technology for the non-linear and multi-dimensional traversal of complex subject matter. In D. Nix & R. J. Spiro (Eds.), *Cognition, education, and multimedia: Explorations in high technology* (pp. 163–205). Hillsdale, NJ: Lawrence Erlbaum.

Suls, J., & Wills, T. A. (1991). *Social comparison: Contemporary theory and research.* Hillsdale, N.J.: Lawrence Erlbaum Associates.

Sweller, J., & Cooper, G. A. (1985). The use of worked examples as a substitute for problem solving in learning algebra. *Cognition & Instruction, 2,* 59–89.

Tennyson, R. D., & Cocchiarella, M. J. (1986). An empirically based instructional design theory for teaching concepts. *Review of Educational Research, 56,* 40–71.

Thorndike, E. L. (1927). The law of effect. *American Journal of Psychology, 39*(1/4), 212–222.

Watson, J. B. (1928). *The ways of behaviorism.* New York: Harper & Brothers.

Whitehead, A. N. (1929). *The aims of education.* New York: Macmillan.

3 Constructivism in an Age of Non-Constructivist Assessments[*]

Daniel L. Schwartz, Robb Lindgren, and Sarah Lewis Stanford University

Constructivism is a theory of knowledge growth and life-long development built on a philosophy of pragmatism (Dewey, 1916). In the context of formal education, it is frequently used as pedagogical label for sense-making activities including discovery, inquiry, exploration, and hands-on learning (Duffy & Jonassen, 1992). It is often set in opposition to behaviorist methods, where external reinforcements regulate learning, as well as direct instruction, where students are told or shown what to do.

Constructivism *writ large* has fared relatively well in education. Lillard and Else-Quest (2006), for example, found that Montessori education leads to better academic and social skills. Russell, Hancock, and McCullough (2007) found that participation in undergraduate research experiences, regardless of specific mentoring styles, increased student interest in pursuing advanced degrees in science. However, constructivism *writ small*—constructivism applied to single lessons or instructional units—has not fared as well. Klahr and Nigam (2004), for example, demonstrated that explicitly telling young children the control of variables strategy led to improved learning compared to having the children simply conduct experiments without guidance. Similar findings have led some scholars to the conclusion that constructivist pedagogies are inconsistent with cognitive architecture because they withhold information that can be readily told or demonstrated (e.g., Kirschner, Sweller, & Clark, 2006). This conclusion cannot be completely warranted, given what we know, for example, about the generation effect (Slamecka & Graf, 1978). Given pairs of synonyms, people will remember a word better if they explicitly have to generate missing information, as in the case of FAST: R_P_D versus reading FAST: RAPID. Nevertheless, their analysis does lend itself to the question, "Wouldn't it be more efficient to simply tell students what they are supposed to do and know?"

Some of the discrepancy between the outcomes of constructivism writ large and constructivism writ small has to do with the nature of the assessments that are used to evaluate pedagogical effectiveness. Constructivist pedagogies writ

[*] The writing of this chapter and the research by Sears (2006) were supported by the National Science Foundation under Grant No. SLC-0354453. Any opinions, findings, and conclusions or recommendations expressed in this material are those of the authors and do not necessarily reflect the views of the National Science Foundation.

small are often evaluated through non-constructivist means. Students receive tests that measure how well they developed their efficiency at remembering facts, executing skills, and solving similar problems. These assessments present something of a mismatch to larger constructivist goals. Dewey (1916) stated, "the aim of education is to enable individuals to continue their education ... the object and reward of learning is continued capacity for growth" (p. 117). Given this, a constructivist-tailored assessment should examine students' abilities and dispositions to construct new knowledge, not just execute old knowledge. This approach would be consistent with the assessments of constructivism writ large, which often indirectly measures students' ongoing abilities to construct knowledge, for example, by examining cumulative effects or by seeing whether students are more inclined to engage new content and new situations both in and out of school (Boaler, 2002).

This chapter shifts the application of constructivism away from instruction and places it instead in the realm of assessment. We begin by noting that constructivism is a sweeping theory so broad that it is difficult for it to dictate specific instructional design decisions. We are not alone in this observation. Mayer (2004) expresses faith in constructivism as a theory of knowledge attainment, but states that "a doctrine based approach to constructivism does not lead to fruitful educational practice" (p. 17). While this may be accurate, we argue that constructivism's breadth is quite valuable when used to assess educational outcomes.

Constructivism is a broad vision of learning; it is not just an approach to instruction. It enables us to consider students' abilities to create new knowledge when they are outside of instruction and we no longer have control over precise instructional variables. By shifting the focus to assessment, we can ask the question, "What experiences prepare students to construct knowledge in the future and in the wild?". This question is important because learning should not end once students leave the classroom and lose a teacher's direct guidance. By creating constructivist assessments, it will be possible to identify the elements of instruction—constructivist or otherwise—that facilitate the development of continued learning.

We justify this shift in focus by presenting three related lines of research. The first demonstrates the significance of constructivist assessments by showing that constructivist-inspired activities prepare students to construct knowledge from direct instruction later. The second line of work shows the value of constructivist assessments for detecting the special benefits of constructivist-inspired instruction. The third line of work demonstrates that targeting constructivist outcomes is compatible with promoting the efficiency outcomes favored by direct instruction, but that direct instruction may not always be compatible with constructivist outcomes. We conclude by tentatively working backward—given constructivist outcome measures, it is possible to start determining which elements of instruction lead to those outcomes.

Specificity in Instructional Theory

Different instructional techniques are suited to different instructional outcomes. If one's instructional goal is the development of sustained interest, then solo drill and practice will probably not fare very well. Instead, instruction that creates a social matrix of participation is likely to be more useful (Barron, 2004). In contrast, if the goal is to create efficiency in highly stable and repetitive contexts, then individual drill and practice may be very effective. One style of instruction does not fit all outcomes.

The relation between instruction and outcomes is mediated by the specific learning processes that are engaged. For instance, simply changing people's beliefs about an interaction can modify the learning processes. Okita, Bailenson, and Schwartz (2007) had people discuss the mechanisms of fever with a graphical human character in virtual reality. By using the virtual-reality set up, the researchers were able to hold all information and interaction constant across participants and conditions. There were two conditions: participants were told the character was either controlled by a person or controlled by a computer. Even though there were no differences in the available information or interaction, people learned more about fever if they thought the character was controlled by a person. People had higher arousal when they thought they were in a social interaction, and arousal levels correlated positively with conceptual learning.

From a psychological perspective, there are many different internal mechanisms that regulate learning, and different instructional conditions can engage learning mechanisms differentially. People can learn by being told; they can learn by observing social models; they can learn through spatial navigation; they can learn through reinforcement; they can learn through deliberate practice; they can learn by exploration; and they can even learn implicitly without any intent or awareness they are learning at all. These pathways of learning engage different brain circuitry (e.g., Seger, Prabhakaran, Poldrack, & Gabrieli, 2000). They are not simply multiple instances of a single "learning module." Each learning process has benefits for particular types of content and outcomes. For example, implicit learning is thought to be important for language acquisition, and direct instruction can interfere with implicit processes (Reber, 1976). The instructional challenge involves deciding which combination of learning processes and environmental supports will yield which desired learning outcomes (Hmelo-Silver, Duncan, & Chinn, 2007). The goal of fitting instruction to outcomes was a major constituent of Gagne's seminal work on the conditions of learning and helped to create the field of instructional design (Gagne, 1985).

In our experience, constructivism tends to be too large and general a philosophy to be useful for the precise handling of the many specific ways and reasons that people learn. Constructivism can be at too macroscopic a level for deriving specific instructional decisions. Sometimes hands-on learning is valuable and sometimes it is not—knowing the microscopic details of when it is valuable is difficult to derive from constructivist philosophies alone.

This is not to say that constructivism does not have an important role to play in the design of instruction. Instructional theories that are more specific tend to focus on one class of learning process and assume "all other things equal." For example, cognitive theories of learning tend to be silent about design decisions involving motivation, but any instructor can testify to the importance of making instructional choices involving student engagement and interest. One way constructivism benefits instruction is that it orients educators toward important values including overall student growth, interest, and agency. This way, when educators consider specific learning processes, they do not lose the bigger picture of education.

Constructivism as a Guide to Assessment

Although we believe that the broad concept of constructivism invites the wrong level of analysis for designing specific instructional moments, we do see constructivism as extremely valuable when applied to learning outcomes. Rather than taking constructivism as an instructional design theory, we suggest that the ideas of constructivism be applied to assessment. We ask the question "Does instruction prepare learners to construct knowledge once we no longer orchestrate specific instructional conditions to target specific learning mechanisms and outcomes?"

At the level of a single lesson, educators are able to offer guidance for specific instructional conditions. Once students leave the confines of formal instruction, however, teachers have no influence over specific instructional decisions and learning processes. In the wild, people need to construct knowledge using whatever resources, internal and external, are available. Because we cannot anticipate and decompose these future opportunities into specific learning mechanisms and situations, the granularity of constructivist theory now becomes appropriate.

A goal of much formal schooling is to provide students a foundation of knowledge on which they can build new knowledge once they leave school. For example, in interviews with school superintendents, we found a unanimous desire for their students to be prepared to learn and adapt so they can make choices on their own once they have left school (Schwartz, Bransford, & Sears, 2005). Except for very narrow training, people will need to continue learning new ideas and skills once they have left the confines of immediate instruction. People grow into their jobs, they change jobs, and the world changes around them.

As we consider constructivist learning outcomes, it is important to note that not all instruction should target the outcome of preparing students to construct new knowledge beyond immediate instruction. This is particularly true for highly stable domains where it is possible to cover nearly every possible combination of skills and performance conditions. For some domains, such as typing, the requisite skills and performance conditions are extremely stable. Keyboards and major keystroke combinations do not change, so there is little reason to prepare students to learn how to type. In this case, the instructional goal should be to make sure people develop good initial habits, so they can become increasingly efficient without having to undo their prior learning.

The typing example is informative when we think of assessment and potential mismatches with the goals of instruction. If we held typing instruction to constructivist outcome measures, for example by evaluating typing instruction based on whether students are prepared to learn the Dvorak keyboard, it would mis-measure the benefits of procedural training for stable environments.

Unfortunately, researchers in education frequently make an analogous mismatch when attempting to assess constructivist-inspired pedagogies by using non-constructivist assessments.

Most end-of-unit tests explicitly block students from constructing new knowledge during the test itself. These tests measure students' abilities at sequestered problem solving (SPS) rather than learning (Bransford & Schwartz, 1999). We say sequestered, because students are shielded from any resources that might help them learn during the test. SPS assessments are ideal when the goal is to determine student efficiency at retrieving and executing well-practiced knowledge and routines in familiar situations. For example, a good typing test would be an SPS test—how fast and accurately can people type. However, SPS assessments are not ideal when evaluating whether students have been prepared to construct knowledge based on what they have learned. During an SPS test, there are typically very slim opportunities and resources for constructing new knowledge.

A more appropriate test for constructivist outcomes is a preparation for future learning (PFL) assessment. In this type of assessment, students have an opportunity to learn during the test itself. Students who have been prepared to construct new knowledge in a domain will learn more during the assessment than those who have not been prepared to learn. PFL measures seem more in line with constructivist outcomes. We provide examples of PFL measures below, but a simple thought experiment can help indicate the need. Imagine a firm wants to hire a financial analyst. Tom has just completed a 2-week course in Excel—his first exposure to spreadsheet software. Sig has not learned Excel, but he has previously taught himself to high levels of expertise with multiple spreadsheet packages over the past several years. The company decides whom to hire by using a paper and pencil test of basic Excel operations that just happen to have been covered in Tom's course. Tom would probably do better on this SPS test. However, we suspect Sig would be more likely to serve the company well in the long run. His deeper understanding of spreadsheet structure and capacity to learn independently will enable him to learn and adapt on the job, for example, when the company switches to a new software package or when the employees are asked to learn advanced features of Excel on their own.

When evaluating instruction it is important to use outcome measures that capture what we want students to achieve. Thus far, most high stakes and experimental assessments have used an SPS format. This format favors direct instruction and repetitive practice, because direct instruction's primary goal is to increase efficiency in well-specified tasks. The SPS format does not favor constructivist pedagogies, which ideally target constructivist outcomes. More importantly, the current lack of PFL assessments means that we cannot know whether constructivist-inspired pedagogies actually achieve constructivist outcomes any better than direct instruction. Simply put, our measures have been misguided. By switching to constructivist assessments, like PFL, we will be in a better position to see which features and styles of instruction promote constructivist outcomes.

What Prepares People to Construct Knowledge from Direct Instruction?

One of the authors (DS) was a remote committee member for a graduate student who was enrolled at one of the premier universities in the United States. Standard tests no longer determined the student's fate. The author told the student at his dissertation proposal that he should explore his theories and conduct loose empirical research until the important structures and themes started to reveal themselves. Only then should he commit his time to exhaustive experimentation and a focused review of the literature. The student's primary advisor had written an important paper favoring direct instruction as a way to improve inquiry skills. In a convivial manner, the advisor stated to the author and graduate student, "You are asking him to follow your theory of education, but your theory is not proven in clinical trials." The author responded wryly, "He should do it your way then. You can tell him exactly what to do, and I am sure he can copy it perfectly. Afterwards, we can see how well the student fares on the job market."

The point of this story is not that one of the committee members was right or wrong, but rather that both pieces of advice, taken to their extremes, are somewhat foolhardy. Over the course of time, people will learn in many ways. Sometimes, it is important to explore and develop one's own ideas. Sometimes, it is important to receive direct guidance. The question is not which method is right; the question is what combination of methods is best for a given outcome.

Direct instruction can be very effective, assuming that people have sufficient prior knowledge to construct new knowledge from what they are being told or shown. In many cases, they do not. For example, a challenge in pre-service teacher education courses is that the students do not have sufficient prior knowledge of teaching in the classroom. In their teacher preparation courses, it is hard for the students to see the significance of the theories and map them into their future pupils' behaviors. Moreover, they lack a repository of personal instances that round out the specific examples used during instruction. Teacher educators have to work very hard to include multiple ideal examples, cases, and videos to help the pre-service teachers understand the significance of theories and lessons presented in the class readings and lectures. In this respect, it is much easier to work with in-service teachers. They can bring to mind relevant cases and juxtapose their own classroom wisdom with the ideas presented by the professor.

If students do not have sufficient prior knowledge to readily make sense of direct instruction, what is the best way to develop it? To address this question empirically, it is important to think in terms of PFL assessments. The empirical question is what types of experiences best prepare students to construct knowledge from direct instruction. A PFL assessment can be used to determine how well students have been prepared to learn, for example, from a lecture, by making learning from the lecture part of the assessment.

A relevant series of studies comes from teaching students in an introductory cognitive psychology course (Schwartz & Bransford, 1998). We describe one of the studies. In this study, the students learned two clusters of cognitive concepts over several lessons. To gather baseline data, all the students received the same instruction to learn the cluster of concepts relevant to encoding theory (what aspects of information people store in long-term memory). The second cluster of concepts was about schema theory (how people organize knowledge). For the second cluster, students completed different treatments so we could compare their learning across instructional treatments and against their own baselines.

The students learned about the encoding concepts first. They received a packet of simplified data sets and experimental descriptions from classic encoding studies. Their task was to analyze the data and make graphs of the most important patterns in 80 minutes. They were not told the point of the experiments they analyzed; it was up to them to decide what patterns were important enough to graph. We will call this activity "Analyze." Two days later, the students heard a 30-minute lecture on encoding. The lecture reviewed the results from the studies and the broader theories that explained them. We will call this activity "Lecture." Thus, for the encoding concepts, all the students received an Analyze+Lecture treatment.

A week later, the students were separated into three treatments for learning about the schema concepts. Two conditions completed Analyze activities for new schema data sets. A third condition received a text passage on the schema concepts. The third condition's task was to write a summary of the passage. We will call this the "Summarize" activity. The chapter included descriptions of the studies and graphs of results, and the chapter developed the broader theories that explained the results. All three groups had 80 minutes to complete their activities. Two days later, one of the Analyze groups received the Lecture, and the other Analyze group was asked to continue the Analyze activity. The Summarize group received the Lecture. Thus, in this phase of the study there was an Analyze+Lecture treatment that was comparable to the way all the students had learned the encoding concepts. There were also the two new learning treatments, Summarize+Lecture and Analyze+Analyze. (We describe what happens when students receive an analog of a Lecture+Analyze treatment in a later section.)

The following week, the students received an assessment to see how much they had learned. They received a written description of a novel experiment. Their task was to predict the outcomes of the experiment. The experiment had eight possible predictions, four based on the encoding concept cluster and four based on the schema cluster. Figure 3.1 shows how many of the concepts appeared in their predictions. The students did better predicting with concepts that they had learned by analyzing the data and then hearing about in the lecture. Students who had summarized the chapter and then heard the lecture did not do very well. The difference was not due to the Summarize students overlooking concepts during the Summarize activity. Graphs and summaries produced by the students during the Analyze and Summarize activities indicated whether or not they had covered a concept prior to the lecture. When Summarize students noted concepts in their summaries, they only made predictions based on those same concepts 23% of the time. In contrast, when the Analyze+Lecture students showed concept-relevant patterns in their graphs, they were likely to make predictions using those concepts 60% of the time.

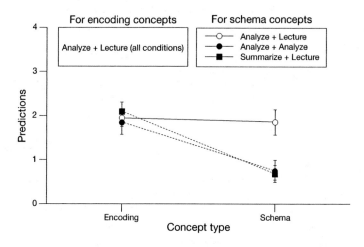

Figure 3.1 Students who explored and graphed data sets on memory experiments demonstrated superior abilities to predict outcomes of a novel experiment, but only if they had a chance to hear an organizing lecture afterwards (source: adapted from Schwartz & Bransford, 1998).

Importantly, students who analyzed the data, but never heard the lecture, also did not do very well. Although the Analyze+Analyze students had graphed the relevant patterns, they only made predictions based on the concepts they graphed 18% of the time. This latter result means that analyzing the data by itself did not lead to effective learning. Instead, the effect of analyzing the data was to prepare students to construct knowledge from the lecture.

From these results, a good way to prepare students for direct instruction is to give them targeted experiences with "exploratory" activities. It was the combination of exploration and telling that led to good learning outcomes. The exploratory activity or the verbal activities by themselves did not yield the desired learning. Monolithic theories that advocate all exploration or all direct instruction do not explain these results.

It is important to note, however, that the benefits of blending instruction only held if the desired outcome was to have students transfer their knowledge to novel situations. Other studies in the series measured recognition memory. Students who heard the lectures without any analysis activity did very well (as did the students who did the analyses-plus-lecture activities). Students who wrote summaries, for example, were able to correctly affirm the encoding concept that people only remember the gist of a passage when they understand it. They just could not apply this declarative fact to the prediction task. If simple memory were the goal of instruction, then lectures may be fine for college students. However, the goal of this psychology course was for students to develop the ability to predict and interpret human behavior. In cases like this, memory assessments are the wrong way to evaluate the quality of instruction or student learning.

Constructivist Activities Yield Constructivist Outcomes

It is not always possible to anticipate when a learning experience will arise. Instruction that targets constructivist outcomes should prepare students to recognize and take advantage of learning opportunities, even when there is no teacher available to say "learn this." In the preceding example, the sheer presence of the lecture format indicated to students that it was important to learn. A more stringent test of pedagogy would examine whether students are prepared to learn without overt prompts.

To examine what types of experiences prepare people to construct knowledge without overt prompting, Schwartz and Martin (2004) conducted a study on learning statistics. Unlike the psychology instruction study which looked at conceptual content, this study examined the acquisition of quantitative ideas and procedures. Multiple classes of ninth-grade students completed invention activities related to the topic of variance. They received data sets, and they had to invent a formula for computing a consumer "reliability index." For example, given data, they had to come up with a value that indicated which of two trampolines produced the most consistent bounce when a ball was dropped repeatedly from a fixed height. Few students invented a correct solution. However, the goal of the instruction was not for students to re-invent what took professional mathematicians many years to articulate. Rather, the goal was to prepare them to understand the formal solution created by mathematicians when it was presented in class. After students completed a series of invention activities, they were taught a formula for variance, and the students were given time to practice using it. Like the case of college students analyzing data on human memory, the invention activities prepared students to form a deep understanding from the content of the lecture. The ninth graders outperformed college students who had a semester of college statistics on a variety of measures ranging from their explicit long-term memory of the formulas to their ability to explain the structure of the formulas (e.g., why variance formulas divide by n). These findings complement the results of the analysis-plus-lecture activities in the preceding study.

The new question in the statistics study was whether students would be prepared to learn spontaneously without overt instruction. The way the experiment worked was that on the last day of several weeks of instruction the students worked in small groups of two to four to learn about standardized scores (e.g., grading on a curve). Half of the students completed a direct instruction treatment we will call "Tell and Copy." The students were told (and shown) a graphical technique for computing standardized scores. They then received a data set and had to answer a question using the technique to find standardized scores (e.g., who broke the world record by relatively more, the high jumper or the long jumper?). The teachers corrected student errors during this practice. The other half of the students completed an invention treatment we will call "Invent a Measure." They received the same data set and question, but they were told to invent their own solution to the problem. They did not receive any specific guidance on how to solve the problem, and they did not receive any feedback on their solutions. No students invented a workable answer, so this would at first seem to be a very inefficient form of instruction. However, by a subsequent PFL assessment (described next), the experience of trying to invent a solution revealed itself as very important. It prepared students to learn from a "hidden" solution later on.

The PFL assessment involved two items within a longer test that occurred about a week after instruction. One item, near the end of the test, was a difficult transfer problem. The target transfer problem did not look like any problems the students had studied. The surface features were novel, and the problem required an application of standardized scores not covered directly in the prior instruction. The other item was a worked example in the middle of the test. Students had to follow the worked example to solve a subsequent problem just below it. Embedded in the worked example was the procedure that would help solve the transfer problem. Nearly all of the students correctly followed the worked example. The question was whether they were prepared to learn from the worked example, such that they could apply it to the target transfer problem.

All the test packets included the target transfer problem, but only half of the tests in each condition included the worked example. This way, it was possible to determine whether students were solving the target transfer problem on the basis of the worked example. Figure 3.2 shows the results. Students who received the direct instruction on standardized scores were not prepared to learn from the worked example. The Tell and Copy students performed roughly the same on the post-test with or without the worked example in their tests. In contrast, students who had tried to invent a way to handle standardized scores were twice as

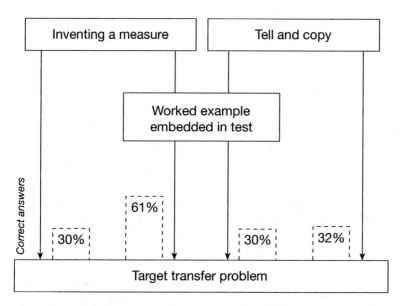

Figure 3.2 Students who tried to invent a solution to learn the concept of standardized scores were more prepared to learn spontaneously from the worked example and transfer it to a subsequent problem than students who had been told and practiced a solution using standardized scores (source: adapted from Schwartz & Martin, 2005).

likely to learn from the worked example and use it to solve the transfer problem. A subsequent study replicated the results with a new set of ninth graders who received the instruction from their regular classroom teachers (Schwartz & Martin, 2004).

The study provides three useful bits of information. The first is that constructivist-inspired activities can lead to constructivist outcomes better than direct instruction, at least in this instance. Students who had unsuccessfully tried to invent solutions to problems involving variance were more prepared to learn spontaneously without explicit support. The second bit of information is that the benefits of the invention activities would have been overlooked if the studies had not used PFL assessments. Students who tried to solve the transfer problem without the benefit of the embedded worked example took an SPS assessment because there were no resources for learning. By this SPS assessment there was little difference between direct instruction and invention. The third bit of information is that worked examples can create effective instruction, but only if students are prepared to construct useful knowledge from the examples. Students in the Tell and Copy condition were able to follow the worked example to solve the immediately following problem, but they did not learn the significance of what the procedure could accomplish.

Issues of Efficiency and Variability in Learning

The efficiency of instruction has always been a central consideration in American pedagogy. Skinner (1986), for example, opposed discovery activities because they do not lead students to produce reinforceable behaviors as quickly as possible. More recently, Chandler and Sweller (1991) pointed to the inefficiency of having students waste time searching for information when it would be more cognitively parsimonious to tell or show them where to look. Even so, it would be a mistake to generalize that exploration is always an inefficient use of time and cognitive resources.

In the preceding studies, we demonstrated that there can be advantages to first letting students experience the complexities of a situation and then providing information that helps them understand expert techniques and concepts in light of their earlier successes, difficulties, and questions. Vollmeyer, Burns, and Holyoak (1996), in a more cognitive paradigm, showed the value of allowing exploration over immediate correction. Even the animal literature shows benefits of slow exploration over getting the right answer as quickly as possible. For example, Verbeek, De Goede, Drent, and Wiepkema (1999) created a set of feeding sites for a species of bird (titmice). Some birds took a slower, more exploratory approach to learning the feeding sites, and others learned the feeding sites more directly. The researchers then changed the feeding sites. The birds that had taken the more exploratory approach were more effective at learning the new feeding sites. In each of these cases, exploration permits the learners to induce more about the structure and variability of the learning space, which enables them to handle new problems in that space more effectively. Effective learning for variable settings is not just about knowledge of routines and concepts; it also demands knowledge about situations to which those routines and concepts apply. Perhaps it is possible to instruct people directly about the structure and variance of a situation, but it is not obvious that the learning processes associated with telling would be the same or as effective as exploration. Obviously they would not be equivalent for the birds.

When people are being instructed for highly stable conditions where efficiency is at a premium, such as typing, then exploring variability is less important. Isolated and stable practice is very useful. But, if there is a possibility that people will need to use their learning in new situations that instruction cannot fully anticipate, then "background" variability becomes important to include in some portion of the instruction. The seminal studies by Gick and Holyoak (1983) provide valuable evidence for this point, and their results can help to overcome the intuition that the best way to teach is to include only relevant information and exclude all "noise" from the instruction. In their studies, people learned how to solve story problems, and then later received a structurally similar story problem with different surface features. For example, the learning problem might have a medical cover story and the target problem might have a military cover story, but both scenarios depend on the same solution of dividing one's forces—radiation beams or troops—and having them converge simultaneously at the target. The question of interest was what conditions of initial learning would help people transfer the convergence solution to the target problem.

Gick and Holyoak explored multiple combinations of initial learning to see which would support transfer. All the combinations worked well for learning the basic solution, but they were not equally effective for supporting transfer. They found that the most effective treatment for achieving transfer was to have subjects read two examples with different cover stories plus an explanation. This combination was more effective than a single example; more effective than an explanation without an example; and, more effective than a single example plus an explanation. It was also more effective than using two examples with similar cover stories plus an explanation. The cover stories of the two different examples were incidental "noise" for the structure of the solution. Yet, by including two different cover stories, it helped the participants learn which features of the problems were relevant (the necessity of dividing a single large force) and which were irrelevant (the medical or military context). In this case, contextual heterogeneity was critical for helping students induce which aspects of the situations were relevant. Working with two similar examples did not help as much as working with two different examples. Figure does not exist without ground. If instruction removes all background variability for the sake of efficiency, students will not be prepared for new situations where they must discern on their own what is relevant and what is extraneous.

Efficient and Constructivist Outcomes Are Not Mutually Exclusive

Thus far, we have considered the issue of efficiency from the perspective of instruction—which combinations of instruction most efficiently help students learn. The same issues of efficiency also suffuse the assessment side of the instructional coin. Are outcomes of high efficiency in knowledge application incompatible with constructivist outcomes? There are merits to this question. One possibility is that people can over-rely on well-learned and efficient routines. They can miss opportunities for learning new ways of doing things that may be even more efficient. Luchins and Luchins' (1959) famous studies of set effect or *einstellung* (rigidity of behavior) demonstrated this problem. People learned a way to solve water jug problems, and they did not let go of this solution even when it became inefficient for new problems. The second possibility is that desired outcomes that emphasize future abilities to construct knowledge will come at the expense of learning efficient solutions, even if students are eventually shown and practice efficient solutions.

A recent study suggests that the former concern is more important than the latter. Premature efficiency is the enemy of subsequent new knowledge construction, whereas early innovation permits both efficiency and constructivist outcomes. Sears (2006) examined whether constructivist outcomes that emphasize abilities to learn are incompatible with outcomes of efficient knowledge application. The study involved college students learning the logic behind the chi-square statistic (i.e., expected versus observed results). Students received a sequence of carefully designed cases. For example, one case focused on determining whether dice were loaded according to the expected probabilities. Students had to invent a procedure for computing a value that indexed their chances of being loaded. Another case asked students to invent a procedure to index whether different groups exhibited different preferences for food, when the expected probabilities are unknown. Figure 3.3 provides this example.

One factor in the study was whether students worked alone or whether they worked in pairs. The second factor involved the sequence of instruction. In one treatment, students were told the relevant procedure for each case, they practiced on that case, plus one more. (This condition would be the analog of a Lecture+Analyze condition had we included it in the studies on learning cognitive psychology.) In the other treatment, students tried to invent a way to handle each case, and then they were told the relevant procedure and practiced on the additional case. This instructional manipulation was very subtle—all the conditions received the exact same cases and the exact same procedural solutions—the only difference was the order they received the materials. The study was conducted in a laboratory so it was also possible to ensure that the time on task was identical in all conditions.

Compute an index to indicate if there are different preferences					
	Candy	Chocolate		Apples	Oranges
Children	6	14	Pigs	14	6
Adults	16	4	Horses	16	4

Figure 3.3 Students needed to derive a single numerical index (value) for each matrix by using the same formula. Students read how to compute the index first, or they tried to invent the index and then they read about the standard solution.

After completing the activities, the students received a post-test. All the students completed the post-test working individually. The test included SPS questions that assessed students' abilities to efficiently apply the procedures to relatively similar problems. The test also included a PFL assessment. The PFL assessment took the same form as the study with high school students learning about variance. Embedded in the test was a worked example that provided hints for how to extend the chi-square logic to determine reliability (per Cohen's Kappa). The question was whether students would spontaneously learn enough from the worked example so they could subsequently solve a very difficult problem that required extending the worked example to a new situation involving instrument reliability.

Figure 3.4 summarizes the relevant results. The left panel shows that students in all four conditions learned the standard procedure to about the same level according to an SPS test. Thus, the invention activities did not interfere with learning and subsequently applying the efficient solution. The right panel shows the results of the PFL assessment. Students who were told the procedure before each case did not do very well by the PFL assessment. They had not been prepared to construct knowledge given the opportunity. The students who tried to invent a solution before hearing the standard approach did better. The PFL benefit was particularly strong for the students who worked in pairs to invent solutions during the initial instruction (they did not work in pairs when completing the test or the worked example in the PFL assessment).

Sears' study provides several informative results. One result is that the seemingly inefficient activity of trying to invent solutions does not entail inefficiency in subsequent performance, *if* students have a subsequent chance to learn the

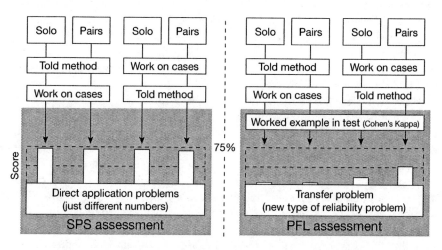

Figure 3.4 Students who tried to invent solutions before learning the canonical solution exhibited equally effective command of the procedures as students who were directly told how to solve the problems and then practiced. However, students who worked in pairs to invent solutions were far superior in their preparation to learn new methods from a worked example embedded in the text and apply them to new problems (source: adapted from Sears, 2006).

standard solution. As in the preceding studies, invention activities prepare students to learn canonical solutions and explanations quite effectively, and in this case, without an appreciable cost in overall instructional time. A second result is that being told an efficient procedure before working with the cases blocked student learning as measured by the PFL assessment. Knowing the procedure beforehand interfered with exploratory behaviors, because the students focused on the procedure rather than the situation presented in the problem. A third informative result is that the use of group discussion has specific benefits. Here we see the benefits of PFL assessments for identifying effective elements of instruction. Working individually or in groups did not make much of a difference for SPS assessments that measure efficiency. However, for constructivist outcomes, group work was beneficial—but only if the groups had an opportunity to invent solutions together. Working in groups in the context of direct instruction had no discernible benefits over working individually. These results make sense. When given direct instruction on how to solve problems, the pairs simply handed off their results to one another to check answers. In contrast, in the invention condition, the paired students talked with one another about their ideas, and this helped them explore their thoughts about the learning space more completely.

Conclusions: What Types of Activities Produce Constructivist Outcomes?

The aim of this chapter was to demonstrate the value of considering constructivist outcomes when evaluating the effectiveness of instruction. We proposed a style of assessment called Preparation for Future Learning (PFL) that seems better suited to one goal of constructivist-inspired pedagogies, which is to enable students to construct knowledge. In a PFL assessment, students receive an opportunity to construct knowledge during the assessment. The studies demonstrated that the PFL measures were sensitive to aspects of constructivist learning that standard assessments would have missed.

While we believe that PFL assessments are powerful tools and that their incorporation into mainstream educational institutions should be seriously considered, we fully acknowledge that there are significant challenges to a widespread conversion. It is a major issue, for instance, whether it will be possible to scale PFL assessments in this era of SPS testing. Establishing reliability at a level that is on a par with current standardized assessments will require a great deal of effort and collaboration among educational institutions and the organizations that oversee them. At a philosophical level, these entities would need to acknowledge the capacity for future learning as an explicit goal of instruction. We should also note that the effects described in the studies above were most likely due to the *content* knowledge the students acquired through the activities of exploring the problem space and inventing solutions. It would likely require longer and more persistent instructional interventions to affect the broader dispositions and the metacognitive capacities of students to regulate their abilities to construct knowledge on their own.

The studies presented in this chapter were specifically designed to demonstrate that PFL assessments, which are consistent with constructivist outcomes, reveal effects missed by SPS assessments. Now that this evidence has been established, at least so far, we hope that others will consider the inclusion of PFL assessments in their own research. It should be relatively easy to add PFL assessments to most instructional studies. Future applications of PFL assessments do not have to use the specialized research designs employed here, which were designed to demonstrate the validity of PFL assessments.

In the examples provided here, the PFL assessments all involved learning from verbal materials such as a lecture or worked example. However, one can imagine PFL assessments that are more interactive and take other forms. For example, technological environments make it possible for students to receive feedback to guide their learning at test. Presumably, good prior instruction would help students learn how to use feedback to construct knowledge. The work of Chen and Klahr (1999) provides an excellent instance. Students learned to conduct experiments in a computer environment, and the outcome measures included how well students arranged and used feedback from their own experiments to keep learning. Chen and Klahr called the most successful condition "direct instruction," but this is a gloss on the intricacy of their intervention which included many elements of exploration coupled with direct explanation.

Given that the constructivist measures revealed unique outcomes in the studies above, we can begin to map backward to discern what learning processes caused the effects. The preceding instructional designs were all variants on a common genre of instruction. This genre, which we describe below, does not include many of the elements that other educators consider important and include in their constructivist-inspired instruction; for example, the instruction presented above was not personally relevant to the students in any interesting way. Therefore, our observations are not meant to say that this genre of instruction is the only or the best model of instruction. Rather, we want to identify the elements and processes that seemed responsible for the current results. Our conclusions are necessarily speculative, because these studies were designed to isolate outcomes of learning not causes.

The successful activities described here share several common design ingredients (for more details, see Schwartz, Martin, & Nasir, 2005). One element was the use of contrasting cases. In each of the activities, students received materials that highlighted important features by using carefully selected contrasts. For example, in the study by Sears (2006), students received materials that juxtaposed cases where the expected values could be known based on probability (e.g., dice) versus cases where the expected values had to be inferred (e.g., by using the marginal means). Other cases contrasted ratio differences versus absolute frequency differences, and so forth. These contrasts helped students notice the important structural features and sources of variability in the learning space, as well as recognize what sources of variability are irrelevant. Although we do not have a hard rule, it has been our experience that adolescents and adults can handle cases that target three to four conceptually central contrasts at a time.

When students engage in the inquiry and exploratory activities that comprise much of constructivist instruction, they are also engaging contrasting cases. For example, they may notice that two different actions lead to two different effects. A risk of poorly developed inquiry activities is that there can be too many contrasts, some less useful than others. While a broad range of possible contrasts will uncover many interesting and useful student ideas, too many contrasts make it difficult for students to discern which variables and interactions are most important. Moreover, in large classes, different students may follow the implications of different contrasts, which will make it difficult to "pull it together" for all the students in a class. In our approach, we pre-figure the contrasts to simplify the instructional task.

A second important feature was that the students were asked to invent representations for the cases, using symbolic procedures or graphs. This was important for four reasons. The first, as demonstrated by Sears, is that students will not notice the structures highlighted by the contrasts if they are told at the outset how to use the correct procedure. They will focus on the procedure rather than the situational structures that make the procedure useful. Inventing the procedure focuses them on the situation and the procedural issues.

The second reason is that invention prepares students to appreciate the "why" captured inside the canonical solution. By working to invent solutions themselves, they begin to understand the issues that led to the design of the expert theory or procedure.

The third reason for having students do representational activities is that the goal of much school instruction is to help students learn to understand and use the compact symbolic representations and theories that experts use to organize complexity. Having students work towards these representations sets the stage for learning the canonical accounts.

A final reason for the invention activities is that students enjoy them, and there appears to be more engaged thinking and positive effects as a result. Students treat these activities as original production activities that promote creative thinking through the exploration of possible solution paths and representational artifacts. The solutions that students produce are sometimes suboptimal, but in general, students are not wrong in their inventions. Rather, their inventions simply do not handle all the cases or generalize to cases yet to be seen. When confronted with their "partial accuracy" students come to appreciate their own work, the work of others, and the standard solution.

Returning to the overall sequence of instruction, the third important feature that we have emphasized here is the eventual delivery of a comprehensive account of the cases. The goal is to prepare students to understand the account. The activities we have described are not discovery activities in the sense of expecting students to discover the canonical solutions on their own. Activities that require "correct" student discovery can place a significant burden on instructors to artfully steer activity without "spilling the beans." Hills (2007), for example, reports that constructivist pedagogies can increase teacher anxiety. By removing the "pressure" of discovering the right answer for a lesson to be successful, students and teachers are liberated to explore the learning space more fully. The canonical solution can be presented after the exploration.

A Final Thought

There are multiple learning mechanisms and outcomes, and different situations can elicit them to varying degrees. Instructional theory can only be improved by understanding the many ways that people learn, how to engage the relevant processes, how these processes interact and how to measure the types of knowledge and performance they yield. Yet, among all the different ways of learning, two clusters have been consistently called out and pitted against each other: constructivist-type learning versus direct-instruction type learning. It did not have to be this way. The instructional debate could instead have centered on other learning processes, for example, spatial versus social. For that matter, the enduring argument could have been about individual differences versus the "average" student, or a host of other issues. Nonetheless, the issue of constructivism versus direct instruction has dominated American educational debates on instructional technique for a very long time (Duffy & Jonassen, 1992).

The debate comes in many forms: passive versus active learning; shaping behavior versus discovery; inquiry versus authority; student centered versus teacher centered; school-as-life versus school-as-preparation-for-life. We suspect that the underlying fuel for much of this debate are (tacit) issues of free choice, expression, and agency as applied to students in classrooms. Through a loose analogy, direct instruction has been associated with controlling students, and constructivism has been associated with self-determination. We are not up to engaging this debate on the basis of evidence. One reason is that—writ large—the merits of being controlled and being self-determined is a normative, cultural question more than it is an empirical question about learning. As Dewey (1916) points out, these issues are deeply related to larger underlying questions in our society. Scientific data cannot prove the principles that define the outcomes we hold most dear. Data can only help us determine how to achieve those outcomes.

Yet, even if we limit ourselves to a narrow empirical question about content learning, we still cannot answer what types of instruction lead to the outcome of helping students construct knowledge (and conceivably, thereby be in a better position to make the choices that determine their lives). Empirical research has been using the wrong outcome measures of instruction. We have being using non-constructivist assessments in an era of constructivist beliefs.

Question: Sweller. *The "learning to learn" goal that is the focus of your chapter is highly desirable and has been pursued for several generations. In this chapter it is seen, correctly I believe, as an aspect of constructivism. My concerns are that I do not believe the goal can be reconciled with any viable cognitive architecture and more importantly, there is no body of supporting evidence that the goal can be attained. My questions concern the experiments claimed to support the basic proposition. As far as I could ascertain, while all of the experiments described were concerned with and indeed demonstrated enhanced learning under various constructivist regimes, none of them demonstrated enhanced learning outside of the content area being taught. If we claim to be preparing students for future* *learning, should we not be able to demonstrate enhanced learning in areas unrelated to those in which the future learning techniques were taught? I do not believe our cognitive architecture supports such teachable/learnable strategies but you presumably do.*

Reply: Schwartz et al. There are two parts to this question. The first is the presumption of a correct theory of cognitive architecture. If true, then the work of cognitive science is done, and all that is left is to draw out a few implications. We are not of this mind. The second part of your question, which we like much more, asks us to differentiate two elements of preparedness for future learning and transfer. One element is the "content" knowledge of a domain that helps people make sense of new related content. This is what our studies developed for the high school students—they learned the deep structure of the important concept of variability that carries through the domain of statistics. It is why they were prepared to transfer these ideas to learn about the more difficult concept of normalizing data. (In this respect, our work differs from the older "learning to learn" literature that focused on abstract skill instruction, for example in logic, that could conceivably transfer to any domain, but psychologically did not.) At the same time, the students were learning to think about a very general phenomenon, namely variance. Unlike learning a procedure about a specific device, there is some hope that they learned powerful content that can affect how they reason about the very many situations where variance is an important feature.

We think it is an incorrect read of the empirical literature to assume that people cannot learn strategies, concepts, and dispositions that transfer to improve learning across a broad class of situations. The evidence is quite clear that people can learn to read well, think in statistical terms, reason by analogy, control variables in research, and so forth. These are not domain general thinking skills in the sense of logic, which can be applied to all topics. Rather, they occupy the middle ground between what Newell and Simon (1972) called (a) weak methods—problem-solving methods that apply to all situations; and, (b) strong methods—methods that arise from knowledge about a specific domain. Perhaps this middle level should be called "protean" methods. They have the potential for flexible use within a domain and related fields that share similar underlying empirical structures.

A good example of a protean method for problem solving and learning might be the construction of visualizations to aid in the management of information. Creating visual representations is a fine way to help learn the structure inherent in complex information, and it can work across many domains. Lee Martin (Martin & Schwartz, in press) found that advanced graduate students in science are more likely to make visual representations to organize novel information than science undergraduates, even when the task has nothing to do with the topic of their graduate studies and the task could be completed without visualizations. Thus, the graduate students exhibited a relatively far transfer of a learning and problem-solving method that was not tied to any specific content, at least in the sense of content about biology or computer science or engineering.

What is notable about Martin's finding is that both the graduate and undergraduate students were very capable of making appropriate visualizations—the undergraduate students just did not bother. Given that it took several years of graduate school for the students to learn it was worth the time to make visualizations of data, it seems that protean learning strategies and their likely transfer take some time to develop. We suspect that given enough time, learners who go through our invention activities would develop some protean skills and dispositions associated with innovating new ideas, which is a type of learning that is quite different from replicating what one is told.

Question: Sweller. *In the research you describe, prior to being presented a lecture or text to read, learners were given several relevant cases that they were asked to analyze in order to attempt to find patterns. Schwartz and Bransford (1998) found that analyzing cases proved superior to summarizing the text while Schwartz and Martin (2004) found that analyzing cases was superior to being explicitly taught how to carry out a relevant calculation. It was concluded that exploration was superior to explicit instruction. My questions concern the appropriateness of the control groups used in these studies. If multiple factors are varied simultaneously, as they were in these experiments, does this procedure not break the "vary one thing at a time" rule essential to all randomized, controlled experiments, resulting in it being impossible to determine exactly what caused the effects? Can the authors of this chapter throw any light on why the obvious control groups seem never to be used?*

Reply: Schwartz et al. This is an important question. Thank you for the opportunity to clarify our approach to cognitive and instructional experimentation, which we see as different endeavors. There are three quick answers. One answer is that the first two studies in the chapter were on measurement and not about isolating singular causes. Until we measure the right thing, studies on causes or conditions of learning are irrelevant. Measurement drives science, and as the current climate of testing in the United States indicates, it also drives instruction.

The second answer is that we very much like the idea of titrating the specifics of our instruction in systematic research, and there are many people who are currently working on this problem. For example, the study by Sears, described at the end of the chapter, is a nice example where information and time on task were held constant, and the only difference was the order of the materials. We believe this is what you asked for in your question.

The third answer is that we do not favor the idea of simultaneously trying to (a) titrate what psychological interactions cause our instruction to be effective, and (b) conduct efficacy research to show that our instruction is more effective than some variant of standard practice. This ends up watering down one or both models of instruction, because people try to make the instruction similar, except for one thing. There are very many examples of this mistake, where researchers end up comparing two sub-optimal models of instruction that have the sole merit of differing on only one variable. For instance, comparisons of learning from diagrams versus animations run into this kind of problem, because people make the animations just like the diagram except that it moves (the one difference); this limits the types of interactions that animations can naturally provide such as pausing, replaying, slow motion, and so forth. Proving what is better and proving the mechanisms that lead to particular outcomes are very different endeavors.

Reaction to Schwartz et al.'s reply: Sweller. *I have two reactions to your reply to the questions. First, you seem to dismiss the importance of using cognitive architecture in instructional design because it presumes "a correct theory of cognitive architecture." Should we really dismiss cognitive architecture from instructional design so easily? Second, I really do not think I am wrong about varying one thing at a time in instructional, cognitive, or any other experiments. That does not prevent factorial experiments to look at interactions nor does it prevent us from investigating the effects of "pausing, replaying, slow motion, and so forth" on animation. It is just that if you vary all of these at once, you do not know which one or which combination caused any observed effects. Running properly controlled experiments that look at individual factors and interactions between factors is essential—and routine— irrespective of whether we are looking at psychological or instructional issues.*

Response to Sweller: Schwartz et al. We certainly did not mean to imply that conducting one-thing-at-a-time experiments is a bad thing to do. We do it a lot. As we have started to move into neuroscience, it has been humbling to see what "control" means in this context. For instance, in a normal behavioral experiment, we would never care about whether the learner turns the worksheet slightly while reading. In the context of a brain scan, different angles of stimulus presentation would be a terrible loss of control. That said, there are other types of productive research designs besides changing only one thing at a time, including fieldwork, epidemiological studies, and so on. Our point is that in the context of classic factorial designs it is important to separate efficacy research from causal research, and it is important to further separate causal research about external conditions of learning from causal research that tests psychological theories.

Why is it important to keep these separate? It has something to do with the rhetoric of the constructivism debate. Can we compare direct instruction and constructivist-inspired instruction by only changing one variable? Imagine you create a model of direct instruction to teach employees about procedures for working with electrical equipment. Now imagine that somebody thinks they can do it better using a more constructivist approach. If they take an efficacy approach and compare their constructivist instruction to your direct instruction approach, you might complain they did not change only one thing at a time, per causal research. On the other hand, if they only study two variations of their own constructivist-inspired instruction, you will complain that they did not prove their method is more effective than yours. No wonder there is so little research that compares direct instruction and constructivism. People should be clear on whether they are testing the features of their own instruction or comparing their instruction against the best version of the other camp. The latter would not vary one variable at a time.

There is also a second, deeper issue: whether the one-variable-at-a-time research is in fact testing a causal theory or only testing whether one feature is more effective than another for a specific model of instruction. For instance, in your own excellent and compelling empirical studies you have confronted this challenge and explicitly acknowledged this issue. Your instructional results are consistent with the theory of cognitive load, but they do not directly test the internal causal mechanisms that give rise to this theory. The evidence is circumstantial with respect to the theory. To demonstrate that working-memory overload is responsible for a decline in performance, it is necessary to do more intrusive designs that involve things like double dissociations, interference paradigms, parametric loads on working memory, working memory covariates, attention tracking, and so on. Moreover, it would also be important to control secondary psychological effects like anxiety, which might confound the isolation of working memory as the causal mechanism. Suddenly one would be doing psychological research that has less and less ecological validity for conditions of instruction.

So, what is the point here? Changing one feature at a time in the context of instructional research is a good way to find out what works for your brand of instruction. It is not a good way to compare different instructional paradigms. It is rarely a good way to gather hard-nosed evidence to prove theories about internal learning mechanisms, *unless* one is willing to leave the realm of effective instruction to implement the very tight and often unnatural learning conditions that can isolate psychological processes in a precise way.

Question: Fletcher. *I appreciated this chapter a lot—especially the focus on PFL and beyond that real data! On constructivist issues! And that's not to overlook some clever designs to produce the data. My question relates to your focus on PFL as an assessment issue. Isn't it just a transfer task—something we know how to do? Is the assessment issue simply a matter of deciding whether or not to do it? It seems to me that an important outcome of your work is that you focus on a constructivist outcome that we actually know how to measure, allowing us to get serious about designing instructional environments that promote it.*

Reply: Schwartz et al. Our work is done! Thank you! Yes, the point is that if we can change our assessments, we will be in a much better position to learn how to design instruction that promotes constructivist outcomes. There is a subtlety in here, however. Most transfer tests have taken a sequestered problem-solving format (SPS), where people can only rely on their prior knowledge to solve the target problem. The typical metrics in an SPS transfer task include speed, accuracy, low variability, first-time correct transfer. SPS transfer measures are often a good way to separate instruction that leads to understanding versus memorization, so they are very useful to include as an assessment. However, SPS measures are about the efficiency with which people can replicate prior behaviors in a new context. In contrast, PFL transfer measures examine whether people can adapt and learn given a new situation. There has not been a tremendous amount of instructional or psychological research that uses PFL measures, but it is increasing. So, at this time, there is no off-the-shelf book of PFL assessments or instructional methods, although we have our beliefs about how to do these things. To make further headway, it will be important to address two key problems of PFL transfer. The first is the knowledge problem: What types of experiences help people develop the knowledge that can transfer to new settings to learn? The second, and more insidious of the two, is the inertia problem: What types of experiences make people feel it is worth the trouble to use what they have learned in new ways? This has not been addressed effectively by the cognitive literature, and we suspect that many demonstrations of failed transfer happen because people did not care enough to see if there were other ways to solve a given problem (cf. Pea et al., 2007). To help address these two problems through research, it would be wonderful if other people started using PFL transfer measures, so the field can start finding out what prepares people to construct knowledge when there is not an instructor telling them what to do.

Question: Fletcher. *I heartily agree that prior knowledge has a big impact on the amount and speed of learning in direct instruction, but doesn't prior knowledge have a far greater impact on constructivist-oriented instruction? Isn't it possible to employ direct instruction given far less prior knowledge on the part of the learner than we need to employ constructivist-oriented instruction? Or does the impact of prior knowledge depend more directly on the different types of instructional objectives likely to be sought with direct instruction, aiming lower in learning taxonomies, versus constructivist instruction, aiming higher in learning taxonomies?*

Reply: Schwartz et al. It is interesting that you predict that direct instruction works better for low prior knowledge. We would have predicted just the opposite. If the goal is to teach kids to tie their shoes, then direct instruction seems like a very good approach, if direct instruction includes opportunities to ask questions, try it out, and get useful feedback. But, if the kids have never seen a shoe, then it might be worth letting them explore shoes and laces a bit. Prior knowledge is not a monolithic construct, and there are different types of prior knowledge. So, we agree with your second option: Different instructional goals interact with different types of prior knowledge, and this interaction requires different instructional techniques.

Let us expand a bit by asking first, do experts or novices learn better from direct instruction? Take the case of giving a lecture. If it is a professional talk you count on the prior knowledge of the audience to make sense of what you are telling them. Despite slips and omissions, the audience can still get something out of the talk. Moreover, they will know the right questions to ask so they can clarify what they are learning. Now imagine you give the same professional talk to novices. There is a good chance they will not gain very much from the talk because they do not have sufficient prior experience of your particular topic. Even if you do a lot of work to ensure that you set up their prior knowledge just right, if you omit some critical information or use a slightly imperfect example, they will not be able to recover. They probably won't even know where to start asking questions.

Now, one might object that this contrast is unfair, because the lecture for a novice should be simpler than a lecture for an expert. Exactly! Experts can learn by being told more effectively than novices, if the content is in their domain.

If we look beyond the immediate lecture, direct instruction done poorly can also have a secondary effect. This involves the "practice" that comes after direct instruction, for example, when doing a problem set. Experts already know something about the structure of the domain, so they can benefit by just practicing the procedure. In contrast, the novices do not. Ideally, during the practice, novices will start to learn something about the structure of the problem space. But, direct instruction (and a lifetime of schooling) tends to focus students' attention to the told-solution procedures, not problem situations, so students learn answers to a problem space they never come to understand.

Next, we ask if novices or experts learn more effectively from "constructivist" activities. Again, the experts win. As one instance, the first author not-so-humbly submits he is better at designing effective psychological inquiry to learn something than first-year undergraduates. Thus, there is a main effect, where experts are better than novices when learning in their domain, regardless of the two types of learning experiences. This main effect is likely to swamp any of the subtle differences in the relative benefits of one type of instruction over another for novices versus experts.

Nevertheless, the relative comparison does help to highlight the challenge of constructivism for novices. Novices do not know how to learn very effectively by these methods. Good inquiry takes some time to develop and differs somewhat across domains (e.g., lawyers engage in a different type of inquiry than geologists do). This means that instructional designers have the substantial burden of making instructional materials that can guide novices to construct knowledge effectively through inquiry, discovery, and what have you. But this does not mean that it is a burden that should be avoided. We think that instructional designers make a mistake when they give in to the contention that making constructivist materials for novices is so difficult that it is better to just directly tell students what to do, because we know how to do that well enough. We also think there are many examples of effective constructivist instruction out there, even if researchers have not compared this instruction to a variant of direct instruction. After all, if the goal is to develop effective constructivist pedagogies, then it seems like an inefficient use of precious resources to mount a direct-instruction comparison. The "what works" standards for this type of racehorse comparison—constructivism versus direct instruction—require a minimum 3-month intervention in schools with very many students and difficult-to-implement sampling schemes. Little of the research that people cite in favor of direct instruction has met these standards of evidence.

Question: Clark. *Thanks for an articulate and entertaining chapter. It seemed balanced, insightful, and focused on moving the discussion to topics more comfortable to advocates of constructivism such as motivation and instructional goals. First a question to clarify your view on the main topic of the debate:*

Since you acknowledge that constructivism has generally not succeeded at supporting learning better than guided instruction ("too large and general," "not at the right level for describing specific instructional decisions"), should we close the door on that argument and move to discuss interventions that influence motivation to learn and reopen the dialogue about the conditions that promote the further transfer of knowledge?

Reply: Schwartz et al. We want to head off the lurking possibility of a presumptive question. If "guided instruction" should be translated into "direct instruction" in this question, then I think we should also point out that direct instruction has generally *not* succeeded at supporting learning better than constructivism. To our knowledge, the studies favoring direct instruction tend to be small-scale, use limited measures and time horizons, pick "skill acquisition" or simple concepts as the learning goals, and distort the constructivist control conditions. This makes sense. How would a person who studies direct instruction know how to make a good constructivist lesson and, of course, vice versa? Perhaps what we need is to find the world's greatest constructivist instructional designer and the world's greatest direct instructional designer and put them head-to-head in a big clinical trial. It is interesting to anticipate their negotiation on the terms of the head-to-head comparison. We guess that the negotiation would stall on the outcomes to be measured. By the end, both designers would concede that each form of instruction is generally better suited to particular outcomes. From there, they could argue on philosophical, economic, or other grounds for why their likely outcomes are more important. If "guided instruction" means a learning situation where there has been a careful arrangement of situations to support learning, whether by discovery, telling, or whatever, then we heartily agree. Well-arranged conditions for learning are going to be better than "sink or swim" versions of constructivism for most outcomes.

We assume that your point is really that terms like "guided instruction," "constructivism," and even the term "direct instruction" are too vague for specific instructional decisions. We agree completely. General theories of knowledge acquisition are too monolithic for moment-to-moment instructional decisions across a variety of contexts. We prefer Gagne's original approach of matching specific learning experiences for specific learning outcomes, and the field has learned a lot since his time that could be very useful in its precision. Even so, we are not sure we want to completely close the door on the debate. As we argued, the significance of constructivism for instruction is that it reminds us that there is more at stake for learners than being able to execute a skill when cued to do so. And, of course, direct instruction reminds us that free-form constructivism is inefficient for some outcomes. We also agree that some form of motivation needs to be let back into the cognitive lexicon, and that transfer is important for domains where students will need to adapt.

Question: Clark. *Isn't it possible that farther transfer is possible when instructivist-guided support employs what has been called varied (or variable) practice and haven't most of the reviews of past research on this issue concluded that the evidence only supported gradual and limited transfer despite claims to the contrary?*

Reply: Schwartz et al. Transfer, transfer, transfer … It is nearly as contentious as constructivism versus direct instruction in some corners of academia. It is too big to handle here, though it is worth noting that if people could not learn for transfer, then they would be awfully stupid every time they walked into a new situation. A repeated finding—one that predates the cognitive revolution—is that a key to transfer is the opportunity to learn the deep structure beneath the surface elements of a situation. This way, the learners can recognize that structure in a new situation that may have different surface features and thereby transfer. "Variable practice" is one approach to this problem, because the hope is that students will learn what is common (i.e., the deep structure) amid the variability of problems and such.

The trick is how to get people to notice the deep structure in situations. Common models of direct instruction can inadvertently block learners from noticing that structure. For example, we just finished gathering data that compared two treatments. In the procedure-given treatment, children were told a formula (density), and they had to apply it to a set of cases to compute the answers. In the invent-the-procedure treatment, children were told to invent a formula to apply to the cases (which they were able to do). The next day, we asked the children from both treatments to remember the cases the best they could. The students in the invent-the-procedure condition recreated the deep structure of the cases. In contrast, the students in the procedure-given condition recreated the formulaic answers. They did not remember the structure of the cases. Moreover, they showed more memory for incidental surface features than the invent-the-procedure condition. Thus, a risk of direct instruction is that learners will focus on the procedure instead of the situation, and they will only notice the eye-catching surface features. This is exactly what prevents people from exhibiting transfer, because they never learn to recognize the structure beneath the surface features. It is notable that many of the instances of failed transfer involved direct instruction; now, we have some evidence why. The study participants learned the solution procedure, but they did not learn about the structure of situations for which that procedure might be useful.

Reaction to Schwartz's reply: Clark. *Transfer is one of the two issues that seem to be raised most often by constructivists when defending discovery and criticizing strong guidance (the other argument has to do with "ill-defined domains" of knowledge). One of the reasons that the transfer issue is so contentious may relate to the fact that transfer studies are most often designed and conducted by people who share a bias about transfer. It is not totally surprising that most of us find evidence for our own theory when we design the treatments that represent not only our approach but also the views of people who disagree with us. I doubt that I'm the best person to design a constructivist treatment in a study examining questions about the transfer potential of guided instruction. What seems to be called for is a series of collaborative studies where people who disagree about what works collaborate on design and implementation and agree ahead to jointly publish the results. It would be productive if we identified and tried to resolve our differences on thorny core issues such as the operational definition (or utility) of different types of transfer and knowledge domains; the metrics for measuring transfer; and the impact of constructivist or guided instruction on transfer. While we will still find opportunities to disagree, the* *disagreements will be based on evidence from studies that we jointly designed and conducted.*

References

Barron, B. (2004). Learning ecologies for technological fluency: Gender and experience differences. *Journal of Educational Computing Research, 31*(1), 1–36.

Boaler, J. (2002). *Experiencing school mathematics: Traditional and reform approaches to teaching and their impact on student learning.* Mahwah, NJ: Erlbaum.

Bransford, J. D., & Schwartz, D. L. (1999). Rethinking transfer: A simple proposal with multiple implications. In A. Iran-Nejad & P. D. Pearson (Eds.), *Review of research in education* (24, pp. 61–101). Washington, DC: American Educational Research Association.

Chandler, P., & Sweller, J. (1991). Cognitive load theory and the format of instruction. *Cognition and Instruction, 8,* 293–332.

Chen, Z., & Klahr, D. (1999). All other things being equal: Acquisition and transfer of the control of variables strategy. *Child Development, 70,* 1098–1120.

Dewey, J. D. (1916). *Democracy and education.* New York: Macmillan.

Duffy, T. M., & Jonassen, D. H. (1992). Constructivism: New implications for instructional technology. In T. M. Duffy & H. H. Jonassen (Eds.), *Constructivism and the technology of instruction: A conversation* (pp. 1–16). Hillsdale, NJ: Erlbaum.

Gagne, R. (1985). *The conditions of learning* (4th ed.). New York: Holt, Rinehart & Winston.

Gick, M. L., & Holyoak, K. J. (1983). Schema induction and analogical transfer. *Cognitive Psychology, 15,* 1–38.

Hills, T. (2007). Is constructivism risky? Social anxiety, classroom participation, competitive game play and constructivist preferences in teacher development. *Teacher Development, 11,* 335–352.

Hmelo-Silver, C. E., Duncan, R. G., & Chinn, C. A. (2007). Scaffolding and achievement in problem-based and inquiry learning: A response to Kirschner, Sweller, and Clark (2006). *Educational Psychologist, 42,* 99–107.

Kirschner, P. A., Sweller, J., & Clark, R. E. (2006). Why minimal guidance during instruction does not work: An analysis of the failure of constructivist, discovery, problem-based, experiential, and inquiry-based teaching. *Educational Psychologist, 41*(2), 75–86.

Klahr, D., & Nigam, M. (2004). The equivalence of learning paths in early science instruction: Effects of direct instruction and discovery learning. *Psychological Science, 15,* 661–667.

Lillard, A., & Else-Quest, N. (2006, September). Evaluating Montessori education. *Science, 313,* 1893–1894.

Luchins, A. S., & Luchins, E. H. (1959). *Rigidity of behavior: A variational approach to the effect of einstellung.* Eugene, OR: University of Oregon Books.

Martin, L., & Schwartz, D. L. (in press). Prospective adaptation in the use of representational tools. *Cognition & Instruction.*

Mayer, R. (2004). Should there be a three-strikes rule against pure discovery learning? The case for guided methods of instruction. *American Psychologist, 59,* 14–19.

Newell, A., & Simon, H. (1972). *Human problem solving.* Englewood Cliffs, NJ: Prentice-Hall.

Okita, S. Y., Bailenson, J., & Schwartz, D. L. (2007). The mere belief of social interaction improves learning. In D. S. McNamara & J. G. Trafton (Eds.), *The proceedings of the*

29th meeting of the Cognitive Science Society (pp. 1355–1360). August, Nashville, TN: Cognitive Science Society.

Pea, R. D., Goldman, S., Martin, L., Blair, K. P., Booker, A., Esmonde, I., & Jimenez, O. (2007). Situations and values in family mathematics. In C. A. Chinn, G. Erkens, & S. Puntambekar (Eds.), *Proceedings of CSCL-2007 (Computer-supported collaborative learning)* (pp. 26–35). Mahwah, NJ: Erlbaum Associates.

Reber, A. S. (1976). Implicit learning of synthetic languages: The role of instructional set. *Journal of Experimental Psychology: Human Learning & Memory, 2*(1), 88–94.

Russell, S. H., Hancock, M. P., & McCullough, J. (2007, April). Benefits of undergraduate research experiences. *Science, 316,* 548–549.

Schwartz, D. L., & Bransford, J. D. (1998). A time for telling. *Cognition & Instruction, 16,* 475–522.

Schwartz, D. L., Bransford, J. D., & Sears, D. L. (2005). Efficiency and innovation in transfer. In J. Mestre (Ed.), *Transfer of learning from a modern multidisciplinary perspective* (pp. 1–51). Greenwich, CT: Information Age Publishing.

Schwartz, D. L., & Martin, T. (2004). Inventing to prepare for learning: The hidden efficiency of original student production in statistics instruction. *Cognition & Instruction, 22,* 129–184.

Schwartz, D. L., Martin, T., & Nasir, N. (2005). Designs for knowledge evolution: Towards a prescriptive theory for integrating first- and second-hand knowledge. In P. Gardenfors & P. Johansson (Eds.), *Cognition, education, and communication technology* (pp. 21–54). Mahwah, NJ: Erlbaum.

Sears, D. (2006). *Effects of innovation versus efficiency tasks on collaboration and learning.* Unpublished dissertation. Stanford University, Stanford, CA.

Seger, C. A., Prabhakaran, V., Poldrack, R., & Gabrieli, J. D. E. (2000). Neuronal activity differs between explicit and implicit learning of artificial grammar strings: An fMRI study. *Psychobiology, 28,* 283–292.

Skinner, B. F. (1986). Programmed instruction revisited. *Phi Delta Kappan, 68,* 103–110.

Slamecka, N. J., & Graf, P. (1978). The generation effect: Delineation of a phenomenon. *Journal of Experimental Psychology: Human Learning and Memory, 6,* 592–604.

Verbeek, M. E. M., De Goede, P., Drent, P. J., & Wiepkema, P. R. (1999). Individual behavioural characteristics and dominance in aviary groups of great tits. *Behaviour, 136,* 23–48.

Vollmeyer, R., Burns, B., & Holyoak, K. (1996). The impact of goal specificity on strategy use and the acquisition of problem structure. *Cognitive Science, 20,* 75–100.

4 Taking Guided Learning Theory to School

Reconciling the Cognitive, Motivational, and Social Contexts of Instruction

Phillip Herman and Louis M. Gomez
University of Pittsburgh

In this chapter we explore the implications of guided learning theory for schooling. Kirschner, Sweller, and Clark (2006) propose a theory of learning based on cognitive-load theory that stresses the limits of working memory. Because of these known limits on human memory, learners need forms of guidance that minimize memory load during instruction. This theory of learning led Kirschner et al. to embrace direct instruction as the most effective pedagogy for schooling. Although guidance may be extremely important for effective instruction, we differ with Kirschner and colleagues in their assertions that inquiry-focused instruction is necessarily unguided and that direct instruction is the only way to provide guidance in schools.

Kirschner et al. are silent on some of the most important challenges of schooling. In particular, they do not explicitly attend to three schooling issues that teachers, administrators, and communities must regularly grapple with: how to motivate students; how instruction needs to be sensitive to the particular social contexts in which instruction unfolds; and how instruction should be consistent with the larger purposes of schooling such as, for example, supporting the development of a scientifically informed citizenry. Without addressing these elements of schooling, the fundamental insights about the importance of guidance in learning may be lost to the world of school practice. To advance the discussion of guided learning theory and its implications for instruction, we will examine ways in which this theory can be reconceptualized and applied to some of these core issues of schooling. We hope our discussion can contribute to clarifying the role that guided learning theory can play in building comprehensive instructional regimes (Cohen, Raudenbush, & Ball, 2003; Lagemann, 2002; Raudenbush, 2005) that are more likely to have an impact on practice in schools.

Kirschner et al. argue that forms of instruction that have variously been labeled inquiry- and problem-based are not and do not seek to be "guided." We disagree. In the domain in which we work, science education, there have been numerous and sustained efforts to design learning environments that are inquiry-focused and work to provide significant guidance to learners. We agree that guidance is critically important to the actions of both learners and, as we will argue, teachers. However, it does not follow from this insight that schools should be limited to direct instructional methods and curricula. We believe inquiry instruction can be guided and still promote the kind of learning and engagement intended by its designers. One key goal of the chapter is to broaden the notion of guidance so that guidance can be better contextualized in instructional routines and tools. Kirschner et al.'s description of guidance is likely too constrained to have a broad impact on instruction in schools. To become useful in schools, any instructional program needs to address some of the core needs and goals of learners and teachers in classrooms. To do so means that, at a minimum, the purposes of schools, student motivation, and the social contexts of instruction should be addressed by the proposed instructional program. These core elements of schooling need to be better accounted for in the discussion of guidance in learning, particularly when Kirschner et al. propose that inquiry instruction should be abandoned. Toward the end of this chapter, we use an example from our own work that we think demonstrates that instruction can be both inquiry-oriented and highly guided. We begin with a description of some of the key elements of the theory of guidance in learning described by Kirschner et al. and their entailments, as we understand them.

Kirschner and colleagues argue that human cognitive architecture and, specifically, the architecture of long-term memory, is now sufficiently understood so as to "provide us with the ultimate justification for instruction. The aim of all instruction is to alter long-term memory" (Kirschner et al., 2006, p. 77). They also claim that evidence from empirical studies over the last decades indicates that minimally guided instruction (whether inquiry, project-based, discovery, etc.) is less effective based on learning outcomes than more guided instruction. Therefore, instructional regimes that offer little guidance to students should be abandoned. Another criticism of minimally guided instruction is that instructional designers have misguidedly equated the goals of learning with the means. For example, Kirschner et al. note that many science programs encourage students to engage in open-ended investigations so as to mimic the work of scientists. They deem this approach, in which students discover the problems they want to study as well as the relevant variables of interest to any particular problem, to be in conflict with what is now known about human cognitive architecture. They warn that the epistemology of science should not be the basis of the pedagogy by which students are taught about science. Methodologically, they argue that only randomized, controlled experiments provide useful evidence about the effectiveness of instruction and that any evidence, if it exists, for the efficacy of minimally guided instruction in learning fails to meet this standard. Finally, they assert that it is the burden of those who advocate for minimally guided programs to explain how such programs are not in conflict with what is known about human cognitive architecture.

Though we will not provide an extended discussion of all aspects of the argument, we next want to analyze and clarify certain key ideas that will be discussed throughout the chapter. Guidance, as others have pointed out, remains somewhat unclear from the discussion to date (Koedinger & Aleven, 2007; Wise &

O'Neill, Chapter 5, this volume). For Kirschner et al., it appears that guidance means something like using worked-out examples in learning. Also, guidance likely translates into direct instruction with minimal "searching of the problem space" by students, which is thought to put an undue burden on working memory. Kirschner et al. are better able to describe and critique minimally guided instructional programs than they are able to provide details about the pedagogical features of a "maximally" guided instructional regime in school settings. For example, Koedinger and Aleven (2007) point out that the work cited by Kirschner and colleagues is not precise enough in describing when, and under what circumstances, more guidance or assistance should be provided to learners. An important goal of this chapter is to think more deeply about what guidance means in schools, not just for students but also teachers. We also want to explore ways in which the concept of guidance can be expanded to address the motivational and social-contextual challenges of schools in more coherent and instructionally practicable regimes.

The Dynamics of Learning in Schools

To meaningfully affect practice, insights from studies about how people learn should be incorporated into larger instructional regimes in schools. Schooling, to a large extent, consists of instructional regimes that are instantiated in and supported by instructional routines and tools. Instructional regimes involve the coherent arrangement of constituent resources of schooling such as content matter, incentives, and teacher and student actions in order to reach specified goals. Instructional regimes unfold in complex school contexts and in some cases can be limited to one classroom or to a particular subject matter. In other cases, instructional regimes stretch across multiple classrooms and domains, as in whole school reform efforts. Implementation of instructional regimes in classrooms is significantly shaped by the development of well-specified instructional routines. Instructional routines are a set of actions that are carried out principally by teachers and students within learning contexts. These routines help teachers and students understand what to do next in instruction. Examples of instructional routines include: working with peers on a problem; interpreting and acting on assessment information; and reading science texts. Instructional routines rely broadly on tools. Tools can be materials like textbooks and software but can also include other supports like posters on the wall which list strategies that students can use to complete learning tasks.

Successful instructional regimes need to address some of the core needs and goals of learners and teachers in classrooms. These regimes do not unfold in isolation; they are often school- or department-wide and encompass much of a school year. Productive instructional regimes leverage all the resources of the school in clearly defined ways to reach specified learning goals. New routines and tools can be difficult to incorporate in schools because teachers do not easily change their practice. Teachers do not simply do what is "most effective" based on rigorous studies of human cognition. Instead, teachers and other stakeholders make complicated appraisals of how well instructional approaches meet their needs and the needs of their students. These appraisals often include teacher preferences such as a desire to stress particular content or use a particular pedagogy. These appraisals also consider the goals of the school in its community, and the social makeup of classrooms. These appraisals may or may not be influenced by the results of controlled studies about effective learning. If they are, teachers must be convinced that the studies translate into regimes that meet many of their needs. In their critique of minimally guided instruction, Kirschner et al. (2006) did not explicitly address important instructional challenges that inquiry approaches were at least partly intended to address. Student motivation, for instance, is absent from the discussion to date. This is particularly worth noting given that proponents of inquiry- or project-based science have stressed the motivational benefits of inquiry as a key affordance of such learning environments (Blumenfeld et al., 1991). For example, "authentic" problems were chosen not necessarily because working on authentic problems directly leads to increased learning but rather because students might be more engaged while working on problems that they perceive to be relevant to their lives. They might therefore persist longer, be more curious about the problem, and think more deeply about authentic versus non-authentic problems. Thus, inquiry regimes were designed in part to address a valid concern of teachers about how to make science instruction more motivating. An important question missing from the debate to date is whether students are more motivated in inquiry settings or in direct-instruction settings. A critique of an instructional regime is stronger when all of the relevant impacts of the regime are explicitly considered. Similarly, the construction of an instructional regime would benefit in this case by fitting discrete ideas about how people learn into school realities.

It is possible to argue that the only thing that matters as an outcome of schooling is learning, that all other elements of schooling are subordinate to learning, so that findings about how people learn are enough to form the basis of an instructional regime. In this view, the other aspects of schooling we mentioned (motivation, social contexts, and purposes) will essentially fall into place and be addressed when learning is optimized. We doubt this is likely to happen for a variety of reasons. First, school personnel are notoriously skeptical about findings from research studies of learning that are not grounded in the realities of classrooms. Teachers need specific ways to incorporate such findings in their instructional choices. Second, student motivation is not a "placeholder" for student achievement. How students affectively understand their school experiences can predict long-term development in schools. For example, a recent report by the Gates foundation (Bridgeland, DiIulio, & Morison, 2006) challenges a core assumption that students who opt to drop out of school are invariably low-achievers who cannot keep up academically. Self-report surveys of high school dropouts indicated that only 35% of the dropouts in their sample reported that "failing in school" was a major factor in dropping out, while 47% reported that a major factor was that they perceived their classes to be "not interesting." Around 70% reported being unmotivated to work hard. Though the report notes that students drop out of school for many reasons, the fact that 65% of the dropouts in their study did not drop out primarily because of low achievement is noteworthy and should challenge beliefs about achievement and persistence. Achievement is not always enough. In some cases students' motivation and affect may better predict lifelong trajectories than achievement (Lau & Roeser, 2002). Third, many educational reformers liken the complexity of the school learning system to a complex living system (cf. Lemke, 2002; Wheatley, 1999). In this perspective, individuals are connected through complex webs of relationships. Another way to understand learning as a living system is to view learning as an ecology (Zhao & Frank, 2003; Deakin Crick, McCombs, & Hadden, 2007). Zhao and Frank describe how efforts to introduce technologies in schools to increase learning have been largely ineffective, in part because such reform efforts have not taken an ecological perspective on schooling in which one must take into account the interactions of parts of a system with each other and their interactions with the whole, as well as the compatibility of reform efforts within existing school environments. For optimal learning, the climate of schools must support the factors inside and outside the learner that influence learning. For all these reasons, instructional regimes must be coherent and address as many elements of school life as possible to have the maximum impact on outcomes. Though motivational and social components of schooling are obviously complex, with a multitude of implications for instruction, we raise them in this chapter to give an idea of how a highly guided instructional regime might at least address core elements of each.

Motivation

Fostering high levels of motivation, however that is operationalized, is a key goal of schools. Motivation must be engaged and sustained for all learners in order to ensure high levels of achievement and to foster a drive toward lifelong participation in learning (Kuhn, 2007). Students vary greatly in their motivational profiles. Achievement goal theory provides one lens to think about motivation in instruction. Goal theory stresses that the purposes that students bring to learning critically determine or relate to their beliefs, behaviors, and cognitions (Ames, 1992). Some students are more intrinsically interested in learning. Others are more interested in outperforming their peers (Kaplan & Maehr, 2007). Self-efficacy is another motivation-related construct that has been shown to predict performance across individuals, tasks, and content domains (Bandura, 1997). Bandura stresses that in some cases, students' self-efficacy beliefs are better predictors of performance than objective measures of ability. Student interest, which some researchers characterize as both a state and disposition of a person, has a powerful positive effect on cognitive functioning (Hidi & Harackiewicz, 2000). Interest influences academic performance across individuals, domains, and subject areas (Hidi & Harackiewicz, 2000). Motivation is an important predictor of academic achievement across grade levels and content areas (Bandura, 1997). Kuhn (2007) notes that contemporary views of motivation try to understand motivated behavior as the interaction of subject matter, trait-like motivation, and state-like, situated motivation that is more likely to impact and be impacted by classroom experiences. Bandura, too, stresses the reciprocal relationship between the motivation-related beliefs that students bring to learning settings, the learning setting itself, and the learning behaviors that students engage in.

Kuhn argues that Kirschner et al. have taken a universalist stance toward learning that does not reflect what we know about individual variation in students' motivational profiles and the motivational affordances of instruction across individuals. If student motivation is not engaged, it is unclear whether minimally or maximally guided instruction leads to different learning outcomes because students may not engage in either guided or unguided learning activities. A fundamental assumption of the guidance argument to date is that it is possible to get students, or a majority of students, to engage in instruction around worked-out examples in classrooms. More research needs to be done to understand the motivational affordances of guidance in instruction before a highly guided instructional regime is offered as the best way of improving learning. If highly guided instruction is less motivating, perhaps because it may be associated with decreases in persistence or intrinsic motivation, learning is less likely to be optimized. An important next step is to integrate guidance more closely with what we know about student motivation. Are worked-out examples motivating to students? Which students? Under what circumstances? What if school were structured so that all activities in every subject area throughout the school day were based on worked-out examples and process sheets, would that be motivating to students? Would they engage in that work consistently? Would they persist? We are not arguing that maximally guided instruction is necessarily less motivating for students; the empirical evidence is lacking to make such a claim. Rather, we are arguing for the importance of explicitly addressing motivation, either theoretically or empirically, when arguing for one kind of instruction over another.

Social Contexts of Instruction

The social context of schools must also be incorporated into effective instructional regimes. By social context we mean, in part, that classrooms always comprise one or more adults with many students of dramatically different characteristics. Individual differences and the resulting social dynamics that arise in classrooms matter in numerous ways. There is growing evidence that students' social networks within and across classrooms have an impact on learning (e.g., Maroulis & Gomez, 2008). For example, the composition of a student's social network can help predict his/her academic achievement. Students who associate with high-achieving peers are much more likely to succeed in school than students whose peers achieve at lower levels. An important instructional question is: How should such social dynamics be addressed instructionally? Teachers, too, are enmeshed in social contexts that have an impact on instruction (e.g., Frank, Zhao, & Borman, 2004). The extent to which all the teachers in a school adopt a common instructional routine such as maximum guidance may affect the overall efficacy of guidance in learning. If the uptake of the approach is haphazard, it may happen in some classrooms and not others, and the impact will likely be relatively muted on long-term learning and development.

Guidance

Many contemporary school-reform efforts stress the role of guidance in instruction, particularly guidance that is informed by evidence from student performance (Bryk, Sebring, Allensworth, Luppescu, & Easton, in press). But, challenging questions remain, not just about the level of guidance, but about the kind of guidance that most matters for learners, when and how guidance should be provided to learners, and which learners benefit from guidance in specific learning tasks. Again, the debate to date seems vague on some of these issues. Kirschner et al. (2006) noted that students with high levels of prior knowledge may not need as much guidance in learning, but that finding does not necessarily provide guidance to teachers who need to determine which students have "high" prior knowledge and how much and what kind of guidance is therefore appropriate in instruction. In a sense, framing the discussion to date as an argument between those who advocate for minimal guidance and those who argue for more guidance perhaps misses many of the nuances of thinking about the important place of guidance in school situations. If guidance is limited to the relatively underspecified description offered by Kirschner et al. (scaffolding, direct instruction, worked-out examples, process sheets, minimal searching of the problem space), we are doubtful whether the call for more guidance in learning is likely to affect schooling in significant ways in the short term because it does not provide enough specification for stakeholders to develop an informed clinical practice in which guidance is more prominent in instruction.

In the next section, we offer a description of our work in high schools designed in part to provide what we would characterize as guidance to teachers and learners as they work to make reading more prominent and more useful in content-area instruction. In particular, this work has focused on providing classrooms with reading-support tools and routines designed to help students better comprehend science texts. We offer this description to help buttress our earlier claims that guidance is most useful when it is integrated into coherent instructional regimes that can be implemented in schools, and that instruction can be both guided and inquiry-focused.

The Adolescent Literacy Support Project

Over the course of 3 years, we have worked in one urban school in Chicago with approximately 1800 students and 13 science teachers who have implemented a reading-support program in their Environmental Science and Biology ninth- and tenth-grade classrooms. All of the work we describe takes place in classrooms that could fairly be characterized as being "inquiry" science classrooms. The National Science Foundation funded the development of the two curricula being used at the school (Investigations in Environmental Science and BSCS Biology: A Human Approach) as part of its effort to support the development of inquiry science materials for high schools. The curricula include extended projects in which students, for example, have to reason about the environmental tradeoffs of locating a new school in a fragile ecosystem so that the school meets the needs of the community and protects an endangered species. Teachers participated in professional development (independently of our project) intended to make their teaching more inquiry-focused. Though there is considerable and often heated debate about what is essential about inquiry instruction and whether any particular classroom is truly "inquiry-focused" or not, such a debate is not germane to our discussion here. Instead, we rely on the fact that the curricula in use are generally understood to be in the family of inquiry-centered approaches. We equipped participants with a suite of electronic and paper-based tools designed to help students learn about, practice, and apply science reading strategies that are designed to increase students' comprehension of science texts. We worked with teachers to develop routines around the reading of text as part of inquiry instruction, including routines around the use of the reading-support tools. In the next sections, we briefly describe some reading challenges in science classrooms, the reading-support tools we introduced, and the professional development we provided for teachers which was intended to introduce and support the development of a new instructional regime around reading in science. Finally, we end this section with an extended example provided by one of our teachers that describes our vision of "guided inquiry" in practice.

Reading in Science

Reading proficiency remains a key roadblock to successful implementation of ambitious science instruction, whether explicitly "inquiry-focused" or not, for too many students in America (Herman, Gomez, Gomez, Williams, & Perkins, 2008). Ambitious science instruction requires students to read texts to learn new content in order to successfully engage in the kinds of practices valued by the science education community including: reasoning from evidence; communicating with others about science; conducting complex investigations; analyzing and representing data; and engaging in cost–benefit analyses (National Research Council, 1996). Students, particularly in traditionally underserved educational settings, too often do not have the opportunity to develop science text reading proficiency that would allow them access to important science content. Teachers, too, are often underprepared to support reading in science in ways that would deepen students' understanding of key science content (Gomez, Herman, & Gomez, 2007). In interviews, the high school science teachers at the school we worked with reported that they have had no pre-service and almost no in-service professional development designed to help them support struggling readers in science. Before the intervention the most common strategy they used when students did not understand a text was to tell the students to "read it again." Other strategies included reading the text aloud or instructing students to use a dictionary. Therefore, texts, a critical learning resource, were often ignored or underutilized in their instruction. The explicit goal of our work was to make texts more prominent in inquiry instruction by providing students and teachers with the guidance to overcome this roadblock.

Reading Support Tools

Science readers should have a corpus of strategies they can use prior to, during, and after reading to better comprehend and learn from text. Students benefit when they learn and practice comprehension strategies when they read (Anderson, 1992; Collins, 1991). Through repeated transactions with texts and by collaborative analysis and discussion with peers, students can better internalize and ultimately take ownership of the strategies (Pressley et al., 1992; Biancarosa & Snow, 2006). When internalized and used frequently, strategy use can lead to large positive effects on text comprehension (Anderson, 1992). We developed three kinds of tools to support reading in science: annotation, double-entry journals, and summarization tools. They are intended to help students recognize the structures of texts, integrate new content with prior knowledge, and increase metacognitive reading skills by having students note what they do and do not understand in texts. Students also learned to write summaries of texts to re-represent their understanding of the gist of texts (Herman et al., 2008). A brief description of each tool follows:

- *Annotation.* Students can select text and indicate whether the selection contains a main or supporting idea, argument or evidence, vocabulary word or definition, transition, conclusion, procedural word, inference, etc. They can identify structures like titles, headings, and subheadings. They can mark words or sections they do not understand.
- *Double-Entry Journals (DEJ).* These tools provide structure for students to monitor and document their understanding. A DEJ has two (or more) columns. On the left, students might identify key concepts, vocabulary, contradictions, or questions about the reading. Students then fill out the right-hand column with evidence, questions, or details as directed by the teacher to coordinate with ideas on the left. What results is a graphic organizer that displays salient information from the article and/or reveals students' misconceptions or lack of understanding.
- *Summarization.* Students must identify main ideas, differentiate secondary ideas, and condense the information while integrating essential elements in a written text. We have in place an electronic summarization tool, Summary Street, which guides students in the production and revision of summaries using Latent Semantic Analysis Technology (Kintsch, Steinhart, Matthews, Lamb, & LSA Research Group, 2000; Landauer, Foltz, & Laham, 1998). Summary Street provides students with feedback about their summaries including redundancy, spelling, and gist scores for each section of a reading.

Teacher Professional Development

For reading to have a more prominent role in inquiry science instruction, teachers need substantial professional development opportunities that focus on helping them develop instructional routines designed to support reading in science. They need to learn about effective reading strategies, including how such strategies can be taught, practiced, and instantiated in tool use. Good professional development is rooted in the content to be taught (Cohen & Hill, 2001), is ongoing, and is practice-based so that teachers can immediately apply what they learn to their practice (Garet, Porter, Desimone, Birman, & Yoon 2001). For 3 years teachers participated regularly in ongoing, practice-based professional development. These sessions took place at the school and focused on ways to support reading in science, including ways to support reading-strategy development through tool use. Teachers learned ways to assess students' strategy development by evaluating student artifacts produced from tool work (summaries, annotations, DEJs). Teachers also learned to be more explicit about their instructional choices around readings. They assigned tools based on purposes and features of specific readings so that in some cases they might have students write a summary while in other cases complete a vocabulary-focused DEJ. We co-developed pacing guides, curricular supports, rubrics to score student work, and assessments. Professional development sessions also included time for teachers to examine student work, practice using the tools, share ideas about how to integrate tool use with science learning goals, and plan upcoming instruction.

Analysis of the Instructional Regime from a Guidance Perspective

The students in these classes are struggling readers. On average, these ninth graders were reading at the fifth- or sixth-grade level based on standardized assessments of reading proficiency (Herman et al., 2008). The readings in these two curricula are clearly written at an advanced level, well beyond students' independent reading ability based on text complexity ratings and student reading scores. Being required to read and understand texts written at a much higher level than one's ability is a good example of a "minimally guided" task that likely challenges the limits of these students' abilities. Teaching students to apply reading strategies as they read the texts is intended to provide them with the guidance they need to make this task more manageable and productive.

When teachers decide to avoid using text because students struggle to read, they are doing a disservice to their students. Learning from texts in ways that allow students to successfully communicate about what has been learned is a critical academic skill for 21st-century citizens (Levy & Murnane, 2004). Reading science texts helps students better understand the domain of science including, for example, how scientists present and value arguments and evidence to support arguments. Reading also directly increases science content knowledge and more generally is a critical component of ambitious instruction. Supporting the development of a scientifically literate populace has to be a key goal of schools generally and science departments in particular. Because the goal is important, reading science texts should not be avoided even though this kind of reading may put a strain on or be in conflict with what we know about human cognitive functioning; the real challenge is to specify ways to make the task possible, meaningful, and useful to learners. We believe our tools provide a way to better specify reading tasks and therefore provide important guidance to learners. Rather than being faced with a long, complicated reading in which they are asked to "understand the reading so you can answer questions about it," the students are directed to more discrete tasks that require them to identify the structures of the reading (titles, headings, transitions, arguments and supporting evidence, etc.), reflect on their understanding of the reading, mark what they do not understand, and represent their understanding by writing a summary of the reading that demonstrates they understand the gist of the text. All along the way they are provided with guidance while reading. They are given information and ways to know what to do next.

Tools and Routines for Instructional Specification

Tools that support instructional routines provide a key form of guidance in learning. The instructional routines also provide guidance to teachers and students about how instruction should occur. When tools and routines are working in sync to support an instructional regime, it is more likely that the regime will guide classroom practice and lead to results that the regime was designed to foster. In the work described above, we wanted teachers to develop instructional routines around reading texts in science class. These routines included: analyzing texts for reading difficulty; explicitly listing their science learning goals for students; integrating the readings and the reading work into larger instructional chunks; assessing understanding of the readings and the science content; using the artifacts that students complete around the tools as a way to represent their understanding of the readings and science; motivating students to engage in the readings by providing clearer purposes for reading; and allowing students to be more strategic in their reading. By increasing comprehension of the texts, we conjectured that students would be more motivated to engage in classroom learning. To make the discussion more concrete, we next provide an example of an instructional routine that was provided to us by a ninth-grade environmental science teacher who worked with us for 3 years. She reports on her efforts to rethink and re-teach a unit that she had taught the year before:

> Working with the literacy tools and professional development has changed my perspective on the role of text in planning and implementing lessons. One lesson where this change was particularly effective was with teaching the greenhouse effect. When I first began teaching, I presented the lesson in the traditional way that the textbook described. The students were assigned to read the text on the greenhouse effect and answer the questions at the end. Then I gave a lecture about what was in the text, with the students passively taking notes. The lab was done after the reading and lecture, where the purpose was to confirm what students had read and been told about the greenhouse effect and how it contributes to global warming.
>
> When considering the reading as part of the inquiry learning, the whole lesson was constructed differently. This year students began by discussing a car on a hot day and the difference between the outside and inside temperature of a car. Then students conducted a lab with 2-liter soda bottles, measuring the temperature difference inside the covered and uncovered bottles.

During the post-lab discussion, I probed students on why the temperature increased. This uncovered the common misconception that light and heat energy are the same thing, and that they both can pass through a barrier like glass (in the case of the car), or plastic wrap (in the lab). The students were perplexed when this did not fit with their observations that the temperature increased in the covered bottles, and the heat could not escape.

The students next used the text to investigate an answer. They read the text and annotated with partners to help dissect the reading. Then as a class, we discussed what they had found to explain the lab results. We worked together as a class to create a DEJ describing the analogy and how it relates to the atmosphere. This tied together the opening example of the car, the 2-L bottles in the experiment, the example of a greenhouse presented in the text, and how these are all analogous to the Earth and the atmosphere. Finally the students returned to their lab group to answer questions that synthesized all of this information and ultimately how the greenhouse effect is the mechanism for global warming.

There are several points worth noting about what she did. In the first position, she was concerned with organizing her instruction so that students understood the greenhouse effect, and specifically the difference between heat and light energy. The goal was not to "get them to understand a text" or to "use the text to give them critical background information," which are common rationales around reading texts in science classrooms. Part of the guidance that teachers can provide to students in inquiry settings is to stress genuine reasons for reading a text such as understanding a phenomenon that is part of an investigation. By reflecting on how she taught the lesson in the past, she realized that students did not necessarily reach her learning goal based on assessments of student understanding. She thought about how to reorganize instruction to increase the likelihood of her students reaching that goal. In the redesigned lesson, students read the text with an authentic and activity-motivated purpose—namely, to get information about energy that might help them explain the phenomenon the lab introduced. This redesign may have increased student motivation to engage in the reading activity. They were authentically curious about their misconceptions and wanted to figure out a solution to the issue raised in the lab. The teacher customized an existing reading support tool to devise an "analogy" DEJ (a new kind of DEJ not envisioned by us) that tied the discussion, lab, and text together. This teacher's redesign of instruction is a good example of the kind of support for reading in science that we hoped for. As an instructional routine, it provides guidance to learners not just through making learning goals explicit but by making learning purposeful, piquing and leveraging student interest, providing customized tools for students to use, and by re-sequencing and re-organizing extant curricular materials. We think the example we detail here shows that guidance can discipline design in inquiry instruction. When this work is considered as a counterpoint to that of Kirschner et al., we think it suggests that "guidance" can discipline design across a broad instructional spectrum.

Some of the hard questions still remain. How does one bound an instructional routine? What are the elements or parts of an instructional routine and how can they be arranged to provide maximum guidance? In the example above, elements included activities that activated prior knowledge, tasks that piqued student interest by highlighting science misconceptions, and opportunities to use tools that encouraged thinking that aligns with learning goals (analogical thinking in this case). For those who care about guidance in learning, it is important to understand how teachers can build specification into instruction through these elements of instructional routines. A taxonomy of the elements of instructional regimes might help in the specification process. Our example is intended in part to highlight elements that might go into such a taxonomy. The next step would be more empirical research to determine which elements of the routine provide adaptive specification to teachers and students that leads to increases in student learning. Koedinger and Aleven (2007) note that understanding the circumstances under which students should be given assistance or when assistance should be withheld to increase "germane" cognitive load remains unclear and is an empirical question for educational researchers. We agree. Understanding this "assistance dilemma" is one example of what teachers must grapple with every day as they design instructional routines to support reading in science.

Final Thoughts

Kirschner et al. (2006) have taken a strong position against many science education reform efforts because they argue that such programs inherently provide insufficient guidance for learners. We agree that guidance is important in learning. However, insights from constrained studies of learning are unlikely to have an impact on instruction unless those insights can be situated in instructional regimes that are instantiated in instructional routines that are supported by useful tools. These regimes, to affect practice, need to be as comprehensive as possible and address the goals and needs of teachers and learners. We raised the issues of student motivation, the social contexts of instruction, and the purposes of schooling to highlight how a finding about the level of guidance required for effective learning does not in itself form the basis of an instructional regime.

Specifying instructional routines designed to increase guidance is hard work and will not happen without considerable effort. Part of what we hope to show from our own work and the work of others, is that many science education reformers are aware of the importance of providing guidance to learners (and teachers), often through tools or explicit routines as part of inquiry instruction. For example, White and Frederiksen (1998) presented a highly scaffolded inquiry cycle that, they argue, allowed underserved elementary students to engage in the study of force and motion, which had been typically thought to be beyond the reach of early-elementary learners. White and Frederiksen's description of inquiry is not the description of a "minimally" guided instructional program in our opinion. They specifically call for a well-specified instructional approach that incorporates questioning, reflection, and metacognitive development. Kuhn and Reiser (2006) have also worked to make inquiry instruction more guided. They argue that students and teachers need explicit instructional routines that support scientific argumentation in inquiry classrooms. Students need practice with explicit routines that show them ways of agreeing, disagreeing, and commenting on scientific arguments. Further, scientific argumentation will not necessarily arise in classrooms without the introduction of explicit routines that support this new practice. Edelson (2006) makes it clear that tools need to be well-specified in their design and use in classrooms. He describes how this can be accomplished by changing the functionality of tools that students would use compared to tools that experts or scientists would use, in order to minimize irrelevant cognitive load and to automate difficult but pedagogically unimportant processes. Edelson describes an explicit rationale for tool design and use that fits comfortably within an inquiry frame. Windschitl, Thompson, and Braaten (2008) propose model-based inquiry as a way to better specify classroom activity and discourse to increase student learning by providing a richer model of scientific inquiry than that often presented in classrooms as the scientific method. This is another example of scholars working to provide teachers with ways to provide guidance to students in inquiry contexts. The conversation might profitably change from one of abandoning instructional approaches whole cloth because of their perceived lack of guidance to specifying how, when, in what form, and under what circumstances guidance is helpful and possible within larger instructional regimes in schools.

It is worth noting that these reform efforts, inquiry and others, did not arise in a vacuum; they came about because of design-based instructional research that revealed deficiencies in more traditional science instructional settings. There are a number of compelling rationales (cognitive, motivational, societal) for approaches to the design of science learning environments whose features include some or all of the following: the study of authentic problems; using real-world datasets in investigations; studying content in depth over breadth; using technologies in learning. Though student achievement is obviously critical to any instructional regime, it is not the only feature of instruction that should be assessed when evaluating the impact of instruction. New approaches to science teaching have come about because many students, particularly those in under-served schools, have had few opportunities to engage in meaningful science learning in schools. We disagree with Kirschner et al. (2006) when they argue that students should absolutely not engage in the practices of science when learning science. We are less sure than they are about the value of such a prohibition. Because of the dire state of Science Technology Engineering and Math (STEM) education in the United States, new approaches to instruction that are based in part on contemporary understandings of learning, motivation, social contexts and the purposes of schools have been and will continue to be developed. To succeed in schools, these instructional programs need to be well-specified in practice. We are not convinced that we should abandon such promising approaches to instruction that potentially offer students access to a rich under-standing of science and perhaps STEM careers. Instead, instructional programs like these may need to be redesigned to provide effective guidance in tools and instructional routines to make desired outcomes more likely. We think this process is already underway. It seems Kirschner et al. completely equate inquiry with unguided or minimally guided learning activities. The assumption seems to be that certain kinds of activities cannot become more guided. It may be that some examples of inquiry are not well-specified and provide minimal guidance. The question for us then is whether it is justified to abandon inquiry before learning whether inquiry activities can be better specified to maximize learning and keep the potentially valuable benefits of inquiry in place. Kirschner et al. seem to be arguing that it cannot be done because, for decades, inquiry regimes have failed to meet high learning standards. We are less certain. We think it is important to learn whether the heterogeneity of activities that make up an inquiry instructional regime, or any instructional regime, can become more specified in practice without losing the proposed benefit of engaging in particular activities. So, if tasks that involve work that scientists do become more guided, is it still possible that engaging in these tasks can foster student interest or curiosity about science as a career while ensuring high achievement? Inquiry regimes, like all instructional regimes, need to be well-specified.

We have seen in our own work that many students in underserved schools have almost no conception of what scientists do. As reformers critically concerned with increasing the representation of these students in STEM fields, we are focused on what should be done. The first step should likely be to ensure quality science instruction for all students. But, an element of that is certainly to make students more aware of and excited by the work of scientists. To better understand the problem, we informally interviewed eighth graders in an underserved Chicago school. Out of one classroom of 30 students, only two could name any science discipline that they might study in high school (Chemistry, Biology, Physics, etc.). They could not offer a description of what a chemist or biologist might actually do. By designing programs that help students better understand and be more interested in the work of scientists, perhaps through guided exposure to the kind of work that scientists engage in, we may increase the likelihood of them choosing to take science classes in high school, perhaps choose science as a major in college, and maybe even enter a STEM career. It is a long haul from middle school classrooms in any educationally underserved environment to a STEM career and we need to continue to explore programs that can work. We disagree with Kirschner et al. that having students engage in the work of scientists means necessarily having them engage in minimally guided instructional activities. The work that scientists do can be highly specified. Scientists are guided by routines and tools in their work. Scientists read about science. Scientists communicate their findings. Scientists conduct constrained investigations. It is not clear why activities that capture the essence of this work cannot be designed in a manner that provides guidance to students while still providing them with authentic experiences that may increase the likelihood that they develop some long-term interest in science as a vocation.

Kirschner and his colleagues have spurred a useful debate. The debate should not really be about guidance versus no guidance. Instead, a more fruitful conversation might center on the most effective ways to design instruction in schools that is shaped by a body of research and practice that shows us when and how to provide guidance within a large range of instructional regimes. We hope we have made a contribution to this debate by arguing for the need to translate findings about guidance into practical instructional routines for students and teachers as part of a large and diverse collection of instructional regimes.

Question: Fletcher. *There seems to be a lot more "work" on the part of teachers in preparing the routines and tools and implementing the guidance you suggest. Or is this a misperception on my part? Given today's teacher workload are your suggestions practicable? Might Fred Keller's lightening strike twice here? Or do the recommended tools and routines lessen the workload sufficiently? Absent time and motion studies, what would you say about the overall practicability of your approach?*

Reply: Herman and Gomez. There is more work for teachers in the approach we advocate but we think that there are a few ways to make the workload more manageable. One way is through better tools and routines like those we described in the chapter. As the tools and routines become well understood and established in instruction, they take less instructional time to implement. Another way, which we have not yet sufficiently developed, is to improve the kind and amount of information that teachers can use from student work to make instruction more effective both in terms of learning outcomes and in use of time.

Initially, science teachers were quite concerned with the additional workload. They stressed the need to cover standards, prepare their students for exams, conduct extended hands-on investigations, etc. We took their concerns seriously while still trying to show the ways in which texts can become more central learning resources in instruction. In particular, we used data to show how well reading comprehension scores predicted a range of science achievement outcomes. This helped teachers think more concretely about the role of reading comprehension in their science classrooms. Perhaps even more powerfully, we demonstrated to teachers that students' proficiency with the reading strategies, as evidenced in their construction of annotation, double-entry journals, and summaries of the texts, predicted science achievement and did so even when reading comprehension scores were included as covariates in regression models (Herman, Gomez, & Gomez, 2008). This finding helped convince teachers that by increasing students' proficiency with the reading strategies, they may be fairly directly increasing science achievement. Thus, we believe they perceived the work as less tangential to their science instruction, which may lessen any ongoing concerns about the additional workload.

Through ongoing professional development, we supported teachers as they worked to integrate the literacy activities into science instruction. The extended example we used in the chapter was designed, in part, to show that the literacy work is not necessarily "additional" work; it can become the grist of science learning if integrated properly. Our experience over 3 years of working to implement this program in schools indicates that it is practicable, though challenging to "get right." Teachers need time to learn about and practice teaching the strategies, learn how to leverage the student work produced around the readings, and learn how to make sure that texts are prominent learning resources in pursuit of their science learning goals. The tools and routines and the formative and summative information that is available from the literacy activities provide guidance to teachers and learners that makes this kind of approach possible in classrooms.

Question: Fletcher. *Your example touches on learning general analytical and evaluative skills—reasoned skepticism, habits of mind, etc.—required for scientific inquiry. For other purposes, I examined available measures of critical, adaptive, and creative thinking and came away dissatisfied. Is there, perhaps, a major problem for constructivist approaches in finding valid measures for the objectives they may be most suited for? These objectives seem not easily amenable to precise measurement, specification, or even articulation. Is there, then, an inherent, endemic, intransigent lack of solid data on the value of constructivist approaches?*

Reply: Herman and Gomez. A real benefit of the current debate about the utility of constructivist approaches should be both a re-articulation of the proposed affordances of constructivist approaches to instruction as well as a focus on the research evidence about the efficacy of such approaches. The evaluation of the impact of constructivist approaches is extremely challenging. As you note, evaluation is often a problem not just of measures but of articulation of impacts. For example, characterizing and assessing learning in constructivist and non-constructivist messy classrooms is hard enough; but how can we evaluate, for example, the motivational affordances of participation? An important reason why it has been deemed important to investigate "relevant" problems to students' lives is not that investigating relevant problems leads directly to increased achievement but that students might be more willing to engage and persist in problems that they perceive as important to their lives. Thus, if studying relevant problems makes a difference, in part, that difference should be articulated and assessed in motivational terms.

Often, the motivational constructs used to measure the impact of constructivist (and other kinds) of classroom implementations are deficient. For example, a common motivation-related measure used to evaluate the impact of participation in learning environments is students' goal orientation (mastery, performance, etc.). However, it is unclear if such constructs are tractable during the relatively short-term implementations of many constructivist learning environments. That is, goals may not change substantially or consistently over half a year but rather over multiple years as students, for example, move from the upper-elementary grades to the middle grades. To evaluate constructivist approaches, at least related to the motivational impact of such approaches, will take not only a re-articulation of the claims and the development of new measures but a careful consideration of the motivational theories themselves to judge how well they capture the kinds of changes likely to occur in these kinds of learning environments which are often of limited duration.

Question: Kintsch. *You describe a program to support reading science texts that is precisely the kind of program that a reading comprehension researcher like me would like to see. You describe the dismal state of much comprehension instruction today* *("read it again," "read it aloud") and contrast it with the approach they have imple-mented in Chicago schools. They don't ask their students to "understand the reading so you can answer questions about it," but give them concrete tasks that support comprehension, together with the guidance the students need to succeed at these tasks. I would like to hear a little more detail about their annotation and double-entry journal tools. How does the teacher provide feedback to the student? Can students work individually, in groups, or as a whole class? Obviously, it is of crucial importance for the student to receive timely feedback—isn't that asking a lot from the busy teacher? In the greenhouse example, the whole class worked on the double-entry journal. One could also think about individualized projects that take even greater advantage of idiosyncratic interests, but in that case one would need to develop a technology that assists the teacher, as in the summarization work you report.*

Reply: Herman and Gomez. We agree that electronic versions of each of the tools could add value for instruction. Teachers and students each need informa-tion about their work with the reading supports in order to self-appraise their progress and improve instruction. We are working to develop electronic versions of the tools that allow students to complete the annotations, double-entry jour-nals, and summaries on computers. For example, we are currently prototyping an electronic annotation tool that aggregates and visually represents the annota-tions of each student's work. These aggregations of student work are visualized by colors so sections of text (words, sentences, paragraphs, etc.) are darker in sec-tions that are frequently included in student annotations and lighter in those sec-tions that fewer students include in their annotations. We call this representation a heat map. If a teacher wants to quickly determine whether all or some students included particular content in their annotations, she could look at this heat map to make a judgment about her next instructional decision. The move toward these electronic versions should also allow teachers to better differentiate instruc-tion. By helping students and teachers track progress, and provide timely feed-back, the electronic versions of the tools should allow for more effective use of the literacy supports over time. Ultimately, our goal is to provide more and better opportunities for guided practice in learning about, practicing, and apply-ing effective reading-comprehension strategies in science.

Acknowledgments

This work was supported in part by the National-Science Foundation under REC No. 0440338.

Parts of this manuscript were prepared while the authors were members of the faculty at Northwestern University in the Learning Sciences Program.

References

Ames, C. (1992). Classrooms: Goals, structures, and student motivation. *Journal of Educa-tional Psychology, 84,* 261–271.

Anderson, V. (1992). A teacher development project in transactional strategy instruction for teachers of severely reading-disabled adolescents. *Teaching & Teacher Education, 8,* 391–403.

Bandura, A. (1997). *Self-efficacy: The exercise of control.* New York: Freeman.

Biancarosa, C., & Snow, C. E. (2006). *Reading Next – a vision for action and research in middle and high school literacy: A report to the Carnegie corporation of New York* (2nd ed.). Washington, DC: Alliance for Excellent Education.

Blumenfeld, P. C., Soloway, E., Marx, R. W., Krajcik, J. S., Guzdial, M., & Palincsar, A. (1991). Motivating project-based learning: Sustaining the doing, supporting the learning. *Educational Psychologist, 26,* 369–398.

Bridgeland, J. M., DiIulio, J. J., Jr, & Morison, K. B. (2006). *The Silent Epidemic.* (Technical Report): The Gates Foundation.

Bryk, A. S., Sebring, P., Allensworth, E., Luppescu, S., & Easton, J. (in press). *Organizing schools for improvement.* Chicago, IL: University of Chicago Press.

Cohen, D. K., & Hill, H. (2001). *Learning policy: When state education reform works.* New Haven, CT: Yale University Press.

Cohen, D. K., Raudenbush, S. W., & Ball, D. L. (2003). Resources, instruction, and research. *Educational Evaluation and Policy Analysis, 25*(2), 1–24.

Collins, C. (1991). Reading instruction that increases thinking abilities. *Journal of Reading, 34,* 510–516.

Deakin Crick, R., McCombs, B., & Hadden, A. (2007). The ecology of learning: Factors contributing to learner-centered classroom cultures. *Research Papers in Education, 22,* 267–307.

Edelson, D. (2006). My world: A case study in adapting scientists' tools for learners. In *Proceedings of the 7th International Conference of the Learning Sciences.* Mahwah, NJ: Erlbaum.

Frank, K. A., Zhao, Y., & Borman, K. (2004). Social capital and the diffusion of innovations within organizations: Application to the implementation of computer technology in schools. *Sociology of Education, 77*(2), 148–171.

Garet, M. S., Porter, A. C., Desimone, L., Birman, B. F., & Yoon, K. S. (2001). What makes professional development effective? Results from a national sample of teachers. *American Educational Research Journal, 38*(4), 915–945.

Gomez, L. M., Herman, P., & Gomez, K. (2007). Integrating text in content-area classes: Better supports for teachers and students. *Voices in Urban Education, 14,* 22–29.

Herman, P., Gomez, L. M., Gomez, K., Williams, A., & Perkins, K. (2008). Metacognitive support for reading in science classrooms. In G. Kanselaar, V. Jonker, P. A. Kirschner, & F. Prins (Eds.), *Proceedings of the 8th International Conference of the Learning Sciences* (342–349). Utrecht, The Netherlands: ICLS.

Hidi, S., & Harackiewicz, J. M. (2000). Motivating the academically unmotivated: A critical issue for the 21st century. *Review of Educational Research, 70*(2), 151–179.

Kaplan, A., & Maehr, M. L. (2007). The contributions and prospects of goal orientation theory. *Educational Psychology Review, 19*(2), 141–184.

Kintsch, E., Steinhart, D., Matthews, C., Lamb, R., and LSA Research Group (2000). Developing summarization skills through the use of LSA-based feedback. In J. Psotka (Ed.). *Special Issue of Interactive Learning Environments, 8*(2), 87–109.

Kirschner, P., Sweller, J., & Clark, R. (2006). Why minimal guidance during instruction does not work: An analysis of the failure of constructivist, discovery, problem-based, experiential, and inquiry-based teaching. *Educational Psychologist, 41,* 75–86.

Koedinger, K., & Aleven, V. (2007). Exploring the assistance dilemma in experiments with cognitive tutors. *Educational Psychology Review, 19,* 239–264.

Kuhn, D. (2007). Is direct instruction an answer to the right question? *Educational Psychologist, 42*(2), 109–113.

Kuhn, L., & Reiser, B. J. (2006). *Structuring activities to foster argumentative discourse.* Paper presented at the annual meeting of the American Educational Research Association. Chicago, IL.

Lagemann, E. C. (2002). Usable knowledge in education. A memorandum for the Spencer Foundation Board of Directors. Retrieved from www.spencer.org/publications/usable_knowledge_report_ecl_a.htm.

Landauer, T., Foltz, P., & Laham, D. (1998). An introduction to latent semantic analysis. *Discourse Processes, 25,* 259–284.

Lau, S., & Roeser, R. W. (2002). Cognitive abilities and motivational processes in high school students' situational engagement and achievement in science. *Educational Assessment, 8*(2), 139–162.

Lemke, J. L. (2002, April). *Complex systems and educational change.* Paper presented at the annual meeting of the American Educational Research Association, New Orleans, LA.

Levy, F., & Murnane, R. J. (2004). *The new division of labor: How computers are creating the next job market.* Princeton, NJ: Princeton University Press.

Maroulis, S., & Gomez, L. M. (2008). Does "connectedness" matter? Evidence from a social network analysis within a small school reform. *Teachers College Record, 110*(9), 1901–1929.

National Research Council. (1996). *National science education standards.* Washington, DC: National Academy Press.

Pressley, M., El-Dinary, P., Gaskins, I., Schuder, T., Bergman, J., Almasi, J., et al. (1992). Beyond direct explanation: Transactional instruction of reading comprehension strategies. *The Elementary School Journal, 92,* 511–555.

Raudenbush, S. (2005). Learning from attempts to improve schooling: The contribution of methodological diversity. *Educational Researcher, 34,* 25–31.

Wheatley, M. J. (1999). *Leadership and the new science: Discovering order in a chaotic world* (2nd ed.). San Francisco, CA: Berett-Koehler.

White, B. Y., & Frederiksen, J. R. (1998). Inquiry, modeling, and metacognition: Making science accessible to all students. *Cognition and Instruction, 16*(1), 3–118.

Winschitl, M., Thompson, J., & Braaten, M. (2008). Beyond the scientific method: Model-based inquiry as a new paradigm of preference for school science investigations. *Science Education, 92*(5), 941–967.

Wise & O'Neill, Chapter 5, this volume.

Zhao, Y., & Frank, K. (2003). Factors affecting technology uses in schools: An ecological perspective. *American Educational Research Journal, 40,* 807–840.

5 Beyond More Versus Less

A Reframing of the Debate on Instructional Guidance

Alyssa Friend Wise and Kevin O'Neill
Simon Fraser University

In this chapter we attempt to reframe the debate surrounding instructional guidance in a way that may be more productive than the one pursued recently. Up till now, the conversation between constructivists and instructionists has largely centered on the adversarial question of whether or not constructivist instructional approaches provide enough guidance to be effective. However, we argue that experimental "high versus low guidance" studies cannot provide a valid basis for making inferences about the fundamental merits of constructivist teaching. Reviewing some of the literature cited in the recent debate (with a particular focus on worked-example studies), we will argue that for constructivists and instructionists alike, the *quantity* of guidance is just one dimension along which guidance can be usefully characterized. We introduce the *context* in which guidance is delivered and the *timing* with which guidance is delivered as two more important concerns. We then make a case for a research agenda that we believe may bring constructivists and instructionists together in exploring questions about the optimal quantity, context, and timing of guidance in ill-defined problem domains.

On one side of the recent debate is a perspective that sees instructional approaches such as problem-based learning (PBL) and guided inquiry as providing too little guidance to support learning effectively (e.g., Kirschner, Sweller, & Clark, 2006). Proponents of this view often cite lab-based findings such as the worked-example effect (e.g., Sweller & Cooper, 1985) as support for the position that "more" guidance, generally given at the outset of instruction, is almost always best for learners. Because of the primacy this perspective places on the delivery of up-front explicit instruction, we refer to it as "instructionism."

On the other side of the debate, there is a perspective that claims that inquiry and PBL approaches do provide a great deal of guidance, and may in fact produce learning outcomes that are superior to up-front explanation (e.g., Hmelo-Silver, Duncan, & Chinn, 2007). Proponents of this view often cite classroom-based studies showing that students in inquiry-based classrooms achieve greater depth of understanding than students in traditional ones (e.g., Hickey, Kindfield, Horwitz, & Christie, 1999) as support for this position, generally referred to as "constructivism."

It appears to us that the two sides are talking past each other. We suspect that this may be due to different ideas about the purpose of guidance, different ambitions with regard to the transfer of learning, and different views about the nature of the evidence needed to justify claims about the merits of *any* instructional approach. In the following sections, we try to unpack these differences and show how these incommensurate views lead us to a methodological catch-22 that, at present, makes the debate irresolvable.

The reader may wonder, if we cannot answer the question of which approach is better, is there still a way to move forward productively? We present one possible path that uses the amount, context, and timing of guidance as a toolkit for thinking about the design of instruction. We explore evidence from both the constructivist and instructionist perspectives regarding the nature of effective instructional guidance, and attempt to develop principles that both instructionists and constructivists may be able to agree to. By using a common language, we hope to engender the possibility of research agendas of interest to both instructionists and constructivists, and to which each group can contribute.

Transfer of Learning and the Purpose of Guidance: Contrasting Instructionism and Constructivism

A logical place to begin is by asking what is meant by the term "guidance." Much of the recent debate seems to have proceeded without a careful definition of the term, nor a well-spelled-out metric of how much of it is provided in a given instructional design. Reviewing the recent debate in *Educational Psychologist* (Kirschner et al., 2006; Hmelo-Silver et al., 2007; Kuhn, 2007; Schmidt, Loyens, van Gog, & Paas, 2007; Sweller, Kirschner, & Clark, 2007), the collection of instructional moves discussed under the rubric of guidance seems to include explanation, feedback, help, modeling, scaffolding, procedural direction, and others. Implicitly, guidance seems to have been taken as a superordinate category that describes *anything* an instructor provides to students to aid their learning and performance.

We find ourselves asking whether this is a useful concept to debate around—to us it seems problematic to meaningfully gauge "amount" across such a broad range of instructional moves. Should a high degree of scaffolding count as more or less guidance than a little explanation? Does a general model given ahead of time constitute more or less guidance than detailed feedback after the fact? Confusion over such questions may help to explain why the current debate has not reached resolution. Despite employing the common language of "guidance," the instructionist and constructivist camps appear to be using the term very differently. An indication that this may be the case can be seen in the different ways that each group approaches the fundamental problem of teaching complex knowledge and skills. Both groups recognize that novices have difficulty navigating large problem spaces (e.g., Sweller, 1988; Mayer, 2004; O'Neill & Weiler, 2006; Polman, 2000). However, the responses of constructivists and instructionists to this challenge are substantially different.

A key difference between instructionist and constructivist perspectives appears to center on the problem of part–whole relationships. In our interpretation, instructionists' main solution to the challenge of teaching a complex body of knowledge or skills is to break it down into smaller, clearer pieces, and provide up-front instruction about how to tackle each one. This way, students are not easily lost amid innumerable details. Eventually, of course, students have to put the pieces together to produce a whole, competent performance; but in the instructionist view, these part–whole relationships are best taught after each of the individual pieces has been mastered. Thus, from an instructionist perspective, a key purpose of instructional guidance is to reduce the extraneous cognitive load borne by the learner in processing each part of the material or task to be learned (Sweller, 1988).

From this perspective, it makes a lot of sense to focus on the amount of guidance provided in an instructional design. It also appears to be a straightforward matter. Having students figure out how to do something themselves entails the least guidance, and the greatest cognitive load. Scaffolding learners by providing a little support along the way entails moderate support, and leads to moderate cognitive load. Telling or showing students exactly how to accomplish a task provides maximum guidance, and introduces minimal cognitive load, which evidence shows can lead to certain kinds of learning gains (Kirschner et al., 2006).

We note, however, that what instructionists take as evidence of learning (at least in the experiments cited in the recent debate) is usually performance on a school-like task performed very shortly after initial training. For example, of the eight worked-example studies reviewed by Kirschner et al. (2006) that looked at transfer, all used transfer tasks that, at best, can be characterized as "very near" on most dimensions of Barnett and Ceci's (2002) transfer taxonomy. In all of these studies, the transfer tasks were identical to the learning tasks in terms of physical context (lab/classroom), modality (written task and problem format), and social context (individual). Most also used a very near temporal context (same session) with one experiment administering a transfer task the following day (Carroll, 1994, Exp. 1).

One important reason for constructivists' very different approach to teaching may come from their greater ambitions where transfer of learning is concerned. The common constructivist sentiment was expressed well by Barnett and Ceci (2005) when they wrote that "no one cares about learning if it stops at the schoolhouse door" (p. 295). This sentiment, so different from that embodied in instructionists' experimental protocols, has a large influence on constructivists' reading of the literature.

Alexander and Murphy (1999) stated that transfer of learning to novel contexts "has long been a problem of Gordian proportions for applied psychologists" (p. 561), and note that very little evidence of transfer to novel problems has been produced in the lab. However, Bransford and Schwartz (1999) have argued that many lab-based transfer studies make people "look dumb" (unable to transfer learning) because they exclusively evaluate sequestered problem solving. They describe sequestered problem solving as a type of testing in which learners are asked to directly apply learned material to a new context without any additional resources or the opportunity to learn in the new context by attempting and revising solutions (Bransford & Schwartz, 1999; Schwartz, Bransford, & Sears, 2005).

Bransford and Schwartz (1999) and Schwartz et al. (2005) describe a series of experiments demonstrating that more encouraging results are obtained when the concept of transfer is expanded beyond a direct application paradigm. They suggest thinking of transfer in terms of "preparation for future learning"—the ways in which a learning experience can prepare students to learn related ideas or skills more quickly or more deeply in the future. They further demonstrate that by measuring students' ability to flexibly respond to and learn from new situations after certain kinds of treatments, one can uncover positive transfer not detected by sequestered problem-solving tasks (Schwartz & Bransford, 1998; Schwartz & Martin, 2004).

These findings make a good deal of sense in relation to constructivist theories of memory, which suggest that better elaborated memories, with more extensive relational networks, will lead to more reliable recall of learned material (Bransford, 1979; Schank, 1982). These same theories suggest that learners will develop more elaborate memories, with more transfer-relevant relational networks, from more authentic experiences, particularly if the experiences are well-scaffolded.

To maximize the chances that worthwhile transfer will occur, constructivists argue that it is important to retain as much of the authenticity (and hence complexity) of the target task as is practical. This position is consistent with current theories of transfer, which suggest (for example) that "the primary job of transfer is the construction [by the learner] of an evolving representation of context that allows the knowledge user to make meaning of contexts" (Royer, Mestre, & Dufresne, 2005, p. xxii). The constructed understanding of a new context allows learners to bring prior knowledge to bear in an appropriate way.

This view of transfer helps to explain famously confusing findings such as those of Carraher, Carraher, and Schliemann (1985). They found that Brazilian children were capable of making sophisticated calculations in their heads when working as street vendors. However, the children could not successfully carry out the same calculations *with the very same quantities* when asked to do so in a lab situation where the problems were represented in writing, such as "5 × 35 = ?". When the same calculations were given in the form of word problems, the additional context helped the children to solve the problems with much greater success (Carraher et al., 1985). These findings illustrate the importance of seeing a context as similar to one previously encountered in order for transfer to occur.

Thus, while instructionists tend to view a complex problem-solving situation as a large problem space filled with extraneous demands on the learner's attention (e.g., Sweller, 1988), a constructivist is more likely to view it as a rich set of contextual cues that may later aid transfer (e.g., Brown, Collins, & Duguid, 1989). In keeping the "pieces" of the skill to be learned together in relation both to each other and a complex macro-context, constructivists aim to teach part–whole relationships throughout the learning process.

Jasper Woodbury is a good illustration of how differently constructivists think about the function of instructional materials. In this mathematics curriculum, students are provided with video case "anchors" that are intended to be authentic to real-life problems (Cognition and Technology Group at Vanderbilt, 1992). The math problems embedded in these video anchors are quite complex, and to an instructionist, likely appear utterly lacking in necessary instructional guidance. No doubt, by *itself* such a situation presents problems for learners, given the limitations of working memory (Cognition and Technology Group at Vanderbilt, 1994). But rather than being designed as a complete plan for instruction, the videos and associated materials were intended to create "teachable moments" in which guidance can be provided in a contextualized way that is responsive to the students' current frame of mind (Schwartz et al., 2005).

Saye and Brush (2002) have aptly described such responsive, real-time guidance from teachers as "soft scaffolding." As Pea (2004) explains, scaffolding is a kind of performance support that is adaptive to the learner's current capability, and gradually fades away. One of the main pedagogical functions of scaffolding is to channel or focus the learner's attention on what is important within a complex learning situation. While directing learner attention is a pedagogical function also endorsed by instructionists (Kirschner et al., 2006), constructivists seek to help learners identify important elements *in situ* rather than extracting them to present to learners.

This overview may help explain why it can appear to instructionists that constructivists are focused on minimizing guidance in instruction. We believe that this is not the case. For their part, constructivists are equally committed to helping novices cope with the limitations of working memory. However, rather than relying exclusively on shrinking the problem space and providing up-front instruction, they aim to help learners manage a large problem space by providing real-time supports that they theorize will make transfer to real-life situations more likely.

To be fair, constructivists have often not been as committed to measuring far transfer as they have been to advocating its importance. A thoroughgoing commitment to measuring unprompted far transfer would entail shadowing research participants in "real life," waiting for transfer to occur—an approach that to our knowledge has never been implemented, for obvious logistical reasons.

The Methodological Issue: Why "High" versus "Low" Guidance Studies Cannot Resolve the Debate

At first blush, judging the "success" of constructivist theory in informing instruction seems to imply a simple horse race: constructivism versus instructionism, winner takes all. In Western culture we seem drawn to contests between two extreme possibilities as a way to get at the truth of a matter, though this approach often does not produce the satisfaction we are after (Tannen, 1999). For example, while comparing test results from a constructivist classroom to those from a more traditional one tells us which class did better in those particular implementations, it does not generate the kind of evidence we need to make generalizable claims about causes. As Kirschner et al. (2006) point out, there are too many different variables at play, including the quality with which each approach is implemented, to make valid inferences about which factors are responsible for the differences. We acknowledge that a great deal of the evidence presented in support of constructivist teaching is subject to this critique. However, we argue that the experimental "high versus low guidance" evidence introduced by scholars such as Kirschner et al. (2006) is also not a valid basis for making inferences about the fundamental merits of constructivist teaching.

Kirschner et al. (2006) use the level of guidance provided in instruction as a proxy by which to compare constructivist and instructionist approaches. The ensuing conversation about the efficacy of constructivist approaches to instruction has thus centered on the question of "how much" guidance is needed for effective instruction, and whether approaches such as guided inquiry and problem-based learning provide enough (Hmelo-Silver et al., 2007; Schmidt et al., 2007; Sweller et al., 2007). If one accepts the assumption that quantity of guidance is the most important difference between constructivist and instructionist designs, it then appears that *any* study comparing "low" and "high" guidance approaches is relevant to the discussion. However, as we have outlined above, the constructivist approach differs from the instructionist one not simply in the amount of guidance provided, but also in how problems are structured and the way in which guidance supports the learner. Importantly, the problem structure and the guidance provided are designed to be mutually supporting—theoretically, we would not expect one to be successful without the other.

Thus, while many of the studies that instructionists have cited in the recent debate are valuable for increasing our understanding about guidance within a particular framework (constructivist or instructionist), we submit that they are not valid evidence for making a judgment between the two frameworks. For example, Mayer (2004) reviewed a set of studies comparing pure-discovery learning with guided inquiry. However, discovery learning and guided inquiry are different forms of *constructivist* instruction. Neither falls under the rubric of explicit, up-front instruction. Thus at best, this study shows that within a constructivist framework, some scaffolding is better than none. It does not compare a constructivist approach with an instructionist one.

Similarly, the worked-example studies which Kirschner et al. (2006) review in detail (e.g., Sweller & Cooper, 1985; Cooper & Sweller, 1987) compare two variations on instructionist designs. One design involves showing students an example of how to do a problem, then gives them many opportunities to practice. The other design replaces a considerable portion of the practice problems with worked-out examples. In both cases, the instruction begins with showing a student exactly how to do a problem. Doing this with one example or with many constitutes a variation of the same instructionist approach. Thus, while useful in other ways, the results of these experiments also do not provide evidence on which to compare the relative success of constructivist and instructionist approaches.

The failure of both constructivists and instructionists to produce evidence that their counterparts find persuasive seems to be caused by a methodological catch-22. To wit: if one conducts a properly designed, classically controlled experiment varying *only* the amount of guidance provided in instruction, they are restricted to making comparisons *within* one of the two frameworks (instructionist or constructivist), or using a very impoverished version of one of the approaches. However, if we attempt to test a "good" instructionist lesson against a "good" constructivist one, we must involve differences in more than one variable, making our results ungeneralizable.

Reframing the Question

The methodological quandary discussed above is not new. The same issues were the focus of the 1987 debate between Papert and Pea around LOGO (Papert, 1987). Back then, Papert argued that it was meaningless to conduct a classical experimental trial of a learning innovation that, by its nature, requires a number of simultaneous and interdependent changes to instruction in order to be effective. The methodological debate remains very much alive today, mostly in the literature surrounding design-based research (Cobb, Confrey, diSessa, Lehrer, & Schauble, 2003; Collins, Joseph, & Bielaczyc, 2004); and there does not appear to be an end in sight.

Instructionists appear to be looking for a grand generalization: is constructivism or instructionism (as characterized by low or high guidance respectively) more effective? But perhaps this is not the most useful question to ask. Putting this in the context of the horse-race analogy, it is like asking which of two horses will win more races *on average*. But instructional designers and teachers deal in specifics. Their natural interest is in predicting what sort of instruction will be most effective in a *particular* situation.

If instructionists find this second question uncompelling, it may be because they believe they can develop a set of inviolate principles with which to predict the performance of instruction across all situations. However, there are a multitude of variables that affect the enactment of an instructional strategy (or a horse race) in a specific situation. For example, the experience of a teacher (Featherstone, 1992), the characteristics of the individual students (Jonassen & Grabowski, 1993), and the type of material to be learned (Stodolsky, 1988) all affect the implementation of instructional strategies in ways that can alter results. In both horse races and classrooms, we suggest that the art of picking a winner is not a matter of figuring out which "horse" has won the most in the past and betting on it in every race, but working to optimize one's chances of a positive outcome given what we know about the conditions in a particular situation.

How would the landscape of research change if instead of seeking rigid, universal *prescriptions*, we sought a tractable set of *considerations* for designing instructional guidance? With such an approach, instead of trying to develop absolute rules that apply to all instructional situations (e.g., more guidance is always better), we would develop principles that characterize successful guidance (e.g., the amount of guidance must be sufficient to support learners in seeing how the different pieces of the task fit together). The principles could then be used to consider a particular instructional context and learning goals, guiding design in a heuristic fashion. Instructionists have started us on this road by identifying one important consideration in instructional design—the amount of guidance provided. To this list, constructivists would add the context in which the guidance is given and the timing with which it is given.

In the following sections, we argue that the amount, context, and timing of instructional guidance are *all* important as factors to consider when planning instruction, regardless of whether one is coming from an instructionist or con-structivist perspective. We do not aspire to provide (now or someday) a set of fully prescriptive rules about the "best" position along each dimension. Rather, as described above, we seek to develop principles for thinking about each factor that can be used to guide choices about guidance in specific learning situations.

Amount of Guidance: From Prescription to Guideline

The way the instructionist case has been argued to date, it would appear that more guidance is bound to be better in every case, regardless of the instructional goals being pursued or the domain in which they are being pursued (e.g., Sweller et al., 2007, p. 117). However, while we agree that amount of guidance is impor-tant to think about, we see the evidence as indicating that it is important in a dif-ferent way. To us, the evidence suggests that the optimal amount of guidance often is an intermediate amount and the *granularity* of the advice provided in a design (i.e., the level of detail) is equally important.

To illustrate this point, we revisit one of the primary sources of evidence cited by Kirschner et al. (2006) for their claim that more guidance is always better, the worked-example effect. Of the nine studies they cite about the effect, five (Carroll, 1994; Cooper & Sweller, 1987; Paas & van Merriënboer, 1994; Sweller & Cooper, 1985; Trafton & Reiser, 1993) only compared *two* levels of guidance: fully worked-out examples and unsolved problems. While these studies can show the relative benefits of two particular "amounts" of guidance, they are not direct evidence of a continuous linear relationship between the two.

Looking at the studies cited that did have more than two conditions, addi-tional guidance did not always result in a commensurate gain in learning (Miller, Lehman, & Koedinger, 1999; Paas, 1992; Quilici & Mayer, 1996). For example, Paas (1992) found that learners in a "completion" condition, who were given a problem only halfway worked out, performed as well on test problems as those given the problems fully worked out. In this case, the additional guidance given by the fully worked-out problem did not seem to provide additional learning benefits. Similarly, in a statistics problem-sorting task, Quilici and Mayer (1996) found that providing learners with three examples of each problem type, as opposed to one, did not result in any differences in students' ability to sort sub-sequent problems into the appropriate types.

This is not to say that additional guidance can *never* lead to learning gains—just that we cannot assume that it will *always* do so. In part, the learning gains achieved may depend on the purpose the additional guidance is serving. For example, in a worked-examples study asking learners to mentally translate between 2-D and 3-D representations of objects, Pillay (1994) found that worked examples showing three intermediate problem stages were more effective than those showing only one. She suggests this may be because in the three-stage rep-resentation, the distance between stages was small enough to "permit subjects to follow the transformation without having to generate [additional] stages them-selves" (Pillay, 1994, p. 110). In a related finding, Catrambone (1994, 1995) found that when there are many individual steps involved, showing how they fit together to achieve sub-goals can make the steps more meaningful and useful. Finally, while not a worked-example study per se, the ninth study cited by Kirschner et al. (2006) looked at guidance in the form of a task for exploring a physics simulation microworld called *Electric Field Hockey* (Miller et al., 1999). They found that it was not the simple absence or presence of a guiding task, but specifically *how* the task influenced students' activities in the microworld that led to learning benefits.

Beyond the worked-example literature, there are other studies that suggest that aiming for the right level of granularity in guidance is a better guideline than "more is always better." For example, Nadolski, Kirschner, and van Merriënboer (2005) found that breaking the task of preparing a legal plea into four steps was more effective in supporting their target population of learners than presenting the task as a whole (one step) or in nine steps. While too few steps may leave learners unclear about what to do, too many seem to overwhelm them or prevent them from seeing the forest for the trees.

These findings are reminiscent of a much earlier study, in which Kittell (1957) compared three strategies for teaching learners to find the word that did not belong in a group, based on some underlying principle. In looking at multiple measures of retention and transfer, the most successful strategy was a medium-guidance one, which gave learners word sets and a general principle to apply. This outperformed both a low-guidance strategy that only gave learners the word sets, and a high-guidance strategy that gave learners the word sets, the general principle *and* an explanation of how the principle applied to each set. In this case, a very high level of guidance was unsuccessful—perhaps because it prompted learners to follow it rotely, without actively making sense of it (Mayer, 2004).

Altogether, this review of the evidence strongly suggests that while the amount of guidance in an instructional design is important to its effectiveness, more is not necessarily better in all cases.

Context of Guidance: Giving Students a Need to Know

As we discussed above, constructivists appear to pay more attention than instructionists to the context in which guidance is offered because they believe it to be important for retention and transfer. As support, constructivists cite studies indicating that when explanations are given in isolation, students learn very little, even when the explanations are well designed (e.g., Wieman & Perkins, 2005; Hrepic, Zollman, & Rebello, 2007). In higher education, for instance, it has been found that even just 15 minutes after a traditional lecture, students recall very little of the material covered (Wieman & Perkins, 2005). This can be the case even when students are given specific prompting about what to focus on (Hrepic et al., 2007). In Hake's (1998) large-scale study of physics learning across 62 universities, he found that students in traditional lecture classes recall an average of less than 30% of the concepts presented.

Several more detailed studies demonstrate how the context of an explanation affects learning results. Schwartz and Bransford (1998), for instance, demonstrated that giving students a lecture on memory led to learning gains when students *first* had the opportunity to analyze results from a real memory experiment. However, when the distinctions between the cases were analyzed for them, or when the prior task involved summarizing a relevant text, the learning from the lecture was significantly less. Similarly, Capon and Kuhn (2004) found that giving students a relevant problem to solve before they heard a lecture on economics made them more likely to explain and apply the concepts on a later examination, instead of simply regurgitating the textbook definition.

We see a strong resonance between these findings and the constructivist perspective as we articulated it earlier. The implication seems to be that learners will construct a different understanding if they are given an explanation in isolation, versus first having an experience that gives them a "need to know." If students are provided with a meaningful goal, or at least the opportunity to develop one, it affects how they construct meaning from instruction, and thus what is learned (Miller et al., 1999; Schank, 1982).

A powerful illustration of the importance of context is provided by Schwartz and Martin (2004). In this study, ninth-grade students were taught statistics. After 2 weeks of instruction, half were asked to invent a method for comparing high scores from different distributions. The other half were shown how to solve the problem graphically and had an opportunity to practice. Students were further subdivided before being given a transfer problem in which they were asked to compute standardized scores numerically. Half the students in each condition were given a worked example for computing standardized scores, while the other half proceeded directly to the transfer test.

The best performers on the transfer post-test were those who were first asked to invent a method for comparing groups, and then given a worked example for computing standardized scores. This group scored twice as highly as each of the other groups, including the group that was given the tell-and-practice instruction followed by the worked example. As Schwartz et al. (2005) explain, the students who had a chance to invent a procedure first were able to learn more from the worked example.

These findings about the role of context in making guidance effective resonate in an interesting way with some of the findings from the worked-example literature. For example, in the original worked-example studies by Sweller and Cooper (1985) and Cooper and Sweller (1987), each worked example was given immediately prior to a similar problem that the student had to solve. While Sweller and Cooper (1985) describe this as a purely motivational strategy, Trafton and Reiser's (1993) work suggests that being able to access the worked example in the context of a problem to be solved is instrumental in achieving the learning benefits.

In the context of teaching LISP programming, Trafton and Reiser found that worked examples only conferred an advantage when they were presented immediately before a similar problem to be solved, and thus available in memory for use during practice (Trafton & Reiser, 1993). This suggests that at least part of the learning occurs when the students use the worked examples as aids in solving the subsequent problems. Further supporting the notion that worked examples provide a benefit as "on-line guides" during problem solving, Carroll (1994) observed that

> students in the worked example condition spent little time examining the worked example before attempting the accompanying practice problem ... instead they proceeded quickly to the practice problem and then referred back to the example as they wrote or completed the equation.
>
> (p. 364)

While the problem-solving context used in these studies is somewhat different than the kinds of context often used by constructivists (e.g., Pea, 1994; Schank & Neaman, 2001), they serve a similar purpose: to provide students with a goal or "need to know" that drives how the students construct an understanding from instruction. Thus, the worked-example literature, as well as the evidence presented by Schwartz and Martin (2004), suggest that the context in which worked examples are given strongly affects their efficacy.

Timing of Guidance: Is Sooner Always Better?

While not always in agreement about *when* guidance should be given, both constructivists and instructionists believe that the timing of instructional guidance is important (e.g., Anderson, 1993; Schwartz & Bransford, 1998). From an instructionist perspective, the best time to provide guidance is as soon as possible—either at the beginning of the instruction or as soon as a learner makes an error. However, the detailed research on intelligent-tutoring systems suggests that depending on the instructional goals being pursued, providing immediate guidance is not always the best strategy (Anderson, Corbett, Koedinger, & Pelletier, 1995; Anderson, 1993; Mathan & Koedinger, 2003).

Intelligent-tutoring systems are computer-based problem-solving environments that pose problems for learners, and offer individualized guidance based on observing every step of their attempts at solving it (Van Lehn, 1988). Intelligent advice from the computer is made possible by an "expert model" that is capable of solving all of the tutorial problems. The tutor thus "knows" whether or not each step taken by the learner is on a path to a valid solution or represents an error.

Early work by Anderson (1993) showed that offering learners guidance as soon as they strayed from a viable solution path increased their problem-solving speed. In a study using an intelligent tutor to teach students LISP programming, learners who were interrupted during their work and offered guidance as soon as they took a step that would not lead to a valid solution completed the programming exercises in about half the time taken by those who received feedback only on request (Anderson, 1993). Anderson et al. (1995) explained that the advantage of immediate feedback is that it is received when the learner's short-term memory retains enough of their attempted solution that they can understand and learn from the feedback.

On the other hand, in a more recent review of the intelligent-tutoring literature, Mathan and Koedinger (2003) suggest that delaying feedback may result in better retention and transfer of learning. As they explain, providing feedback as soon as an error is detected can rob learners of the opportunity to develop the evaluative skills needed to examine the effects of a problem-solving step, and attempt to repair it in case of error.

In an effort to test this hypothesis, Mathan and Koedinger (2003) conducted an experiment using two different feedback conditions. In one condition, the tutor offered immediate feedback on errors. In the other, the tutor waited to see whether learners detected their own errors, and attempted to guide them through detecting and correcting their mistakes *only* if they attempted to move on to a new problem. Findings from this study indicated that while the learners in the two groups performed similarly on the first problem, those in the delayed feedback condition learned at a faster rate on all subsequent problems (Mathan & Koedinger, 2003).

Together, the Anderson (1993) and Mathan and Koedinger (2003) studies suggest two things about the timing of instructional guidance. First, it clearly matters. When the type of feedback is held constant, timing strongly affects short-term outcomes. Second, the timing of feedback should vary according to instructional goals. While immediate feedback promotes more rapid problem solving in the short term, delaying feedback can result in better long-term retention and transfer.

The Possibility of a Joint Research Agenda

In the previous section we argued that amount, context, and timing are all important factors to attend to when planning instruction, whether one is coming from an instructionist or constructivist position. If we can talk about instructionist and constructivist instructional designs in similar terms, there may be potential for intellectual transfer between the groups.

Up till now, it seems that little cross-fertilization has occurred. Each group has been content to draw on and contribute to work by like-minded colleagues. For their part, instructionist scholars have expressed frustration that constructivists have "mostly ignored" the detailed findings of worked-example studies (Sweller et al., 2007, p. 119). Similarly, we are unaware of any major instructionist attempts to draw on constructivist findings. Despite this lack of crossover, the two camps often create guidance that is similar in its pedagogical functions. For example, both groups use some form of explanation (e.g., Garner, 1987; Schwartz & Bransford, 1998), procedural direction (e.g., van Merriënboer, 1997; McNeill, Lizotte, Krajcik, & Marx, 2006), and feedback (e.g., Phye & Sanders, 1994; Kolodner & Guzdial, 2000).

Looking at one example in particular, both Hmelo-Silver et al. (2007, p. 102) and Sweller et al. (2007, p. 118) note that instructionists' worked examples serve a similar function to real-time modeling in inquiry environments. Each kind of guidance shows learners how domain experts break down a problem to make it more soluble, and how the different concepts, strategies, and procedures they use are combined to achieve working solutions. Thus, perhaps the lack of crossover between the camps occurs not because there is no relevance, but because the findings of each are so ensconced in the language of their particular framework that these connections are difficult to make.

As a case in point, worked-example studies deal almost exclusively with well-structured problems in technical domains such as science and mathematics (see reviews by Sweller, van Merriënboer, & Paas, 1998; Atkinson, Derry, Renkl, & Wortham, 2000). The guidelines for the design of worked examples that have emerged from the research are thus worded specifically for the creation of algorithmic, written-out problem solutions. It is difficult for constructivists to transfer these findings to real-time guidance, and to the ill-defined problem domains (e.g., social studies, history, writing) with which many of them are concerned. Attempts to make such translations (e.g., Atkinson et al., 2000) run the risk of distorting the original approach. For example, Atkinson et al. (2000) describe how the guidelines for worked examples could be translated for use in the PBL environment of the Secondary Teacher Education Project (STEP). However, in many respects this description (for example, providing an expert solution before each case that students are given to solve) sounds more like up-front instruction than a problem-based approach.

We believe that the categories of amount, context, and timing may allow us to translate the worked-example findings in a more appropriate way and create an interesting and testable research agenda that could bring instructionists and constructivists together. We illustrate this in the following section. For instructionists, this agenda offers the opportunity to expand their work into new domains. For constructivists, it offers a strategy for drawing on a body of highly detailed findings that, as Kirschner et al. (2006) point out, have not been used much by constructivists in the past. Our example is just one of the many possible ways in which using the general language of amount, context, and timing may support productive conversations between instructionists and constructivists.

Applying Worked-Example Guidance Principles to Real-Time Modeling: Thinking about Amount, Context, and Timing

Earlier we noted that worked examples seem to be most effective when the *amount* of guidance they provide is sufficient to show learners how to get from one stage to the next (Pillay, 1994) and when individual steps are grouped together to show sub-goals along the way (Catrambone, 1994, 1995). In addition, it appears valuable to provide worked examples in the *context* of a problem to be solved (e.g., Trafton & Reiser, 1993) and perhaps *after* students have had a chance to attempt problems in the domain (Schwartz & Martin, 2004). What might such principles look like for real-time modeling? To give a concrete illustration, we consider the problem of teaching students to analyze the historical significance of a document. The first phase of the new research we envision could take an observational form. Outstanding history teachers could be identified (perhaps through large-scale test data) and observed over the course of several days. Observers would note the degree to which they use modeling to teach the analysis of historical documents, and whether the characteristics set forth in the worked-example literature are useful (and sufficient) to describe their practice.

This observational data would help us to describe more precisely how the principles described above are instantiated for modeling problem solving in complex and ill-defined domains. For example, when is the modeling provided, in what context is it provided, and how much of it is provided at one time?

The second phase of the research would use an experimental approach to build on the findings of the first. Systematic variations could be made in the amount, context, and timing of the modeling guidance. For example, in terms of timing, is it best for the teacher to model the analysis process (a) as a whole up-front; (b) as separate pieces before the students get to each part; (c) after students have had a chance to explore the problem; (d) only when learners commit an error (either immediately or after they have a chance to detect and correct their mistake); or (e) some combination of the above? In terms of the problem context, we could compare the following conditions: (a) simply providing a model; (b) providing the model in the context of another document to be analyzed; and (c) providing the model as guidance to help students use historical documents as evidence in a debate on a current governmental policy. For amount, we might look at variations in (a) the size of the sub-goals used; (b) how this structure is highlighted for students; and (c) the ways in which skilled teachers illustrate the transition from one stage of analysis to the next.

For each comparison outlined, research could examine both the learning process and learning outcomes. One outcome measure to examine would be students' ability to analyze other historical documents. Following Bransford and Schwartz's (1999) notion of transfer as preparation for future learning, this should be evaluated not only in terms of success in producing sophisticated solutions, but also how students go about attacking novel problems. For example, how do students adapt to analyze a *foreign* historical document? Are some groups more able to learn from initial mis-steps than others? In addition, we could examine the different ways in which students interacted with the teacher's modeling. Did they ask questions of the teacher? If so, what kind? If given the opportunity to access a video of the teacher's modeling, did they choose to use it? If so, when did they access it, what parts did they look at, and how did they try to use them?

Together, the kinds of studies we have outlined above may help to articulate principles for successful modeling of complex problem solving in ill-defined domains. Whether we can generate such principles more quickly by drawing on the worked-example findings is an interesting and potentially fruitful question. We would also expect such research to generate new avenues for investigation into the principles that make worked examples themselves effective. While there may be differences in what makes modeling and worked examples effective, we should be able to discuss them in similar terms. Such a research agenda could be of interest to instructionists and constructivists alike, and is just one example of how using a more general language can help to build common ground in the conversation on instructional design.

Conclusion

We have argued above that instructionists and constructivists may be talking past each other due to different ambitions with regard to transfer, and different assumptions about how best to make it happen. Instructionists seem to be interested primarily in transfer to formally similar problems in school-like situations, while constructivists are more interested in cross-contextual transfer and transfer between school-like and real-world situations. These very different commitments may have led them to different readings of the literature, different demands on theory and research methods, and different approaches to supporting novices in complex problem spaces.

In our view, the multiple differences in the way guidance is conceived by each group has led to a methodological stalemate, in which each group brings forth evidence that the other group does not find convincing. We suggest that it is time to move away from the unproductive adversarial question of "which approach is better overall" to a collaborative agenda in which we seek to understand principles for designing the amount, context, and timing of guidance that is suitable for particular goals and situations. To illustrate what this might mean, we have sketched the outlines of a research agenda that we believe may bring instructionists and constructivists together in a productive partnership.

We note that some important factors in the design and effectiveness of instructional guidance have been overlooked in this chapter, including how the principles outlined may interact with individual differences between learners (Jonassen & Grabowski, 1993). We expect that as research progresses, these will be elucidated. We also note that proceeding down the path we have outlined leaves a greater degree of inference to the designer in translating principles to practice. We feel that this flexibility is necessary to design instruction that meets the needs of particular learning situations; however, we wonder how willing instructionists will be to slacken their commitment to generating deterministic prescriptions for instruction.

We hope that this discussion has provided a helpful way to think about the current debate surrounding instructional guidance. As we move forward in the 21st century, educational researchers are recognizing the inherent complexity involved in many of the most important educational issues. Answers seem to lie not in contests between two extreme possibilities, but in the fine distinctions that emerge from a detailed and multidimensional examination of the evidence. This framework presents one tool to help researchers make progress on this long-term endeavor.

Question: Clark. *I enjoyed reading your chapter. We all hope that a clearer conception of instructional guidance will be the main product of the debate. In the 1970s Lee Cronbach complained that we measure individual differences in micrometers and instructional methods with divining rods. The situation is more or less the same today. You argue persuasively for systematic research that clarifies issues such as the amount, context, and timing of guidance. Yet it also seems that there is no agreement about the cognitive functions of the various operations that are offered to define* *guidance in research or practice. How can we accomplish what you propose without considering the function of the enormous range of instructional support activities that are considered to be examples of "guidance" by various groups in education?*

Reply: Wise and O'Neill. We agree completely that a better theorization (and testing) of the functions that different types of guidance play in supporting the learning process is needed. In fact, in an earlier version of our chapter we used pedagogical function as a grouping category to show commonalities in the different kinds of guidance favored by the two camps. To us, this seems like a very productive avenue for starting to make sense of the large range of instructional support activities currently employed and studied. Furthermore, once function is used to organize the various types of guidance, it appears that much of the debate is not about *whether* a particular type of guidance (pedagogical function) should be given but *how* it should be given. For example, we discussed how both worked examples and real-time modeling in inquiry environments serve the function of showing learners how domain experts break down a problem to make it more soluble and how the different concepts, strategies, and procedures they use are combined to achieve working solutions. To us, it appears that the difference between worked examples and real-time modeling is not the pedagogical function served, but whether the guidance is given before or in the course of problem solving and in the set up of the problem-solving situation itself (i.e., the timing and context of the guidance).

Similarly, both instructionists and constructivists employ some form of guidance to provide procedural direction to students, either in the form of process worksheets or as scaffolds to support the inquiry process. Again, the pedagogical function in both cases seems the same: to provide students with steps, rules, or guidelines to follow in completing a task; the difference lies in the level of granularity with which the guidance is given and the larger task structure in which the guidance is embedded (i.e., the amount and context of the guidance).

We do not assume that the most effective way to give guidance will be the same across types of guidance (or across learning goals for a particular kind of guidance). Thus, identifying a pedagogical function and the various forms of guidance that seem to be fulfilling this function is an important prerequisite to conducting this kind of research. Additionally, in conducting the research on how students interact with the guidance, we can examine if the guidance is indeed serving the pedagogical function we anticipated, or if there are other function(s) being served.

Question: Clark. *Isn't it possible that farther transfer is possible when instructionist-guided support employs what has been called varied (or variable) practice and haven't most of the reviews of past research on this issue concluded that the evidence only supported gradual and limited transfer despite claims to the contrary?*

Reply: Wise and O'Neill. The reviews of research on this topic, including the ones we cover in our chapter, do recommend caution in our expectations of transfer. As Anderson, Reder, and Simon (1996) point out, depending on the relationship between the learning and transfer materials (and, we would add, learning and transfer situations) "there can be either large amounts of transfer, a modest amount, no transfer at all or even negative transfer" (pp. 7–8). As we read the reviews, however, they do not argue that only small, gradual transfer is possible. On the contrary, Anderson et al. (1996) present evidence to *contest* the claim that knowledge does not transfer between tasks. Similarly, Perkins and Salomon (1989) sum up their review by stating that "Given appropriate conditions, such as cueing, practicing, generating abstract rules, socially developing explanations and principles, conjuring up analogies ... and the like, transfer from one problem domain to another can be obtained" (p. 22).

We do take issue with one small point in Perkins and Salomon's summation: the idea that what is transferred are "general skills." In our view, there is not good evidence for the existence of cognitive skills that are truly general from the time that they are mastered, though there is great evidence that such skills can be *generalized* over time with appropriate kinds of practice, in the appropriate contexts, and with appropriate scaffolding and feedback. To borrow Perkins and Salomon's example, the chess master *can* potentially learn to transfer his skill in chess to battlefield strategy; but this will not necessarily be a quick process, however straightforward the analogies may seem to an outside observer.

As you suggest, part of the training that may help to generalize skill is variable practice—though we don't see this as an instructional technique that instructionists have a monopoly on. However, from a constructivist perspective the practice should include not only variations in the cognitive features of the task, but also variation across a range of appropriate situations of use. So, the bookish chess master may need considerable practice not only in working a range of military strategy problems, but working them in a variety of appropriate social settings (such as a hotly contested argument in a battlefield tent with a group of gruff generals) before he can reliably transfer his strategic thinking to be productive in a military context.

Question: Rosenshine. *I was very impressed with the examples of instructional procedures related to the amount of guidance, the context of guidance, and the timing of guidance. The example of giving students a problem to solve before they hear a lecture is a lovely and inventive idea. But every one of the examples in these three sections came from a study in which the criterion was "gain in learning." I see absolutely no conflict between constructivists and direct-instruction advocates when we read, discuss, or conduct research in which "gain in learning" is the criterion. Do you agree that when constructivists and direct-instruction advocates are both interested in the outcome of a gain in learning there is no longer any conflict between the two groups?*

Also, in the opening section, you note that constructivists are interested in "worthwhile transfer," "preparation for future learning," the "ability to learn from new situations," and "transfer to real-life situations." But, you also note that "constructivists have not been as committed to measuring far transfer as they have been to advocating its importance." If constructivists can't measure far transfer and worthwhile transfer, why do you have a section on this topic? Wouldn't it be more honest to drop these unsupported claims and focus only on constructivist instructional procedures that lead to gains in learning? Would your argument suffer if inferences about "worthwhile transfer" were removed from your chapter?

Reply: Wise and O'Neill. In our minds there is a difference in what instructionists and constructivists are talking about when they refer to a gain in learning. As we wrote in our chapter, it seems to us that constructivists are more ambitious with respect to transfer, and link their understanding of "learning gain" very closely with it. In this vein, we aim to optimize instructional activities for depth of understanding and far transfer rather than quick learning and near transfer. We feel that there are two very compelling reasons why we need to include a consideration of far transfer when we talk about gains in learning: first, this is the ultimate goal of education—to prepare students to use the knowledge they learn in school in real-world contexts at some point in the future; second, instructional techniques that lead to the quickest initial learning may not necessarily be the same as those that lead to the best retention and long-term transfer. For example, we discuss the intelligent-tutoring literature in which immediate feedback has been found to produce more rapid learning initially, while delayed feedback has led to better retention and transfer. Thus, tasks that test students on exactly what they learned or provide a weak measure of near transfer cannot be used as a proxy for far-transfer results, and more far-transfer measures need to be included in future studies.

It seems that you over-interpret the statement we made in our chapter about the difficulties constructivists have had in assessing far transfer. We certainly did not intend to say that far transfer is unmeasurable. Nor did we intend to say that constructivists have entirely failed to measure far transfer. Our comments in this section were meant to point out the logistical, conceptual, and monetary challenges of measuring the extreme end of the transfer continuum—unprompted use of knowledge in everyday settings, long after the initial learning. Barnett and Ceci (2002) have devised a useful taxonomy for thinking about the different ways a transfer situation can differ from the original learning situation in terms of six dimensions: the knowledge domain; physical context; temporal context; functional context; social context; and task modality. In the great majority of the instructionist studies we have reviewed, "transfer" is operationalized as testing performance in a context that differs on only one of these dimensions, knowledge domain, and only slightly at that. The other five dimensions are virtually the same in the training and testing scenarios: physical context (lab/classroom); functional context (academic, evaluative); social context (individual); temporal context (same day or next day); and modality (written/typed task, same problem format). Even within the knowledge domain, what instructionists seem to consider "far" transfer is quite different from what constructivists do.

While we think that both instructionists and constructivists could and should go farther in terms of measuring transfer along all of Barnett and Ceci's dimensions, there are some notable examples of far-transfer measurements that have been done. In science, researchers have looked for evidence of transfer from project-based learning in the quality of their written reports, and their ability to plan novel investigations (O'Neill & Polman, 2004). Klahr and Nigam (2004) used a similar strategy when they asked students who had been learning a control-of-variables strategy to critique other students' (problematic) science fair posters. Fong, Krantz, and Nisbett (1986) conducted one of the few studies that looked at transfer outside the classroom, by calling research participants at home and conducting a "survey" that asked them questions that involved the statistical knowledge they had been learning in school. Studies like these demonstrate that it is neither impossible nor impractical to devise and implement far-transfer measures in educational research.

Question: Rosenshine. *I enjoyed reading your example about learning how to teach students to analyze historical documents. You wrote that the first step would be to find outstanding history teachers and observe their instructional procedures. The second step would be experimental studies where students were taught to analyze documents using ideas learned from observing these teachers and, within the intervention, there might be variations in the timing and use of models. These two steps seemed very similar to direct instruction and process–product research where the researchers also identified outstanding teachers, studied their instructional procedures, and then used these procedures in experimental studies where a measure of student achievement was the criterion. In other words, if I were interested in training students to analyze historical documents I would want to use the same procedures that you describe. So if the goal is to train students to become more proficient at analyzing historical documents, do you see any conflict, or any difference, in how constructivism and direct-instruction advocates would try to achieve this goal?*

Reply: Wise and O'Neill. We thank you for pointing out the (unintentional) similarities between our proposed new line of research on modeling in history instruction and the procedures of process–product research of 30 years ago. In addition to the important similarities you point out, we think that what we are proposing in our chapter is different in some key ways from that earlier work. Perhaps it would be fair to say that our proposal adopts characteristics of the successful process–product research design, while adapting them to address current research problems. For example, the process–product research appears to be largely domain general and to have examined the presence or absence of a wide array of instructional procedures. In contrast, the work we propose is domain-specific, focuses on one particular form of instructional guidance (modeling), and examines the enactment (the "how") rather than the simple presence or absence. These are important differences in our view since the past three decades of cognitive science have shown how powerful domain-specific influences are on thinking and learning. Further, the series of experiments we are suggesting appear (from our understanding) to address questions of a more specific nature than the process–product research.

Finally, we believe some important changes have taken place in history instruction which would likely have substantial influence on both the implementation and effectiveness of modeling in history classrooms. The original process–

product research seems to have compared various forms of teacher-centered classrooms. Until the late 1980s or early 1990s, relatively little attention was paid in North America to teaching historical interpretation; emphasis on the mastery of textbook narratives seems to have prevailed. That situation has now changed— the 1996 revision of the US National Standards for History included substantial recommendations for conveying and understanding the nature of historical knowledge. Today, regular publications for teachers frequently contain articles on teaching history using primary-source evidence.

To sum up, we want to highlight that our goal in suggesting this program of research was not to create a "constructivist" approach to teaching students how to analyze historical documents, but to suggest a joint research agenda that both constructivists and instructionists could pursue. The goal would be to catalog the many ways in which modeling guidance is given in history classrooms, with the aim of optimizing the use of this powerful instructional strategy for different instructional contexts and goals.

Question: Rosenshine. *When students construct knowledge on their own, or with minimal supervision, they are also likely to also construct errors. How do constructivists handle this possibility of students making unintentional but persistent errors under conditions of minimal supervision?*

Reply: Wise and O'Neill. Given the constructivist belief that students inevitably construct their own understandings (regardless of what form of instruction is used), it is certainly possible that at some points they will construct problematic understandings. We agree that this is an important issue. Your question seems to imply, however, that this is a special problem for constructivist classrooms because they leave students alone with instructional materials and activities for too long. While students in a constructivist classroom may spend a great deal of their time working on a problem with their classmates, this does not mean that they are without teacher supervision. As we pointed out in our chapter, constructivists are not advocating "minimal guidance," we are advocating that guidance be more situated, flexible, and responsive.

We expect three features of a well-designed constructivist classroom to safeguard against students holding on to misinterpretations that arise during instruction. First, a well-designed constructivist activity will give students opportunities to test the viability of their understandings as they develop. For example, in the case of science, the instructional design may include specific experimentation that targets common student preconceptions. Second, a constructivist classroom that promotes valued forms of student discussion, justification, and testing of ideas (scientific argumentation), will provide additional opportunities for problematic ideas to surface and be transformed. Third, in both cases, a skilled teacher circulating in the classroom will be able to provide just-in-time guidance (in the moment it is needed) to help students understand their errors or misunderstandings, and correct them.

References

Alexander, P. A., & Murphy, P. K. (1999). Nurturing the seeds of transfer: A domain-specific perspective. *International Journal of Educational Research, 31*, 561–576.

Anderson, J., Corbett, A. T., Koedinger, K. R., & Pelletier, R. (1995). Cognitive tutors: Lessons learned. *The Journal of the Learning Sciences, 4*(2), 167–207.

Anderson, J. R. (1993). *Rules of the mind.* Hillsdale, NJ: Erlbaum.

Anderson, J. R., Reder, L. M., & Simon, H. A. (1996). Situated learning and education. *Educational Researcher, 25*(4), 5–11.

Atkinson, R. K., Derry, S. J., Renkl, A., & Wortham, D. (2000). Learning from examples: Instructional principles from the worked examples research. *Review of Educational Research, 70*, 181–214.

Barnett, S. M., & Ceci, S. J. (2002). When and where do we apply what we learn? A taxonomy for far transfer. *Psychological Bulletin, 128*(4), 612–637.

Barnett, S. M., & Ceci, S. J. (2005). Reframing the evaluation of education: Assessing whether learning transfers beyond the classroom. In J. P. Mestre (Ed.), *Transfer of learning from a modern multidisciplinary perspective* (pp. 295–312). Greenwich, CT: Information Age Publishing.

Bransford, J. D. (1979). *Human cognition: Learning, understanding, and remembering.* Belmont, CA: Wadsworth.

Bransford, J. D., & Schwartz, D. L. (1999). Rethinking transfer: A simple proposal with multiple implications. *Review of Research in Education, 24*, 61–100.

Brown, J. S., Collins, A., & Duguid, P. (1989). Situated cognition and the culture of learning. *Educational Researcher, 18*(1), 32–42.

Capon, N., & Kuhn, D. (2004). What's so good about problem-based learning? *Cognition and Instruction, 22*, 61–79.

Carraher, T. N., Carraher, D. W., & Schliemann, A. D. (1985). Mathematics in the streets and in the schools. *British Journal of Developmental Psychology, 3*, 21–29.

Carroll, W. (1994). Using worked examples as an instructional support in the algebra classroom. *Journal of Educational Psychology, 86*, 360–367.

Catrambone, R. (1994). Improving examples to improve transfer to novel problems. *Memory and Cognition, 22*, 606–615.

Catrambone, R. (1995). Aiding subgoal learning: Effects on transfer. *Journal of Educational Psychology, 87*, 5–17.

Cobb, P., Confrey, J., diSessa, A., Lehrer, R., & Schauble, L. (2003). Design experiments in educational research. *Educational Researcher, 32*(1), 9–13.

Cognition and Technology Group at Vanderbilt. (1992). The Jasper experiment: An exploration of issues in learning and instructional design. *Educational Technology Research & Development, 40*(1), 65–80.

Cognition and Technology Group at Vanderbilt. (1994). *The Jasper project: Lessons in curriculum, instruction, assessment, and professional development.* Mahwah, NJ: Lawrence Erlbaum Associates.

Collins, A., Joseph, D., & Bielaczyc, K. (2004). Design research: Theoretical and methodological issues. *The Journal of the Learning Sciences, 13*(1), 15–42.

Cooper, G., & Sweller, J. (1987). The effects of schema acquisition and rule automation on mathematical problem-solving transfer. *Journal of Educational Psychology, 79*, 347–362.

Featherstone, H. (1992). *Learning from the first years of classroom teaching: The journey in, the journey out* (NCRTL Special Report). East Lansing, MI: National Center for Research on Teacher Learning, Michigan State University.

Fong, G. T., Krantz, D. H., & Nisbett, R. E. (1986). The effects of statistical training on thinking about everyday problems. *Cognitive Psychology, 18*, 253–292.

Garner, R. (1987). Strategies for reading and studying expository text. *Educational Psychologist, 22*(3–4), 299–312.

Hake, R. R. (1998). Interactive-engagement versus traditional methods: A six-thousand-student survey of mechanics test data for introductory physics courses. *American Journal of Physics, 66*(1), 64–74.

Hickey, D. T., Kindfield, A. C. H., Horwitz, P., & Christie, M. (1999). Advancing educational theory by enhancing practice in a technology supported genetics learning environment. *Journal of Education, 181*(2), 25–55.

Hmelo-Silver, C. E., Duncan, R. G., & Chinn, C. A. (2007). Scaffolding and achievement in problem-based and inquiry learning: A response to Kirschner, Sweller, and Clark (2006). *Educational Psychologist, 42*(2), 99–107.

Hrepic, Z., Zollman, D. A., & Rebello, N. S. (2007). Comparing students' and experts' understanding of the content of a lecture. *Journal of Science Education and Technology, 16*(3), 213–224.

Jonassen, D. H., & Grabowski, B. L. (1993). *Handbook of individual differences, learning, and instruction.* Hillsdale, NJ: Lawrence Erlbaum Associates.

Kirschner, P. A., Sweller, J., & Clark, R. E. (2006). Why minimal guidance during instruction does not work: An analysis of the failure of constructivist, discovery, problem-based, experiential, and inquiry-based teaching. *Educational Psychologist, 41*(2), 75–86.

Kittell, J. E. (1957). An experimental study of the effect of external direction during learning on transfer and retention of principles. *Journal of Educational Psychology, 48*(7), 391–405.

Klahr, D., & Nigam, M. (2004). The equivalence of learning paths in early science instruction: Effects of direct instruction and discovery learning. *Psychological Science, 15*, 661–667.

Kolodner, J. L., & Guzdial, M. (2000). Theory and practice of case-based learning aids. In D. H. Jonassen & S. M. Land (Eds.), *Theoretical foundations of learning environments* (pp. 215–242). Mahwah, NJ: Lawrence Erlbaum Associates.

Kuhn, D. (2007). Is direct instruction an answer to the right question? *Educational Psychologist, 42*(2), 109–113.

Mathan, S., & Koedinger, K. R. (2003). Recasting the feedback debate: Benefits of tutoring error detection and correction skills. In U. Hoppe, F. Verdejo, & J. Kay (Eds.), *Artificial intelligence in education: Shaping the future of learning through intelligent technologies* (pp. 13–20). Amsterdam: IOS Press.

Mayer, R. (2004). Should there be a three-strikes rule against pure discovery learning? The case for guided methods of instruction. *American Psychologist, 59*, 14–19.

McNeill, K. L., Lizotte, D. J., Krajcik, J., & Marx, R. W. (2006). Supporting students' construction of scientific explanations by fading scaffolds in instructional materials. *Journal of the Learning Sciences, 15*(2), 153–191.

Miller, C., Lehman, J., & Koedinger, K. (1999). Goals and learning in microworlds. *Cognitive Science, 23*, 305–336.

Nadolski, R. J., Kirschner, P. A., & van Merriënboer, J. J. G. (2005). Optimizing the number of steps in learning tasks for complex skills. *British Journal of Educational Psychology, 75*, 223–237.

O'Neill, D. K., & Polman, J. L. (2004). Why educate "little scientists"? Examining the potential of practice-based scientific literacy. *Journal of Research in Science Teaching, 41*(3), 234–266.

O'Neill, D. K., & Weiler, M. J. (2006). Cognitive tools for understanding history: What more do we need? *Journal of Educational Computing Research, 35*(2), 179–195.

Paas, F. (1992). Training strategies for attaining transfer of problem-solving skill in statistics: A cognitive-load approach. *Journal of Educational Psychology, 84*, 429–434.

Paas, F., & van Merriënboer, J. J. G. (1994). Variability of worked examples and transfer of geometrical problem solving skills: A cognitive-load approach. *Journal of Educational Psychology, 86*, 122–133.

Papert, S. (1987). Computer criticism vs. technocentric thinking. *Educational Researcher, 16*(5), 22–30.

Pea, R. D. (1994). Seeing what we build together: Distributed multimedia learning environments for transformative communications. *The Journal of the Learning Sciences, 3*(3), 285–299.

Pea, R. D. (2004). The social and technological dimensions of scaffolding and related concepts for learning, education and human activity. *The Journal of the Learning Sciences, 13*(3), 423–451.

Perkins, D. N., & Salomon, G. (1989). Are cognitive skills context-bound? *Educational Researcher, 18*(1), 16–25.

Phye, G. D., & Sanders, C. E. (1994). Advice and feedback: Elements of practice for problem solving. *Contemporary Educational Psychology, 19*(3), 286–301.

Pillay, H. (1994). Cognitive load and mental rotation: Structuring orthographic projection for learning and problem solving. *Instructional Science, 22*, 91–113.

Polman, J. L. (2000). *Designing project-based science: Connecting learners through guided inquiry.* New York: Teachers College Press.

Quilici, J. L., & Mayer, R. E. (1996). Role of examples in how students learn to categorize statistics word problems. *Journal of Educational Psychology, 88*, 144–161.

Royer, J. M., Mestre, J. P., & Dufresne, R. J. (2005). Introduction: Framing the transfer problem. In J. P. Mestre (Ed.), *Transfer of learning from a modern multidisciplinary perspective* (pp. vii–xxvi). Greenwich, CT: Information Age Publishing.

Saye, J. W., & Brush, T. (2002). Scaffolding critical reasoning about history and social issues in multimedia-supported learning environments. *Educational Technology Research & Development, 50*(3), 77–96.

Schank, R. C. (1982). *Dynamic memory: A theory of reminding and learning in computers and people.* Cambridge: Cambridge University.

Schank, R. C., & Neaman, A. (2001). Motivation and failure in educational simulation design. In K. D. Forbus & P. J. Feltovich (Eds.), *Smart machines in education: The coming revolution in educational technology* (pp. 37–69). Cambridge, MA: MIT Press.

Schmidt, H. G., Loyens, S. M. M., van Gog, T., & Paas, F. (2007). Problem-based learning is compatible with human cognitive architecture: Commentary on Kirschner, Sweller, and Clark (2006). *Educational Psychologist, 42*(2), 91–97.

Schwartz, D. L., & Bransford, J. D. (1998). A time for telling. *Cognition and Instruction, 16*, 475–522.

Schwartz, D. L., Bransford, J. D., & Sears, D. (2005). Efficiency and innovation in transfer. In J. P. Mestre (Ed.), *Transfer of learning from a modern multidisciplinary perspective* (pp. 1–51). Greenwich, CT: Information Age Publishing.

Schwartz, D. L., & Martin, T. (2004). Inventing to prepare for learning: The hidden efficiency of original student production in statistics instruction. *Cognition and Instruction, 22*, 129–184.

Stodolsky, S. S. (1988). *The subject matters: Classroom activity in math and social studies.* Chicago, IL: University of Chicago Press.

Sweller, J. (1988). Cognitive load during problem solving: Effects on learning. *Cognitive Science, 12,* 257–285.

Sweller, J., & Cooper, G. A. (1985). The use of worked examples as a substitute for problem solving in learning algebra. *Cognition and Instruction, 2,* 59–89.

Sweller, J., Kirschner, P. A., & Clark, R. E. (2007). Why minimally guided teaching techniques do not work: A reply to commentaries. *Educational Psychologist, 42*(2), 115–121.

Sweller, J., van Merriënboer, J. G., & Paas, F. G. (1998). Cognitive architecture and instructional design. *Educational Psychology Review, 10,* 251–296.

Tannen, D. (1999). *The argument culture: Stopping America's war of words.* New York: Ballantine Books.

Trafton, J. G., & Reiser, B. J. (1993). *The contribution of studying examples and solving problems to skill acquisition.* Paper presented at the 15th Annual Conference of the Cognitive Science Society.

Van Lehn, K. (1988). Student modeling. In M. C. Polson & J. J. Richardson (Eds.), *Foundations of intelligent tutoring systems* (pp. 55–78). Hillsdale, NJ: Erlbaum.

Van Merriënboer, J. J. G. (1997). *Training complex cognitive skills.* Englewood Cliffs, NJ: Educational Technology Publications.

Wieman, C., & Perkins, K. (2005). Transforming physics education. *Physics Today, 59*(11), 36–41.

6 Constructivism

When It's the Wrong Idea and When It's the Only Idea*

Rand J. Spiro and Michael DeSchryver
Michigan State University

Overview: Constructivist Approaches as Necessary in Ill-Structured Domains and Desirable for Deep Learning on the Web

Constructivist approaches to learning and instruction have been roundly criticized in several prominently placed articles in recent years (e.g., Mayer, 2004; Kirschner, Sweller, & Clark, 2006). A key to the power of the critiques has been the predominance of empirical findings indicating the greater effectiveness of highly guided instruction when compared to constructivist approaches that have a relative lack of direct instructional guidance. It is not a coincidence that these empirical findings have come almost exclusively from well-structured domains within mathematics and science and a few outside those areas (e.g., more orderly aspects of reading development related to the graphophonemic code). We have no objection to the argument that highly guided learning and direct instruction can be maximally effective in such domains, where by their very nature it is possible to determine what information "fully explains the concepts and procedures that students are required to learn" (Kirschner et al., 2006, p. 75).

The argument of this chapter is a simple one: the success of direct instructional guidance approaches in well-structured domains (WSDs) cannot extend to ill-structured domains (ISDs), *in principle*, because of the very nature of those domains. That which would be directly instructed and explicitly guided *does not exist* in ill-structured domains—hence the claim that it is *not* a coincidence that direct instructional guidance approaches lack a corpus of supporting data in ISDs like they have in WSDs. Given that the debate between these approaches is unsettled on empirical grounds for ISDs, this chapter aims to provide some conceptual clarification of key issues of learning and instruction in such domains. The hope is that such clarification would contribute toward forming a basis for empirical work that would directly address the debated issues of this volume.

The argument will be developed by first discussing the nature of ISDs and the kinds of learning and instruction that that nature would seem to exclude by

* The writing of this chapter was supported in part by the Literacy Achievement Research Center, Michigan State University. An earlier version of this chapter was presented by the first author at a debate on constructivism at the 2007 meeting of the American Educational Research Association. This Chapter contains the arguments presented there and extends them.

definition. Then we will present quotes from papers by direct instructional guidance advocates in order to make their goals and recommendations explicit. It will be shown that those explicitly stated goals could not be achieved given the very nature of learning in ISDs. That is, what *makes* a domain ill structured is the absence of the very features that are supposed to be directly instructed and supported. Further, empirical evidence will be cited for the hazards of treating ISDs as if they were WSDs in the kinds of guidance and support provided. The differing nature of guidance and support in a constructivist framework developed for learning and instruction in ISDs is briefly addressed. In the penultimate section, an argument is presented for the Web as an ideal environment for deep learning in ISDs, but one that requires relatively open exploration unfettered by direct instructional intervention for that potential to be achieved. In the final section, we make the claim that treating ISDs as if they were well-structured is no longer just an academic argument with implications for such things as test scores (as important as the latter may be), but rather has potentially significant societal consequences.

The Problem of Ill-Structured Domains

We will argue that direct instructional guidance approaches are *necessarily* "misguided"—in several ways—in ill-structured domains. Let us begin, then, with a discussion of ISDs.

Wittgenstein (1953) famously provided the following example of an ill-structured concept. He analyzed the concept of games and demonstrated that for the set of all consensually accepted instances of games, there was no feature common to all. Any attempt to identify the necessary and sufficient conditions for something to be called a game fails. This is true of any ill-structured concept and, by extension and to an even greater extent (and with profound implications for knowledge application), for ill-structured *domains* (or, more precisely, those *parts* of domains that are ill structured). Ill-structured domains are characterized by being indeterminate, inexact, noncodifiable, nonalgorithmic, nonroutinizable, imperfectly predictable, nondecomposable into additive elements, and, in various ways, disorderly (Spiro, Vispoel, Schmitz, Samarapungavan, & Boerger, 1987; Spiro, Collins, & Ramchandran, 2007). An important feature of ISDs is that one cannot have pre-packaged prescriptions in long-term memory for how knowledge in those domains is to be applied across any reasonably large range of situations. This is because *irregularity* is a crucial feature of ISDs. That is, the circumstances for knowledge application in ISDs are characterized by considerable variability from one instance to another, and thus pre-specifiability of the conditions for knowledge use is not possible.

Ill-structuredness should not be confused with *complexity*. Complexity alone does not connote ill-structuredness. In fact, many well-structured domains demonstrate complexity. A key feature in separating well-structured complexity from ill-structured, as we have said, is the regularity (or lack thereof) demonstrated by same-named concepts and phenomena across instances. For example, the physiology of force production by muscle fibers is complex. Many hundreds of thousands of fibers perform processes involving intricate anatomical mechanisms (e.g., the sliding and ratcheting of actin and myosin filaments) and even more intricate interactions of calcium ion pumps in the activation (recruitment) of muscle cells. However, given that each fiber of a given sort (e.g., skeletal muscle) produces force in the *same* (complex) way, there is *regularity* in the application of this concept (Coulson, Feltovich, & Spiro, 1989; Feltovich, Spiro, & Coulson, 1989). As such, the domain is not ill structured, and is instead one of "well-structured complexity."

Consider, on the other hand, concepts such as core democratic values in social studies. Ideas like "justice" or "the common good" are ill structured because they are complex and because instances of their application vary considerably in *how* they are understood (Spiro et al., 2007). Because of this irregularity, definitions and explicit guidance work for too small a set of possible applications and miss too many legitimate ones, while at the same time seducing the learner to rely on the explicit guidance.

Examples of ill-structured domains include the obvious ones: social studies, humanities, and the arts. But many aspects of more "scientific" domains have an ill-structured quality (e.g., most "macro" concepts of evolutionary biology, such as "adaptation"; Mayr, 1988). Further, all areas of knowledge application in unconstrained, real-world situations tend to have substantial aspects of ill-structuredness. Think of the difference between experimental design as sequentially and incrementally taught in a statistics course versus decision-making when trying to design a test of a theory-driven hypothesis "in the wild." Similarly, consider the difference between basic biomedical science and clinical practice, or between engineering practice and its underlying physical and mathematical principles. All professional domains present challenges of ill-structuredness. Whereas biomedical cognition clearly has some well-structured, basic science components in anatomy and physiology, as well as in many aspects of diagnosis, treatment/management decisions are affected by so many contextual factors that they are inevitably characterized by considerable indeterminateness. Such decisions depend on myriad unanticipatable interactions of those contextual variables, each of which can take on many values—for example, the severity of patients' primary conditions; the presence or absence of secondary conditions; individual preferences that affect trade-offs between, say, pain reduction and clarity of thought; effects of treatments on differing job-performance requirements; and many, many others.

That professional domains are ill structured becomes especially clear when one considers teaching (e.g., Lampert, 2001; Palincsar et al., 2007; Shulman, 1992; Sykes & Bird, 1992). A prospective teacher can take a dozen courses on "methods," but once in the field it becomes clear that "it's not that simple," "it depends," "it's not either–or" are watchwords of practice. For example, how does one teach the appropriate situation-specific application of a ubiquitous teaching concept like "scaffolding" (Palincsar et al., 2007)? Not by providing a pre-specified set of rules for the application of the concept. That is not possible, and any candidate rules that help in some situations will mislead in others. The way such a concept is learned for application is through the accumulation of considerable experience, the exposure to many examples, and an appreciation for multiple interacting contextual features (Palincsar et al., 2007). That is the reason for the oft-cited "10-year rule" for the attainment of expertise in complex domains (Ericsson, Charness, Hoffman, & Feltovich, 2006; see also Sternberg, 2001). This leads to the ability to detect patterns of *family resemblance* in much the same way as Wittgenstein illustrated for the application of the concept of games. Absent defining conditions for knowledge use and generalizable procedures for knowledge application, constructivist approaches are not just *nice*, they are *necessary*. Yes, the cognitive load of such learning will be high, and support will be required. But that support will have to be different from the kind recommended by Kirschner, Sweller, and Clark (see the treatment of their explicit recommendations in the next section).

Direct Instructional Guidance and the Idea of Full Explanation of Essential Information, Concepts, and Procedures

Kirschner et al. (2006) elegantly demonstrate the appropriateness of direct instructional guidance in well-structured domains. However, as we will see, the very arguments that elucidate best practice for WSDs at the same time demonstrate why direct instructional methods do not apply in ISDs, and indirectly provide insights into why constructivist methods do. In this section we will examine several aspects of the *explicit* direct instructional guidance argument.

It should be noted that this section is built around *quotes* from direct instructional guidance theorists that may be seen as *defining* their position. The quotes are drawn from Kirschner, Sweller, and Clark's very influential piece in *Educational Psychologist*. In relying on these quotes it should be added that it is not always clear in private conversations and public discussions that these authors faithfully adhere to the letter of their published assertions. Further, there is evidence of some movement away from the more extreme stances they have taken (e.g., van Merriënboer & Sweller, 2005, where Cognitive Load Theory is taken in some new directions involving more complex kinds of learning, as has occurred with van Merriënboer & Kirschner's very useful and insightful new book, 2007). It should also be said that these steps have been very much within the same family as their past work on WSDs and thus do not address the special needs of ISDs articulated in this chapter. It is a tribute to them and the quality of their work—and the work of other long-term, careful advocates of direct instructional approaches (e.g., Rosenshine & Stevens, 1986; Rosenshine, 2002)—that their *words* are taken so seriously. So, in this chapter, as the first author did in the AERA debate that is the antecedent of this volume, we will hold them to their literal claims and hold those claims up for scrutiny through the lens of the requirements of learning in ISDs.

Again, the intention is not in any way to devalue the landmark work that has been done in the framework of Sweller's Cognitive Load Theory, say, or by Kirschner in his leading-edge work on complex learning or by direct instructional guidance theorists such as Rosenshine. Rather, we are addressing—and, yes, *rejecting*—the application of central aspects of their *explicit* recommendations when they are applied to ISDs.

Essential Information

Kirschner et al. (2006) discuss the importance of learners "being presented with *essential* information" (p. 75; italics added). In an ill-structured domain, it is the absence of information that could be considered "essential" that makes the domain ill structured. Any sort of Platonist *essentialism* (or, less formally, any attempt to claim essential qualities across situations) is inapplicable in ISDs. If it could be done, they would be WSDs. Present essential information if you can; but if you cannot, do not present a *fiction* that students will take as fact. Information will be treated as essential if presented thus, and will end up interfering with performance in whatever contexts some other calculus of "essentialness" is required.

For example, if a student is in a social studies class and is learning about core democratic values, what is essential about the concept of "justice" for the application of that concept in new contexts? The answer is almost *nothing*. Students who take the Michigan Educational Assessment Program (MEAP) test are required to use two core democratic values in a letter to the editor on a topic they are assigned. They do very poorly at this task and the authors have heard many social studies teachers report that this is a very difficult topic to teach. The reason is that teachers try to give them—and students try to learn—essential qualities of these concepts. However, any purported essential qualities will hit only a small fraction of the contexts in which the concept may be applied (Spiro et al., 2007). Think about all the different ways the concept of "justice" or "the common good" or "liberty" or "equality" are applied, with equal validity, by people with different ideological stances, in the context of different social issues, and so on. When there are so many different ways that a concept may be used, or a concept must be subtly tailored to different contexts, explicitly supporting any one or a small subset of those will provide a crutch that learners and teachers will too readily (over)rely upon.

Lest one think that we are only talking about domains in social studies and humanities, let us reiterate that features of ill-structuredness occur in science domains (for example, the concept of adaptation in biology mentioned earlier), in places where social science concepts intersect with science concepts (e.g., understanding the issue of "sustainability" in climate change discussions), and in *all* professional domains. Consider engineering, for so long thought to be essentially a mathematics- and physics-based discipline, and where it is now widely recognized that, for example, every bridge that is built has its own idiosyncratic "personality" with different span lengths, climatological conditions, terrain features, traffic patterns, etc. The intersection of these features in highly varying combinations across bridge-building makes the reliance on essentialist formulations maladaptively reductive (Petroski, 1992). All professional domains, however much they contain well-structured basic science and mathematics components, become ill structured when those generalizable principles have to be combined and tailored in the context of highly variable cases of application in the real world. Finding "essential information" to present in ISDs is not as easy as studies by direct instructional guidance advocates in math, science, and parts of reading acquisition would lead one to expect (Rosenshine & Stevens, 1986, have noted this).

In general, many more domains have substantial aspects of ill-structuredness than is generally thought. The extent to which ISDs must be dealt with has been *vastly underrated.*

Full Explanation

Direct instructional guidance is partially defined as "providing information that *fully explains* the concepts and procedures that students are required to learn" (Kirschner et al., 2006, p. 75; italics added). In an ill-structured domain, the ideal of full explanation is simply impossible. Otherwise it would be a well-structured domain. Furthermore, providing information advertised as "essential" and "fully explanatory" creates a mindset in which the learner comes to believe that this *dependent* way of thinking will work, and that the particular information they are provided with really is essential and does fully explain, leaving them nothing more that they have to do. The problem is that they have a lot more that they have to do in an ill-structured domain than whatever was supposedly "fully explained." Going along with the direct instructional guidance way of thinking makes students' and teachers' cognitive tasks easier and thus more attractive. We have referred to the artificial neatening of ill-structured concepts as "seductive reductions," and have empirically demonstrated how they are quickly latched onto to deleterious effect and are very difficult to undo (Feltovich et al., 1989; Feltovich, Coulson, & Spiro, 2001). There is a large body of empirical evidence that early simplifications impede the later acquisition of complexity (Feltovich et al., 1989, 2001; Feltovich, Spiro, & Coulson, 1997; Spiro, Coulson, Feltovich, & Anderson, 1988; Spiro, Feltovich, Coulson, & Anderson, 1989). To take one example, Spiro et al. (1989) provided evidence for nine different ways that the early use of powerful instructional analogies interfered with conceptual mastery in later treatments of the same topic *just* where the source analogy was missing key information or was misleading about the target concept—later learning was *reduced* to the initial explicit guidance and support (even though the limitations of the early models were explicitly mentioned). In the absence of essential information that can be directly instructed and fully explainable procedures, the learner's task in acquisition and application is more difficult, but that difficulty cannot be avoided, only ameliorated. It is a difficulty that must be faced and supported; but the nature of the support that is required cannot be the presentation of essential information and full explanations like that which works so well in direct instructional guidance in well-structured domains.

Direct Instruction on Procedures

Kirschner, Sweller, and Clark also state that "novice learners should be provided with direct instructional guidance on the concepts and procedures required by a particular discipline, and should not be left to discover those procedures by themselves" (2006, p. 75). Yes, known procedures should be directly instructed and maximally guided. But, in an ill-structured domain, repeatable "procedures" do not exist to be provided to the learner. Rather procedures *must* be inferred to fit the situation at hand based on a fresh compilation from existing procedural fragments and other related knowledge.

Of course, this also means there is no *thing* to be "discovered." Here, the advocates of discovery learning are as much on the wrong track in ill-structured domains as the direct instructional guidance theorists. The only thing to be "discovered" is the many vagaries, the subtleties and nuances, the family-resemblance relationships that determine how knowledge from ISDs is legitimately used.

By the way, when we said earlier that direct instructional guidance approaches are generally preferable in WSDs, we did not mean to imply that less-supported constructivist or discovery processes are *never* appropriate in WSDs. For certain concepts and procedures that are central to a domain and for which more active cognitive processing will activate connections that might have been dormant otherwise, the greater cognitive effort associated with discovery learning may be quite fruitful. Thus, we take no stand on the debate between direct instructional guidance and constructivism in WSDs other than to say the direct instructional guidance theorists are probably right that their approach is often the most effective and efficient one given load and time constraints. In the extreme, of course, it is ludicrous to wish for all the acquired knowledge of centuries past to have to be constructed afresh or, worse, *(re-)discovered*. On the other hand, it seems likely that practicing discovery processes in problem solving leads to the acquisition of a useful skill.

The Central Role of Retrieval from Long-Term Memory

Kirschner et al. (2006) say that

> expert problem solvers derive their skill by drawing on the extensive experience stored in their long-term memory and then quickly select and apply the best procedures for solving problems. The fact that these differences [in novice versus expert chunking of familiar situations] can be used to fully explain problem solving skill emphasizes the importance of long-term memory to cognition.
>
> (p. 76)

However, in ill-structured domains, the reliance on chunks, templates, and other pre-packaged prescriptions from long-term memory for how to think and act is the *problem* not the solution. In ISDs, because of the non-overlap of features from case to case (for cases/examples/events/occurrences categorized together), cognitive processing emphasis must shift from retrieval of intact structures to ongoing assemblage of new structures from pieces that were *not* pre-stored together in long-term memory.

For some non-routine problems, reliance on retrieval of templates from an ample library in long-term memory can *interfere* with problem solution. For example, Feltovich et al. (1997) found that expert radiologists who relied on template retrieval (and who had far more of those templates than novices and were able to use them with great success in routine problems) performed more poorly on a non-routine problem than an expert who recognized the need for a novel solution. The latter expert realized that reliance on long-term memory was *limiting* rather than productive (see also Hatano & Inagaki, 1986). To the extent a domain is ill structured, there will be a greater need for creative or emergent problem-solving processes. Overreliance on retrieval of explicit guidance from long-term memory is counter-productive in those situations. The claim that the availability of pre-stored chunks in long-term memory "fully explain problem solving skill" (p. 76) is simply false for non-routine problems and in ISDs generally.

In addition, the role of long-term memory itself is undergoing a transformation with the ready availability of external media capable of extensive storage, efficient retrieval, and the speedy execution of routinized tasks. Kirschner et al. (2006) claimed, "long-term memory is now viewed as the central, dominant structure of human cognition. Everything we see, hear and think about is critically dependent on and influenced by our long-term memory" (p. 76). And, "The aim of all instruction is to alter long-term memory. If nothing has changed in long-term memory, nothing has been learned" (p. 77). Even if technological developments go no further than the widespread use of Google, it can be fairly said that all bets may be off with respect to the role of long-term memory in cognition. That extensive external "memories" will require a re-calibration of cognitive theory is a commonplace, with an accompanying belief that this will free capacity for more inferential and creative (i.e., constructive) activity (e.g., Pink, 2006).

In Sum: The Case Against Direct Instructional Guidance in Ill-Structured Domains

In well-structured domains, we agree that concepts can be directly instructed, fully explained, and simply supported—and more often than not they should be. Yes, the data favor direct instructional guidance (Mayer, 2004; Kirschner et al., 2006), but most of this data is from well-structured domains like physics and mathematics, with a sprinkling of other domains (e.g., aspects of early reading development, but not as many aspects of reading comprehension; Rosenshine & Stevens, 1986). It could be said that direct instructional guidance approaches have been validated for just those domains where essential information was most identifiable and full explanation most viable—i.e., where those approaches were most likely to work. Early graphophonemic development, beginning math, and introductions to the orderly foundations of some areas of science can all benefit from direct instruction. But, this is not *possible* in an ill-structured domain. Therefore, the argument in this chapter is that there is *no alternative, in principle,* to constructivist approaches in learning, instruction, mental representation, and knowledge application for ill-structured domains. This argument is not made on an empirical basis, that such approaches work better than direct instructional guidance approaches. Rather the argument is made *in principle.* That which direct instructional guidance advocates call for is just that which is absent, that which makes domains ill structured. Any identified absence of supporting empirical data for constructivist approaches in ill-structured domains—these *have* been less studied—is irrelevant. Even if constructivist approaches had been widely shown not to work in ill-structured domains (though there is empirical evidence from controlled experiments for some success inducing transfer using the constructivist approach of Cognitive Flexibility Theory in ISDs; e.g., Jacobson & Spiro, 1995), it does not matter. We have no other choice. The principles of direct instruction—at least in the strong presentation of those principles in the quotes above—do not apply to ill-structured domains (and, again, the reviews arguing for direct instructional guidance in instruction do not cite studies in ISDs, on the whole, so there is no evidence of a better way on the direct instruction side). We cannot teach something the wrong way just because we have not perfected the right way. We need to find a way to teach ISDs that respects and reflects the nature of those domains. We as researchers need to *try harder*. Too much direct instructional guidance produces dependence on support, when what is most needed in ISDs—where anticipating all the guidance that might be needed is impossible and best efforts to do so can not help but misdirect learners—is *independence*. This will mean some kind of constructivist approach. The question is what kind, and how will it provide its own unique kind of support different from the kinds direct instructional guidance approaches provide for WSDs.

An example of a moderate (or "middle path") kind of constructivist approach to learning and instruction in ISDs is Cognitive Flexibility Theory (CFT). CFT is not a direct instructional guidance approach. But neither is it a discovery approach or a more extreme form of constructivism that opposes the provision of guidance. CFT provides guidance ... because it *must*. Learning in ISDs would be overwhelming otherwise. It is the particular way that CFT instruction and the associated guidance is tailored to the needs of learning in ISDs that distinguishes it in fundamental ways from direct instructional guidance approaches. (Other constructivist approaches also take a "middle path" between direct instructional guidance and more radical forms of constructivism; see, for example, Bransford & Schwartz, 2000; Duffy & Jonassen, 1992; Tobias, 1991.)

Space does not permit (and this is not the appropriate venue) for a detailed presentation of CFT. The interested reader can find many discussions of CFT, the associated learning environments based on CFT over the theory's 20-year history, and empirical tests of the theory (e.g., Jacobson & Spiro, 1995; Spiro et al., 1988, 2007; Spiro, Feltovich, Jacobson, & Coulson, 1992; Spiro & Jehng, 1990; Spiro, Collins, Thota, & Feltovich, 2003; Spiro, Collins, & Ramchandran, 2006). Suffice it for present purposes to say that CFT was developed as a reaction to difficulties Spiro and his colleagues sensed with schema-theoretic approaches (including his own; for that critique of schema theories, see Spiro, 1980; Spiro & Myers, 1984; Spiro et al., 1987). The problem was the one we have been discussing, domain ill-structuredness. In an ISD, one cannot have a prepackaged prescription for how to think and act. You cannot have a precompiled schema that can be instantiated for whatever the situation at hand may be if those situations vary too much, one to the next. Rather, in ISDs, a schema-of-the-moment for a new situation has to be built out of fragments of knowledge and experience that may never have been combined before. To prepare for that kind of situation-sensitive knowledge assembly drawing upon a wide range of unanticipatable knowledge-activation patterns, CFT-based systems facilitate a nonlinear criss-crossing of knowledge terrains to resist the development of oversimplified understandings and to develop connections between fragmentary knowledge sites on multiple dimensions to support maximum adaptive flexibility in the later situation-sensitive assembly of knowledge and experience to suit the needs of a new comprehension or problem-solving event.

A key feature of CFT is that its recommendations for ill-structured aspects of knowledge domains are in most ways the *opposite* of what works best in WSDs. Dimensions for which this is so include the following (again, see the cited CFT papers for explanations). Instead of narrowing to some ideal schema, explanation, or prototype example, *expand* to *multiple representations* (because some will be better in some situations and others will work best in other places); rigidly specified, pre-defined representations need to be replaced by open ones (for increased adaptability across highly variable contexts of application in ISDs); the *atomistically decomposable* knowledge of WSDs does not work, by definition, in ISDs, and must be replaced by the naturally occurring integration of components and ecologically based interconnectedness and non-additivity that occurs when real-world cases are the starting points for all instruction; adaptive assembly of knowledge is cultivated as a primary alternative to the retrieval of intact structures from long-term memory. These are just a few of the opposite directions of instruction from WSDs that CFT promotes.

Not surprisingly, these differences in instructional tendencies will be accompanied by differences in the nature of guidance and support. The point of agreement with Kirschner, Sweller, and Clark (2006) is that support is needed. The point of disagreement is what kind of support is required. CFT *balances* the acceptance of the necessary additional cognitive *complexity* and the effort to make the mastery of that complexity cognitively *manageable*. This has always been the primary challenge at the center of learning-environment design based on CFT. Space does not permit a description of the many ways that CFT-based systems achieve the aforementioned balance, so the reader is directed to the cited papers (all of which are available at www.cogflex.org).

The Future of Constructivist Learning: The Post-Gutenberg Mind and Deep Learning on the Web

We are just beginning to enter a new world of learning that is potentially available with the Web. The authors have been contending (see Spiro, 2006a, 2006b, 2006c for a summary of the argument) that more advanced forms of complex learning in ill-structured domains are becoming possible with:

1. advanced Web-exploration skill, especially in the development of the ability to dynamically generate complex search queries that permit a learner to

navigate with a fair degree of precision through the world of interrelated knowledge on the Web without having to rely on precompiled hotlinks or on sequential clicks through a Google list;

2.   an *opening mindset*, as contrasted with the too-typical mindset of closing toward the finding of facts and "answers" on the Web; and further with

3.   high-speed connections and increasingly more precisely targetable search engines that permit pertinent (though often unexpected and thus *serendipitous*) connections to be found, to be more likely to be noticed, and to stick in memory.

We refer to this constellation of learning developments as the New Gutenberg Revolution, with the associated nonlinear ways of thinking so suited to ISDs called the Post-Gutenberg Mind (see Spiro, 2006a, 2006b, 2006c, 2006d, 2006e and Spiro et al., 2007). This learning can be both *deep* and *fast* (as empirically demonstrated in DeSchryver & Spiro, 2008). Reading a single book on a topic that would present only that author's *swath* through the subject matter does not present the multiple perspectives and many alternative points of connection that criss-crossing a Web landscape permits and can to an ever-increasing degree support (with the aid often coming for free in Web environments themselves with such tools as Google History and ClipMarks). This multiplicity and interconnectedness makes possible many potential situation-sensitive knowledge-assembly paths to build "schemas of the moment" to suit the needs of unforeseeable future situations, as is required in ISDs.

Space will not permit us to go into extensive detail on these arguments or the impressive findings so far from the empirical research that has begun to test the arguments. Detailed reports are available (DeSchryver & Spiro, 2008, and the Spiro, 2006 papers cited above) and others are forthcoming. The point for the present chapter is that the affordances of the Web for deep learning in ISDs are unlikely to occur without unfettered searching that unfolds dynamically over time as a function of what is being found and the proclivity to have future learning moves be shaped in turn by those findings in continuous and reciprocal interaction of learner and Web. Direct instructional guidance would interfere with the latter ideal.

Further, the Web allows each learner to find their own way into the web of knowledge they are trying to master, with everything then reachable from wherever that learner had found the ideal entry point for him or her. This is a kind of spontaneous customizability of learning. Direct instructional guidance approaches would militate against this free adaptive personalization of naturally occurring "instruction" that the Web can offer. (It is "natural" in the sense that one learns eventually to "drive" through the landscape of knowledge with as little attention to the steering wheel—Google in this analogy—as is paid to steering a car through a real landscape.)

Of course, all of this depends not only on learners having appropriate mindsets for complex learning in ISDs, as described in the preceding sections, and advanced skill in Web exploration, but also on the use of critical evaluation skills to determine the trustworthiness of information (something that could be partly taught with direct instruction). Even here, however, our findings are surprising. For example, blogs, unreliable as they are, turn out to be very useful for learning once the learner has acquired enough knowledge to realize where the blogger is on shaky ground. The learner can then use the opportunity of virtually counter-arguing to strengthen knowledge in the domain rather than threaten it (DeSchryver & Spiro, 2008).

We argue that the more explicit and detailed the subject-matter guidance provided, the less likely the potentially salutary effects of Web-based learning are to occur. We are confident that it will soon be definitively shown that the Web can make possible orders of magnitude increases in usable knowledge per unit of learning time. That definitive demonstration has not yet been made. *However*, given that the availability of so much of the world's knowledge, in easily accessible *random-access* form, has only within the last few years become a fact, and given the plausibility of the arguments for new kinds of learning tied to the affordances of this new medium, the *possibility* of radical improvements in learning in a constructivist mode becomes a pressing hypothesis to be put to rigorous empirical test.

The world does not go in a line, and now learning media can opportunistically follow the natural, nonlinear contours of the world rather than artificially straightening those contours and then hoping the learner can independently bend them back later as needed. We believe the Web is the efficient learning medium of the future for constructing adaptively flexible knowledge in ISDs. We also believe direct instructional guidance would interfere with the independence, opportunism, and ongoing flexible response that learning in reciprocal interaction with the Web seems to require.

Concluding Remarks: The High Stakes of Learning in Ill-Structured Domains

The central argument of this chapter is that successful learning with direct instructional guidance approaches is *impossible in principle* for ill-structured aspects of knowledge domains. This is because direct instructional guidance approaches, as explicitly characterized by Kirschner et al., emphasize kinds of guidance and support that are antithetical to the needs of learning in ISDs. There is little if any empirical backing for direct instructional guidance in ISDs, and it is unlikely that any will be forthcoming. ISDs do not have essential and routinized features to provide by direct instruction by the very nature of their ill-structuredness. The only alternative is constructivist, notwithstanding any difficulty in learning and instruction that *may* be a concomitant. Alternative forms of guidance and support for constructivist learning and instruction in ISDs must continue to be developed and studied, especially in the context of what might be the ultimate—and free—constructivist learning environment, the Web. The fact that this may be hard is all the more reason to proceed with speed and determination.

We conclude simply with the contention that this problem matters *a lot*. Not only is the prevalence of ISDs significantly underestimated, but the most important challenges we face as a society (e.g., the tradeoff between security and civil liberties in an age of terrorism; the achievement gap in education; health care) and even as a species that hopes to survive (e.g., climate change) are riddled with complex ill-structuredness. How can we expect people to make informed decisions about, say, supporting different candidates' positions on these issues if we do not find better ways of fostering understanding at this level?

So, we issue a "call to arms." Between the affordances of nonlinear digital media, including the Web, for learning in ill-structured domains, and the societal need at the professional and especially the "grand social challenge" level, the ultimate constructivist story is unfolding. The kind of learning that is most needed at this time in history can meet the coincidentally available new media with the potential to meet those needs. A generation of children is growing up immersed in nonlinear, random-access environments and is thus better prepared than previous generations for this form of processing, if they are better directed to use it than they have been so far. Even if only a *fraction* of the epochal claims of this New Gutenberg Revolution/Post-Gutenberg Mind hypothesis (Spiro, 2006a, 2006b, 2006c, 2006d, 2006e) turn out to be true, it would still be the learning event of our age, and one that deserves the full attention of educational psychologists and learning-science researchers before it happens without us, causing the world to ask how we missed so large a story that was right under our nose.

So, there is no choice. Learning in ISDs must be done right, and direct instructional guidance approaches are the wrong tools for the task. If that is a difficult challenge, it is nevertheless one we must face. We as a field must find ways to guide and support learning in ISDs that is tailored to the special needs of those domains. This is much more than an academic debate on the merits of different instructional approaches. The more critical the societal issue, the more likely it is to be an ISD. We can do better at teaching toward these "grand social challenges." We *must* do better. The stakes are incredibly high.

Question: Rosenshine. *Reading comprehension, as you noted, is not a well-structured domain. Yet, as I wrote in the article that you cited (Rosenshine, 2002) as well as in my chapter in this volume, there have been a number of intervention studies that have successfully helped students make gains in comprehension as measured by standardized tests or experimenter-developed tests on reading. These studies did not teach reading comprehension skills directly, rather, the investigators provided students with prompts and supports and provided practice and feedback as the students learned to use these prompts and supports. And, as a result of this support and guidance, student scores in reading comprehension improved compared to the scores of the control students. Many authors referred to their procedures as "direct instruction." Would you say that this use of scaffolding and prompts is an example of "direct instructional guidance"? How do constructivists teach reading comprehension?*

Reply: Spiro and DeSchryver. We think it is fine to call this "direct instruction." Much of the problem in this debate has been attributable, we think, to semantic confusion about the use of that term, which we think is a red herring. Unless one is talking about pure discovery learning, most constructivist instruction—definitely including Cognitive Flexibility Theory!—calls for some form of learner support and instructors telling learners *something*. The problem occurs when this generic reference to direct instruction becomes conflated with a more specific recommendation for the form direct instruction should take. In our chapter we point to Kirschner et al. (2006) and their strong and clear dicta to provide "essential information" and "full explanations." There is no question this is just the ticket for teaching, say, Newtonian mechanics or how to use a complex piece of equipment. However, in ill-structured domains (more precisely, ill-structured *aspects* of knowledge domains), which are ill structured precisely because their common core of essential information accounts for only a small part of the knowledge needed and because a priori full explanations must be replaced by situation-sensitive assembly of explanations out of explanatory fragments, the Kirschner et al. recommendations militate against successful learning (see references to empirical studies in our chapter). Where there isn't a substantial core of essential information across occasions of knowledge application, and explanations fully provided in advance don't generalize adequately across situations, constructivist approaches are the only alternative to the aforementioned strong form of instructional advice offered by Kirschner et al. (because the domains wouldn't be ill structured if their advice *could* be followed!).

So what about reading comprehension strategy instruction? Look at some of those strategies, for example, "connect the text to prior knowledge and experience." As has been amply shown, the use of background knowledge in comprehension is a process that is highly ill structured. It happens in so many ways that you could never reduce it to its essentials or fully explain how to do it. So you will need to directly instruct, as you point out, but that instruction will start to look more like *"instruction to construct"* (accompanied, as you say, by feedback, prompts, and supports) than it will resemble the strong form of the Kirschner et al. recommendation.

How do constructivists teach reading comprehension? From the point of view of Cognitive Flexibility Theory (CFT), you will have to see our cited papers for details, given space limits here. Here we will simply note a few examples of first steps CFT takes in its instructional systems that differ from the Kirschner et al. recommendations. At the level of "ways of thinking" or "epistemic stance" or "mindset" (Spiro, Feltovich, & Coulson, 1996), a starting point of instruction in CFT for ill-structured domains is that it tells learners to *not* expect to find too much essential information and supports them in beginning to see, for example, how concepts *vary* across their permissible family of applications. The mindset that is instilled by demonstration encourages learners to begin with presuppositions (for ill-structured aspects of domains) like: "It's not that simple"; "It depends"; "piece together explanations and information from different parts of memory and don't count on retrieving schemas that provide full explanations or prepackaged prescriptions for how to think and act"; and so on.

Question: Klahr. *You use Wittgenstein's famous example of games as an ill-structured concept, and then go on to argue that "there is no alternative, in*

principle, *to constructivist approaches in learning, instruction, mental representation, and knowledge application for ill-structured domains" (your emphasis).* But
how could someone without knowledge of any games understand Wittgenstein's
point? Wouldn't someone with a detailed understanding of the rules of, say, baseball,
poker, squash, chess, Nim, pattie-cake, Tetris, and rock-scissors-paper be in a much
better position to understand games as an ill-structured concept than a space traveler
with no knowledge of any game who happened to pick up Philosophical Investigations *and browse through it while refueling his spaceship? And wouldn't a few hours
of direct instruction in the rules of each of those games put our intergalactic visitor in
a better position to understand this particular ill-structured domain than would an
equal amount of time wandering around a Pirates–Cubs game trying to discover
what all those earth-creatures were doing on the field?*

Reply: Spiro and DeSchryver. Our answer is absolutely yes to all of it. But we
don't see how this poses any problems for us. As we said in our chapter, any
essential information that can be explicitly provided and any procedures that can
be fully explained, should be. The chapter is also very clear on not being supportive of pure discovery procedures in most cases. So, we're in agreement: no wandering around at a Pirates–Cubs game for your intergalactic visitor. Teach the
rules of lots of games (that have rules; not all games do). Provide full explanations and worked examples for rock-scissors-paper. Just don't teach the "rules"
for what makes something a game *in general,* don't overly rely on the "essential
information" to know about "games," etc.

Now, in the preceding sentences substitute for the word "games" domain
names such as "Renaissance" (or "Renaissance Art," or "Da Vinci's Paintings,"
or "*Mona Lisa*"). Or, if you prefer something seemingly more solid, substitute
the biological concept "Adaptation" (a topic of similar dispute as to its
well-structuredness). For all of these, the problems with teaching "games" *as a
domain* that we discussed in the preceding paragraph become greatly magnified.
Now you will find a lot less in the way of rule-based regularity for the individual
cases than we found for instances like rock-scissors-paper. And the variability
across instances of, say, "Renaissance Artifacts," will be greater, making the
learner's *reliance* on having essential information and generalizable full explanations an even greater danger. Yes, there is *some* essential information. But it must
be presented along with the proviso that that information be treated as only a
part of what learners need to be thinking and doing—and that substantial
remainder will involve more constructivist support.

There is some essential information that can be provided to help learners
learn about Michelangelo's *David.* But that will barely scratch the surface. Look
at one further example: Sweller, in his response to our questions, points to some
new work from his lab on explicit instruction in ill-structured domains. That
work is in domains like music. Looking at the dissertation referred to, the problems of pitch, timing, and so on that that study looked at are clearly
well-structured aspects of the music domain, amenable to Kirschner et al.'s.
approach. However, what would happen with the ill-structured aspects seems
not to be addressed in that study. Let's make sure we don't overgeneralize from

empirical results that deal only with the well-structured aspects of domains that may be largely ill-structured and prematurely write off constructivist instruction on that basis.

References

Bransford, J. D., & Schwartz, D. L. (2000). Rethinking transfer: A simple proposal with multiple implications. *Review of Research in Education, 24,* 61–100.

Coulson, R. L., Feltovich, P. J., & Spiro, R. J. (1989). Foundations of a misunderstanding of the ultrastructural basis of myocardial failure: A reciprocating network of oversimplifications. *Journal of Medicine and Philosophy, 14,* 109–146 [Special issue on "The structure of clinical knowledge."].

DeSchryver, M., & Spiro, R. (2008). New forms of deep learning on the Web: Meeting the challenge of cognitive load in conditions of unfettered exploration. In R. Zheng (Ed.), *Cognitive effects of multimedia learning* (pp. 134–152). Hershey, PA: IGI Global, Inc.

Duffy, T., & Jonassen, D. (1992). *Constructivism and the technology of instruction: A conversation.* Hillsdale, NJ: Erlbaum.

Ericsson, A., Charness, N., Hoffman, R., & Feltovich, P. J. (Eds.) (2006). *Expertise and expert performance.* Cambridge: Cambridge University Press.

Feltovich, P. J., Coulson, R. L., & Spiro, R. J. (2001). Learners' understanding of important and difficult concepts: A challenge to smart machines in education. In P. J. Feltovich & K. Forbus (Eds.), *Smart machines in education* (pp. 349–376). Cambridge, MA: MIT Press.

Feltovich, P. J., Spiro, R. J., & Coulson, R. L. (1989). The nature of conceptual understanding in biomedicine: The deep structure of complex ideas and the development of misconceptions. In D. Evans & V. Patel (Eds.), *The cognitive sciences in medicine* (pp. 113–172). Cambridge, MA: MIT Press.

Feltovich, P. J., Spiro, R. J., & Coulson, R. L. (1997). Issues of expert flexibility in contexts characterized by complexity and change. In P. J. Feltovich, K. M. Ford, & R. R. Hoffman (Eds.), *Expertise in context: Human and machine* (pp. 125–146). Cambridge, MA: MIT Press.

Hatano, G., & Inagaki, K. (1986). Two courses of expertise. In H. Stevenson, H. Azuma, & K. Hakuta (Eds.), *Child development and education in Japan* (pp. 262–272). New York: W.H. Freeman.

Jacobson, M. J., & Spiro, R. J. (1995). Hypertext learning environments, cognitive flexibility, and the transfer of complex knowledge: An empirical investigation. *Journal of Educational Computing Research, 12,* 301–333.

Kirschner, P. A., Sweller, J., & Clark, R. E. (2006). Why minimal guidance during instruction does not work: An analysis of the failure of constructivist, discovery, problem based, experiential, and inquiry-based teaching. *Educational Psychologist, 41*(2), 75–86.

Lampert, M. (2001). *Teaching problems and the problems of teaching.* New Haven, CT: Yale University Press.

Mayer, R. E. (2004). Should there be a three-strikes rule against pure discovery learning? *American Psychologist, 59*(1), 14–19.

Mayr, E. (1988). *Toward a new philosophy of biology: Observations of an evolutionist.* Cambridge, MA: Harvard University Press.

Palincsar, A. P., Spiro, R. J., Kucan, L., Magnusson, S. J., Collins, B. P., Hapgood, S., et al. (2007). Research to practice: Designing a hypermedia environment to support elementary teachers' learning of robust comprehension instruction. In D. McNamara (Ed.),

Reading comprehension strategies: Theory, interventions, and technologies (pp. 441–462). Mahwah, N.J.: Lawrence Erlbaum.

Petroski, H. (1992). *To engineer is human: The role of failure in successful design*. New York: Vintage Books.

Pink, D. (2006). *A whole new mind: Why right-brainers will rule the future*. New York: Penguin Group.

Rosenshine, B. (2002). Converging finding on classroom instruction. In A. Molnar (Ed.), *School reform proposals: The research evidence* (pp. 175–196). Greenwich, CT: Information Age Publishing, Inc.

Rosenshine, B., & Stevens, R. (1986). Teaching functions. In M. C. Wittrock (Ed.), *Handbook of research on teaching* (pp. 376–391). New York: Macmillan.

Shulman, L. S. (1992). Toward a pedagogy of cases. In J. H. Shulman (Ed.), *Case methods in teacher education* (pp. 1–29). New York: Teachers College Press.

Spiro, R. J. (1980). Constructive processes in prose comprehension and recall. In R. J. Spiro, B. C. Bruce, & W. F. Brewer (Eds.), *Theoretical issues in reading comprehension* (pp. 245–278). Hillsdale, NJ: Lawrence Erlbaum Associates.

Spiro, R. J. (2006a). The "New Gutenberg Revolution": Radical new learning, thinking, teaching, and training with technology ... bringing the future near. *Educational Technology, 46*(1), 3–4.

Spiro, R. J. (2006b). The post-Gutenberg world of the mind: The shape of the new learning. *Educational Technology, 46*(2), 3–4.

Spiro, R. J. (2006c). Old ways die hard. *Educational Technology, 46*(3), 3–4.

Spiro, R. J. (2006d). Approaching the post-Gutenberg mind: The revolution is in progress. *Educational Technology, 46*(4), 3–4.

Spiro, R. J. (2006e). What does it mean to be "post-gutenbergian"? And why doesn't Wikipedia apply? *Educational Technology, 46*(6), 3–5.

Spiro, R. J., Collins, B. P., & Ramchandran, A. R. (2006). Modes of openness and flexibility in "Cognitive Flexibility Hypertext" learning environments. In B. Khan (Ed.), *Flexible learning in an information society* (pp. 18–25). Hershey, PA: Information Science Publishing.

Spiro, R. J., Collins, B. P., & Ramchandran, A. R. (2007). Reflections on a post-Gutenberg epistemology for video use in ill-structured domains: Fostering complex learning and cognitive flexibility. In R. Goldman, R. D. Pea, B. Barron, & S. Derry (Eds.), *Video research in the learning sciences* (pp. 93–100). Mahwah, NJ: Lawrence Erlbaum Associates.

Spiro, R. J., Collins, B. P., Thota, J. J., & Feltovich, P. J. (2003). Cognitive flexibility theory: Hypermedia for complex learning, adaptive knowledge application, and experience acceleration. *Educational technology, 44*(5), 5–10. [Reprinted in A. Kovalchick & K. Dawson (Eds.). (2005). *Education and technology: An encyclopedia* (pp. 108–117). Santa Barbara, CA: ABC-CLIO.]

Spiro, R. J., Coulson, R. L., Feltovich, P. J., & Anderson, D. (1988). Cognitive flexibility theory: Advanced knowledge acquisition in ill-structured domains. *Tenth Annual Conference of the Cognitive Science Society*. Hillsdale, NJ: Erlbaum. [Reprinted in R. B. Ruddell (Ed.), *Theoretical models and processes of reading* (5th ed.). Newark, DE: International Reading Association, pp. 602–616.].

Spiro, R. J., Feltovich, P. J., & Coulson, R. L. (1996). Two epistemic world-views: Prefigurative schemas and learning in complex domains. *Applied Cognitive Psychology, 10*, 52–61.

Spiro, R. J., Feltovich, P. J., Coulson, R. L., & Anderson, D. (1989). Multiple analogies for complex concepts: Antidotes for analogy-induced misconception in advanced knowledge acquisition. In S. Vosniadou & A. Ortony (Eds.), *Similarity and analogical reasoning* (pp. 498–531). Cambridge: Cambridge University Press.

Spiro, R. J., Feltovich, P. J., Jacobson, M. J., & Coulson, R. L. (1992). Cognitive flexibility, constructivism, and hypertext: Random access instruction for advanced knowledge acquisition in ill-structured domains. In T. Duffy & D. Jonassen (Eds.), *Constructivism and the technology of instruction* (pp. 57–75). Hillsdale, NJ: Erlbaum. [Reprinted from a special issue of the journal *Educational Technology* on *Constructivism*, 1991.]

Spiro, R. J., & Jehng, J. C. (1990). Cognitive flexibility and hypertext: Theory and technology for the nonlinear and multidimensional traversal of complex subject matter. In D. Nix, & R. J. Spiro (Eds.), *Cognition, education, and multimedia: Explorations in high technology* (pp. 163–205). Hillsdale, NJ: Lawrence Erlbaum.

Spiro, R. J., & Myers, A. (1984). Individual differences and underlying cognitive processes in reading. In P. D. Pearson (Ed.), *Handbook of research in reading* (pp. 471–502). New York: Longman.

Spiro, R. J., Vispoel, W. L., Schmitz, J., Samarapungavan, A., & Boerger, A. (1987). Knowledge acquisition for application: Cognitive flexibility and transfer in complex content domains. In B. C. Britton, & S. Glynn (Eds.), *Executive control processes* (pp. 177–199). Hillsdale, NJ: Lawrence Erlbaum Associates.

Sternberg, R. J. (2001). *Complex cognition: The psychology of human thought.* Oxford: Oxford University Press.

Sykes, G., & Bird, T. (1992). Teacher education and the case idea. *Review of Research in Education, 18,* 457–521.

Tobias, S. (1991). An electric examination of some issues in the constructivist–ISD controversy. *Educational Technology, 31*(10), 41–43.

Van Merriënboer, J. J. G., & Kirschner, P. A. (2007). *Ten steps to complex learning.* Mahwah, NJ: Lawrence Erlbaum.

Van Merriënboer, J. J. G., & Sweller, J. (2005). Cognitive load theory and complex learning: Recent developments and future directions. *Educational Psychology Review, 17*(2), 147–177.

Wittgenstein, L. (1953). *Philosophical investigations.* New York: Macmillan.

Part III

Challenges to the Constructivist View

7 What Human Cognitive Architecture Tells Us About Constructivism

John Sweller University of New South Wales

Human cognitive architecture constitutes a natural information-processing system whose evolution has been driven by another natural information-processing system, evolution by natural selection. Considering human cognition from an evolutionary perspective has considerable instructional consequences. Those consequences can be used by theories such as cognitive-load theory to generate instructional procedures. Procedures generated by cognitive-load theory place their emphasis on explicit instruction rather than versions of discovery learning or constructivist teaching. Discovery-learning techniques were developed prior to our current understanding of human cognitive architecture and, it is argued, are incompatible with that architecture. As a consequence and unsurprisingly, the field has failed to produce a large body of empirical research based on randomized controlled experiments demonstrating the effectiveness of constructivist teaching techniques.

Constructivist teaching techniques that guide students to find information for themselves rather than presenting that information explicitly have provided a favored instructional technique among education researchers for several decades. The popularity of such techniques can probably be sourced back to Bruner (1961) who used Piagetian theory (e.g., Piaget, 1928) to emphasize discovery learning. Minimally guided instructional techniques (see Kirschner, Sweller, & Clark, 2006) were developed prior to our current understanding of human cognitive architecture. In this chapter, I will argue that such techniques make little sense in light of our current understanding of human cognition.

There are many aspects of constructivism that are unobjectionable. For example, we surely must construct mental representations of the external world that we can use to function in that world. In that sense, all learning is essentially constructivist and I am not aware of any theorist who objects to this characterization of learning. Constructivist teaching intended to teach people how to construct knowledge by withholding information from learners is another matter entirely. Withholding easily presented information from learners is a major characteristic of constructivist teaching, inquiry and problem-based learning. Requiring students to discover knowledge rather than explicitly providing them with essential information has become a dominant teaching paradigm. It is a paradigm based on the assumption that knowledge acquired during a problem-solving search is more useful than the same knowledge presented explicitly by an instructor. The purpose of this chapter is to indicate that there is nothing in our cognitive architecture suggesting that it might be beneficial to withhold readily presentable information from students so that they can discover it themselves.

Why are Constructivist Teaching Techniques so Popular?

For someone who is not already committed to a constructivist teaching approach, it can be difficult to find a theoretical or practical justification for the procedure. If a student needs to learn to solve a particular category of problem, for example, why would we not explicitly demonstrate how that problem can be solved? What can conceivably be gained by leaving the learner to search for a solution when that search is usually very time consuming, may result in a suboptimal solution, or even no solution at all? There are at least two possible answers that probably explain the rise and continuing popularity of constructivist, discovery-based, problem-based teaching techniques.

In the 1980s and early 1990s, most researchers in the area of cognitive processes and instructional design assumed that the acquisition of general problem-solving strategies was a critical component of human cognitive skill. The earlier publication of Newell and Simon's (1972) book on human problem solving was immensely influential and had emphasized domain-general problem-solving strategies such as means–ends analysis. A means–ends strategy required problem solvers to consider their current problem state, consider the goal state, extract differences between the two states and find problem-solving operators to reduce those differences. This strategy could be used on a wide range of transformation problems and it was clearly hoped by many in the field that if a large number of such general strategies could be isolated, they could be taught to learners who would then become superior problem solvers.

The quest failed. No other sophisticated, general strategies were isolated and means–ends analysis seemed unteachable because we all use the strategy automatically from a very young age. While the quest to find general problem-solving strategies has ended for most researchers, the implication of that quest was retained: If we have people solve lots of problems they will acquire general problem-solving strategies even if we cannot specify those strategies, as yet. In other words, it seems to be assumed that our failure to find general problem-solving strategies is only temporary and they will, in due course, be found. There is, of course, another possibility. It is possible there are no general, teachable/learnable problem-solving strategies and all problem-solving skill is based on domain-specific knowledge. If so, having learners search for problem solutions is a waste of everyone's time. The reasons why there are no teachable, general problem-solving strategies lie in our basic cognitive architecture and will be discussed below.

There may be another reason for the enduring popularity of constructivist, problem-based teaching techniques that reduce an emphasis on explicit teaching. Huge amounts of the information acquired by humans are not explicitly taught. We are not taught the means–ends problem-solving strategy discussed above and yet all people use it automatically and effortlessly. Similarly, we are not explicitly taught to listen to and speak our first language. Immersion in a language group is all that is needed to enable us to learn a first language, including the immensely complex motor movements required to speak. The complex tasks of recognizing faces and learning appropriate social interactions are similarly learned simply by immersion in a culture.

Given the ease with which we learn the above tasks and the difficulty many of us have acquiring the information dealt with in schools and other education and training contexts, it seemed natural to assume that the effortlessness with which we acquired information out of class and the difficulty of acquiring most education-based information was entirely due to inappropriate teaching strategies. If we duplicated the learning environment within educational institutions that occurred outside those institutions, surely learning could be just as smooth and automatic. By immersing people in a learning area rather than explicitly teaching them, they should learn just as easily as in the external world.

While I know of no body of evidence based on randomized, controlled experiments able to support this view, there does not seem to be a flaw in the basic argument. We do seem to learn much more readily outside than within educational contexts and it is quite plausible to assume that the difficulty we have learning in educational institutions is caused by inappropriate pedagogical procedures (Brown, Collins, & Duguid, 1989; Collins, Brown, & Newman, 1989; Resnick, 1987). Nevertheless, new theoretical advances proposed by David Geary based on evolutionary psychology have provided us with an explanation (Geary, 2002, 2005, 2007). Geary distinguishes between biologically primary and biologically secondary knowledge. Primary knowledge is knowledge that we have evolved to acquire over lengthy, evolutionary time periods. We are hard-wired to acquire that knowledge easily, effortlessly, and, indeed, unconsciously, simply as a consequence of being immersed in a functioning human society. We do not need to be taught how to construct knowledge or solve a problem by mean–ends analysis any more than we need to be taught to understand and speak our first language. We do not need to consciously set out to learn these tasks. A normally functioning human in a normally functioning society (and, indeed, in many dysfunctional societies) will automatically acquire these skills because we have evolved to acquire them over many millennia.

In contrast, biologically secondary information has only been required very recently and only by relatively advanced societies. While it relies on evolutionary primary knowledge to act as a base, it is different from primary knowledge. Reading and writing are relatively recent inventions of advanced societies and only became widespread a few generations ago. We have not evolved to read and write in the same way we have evolved to listen and speak. Most of us would have no idea how to teach people how to organize their tongue, lips, and breath in order to speak and do not need to do so. It is a skill we have evolved to acquire simply by being immersed in a listening/speaking society. In contrast, learning to write needs to be taught because we have not evolved to learn writing automatically. Simply being immersed in a reading/writing society will not guarantee that someone will learn to read or write. We need to be explicitly taught.

Educational institutions are relatively new inventions that were developed precisely because evolutionary secondary knowledge must be taught differently from evolutionary primary knowledge. Secondary knowledge must be explicitly taught because simple immersion will result in minimal learning by the vast majority of any population. The inquiry learning of constructivist, discovery, and problem-based procedures usually includes some scaffolding and structure (Hmelo-Silver, Duncan, & Chinn, 2007; Schmidt, Loyens, van Gog, & Paas, 2007) but by definition, also includes elements that require learners to engage in "inquiry" without explicit instruction. For some, immersion in a discipline with minimal explicit instruction concerning the findings of the discipline is paramount (Kuhn, 2007). The absence of explicit instruction that works perfectly in the case of biologically primary knowledge is likely to fail abysmally when dealing with secondary knowledge. Our cognitive architecture relevant to dealing with biologically secondary knowledge explains why.

Human Cognitive Architecture and Natural Information-Processing Systems

The procedures we use to acquire biologically secondary knowledge can be described by a series of principles that have as their core the sensory memory, working memory, and long-term memory cognitive architecture of Atkinson and Shiffrin (1968). That cognitive architecture can be characterized as a natural information-processing system that has evolved according to the principles of another, much more pervasive natural information-processing system, evolution by natural selection. A natural information-processing system is described as any information-processing system that occurs in nature rather than in a laboratory or in a machine such as a computer. Both human cognition and evolution by natural selection have essentially the same function of creating, remembering, and disseminating information across space and time and, accordingly, rely on the same underlying principles. In the case of human cognition, these principles constitute a human cognitive architecture that is organized to deal with biologically secondary knowledge (Sweller, 2003; Sweller & Sweller, 2006). It is not surprising that the principles that underlie human cognitive architecture are the same as the principles underlying biological evolution since, of course, evolutionary biology drove the development of human cognitive architecture. That architecture, with its clear implications for the instructional design concerns associated with the issue of direct versus indirect teaching, will be described next.

Information Store Principle

In order to function in a complex environment, natural information-processing systems require an enormous store of information. A genome provides that store in the case of evolutionary biology. Long-term memory provides an equivalent function in human cognition. De Groot's (1965) finding that chess grand masters differed from less able players only in their ability to reconstruct briefly seen board configurations taken from real games followed by Chase and Simon's (1973) finding that the result could be replicated, but not for random board configurations, changed our conceptions of the function of long-term memory and of human cognition. Long-term memory was not simply an adjunct of thought and problem solving, but a central structure. Competent problem solvers in a given area were competent because they had stored an enormous amount of information in long-term memory. While quantifying knowledge is difficult, it has been estimated that chess grand masters have stored tens of thousands of board configurations and the best move associated with each configuration in long-term memory (Simon & Gilmartin, 1973) and it is that store of information that accounts for chess skill. A large store of information in long-term memory can similarly explain acquired skill in any field including educationally relevant areas. A mathematician is good at solving mathematics problems because he or she has stored innumerable mathematics problem states and the moves appropriate to those states in long-term memory; lawyers are good at arguing legal cases because they are familiar with legal precedents and the consequences of those precedents, etc.

The well-known findings associated with the game of chess can be used to provide a definition of learning and should have provided a focus for instructional research. Instead of providing that central focus, the chess findings were largely ignored by many of those interested in instructional issues. Learning, which in the Behaviorist era was defined as a change in behavior, should now have been defined as a positive change in long-term memory. Instead, learning tended not to be defined at all. By failing to define learning, it was open to those pursuing a discovery or problem-based learning agenda, to ignore what was supposed to change when students learned. Constructivist teaching techniques could be advocated with no risk of conflicting with any structures or processes of human cognitive architecture such as long-term memory because the agenda was pursued as though human cognitive architecture did not exist.

If nothing has changed in long-term memory, nothing has been learned. Based on the work using chess and other, educationally relevant, tasks, in the many learning domains requiring problem-solving skill, a skilled problem solver has learned to recognize a large number of problem states and the problem-solving moves appropriate to those states. These states and the relevant moves needed to transform them into other states are stored in long-term memory. Accordingly, the purpose of instruction is to increase knowledge in long-term memory. Procedures that do not specify what should change in long-term memory due to instruction run the risk that little is being learned. If requiring learners to discover information for themselves has beneficial consequences for storing knowledge in long-term memory, the reasons and processes of this advantage need to be specified. They rarely are specified and, indeed, empirical evidence suggests there are no beneficial consequences to discovery over explicit instruction (e.g., Klahr & Nigam, 2004).

Borrowing and Reorganizing Principle

How does a natural information store accumulate its large store of information? The vast bulk of information comes from other stores. In the case of a genome, asexual reproduction results in an exact copy, apart from mutations, of the genome being transferred from one generation to the next. Sexual reproduction also results in transfer but the mechanism is structured to ensure that an exact copy from one generation to the next is impossible with reorganization being a necessary part of the process. Sexual reproduction ensures that all offspring differ from all of their male and female ancestors and, apart from monozygous siblings, differ from each other as well.

Humans have evolved to acquire both biologically primary and biologically secondary knowledge from other humans and, as a consequence, the bulk of information in long-term memory has been acquired from others. Just as most of an individual's genomic information is acquired from others, so is most of our cognitive information. We imitate what other people do, especially in the case of biologically primary knowledge but also biologically secondary knowledge, listen to what they say and read what they write. We engage in these activities in order to obtain knowledge held in other people's long-term memories. Analogically with sexual reproduction, we do not precisely copy information from other people but rather combine it with previous information in long-term memory in a process that can create novel information.

Preliminary neurological evidence for the importance of imitation comes from work on the mirror-neuron system. Mirror neurons fire when we make a movement, imagine making the movement, listen to sentences about the movement or when we observe someone else making the same movement (Grafton, Arbib, Fadiga, & Rizzolatti, 1996; Iacoboni et al., 1999; Tettamanti et al., 2005). While this work primarily deals with biologically primary information, it may be reasonable to speculate that we have evolved to imitate others when they are engaged in biologically secondary tasks as well. The ease with which we assimilate the culture into which we are born provides some evidence. We seem to have evolved to imitate others and learning by imitation results in information held in the long-term memory of one person being transferred to the long-term memory of someone else (Bandura, 1986).

When dealing with secondary knowledge, the vast bulk of information is obtained via listening and reading. Cognitive-load theory has been designed to provide techniques to assist in the design of written, drawn, and spoken information (Sweller, 2003, 2004; Sweller, van Merriënboer, & Paas, 1998), and those specific techniques will not be discussed in this chapter other than in general terms with respect to constructivist teaching techniques.

It needs to be emphasized that while the borrowing and reorganizing principle involves the direct transmission of information, it is a major source of novelty and creativity. Just as sexual reproduction ensures that all offspring with the exception of monozygous siblings are unique, so the borrowing and reorganizing principle ensures that all cognitive information is reorganized into a unique form. When we obtain information from someone else, we are likely to adapt it to information already present in long-term memory resulting in a unique form of that knowledge.

If, as suggested by the borrowing and reorganizing principle, we have evolved to obtain information from others, deliberately withholding that information under a discovery, problem-based, constructivist agenda is bizarre. It can be very difficult to see how it can be beneficial to have learners attempt to discover information that could be explicitly presented to them if, as suggested by the borrowing and reorganizing principle, we have evolved to acquire information from others. It becomes even more difficult to understand when we consider the processes we must use to discover novel information, the topic of the next principle.

Randomness as Genesis Principle

While the borrowing and reorganizing principle can be used to explain the transmission of information, a procedure is required for the initial creation of that information. The randomness as genesis principle provides that mechanism. In genetics, the ultimate source of all variability both between and within species can be sourced to random mutation. Evolution by natural selection is a creative process that has created all life and random mutation is the initial source of that creativity. In more detail, it can be described as a random generation followed by tests of effectiveness process. While the initial mutation is random, the process is able to function only because it is followed by a test of effectiveness in which effective mutations that increase the adaptivity of the organism to the environment are more likely to survive and reproduce than organisms with mutations that stay constant or decrease the probability of survival and reproduction.

The creation of novelty by the human cognitive system during problem solving uses an identical random generation followed by tests of effectiveness process. When solving a problem, there are two separate sources by which moves can be generated, with most moves requiring a combination of both sources. To the extent that information is available in long-term memory, that information will be used to generate moves. The available information may be partial in the sense that it does not indicate explicitly which move should be made, but rather allows the problem solver to rank moves in terms of the probability of effectiveness. In the case of novel problems, there may be insufficient information available either to make a decision concerning a move or to even rank moves. In other words, relevant information may be unavailable in either the problem solver's long-term memory or the long-term memory of others to which the problem solver has access either through spoken or written material. There may be multiple available moves with the problem solver having no information indicating which moves might be preferable. Under those circumstances, a random generate and test strategy is unavoidable.

Some evidence for the use of a random generate and test strategy comes from the dead-ends at which problem solvers arrive when presented with a difficult, novel problem. Random generate and test easily explains such dead-ends because using random generate and test, we cannot know the outcome of a particular move until after it has been made, either mentally or physically, and so many moves will result in dead-ends. If we know the probable outcome of a move, we are using knowledge from long-term memory, not random generate and test, and knowledge will reduce the number of potential dead-ends. Random generate and test can allow us to acquire knowledge of a problem space but that knowledge only becomes available after the random generate and test process has occurred. Knowledge of the outcome of a randomly generated move can only be acquired after it is made, frequently mentally, not before.

While the arrival at dead-ends by problem solvers provides some evidence of the use of a random generate and test strategy, ultimately the argument relies on logic more than empirical evidence. When generating problem-solving moves, there seems no alternative to a combination of knowledge from long-term memory and random generate and test. In the absence of alternatives and until those alternatives are proposed, we seem to have no choice but to accept that problem solving consists of a combination of knowledge from long-term memory and random generate and test. Furthermore, we know that an equivalent to knowledge and random generate and test can explain the massive creativity of evolution by natural selection and appears quite sufficient to explain human creativity. Accordingly, in this chapter, random generate and test will be assumed to provide the genesis of human creativity.

It might be noted that the basic random generate and test processes used by the randomness as genesis principle apply to all examples of creativity, including those that depend heavily on knowledge held in long-term memory. Consider a person engaged in analogical problem solving (Gick & Holyoak, 1980, 1983). A new problem is presented that may appear to be similar to one for which solution knowledge is available in long-term memory. The processes used to decide whether the source problem should be used to assist in solving the target problem are identical to the processes used to determine any problem move. Where knowledge is available to, for example, rank possible source analogues, that knowledge will be used. Where knowledge is incomplete, as it normally is during problem solving, the only certain way of testing whether analogical problem solving will work is to attempt to solve the target problem (mentally or physically) using the known solution of the source problem. In other words, whether the analogy will work can only be tested by attempting to actually solve the target problem analogically. Until that point, the problem solver cannot know whether analogical problem solving will yield a solution and of course, to the extent that knowledge is unavailable, making a particular decision has random components in the same way that making any particular problem-solving move based on insufficient knowledge has random components. Once tested for effectiveness, information concerning the usefulness of the analogy becomes available, eliminating the random component of random generate and test. *Einstellung* (Fingerman & Levine, 1974; Luchins, 1942; Sweller, 1980; Sweller & Gee, 1978), which can render simple problems difficult or even insoluble due to inappropriate attempts at analogical problem solving, provides evidence for the random components inherent in analogical problem solving.

Instructional implications for any inquiry-based, discovery learning, or constructivist teaching procedure that withholds information from learners so that they can find the information themselves, appears to flow from the randomness as genesis principle. If learners are required to discover problem solutions for themselves, and to the extent that those solutions are not available in long-term memory or from instruction, then according to the randomness as genesis principle, a random generate followed by tests of effectiveness procedure is the only available procedure. It is difficult to see what can conceivably be learned by forcing learners to engage in such a procedure. Because random generate and test is probably acquired early as a biologically primary skill, it is likely to be unteachable and unlearnable beyond the first few years of life. To this point, there is no evidence that it is teachable. Furthermore, as indicated previously, there is no evidence that other general problem-solving strategies are learned, and if the randomness as genesis principle is valid, random generation does not leave scope for general problem-solving strategies. The failure to find such strategies after decades of effort suggests they will not be found.

Of course, using a random generate and test procedure may have other advantages. While we may not learn general problem-solving strategies by inquiry-learning techniques, we may learn domain-specific knowledge more rapidly and easily during problem solving than during explicit instruction. Nevertheless, there seems nothing in our cognitive architecture to suggest this possibility and neither is there empirical support for it (e.g., Klahr & Nigam, 2004). The randomness as genesis principle appears incompatible with efficiently acquiring knowledge via inquiry-learning techniques. It does, on the other hand, have important structural consequences for human cognitive architecture as exemplified in the next principle.

Narrow Limits of Change Principle

In biological systems, the epigenetic system (Jablonka & Lamb, 2005) controls the flow of environmental information to the genetic system (Sweller & Sweller, 2006). Environmental factors can increase or decrease mutations in particular parts of a genome. They can massively alter a phenotype without altering a genotype but in the process alter the consequences of mutations in particular sections of a genome. Thus, the epigenetic system can determine what aspects of an environment affect particular aspects of a genome (West-Eberhard, 2003).

Working memory plays the same role in human cognition as the epigenetic system plays in biological evolution. Information flowing from the environment to working memory determines what aspects of the environment are considered and what aspects of long-term memory are likely to be altered. Problem solving occurs in working memory but the environment, in conjunction with information already in long-term memory, determines which problems will be considered for solution and which novel, environmental information will be attended to.

Because of the randomness as genesis principle, there are severe limits to the extent to which change is possible when dealing with novel information. Natural information-processing systems can only change slowly and incrementally, leading to the narrow limits of change principle. Large, rapid, random changes to an information store are likely to destroy its functionality, whereas smaller changes, each tested for effectiveness, are more likely to be effective. For this reason, changes to both a genome and long-term memory tend to be slow and incremental.

The reason changes to long-term memory are slow and incremental is because working memory is structured to ensure that outcome. When dealing with novel information, and only when dealing with novel information, working memory is limited in both capacity (Miller, 1956) and duration (Peterson & Peterson, 1959). We can hold no more than about seven novel elements of information in working memory and can process no more than about four elements depending on the nature of the processing required (Cowan, 2001). In this manner, working memory, via the narrow limits of change principle, prevents substantial, possibly destructive changes to long-term memory that might be generated by the randomness as genesis principle.

The implications of a limited working memory for inquiry-based instructional procedures is critical and indeed, as indicated by cognitive-load theory (Sweller, 2003, 2004; Sweller et al., 1998), our limited working memory when dealing with novel information has implications for a variety of instructional procedures. Inquiry-based instruction (Hmelo-Silver et al., 2007) that reduces information made available to learners so that they can discover it themselves tends to be designed as though we either do not have a limited working memory or if we do, working-memory limitations are irrelevant to instructional issues. Problem-solving search, especially means–ends search, places a huge burden on working memory (Sweller, 1988). There is a large research literature demonstrating that when novices study worked examples, their problem-solving skills improve more than by merely trying to solve the equivalent problems by themselves (Paas & van Gog, 2006; Renkl, 2005). Studying a worked example reduces extraneous cognitive load compared to solving a problem by oneself. Advocates of constructivist teaching techniques need to consider the consequences of a severely limited working memory for learning through problem-based search.

Environmental Organizing and Linking Principle

The limitations of working memory only apply when we deal with novel information from the environment. For both biological evolution and human cognition, there must be limits to the amount of novel information, randomly generated, that can be processed and that can alter the information store. Those limits disappear when information from the information store directs activity within an environment. In the case of biological evolution, the epigenetic system not only acts as an intermediary that permits environmental information to influence a genome, it also allows genomic information to direct activity. There is no limit to the amount of previously organized, genomic information that can be used by the epigenetic system to direct biological activity. For example, different cells in the body such as liver cells and skin cells have vastly different structures and functions despite having an identical DNA-based genetic code in their nuclei. The different structures and functions are caused by the epigenetic system using environmental factors to marshal vast amounts of differential genetic information for differential purposes. There appear to be no limits to the amount of genetic information used by the epigenetic system for a particular purpose (Jablonka & Lamb, 2005; West-Eberhard, 2003).

Working memory has an identical function in human cognition. It not only processes novel information from the environment as indicated by the narrow limits of change principle, it also processes familiar information from long-term memory. But the characteristics of working memory change dramatically when it is dealing with the previously organized, familiar information from long-term memory rather than the unorganized, random information from the environment. There may be no effective limits to the amount or duration of organized information from long-term memory with which working memory can deal. Ericsson and Kintsch (1995) coined the term "long-term working memory" to discuss working memory when dealing with information retrieved from long-term memory, because working memory has such vastly different characteristics when dealing with familiar information from long-term memory compared to novel information encoded from the environment.

In some ways, the environmental organizing and linking principle provides the ultimate justification for the human cognitive system. We process information in working memory for storage in long-term memory so that under appropriate environmental conditions it can be brought back into working memory and used to govern our cognitive activity. For many, very complex activities, very large amounts of stored information from long-term memory must be brought into working memory to govern our activity. Highly skilled performance may require vast amounts of information from long-term memory to be brought into working memory for indefinite periods. The capacity and duration limits of working memory when dealing with novel information from the environment are replaced by a seemingly unlimited capacity and duration structure when working memory deals with familiar information from long-term memory.

On this argument, the function of learning is to store large amounts of information in long-term memory so that it can be brought effortlessly into working memory enabling us to function in a large variety of complex environments. Explicit instruction is intended to directly facilitate this process. It is quite unclear, and rarely, if ever, specified, how inquiry-based learning procedures assist in either storing information in long-term memory or in using that information to subsequently direct activity.

Empirical Evidence

The cognitive architecture described in this chapter has been used by cognitive-load theory to generate a large range of instructional procedures (Sweller, 2003, 2004). The effectiveness of those procedures has been validated using randomized, controlled experimental designs, replicated by many researchers under many conditions from around the world. The worked-example effect (Paas & van Gog, 2006; Renkl, 2005) is particularly relevant to the present argument. The effect occurs when students learn more from studying worked examples than solving the equivalent problems. Many studies have demonstrated this effect with novice learners. The effect indicates the critical importance of explicit instruction when dealing with novice learners.

It is only with increased expertise that the importance of explicit instruction decreases. Over longer periods, as expertise increases, the worked-example effect first disappears and then reverses with problem solving proving superior to studying worked examples (Kalyuga, Chandler, Tuovinen, & Sweller, 2001). That reversal is due to another cognitive-load effect, the redundancy effect (Sweller, 2005). For more expert problem solvers, studying an example constitutes a redundant activity that imposes an extraneous cognitive load. The ability of cognitive-load theory, or indeed any theory, to generate applications such as these provides strong evidence for the validity of the theory.

Discussion and Conclusions

The cognitive architecture discussed in this chapter has obvious implications for the amount of guidance and assistance provided to learners. Instruction should be explicit and clear. Based on this architecture, there seems no purpose or function to withholding information from learners so that they can discover it for themselves. Attempting to discover information is unavoidable when that information is unavailable from other sources as occurs when investigators engage in research. In addition, of course, the manner in which research is carried out in various disciplines needs to be taught—explicitly. We should not assume that because research activities are valuable they should be engaged in by people who are attempting to learn and so are in no position to discover anything novel. At the very least, if research is considered a valuable learning tool rather than as a means of discovering novel information, we need to be able to specify exactly what is learned during the research process—in other words, what has changed in long-term memory. From the perspective of cognitive architecture discussed in this chapter, engaging in research based on ignorance of information already available to others will result in no advantages whatsoever.

Of course, the cognitive architecture described here may be invalid. While the logic that underlies this architecture also underlies evolution by natural selection, it does not follow that they must have an identical structure. It is possible that human cognitive architecture functions in an entirely different manner from evolution by natural selection. Nevertheless, at the very least it is intriguing that both human cognitive architecture and evolution by natural selection are natural information-processing systems able to create, remember, and disseminate novel information over space and time. Furthermore, since evolution by natural selection drove the structures and functions of human cognition, it may not be surprising if the logic underlying both systems is similar. That similarity and the fact that empirical evidence concerning long-term memory and working memory support the cognitive architecture outlined here suggest the current conceptualization is accurate. If it is considered not to be accurate, the onus is on those who support inquiry-based learning techniques to indicate an alternative architecture that supports withholding information from learners. That architecture will need to not only specify new principles but in addition exclude all of the principles discussed in this chapter because each of these principles seems to be antithetical to an inquiry-based regime.

Question: Duschl and Duncan. *The analogy between the genetic system and the cognitive system is interesting. However, it is unclear what the evidentiary base is for drawing the parallels and assumptions on which your argument is based. For example, you note that based on the borrowing and reorganizing principle (which in genetics amounts to sexual reproduction and genetic recombination) we have "evolved to obtain information from others, deliberately withholding that information under a discovery, problem-based, constructivist agenda is bizarre." It is unclear how one makes the jump from the borrowing and reorganizing principle to your assumption that we have evolved to obtain information. Nor is it clear what the evidence is for such a speculation.*

Reply: Sweller. Duschl and Duncan ask an important and interesting question. Primary evidence for the borrowing and reorganizing principle comes from the overwhelming number of studies demonstrating the worked-example effect. Those studies indicate how worked examples should be structured, when they should be used, and which categories of students should study worked examples. The effect provides powerful, direct evidence for the borrowing and reorganizing principle. There is additional evidence. Psychological evidence of a human propensity to imitate other humans was provided by Bandura (1986). We habitually observe other people and mimic their actions and procedures. The fact that we automatically assimilate the culture in which we live provides strong evidence for the importance and strength of this propensity to imitate. The knowledge acquired through imitation is presumably stored in long-term memory. Recent biological evidence strengthening this argument comes from the discovery of the mirror-neuron system (e.g., Tettamanti et al., 2005) that not only fires when we act but also when we think of acting, observe someone else acting, or even when we hear someone talking of acting. We seem to have evolved particular neurological pathways to facilitate using other people's knowledge.

Question: Duschl and Duncan. *Much of the research cited in support of direct instruction compared direct instruction with unguided discovery. This comparison misses the boat somewhat as no one is arguing for a pedagogy based on a free-for-all discovery environment. The argument is focused on the nature and amount of scaffolding necessary. Are there any studies that compare guided-inquiry pedagogies with direct instruction that would support your claims?*

Reply: Sweller. I do not know of any experiment that has used totally unguided discovery compared to explicit instruction, possibly because the results of such an experiment are assumed by most researchers to be a foregone conclusion. Unfortunately, nor do I know of a body of research based on properly designed (altering one variable at a time) randomized, controlled experiments demonstrating the advantages of guided discovery over explicit instruction. In fact, the empirical evidence for my argument advocating explicit instruction is based on the worked-example effect. Constructivist teaching techniques ignore both the worked-example effect and the working-memory implications of problem-solving search. The worked-example effect seems to provide a direct test of the constructivist position but with results counter to that position. I am distressed that the field has successfully advocated the introduction of constructivist techniques into educational practice with no body of justifying evidence using controlled experiments.

Question: Duschl and Duncan. *You note that, "we should not assume that because research activities are valuable they should be engaged in by people who are attempting to learn and so are in no position to discover anything novel." This statement suggests a view of science education as endowing students with content knowledge. However, many science education researchers, and policy makers, have been arguing for dual goals for science education: (a) understanding scientific concepts, models, theories; and (b) understanding how such scientific knowledge is developed. Inquiry approaches target both goals. How does direct instruction target the second goal?*

Reply: Sweller. I agree entirely that science education should result not only in students understanding the theories and findings of science but also the processes by which scientific knowledge is developed—but both should be taught explicitly. I disagree with the suggestion that science research methodology can only be taught adequately using inquiry procedures. There is nothing to prevent explicit instruction on the goals, history, and procedures used by science to advance knowledge. While I disagree with the hypothesis that the processes by which science develops should be taught by inquiry methods, I do not, of course, have any problem with the hypothesis being proposed. But it needs to be tested. I think the hypothesis is unlikely to be supported by any fair test because I do not see why knowledge concerning scientific theories and findings should be taught in a different manner from knowledge concerning the methods by which science proceeds, as seems to be implied by the third question. Again, I am concerned that the required body of research using randomized, controlled experiments and demonstrating an advantage for inquiry-learning techniques does not exist and yet inquiry-learning procedures have been adopted in classrooms. Advocacy should be based on data, not hypotheses.

Question: Spiro and DeSchryver. *We agree with you that teaching should not withhold "easily presented information" and should explicitly provide "essential information" for well-structured aspects of domains but wonder about those ill-structured aspects or ill-structured domains. Is it not the case that what makes them ill structured is that those aspects lack any essential qualities that can be easily presented in explicit fashion? Is there a danger that, for ill-structured aspects of knowledge, explicitly presented information will apply to some but not a majority of situations but may be treated by learners as if it were essential, thus producing some harm in learning due to over-extension?*

Reply: Sweller. I will divide this response into two sections: A theoretical analysis of the distinction between ill-structured and well-structured problems and a discussion of the empirical evidence concerning explicit instruction in ill-structured domains. The first theoretical point to make is that much of the field has assumed, correctly I suspect, that when dealing with problem-solving strategies, a distinction between well-defined and ill-defined problems is not sustainable. The sub-goals set up to assist in solving well-defined problems are just as indefinite as when dealing with ill-defined problems. Accordingly, even when dealing with well-defined problems, instructors must determine which problem paths should be taught and, frequently, multiple paths may need to be presented to learners. The second theoretical point to make is that in any problem-solving domain, some solutions may be considered superior (shorter, more elegant, take into consideration more problem goals, etc.) to others under some circumstances. If instructors have difficulty determining what is important under various circumstances, novice problem solvers are likely to find it impossible.

While these theoretical points may be important, empirical evidence provides the ultimate criterion. If, for example, the presentation of worked examples is superior to problem solving in ill-structured domains, then theories must be adjusted to take the evidence into account. In the early days of cognitive-load theory, most research used mathematics, science, and technology curriculum materials. More recently, a flood of experiments has been published using materials from ill-structured domains such as language, music, and art. Because I am more familiar with them, I will use a few examples from experiments carried out at UNSW, but there are others, and today the use of ill-structured domains is anything but rare.

Yeung, Jin, and Sweller (1998) looked at the problem-solving consequences of providing explanatory notes during reading comprehension tasks for both native English speakers and English as a second language learners and found improvements in comprehension as appropriately structured explicit instruction increased. Diao, Chandler, and Sweller (2007) and Diao and Sweller (2007) confirmed the importance of appropriately structured explicit instructions when learning English as a second language. Problem-solving tests were used as the dependent variables. Using explicit-instruction techniques, Owens and Sweller (2008) demonstrated a variety of cognitive-load effects in the domain of music instruction. Next, and coincidentally, Rourke and Sweller (in press) have directly tested whether the worked-example effect could be obtained in an ill-defined domain. They used art students learning to recognize furniture designers' styles and found the same worked-example effect as commonly obtained using well-defined problems in technical domains. While the hypothesis that ill-defined problem domains yield different results from well-defined domains may have been viable one or two years ago, the flood of data recently published or becoming available renders the hypothesis problematic.

References

Atkinson, R. C., & Shiffrin, R. M. (1968). Human memory: A proposed system and its control processes. In K. W. Spence & J. T. Spence (Eds.), *The psychology of learning and motivation* (Vol. 2, pp. 89–195). Oxford: Academic Press.

Bandura, A. (1986). *Social foundations of thought and action: A social cognitive theory.* Englewoods Cliffs, NJ: Prentice Hall.

Brown, J. S., Collins, A., & Duguid, P. (1989). Situated cognition and the culture of learning. *Educational Researcher, 18*, 32–42.

Bruner, J. (1961). The art of discovery. *Harvard Educational Review, 31*, 21–32.

Chase, W. G., & Simon, H. A. (1973). Perception in chess. *Cognitive Psychology, 4*, 55–81.

Collins, A., Brown, J. S., & Newman, S. E. (1989). Cognitive apprenticeship: Teaching the crafts of reading, writing, and mathematics. In L. B. Resnick (Ed.), *Knowing, learning, and instruction: Essays in honor of Robert Glaser* (pp. 453–494). Hillsdale, NJ: Lawrence Erlbaum Associates.

Cowan, N. (2001). The magical number 4 in short-term memory: A reconsideration of mental storage capacity. *Behavioral and Brain Sciences, 24*, 87–114.

De Groot, A. (1946/1965). *Thought and choice in chess*. The Hague: Mouton.

Diao, Y., Chandler, P., & Sweller, J. (2007). The effect of written text on learning to comprehend spoken English as a foreign language. *American Journal of Psychology, 120*, 237–261.

Diao, Y., & Sweller, J. (2007). Redundancy in foreign language reading instruction: Concurrent written and spoken presentations. *Learning and Instruction, 17*, 78–88.

Ericsson, K. A., & Kintsch, W. (1995). Long-term working memory. *Psychological Review, 102*, 211–245.

Fingerman, P., & Levine, M. (1974). Nonlearning: The completeness of the blindness. *Journal of Experimental Psychology, 102*, 720–721.

Geary, D. (2002). Principles of evolutionary educational psychology. *Learning and Individual Differences, 12*, 317–345.

Geary, D. (2005). *The origin of mind: Evolution of brain, cognition, and general intelligence*. Washington, DC: American Psychological Association.

Geary, D. (2007). Educating the evolved mind: Conceptual foundations for an evolutionary educational psychology. In J. S. Carlson & J. R. Levin (Eds.), *Psychological perspectives on contemporary educational issues* (pp. 1–99). Greenwich, CT: Information Age Publishing.

Gick, M. L., & Holyoak, K. J. (1980). Analogical problem solving. *Cognitive Psychology, 12*, 306–355.

Gick, M. L., & Holyoak, K. J. (1983). Schema induction and analogical transfer. *Cognitive Psychology, 15*, 1–38.

Grafton, S., Arbib, M., Fadiga, L., & Rizzolatti, G. (1996). Localization of grasp representations in humans by positron emission tomography: 2. Observation compared with imagination. *Experimental Brain Research, 112*, 103–111.

Hmelo-Silver, C., Duncan, R., & Chinn, C. (2007). Why problem-based learning and inquiry learning are not minimally guided: On assumptions and evidence. *Educational Psychologist, 42*, 99–107.

Iacoboni, M., Woods, R., Brass, M., Bekkering, H., Mazziotta, J., & Rizzolatti, G. (1999). Cortical mechanisms of human imitation. *Science, 286*, 2526–2528.

Jablonka, E., & Lamb, M. J. (2005). *Evolution in four dimensions: Genetic, epigenetic, behavioral, and symbolic variation in the history of life*. Cambridge, MA: MIT Press.

Kalyuga, S., Chandler, P., Tuovinen, J., & Sweller, J. (2001). When problem solving is superior to studying worked examples. *Journal of Educational Psychology, 93*, 579–588.

Kirschner, P., Sweller, J., & Clark, R. (2006). Why minimal guidance during instruction does not work: An analysis of the failure of constructivist, discovery, problem-based, experiential, and inquiry-based teaching. *Educational Psychologist, 41*, 75–86.

Klahr, D., & Nigam, M. (2004). The equivalence of learning paths in early science instruction: Effects of direct instruction and discovery learning. *Psychological Science, 15*, 661–667.

Kuhn, D. (2007). Is direct instruction the answer to the right question? *Educational Psychologist, 42*, 109–113.

Luchins, A. (1942). Mechanisation in problem solving: The effect of Einstellung. *Psychological Monographs, 54* (Whole No. 248).

Miller, G. A. (1956). The magical number seven, plus or minus two: Some limits on our capacity for processing information. *Psychological Review, 63*, 81–97.

Newell, A., & Simon, H. A. (1972). *Human problem solving.* Englewood Cliffs, NJ: Prentice Hall.

Owens, P., & Sweller, J. (2008). Cognitive load theory and music instruction. *Educational Psychology, 28*, 29–45.

Paas, F., & van Gog, T. (2006). Optimising worked example instruction: Different ways to increase germane cognitive load. *Learning & Instruction, 16*, 87–91.

Peterson, L., & Peterson, M. J. (1959). Short-term retention of individual verbal items. *Journal of Experimental Psychology, 58*, 193–198.

Piaget, J. (1928). *Judgment and reasoning in the child.* New York: Harcourt.

Renkl, A. (2005). The worked out example principle in multimedia learning. In R. E. Mayer (Ed.), *The Cambridge handbook of multimedia learning* (pp. 229–245). New York: Cambridge University Press.

Resnick, L. B. (1987). Learning in school and out. *Educational Researcher, 16*, 13–20.

Rourke, A., & Sweller, J. (in press). The worked-example effect using ill-defined problems: Learning to recognise designers' styles. *Learning and Instruction.*

Schmidt, H., Loyens, S., van Gog, T., & Paas, F. (2007). Problem-based learning *is* compatible with human cognitive architecture: Commentary on Kirschner, Sweller, and Clark (2006). *Educational Psychologist, 42*, 91–97.

Simon, H., & Gilmartin, K. (1973). A simulation of memory for chess positions. *Cognitive Psychology, 5*, 29–46.

Sweller, J. (1980). Transfer effects in a problem solving context. *Quarterly Journal of Experimental Psychology, 32*, 233–239.

Sweller, J. (1988). Cognitive load during problem solving: Effects on learning. *Cognitive Science, 12*, 257–285.

Sweller, J. (2003). Evolution of human cognitive architecture. In B. Ross (Ed.), *The psychology of learning and motivation* (Vol. 43, pp. 215–266). San Diego: Academic Press.

Sweller, J. (2004). Instructional design consequences of an analogy between evolution by natural selection and human cognitive architecture. *Instructional Science, 32*, 9–31.

Sweller, J. (2005). The redundancy principle. In R. E. Mayer (Ed.), *The Cambridge handbook of multimedia learning* (pp. 159–167). New York: Cambridge University Press.

Sweller, J., & Gee, W. (1978). Einstellung, the sequence effect, and hypothesis theory. *Journal of Experimental Psychology: Human Learning & Memory, 4*, 513–526.

Sweller, J., & Sweller, S. (2006). Natural information processing systems. *Evolutionary Psychology, 4*, 434–458.

Sweller, J., van Merriënboer, J. J., & Paas, F. G. (1998). Cognitive architecture and instructional design. *Educational Psychology Review, 10*, 251–296.

Tettamanti, M., Buccino, G., Saccuman, M., Gallese, V., Dana, M., Scifo, P., et al. (2005). Listening to action-related sentences activates fronto-parietal motor circuits. *Journal of Cognitive Neuroscience, 17*, 273–281.

West-Eberhard, M. (2003). *Developmental plasticity and evolution.* New York: Oxford University Press.

Yeung, A. S., Jin, P., & Sweller, J. (1998). Cognitive load and learner expertise: Split-attention and redundancy effects in reading with explanatory notes. *Contemporary Educational Psychology, 23*, 1–21.

8 Epistemology or Pedagogy, That Is the Question

Paul A. Kirschner *Utrecht University*

Epistemology or Pedagogy, That IS the Question

At the time of writing, there is an animated debate which has apparently split the educational world—both teachers and researchers—into two ideological factions. The first faction is depicted as old-school pedagogues who believe that all teaching and instruction should be based upon classical, sage-on-the-stage, expository and didactic approaches of universal truths. The second faction is depicted as fuzzy-brained social constructivists who believe that nothing is true and that learners can only learn by constructing their own knowledge and behaviors through undirected experiences. This debate has infiltrated every pore of our discussions on teaching, learning, and education at scientific and professional conferences, in scientific and professional journals, and, in many countries, even the mass media and national politics.

Of course we, as rational right-minded people, know that neither faction is correct and that the "truth" lies in the middle. For this reason I will try to avoid this ideological discussion and concentrate on a deeper underlying question, namely whether we are selling ourselves and our children short when we use or substitute an epistemology of a domain for a pedagogy for teaching in that domain. Before beginning, I need to define these two terms.

Epistemology and Pedagogy

Epistemology is the study of knowledge and what it means to know something (Shaffer, 2007). It is a branch of science that studies the nature, methods, limitations, and validity of knowledge and belief and addresses questions such as: What is knowledge? How is knowledge acquired? What do people know? In more pedestrian terms, it studies the way someone practicing a profession understands her or his profession and gains new knowledge in that profession. For the natural scientist, it could be the "scientific method" often carried out in teams. For the anthropologist it could be ethnographic or descriptive/deductive research from within, as part of a group or society being studied. And for the philosopher it could be dialogic in debate with others.

Pedagogy, on the other hand, is the art or science of being a teacher, generally referring to strategies or styles of instruction. A pedagogy can be (1) *general*, as in the strategies, techniques, and approaches that teachers use to facilitate learning in general; (2) *specific to a domain*, such as the application of specific strategies, techniques, and approaches belonging to a domain (i.e., professional or pedagogical content knowledge) to the instruction of that specific domain (e.g., mathematics, English as a second language, music); or (3) *specific to a certain approach to teaching* that may or may not be domain specific, such as work-based pedagogy (i.e., the organization of the social activities, organizational structures, and cultural practices by which newcomers, such as student interns, come to acquire and engage that knowledge (Hughes & Moore, 1999)), problem-based pedagogy (i.e., "an approach to structuring the curriculum which involves confronting students with problems from practice which provide a stimulus for learning" (Boud & Feletti, 1991, p. 21)), or even constructivist pedagogy (i.e., the "creation of classroom environments, with goals that focus on individual students developing deep understandings in the subject matter of interest and habits of mind that aid future learning" (Richardson, 2003, p. 1627)).

Having made this distinction, the next step is to look at learners. The next section will deal with learners and their characteristics (i.e., their cognitive development and their expertise) and why the epistemology of practicing in a domain is not a good pedagogy for learning that domain.

Learners

There are two major problems with using a domain's epistemology as its pedagogy. The first is rooted in developmental psychology and biology where Luria and Piaget long ago made clear that children or adolescents (i.e., typical learners in initial education: preschool through university) are not miniature adults. Luria discussed the metamorphosis of a child into an adult as follows:

> The incorrect belief that children and adults differ only in quantitative terms has become firmly entrenched in the general consciousness. Its proponents argue that if you take an adult, make him [*sic*] smaller, somewhat weaker and less intelligent, and take away his knowledge and skills, you will be left with a child. This notion of the child as a small adult is very widespread ... essentially the child is ... in many respects radically different from the adult, and [that he] is a very special creature with his own identity ... qualitatively different from the adult.
>
> (Vygotsky & Luria, 1930/1992, Chapter 2)

In Piaget's view (1955), cognitive development, which he called development of intelligence, is based upon *assimilation* of newly experienced phenomena in already existing cognitive schemata and *accommodation* of those schemata in cases where the new information does not match the existing schemata. In his words, intelligence "progresses from a state in which accommodation to the environment is undifferentiated from the assimilation of things to the subject's schemata to a state in which the accommodation of multiple schemata is distinguished from their respective and reciprocal assimilation" (n.p.). This process proceeds through a series of what he called *cognitive stages*, each characterized by a general cognitive structure that affects all thinking. Each stage represents how reality is understood during that stage, and each stage, except the last one, is an inadequate approximation of reality. In other words, learners—at least those in initial education—see the word differently from practitioners, interpret and understand it differently, and are not capable of carrying out the abstract cognitive transformations necessary for true knowledge construction. Such learners apply inadequate, often faulty novice theories that differ greatly from the sophisticated theories of a domain or the world held by practitioners (Chi, Feltovich, & Glaser, 1981; Mazens & Lautrey, 2003; Partridge & Paap, 1988). As Hannust and Kikas (2007) state in their research on experimentation for teaching children astronomy, children

> acquire factual information rather easily and therefore early instruction should introduce the core facts related to the topics. Some children over-generalized new knowledge very easily, indicating that the materials used in teaching may promote the development of non-scientific notions and that those notions must be addressed promptly to avoid the development of coherent non-scientific models.
>
> (p. 89)

Even if we concentrate on teaching for and learning by those who might be able to think abstractly and carry out the necessary cognitive transformations to think inductively and construct theories, we are confronted with a second problem when using epistemology as pedagogy, namely that learners or novices are not miniature professionals or experts. Experts not only know more and work faster than novices, they also deal differently with problems and solve them in different ways. Here follows a number of ways that novices and experts differ.

De Groot (1946, 1978) determined that chess grand masters, when determining what the next move should be, do not consider more moves than less highly ranked expert chess players, but "zoom in" on potentially good moves earlier in their search than "weaker" players. As Gobet and Simon (1996) state, "stronger and weaker players examine nearly the same number of branches, but ... the stronger players select more relevant and important branches ... because of their greater ability to recognize significant features" (p. 53). This ability to better recognize significant features was also found by Boucheix, Lowe, and Soirat (2006), noting that when viewing animations of the working of a defective piano, expert piano tuners fixate on areas of the animations that contain crucial but less-conspicuous content more frequently than novices who tend to fixate on high-salience information, neglecting less-conspicuous aspects necessary for building high-quality mental models.

> Cuthbert, du Boulay, Teather, Teather, Sharples, and du Boulay (1999) in their review on expert-novice differences in diagnostic medical cognition, determined that: experts produce fewer, but more general hypotheses ... at an earlier stage of problem formulation than novices. Furthermore, experts

work from findings to a hypothesis (forward reasoning) using a breadth first approach (considering and evaluating several hypothesis at once) ... novice reasoning is characterised as backwards (from hypothesis to data), and furthermore, depth first (considering and evaluating a single hypothesis at a time). Experts also demonstrate superior hypothesis evaluation skills, in particular, they are better able to disregard discredited hypotheses and are more likely to change their hypothesis to fit the data than to change the data to fit their hypothesis or to ignore inconsistent findings altogether.

(pp. 23–24)

In other words, the differences between experts and novices manifest themselves not only at the conceptual level, but also at the level of epistemology and ontology (Jacobson, 2000).

Other areas where much research has been carried out on expert–novice differences are physics (Chi et al., 1981; Hardiman, Dufresne, & Mestre, 1989), computer programming (Adelson, 1981), mathematical problem solving (Shoenfeld & Herrmann, 1982), and teaching (Hogan, Rabinowitz, & Craven, 2003). Bransford, Brown, and Cocking (1999) conclude that this body of research shows that:

it is not simply general abilities, such as memory or intelligence, nor the use of general strategies that differentiate experts from novices. Instead, experts have acquired extensive knowledge that affects what they notice and how they organize, represent, and interpret information in their environment. This, in turn, affects their abilities to remember, reason, and solve problems.

(p. 19)

Donovan, Bransford, and Pellegrino (1999) present six major differences between experts and novices, four of which have concrete bearing on how we teach and learn. The first is that experts *attend to* and *notice* more important features or meaningful patterns of information in a problem or a situation than novices. As stated, eye-movement research has shown that experts fixate on crucial though less-conspicuous content more frequently than novices who fixate on high-salience information, neglecting less-conspicuous aspects that are necessary for building high-quality mental models (Boucheix et al., 2006). Learners miss the necessary basic domain knowledge to do this, and concentrate on superficially conspicuous information, regardless of its actual importance (Lowe, 1999, 2004).

This variation in attending is most probably due to the second major difference, namely that experts have a great deal of *accessible content knowledge* organized to reflect deep understanding of the subject matter. In other words, what experts already know determines what they see and how they see it. Because novices know little about a subject or a domain, they do not know where to look and, having looked at something, have trouble correctly interpreting what they see.

The third difference is that the experts' knowledge is not simply reducible to sets of isolated facts or propositions, but reflects "*contexts of applicability*" of that knowledge. Donovan et al. (1999) called this *conditionalized* knowledge, though it could also be called *contextualized* or *situated*. It means that experts have a type of knowledge that includes knowledge of the contexts and/or situations in which it is or will be useful. In contrast, a novice's knowledge is often *inert* (Whitehead, 1929); it has been learned but cannot be accessed for problem solving.

The fourth difference (Donovan et al., 1999) is that experts *retrieve* important aspects of their knowledge with *little effort* whereas novices spend a great deal of effort attempting to remember and process individual knowledge elements. Experts have many and varied rich cognitive schemas at their disposal in which their knowledge is organized and from which needed aspects of that knowledge can be easily and quickly retrieved (Glaser & Chi, 1988; Schneider & Shiffrin, 1977). Larkin (1979) found that physics experts remember sets of related equations while novices retrieve a series of single equations, suggesting sequential memory search. "Experts appear to possess an efficient organization of knowledge with meaningful relations among related elements clustered into related units that are governed by underlying concepts and principles" (Bransford et al., 1999, p. 26).

In other words, applying an epistemology used by domain experts or practitioners as a pedagogy for learning in that domain will not work. In the following, I will look at this problem within a specific and well-studied domain, namely the natural sciences.

Practicing Science or Learning to Practice Science?

Curriculum reform in the natural sciences has emphasized the experience of the processes and procedures of science, moving away from the teaching of science as a body of knowledge (Bybee, 2003; Harmer & Cates, 2007; Hodson, 1988). Bybee stated that

> students learn by constructing their own meaning from experiences [and] ... that science teaching should consist of experiences that exemplify the spirit, character, and nature of science and technology ... inquiry-oriented laboratories are infrequent experiences for students, but they should be a central part of their experience in science education.
>
> (Bybee, 2003, n.p.)

In 1996, the National Research Council declared that inquiry into authentic questions generated from student experiences should be the central strategy for teaching science. In 2005, Gabric, Hovance, Comstock, and Harnisch stated that

> the ultimate goal was to provide a learning environment in which students could feel like scientists in their own classrooms. This meant that our students would need to be involved in the acquisition of their scientific knowledge by—not only reading and writing about—but actually doing science.
>
> (p. 80)

This focus is coupled to the assumption that to teach the process of science (i.e., the pedagogy), we can best confront learners with experiences either based on or equivalent to science procedures (i.e., the epistemology). This has led to a tenacious commitment by educators, instructional designers, and educational researchers to discovery and inquiry methods of learning which is based upon confusing teaching science *as* inquiry (i.e., an emphasis in the curriculum on the processes of science) with teaching science *by* inquiry (i.e., using the process of science to learn science). The error here is that no distinction is made between the behaviors and methods of the scientist—who is an expert practicing her or his profession—and those of a student who is essentially a novice.

Even if this were true—and now I play devil's advocate—the epistemology used in school science is that of the inductive, positivist scientist. Cawthron and Rowell (1978) described this as a "conception of scientific method as ... a well defined, quasi-mechanical process consisting of a number of characteristic stages" (p. 33). It is as though scientists look at the world with no a priori ideas and that they objectively observe, collect, record, analyze, and interpret without underlying hypotheses or preconceptions except those relating to the logic of thought processes. This objective, impartial, and unbiased scientist finally draws conclusions about relationships and makes generalizations about an observed phenomenon based upon the facts collected. It seems as though "constructivist" educators and curriculum designers see the domain taught as being "positivist," containing general and identifiable truths. Southerland and Gess-Newsome (1999) confirmed this, describing even those teachers who had learned science through modern, discovery-based curricula as a form of discovery maintain positivist views of knowledge, learning, and teaching. Discovery, thus, becomes trivialized to "stage-managed pseudo-discovery of the inevitable" (Hodson, 1985, p. 40).

But I digress. Returning to the main point, it is clear that many curriculum developers and instructional designers either are not aware of or do not see the distinction between the epistemological basis of the natural sciences and the pedagogic basis for teaching the natural sciences. Because experiments are widely used in science, science teachers are conditioned to regard them as a necessary and integral part of science education. But students do not practice science. They are learning about science and/or learning to practice science. It is the teacher's job to teach science, teach about science, and teach how to do science.

A student, as opposed to a scientist, is still learning about the subject area in question and, therefore, possesses neither the theoretical sophistication nor the wealth of experience of the scientist. Also, the student is learning science—as opposed to doing science—and should be aided in her/his learning through the application of an effective pedagogy and good instructional design.

We find these concerns in educational and psychological literature as far back as Ausubel (1964) and as recently as Klahr and Nigam (2004) and Mayer (2004). Ausubel expressed problems that accompany the failure to differentiate between the scientist and the student. According to him, scientists are engaged in a full-time search for new, general, or applied principles in a field, whereas students are engaged in learning the basic subject matter of a field which scientists learned in their student days plus the way in which scientists practice. If students are ever to discover scientifically, then they must first learn both the content as well as how to discover! The student "cannot learn adequately by pretending [to be] a junior scientist" (p. 298). According to Mayer, many phenomena associated with using discovery make it relatively ineffective as an instructional method. Klahr and Nigam state that

> children in discovery situations are more likely than those receiving direct instruction to encounter inconsistent or misleading feedback, to make encoding errors and causal misattributions, and to experience inadequate practice and elaboration. These impediments to learning may overwhelm benefits commonly attributed to discovery learning—such as "ownership" and "authenticity".
>
> (p. 661)

Kyle (1980) described scientific inquiry as a systematic and investigative performance ability which incorporates unrestrained thinking capabilities after a person has acquired a broad, critical knowledge of the particular subject matter through formal learning processes. This same idea is posed as an apparent anomaly by Klahr and Nigam (2004) when they note that "most of what students (and teachers and scientists) know about science was taught to them, rather than discovered by them" (p. 661).

This lack of clarity about the difference between learning and doing science has led many educators to advocate the discovery method as the way to teach science (Allen, Barker, & Ramsden, 1986; Bybee, 2003; Kirschner, Sweller, & Clark, 2006). This approach fits well in contemporary learner-centered pedagogies emphasizing direct experience and individual inquiry (e.g., experiential learning (Kolb & Fry, 1975; Itin, 1999), authentic learning (Downes, 2007), inquiry-based learning (Dewey, 1997), and problem-based learning (Barrows & Tamblyn, 1980; Hmelo-Silver, 2004; Hmelo-Silver & Barrows, 2006)). Cawthron and Rowell—in 1978—had the prescience to characterize this as the coalescing of the logic of knowledge and the psychology of knowledge under the mesmeric umbrella term "discovery."

But to discover (i.e., notice) anything, learners need a prior conceptual framework—as discussed earlier in this chapter when the differences between experts and novices were discussed—as well as the ability to think in abstract ways about what they have noticed (see the earlier discussion on the development of thinking). Discovery, thus, presupposes a prior conceptual framework and the ability to interpret and sometimes reinterpret what has been seen or experienced in abstract terms, but there is no guarantee that it will lead to new concepts, much less correct ones. This is because, first, novices have little knowledge and experience in a domain which causes them to encode information at a surface or superficial level, while experts have much knowledge and experience in a domain and are, thus, able to encode information at a deeper, more structural level (Chi et al., 1981; Novick, 1988; van Gog, Paas, & van Merriënboer, 2005). Second, novices do not simply produce random guesses in the absence of knowledge, "but rather as systematically off the mark in a particular way that makes sense given a particular misconception" (Means, 2006, p. 508).

The strangest and possibly most unfortunate aspect of this whole problem is that this is not new. Novak (1988), in noting that the major effort to improve secondary school science education in the 1950s and 1960s fell short of expectations, stated that the major obstacle in the way of "revolutionary improvement of science education ... was the obsolete epistemology that was behind the emphasis on 'inquiry' oriented science" (pp. 79–80). More recently, Chen and Klahr (1999; see also Klahr, this volume) demonstrated that direct instruction was significantly better than discovery learning on children's ability to design simple, unconfounded experiments, and even more important, those receiving direct instruction were also superior on a far-transfer test of experimental design administered 7 months later.

Conclusion

For designing instruction, Vamvakoussi and Vosniadou (2004) warn that "presuppositions that constrain learning are not under the conscious control of the learner. It is important to create learning environments that allow students to express and elaborate their opinions, so that they become aware of their beliefs" (p. 466). Van Merriënboer and Kirschner (2007) note that there are considerable differences between domain models that describe the effective mental models used by competent task performers and the intuitive or naive mental models of novice learners in that domain. Such intuitive or naive mental models are often fragmented, inexact, and incomplete; reflecting misunderstandings or misconceptions where learners are unaware of the underlying relationships between the elements.

As such, how to learn or be taught in a domain is quite different from how to perform or "do" in a domain (i.e., learning science vs. doing science). The epistemology of most sciences, for example, is often based upon experimentation and discovery and, since this is so, experimentation and discovery should be a part of any curriculum aimed at "producing" future scientists. But this does not mean that experimentation and discovery should also be the basis for curriculum organization and learning-environment designing (Bradley, 2005; Kirschner, 1992). Modern curriculum developers and instructional designers confuse the epistemological nature of a domain with the psychological bases of learning and the pedagogic bases for teaching. Epistemology refers to how knowledge is acquired and the accepted validation procedures of that knowledge; pedagogy refers to how something is taught.

In the natural and social sciences, for example, the epistemology is often based upon experimentation, discovery, and testing. Curriculum designers using a discovery or inquiry-learning approach operate on the belief that how science is practiced is also the best way to teach and/or learn it. Critics of such inquiry-based instruction such as Sewall (2000), caution that such approaches are over-emphasized at the expense of "carefully prepared lesson(s) ... focused and guided...; interspersed with small group work when appropriate; and with a clear sense of direction at the beginning and summary at the end, leaving all participants with a feeling of completion and satisfaction" (p. 6).

This ambiguity about the difference between learning and doing science, coupled with the current societal prioritization of knowledge construction has led educators to advocate discovery as the way to teach science. But discovery presupposes a prior conceptual framework (Vosniadou, 2002). Via discovery, one can investigate relationships between concepts, but whether this leads to new concepts depends upon the structure and content of existing knowledge. Klahr and Nigam (2004) conclude, based on their empirical findings, that there is a "need to reexamine the long-standing claim that the limitations of direct instruction, as well as the advantages of discovery methods, will invariably manifest themselves in tasks requiring broad transfer to authentic contexts" (p. 666).

The origin of these teaching approaches lies in a failure to distinguish between learning and doing; in overlooking that students are not experts practicing something, but rather novices learning about something. It is the teacher's job to teach science, teach about science, and teach how to do science. It is not the teacher's job to practice science as part of the teaching exercise; leave that to the scientists.

Question: Duschl and Duncan. *A big part of scientific literacy is learning to distinguish scientific claims from pseudoscience and hoax claims. What are the pedagogical strategies that develop learners' abilities to assess the status of knowledge claims presented by the popular media?*

Reply: Kirschner. Van Merriënboer and Kirschner (2007) present a series of pedagogic/instructional-design approaches that are based on realistic (i.e., authentic) whole tasks and that contain the support and guidance needed to achieve the type of learning and abilities that you ask about.

To begin, a well-designed case study could/would present learners with descriptions of actual or hypothetical problem situations situated in the real world (i.e., a claim presented in the popular media) and require them to actively participate in the determination of the validity of that claim. For learning to distinguish scientific claims from pseudoscience and hoax claims, a case study would confront learners with a claim that the popular media has presented (the "given state"), a list of possible research results and/or scientific "facts" that is not too long and that is directly relevant for determining the validity/truth of the claim (criteria for the "goal state"), and worked-out examples of the thinking and possible further search queries for new information necessary to determine the validity/truth of the claim (the "solution"). In order to arouse the learners' interest, it may be desirable to use a case study that describes a spectacular event, such as an accidental discovery, a success story, or a disputed result, et cetera. In a well-designed case study, learners would be required to answer questions that provoke deep processing of the problem state and of the associated operators (i.e., solution steps) so that they can compare that case with other cases in order to induce generalized solutions. By studying the—intermediate—solutions, learners get a clear idea of how a particular domain is organized and what determines "proof" or "refutation."

In our book (van Merriënboer and Kirschner, 2007) we discuss many other learning tasks that could be used such as imitation tasks, non-specific goal problems, completion tasks, reverse troubleshooting, et cetera. The common element of all of the learning tasks is that they direct the learners' attention to problem states, acceptable solutions, and useful solution steps. This helps them mindfully abstract information from good solutions or use inductive processes to construct cognitive schemas that reflect generalized solutions for particular types of tasks. The bottom line is that having students solve many problems on their own is often not the best thing for teaching them problem solving! For novice learners, studying useful solutions together with the relationships between the characteristics of a given situation and the solution steps applied is much more important for developing problem-solving and reasoning skills than solving equivalent problems.

Question: Duschl and Duncan. *Without the inclusion of some epistemological elements used by domain experts or practitioners, how do learners progress from novice to expert? When and how do you recommend epistemological elements enter the learning environment?*

Reply: Kirschner. As should be clear by the answer to the previous question, epistemological elements can enter the learning environment very early in the learning process. The clue here is that the epistemology of the expert is not the guiding principle for the pedagogy, but rather that the learning, (i.e., the acquisition of that epistemology), is the goal and leading principle.

Question: Herman and Gomez. *What is the relationship between epistemology and pedagogy? Do you mean that no domain-based epistemology can inform classroom pedagogy? Or do you mean something more radical, that classroom-based instruction is (should be) divorced from any coherent epistemology?*

Reply: Kirschner. The "only" relationship between epistemology and pedagogy is based not upon the translation or mapping of an epistemology (on) to a pedagogy, but rather the selection of a fitting pedagogy to "teach" (i.e., help the learner acquire) the epistemology. In other words, the choice of a pedagogy can and possibly must be "informed" by the epistemology that the learner should acquire, but is not the same as making use of that epistemology as a pedagogy.

In addition to the pedagogies discussed in answer to Duschl and Duncan's question is the experimental seminar, a pedagogy specifically designed for undergraduate students in natural sciences to support the acquisition of the epistemology of the natural scientist, first proposed by Conway, Mendoza, and Read (1963). Here, students collectively perform an experiment or watch an expert perform an experiment. This way they gain a clear concept of how a well-performed experiment progresses. Collective experimentation or demonstration is followed by group discussion, where necessary stimulated by an "expert," such as teacher, lecturer, or professor, and in which students can help each other. An experiment which is routine and uninteresting to one or two students can trigger a valuable discussion in a group. This provides the student with a model for problem identification, experimental design, assembling, testing, and calibrating equipment, data collection, analysis, interpretation, and reporting results. The possibility to model, discuss, reason, and compare methods and results with others is characteristic for this type of practical. An important aspect of the experimental seminar is that it makes use of modeling to facilitate the development of a template necessary for the learner (see answer to Duschl and Duncan).

A second integral aspect of the experimental seminar is discussion. This is what Kollard (1985) calls the didactic translation of observations. To counteract any misconceptions arising from a demonstration, a discussion must round off the demonstration. In this way both relevant and irrelevant observations can be noted and discussed. Discussion also helps promote conceptualization and deeper understanding of what has occurred. Support and guidance in the form of scaffolding the discussion can be seen as the addition of an additional informed opinion. Such discussion encourages students to reflect upon past personal experience and to use it as a means to discover and evaluate solutions to present problems.

References

Adelson, B. (1981). Problem solving and the development of abstract categories in programming languages. *Memory & Cognition, 9*, 422–433.

Allen, J. B., Barker, L. N., & Ramsden, J. H. (1986). Guided inquiry laboratory. *Journal of Chemical Education, 63*, 533–534.

Ausubel, D. P. (1964). Some psychological and educational limitations of learning by discovery. *The Arithmetic Teacher, 11*, 290–302.

Barrows, H. S., & Tamblyn, R. M. (1980). *Problem-based learning: An approach to medical education.* New York: Springer Publishing Company.

Boucheix, J.-M., Lowe, R., & Soirat, A. (2006, August/September). *One line processing of a complex technical animation: Eye tracking investigation during verbal description.* Paper presented at the EARLI SIG 2 Bi-annual meeting Text and Graphics Comprehension (pp. 14–17). Nottingham: University of Nottingham. Retrieved December 8, 2008, from www.lsri.nottingham.ac.uk/SIG2/proceedings.pdf.

Boud, D., & Feletti, G. (Eds.). (1991). *The challenge of problem-based learning.* London: Kogan Page.

Bradley, D. (2005). *Practicals in science education.* Unpublished doctoral thesis, Curtin University, Australia.

Bransford, J. D., Brown, A. L., & Cocking, R. R. (Eds.). (1999). *How people learn: Brain, mind, experience and school.* Washington, DC: National Academies Press.

Bybee, R. W. (2003). *Science curriculum reform in the United States.* Washington, DC: National Academy of Sciences. Retrieved February 20, 2008, from www.nas.edu/rise/backg3a.htm.

Cawthron, E. R., & Rowell, J. A. (1978). Epistemology and science education. *Studies in Science Education, 5*, 51–59.

Chen, Z., & Klahr, D. (1999). All other things being equal: Children's acquisition of the control of variables strategy. *Child Development, 70*, 1098–1120.

Chi, M. T. H., Feltovich, P. J., & Glaser, R. (1981). Categorization and representation of physics problems by experts and novices. *Cognitive Science, 5,* 121–152.

Conway, R. G., Mendoza, E., & Read, F. H. (1963). The seminar method of teaching experimental physics. *Bulletin of the Institute of Physical Society, 14,* 330–332.

Cuthbert, L., du Boulay, B., Teather, D., Teather, B., Sharples, M., & du Boulay, G. (1999). *Expert/novice differences in diagnostic medical cognition: A review of the literature* (Cognitive Sciences Research Paper 508). Brighton, UK: University of Sussex.

Dewey, J. (1997). *How do we think.* New York: Dover Publications.

De Groot, A. D. (1946). *Het denken van den schaker* [Thinking Processes in Chess Players]. Amsterdam: Noord Hollandsche.

De Groot, A. D. (1978). *Thought and choice in chess* (Revised translation of De Groot, 1946; 2nd ed.). The Hague: Mouton Publishers.

Donovan, M. S., Bransford, J. D., & Pellegrino, J. W. (1999). *How people learn: Bridging research and practice.* Washington, DC: National Research Council.

Downes, S. (2007). *Emerging technologies for learning.* Coventry: Becta. Retrieved September 22, 2007, from http://partners.becta.org.uk/page_documents/research/emerging_technologies07_chapter2.pdf.

Gabric, K., Hovance, C., Comstock, S., & Harnisch, D. (2005). Scientists in their own classroom: The use of type II technology in the science classroom. *Computers in the School, 22*(3/4), 77–91.

Glaser, R., & Chi, M. (1988). Overview. In M. Chi, R. Glaser, & M. J. Farr (Eds.), *The nature of expertise* (pp. xv–xxviii). Hillsdale, NJ: Erlbaum.

Gobet, F., & Simon, H. A. (1996). The roles of recognition processes and look-ahead search in time-constrained expert problem solving: Evidence from grandmaster level chess. *Psychological Science, 7,* 52–55.

Hannust, T., & Kikas, E. (2007). Children's knowledge of astronomy and its change in the course of learning. *Early Childhood Research Quarterly, 22,* 89–104.

Hardiman, P. T., Dufresne, R., & Mestre, J. P. (1989). The relation between problem categorization and problem solving among experts and novices. *Memory and Cognition, 17,* 627–638.

Harmer, A. J., & Cates, W. M. (2007). Designing for learner engagement in middle school science: Technology, inquiry, and the hierarchies of engagement. *Computers in the Schools, 24*(1/2), 105–124.

Hmelo-Silver, C. E. (2004). Problem-based learning: What and how do students learn? *Educational Psychology Review, 16,* 235–266.

Hmelo-Silver, C. E., & Barrows, H. S. (2006). Goals and strategies of a problem-based learning facilitator. *Interdisciplinary Journal of Problem-based Learning, 1,* 21–39.

Hodson, D. (1985). Philosophy of science, science and science education. *Studies in Science Education, 12,* 25–57.

Hodson, D. (1988). Experiments in science and science teaching. *Educational Philosophy and Theory, 20,* 53–66.

Hogan, T. M., Rabinowitz, M., & Craven, J. (2003). Problem representation in teaching: Inferences from research on expert and novice teachers. *Educational Psychologist, 38,* 235–247.

Hughes, K. L., & Moore, D. T. (1999). *Pedagogical strategies for work-based learning* (IEE Working Paper No. 12). New York: Institute on Education and the Economy, Columbia University. Retrieved from www.tc.columbia.edu/iee/PAPERS/workpap12.pdf.

Itin, C. M. (1999). Reasserting the philosophy of experiential education as a vehicle for change in the 21st century. *The Journal of Experiential Education, 22*(2), 91–98.

Jacobson, M. J. (2000). Problem solving about complex systems: Differences between experts and novices. In B. Fishman & S. O'Connor-Divelbiss (Eds.), *Fourth International Conference of the Learning Sciences* (pp. 14–21). Mahwah, NJ: Erlbaum.

Kirschner, P. (1992). Epistemology, practical work and academic skills in science education. *Science and Education, 1*, 273–299.

Kirschner, P., Sweller, J., & Clark, R. (2006). Why minimal guidance during instruction does not work: An analysis of the failure of constructivist, discovery, problem-based, experiential, and inquiry-based teaching. *Educational Psychologist, 41*(2), 75–86.

Klahr, D., & Nigam, M. (2004). The equivalence of learning paths in early science instruction: Effects of direct instruction and discovery learning. *Psychological Science, 15*, 661–667.

Kolb, D. A., & Fry, R. (1975). Toward an applied theory of experiential learning. In C. Cooper (Ed.), *Theories of group process* (pp. 33–57). London: John Wiley.

Kollard, U. H. (1985). *Didactischvertalen: Vakstructuur en leerstofordening in de natuurwetenschappelijkevakken* [Didactic translation: Structure and ordering in the natural sciences]. Unpublished doctoral thesis, VrijeUniversiteit, Amsterdam.

Kyle, W. C., Jr. (1980). The distinction between inquiry and scientific inquiry and why high school students should be cognizant of the distinction. *Journal of Research on Science Teaching, 17*, 123–130.

Larkin, J. H. (1979). Processing information for effective problems solving. *Engineering Education*, 285–288.

Lowe, R. K. (1999). Extracting information from an animation during complex visual learning. *European Journal of Psychology of Education, 14*, 225–244.

Lowe, R. K. (2004). Interrogation of a dynamic visualisation during learning. *Learning and Instruction, 14*, 257–274.

Mayer, R. (2004). Should there be a three-strikes rule against pure discovery learning? The case for guided methods of instruction. *American Psychologist, 59*, 14–19.

Mazens, K., & Lautrey, J. (2003). Conceptual change in physics: Children's naïve representations of sound. *Cognitive Development, 18*, 159–176.

Means, B. (2006). Prospects for transforming schools with technology-supported assessment. In R. K. Sawyer (Ed.), *Cambridge handbook of the learning sciences* (pp. 505–520). New York: Cambridge University Press.

Novak, J. (1988). Learning science and the science of learning. *Studies in Science Education, 15*, 77–101.

Novick, L. R. (1988). Analogical transfer, problem similarity and expertise. *Journal of Experimental Psychology: Learning, Memory and Cognition, 14*, 510–520.

Partridge, D., & Paap, K. (1988). An introduction to learning. *Artificial Intelligence Review, 2*, 79–102.

Piaget, J. (1955). *The construction of reality in the child* (M. Cook, Trans.). London: Routledge and Kegan Paul Ltd. Retrieved September 6, 2007 from: www.marxists.org/reference/subject/philosophy/works/fr/piaget2.htm.

Richardson, V. (2003). Constructivist pedagogy. *Teachers College Record, 105*, 1623–1640.

Schneider, W., & Shiffrin, R. M. (1977). Controlled and automatic human information processing: Detection, search, and attention. *Psychological Review, 84*, 1–66.

Sewall, G. (2000). Lost in action. *American Educator, 24*(2), 4–9.

Shaffer, D. W. (2007). *How computer games help children learn.* New York: Palgrave.

Shoenfeld, A. H., & Herrmann, D. J. (1982). Problem perception and knowledge structure in expert and novice mathematical problem solvers. *Journal of Experimental Psychology: Learning, Memory & Cognition, 8*, 484–494.

Southerland, S. A., & Gess-Newsome, J. (1999). Preservice teachers' views of inclusive science teaching as shaped by images of teaching learning, and knowledge. *Science Education, 83*(2), 131–150.

Vamvakoussi, X., & Vosniadou, S. (2004). Understanding the structure of the set of rational numbers: A conceptual change approach. *Learning and Instruction, 14*, 453–467.

Van Gog, T., Paas, F., & van Merriënboer, J. J. G. (2005). Uncovering expertise-related differences in troubleshooting performance: Combining eye movement and concurrent verbal protocol data. *Applied Cognitive Psychology, 19*, 205–221.

Van Merriënboer, J. J. G., & Kirschner, P. A. (2007). *Ten steps to complex learning.* Mahwah, NJ: Lawrence Erlbaum.

Vosniadou, S. (2002). Exploring the relationships between conceptual change and intentional learning. In G. Sinatra & P. Pintrich (Eds.), *Prospects and problems for modes of intentional conceptual change* (pp. 377–406). Mahwah, NJ: Lawrence Erlbaum.

Vygotsky, L. S., & Luria, A. R. (1992). *Ape, primitive man, and child: Essays in the history of behaviour* (Evelyn Rossiter, Trans.). Sydney: Harvester Wheatsheaf. (Original work published in 1930 in Russian.) Available at www.marxists.org/archive/luria/works/1930/child/ch02.htm.

Whitehead, A. N. (1929). *The aims of education and other essays.* New York: The Free Press.

9 How Much and What Type of Guidance is Optimal for Learning from Instruction?[*]

Richard E. Clark University of Southern California

This chapter summarizes evidence relevant to the debate about the amount and type of instructional guidance that is most effective and efficient for learning, performance, and transfer. Arguments about the disputed benefits of "constructivist" versus "instructivist" or "objectivist" approaches (e.g., Duffy & Jonassen, 1992; Jonassen, 1991; Kirschner, Sweller, & Clark, 2006) or "problem-based learning" versus "transmission models" (e.g., Schwartz & Bransford, 1998; Sweller, 2006) focus primarily on different views about how much and what type of guidance needs to be offered when and to whom with what impact. All of the participants in the debate seem to agree about many of the forms of instructional support that must be offered to most students in most educational environments. The disagreement that fuels the debate stems from different views about the necessity and consequences of forcing specific procedural guidance in situations where learners may be able to discover solutions to unfamiliar problems and tasks. It will be argued that all evidence supporting the discovery elements of constructivist theory is based on studies that failed to vary the type and amount of guidance provided. It is also argued that the debate can be resolved by reference to research that systematically varies the type, amount, and beneficiaries of instructional guidance needed to solve problems or perform tasks.

Any attempt to explicate a construct such as "guidance" or "discovery" is hampered by the fact that advocates of different instructional theories and models tend to define and operationalize instructional support in very different ways. These different theories often spring from different models of learning and sometimes different belief systems, inquiry methods, and philosophies (Cronbach & Snow, 1977; Jonassen, 1991; Merrill, 2002; Romiszowski, 2006). To some extent, these differences reflect the increased specialization and fragmentation in educational research and theory over the past half-century (Winthrop, 1963; Ravitch & Viteretti, 2001) and a growing fragmentation among various sub-specializations in educational research. One result of this phenomenon is that researchers who favor a specific theory or point of view tend to isolate them-

[*] The project or effort described here has been sponsored by the US Army Research, Development, and Engineering Command (RDECOM). Statements and opinions expressed do not necessarily reflect the position or the policy of the United States Government, and no official endorsement should be inferred.

selves and limit their research, reading, and collaboration to the journals and professional associations or divisions of associations that emphasize their perspective. Attempts to encourage dialogues between the diverse groups who are concerned with instruction and learning will help bridge the gaps and resolve important disagreements.

This chapter begins with the assumption that those participating in this discussion want to improve instruction in the educational system we have inherited rather than to change our approach to guidance in order to impose ideological changes on our educational system. With this exception in mind, the discussion turns next to a description of the types of instructional support that many of the parties to the debate seem to accept as valid and those that have caused disagreement.

Guidance and Discovery in Learning from Instruction

In the past century the instructional support provided during learning has been referred to by terms such as instructional methods (Cronbach & Snow, 1977; Tobias, 1982; Clark, 1982), instructional strategies or teaching strategies (e.g., Merrill, 2002; Weston & Cranton, 1986), direct instruction (Klahr and Nigam, 2004), and scaffolding (e.g., Pea, 2004). Salomon (1994), in a very engaging discussion of the way that instructional methods influence learning, hypothesized that instructional support either activated or supplanted cognitive processes necessary for performance. Yet a large number of operationally different treatments have been offered as examples of each of these types of support. The variability in definition has made it nearly impossible to develop a coherent system for understanding instructional treatments. Three decades ago, Cronbach and Snow (1977) complained that "taxonomies of instructional treatments ... are almost totally lacking ... we [need] to identify the significant underlying dimensions along which complex treatments vary" (pp. 164–165). Three decades later, we continue to lack a systematic way to describe differences between the varieties of instructional support activities examined in research and used in practice. This lack of a system for describing instructional treatments does not imply that those concerned with instruction disagree about all activities that are required to support instruction. For example, many of the participants on both sides in the debate about constructivism would agree in general about the usefulness of some of the types of support that Pea (2004) characterized as aspects of instructional "scaffolding."

Contrasting Scaffolding and Guidance

Pea (2004) and others have adopted the term "scaffolding" to describe one approach to instructional support. Scaffolding is an engineering term that refers to an external frame placed to support a building during the early stages of construction and gradually withdrawn or "faded" as the building becomes stronger. In an educational context, scaffolding provides learning support that is faded as student learning becomes stronger. Pea describes scaffolding as "modeling more advanced solutions to the task – [and] reducing the degrees of freedom for the task ... by recruiting and focusing the attention of the learner by marking relevant task features" (p. 432). Further, he characterizes scaffolded situations as "those in which the learner gets assistance or support to perform a task beyond his or her own reach if pursued independently when *unassisted* ... [and gradually] fading [support] as the learner becomes more proficient" (pp. 430, 431; emphasis in the original text).

These descriptions are general and so open the door to discussions about the specific types of measures employed to gauge learning progress or exactly when, how, and how much support should be faded without cognitively overloading "unassisted" learners—and exactly how we should model solutions or focus attention most effectively and efficiently. Yet there is wide agreement about the benefits of fading, modeling, and directing attention. The devil is in the details in arguments about these general categories of support. A critical detail for the debate about guidance concerns whether unassisted learners should be required to construct or discover their own solutions to problems or ways to accomplish a task or whether they should be required to use procedures that are demonstrated for them. Pea (2004) suggests that a scaffolding theory must demonstrate that scaffolding is only provided when we have "independent evidence that the learner cannot do the task or goal unaided" (p. 443). Guidance advocates suggest that learners must be provided with a complete demonstration of how to perform all aspects of a task that they have not learned and automated previously. So even if a learner could solve a problem with adequate mental effort, guidance advocates provide evidence that it is more effective and efficient to provide a complete description of "when and how" (Kirschner, Sweller, & Clark, 2006; Sweller, Kirschner, & Clark, 2007). This is the key issue that separates many of the participants in this debate.

Contrasting Problem-Based Learning and Guidance Theories

Similarly, many of those who disagree with some aspects of the constructivist approach can agree with advocates of problem-based or inquiry learning (PBL) who recommend providing learners with a description of an "authentic" problem or task during instruction (e.g., Barrows, 1986; Savery and Duffy, 2001). Problems are presented in advance of instruction in order to motivate learners, focus their attention and help connect with their prior relevant experience, and again when learners are learning to solve a class of problems. For example, when teaching a history lesson, problem-based learning advocates would have us describe history problems that represent "the use of history in ways that ... a good citizen would [use their knowledge of history]" (Savery & Duffy, 2001, p. 4). The agreement about problem or task authenticity extends also to the measures that are used to validate learning. In most PBL courses, outcome measures test students' ability to apply what they have learned to solving problems in realistic settings rather than memorizing arbitrary facts or procedural steps (e.g., Merrill, 1983, 2002).

Yet some of us part company with problem-based learning advocates when they require learners to invest effort in order to construct a solution to an authentic problem when an effective solution is available. Savery and Duffy (2001) want students to "engage in the construction of history" in order to learn historical analysis and when learning science, "we do not want the learner to [learn to] ... execute scientific procedure as dictated – but rather to engage in scientific problem solving [designed for the developmental level of the learner]" (p. 4). They suggest, "The teacher's role should be to challenge the learner's thinking – not to dictate or attempt to proceduralize that thinking" (p. 5). The key issue is whether learners will be required (forced, dictated) to discover or invent any part of their own learning support or the curriculum they are learning. This issue is subtle but vital in understanding what Mayer (2004) and Kirschner, Sweller, and Clark (2006) believe to be the reason why many instructional treatments in the past have failed to show adequate benefits. It is also the issue that dominated discussions about the design of experiments offered as evidence in rejoinders by Hmelo-Silver, Duncan, and Chinn (2007) and Schmidt, Loyens, van Gog, and Paas (2007) and a reply to the rejoinders by Sweller, Kirschner, and Clark (2007).

What is Guidance and Why Is It Preferable to Discovery During Learning?

Instructional "guidance" is defined as providing students with accurate and complete procedural information (and related declarative knowledge) that they have not yet learned in a demonstration about how to perform the necessary sequence of actions and make the necessary decisions to accomplish a learning task and/or solve a problem. Guidance also forces students to practice by applying the demonstrated procedure to solve problems or accomplish tasks that represent the performance expected in an application environment and receive supportive and corrective feedback during their practice.

This approach to guidance is based on three defining criteria:

1. Guidance must provide an accurate and complete demonstration of how (decisions and actions) and when (conditions) to perform a task or solve a class of problems;
2. When adaptive transfer is required, guidance must also provide the varied practice and declarative knowledge that permits learners to adapt a procedure to handle a novel situation;
3. Guidance requires forced individual application practice of procedures accompanied by immediate corrective feedback on part- and whole-task versions of problems and tasks that represent those to be encountered in the transfer environment.

The evidence and theoretical rationale for each of these three criteria are discussed next.

1 Guidance Must Provide an Accurate and Complete Demonstration of How (Decisions and Actions) and When (Conditions) to Perform a Task or Solve a Class of Problems

Mayer (2004) and Kirschner, Sweller, and Clark (2006); Sweller, Kirschner, and Clark (2007) have reviewed a combination of laboratory and field-based studies of the effects of variations in guidance on learning. Mayer (2004) offered evidence that this finding has been clearly evident in research that stretches back at least a half-century. Merrill (2002, 2006) provides a description of the way a number of evidence-based contemporary instructional design systems implement guidance. These research reviews conclude that the most effective instructional guidance provided complete information in the form of a demonstration that depicted how to perform a task or solve a class of problems. Effective treatments also provided an opportunity for application practice accompanied by corrective feedback.

In order to describe why procedural instruction is more effective than requiring students to discover or construct a procedure, and why it has been difficult to provide both accurate and complete demonstrations of how to accomplish complex tasks, the discussion turns next to a brief review of research on the impact of knowledge types in learning and the way that automated expertise affects the development and delivery of instruction.

Declarative and Procedural Knowledge

Schneider and Shiffrin (1977) and others (Anderson, 1983, 1996; Newell, 1990; Schneider & Chein, 2003) have provided a theoretical rationale for strong guidance with evidence that two types of knowledge are involved in the performance of a complex task: controlled knowledge (often called declarative) and automated (also called procedural, implicit, or production) knowledge.

Complex learning (Clark & Elen, 2006) requires that these two types of knowledge interact in ways that we seldom acknowledge in either instructional research or practice. Understanding the way that knowledge types interact during learning and performance is critical to advancing our understanding of instruction. Anderson's (1983, 1996; Anderson & Lebiere, 1998) ACT-R (Adaptive Control of Thought-Revised) theory is an example of a systematic body of research on the learning and cognitive operation of these two types of knowledge and is based on cognitive information-processing theories of cognition. He and his colleagues present evidence that all learning and performance is supported by a combination of declarative knowledge—which is an abstract representation of facts, concepts, processes, and principles in episodic or semantic form—and procedural knowledge in the form of mental "productions" which consist of goal statements and the overt actions and cognitive operations that will achieve the goals under specified conditions. Each type of knowledge is stored in separate long-term memory systems.

Research based on ACT-R provides evidence that performance on complex tasks such as advanced mathematics problem solving requires productions in the form of procedures that accomplish goals and that declarative knowledge is sometimes useful to fill in the missing steps of already-learned productions. ACT-R also suggests that with use over time, productions become automated and unconscious but declarative knowledge is processed in working memory where activity is consciously recognized. ACT-R specifies that whenever we recognize the conditions that reflect a performance goal, performance is initiated that draws on available productions. When the goal is to learn or solve a problem, we apply the goal-directed productions we have available and if available productions are incomplete or inadequate we use declarative knowledge to fill in the missing steps. If instruction provides the necessary steps to fill the gap, learning occurs faster and more effectively (e.g., with fewer performance errors) than if we must fill in the gaps using declarative knowledge (Velmahos et al., 2004; Clark & Elen, 2006). Yet our awareness of performance is limited to the declarative knowledge we have processed in working memory because productions are automated and unconscious so that they circumvent the limits on working memory (see, for example, an engaging discussion of this process in a chapter on consciousness by Kihlstrom, 1987, and in Sweller's 2006 description of Cognitive Load Theory).

Self-awareness is, in part, the capacity to observe our thinking about and remembering declarative knowledge. Yet we are only indirectly aware of our constant use of automated, unconscious procedural knowledge, which we can observe only by noticing the consequences of its operation. For example, most adults, when asked for the product of 6 × 108 will respond "648" without an awareness of how they solved the problem. Only the unautomated portions of the solving procedure are conscious and therefore open to conscious inspection. Some readers may have multiplied 100 by 6 and added the automated product of 6 times 8 to get the solution; others may have immediately realized the answer "648." Those who performed the operation in two conscious steps are more likely to be aware of their cognitive processing than those who have automated the entire solution process for this type of problem.

Important to this discussion is recent evidence that the declarative components of learning or problem solving may only be the "tip of the iceberg." It is likely that the teaching and learning of most tasks and the solving of complex problems require an understanding of a large number of task-specific automated processes that support the handling of the conscious components of tasks. These unconscious components may be unknown and/or ignored by instructional researchers, teachers, or trainers. Because of the severe limits on our working memory, it is likely that most mental processes supporting problem solving and learning are automated and unconscious (Cowen, 2001; Clark & Elen, 2006; Sweller, 2006; Feldon, 2007). One way to interpret the evidence from the past half-century of research on discovery learning (Mayer, 2004) is that the type of learning that most effectively supports performance on complex tasks is almost completely procedural and that experts are largely unaware of how they perform tasks and solve problems because expertise is largely automated and unconscious (Clark & Elen, 2006; Clark, Feldon, van Merriënboer, Yates, & Early, 2007).

Experts Are Largely Unaware of How They Perform—The 70% Principle

One component of instruction is a curriculum, which is, in part, a description of the knowledge required to accomplish a set of tasks. Experts who most often have both practical experience and a formal education in the field to be taught prepare curricula. When experts develop instructional materials they attempt to share what they know about the tasks students must learn. Yet there is evidence that while most experts are successful at solving even very complex problems within their area of expertise, they are largely unaware of the operation of their own expertise (Besnard, 2000). For example, Feldon (2004) studied the self-awareness of personal research design strategies used by a number of well-published psychologists who teach research design. He found that these experts who serve as mentors for young researchers were approximately 70% unaware of the primary analytical strategies they were using when designing experiments.

Additional evidence for the hypothesis that expertise is largely automated and unconscious comes from studies of task analysis and other self-report protocols conducted with experts. For example, Chao and Salvendy (1994) studied the errors made by a number of top programming experts during systematic task-analysis interviews. The steps suggested by the experts to solve and debug specific programs were collected and used to develop a master protocol. Their analysis suggested that the debugging strategies suggested by each expert were only approximately 31% accurate. These experts could debug programs but were not aware of about 70% of the steps they used. Besnard (2000), Clark et al. (2007), and Hoffman, Crandall, and Shadbolt (1998) have described other studies that report similar data.

Teachers and Trainers May Often Provide Wrong or Incomplete Information

The evidence for our lack of awareness of our own automated procedural knowledge sheds doubt on many of our most closely held assumptions about instruction and learning. Teachers are selected for their expertise at all educational levels from early schooling to the most advanced doctoral programs. Cognitive apprenticeships (Brown, Collins, & Duguid, 1989) and communities of practice (Brown & Duguid, 1991) are both popular strategies for teaching complex knowledge. Teachers, mentors, and collaborative colleagues are expected to "teach what they know." If experts who teach are an average of 70% unaware of their procedural knowledge, what might be the consequence for their students or collaborators? For the past half-century, studies examining the interaction between student aptitudes and different forms of instructional treatments (most often called aptitude x treatment or ATI studies) have consistently reported that students with lower ability levels and/or less prior knowledge and/or lower motivation are more vulnerable to learning difficulties when instruction is incomplete, unstructured, or gives inaccurate information (e.g., Cronbach & Snow, 1977; Kyllonen & Lajoie, 2003).

Guidance in Poorly Defined or Ill-Structured Domains of Knowledge

Some instructional researchers and developers argue that accurate and complete guidance is not possible for many tasks required in modern curricula that come from ill-structured domains of knowledge (Jonassen, 1997; Spiro, Feltovich, Jacobson, & Coulson, 1992). Poorly structured problems are those that "possess multiple solutions, solution paths, fewer parameters which are less manipulable, and contain uncertainty about which concepts, rules, and principles are necessary for the solution or how they are organized and which solution is best" (Jonassen, 1997, p. 65). Examples include medical diagnosis, historical analysis, leadership or organizational management and counseling psychology. It is also argued that the research tasks used to demonstrate the benefits of procedural instruction, such as Anderson's ACT-R theory, tends to be drawn from more structured domains such as mathematics, and therefore may not generalize to poorly structured domains.

Describing a domain as "ill structured" most often means that either domain experts do not agree or that there are no solutions to some problems. Nearly all problems contain "multiple solution paths," many of which achieve an acceptable resolution to a problem. In this case, the best option is to teach the most direct and simple solution path to novices. In general, when experts fail to consistently solve complex problems we can hardly expect students to discover solutions during instruction. In the case where students are expected to invent a solution, the preferable instructional approach is to provide expert-based procedures for inventing solutions to problems in the domain. In this case the focus of the instruction shifts from students discovering solutions to students learning a procedure for discovering solutions. The important issue for those designing problem-solving instruction is whether there are experts in a knowledge domain who consistently succeed at solving problems or performing tasks in that domain. Expert solutions to problems can be captured using cognitive task analysis and taught to novices.

Cognitive Task Analysis for Capturing Expertise

Research on the use of cognitive task analysis (CTA) to capture and identify the automated knowledge used by experts has grown in recent years (Clark & Estes, 1996; Schraagen, Chipman, & Shalin, 2000; Clark et al., 2007). As evidence of the instructional value of using CTA to identify automated and unconscious expert knowledge, Lee (2004) performed a meta-analytic study of the effectiveness of CTA-based training and performance-improvement studies in a variety of organizations and focused on different types of tasks. She reported an overall median percentage of post-training performance gain effect size of 1.72 (an average increase of 44% on outcome performance measures) for CTA-based instruction when compared to more traditional instructional design using behavioral task analysis. Most of the outcome measures reviewed emphasized application of learning rather than recall or recognition tasks.

Velmahos et al. (2004) studied the expertise of emergency medicine experts who teach in a medical school. In a controlled study, half of a randomly assigned group of 24 medical students were taught a routine emergency procedure in a traditional modeling and practice strategy by expert emergency physicians who teach. The established teaching strategy employed is called "see one–do one –teach one." The student first watches a procedure performed by an expert who explains it in a "think aloud" fashion, and then practices the procedure while getting feedback from the same expert. Finally the student teaches another student to perform the procedure while the expert observes. While this instructional method has served medicine for decades, recent concerns about medical mistakes have refocused interest on the way medical students are trained and have encouraged attempts to close the gaps identified in the way complex procedures are taught (Starfield, 2000). The "see-do-teach" students' post-training performance was compared with the other half of the medical students who were trained with information gathered in a "cognitive task analysis" or CTA (Clark & Estes, 1996; Schraagen et al., 2000; Clark et al., 2007) on the same emergency procedure. The CTA interview is designed to expose automated decisions made by experts and make them available for training. The CTA-trained students were required to use the procedures they saw demonstrated. The emergency medicine experts who were interviewed with CTA also served as the instructors for the see-do-teach condition. All students received both memory and performance tests. It was clear from the analysis that the information provided to the see-do-teach students contained significant omissions and errors.

After training, whenever the medical students performed the routines with patients in the following year, they were observed and evaluated with checklists by judges who were unfamiliar with the instructional method they had experienced. The experimental group who received training based on cognitive task analysis outperformed the expert-taught control group on all analytical (diagnostic) and many performance items by over 50% during the year following training. Velmahos (personal communication) also reported that the traditionally trained doctors caused three serious medical emergencies applying the medical protocol with patients (average for new physicians) and those with CTA training made no life-threatening mistakes.

Research Suggestions

Disputes about variations in guidance can best be determined by reference to evidence from "randomized, controlled tests of competing instructional procedures [where] altering one [relevant] variable at a time is an essential feature of a properly controlled experiment" (Sweller, Kirschner, & Clark, 2007, p. 115). In addition, the hypothesized operation of the strategies selected for examination should be drawn from an evidence-based view of human cognitive architecture. A balanced review of existing studies will indicate that most of the disputes about guidance may stem from different strategies for designing guidance experiments. Design issues appear to be the root of the disagreements with Kirschner, Sweller, and Clark's (2006) argument about the "failure" of constructivism, discovery, and problem-based learning. Rejoinders to this review (for example, Hmelo-Silver et al., 2007; Schmidt et al., 2007) pointed to evidence from studies where lower or mid-level guidance conditions typically found in problem-based learning experiments were compared with no guidance or very minimal levels of guidance. Research protocols that examine the amount and type of guidance required for application learning must systematically vary the completeness of steps in instructional demonstrations and whether students are required to learn and apply procedures for completing tasks and solving problems. All models or demonstrations of problem solving and "worked examples" of ways to perform tasks are not equally complete or accurate (Clark et al., 2007; Velmahos et al., 2004). There is considerable evidence that incomplete demonstrations, models, or worked examples place unnecessary and sometimes overwhelming amounts of irrelevant cognitive load on learners (Mayer, 2004; Sweller, 2006). Yet all researchers must validate claims that the cognitive load imposed by requiring students to construct missing steps or sections of procedures or complete routines for solving problems are beneficial, harmful, or inconsequential. DeLeeuw and Mayer (2008) have examined various approaches to measuring different types of cognitive load and have provided evidence that different types of cognitive load imposed during instruction are sensitive to different types of measures.

We must clearly describe the operations, decision rules, and psychological reasoning used to construct treatments where guidance is varied. Critics and consumers of research on guidance must go beyond labels such as scaffolding, problem-based, or direct instruction and instead look carefully at the operations used to design and implement treatments.

Yet demonstrations are not the only type of support required for guidance. The discussion turns next to elements of guidance that are included to support the transfer of learning to novel contexts after instruction.

2 When Adaptive Transfer is Required, Guidance Must Also Provide the Varied Practice and Declarative Knowledge that Permits Learners to Adapt a Procedure to Handle a Novel Situation

There is considerable disagreement about whether people can be taught to become adaptable (see for example, Anderson, Reder, & Simon, 1996; Singley & Anderson, 1989) and yet most educators view adaptability as a desirable goal of education. Procedural knowledge is considered by some to be bound to the context where it was learned and thus some researchers reject the notion of adaptability entirely (Anderson et al., 1997). This section of the discussion begins with a brief description of the evidence for adaptable expertise and then considers the disagreements about the types of instructional support that foster adaptable expertise.

Different instructional theories propose different ways to achieve adaptable expertise. Foremost among those differences is the question of whether forced compliance with a specific procedure for solving problems or accomplishing tasks supports or inhibits adaptable performance. This concern is one of the main reasons why Pea (2004) stipulated that scaffolding provided learning support only until the problem or task was "beyond his or her own reach if pursued independently when *unassisted*" (p. 430) and required that instructional designers and teachers have "independent evidence that the learner cannot do the task or goal unaided" (p. 443). It is also part of the reason why Savery and Duffy (2001) were concerned that teachers do not "dictate or attempt to proceduralize ... thinking" (p. 5) but instead that learners be required to "engage in ... construction ... we do not want the learner to ... execute scientific procedure as dictated" (p. 4). Those who recommend the teaching of procedures argue that adaptable expertise results when procedures are demonstrated in conjunction with varied practice.

Does Forced Procedural Knowledge Inhibit Adaptability?

A large body of empirical research on expertise and transfer supports the conclusion that procedures do not inhibit (but instead support) adaptability. Hatano and Inagaki (1986, 2000), Besnard and Bastien-Toniazzo (1999), Bereiter and Scardamalia (1993), Gott, Hall, Pokorny, Dibble, and Glaser (1993), Perkins and Grotzer (1997), De Corte (2003), Masui and De Corte (1999), and Klahr and Nigam (2004), among others, have offered evidence that more flexible experts acquire and apply both procedural and conceptual knowledge differently than less flexible experts. In a recent review of research on the development of advanced expertise, Feldon (2007) tackles the flexibility question and states:

> careful empirical studies of acquisition and transfer for automated skills demonstrate that limited transfer of automated procedures to novel cues and circumstances can occur ... Further, because complex skills are inherently compilations of many distinct subskills, any particular performance may represent one of three possible paths. These paths are (1) fully automated processes, (2) serial execution of automated and consciously mediated subskills, or (3) simultaneous execution of both automatic and conscious elements.
>
> (p. 97)

Feldon goes on to suggest that when experts learn and automate procedures, they are able to apply them without "thinking" while using their conscious, conceptual knowledge to adjust "sub-skills" (chunks of larger procedures) to solve novel problems by enlarging and varying the conditions under which they apply a procedure. Without automated procedures, the complexity involved in handling the novelty involved in enlarging the application conditions for a procedure has been found to cause "cognitive overload" and defeat performance (Clark, 2001; Sweller, 2006).

Declarative and Procedural Knowledge Interactions

Anderson's ACT-R theory is supported by many years of studies that demonstrate the role of conscious, declarative knowledge in the development of productions (procedures) that support performance (Anderson & Lebiere, 1998). ACT-R hypothesizes that when existing automated knowledge (in the form of condition-action sequences) is not adequate to achieve a goal, learners rely on declarative knowledge to construct new steps and extend the conditions under which prior knowledge is applied to achieve a goal. While the construction process is not well understood, it is reasonable to assume that declarative knowledge is often involved in the construction process. Anderson and Lebiere (1998) claim, "production rules specify how to retrieve and use ... declarative knowledge to solve problems" (p. 5). And "productions are created from declarative chunks in a process called production compilation" (p. 11). In Anderson's ACT-R "flow of information" figure (Figure 9.1), he notes that declarative knowledge can modify a production but all performance is based on productions.

During instruction it is simply not possible to provide practice exercises that represent the entire range of transfer situations where knowledge will need to be applied. Identifying the declarative knowledge needed for transfer to novel situations is challenging because we have no widely shared approach to categorizing declarative knowledge in a way that relates the categories to the development of procedural steps.

Clark and Elen (2006) have described one possible system drawn from Merrill's (1983) taxonomy of declarative knowledge that has since been used by many instructional designers and researchers. His system proposes three types of declarative knowledge, each of which supports a different kind of procedure. For example, learning "concepts" (any term with a definition and at least one example) supports the development of classification procedures that permit people to identify common, culturally appropriate examples of a concept. For example, a classification procedure for anger would include steps where people

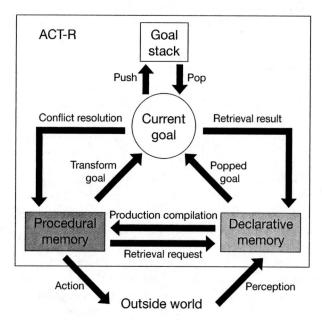

Figure 9.1 Flow of information among the components of ACT-R (source: taken from Anderson & Lebiere, 2004).

are asked to determine whether the defining attributes of anger are present in a typical situation. Relevant declarative knowledge in this situation might be to offer a psychological definition of "anger" which should permit someone to identify anger expressed in novel ways (such as a very angry person from a culture where anger is expressed with smiles or laughter). They would presumably construct steps that allow them to identify anger even when it is expressed in novel ways and settings. Providing declarative principles (cause-and-effect relationships) permit people to develop steps that enable them to change something in order to achieve a goal. If we describe anger as a principle (e.g., by describing factors that have been found to increase and decrease anger responses in most people) it is hypothesized that students should be able to develop steps that permit them to modify anger responses when interacting with others in a novel situation.

One additional type of support called "varied practice" has been found to increase adaptability and the discussion turns next to a brief description.

Varied Practice and Adaptability

In order to foster adaptable performance during instruction,

> it is important that all learning tasks differ from each other on all dimensions that also differ in the real world, such as the context or situation in which the task is performed, the way in which the task is presented, the saliency of the defining characteristics, and so forth. This allows the learners to abstract more general information from the details of each single task.
>
> (van Merriënboer & Kirschner, 2007, p. 19)

Requiring students to apply what they are learning to increasingly novel contexts or situations has been found to increase their adaptability, even to post-instructional transfer situations that do not mirror the actual contexts that were practiced (Cohen, Bloomberg, & Mulavara, 2005; Salomon & Perkins, 1989). Varied (or variable) practice is presumed to broaden the transfer conditions where students are able to apply the new procedure being learned (Salomon & Perkins, 1989).

Research Suggestions

It is possible to point to considerable evidence that forced procedures are more effective than constructed routines at supporting adaptable performance when procedures are accompanied by relevant declarative knowledge and varied practice. It is also possible to point to evidence that, for example, students in a collaborative learning setting who are required to construct a solution to a problem at the start of instruction may learn more and become more adaptable than those who receive only forced procedures (e.g., Schwartz, Bransford, & Sears, 2005; Sears, 2006). Yet it is possible that the Sears and Schwartz studies only examined "problem first" conditions which are considered to be a motivational treatment (e.g., Pintrich & Schunk, 2002) and did not test hypotheses concerning the impact of increasing amounts of varied practice or declarative knowledge. Additional research on these two variables would be valuable if they were systematically varied in future studies.

Varied practice must also be accompanied by corrective and supportive feedback so that students do not acquire misconceptions that must be unlearned later.

3 Guidance Requires Forced Individual Application Practice of Procedures Accompanied by Immediate Corrective Feedback on Part- and Whole-Task Versions of Problems and Tasks that Represent Those to be Encountered in the Transfer Environment

Guidance advocates suggest that effective instruction must provide the opportunity for students to apply the procedures they have seen demonstrated in forced and guided practice exercises where they receive immediate corrective feedback on their performance. Clark and Blake (1997) and Feldon (2007) argue that adaptability can be taught in a way that facilitates the solution of novel and challenging problems. De Corte (2003); Druckman and Swets (1988); Masui and De Corte (1999); Merrill (2002); Perkins and Grotzer (1997); Rosenshine and Meister (1997); Slavin (2006); Rosenshine and Meister (1997) and Rosenshine and Stevens (1986) have described the research base supporting guided practice with feedback and have provided guidelines for constructing demonstration and practice exercises in classroom settings.

The problems and tasks provided during practice exercises must be representative of the population of problems and tasks they will be expected to tackle after instruction. Since most transfer environments require task performance rather than the recall of facts, practice must follow a demonstration or worked example of a forced procedure and require the application of the procedure in order to complete a task and/or solve a problem. Corrective feedback must be frequent enough so that students do not learn errors. In addition, a meta-analysis of feedback studies conducted in many nations by Kluger and DiNisi (1998) indicated that the most feedback must be focused on the effectiveness of the strategy being used by a student during practice and not comment on whether a student is "wrong."

Constructivist Views on Practice and Feedback

Constructivist approaches to learning environments support practice and feedback but in a more limited form, often depending on the type of learning task. In their description of constructivism, Savery and Duffy (2001) suggest that the use of practice and feedback depend on the goal of a learning experience:

> Thus if domain-specific problem solving is the skill to be learned then a simulation which confronts the learner with problem situations within that domain might be appropriate. If proficient typing is required for some larger

context, certainly a drill and practice program is one option that might be present.

(p. 6)

Shabo (1997) describes a series of constructivist hypermedia projects where teachers found it necessary to increase the feedback provided to students because "The problem was that learners received little feedback to guide them on how to use the non-linear structure, and not all could acquire important skills and knowledge of the subject matter" (p. 231). Goodman, Wood, and Hendrickx (2004) present evidence from a large study where the prior knowledge of students was assessed and many different types of outcome measures were employed. They conclude that "increasing the specificity of feedback positively affected practice performance" (p. 248), but noted that feedback had to be accompanied by varied practice in order to promote transfer of learning.

The difference between constructivist and guidance advocates appears to be about whether practice and feedback is task-specific and at what point practice and feedback should be faded or eliminated as expertise develops. The suggestion that only certain types of learning tasks require practice and feedback requires more systematic research. Both constructivist and guidance advocates agree that as students gain more prior knowledge they sometimes require a gradual fading of practice and feedback, but the research and measurement technology available to support fading makes clear prescriptions difficult.

Fading Guidance and the Measurement of Prior Knowledge and Expertise

Many instructional theories recommend the fading of guidance and scaffolding as expertise increases. These same theories recommend against providing procedural guidance including practice and feedback to learners who have already achieved advanced expertise on the class or domain of tasks and problems that characterize new skills to be learned. Since the 1920s we have had evidence that guidance interacts with prior knowledge (Shulman & Keisler, 1966). In a comprehensive review of studies where aptitudes interact with instructional methods, Cronbach and Snow (1977) and Gustafsson and Undheim (1996) described many studies where the amount of "structure" in instruction interacted with prior knowledge and general ability. In fact, after reviewing hundreds of studies spanning a half-century, they concluded that the most robust interactions occurred between prior knowledge and general ability on the one hand, and prior knowledge and instructional structure on the other. According to Gustafsson and Undheim (1996),

> Treatments with a high degree of structure exercise a high level of external control of the learning activities through control of the sequence of pacing, feedback and reinforcement ... tasks are broken down into small units and presentations are concrete and explicit. Instructional methods characterized as expository, direct instruction, teacher controlled or drill-and-practice are instances of high structure.

(p. 227)

This definition of the term "structure" is similar to the definition of guidance used in this discussion. Some of these "aptitude-treatment interactions" were disordinal which suggests that in some instances, as the amount of guidance increased, students with higher levels of prior knowledge experienced a gradual decrease in learning. Both Cronbach and Snow (1977) and Gustafsson and Undheim (1996) suggest that more structured treatments tend to interfere with automated routines that had been developed by learners with higher levels of general ability and/or more task experience. This finding clearly indicates that under some conditions, instructional guidance might also have negative effects.

Possible Negative Effects of Forced Practice

Kayluga, Ayres, Chandler, and Sweller (2003) describe a number of studies where instructional media and methods cause cognitive overload for novices but are either neutral or beneficial for more experienced students. They also describe studies where strong guidance in the form of forced practice and feedback on specific procedures or worked examples during learning led to less learning for students with higher levels of prior knowledge. Their findings about the interaction between prior knowledge and forced practice mirror those described earlier by Cronbach and Snow (1977) and by Gustafsson and Undheim (1996). One way to summarize these studies is to suggest that more experienced students are sometimes helped, sometimes neither helped nor hurt, and sometimes their learning is harmed by forced practice. One of the difficulties encountered by researchers in this area is that our technology for measuring prior knowledge is inadequate and tends to focus more on declarative than on procedural knowledge. Since we have defined prior knowledge as declarative and do not yet have an adequate technology for measuring the extent of automation of task-relevant procedural knowledge, the evidence about interactions between prior knowledge and guidance is suspect. Yet we have evidence (e.g., Kayluga et al., 2003) that some students with higher levels of prior knowledge apparently learned less from complete guidance in the form of worked examples. In the "direct instruction" studies by Klahr and Nigam (2004), about 10–15% of subjects who received lower levels of guidance outperformed students who received very complete guidance. It is possible that these findings will make more sense when better measures of automated, task-relevant knowledge are available. An interesting exception is a promising strategy for measuring application knowledge suggested by Kayluga and Sweller (2004).

Other uncontrolled factors might also be influencing the outcome of these studies. In a meta-analysis of instructional ATI research, Whitener (1989) noted that

> Results are consistent with the interpretation that there are greater differences in learning achievement between Ss with high prior achievement and Ss with low prior achievement when structuring and organizing support are provided and smaller differences between these Ss when instruction is self-paced.

> (Whitener, 1989, p. 65)

Her results suggest that when instruction provides forced procedures and specific feedback, learner control over pacing reduces (but does not eliminate) the benefits of prior knowledge. Other reviews of this issue (e.g., Clark, 1982, 1989) have found similar results. Self-pacing apparently allows lower-prior-knowledge students to avoid cognitive overload caused by the speed of processing demanded when pacing is externally controlled.

Conclusion

Advocates for various forms of constructivism and guidance appear to agree about the utility of many forms of instructional support. For example, both groups recommend the "modeling of more advanced solutions of the task" and "focusing the attention of the learner by marking relevant task features" (Pea, 2004, p. 432), as well as providing students with authentic problems that represent those found in the setting where we expect students to use the knowledge they have learned (e.g., Savery & Duffy, 2001) and using outcome measures that require students to apply what they have learned (not simply memorize facts). We seem also to agree about the benefits of varied practice and the teaching of declarative knowledge when performance requires that students adapt the skills being learned to handle novel contexts or problems (e.g., Jonassen, 1997; van Merriënboer & Kirschner, 2007) and providing supportive and corrective feedback during part- and whole-task practice exercises on some (not all) learning tasks (e.g., Savery & Duffy, 2001). Finally, there appears to be widespread agreement that all instructional support should be gradually faded when students' expertise reaches the level where additional support damages learning (Kayluga et al., 2003; Kayluga & Sweller, 2004).

Disagreement

The main source of disagreement between constructivist and guidance advocates appears to be focused primarily on one issue—whether students who are able to construct a procedure for performing a task or solving a problem (but have not yet done so) should be directed to apply an "advanced solution" presented in a demonstration or worked example and engage in forced part- and whole-task practice while receiving corrective and supportive feedback.

Guidance advocates (e.g., Mayer, 2004; Kirschner, Sweller, & Clark, 2006; Sweller, Kirschner, & Clark, 2007) argue that cognitive architecture places severe restrictions on working-memory capacity and so forced guidance allows students to allocate limited cognitive capacity to learning a successful performance routine without limiting transfer. They present consistent evidence from the past half-century where guidance results in significantly more learning than constructing solutions to problems and tasks.

Constructivism advocates believe that "the teacher's role is to challenge the learners thinking ... and not to dictate or attempt to proceduralize that thinking" (Savery & Duffy, 2001, p. 5) and require that instructional support not be provided "unless we have independent evidence that the learner cannot do the task or goal unaided" (Pea, 2004, p. 443). Constructivism advocates point to studies where students who construct solutions to problems and tasks achieve not only immediate learning but also longer-term transfer benefits (e.g., Hmelo-Silver et al., 2007).

Resolution

A balanced view of the evidence offered on both sides of the debate would conclude that at this point, support for the guidance position appears to be stronger than for the constructivist position—but some of the constructivist evidence is promising nonetheless. It is clear that many advocates of the constructivist position have moved far beyond the radical views advocating total discovery suggested in the past and that considerable agreement exists between the parties to this debate. Yet current studies used to support both sides tend to examine gross comparisons between forced guidance and no guidance rather than situations where students are able to construct solutions but have not yet done so. Future research studies must systematically explore clearly operationalized variations in guidance that reflect the disagreements. Outcome measures must examine the short- and longer-term learning of declarative and application knowledge. In addition, adequate tests of existing hypotheses about fading instruction and the negative effects of guidance on farther transfer and adaptability require the development of improved measures of automated prior knowledge that include both declarative and procedural forms. We must be able to distinguish between how much and what kind of declarative and procedural knowledge students bring to instruction as well as an adequate technology for tracking their learning in real time during and after instruction. Equally important for the resolution of this and other disagreements is a commitment to increased communication and collaboration between those who advocate very different kinds of instructional support. We must collaborate to produce a clear taxonomy of instructional support that specifies the appropriateness of each type for different learning goals, tasks, and learners. In order to achieve any of those goals, we must be willing to give up the comfortable isolation of like-minded groups and welcome disagreements that can be solved by collaborative, evidence-based inquiry.

Question: Jonassen. *Direct instruction, including worked examples, is clearly effective for supporting learning how to solve well-structured problems. However, ill-structured problems, by definition, are not amenable to direct instruction. How can you design direct instruction to support learning how to solve emergent, interdisciplinary problems with multiple solutions, solution criteria, and solution paths, or no solutions at all? Should we ignore ill-structured problems because direct instruction, other than general heuristics, cannot be used to teach learners how to solve them?*

Reply: Clark. This question touches on one of the most important issues that separate constructivists from guidance advocates. The issue of structure in knowledge domains stems from a concern that strong guidance may not be possible in emergent or established domains where experts disagree about what students need to learn (e.g., counseling psychology, history). I want to suggest a different view of this issue and propose that the problem described in the question can be handled with direct instruction provided it is accompanied by cognitive task analysis. When attempting to design instruction for "ill-structured" domains we are most often in one of two situations—either domain experts can reliably solve emergent or long-standing problems but do not agree about how they do it, or experts have not yet succeeded in solving problems or accomplishing complex tasks. For solvable problems and complex tasks that experts succeed in performing, the goal is to identify and capture the simplest and most effective solutions and then employ procedurally guided instruction to teach those solutions to novices. The goal is to use cognitive task analysis interviews with experts and the literature of the domain to identify the most robust and simplest solution path and teach it to students. In some instances different solution paths indicate important variations in the problems being solved. Often, variations in the initial conditions or values assigned to different variables in a problem will lead to different solution paths.

The second alternative occurs when domain experts have not succeeded in inventing effective solutions that can be demonstrated to students. In this instance, it seems unrealistic to expect that even the most intelligent and motivated students would be able to discover minimally acceptable solutions during instruction. In the case where students are expected to invent a solution, the preferable instructional approach is to provide expert-based, domain-specific procedures for inventing solutions to problems through procedurally guided instruction. In this case the focus of the instruction shifts from students discovering solutions to students learning a protocol for discovering solutions in a domain. In this case, it is also necessary to teach the important conceptual knowledge in a domain (facts, concepts, processes, and principles) so that students will be able to use knowledge-invention procedures effectively. For example, if students want to learn how to develop solutions to counseling psychology problems that have not yet been solved, they need to be able to implement theory-development and research-design procedures that are appropriate to that area and they must be able to apply current concepts and principles as they plan and conduct research. The bottom line in this approach is that there are no "ill-structured domains" if we use cognitive task analysis and/or "how to solve this type of problem" as a basis for guided instruction.

Question: Jonassen. *Experts organize their knowledge around cases, rather than declarative knowledge, and they reason using forward chaining. Experts rarely agree, and they have difficulty unpacking what they know. How can you justify using experts in cognitive task analysis for the purpose of designing instruction for novice learners?*

Reply: Clark. We probably agree that novice reasoning and problem-solving strategies change as expertise develops. Without adequate learning support, novices initially start reasoning backward based on the surface characteristics of problems to choose a solution strategy and then reason forward as they use trial and error to check successive solutions to solve problems. This approach is very inefficient and not very effective for most performance objectives. Experts instantly classify problems into principled categories and reason forward as they implement effective and efficient solution strategies connected to the categories. If some novices can learn to solve problems like experts, why not accelerate this process for all novices by showing them how experts solve domain problems and give them the necessary declarative and procedural knowledge to imitate expert protocols? I appreciate the opportunity to make clear what I only implied in my chapter—that fully guided instruction based on newer cognitive task analysis (CTA) strategies is intended to teach novices to reason like domain experts.

Question: Wise and O'Neill. *Constructivists propose that simplifying a complex domain for the purpose of teaching may encourage learners to take inappropriately simple approaches to complex problems. True domain experts are aware of the limits of the knowledge they work with; is this not a facet of expertise that should be represented in instruction?*

Reply: Clark. You ask two questions—one about inappropriate simplification and another about domain experts. I respect your concern about inappropriate simplification of complex problems. No one wants to make the mistake you describe. I changed my mind slowly about this issue by looking at evidence from the systematic programs of inquiry by instructional researchers such as John Anderson. Anderson's ACT-R model includes the cognitive and neural mechanisms that support learning from instruction and he has applied it to the teaching of math, language, problem-solving, reasoning, and visual perception. His model has been translated into instructional programs that successfully support student learning and transfer of some of the most complex instructional tasks and problems.

Anderson's view is that all complex learning is a product of the gradual accumulation or "scaling" of simple learning into more complex assemblies of knowledge. For example, Lee and Anderson (2001) re-analyzed learning data collected from the very complex Kanfer–Ackerman Air Traffic Controller Task (Ackerman, 1988; Ackerman & Kanfer, 1994) and demonstrated convincingly that the learning in this complex task reflects the gradual build-up of small, procedural-knowledge chunks starting at the keystroke level. They also demonstrated that a large portion of the learning at the keystroke level reflected learning at an even lower, attentional level. The overall execution speed of the necessary complex cognitive skills increased according to Anderson's power law of practice. What was most interesting in this (and many of Anderson's other studies) is that the process by which trainees first learned and then assembled the individual sub-skills explained more of the variance in whole-task performance than fitting any single subtask to the overall task. So the sequential learning and gradual automating and interconnecting of larger sets of component attention and cognitive subskills was a necessary and sufficient condition for optimal performance at a highly complex task.

Assembling procedural components of complex cognitive routines is a function of sequencing rules, accurate problem-solving procedures including those used to make decisions, and "hands on" practice. In my chapter I stressed the need for "whole-task practice" following "part-task" practice instruction—and the need to introduce increasingly novel features in authentic practice problems to promote "varied practice." I have also become an advocate for training using multimedia immersive simulations and serious games as vehicles for whole-task practice since varied practice and knowledge automation is a gradual process that requires many hours of exercises.

Your second question proposes that "true domain experts are aware of the limits of the knowledge they work with" and ask whether that awareness should be included in instruction. I don't think that anyone has addressed this issue systematically. Over the past 20 years I've conducted cognitive task analysis interviews with many experts in different domains. My experience is that the majority of experts seem equally overconfident about their knowledge of areas both inside and outside their area of expertise. Yet if the issue you raise is intended to suggest that we should clearly describe to students the application limits of the knowledge being taught, I certainly agree. It seems that the difficulty for all of us is not our inclination to specify application limits but a lack of agreement about how to define those limits and what pedagogical approaches achieve different application limits.

Question: Wise and O'Neill. *We appreciate your effort to define instructional guidance from your perspective and agree that a clear definition around which to converse has been lacking in the recent dialogue. However, we are unclear how guidance, as you define it, relates to other commonly used terms such as scaffolding and instructional support. For example, are guidance and scaffolding two kinds of instructional support, useful in different situations? Or are demonstrations and feedback two kinds of instructional support that combine to become guidance? This is a question of more than just semantics, since you seem to critique Pea's (2004) discussion of scaffolding as referring to guidance or instructional support more generally, when we believe his intent was to set scaffolding (in its Vygotskian sense) apart from related guidance practices.*

Reply: Clark. Apparently I could have done a better job communicating my acceptance of nearly all of Pea's descriptions of the elements of scaffolding as shared elements of guidance—except for the requirement that learners discover or invent any part of the solutions to problems or steps necessary to perform a task. Nearly all of the elements of scaffolding, except for discovery, have a long and positive history in instructional research and practice.

Question: Wise and O'Neill. *We value your observation that instructionists and constructivists have largely kept to their corners, working with like-minded researchers for some time. However, there are clearly points of intersection between these camps in the literature. For example, like us, you reference the literature on intelligent-tutoring systems (ITS) to support your argument. Because of this, we were* surprised to see you insist on the importance of immediate feedback in your defini- tion of instructional guidance. In the ITS literature there appears to be some debate around the merits of immediate feedback (see Mathan & Koedinger, 2003 and the discussion in our chapter). How do you view this debate, and do you think it needs to be factored into your definition of instructional guidance somehow?

Reply: Clark. Evidence about feedback has not been the exclusive domain of ITS researchers. It extends back at least a century and has been reconceptualized by many researchers over the years. Mathan and Koedinger clearly state that delayed feedback can sometimes result in the learning of incorrect information. They also describe a study where delayed feedback produced greater conceptual under- standing and farther transfer but caution that the design of effective delayed feedback is difficult. Their conclusion was similar to the advice provided by Druckman and Bjork (1994) in their review. Applying the conflicting evidence about the timing of feedback is risky and so I believe that the most secure pre- scription is that well-designed immediate feedback prevents the learning of incorrect knowledge that must later be corrected. I've seen little evidence that delayed feedback typically enhances conceptual learning or farther transfer or that it is the only way to support adaptable learning—but I'm open to new evidence.

References

Ackerman, P. L. (1988). Determinants of individual differences during skill acquisition: Cognitive abilities and information processing. *Journal of Experimental Psychology: General, 117*, 288–318.

Ackerman, P. L., & Kanfer, R. (1994). *Kanfer–Ackerman air traffic controller task, CD-ROM database, datacollection program, and playback program.* Office of Naval Research, Cog- nitive Science Program.

Anderson, J. R. (1983). *The architecture of cognition.* Cambridge, MA: Harvard University Press.

Anderson, John R. (1996). ACT: A simple theory of complex cognition. *American Psychol- ogist, 51*(4), 355–365.

Anderson, J. R., & Lebiere, C. (1998). *The atomic components of thought.* Mahwah, NJ: Erlbaum.

Anderson, J. R., Reder, L. M., & Simon, H. A. (1996). Situated learning and education. *Educational Researcher, 25*, 5–11.

Anderson, J. R., Reder, L. M., & Simon, H. A. (1997). Situative versus cognitive perspec- tives: Form versus substance. *Educational Researcher, 26*, 18–21.

Barrows, H. S. (1986). A taxonomy of problem based learning methods. *Medical Educa- tion, 20*, 481–486.

Bereiter, C., & Scardamalia, M. (1993). *Surpassing ourselves: An inquiry into the nature and implications of expertise.* Chicago, IL: Open Court.

Besnard, D. (2000). Expert error. The case of trouble-shooting in electronics. In *Proceed- ings of the 19th International Conference SafeComp2000* (pp. 74–85). Rotterdam, The Netherlands.

Besnard, D., & Bastien-Toniazzo, M. (1999). Expert error in trouble-shooting: An explor- atory study in electronics. *International Journal of Human–Computer Studies, 50*, 391–405.

Brown, J. S., Collins, A., & Duguid, P. (1989). Situated cognition and the culture of learning. *Educational Researcher, 18*(1), 32–42.

Brown, J. S., & Duguid, P. (1991). Organizational learning and communities of practice: Toward a unified view of working, learning and innovation. *Organizational Science, 2*(1), 40–57.

Chao, C.-J., & Salvendy, G. (1994). Percentage of procedural knowledge acquired as a function of the number of experts from whom knowledge is acquired for diagnosis, debugging and interpretation tasks. *International Journal of Human–Computer Interaction, 6,* 221–233.

Clark, R. E. (1982). Antagonism between achievement and enjoyment in ATI studies. *Educational Psychologist, 17*(2), 132–148.

Clark, R. E. (1989). When teaching kills learning: Research on mathematics. In H. Mandl, E. De Corte, N. Bennett, & H. F. Friedrich (Eds.), *Learning and instruction. European research in an international context* (Vols 2 & 3, pp. 1–22). Oxford: Pergamon.

Clark, R. E. (2001). *Learning from media: Arguments, analysis and evidence.* Greenwich, CT: Information Age Publishing.

Clark, R. E., & Blake, S. (1997). Analyzing cognitive structures and processes to derive instructional methods for the transfer of problem solving expertise. In S. Dijkstra & N. M. Seel (Eds.), *Instructional design perspectives. Volume II, Solving instructional design problems* (pp. 183–214). Oxford: Pergamon.

Clark, R. E., & Elen, J. (2006). When less is more: Research and theory insights about instruction for complex learning. In J. Elen & R. Clark (Eds.), *Handling complexity in learning environments: Research and theory* (pp. 283–297). Oxford: Elsevier Science Limited.

Clark, R. E., & Estes, F. (1996). Cognitive task analysis. *International Journal of Educational Research, 25,* 403–417.

Clark, R. E., Feldon, D., van Merriënboer, J., Yates, K., & Early, S. (2007). Cognitive task analysis. In J. M. Spector, M. D. Merrill, J. J. G. van Merriënboer, & M. P. Driscoll (Eds.), *Handbook of research on educational communications and technology* (3rd ed., pp. 577–593). Mahwah, NJ: Lawrence Erlbaum Associates.

Cohen, H. S., Bloomberg, J. J., & Mulavara, A. P. (2005). Obstacle avoidance in novel visual environments improved by variable practice training. *Perceptual and Motor Skills, 101*(3), 853–861.

Cowen, N. (2001). The magical number 4 in short term memory: A reconsideration of mental storage capacity. *Behavioral and Brain Sciences, 24,* 87–114.

Cronbach, L. J., & Snow, R. E. (1977). *Aptitudes and instructional methods.* New York: Irvington.

De Corte, E. (2003). Transfer as the productive use of acquired knowledge, skills, and motivations. *Current Directions in Psychological Science, 12*(4), 143–146.

DeLeeuw, K. E., & Mayer, R. E. (2008). A comparison of three measures of cognitive load: Evidence for separable measures of intrinsic, extraneous and germane load. *Journal of Educational Psychology, 100*(1), 223–234.

Druckman, D., & Bjork, R. A. (1994). *Learning, remembering and believing.* Washington DC: National Academy Press.

Druckman, D., & Swets, J. A. (Eds.). (1988). *Enhancing human performance: Issues, theories and techniques.* Washington, DC: National Academy Press.

Duffy, T. M., & Jonassen, D. H. (Eds.). (1992). *Constructivism and the technology of instruction, a conversation.* Mahwah, NJ: Lawrence Erlbaum Associates.

Feldon, D. F. (2004). *Inaccuracies in expert self-report: Errors in the description of strategies*

Feldon, D. F. (2007). Implications of research on expertise for curriculum and pedagogy. *Educational Psychology Review, 19*(2), 91–110.

Goodman, J. S., Wood, R. E., & Hendrickx, M. (2004). Feedback specificity, exploration and learning. *Journal of Applied Psychology, 89*(2), 248–262.

Gott, S. P., Hall, E. P., Pokorny, R. A., Dibble, E., & Glaser, R. (1993). A naturalistic study of transfer: Adaptive expertise in technical domains. In D. K. Detterman & R. J. Sternberg (Eds.), *Transfer on trial: Intelligence, cognition, and instruction* (pp. 258–288). Norwood, NJ: Ablex.

Gustafsson, J.-E., & Undheim, J. O. (1996). Individual differences in cognitive functions. In D. Berliner & R. C. Calfee (Eds.), *Handbook of educational psychology* (pp. 186–242). New York: Simon & Schuster Macmillan.

Hatano, G., & Inagaki, K. (1986). Two courses of expertise. In H. Stevenson, H. Asuma, & K. Hakauta (Eds.), *Child development and education in Japan* (pp. 262–272). San Francisco, CA: Freeman.

Hatano, G., & Inagaki, K. (2000, April). *Practice makes a difference: Design principles for adaptive expertise*. Paper presented at the Annual Meeting of the American Education Research Association. New Orleans, LA.

Hmelo-Silver, C. E., Duncan, R. G., & Chinn, C. A. (2007). Scaffolding and achievement in problem-based and inquiry learning: A response to Kirschner, Sweller, and Clark (2006). *Educational Psychologist, 42*(2), 99–107.

Hoffman, R., Crandall, B., & Shadbolt, N. (1998). Use of the critical decision method to elicit expert knowledge: A case study in the methodology of cognitive task analysis. *Human Factors, 40,* 254–276.

Jonassen, D. H. (1991). Evaluating constructivist learning. *Educational Technology, 31*(9), 28–33.

Jonassen, D. H. (1997). Instructional design models for well-structured and ill-structured problem-solving learning outcomes. *Educational Technology Research and Development, 45*(1), 65–94.

Kayluga, S., Ayres, P., Chandler, P., & Sweller, J. (2003). The expertise reversal effect. *Educational Psychologist, 38*(1), 23–31.

Kalyuga, S., & Sweller, J. (2004). Measuring knowledge to optimize load factors during instruction. *Journal of Educational Psychology, 96*(3), 558–568.

Kihlstrom, J. F. (1987). The cognitive unconscious. *Science, 237*(4821), 1445–1452.

Kirschner, P. A., Sweller, J., & Clark, R. (2006). Why minimal guidance during instruction does not work: An analysis of the failure of constructivist, discovery, problem-based, experiential and inquiry-based teaching. *Educational Psychologist, 41,* 75–86.

Klahr, D., & Nigam, M. (2004). The equivalence of learning paths in early science instruction: Effects of direct instruction and discovery learning. *Psychological Science, 15*(10), 661–667.

Kluger, A., & DeNisi, A. (1998). Feedback interventions: Toward the understanding of a double-edged sword. *Current Directions in Psychological Science, 7*(3), 67–72.

Kyllonen, P., & Lajoie, S. P. (2003). Reassessing aptitude: Introduction to a special issue in honor of Richard E. Snow. *Educational Psychologist, 38*(2), 79–83.

Lee, F. J., & Anderson, J. R. (2001). Does learning a complex task have to be complex? A study in learning decomposition. *Cognitive Psychology, 42,* 267–316.

Lee, R. L. (2004). *The impact of cognitive task analysis on performance: A meta analysis of comparative studies*. Unpublished Ed.D. dissertation, Rossier School of Education, University of Southern California, USA.

Masui, C., & De Corte, E. (1999). Enhancing learning and problem solving skills: Orienting and self-judging, two powerful and trainable learning tools. *Learning and Instruction, 9,* 517–542.

Mathan, S., & Koedinger, K. R. (2003). Recasting the feedback debate: Benefits of tutoring error detection and correction skills. In U. Hoppe, F. Verdejo, & J. Kay (Eds.), *Artificial intelligence in education: Shaping the future of learning through intelligent technologies* (pp. 13–20). Amsterdam: IOS Press.

Mayer, R. (2004). Should there be a three-strikes rule against pure discovery learning? The case for guided methods of instruction. *American Psychologist, 59*(1), 14–19.

Merrill, M. D. (1983). Component display theory. In C. Reigeluth (Ed.), *Instructional design theories and models* (pp. 279–333). Hillsdale, NJ: Erlbaum.

Merrill, M. D. (2002). First principles of instruction. *Educational Technology Research and Development, 50*(3), 43–59.

Merrill, M. D. (2006). Hypothesized performance on complex tasks as a function of scaled instructional strategies. In J. Elen & R. Clark (Eds.), *Handling complexity in learning environments: Research and theory* (pp. 265–282). Oxford: Elsevier Science Limited.

Newell, A. (1990). *Unified theories of cognition.* Cambridge, MA: Harvard University Press.

Pea, R. (2004). The social and technological dimensions of scaffolding and related theoretical concepts for learning, education and human activity. *Journal of the Learning Sciences, 13*(3), 423–451.

Perkins, D. N., & Grotzer, T. A. (1997). Teaching intelligence. *American Psychologist, 52*(10), 1125–1133.

Pintrich, P. R., & Schunk, D. H. (2002). *Motivation in education-theory, research, and applications* (2nd ed.). New Jersey: Merrill Prentice Hall.

Ravitch, D., & Viteritti, J. P. (2001). *Making good citizens: Education and civil society.* New Haven, CT: Yale University Press.

Romiszowski, A. J. (2006, November–December). Topics for debate. *Educational Technology*, 61–63.

Rosenshine, B., & Meister, C. (1997). Reciprocal teaching: A review of the research. *Review of Educational Research, 64*(4), 479–530.

Rosenshine, B., & Stevens, R. (1986). Teaching functions. In M. C. Wittrock (Ed.), *Handbook of research on teaching* (3rd ed., pp. 376–390), 3rd Edition. New York: Macmillan.

Salomon, G. (1994). *Interaction of media, cognition and learning.* Hillsdale, NJ: Lawrence Erlbaum Associates.

Salomon, G., & Perkins, D. N. (1989). Rocky roads to transfer: Rethinking mechanisms of a neglected phenomenon. *Educational Psychologist, 24*(2), 113–142.

Savery, J. R., & Duffy, T. M. (June 2001). *Problem Based Learning: An instructional model and its constructivist framework* (technical report no. 16–01). Center for Research on Learning and Technology.

Schmidt, H. G., Loyens, S. M. M., van Gog, T., & Paas, T. (2007). Problem-based learning is compatible with human cognitive architecture: Commentary on Kirschner, Sweller, and Clark (2006). *Educational Psychologist, 42*(2), 91–97.

Schneider, W., & Chein, J. W. (2003). Controlled & automatic processing: Behavior, theory, and biological mechanisms. *Cognitive Science, 27*, 525–559.

Schneider, W., & Shiffrin, R. M. (1977). Controlled and automatic human information processing: 1. Detection, search, and attention. *Psychological Review, 84*, 1–66.

Schraagen, J. M., Chipman, S. F., & Shute, V. J. (2000). State-of-the-art review of cognitive task analysis techniques. In J. M. Schraagen, S. F. Chipman, & V. J. Shute (Eds.), *Cognitive Task Analysis* (pp. 467–487). Mahwah, NJ: Lawrence Erlbaum.

Schwartz, D. L., & Bransford, J. D. (1998). A time for telling. *Cognition and Instruction, 16*, 475–522.

Schwartz, D., Bransford, J., & Sears, D. (2005). Efficiency and innovation in transfer. In

J. Mestre (Ed.), *Transfer of learning from a modern multidisciplinary perspective* (pp. 1–51). Greenwich, CT: Information Age Publishing.

Sears, D. (2006). *Effects of innovation versus efficiency tasks on collaboration and learning.* Unpublished Ph.D. dissertation, School of Education, Stanford University, CA.

Shabo, A. (1997). Integrating constructivism and instructionism in educational hypermedia programs. *Journal of Educational Computing Research, 17*(3), 231–247.

Shulman, L., & Keisler, E. (Eds.). (1966). *Learning by discovery: A critical appraisal.* Chicago, IL: Rand McNally.

Singley, M. K., & Anderson, J. R. (1989). *Transfer of cognitive skill.* Cambridge, MA: Harvard University Press.

Slavin, R. (2006). *Educational psychology* (8th ed.). Boston, MA: Pearson/Allyn & Bacon.

Spiro, R. J., Feltovich, P. L., Jacobson, M. J., & Coulson, R. L. (1992). Cognitive flexibility, constructivism, and hypertext: Random access for advanced knowledge acquisition in ill-structured domains. In T. M. Duffy & D. Jonassen (Eds.), *Constructivism and the technology of instruction: A conversation* (pp. 57–75). Hillsdale, NJ: Lawrence Erlbaum Associates.

Starfield, B. (2000). Is U.S. medical care really the best in the world? *Journal of the American Medical Association, 284*(3), 483–485.

Sweller, J. (2006). How the human cognitive system deals with complexity. In J. Elen & R. E. Clark (Eds.), *Handling complexity in learning environments: Research and theory* (pp. 13–26). Oxford: Elsevier Science Ltd.

Sweller, J., Kirschner, P. A., & Clark, R. E. (2007). Why minimally guided teaching techniques do not work: A reply to commentaries. *Educational Psychologist, 42*(2), 115–121.

Tobias, S. (1982). When do instructional methods make a difference? *Educational Researcher, 11*(4), 4–9.

Van Merriënboer, J. J. G., & Kirschner, P. A. (2007). *Ten steps to complex learning: A systematic approach to four component instructional design.* Mahwah, NJ: Lawrence Erlbaum Associates.

Velmahos, G. C., Toutouzas, K. G., Sillin, L. F., Chan, L., Clark, R. E., Theodorou, D., & Maupin, F. (2004). Cognitive task analysis for teaching technical skills in an inanimate surgical skills laboratory. *The American Journal of Surgery, 18*, 114–119.

Weston, C., & Cranton, P. A. (1986). Selecting instructional strategies. *Journal of Higher Education, 57*(3), 259–288.

Whitener, E. M. (1989). A meta-analytic review of the effects on learning of the interaction between prior achievement and instructional support. *Review of Educational Research, 59*(1), 65–86.

Winthrop, H. (1963). Some considerations concerning the status of phenomenology. *Journal of General Psychology, 68*, 127–140.

10 Constructivism as a Theory of Learning Versus Constructivism as a Prescription for Instruction[*]

Richard E. Mayer University of California, Santa Barbara

Constructivism[1] has long been recognized as a useful theory of learning in which learners build mental representations by engaging in appropriate kinds of active cognitive processing during learning. It is tempting to also view constructivism as a prescription for instruction in which learners must be behaviorally active during learning. While accepting constructivism as a theory of learning, this chapter examines what is wrong with this view of constructivism as a prescription for instruction. In particular, the thesis of this chapter is that it is inappropriate to assume that active cognitive learning requires teaching methods that promote hands-on behavioral activity during learning—such as discovery methods. Similarly, it is inappropriate to assume that passive instructional methods—such as multimedia presentations—cannot promote active cognitive learning.

In this introduction, I explore the *constructivist teaching fallacy* by drawing on a distinction between high cognitive activity during learning (which according to constructivist learning theory leads to deeper learning) and high behavioral activity during learning (which according to a constructivist teaching theory leads to deeper learning). Second, the chapter reviews exemplary research on when active instructional methods lead to passive cognitive learning (i.e., high behavioral activity and low cognitive activity), including ways that discovery methods can fail. Third, the chapter reviews exemplary research concerning when passive instructional methods lead to active cognitive learning (i.e., low behavioral activity and high cognitive activity), including ways of designing multimedia lessons that promote active learning. Overall, constructivism can be successful as a theory of active learning but not as a prescription for active instruction.

An Example of the Constructivist Teaching Fallacy

Consider two scenarios for helping students learn to solve algebra equations. In one scenario, we show the learner how to solve problems using worked-out examples and then let them apply the solution procedure to a new problem. This

[*] Writing of this chapter was supported by a grant from the Office of Naval Research. The author's mailing address is: Richard E. Mayer, Department of Psychology, University of California, Santa Barbara, CA 93106–9660. The author's email address is: mayer@psych.ucsb.edu.

can be considered a passive instructional method because the learner is being shown what to do. In another scenario, we ask the learner to solve equations. This can be considered an active instructional method because the learner is behaviorally active. According to constructivist theories of learning, learning is an active process in which the learners actively construct mental representations in their working memories. Based on constructivist theories of learning, you might suppose that students would learn better in the second scenario because they are engaging in what appears to be active learning.

What is wrong with this analysis? An empirical problem with this analysis is that it conflicts with the empirical research base. When researchers compared instructional methods that included worked-out examples (i.e., a passive method) versus those that relied exclusively on hands-on problem solving (i.e., an active method), they found that students—particularly novices—tended to learn better with the more passive instructional method than the more active one (Cooper & Sweller, 1987; Sweller, 1999; Sweller & Cooper, 1985). Thus, there is consistent empirical evidence that contradicts the call to favor active over passive methods of instruction (Klahr & Nigam, 2004; Kirschner, Sweller, & Clark, 2006; Mayer, 2004).

Why is this analysis wrong? A theoretical problem with this analysis is that it conflicts with research-based theories of how people learn (Bransford, Brown, & Cocking, 1999; Mayer, 2001; Sweller, 1999). This analysis confuses constructivism as a theory of learning (which emphasizes cognitive activity during learning) and constructivism as a prescription for instruction (which emphasizes behavioral activity during learning). According to constructivist theories of learning, active learning occurs when learners engage in appropriate cognitive processing during learning, resulting in the construction of cognitive representations (Mayer, 2001, 2008). The goal of instruction—according to constructivist learning theory—is to promote appropriate cognitive processing during learning (Mayer, 2001, 2008). The thesis of this chapter is that instructional methods should promote appropriate cognitive processing during learning. Researchers should focus on identifying the conditions under which this goal can be accomplished. Behavioral activity during learning does not guarantee that the learner will engage in appropriate cognitive processing, and behavioral inactivity during learning does not guarantee that the learner will not engage in appropriate cognitive processing.

In short, this analysis is an example of what I have called the *constructivist teaching fallacy* (Mayer, 2004)—the idea that active instructional methods (e.g., discovery) are required to produce active learning (i.e., engaging in appropriate cognitive processing during learning). Figure 10.1 lays out four quadrants based on the distinction between behavioral activity during learning and cognitive activity during learning—high behavioral activity and low cognitive activity (as exemplified by discovery methods of instruction); high behavioral activity and high cognitive activity (as exemplified by guided discovery methods of instruction); low behavioral activity and high cognitive activity (as exemplified by what I call principled presentations); and low behavioral activity and low cognitive activity (as exemplified by what I call unprincipled presentations).

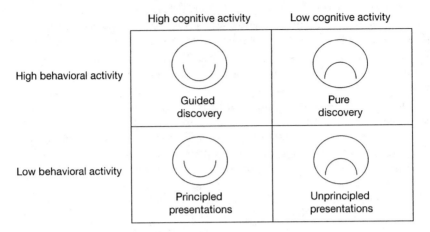

Figure 10.1 Four kinds of instructional methods based on cognitive and behavioral activity.

Active Versus Passive Learning

The top portion of Table 10.1 provides definitions and examples of active versus passive learning.

What Is Learning? Learning is attributable to experience change in the learner's knowledge due to experience. This definition has three parts: (a) learning involves a change; (b) the change is relatively permanent; and (c) the change is in what the learner knows (Mayer, 2008). This definition is broad enough to include all forms of academic learning ranging from learning to solve algebra equations such as "$2x - 6 = 4$, Solve for x," to learning to read printed words such as "cat," to learning to write an essay, to learning Newton's laws of motion.

What Is Active *Learning?* Constructivist learning theory is the idea that learning involves actively building knowledge representations in working memory by applying appropriate cognitive processes. Constructivist learning theories have a

Table 10.1 Distinctions Between Two Kinds of Learning and Two Kinds of Instruction

Name	Definition
Active learning	Learner engages in appropriate cognitive processing during learning (e.g., selecting relevant incoming information, organizing it into a coherent mental structure, and integrating it with relevant prior knowledge).
Passive learning	Learner does not engage in appropriate cognitive processing during learning (e.g., selecting only).
Active instruction	Learner is required to engage in behavioral activity during learning (e.g., discovering a solution to a problem).
Passive instruction	Learner is not required to engage in behavioral activity during learning (e.g., reading a passage or watching a presentation).

long history in psychology and education, with roots in Piaget's (1970) classic theory of how knowledge develops in children and Bartlett's (1932) classic theory of how people learn from prose. Today, constructivist theories of learning play a dominant role in psychology and education (Bransford, Brown, & Cocking, 1999; Mayer, 2008) and have useful implications for instructional design (Mayer, 2005).

As an example of a constructivist theory of learning, consider the cognitive theory of multimedia learning, which we have been testing over the past 20 years (Mayer, 2001, 2005; Mayer & Moreno, 2003). As is summarized in Figure 10.2, learning takes place in the human cognitive system, which consists of three memory stores and three cognitive processes.

The three memory stores in Figure 10.2 are:

- *sensory memory*—Information from the outside world enters your cognitive system through your eyes (such as when you view an animation) and/or your ears (such as when you listen to narration). Information entering via the ears is temporarily held in an auditory sensory memory, and information entering via the eyes is temporarily held in a visual sensory memory. This information fades rapidly but if you pay attention, some of it can be transferred to working memory for further processing.
- *working memory*—In working memory, you can process only a limited amount of the incoming information at any one time, including mentally reorganizing the incoming information and integrating it with other information transferred from long-term memory. Knowledge construction occurs in working memory, but limits on the capacity of working memory represent a major challenge for instructional design.
- *long-term memory*—Long-term memory is your storehouse of existing knowledge. It is not limited in capacity or duration, but you can only be aware of its contents when you transfer information to working memory. Only a limited amount of information from long-term memory can be transferred to working memory at any one time.

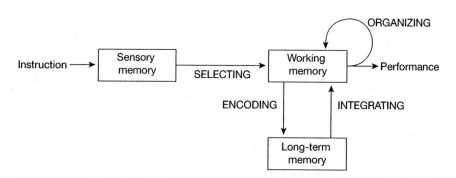

Figure 10.2 How learning works.

The three cognitive processes listed in Figure 10.2 are:

- *selecting*—Selecting refers to paying attention to relevant aspects of the incoming information, as indicated by the arrow from sensory memory to working memory.
- *organizing*—Organizing refers to mentally arranging pieces of information into a coherent cognitive structure, as indicated by the arrow from working memory to working memory.
- *integrating*—Integrating refers to mentally combining incoming information with relevant knowledge retrieved from long-term memory, as indicated by the arrow from long-term memory to working memory.

According to constructivist learning theory, active learning occurs when the learner engages in appropriate cognitive processing during learning, which includes attending to relevant incoming information, mentally organizing it into a coherent cognitive structure, and mentally relating it with relevant prior knowledge from long-term memory (Mayer, 2001, 2008). Also, according to constructivist learning theory, passive learning occurs when the learner engages in minimal cognitive processing during learning—such as failing to engage in the deeper processes of organizing and integrating (Mayer 2001, 2008).

Active Versus Passive Instruction

The bottom portion of Table 10.1 provides definitions and examples of active versus passive instruction.

What is Instruction? Instruction refers to the teacher's construction of a learning environment that is intended to foster changes in the learner's knowledge. In short, instruction refers to external events arranged by the teacher that are intended to cause internal cognitive processing in the learner during learning. This definition contains two parts: (a) instruction is something the teacher (or instructional designer) does; and (b) the goal of instruction is to promote learning (Mayer, 2008). This definition is broad enough to include active methods—such as giving learners a problem to solve on their own—and passive methods—such as providing a worked-out example of the steps in how to solve a problem.

What is Active Instruction? On the most straightforward level, active instruction refers to instructional methods in which the learner is behaviorally active—such as discovery methods or methods that require discussion. Similarly, passive instructional methods refer to instructional methods in which the learner is not behaviorally active—such as reading a book or watching a presentation. The constructivist teaching fallacy is the idea that constructivist learning is caused by active methods of instruction rather than by active learning (i.e., active cognitive processing during learning) and that non-constructivist learning is caused by passive methods of instruction rather than by passive learning (i.e., lack of appropriate cognitive processing during learning).

According to constructivist theories of learning such as the cognitive theory of multimedia learning (Mayer, 2001, 2005; Mayer & Moreno, 2003), which is consistent with Sweller's (1999, 2005) cognitive load theory, instructional manipulations can prime three kinds of cognitive processing during learning:

- *Extraneous processing* (or extraneous cognitive load) is cognitive processing that does not serve the instructional goal and is caused by poor instructional design. It does not correspond to any of the arrows in Figure 10.2 but does consume precious cognitive capacity.
- *Essential processing* (or intrinsic cognitive load) is cognitive processing aimed at attending to and encoding the main elements of the presented information and their relations, and depends on the inherent complexity of the material. It corresponds to selecting and a small amount of organizing in Figure 10.2.
- *Generative processing* (or germane cognitive load) is cognitive processing aimed at making sense of the incoming material and depends on the learner's efforts to understand the material. It corresponds to organizing and integrating in Figure 10.2.

Meaningful instruction enables the learner to engage in essential and generative processing during learning, leading to superior performance on transfer tests (Mayer, 2001, 2008). In contrast, rote instruction does not prime much essential processing and generative processing, leading to poor performance on transfer tests (Mayer, 2001, 2008). The major challenge for instructional design concerns the limited processing capacity available in the learner's working memory. Accordingly, meaningful instructional methods should reduce extraneous processing in order to free up capacity for essential and generative processing. In addition, meaningful instructional methods should manage essential processing—that is, seek ways to accommodate the demands for essential processing—when the material is complex.

The remainder of this chapter explores research concerning each of the four quadrants in Figure 10.1. Along the columns, we can consider the level of cognitive activity during learning, which can range from low to high. Along the rows, we can consider the level of behavioral activity, which can range from low to high. In particular, I examine when active instructional methods lead to passive learning, when active instructional methods lead to active learning, when passive instructional methods lead to active learning, and when passive instructional methods lead to passive learning.

Quadrant 1: When Active Instructional Methods Lead to Passive Learning

In Figure 10.1, the upper-right quadrant represents a situation in which the learner is behaviorally active but not cognitively active. According to the constructivist teaching fallacy, this situation should lead to deep learning because the learner is behaviorally active during learning.

As an example of an active instructional method, let's consider discovery learning methods. In discovery learning methods, students are given a problem to solve on their own so they can learn by doing. Discovery learning is considered an active instructional method because the learner is behaviorally active during the learning process. The intended learning outcome of discovery learning methods is deep learning, as indicated by the ability to use the learned material in new situations. In this section, I review three recent papers that summarized the evidence against discovery methods in which active instruction leads to passive learning (Mayer, 2004; Kirschner et al., 2006; Klahr & Nigam, 2004).

Three Strikes Against Pure Discovery

What does the research tell us about the effectiveness of discovery-learning methods? In a recent review (Mayer, 2004), I examined three bodies of literature on discovery—research on teaching of problem-solving rules culminating in the 1960s, research on teaching of Piagetian conservation strategies culminating in the 1970s, and research on teaching of LOGO programming culminating in the 1980s. In each case, students who learned with minimal guidance under a pure-discovery method tended to perform more poorly on retention and transfer tests than students who learned with substantial amounts of guidance under a guided-discovery method.

First, consider students' learning of problem-solving principles. For example, Kittel (1957) taught students to solve oddity problems such as marking the word that does not belong in the set: GONE START GO STOP COME. In this case the principle is "form two pairs of opposites" so the correct answer is GONE. Overall, students learned to solve oddity problems based on 15 different principles. In the pure-discovery group, students were given problems to solve on their own. In the guided-discovery group, students were given the principle (e.g., "form two pairs of opposites") before each problem and asked to solve it. In the expository group, students were given the principle and shown the correct answer for each problem. The guided-discovery group (and the expository group) outperformed the pure-discovery group on subsequent tests of retention and transfer. Similar results were obtained by other researchers who focused on teaching of problem-solving principles (Mayer, 2004). In the first major review of empirical research on discovery learning, Shulman and Keislar (1966) concluded: "Many strong claims for learning by discovery are made in educational psychology. But almost none of these claims has been empirically substantiated or even clearly tested in an experiment" (p. 33).

A second line of research on discovery learning involves teaching children to solve Piagetian conservation problems, such as conservation of number tasks. For example, Gelman (1969) found that kindergarteners who were asked to solve conservation problems without any guidance from the teacher did not tend to show improvement on subsequent tests. However, Gelman found improvements for kindergarteners who received guided practice in which the teacher directed their attention to the relevant aspects of the task and showed how paying attention to irrelevant aspects led to incorrect answers. Similar results were obtained by other researchers throughout the 1970s, indicating that guided discovery resulted in deeper learning than did pure discovery (Mayer, 2004).

As a third test, consider the best way to help students learn a computer programming language called LOGO, in which students can program an onscreen turtle to draw. For example, Kurland and Pea (1985) reported that students who had more than 50 hours of hands-on experience using LOGO under pure discovery conditions did not perform well on tests in which they had to write new programs. In contrast, Fay and Mayer (1994) found large improvements in program-planning skill for students who learned LOGO through a systematic guided approach in which they received guidance and feedback on a set of prescribed tasks as compared to students who learned LOGO by pure discovery. In a review of research through the 1980s, Littlefield et al. (1988) concluded "mastery of the programming language has not been achieved when LOGO has been taught in a discovery-oriented environment" (p. 17).

In reviewing these three classic bodies of literature, I concluded that they constituted "three strikes against pure discovery" and that they showed "the formula *constructivism = hands-on activity* is a formula for educational disaster" (Mayer, 2004, p. 17).

Why Minimal Guidance During Instruction Does Not Work

In a recent review, Kirschner et al. (2006) systematically spelled out the case against discovery methods of instruction by summarizing "empirical studies over the past half-century that consistently indicate that minimally guided instruction is less effective and less efficient than instructional approaches that place a strong emphasis on guidance of the student learning process" (p. 75). For example, Sweller and Cooper (1985; Cooper & Sweller, 1987) were the first to report a *worked-example effect* in which students learned less from practice in actually solving algebra than from studying worked examples of the same problems. In a more recent review, Renkl (2005) and Kirschner et al. (2006) reported that the worked-example effect could be enhanced by providing an appropriate mix of guidance and discovery. Similarly, Clark (1989) reviewed studies in which students who were allowed to choose or were assigned an unguided method of instruction actually showed a loss of learning even though they tended to like the experience. Kirschner et al. (2006) conclude that discovery methods appear to be particularly disadvantageous for lower aptitude and less experienced students.

Critics of the Kirschner et al. position acknowledge that many students benefit from some balance of guidance and discovery (Schmidt, Loyens, van Gog, & Paas, 2007; Hmelo-Silver, Duncan, & Chinn, 2007), although in rebuttal, Sweller, Kirschner, and Clark (2007) call for well-controlled experiments to determine how much guidance is needed. In another critique, Kuhn (2007) argues for the value of problem-solving inquiry in science learning but Sweller et al. (2007) note that inquiry-based curricula have generally fallen far short of expectations.

Teaching Scientific Reasoning by Discovery

Klahr and Nigam (2004) taught scientific reasoning skills to elementary school children through a discovery approach or a direct-instruction approach. In the discovery method, children were given a control-of-variables problem and asked to design experiments to test hypotheses. In the direct-instruction method, children were given a control-of-variables problem and asked to study examples of confounded and unfounded ways to test hypotheses. Of low-performing students, only 15% developed appropriate scientific reasoning skills under a discovery method, whereas 69% developed scientific reasoning skills under direct instruction. Similar results were reported by Chen and Klahr (1999). Although Kuhn and Dean (2005) conducted research purporting to demonstrate the value of discovery in learning to solve control-of-variables problems, Klahr (2005) notes that their instructional method was not particularly effective in promoting transfer.

In reviewing research on computer-based systems that employ discovery methods of instruction, de Jong and van Joolingen (1998) identified several difficulties that learners encounter in discovery learning in scientific reasoning tasks: "learners (even university students) simply do not know what a hypothesis should look like" (p. 183); "learners may not be able to state or adapt hypotheses on the basis of data collected" (p. 183); "in stating hypotheses ... learners can be led by considerations that do not ... help them" (p. 184); learners tend to "seek information that confirms their hypothesis" (p. 184), "design inconclusive experiments" (p. 185), design "the same experiment several times" (p. 185), and "construct experiments that are not intended to test a hypothesis" (p. 185); and learners tend to mis-encode and misinterpret the data. De Jong (2005) concludes that students need guidance in learning how to think scientifically, which can be called the *guided-discovery principle.*

Overall, there is a consistent research base demonstrating the ineffectiveness of pure-discovery methods of instruction, particularly for learners with low levels of experience and prior knowledge. This empirical database—dating back 50 years—provides compelling evidence that it is possible to design active instructional methods that lead to passive learning—that is, low levels of cognitive processing during learning. A theoretical explanation for this quadrant is that hands-on activity can create so much extraneous cognitive processing that learners do not have enough remaining cognitive capacity to engage in the essential and generative processing needed for active learning (Mayer, 2001; Mayer & Moreno, 2003; Sweller, 1999).

Quadrant 2: When Active Instructional Methods Lead to Active Learning

You should not interpret the foregoing review to mean that active instructional methods are always ineffective. The upper-left quadrant of Figure 10.2 represents situations in which active instructional methods lead to active learning. The research reviewed in the prior section indicates several conditions under which active instructional methods can prime appropriate cognitive processing during learning, including (1) when appropriate guidance is incorporated into the lesson (i.e., guided discovery), and (2) when the learner is experienced or has high aptitude.

When guidance is incorporated into a hands-on lesson, this can reduce the learner's extraneous processing so more cognitive capacity is available for essential and generative processing. The hands-on activity may be motivating enough to foster essential and generative processing. De Jong (2005) refers to instruction that balances discovery and guidance as the *guided-discovery principle*.

When learners have appropriate experience or aptitude they may be able benefit from discovery environments because they know how to control their learning process in a way that minimizes extraneous processing. Kalyuga (2005) uses the term *expertise-reversal effect* to refer to situations in which an instructional method that disadvantages low-knowledge learners (such as discovery) can actually be helpful for high-knowledge learners.

Quadrant 3: When Passive Instructional Methods Lead to Active Learning

Consider a short narrated animation that explains how lightning storms develop. The lightning lesson is an example of a passive instructional method because the learner does not have to engage in any hands-on activity. Yet, students can engage in active learning, as indicated by their being able to generate solutions to transfer problems based on the lesson, such as explaining what you could do to reduce the intensity of a lightning storm.

The lower-left quadrant of Figure 10.2 represents a situation in which a passive instructional method leads to active learning. For example, research on the design of multimedia lessons shows that learners can achieve deep understanding—as indicated by performance on a transfer test—from reading well-designed illustrated passages on paper or viewing well-designed narrated animations on a computer screen (Clark & Mayer, 2008; Mayer, 2005). I refer to these lessons as *principled presentations* because they are designed in ways that are consistent with how people learn and with research evidence. On the basis of more than 100 experimental tests conducted during the past 25 years, my colleagues and I have developed a core of evidence-based principles for how to design multimedia lessons that will promote active learning (Mayer, 2001, 2005; Mayer & Moreno, 2003). Some of the principles are intended to reduce extraneous cognitive processing during learning (or extraneous cognitive load):

- *coherence principle*—People learn better when extraneous material is excluded.
- *signaling principle*—People learn better when essential material is highlighted.
- *spatial contiguity principle*—People learn better when corresponding words and pictures are near each other on the page or screen.
- *temporal contiguity principle*—People learn better when corresponding narration and pictures are presented simultaneously.
- *redundancy principle*—People learn better from narration and animation than from narration, animation, and onscreen text.

Some of the principles are intended to manage essential cognitive processing during learning (or intrinsic cognitive load):

- *segmenting principle*—People learn better when a continuous presentation is broken down into learner-paced segments.
- *pretraining principle*—People learn better when a continuous presentation is preceded by training in the names and characteristics of the key components.
- *modality principle*—People learn better from a multimedia presentation when the words are spoken rather than printed.

Some of the principles are intended to foster generative cognitive processing during learning (or germane cognitive load):

- *multimedia principle*—People learn better from words and pictures than from words alone.
- *personalization principle*—People learn better when the words are in conversational style rather than formal style.
- *voice principle*—People learn better from narration and animation when the narration involves a human voice rather than a machine voice.

We evaluate active learning by testing learners on problem-solving transfer questions in which they must apply what was presented to new situations. Active learning involves the cognitive processes of selecting, organizing, and integrating during learning whereas passive learning involves mainly selecting. Our research shows that people perform better on transfer tests when multimedia lessons are based on these design principles than when they are not (Mayer, 2001, 2005; Mayer & Moreno, 2003). Thus, passive instruction such as viewing multimedia presentations can lead to active learning when the passive instruction is designed to reduce extraneous processing, manage essential processing, and foster generative processing.

Quadrant 4: When Passive Instructional Methods Lead to Passive Learning

Of course, it is possible to design passages or presentations in ways that do not prime deep cognitive processing during learning. This situation is represented in the bottom-right quadrant of Figure 10.2. Quadrant 4 is epitomized by what I call *unprincipled presentations*—presentations that violate research-based design principles. For example, failing to coordinate corresponding graphics and text or failure to exclude extraneous material can lead to passive learning—that is failure to engage in deep cognitive processing during learning.

Conclusion

What can we conclude from our tour of the four quadrants in Figure 10.1? The main point of this chapter is that active methods of instruction do not necessarily lead to active learning and passive methods of instruction do not necessarily lead to passive learning. Constructivism is a theory of learning—more specifically, a theory of active learning—in which active learning involves engaging in appropriate cognitive processing during learning. These active learning processes can be caused by passive instructional methods (such as principled presentations) and can be hindered by active instructional methods (such as pure discovery).

When the instructional goal is to promote constructivist learning, instructional methods should be used that prime appropriate cognitive processing during learning—such as selecting relevant material, mentally organizing the material into a coherent cognitive representation, and integrating the material with relevant prior knowledge. Constructivist theories of learning describe how this process of active learning takes place. The constructivist teaching fallacy occurs when someone assumes that active learning is caused by active instructional methods and passive learning is caused by passive methods of instruction. My goal in this chapter is to discourage educators and researchers from committing the constructivist teaching fallacy. Instead, instructional design should be based on evidence-based principles for how instructional methods affect aspects of active cognitive processing during learning.

Question: Duschl and Duncan. *If learning sequences are carefully and thoughtfully coordinated, then doesn't this make the existence of novice learners a consequence of either poorly focused and non-coherent lesson sequences, poor instruction/implementation, or both? If we adopt learning progressions or planned instructional sequences that follow empirically established developmental trajectories coupled with effective formative assessments and teaching to keep learning on track, doesn't the problem of novice learners become a moot point? Why are we not seeking such curriculum designs as an educational research goal in conjunction with the generalized pedagogical practices you advocate?*

Reply: Mayer. A novice is someone who does not have much domain knowledge. Based on this definition, most K–12 students are novices for most topics they are studying in school. The existence of novice learners is not necessarily a consequence of poor instruction. Thus I do not understand what you mean by the "problem of novice learners." I think the fundamental point is that instructional designers should take the learner's prior knowledge into account. Prior knowledge is not a dichotomous variable in which students are either novices or experts. Effective instruction can help students develop domain knowledge in a way that helps them move along the path towards expertise. However, the consensus among cognitive scientists is that it takes 10 years of sustained study to become an expert in a domain, so it is unlikely that many K–12 students have reached expert status in many school domains. Similarly, I do not understand exactly what you mean by "such curriculum designs" but I certainly agree that it would be useful to have clear instructional objectives.

Question: Duschl and Duncan. *What do you mean by discovery? Please give an example of the kind of instructional practices that involve only discovery.*

Reply: Mayer. Pure discovery refers to instructional methods in which the student works on a learning task with minimal teacher guidance. I provide the following examples based on my observations of K–12 classrooms over the years. First, in an elementary school computer lab a teacher shows students how to use some basic LOGO commands such as FORWARD, BACK, RIGHT, LEFT, PENUP and PENDOWN. Then, students are seated in front of a computer and told to make some drawings and save their programs. The goal of the lesson is to help students learn how to write efficient computer programs that include modularity, although good programming design is never explicitly taught. Research on LOGO learning shows that when students are allowed to interact with the LOGO machine without much guidance, they generally do not learn how to write efficient programs. Second, in a junior high school mathematics class, the teacher spends a few minutes describing graphing of linear functions. Then, students are seated in groups of four and given a set of graphing problems to solve through group discussion without teacher intervention for the next 30 minutes. Research on cooperative learning shows that this form of discovery learning is not particularly effective. My point is that teachers sometimes interpret the call using for constructivist methods to mean that they should proudly use ineffective methods such as those I described above.

Question: Duschl and Duncan. *You also have little to say about motivation for learning. Why is your approach devoid of scientific practices that involve (1) stimulating and motivating cognitive activities addressing scientific reasoning (e.g., asking questions, choosing measurements, distinguishing evidence from explanations, refining explanations), and (2) making decisions about or evaluating the status of competing knowledge claims (e.g., establishing criteria to critique scientific methods, measurements, models, and/or explanations)?*

Reply: Mayer. I agree that motivation is a crucial factor in learning, and that any complete theory of learning and instruction must incorporate the role of motivation. We have done some research involving motivation (and metacognition), and I appreciate the friendly suggestion to do more. I am certainly not opposed to "stimulating and motivating cognitive activities." I am simply pointing out that all hands-on activities are not necessarily "stimulating and motivating cognitive activities" (and in fact, many hands-on activities can be unproductive), whereas all passive instruction methods (such as reading this dialogue) are not necessarily "unstimulating and unmotivating cognitive activities." Similarly, I am all for "making decisions about or evaluating the status of competing knowledge claims," but again I am simply pointing out that when the learners are novices they may need considerable guidance from the teacher in the course of developing these scientific reasoning skills.

Question: Wise and O'Neill. *In your chapter, you make the important point that in designing instruction from a constructivist perspective on learning, our focus* should be on the cognitive interactions that we want students to engage in, not on surface indications of behavioral activity. On that point we think all would agree—learners can certainly participate in a behavioral activity (for example, a class discussion) without engaging in the kinds of cognitive activities that lead to desired learning. But many constructivists would point out that this doesn't mean that learners are being cognitively inactive—learners will construct some understanding of a situation, regardless of how well or poorly it is designed. The question is whether or not it is a viable understanding that is relevant to the learning goals for the environment.

Following from this perspective, we believe that two important factors to consider in instruction are (a) support for developing appropriate learner goals, and (b) opportunities for learners to test the viability of their constructed understanding. To our way of thinking, these two factors may be important in distinguishing a constructivist perspective from an information-processing one. How do you see it?

Reply: Mayer. I certainly agree with everything you say in the first paragraph. However, regarding the core question, in the second paragraph, I am not sure what you mean by "support for developing appropriate learner goals" and "opportunities for learners to test the viability of their constructed understanding." I am also not sure what you mean by saying that "these two factors may be important in distinguishing between the constructivist perspective and an information-processing one." Finally, my major problem with this question is that it does not specify the difference between the constructivist and information-processing perspective, as there are many versions of each perspective. In my own writing on the information-processing perspective, I distinguish between the classic view and the constructivist view; in my own writing on constructivism, I distinguish between cognitive constructivism and radical constructivism. I show that the constructivist and information-processing perspectives can be reconciled with one another, so perhaps there is no need to try to distinguish the perspectives. Overall, the search for "schools of learning" has been an unproductive approach for the science of learning. In my opinion, our field would be better served by trying to figure out research-based answers to how learning and instruction work rather than by engaging in high-level philosophical arguments about which "ism" is best.

Question: Wise and O'Neill. *Your chapter focuses on the design of instructional materials. However, we and others have argued that a constructivist approach to instruction is not defined primarily by the kind of instructional resources involved, but more importantly by the context framing their use—for instance setting up goals for students in working with the materials and having teachers give real-time responsive support. In our chapter, we discuss the Jasper Woodbury series as a good illustration of constructivist instructional design in which the materials are not intended to be complete and self-sufficient. What do you see as an ideal context of use for the kind of multimedia learning resources you design? How do you see this context as important in determining what students learn from these multimedia learning resources?*

Reply: Mayer. I agree that context is an important consideration in instructional design, and that anchored instruction, for example, is an intriguing idea. You mention the Jasper Woodbury series as a good illustration of constructivist instructional design, and I agree that it received a lot of attention. In many ways it epitomizes what many scholars see as constructivist teaching; however, the instruction requires a lot of valuable class time (including a lot of discussion within peer groups). In my opinion, it is fair to ask, "Does it work better than well-designed direct instruction?" In short, it is fair to ask, "Where is the scientific evidence that using the Jasper series helps students to understand mathematical problem solving better than other kinds of well-designed instruction?". An important—but unanswered—question about Jasper concerns how and when to incorporate teacher guidance into the lesson.

Question: Wise and O'Neill. *Do you agree that there are important limits to what can be taught explicitly? Do you see a unique value for social interaction in the learning process that is not replicable by static tools and materials? If so, how would you describe it?*

Reply: Mayer. This is a worthwhile research question. To date, I am not impressed with the available evidence concerning the instructional value of social interaction.

In conclusion, the research community represented in this book is engaged in the worthwhile task of understanding how learning works and how to foster learning. In my opinion, we are most likely to make progress (a) if we attempt to test specific theories of how learning and instruction work rather than by seeking to determine which "ism" is best, and (b) if we base our arguments on evidence from rigorous scientific research rather than on quotations based on the opinions of experts.

[Mayer's replies were shortened and edited by the editors.]

Note

1   There are many varieties of constructivism, ranging from cognitive constructivism to social constructivism to radical constructivism but in my opinion searching for the perfect "ism" is an unproductive activity for educational researchers (Mayer, 1997). In this chapter, I focus on a basic version of cognitive constructivism that I define as a "theory of learning in which learners build knowledge in their working memory by engaging in appropriate cognitive processing during learning" (Mayer, in press). For purposes of this chapter, the main features of constructivism are:

- who—the learner
- what—builds knowledge structures
- where—in working memory
- how—by engaging in active cognitive processing
- when—during learning.

In short, constructivism is a theory of learning in which the learner builds knowledge structures in working memory by engaging in active cognitive processing during learning.

This vision of how learning works has its roots in the classic cognitive constructivist theories of Piaget (1970), Bartlett (1932), and Wertheimer (1959), particularly their emphasis on schema construction. Similarly, this vision of how learning works is reflected in modern learning theories such as the cognitive theory of multimedia learning (Mayer, 2001; Mayer & Moreno, 2003) and cognitive-load theory (Sweller, 1999, 2005), particularly their emphasis on active cognitive processing in working memory during learning. For example, Mayer (2001, 2008) identified three major cognitive processes in this view of learning as knowledge construction: (a) *selecting*—attending to relevant information that enters the cognitive system through the eyes and ears; (b) *organizing*—mentally arranging the selected material into coherent cognitive structures; and (c) *integrating*—mentally integrating the incoming material with prior knowledge activated from long-term memory. According to this basic version of constructivist learning theory, active learning (or meaningful learning) requires all three of these processes whereas passive learning (or rote learning) requires only a minimal amount of selecting and organizing.

References

Bartlett, F. C. (1932). *Remembering: A study in experimental and social psychology.* Cambridge: Cambridge University Press.

Bransford, J. D., Brown, A. L., & Cocking, R. R. (Eds.). (1999). *How people learn.* Washington, DC: National Academy Press.

Chen, Z., & Klahr, D. (1999). All other things being equal: Acquisition and transfer of the control of variable strategy. *Child Development, 70,* 1098–1120.

Clark, R. C., & Mayer, R. E. (2008). *e-Learning and the science of instruction* (2nd ed). San Francisco: Pfeiffer.

Clark, R. E. (1989). When teaching kills learning: Research on mathematics. In H. N. Mandl, N. Bennett, E. de Corte, & H. F. Freidrich (Eds.), *Learning and instruction: European research in an international context* (Vol. 2, pp. 1–22). London: Pergamon.

Cooper, G., & Sweller, J. (1987). Effects of schema acquisition and rule automation on mathematical problem-solving transfer. *Journal of Educational Psychology, 79,* 347–362.

de Jong, Ton (2005). The guided discovery principle in multimedia learning. In R. E. Mayer (Ed.), *The Cambridge handbook of multimedia learning* (pp. 215–228). New York: Cambridge University Press.

de Jong, T., & van Joolingen, W. R. (1998). Scientific discovery learning with computer simulations of conceptual domains. *Review of Educational Research, 68,* 179–203.

Fay, A. L., & Mayer, R. E. (1994). Benefits of teaching design skills before teaching LOGO computer programming: Evidence for syntax-independent learning. *Journal of Educational Computing Research, 11,* 185–208.

Gelman, R. (1969). Conservation acquisition: A problem of learning to attend to relevant attributes. *Journal of Experimental Child Psychology, 7,* 167–187.

Hmelo-Silver, C. E., Duncan, R. G., & Chinn, C. A. (2007). Scaffolding and achievement in problem-based and inquiry learning: A response to Kirschner, Sweller, and Clark (2006). *Educational Psychologist, 42,* 99–108.

Kalyuga, S. (2005). The prior knowledge principle in multimedia learning. In R. E. Mayer (Ed.), *The Cambridge handbook of multimedia learning* (pp. 325–338). New York: Cambridge University Press.

Kirschner, P. A., Sweller, J., & Clark, R. E. (2006). Why minimal guidance during instruction does not work: An analysis of the failure of constructivist, discovery, problem-based, experiential, and inquiry-based teaching. *Educational Psychologist, 41,* 75–86.

Kittel, J. E. (1957). An experimental study of the effect of external direction during learning on transfer and retention of principles. *Journal of Educational Psychology, 48,* 391–405.

Klahr, D. (2005). Early science instruction: Addressing fundamental issues. *Psychological Science, 16,* 871–872.

Klahr, D., & Nigam, M. (2004). The equivalence of learning paths in early science instruction. *Psychological Science, 15,* 661–667.

Kuhn, D. (2007). Is direct instruction an answer to the right question? *Educational Psychologist, 42,* 109–114.

Kuhn, D., & Dean, D. (2005). Is developing scientific thinking all about learning to control variables? *Psychological Science, 16,* 866–870.

Kurland, D. M., & Pea, R. D. (1985). Chidren's mental models of recursive LOGO programs. *Journal of Educational Computing Research, 1,* 235–244.

Littlefield, J., Delclos, V. R., Lever, S., Clayton, K. N., Bransford, J. D., & Franks, J. J. (1988). Learning LOGO: Method of teaching, transfer of general skills, and attitudes toward school and computers. In R. E. Mayer (Ed.), *Teaching and learning computer programming* (pp. 111–136). Hillsdale, NJ: Erlbaum.

Mayer, R. E. (1997). Searching for the perfect ism: An unproductive activity for educational research. *Issues in Education, 3,* 225–228.

Mayer, R. E. (2001). *Multimedia learning.* New York: Cambridge University Press.

Mayer, R. E. (2004). Should there be a three-strikes rule against pure discovery learning? The case for guided methods of instruction. *American Psychologist, 59,* 14–19.

Mayer, R. E. (2005). Cognitive theory of multimedia learning. In R. E. Mayer (Ed.), *The Cambridge handbook of multimedia learning* (pp. 31–48). New York: Cambridge University Press.

Mayer, R. E. (2008). *Learning and instruction* (2nd ed). Upper Saddle River, NJ: Pearson Merrill Prentice Hall.

Mayer, R. E. (in press). Constructivism: Discovery learning. In E. M. Anderman (Ed.), *Psychology of classroom learning: An encyclopedia.* Farmington Hills, MI: Thompson Gale.

Mayer, R. E., & Moreno, R. (2003). Nine ways to reduce cognitive load in multimedia learning. *Educational Psychologist, 38,* 43–52.

Piaget, J. (1970). *Science of education and psychology of the child.* New York: Oxford University Press.

Renkl, A. (2005). The worked-out example principle in multimedia learning. In R. E. Mayer (Ed.), *The Cambridge handbook of multimedia learning* (pp. 229–245). New York: Cambridge University Press.

Schmidt, H. G., Loyens, S. M. M., van Gog, T., & Paas, F. (2007). Problem-based learning is compatible with human cognitive architecture: Commentary on Kirschner, Sweller, and Clark (2006). *Educational Psychologist, 42,* 91–98.

Shulman, L. S., & Keislar, E. R. (1966). *Learning by discovery: A critical appraisal.* Chicago, IL: Rand-McNally.

Sweller, J. (1999). *Instructional design in technical areas.* Camberwell, Australia: ACER Press.

Sweller, J. (2005). Implications of cognitive load theory for multimedia learning. In R. E. Mayer (Ed.), *The Cambridge handbook of multimedia learning* (pp. 19–30). New York: Cambridge University Press.

Sweller, J., & Cooper, G. A. (1985). The use of worked examples as a substitute for problem solving in learning algebra. *Cognition and Instruction, 2,* 59–89.

Sweller, J., Kirschner, P. A., & Clark, R. E. (2007). Why minimally guided teaching techniques do not work: A reply to commentaries. *Educational Psychologist, 42,* 115–121.

Wertheimer, M. (1959). *Productive thinking.* New York: Harper & Row.

11 The Empirical Support for Direct Instruction

Barak Rosenshine University of Illinois, Champaign Urbana

In the article that stimulated the debate at the 2007 meeting of the American Educational Research Association which, in turn, led to this volume, Kirschner, Sweller, and Clark (2006) concluded that direct instructional guidance was superior in effects to "minimal guidance during instruction." But Kirschner et al. (2006) only gave a few examples of direct instructional guidance. They noted the value of modeling, of teaching self-checking procedures, of including many examples, of using worked examples, and of using process worksheets.

However, in addition to these examples, there is a large research-based literature on the instructional procedures that comprise direct instruction and direct instructional guidance and I believe that these procedures fit the cognitive theory on information processing described by Kirschner et al. (2006). These instructional procedures come from two areas of research: the process–product studies of classroom instruction (Medley & Mitzel, 1963; Brophy & Good, 1986; Rosenshine & Stevens, 1986) and the research on teaching cognitive strategies (Rosenshine & Meister, 1992).

Process–Product Studies of Classroom Instruction

Process–product research on teaching (Medley & Mitzel, 1963) refers to a series of observational studies of classroom instruction. The original research studied the correlations between teacher behavior and measures of student achievement gain (Brophy & Good, 1986; Rosenshine & Stevens, 1986) and this correlational research has been followed by experimental studies (Gage & Needles, 1989). The work has been called process–product research on teaching (Medley & Mitzel, 1963) because of the original focus on correlations. Although this research was primarily conducted from 1955 to 1985, there has been no observational or correlational research on instruction since that time that has invalidated these findings.

The goal of the process–product research on instruction was to identify the instructional procedures that were used by those teachers whose students made the highest gains on standardized tests or tests developed by the research team and to compare these instructional procedures with the procedures used by those teachers whose students made the smallest gains on the same tests.

Design of the Studies

In this research (see Brophy & Good, 1986; Rosenshine & Stevens, 1986) the investigators first gave pretests to students and after a period of instruction, such as a semester, post-tests were administered to a number of classrooms, usually 20 to 30. These assessments were usually in reading or mathematics. Some of the tests were standardized and others were developed by the experimenter (Brophy & Good, 1986). After making appropriate adjustments for the initial ability of the students, the investigators identified those teachers whose classes made the highest achievement gain in the subject being studied and those teachers whose classes made the least gain.

During the study, observers sat in these classrooms, and observed and recorded the frequency with which those teachers used various instructional behaviors. The observers usually recorded the number and type of questions, the quality of the student answers, and the responses of a teacher to a student's answers. Many investigators also recorded how much time was spent in activities such as review, presentation, guided practice, and supervising seatwork. Some investigators recorded how the teachers prepared students for seatwork and homework. Other observers recorded the frequency and type of praise, and the frequency, type, and context of criticism. The overall attention level of the class, and sometimes of individual students, was also recorded. This information was then used to describe how the most successful teachers were different from their less successful colleagues, and these results are described in this chapter.

These correlational studies were sometimes followed by experimental studies (Gage & Needles, 1989; Brophy & Good, 1986; Rosenshine & Stevens, 1986) in which the investigators developed a manual for teaching based, in part, on findings from the correlational studies. For example, the work of Good and Grouws began with a correlational study (Good & Grouws, 1977), and they then applied their findings in an experimental study (Good & Grouws, 1979). One group of teachers in this study received a manual that contained a set of instructional procedures that were found to be correlated with student achievement gains in the process–product study. The experimental teachers were taught to use these behaviors in their teaching while the control teachers were asked to continue their regular teaching. These studies have shown that the teachers who received the manual performed many of the suggested instructional procedures. For example, in the study by Good and Grouws (1979) teachers in the experimental group assigned homework 66% of the time compared to 13% of the time for the control group.

The majority of these experimental studies (Gage & Needles, 1989) showed that the teachers in the experimental groups used more of the new behaviors they were taught to use, and student post-test scores in their classrooms, adjusted by regression for their initial scores, were significantly higher than scores in classrooms taught by the control teachers. Those who observed classrooms did not begin with any specific theoretical orientation.

Direct Instruction

McDonald and Elias (1976) looked at patterns of the results in one of their studies and wrote that the successful teachers used a pattern that they called "direct instruction," a term which Rosenshine (1976) also used to describe the actions of teachers in these studies whose students were high achievers. Others (e.g., Stanovich, 1980) have used the term "explicit teaching." Morrison (1926) used the term "systematic teaching" to refer to a method of instruction that included corrective teaching and re-teaching to mastery. Katz (1994) also used the term "systematic instruction" to refer to the explicit sequencing of instruction and the emphasis upon providing guided practice.

Unfortunately, however, some contemporary authors (e.g., Kuhn, 2007; Stein, 1999) have used direct instruction to refer to any instruction led by a teacher regardless of how systematic or unsystematic the instruction was. They may not be aware of the specific, research-based use of the term direct instruction.

Six Teaching Functions

Rosenshine and Stevens (1986) grouped the results from the process–product research on teaching into six functions.

1 Daily Review

Effective teachers in these studies began their lesson with a 5–8 minute review which included a short review of previously covered material, correction of homework, and determining the prior knowledge relevant to the day's lesson. These reviews ensured that the students have a firm grasp of the prerequisite skills for the day's lesson. The teachers' activities included reviewing the concepts and skills necessary to do the homework; having students correct each other's papers; asking about points at which the students had difficulty or made errors; and reviewing or providing additional practice on facts and skills that need overlearning.

One example of effective daily review is in the Exemplary Center for Reading Instruction (ECRI) reading program (American Federation of Teachers, 1998). In this program, 5 minutes are spent in daily review of sight words—words from prior stories and words from forthcoming stories in their reader. The teacher presents the word lists and the students say the words, in unison, and, when necessary, they re-read the lists until the reading is fluent. The students read at the rate of a word a second, which makes it possible for a class to review 150 sight words in less than 4 minutes.

Daily review was also part of a successful experiment in elementary-school mathematics (Good & Grouws, 1979). It was found, in this study, that teachers in the control group, who had said that they conducted review every day, actually did so on only 50% of the days they were observed. The teachers in the more successful experimental group, who had received training in daily review, conducted review and checked homework on 80% of the days they were observed.

The importance of daily review can also be justified by the research on human cognitive architecture. As Chase and Chi (1980) noted, the development of expertise requires practice, thousands of hours of practice. The practice of recalling previous learning can serve to strengthen the connections in our knowledge structures, and can thus help us to recall that material effortlessly and automatically.

Daily practice of vocabulary can lead to seeing the words as a unit, rather than as individual letters (Laberge & Samuels, 1974). Developing automatic recall in reading and other areas also means that more space is now available in working memory, space that can be used for comprehension. Similarly, Greeno (1978) noted that mathematical problem solving is improved when the basic skills (addition, multiplication, etc.) are overlearned and become automatic, thus freeing processing capacity.

2 Presenting New Material

The most effective teachers in these studies spent more time presenting new material and guiding student practice than the less effective teachers (Evertson, Anderson, Anderson, & Brophy, 1980; Good & Grouws, 1979). Evertson et al. (1980) found that the most effective mathematics teachers spend about 23 minutes per day in lecture, demonstration, and discussion, in contrast to 11 minutes for the least effective teachers. The more effective teachers used this extra time to provide explanations, give examples, ask questions to check for student understanding, and re-teach material when necessary. In contrast, Evertson et al. (1980) and Good and Grouws (1979) found that the less effective teachers gave shorter presentations and explanations and asked fewer questions. The result of this insufficient preparation showed up during the seatwork. It was found that the students who were not sufficiently prepared made more errors during independent practice.

The more effective teachers also presented new material in small steps (Brophy & Good, 1986). These teachers gave short presentations, provided many examples, and followed this material with guided practice. Only after the students had mastered this material did they proceed to the next step. Dorothy DeLay, an esteemed teacher of violin whose students included Itzhak Perlman, Nadja Salerno-Sonnenberg, and Gil Shaham, made this same point (Kozinn, 2002) when she recommended to violin teachers that they should first analyze the problem, and then simplify the task into steps so that the student can succeed and not be overwhelmed by its difficulties.

Effective teachers also stopped to check for student understanding. They did this by asking questions about the material; they asked students to summarize the presentation to that point or to repeat directions or procedures, or asked students whether they agreed or disagreed with other students' answers. This checking has two purposes: answering the questions might cause the students to elaborate upon the material they learned and augment connections to other learning in their long-term memory; checking for understanding can also tell the teacher when parts of the material need to be re-taught.

Limiting the amount of material the students receive at one time and facilitating the processing of the new material fits the research on the limitations of our working memory (Miller, 1956; Norman & Brokow, 1975) so that it will not be taxed by too much material at one time.

3 Guiding Student Practice

As Chase and Chi (1980) and Frederiksen (1984) have noted, we need to spend time rephrasing, elaborating, and summarizing new material so that it can be stored in long-term memory. Making connections with prior knowledge in long-term memory through tasks such as rephrasing and summarization facilitate later retrieval and use of this information.

Brophy and Good (1986), Rosenshine and Stevens (1986), and Good and Grouws (1979) found that the most effective teachers met this need for processing new material by providing guided and supervised practice. During guided practice the teachers supervised students' initial practice on a skill, corrected errors, and provided the active practice and elaboration that are necessary to move new learning into long-term memory. Teacher questions and student discussion were a major way of providing this practice. Questions also allowed a teacher to check for understanding, that is, to determine how well the material has been learned and whether there is a need for additional instruction.

A number of correlational studies (e.g., Stallings & Kaskowitz, 1974) have shown that the more effective teachers asked more questions than were asked by the less effective teachers. In a correlational study of junior high school mathematics instruction (Evertson et al., 1980), the most effective teachers asked an average of 24 questions during a 50-minute period, whereas the least effective teachers asked only 8.6 questions. The most effective teachers asked six process questions (questions that ask the students to explain the process they used to answer the question) during each observed period, whereas the least effective teachers asked only 1.3 process questions.

In the experimental study by Good & Grouws (1979), teachers were taught to use a high frequency of questions during guided practice. The students of teachers in the experimental classes in this study achieved higher scores on the post-test than did students of teachers in the control groups. Although most teachers provided some guided practice, the most effective teachers spent more time in guided practice, more time asking questions, more time checking for understanding, more time correcting errors, and more time having students work out problems with teacher guidance.

High Percentage of Correct Answers

Effective teachers had a high success rate when they asked questions (Fisher et al., 1978). In a study of fourth-grade mathematics, Good and Grouws (1979) found that 82% of students' answers were correct in the classrooms of the most successful teachers, whereas the least successful teachers had a success rate of 73%. The optimal success rate appears to be about 75–80% during guided practice (Brophy

& Good, 1986), suggesting that the effective teachers combine both success and sufficient challenge. The most effective teachers obtained this success level by "teaching in small steps" (Brophy & Good, 1986), that is, by using a combination of short presentations and supervised student practice and by providing sufficient practice on each part before proceeding to the next step.

4 Provide Feedback and Corrections

Student errors are a particular problem in instruction because early errors that are not corrected might be stored as errors in long-term memory and, later, retrieved as errors (Guzzetti, Snyder, Glass, & Gamas, 1993). When students made an error the more effective teachers helped them by simplifying the question, providing hints, or re-teaching the material. The less effective teachers, however, often supplied the correct answer and then moved on to the next student. Apparently, such practice may not be sufficient to correct the error.

During questioning, when a student was correct but hesitant, many of the more successful teachers also provided process feedback (Good & Grouws, 1979). Teachers might say such things as "Yes that's right, because ..." and then the teacher would re-explain the process needed to arrive at the correct answer. By providing an additional explanation or repetition of the process in this manner, the teacher provided students with the additional learning that the hesitant student appeared to need.

In a review of effective college teaching, Kulik and Kulik (1979) found that instruction is more effective when (a) students receive immediate feedback on their examinations, and (b) students have to do additional study and take another test when their quiz scores do not reach a set criterion.

5 Conduct Independent Practice

In typical teacher-led classrooms, guided practice is followed by independent practice—by students working alone and practicing the new material. This independent practice is necessary because a good deal of practice (overlearning) is needed in order to attain fluency and automaticity in a skill (Laberge & Samuels, 1974; Anderson, 1982). When students become fluent, automatic working memory is taxed minimally and students can then devote more attention to comprehension and application. Independent practice provides students with the additional review and elaboration they need to become fluent in a skill, such as dividing decimals, reading a map, conjugating a regular verb in a foreign language, completing and balancing a chemical equation. This need for fluency also applies to facts, concepts, and discriminations that must be used in subsequent learning. Students usually work alone during this seatwork. But unfortunately, Stallings and Kaskowitz (1974) and others found that students were least engaged when they were working alone and more engaged when they were in a setting led by a teacher.

Fisher et al. (1978), who conducted an extensive process–product study of second-grade reading and mathematics instruction, found that teachers who spent more time in guided practice also had students who were more engaged during seatwork. This finding suggests that when teachers provided sufficient instruction during guided practice the students were better prepared for the seatwork. Similarly, Fisher et al. (1978) also found that classrooms where the teachers had to stop at students' desks and provide a great deal of explanation during seatwork were also classrooms where the error rates on students' papers were highest. Having to stop and provide explanations during seatwork suggests that the initial explanation and guided practice were not sufficient. Sometimes, it may be appropriate for a teacher to practice some of the homework problems with the entire class before the students take the work home or engage in independent practice. Fisher et al. (1978) also found that students were more engaged when their teacher circulated around the room and monitored and supervised their seatwork. However, the optimal time for these contacts was 30 seconds or less. The need for longer contacts, as noted, was a sign that the guided practice had not been sufficient. But such independent practice may not be effective unless students receive sufficient instruction before this practice begins.

6 Weekly and Monthly Review

Some of the successful programs in elementary schools provided for frequent review. In the successful experimental study that Good and Grouws (1979) conducted, teachers in the experimental group were asked to review the previous week's work every Monday and the previous month's work every fourth Monday. These reviews and tests were intended to provide the additional practice that students needed (Frederiksen, 1984; Laberge & Samuels, 1974; Pellegrino & Glaser, 1980) in order to become skilled and successful performers. Review can serve to reinstate and elaborate prior learning, and can also strengthen and extend connections within cognitive structure. Review, then, may help students develop patterns and unify their knowledge, and review can enhance the development of automaticity (Laberge & Samuels, 1974). When discussing how expertise is acquired, Chase and Chi (1980) wrote: "The most obvious answer is practice, thousands of hours of practice ... for the most part practice is by far the best predictor of performance" (p. 12).

Summary

In this research, the more effective teachers typically began a class with a review of prior material and practice of prerequisite skills. Then, new material was taught in small steps, with short presentations that were followed by practice or questions. After the presentation, the teacher guided the students as they practiced the new skill and continued this guidance until all students had been checked and received feedback. Guided practice was followed by independent practice, which was continued until students could perform the new skill independently and fluently.

Instruction in new material begins with full teacher control, and the teacher diminishes control throughout the lesson so that at the end students are working independently. This progression moves from teacher modeling, through guided practice using prompts and cues, to independent and fluent performance by the students. At each step there is a need to monitor student learning, guide student practice, and provide additional support when they need it. But as students exhibit more mastery, the teacher increasingly diminishes control. Palincsar and Brown (1984) also applied this progression of diminishing control in their work on reciprocal teaching.

The Teaching of Ill-Structured Tasks

These findings from the process–product research on classroom instruction are very useful when we can divide a task into series of explicit steps and guide students as they practice on those steps. But how does one teach tasks that cannot be broken into explicit steps, such as reading comprehension, writing, and mathematical and scientific problem solving?

A new line of research, aimed at teaching these ill-structured tasks, began in the 1970s and flourished in the 1980s (Pressley et al., 1995). The emphasis in this new approach was on providing students with guides and supports that can help them master the task. As shown in Pressley et al. (1995), many of the studies that provided and taught these guides and supports were quite successful—as measured by standardized tests and experimenter-developed tests—in helping students improve their abilities in ill-structured tasks such as reading comprehension, writing, and the ability to learn new science material.

Identifying Expert Processes

One approach to developing these guides and supports was to identify the cognitive strategies that experts used (Kintsch & van Dijk, 1978; Bereiter & Bird, 1985; Larkin & Reif, 1976) and then teach these strategies to students. The strategies were identified by giving experts problems to solve and asking them to think aloud as they attempted to solve these problems. Kintsch and van Dijk (1978) studied the processes experts were using to summarize text. Bereiter and Bird (1985) presented difficult and ambiguous reading passages to expert readers and then asked these readers to think aloud as they attempted to comprehend the passages. Larkin and Reif (1976) studied expert problem solvers in physics and identified the procedures they used.

The researchers then developed and tested an instructional program based on these expert responses. Kintsch and van Dijk (1978) successfully taught the summarizing procedures they identified to new students, and many other investigators (e.g., Palincsar & Brown, 1984) have taught these same procedures in their studies. Bereiter and Bird developed a program based on the strategies the experts used, and they taught these strategies to one group of average readers. At the end of the study, the trained readers significantly outperformed the control students on a standardized test in reading. Bereiter and Bird's (1985) guides were also taught as part of Anderson's (1991) reading program for teenage problem readers, and her program has obtained similar significant results on standardized tests. Larkin and Reif (1976) taught the expert procedures they identified to physics students. In all three studies the achievement scores of novices who were taught these procedures were superior to scores of students in a control group.

In another effort to improve reading comprehension, many investigators taught students to ask themselves questions starting with "who," "how," "what," "why," and "when" about the material in the paragraphs and passages they were reading. It was hoped that in the process of asking questions students would learn to search the text, read more carefully and, thus, improve their reading comprehension. Palincsar and Brown (1984) suggested that students who participated in asking questions were engaging in "comprehension-fostering activities." Thus, although reading comprehension is an ill-structured task, investigators attempted to overcome this problem by modeling and teaching comprehension-fostering strategies to the students. As a result of this instruction and practice in asking questions, a number of studies showed that student reading-comprehension scores improved when students were tested on new passages (Rosenshine, Chapman, & Meister, 1996).

Scaffolds and Instructional Supports

Investigators also attempted to teach ill-structured tasks by providing students with additional scaffolds, or instructional supports (Tobias, 1982), in order to reduce the initial difficulty of the task (Collins, Brown, & Newman, 1990). Scaffolds help bridge the gap between the students' current abilities and the goal. These scaffolds are gradually withdrawn as learners become more independent, although students may continue to rely on scaffolds when they encounter particularly difficult problems. One might look at scaffolds as an extended form of guided practice for the teaching of ill-structured tasks. Kirschner et al. (2006) referred to this practice as "direct instructional guidance."

A teacher modeling how to ask a question is an example of a scaffold. This modeling, and support for students when they attempt the task, helps students to develop their own questions. This modeling is withdrawn as students become more competent. Thinking aloud by the teacher is another scaffold. A list of scaffolds that have been used in these studies and the citation of studies in which they appeared are listed below. In each of these studies the outcome measure was student achievement on either a standardized test or an experimenter-developed test. Significant results, favoring the experimental group, were obtained in each of the 13 studies associated with these 10 instructional procedures.

1. Modeling the use of strategy by the teacher (King, 1994; Raphael & Pearson, 1985).
2. Thinking aloud by the teacher as choices were made (Anderson, 1991; Schoenfeld, 1985).
3. Providing cue cards of specific prompts to help students carry out the strategy (Englert, Raphael, Anderson, Anthony, & Stevens, 1991; Singer & Donlan, 1982).
4. Dividing the task into smaller components, teaching each component

separately, and gradually combining the components into a whole process (Palincsar, 1987; Dermody, 1988).
5. Anticipating student errors (Brady, 1990).
6. Completing part of the task for students (King, 1991; Blaha, 1979).
7. Providing models of completed work (Palincsar & Brown, 1984).
8. Providing for reciprocal teaching by teacher and students (Palincsar, 1987).
9. Providing check lists (Rinehart, Stahl, & Erickson, 1986).
10. Suggesting fix-up strategies when errors were made (Bereiter & Bird, 1985).

This new focus on cognitive strategies and scaffolding resulted in a number of studies that were successful in improving students' achievement on the complex tasks of reading comprehension, mathematical problem solving, writing, science problem solving, and study skills (Pressley et al., 1995).

Rosenshine et al. (1996) summarized the results of 26 studies in which students were taught to generate questions about their reading and then practiced using this procedure as they read. Students in the control group continued their normal classroom reading activities. The results of this treatment were assessed using standardized tests or experimenter-developed tests. Rosenshine et al. (1996) found that when teaching students to generate questions about their reading, the studies had a median effect size of 0.82 when experimenter-developed comprehension tests were used as an outcome measure. Such an effect size means that a student at the 50th percentile of the experimental group would have scored in the 80th percentile of the control group. When standardized tests were used, the median effect size was 0.32, which means that the average student in the 50th percentile of the experimental group would have scored in the 63rd percentile of the control group.

Palincsar and Brown (1984, 1989) suggested that reading comprehension might be improved if students learned and practiced four "comprehension-fostering" strategies: asking questions, summarizing, using the text to predict what might happen next, and attempting to clarify unclear words. The students were taught these four strategies and then worked in groups to practice the four strategies on new material using a method they called "reciprocal teaching." A number of subsequent studies used the reciprocal-teaching format. When experimenter-developed tests were used in these studies, the results were usually statistically significant and the average effect size was 0.88 (which means that the average student in the experimental group would have scored at the 81st percentile in the control group) (Rosenshine & Meister, 1994). When standardized tests were used, the average effect size was 0.32 (which means that the average student in the experimental group would have scored in the 63rd percentile of the control group).

Hirsch (2006), however, noted that in the reciprocal-teaching studies reviewed by Rosenshine and Meister (1994) the number of instructional sessions ranged from 6 to 25, and teaching more sessions did not result in higher achievement gain (see Rosenshine & Meister, 1994, pp. 500, 506). And although 4 to 12 comprehension strategies were taught in the reciprocal-teaching studies, teaching 12 strategies was no more effective than teaching the two strategies of question generation and summarization (Rosenshine & Meister, 1994, pp. 495–496). Hirsch wrote that although teaching reading-comprehension strategies is useful, "Formal comprehension skills can only take students so far. Without broad knowledge, children's reading comprehension will not improve and their scores on reading comprehension tests will not bulge upwards" (Hirsch, 2006, p. 8).

Direct Instruction

A number of investigators referred to their work on the teaching of cognitive strategies as "direct instruction." Dermody (1988) called her work "direct instruction of the specific comprehension strategies of predicting, clarifying, question-generating, and summarizing" (p. 57); and Grajia (1988) referred to her work as "direct instruction of a summarization strategy" (p. 89).

Similar uses of the term "direct instruction" appeared in the descriptions of a number of additional studies in reading comprehension (Berkowitz, 1986; Lonberger, 1988; Weiner, 1978; Baumann, 1984). Students have also received direct instruction in scientific reasoning (Linn, 1977), and in solving physics problems (Larkin & Reif, 1976).

Thus there is an extensive body of research for teaching higher-level tasks and special instructional procedures that were developed to facilitate and support this instruction. These facilitators included the cognitive processes that were used by experts, as well as specific scaffolds and supports that were developed by a number of investigators. These instructional procedures have sometimes been called "direct instruction."

Summary

Kirschner et al. (2006) have argued that constructivist types of teaching do not fit the findings on human cognitive architecture. I have attempted to show that there are two sets of instructional procedures—both of which have been called "direct instruction"—that fit human cognitive architecture and that have been successfully used to teach students both well-structured and ill-structured tasks (Newell & Simon, 1972). One set of instructional procedures, called "process–product" results and "direct instruction," came from the study of the instructional procedures used by those teachers whose students made the highest gains as measured by standardized tests and experimenter-developed tests. The second set of instructional procedures has also been called "direct instruction." These procedures come from the large body of experimental studies, all involving teacher-led instruction, that have been successful in teaching reading comprehension, mathematical problem solving, writing, science problem solving, and study skills as measured by standardized tests and experimenter-developed tests.

There is no conflict between these two sets of instructional procedures, and there is a great deal of overlap. Many of the scaffolds that were used in the cognitive strategy research could be used to facilitate guided practice when teaching topics in well-structured areas. Modeling, thinking aloud, completing part of the task, suggesting fix-up strategies, and anticipating student errors could certainly be used during guided practice when well-structured tasks are being taught.

It should be noted that many of these studies are 30 or more years old and probably predate the graduate study of many constructivist investigators, perhaps explaining why some researchers are unfamiliar with them and cite them so rarely. It should also be noted that the results of these studies have not been refuted, and that many of the procedures can be applied in both traditional and constructivist classrooms.

When the goal is student achievement as measured by standardized tests and experimenter tests then the instructional procedures labeled direct instruction have been shown to be more effective than comparison practices. These instructional procedures are also in harmony with current cognitive theoretical views of learning. The procedures call for instruction in small steps in order to meet the constraints of our working-memory capacity (Miller, 1956). These procedures provide for guidance and scaffolding as students learn new material (Kirschner et al., 2006). They promote high-quantity and high-quality practice, activities that facilitate the development of automatic processing (Laberge & Samuels, 1974). These procedures also promote the accumulation of the vast amounts of information that are a prerequisite of expertise (Chase & Simon, 1973; Chase & Chi, 1980; Frederiksen, 1984; Hirsch, 2006).

Question: Gresalfi and Lester. *You make an important claim that the term "direct instruction" is often used without connecting to the established literature documenting practices that are considered to be elements of this instructional method. We agree that such documentation is crucially important. However, in the review we were surprised that there was no mention of the students themselves in these classrooms. A fervent debate currently rages about the kinds of classroom practices that are associated with teaching diverse communities of students equitably. Echoing the debates in this chapter, some scholars argue that direct instruction is most effective for low SES or minority students. In contrast, others argue that practices involving collective engagement with complex, open problems connected to real-world contexts are more likely to lead to equitable outcomes. The findings you described regarding "effective" practice immediately raised the question of whether direct instruction was beneficial for some students in some schools, but not others.*

Reply: Rosenshine. The report on mathematical education by the National Mathematics Advisory Panel (2008) agrees with Delpit's (1986) position that direct instruction is particularly important for students from low SES backgrounds. The NMAP report noted that "Explicit instruction with children who have mathematical difficulties has shown consistently positive results on performance with word problems and computation." The panel defined explicit instruction to mean

> that teachers provide clear models for solving a problem using an array of examples, students receive extensive practice in the use of newly learned

strategies and skills, students are provided with opportunities to think aloud ... and students are provided with extensive feedback.

(*Education Week*, 2008)

So I believe this report sides with Delpit's (1986) conclusions about the value of direct or explicit instruction. As a result of this report, I wonder whether constructivists would now advocate these explicit instruction practices for children from low SES homes who are learning how to solve word problems in mathematics?

You also asked about the effectiveness of direct instruction for different learners. For reasons of space I did not address that topic in my chapter. In brief, when students are faster or older, or when the material is less difficult, then less time needs to be spent in review and more time can be spent on new material (although we often overestimate how much new material can be learned at a given time). Similarly, in such cases there is less need for guided practice and less need for independent practice in class. More of the independent practice can be done as homework because the students do not need as much help. But even in these situations, it is more efficient to return to small-step instruction when the material becomes difficult.

When learners are younger and slower, or when the material is difficult for all students, then more time ought to be spent in review, less time in presentation of new material, and more time in both guided and independent practice. During independent practice, there should be more supervision and a greater emphasis on all students becoming quick and accurate. When material is particularly difficult, some teachers use a series of cycles of short presentation, guided practice, and independent practice.

Question: Gresalfi and Lester. *It seems crucial that discussions of instructional practice consider learning and performance goals as a central focus. Yet, your discussion of effective teaching practice barely touches on the nature of the learning outcomes that were targeted. In neglecting this topic, the findings that we are comparing are likely to be targeting quite different things. For example, in supporting your argument that frequent review is an important instructional practice, you cite Chase and Chi (1980) who stated that "the most obvious answer is practice, thousands of hours of practice ... for the most part practice is by far the best predictor of performance" (p. 12). Interestingly, nowhere is the nature of this practice discussed. Expert chess players do not become expert by spending many hours reviewing the rules governing the movement of pieces. Indeed, many have been able to master this procedural aspect of the game without ever winning a match. Instead, the nature of the practice involves engagement in the complexities of the actual task; that is, the game of chess, which includes but is not limited to procedural elements. An important question to be addressed therefore relates to whether the kinds of instructional practices that are cited are likely to be related to the kinds of performance that are targeted.*

Reply: Rosenshine. I'm sorry that you concluded that my chapter "barely touches on the nature of the learning outcomes." In fact, my chapter was about instructional behaviors and instructional procedures that were related to student achievement, as measured by standardized tests and experimenter-developed tests. However, I re-read my chapter and I now see that I should have explicitly noted that achievement tests were used in all of the studies I cited in the section "The teaching of ill-structured tasks." I thank Prof. Gresalfi for the opportunity to emphasize that point.

You appear to believe that direct instruction is limited to teaching rules, to teaching well-structured topics, and nothing more. In fact, direct instruction has been and can be a major component in the teaching of ill-structured tasks. For example, there is a plethora of books on chess to help chess players get started. One reason chess books are written and sold is because many believe that the quality of their chess playing, the "nature of practice," can be improved through direct instruction in chess strategies. Of course, such direct instruction is not sufficient to teach winning chess, but the direct instruction in chess books is much more simply stating rules. Direct instruction in chess and other areas can serve to provide the background knowledge and rehearsal that is necessary, although not sufficient, for expert performance.

Reading comprehension is an ill-structured task that cannot be taught directly. But, as I noted in the second part of my chapter, many investigators have attempted to improve students' reading comprehension by developing and teaching cognitive strategies in the hope that learning to use these strategies might lead to improved reading comprehension. These strategies were usually taught to the students using direct instruction.

I agree with you that it is important that students practice "the complexities of the task." But there is a danger that students will learn and practice errors if they practice difficult and complex tasks before they are sufficiently prepared for the activity. The direct-instruction model that emerged from the process–product research suggests that students will do better if they receive extensive guided practice and scaffolding before they practice complex tasks on their own. Reciprocal teaching shows how guided practice can be used to help students learn an ill-structured task and how the guidance is reduced and the demands on the student increased as competency develops.

Guided practice is a major component of the direct-instruction model that emerged from the process–product research. This same guided practice has also been used extensively, in studies where student achievement was the outcome measure, to help students learn ill-structured tasks. This guidance included providing students with scaffolds and supports, with models of completed work, and with suggestions for fix-up strategies. The guidance also included thinking aloud by the teacher, initial completion of part of the task by the teacher, and suggestions for fix-up strategies. Kirschner et al. (2006) referred to this expansion of guided practice as "direct instructional guidance." Other researchers, as I noted in the second half of my chapter, referred to these practices as "direct instruction." Whatever the label, the use of extensive and supervised guided practice has served as a major component, in many studies, for the teaching of ill-structured tasks.

Question: Jonassen. *In your chapter, you reviewed research on the efficacy of questions, review, practice, discovery, and guidance. These are all components that I regularly use in designing problem-based learning environments, albeit in different forms. Why then does our discourse have to devolve into dualistic debates?*

Reply: Rosenshine. I agree. I think we are all using the same mix of instructional procedures. At present, I don't see any inherent conflict between us when we are both interested in helping students obtain gains in achievement on the same standardized test or experimenter-developed test. In reading comprehension, for example, I wonder if there is any difference in principle between the instructional procedures used in reciprocal teaching and those that a constructivist would use to help students improve their reading-comprehension skills.

Question: Jonassen. *The methods that you espouse are effective, in part, because we can isolate the convergent knowledge and/or skills using some form of task analysis. How do you do that for ill-structured problems and tasks that require the integration of different content domains, possess multiple solutions, solution paths, or no solutions at all, and possess multiple criteria for evaluating solutions? Should we simply ignore those in favor of that which we can confidently teach?*

Reply: Rosenshine. I believe that your question reflects a widespread misconception that direct instruction is limited to breaking skills down into specific parts, and that direct instruction is not useful for teaching ill-structured tasks. But the direct-instruction model that emerged from the process–product studies also included guided practice, responses to students, independent practice, and review and, I suggest, all these components are also useful for teaching ill-structured tasks.

There are three areas, in particular, where direct instruction has been used successfully to help students learn ill-structured tasks: providing background knowledge, providing and teaching procedural prompts, and guiding student practice.

- *Providing background knowledge.* A great deal of accessible background knowledge is required for working in ill-structured domains. Frederiksen (1984) wrote that "For medical problems ... good performance was associated primarily with knowledge of medicine" (p. 387) and Chase and Chi (1980) wrote that "long term knowledge underlies skilled performance" (p. 11). Direct instruction has been consistently shown to be an effective way for providing that background knowledge.
- *Providing and teaching the use of procedural prompts.* As I tried to show in the second part of my chapter, there were a number of studies where students were taught prompts and strategies that were intended to serve as supports to help them learn ill-structured tasks such as reading comprehension and writing. I believe that these prompts and the methods used to teach them represent direct instruction.

  For example, in a number of studies students were taught to ask questions about the material they were reading. Rosenshine et al. (1996) reviewed these studies and found that students who were taught to generate questions had higher comprehension scores on standardized tests and experimenter-developed tests than did students in the control groups. Perhaps the process of asking questions led students to read differently, perhaps the process of asking questions led them to search for meaning as they read the paragraph. Students were taught to ask questions through the use of "procedural prompts" (Rosenshine & Meister, 1992). In some studies (e.g., Palincsar & Brown, 1984), students were given the prompts of "who," "what," "why," and "where" as guides to help them ask questions. I believe that these prompts are a form of direct instruction.

I contend that the development of these prompts, and instruction in the use of these prompts, represents a form of direct instruction that has been successful in helping students learn new skills in the ill-structured areas of reading, writing, and learning science material.

- *Guiding student practice.* A good deal of guided practice occurred as students were learning to use these prompts. Guided practice, as I noted, was part of the process–product model of direct instruction. King (1994) developed questioning prompts and wrote that "direct explanation, modeling, cognitive coaching, scaffolding, and feedback" (p. 33) was used to guide student practice in the use of these prompts. In King's studies, teachers guided students and gradually shifted responsibility to the students through four steps: the teacher thought aloud and modeled using the prompt to ask a question; the teacher asked for student input while she used a prompt to ask a question; students generated several questions with teacher help; and students generated questions independently. Thus, even when the components of a task cannot be broken down with task analysis, the prompts, guided practice, corrections, independent practice, and overlearning functions of direct instruction are still available and useful to help students learn ill-structured tasks. Kirschner et al. (2006) labeled this focus on guiding student practice during the learning of ill-structured tasks as "direct instructional guidance."

Reaction to Rosenshine's response: Jonassen. *First, my assumptions. I have argued that constructive learning is most likely engaged and embodied in problems to be solved. The conceptual glue that binds constructionist, project-based, and inquiry-based learning is a problem to solve. That is why all of my research focused on problem solving. Given that, I certainly agree with you that "direct instruction is much more than the analysis of a task." However, direct instruction, by its very nature, relies on some form of task analysis. Direct instruction aims to teach an articulated skill or body of information. How can you teach what you cannot identify? However, many problems, such as dilemmas, have no known solution at all. I question whether it is possible to directly teach such ambiguous outcomes. Although it is possible to analyze and articulate the many perspectives on such problems, their solution requires learner commitments and knowledge construction.*

The reality is that direct instruction and inquiry-based learning are more analogous than polemicists believe. I advocate multiple forms of analysis for designing problem-based learning environments, including analysis of causal relationships, analogous case structures, activity systems, and so on. And a number of our recent studies have examined the use of question prompts for engaging different forms of reasoning. Perhaps the most significant difference between direct and problem-based learning (especially for ill-structured problems) is the way that learning is assessed. When no accepted or "correct" answer exists, how can we assess student production or reproduction? Instead, we assess students' ability to generate an argument supporting the viability of their solution. Because multiple solutions to a problem may exist, we can best infer students' understanding by their abilities to make predictions and inferences and assemble those into an argument justifying their solution. I am focusing more on supporting basic cognitive skills, including analogical and causal reasoning and argumentation. Those skills may be direct taught or may be scaffolded in learning environments with various tools. The irony of this dialectic is that we seem to be using different lexicons to describe similar processes. So rather than crossing sophomoric swords, we should explore how we can collaborate to resolve the genomic complexities of learning.

References

American Federation of Teachers. (1998). *Building on the best, learning from What Works: Seven promising reading and English language arts programs.* Washington, DC: American Federation of Teachers.

Anderson, J. R. (1982). *Cognitive skills and their acquisition.* Hillsdale, NJ: Erlbaum.

Anderson, V. (1991, April). *Training teachers to foster active reading strategies in reading-disabled adolescents.* Paper presented at the annual meeting of the American Educational Research Association, Chicago.

Baumann, J. F. (1984). The effectiveness of a direct instruction paradigm for teaching main idea comprehension. *Reading Research Quarterly, 20*(1), 93–115.

Bereiter, C., & Bird, M. (1985). Use of thinking aloud in identification and teaching of reading comprehension strategies. *Cognition and Instruction, 2,* 131–156.

Berkowitz, S. (1986). Effects of instruction in text organization on sixth-grade students memory for expository reading. *Reading Research Quarterly, 21,* 161–178.

Blaha, B. A. (1979). *The effects of answering self-generated questions on reading.* Doctoral dissertation, Boston University.

Brady, P. L. (1990). *Improving the reading comprehension of middle school students through reciprocal teaching and semantic mapping strategies.* Doctoral dissertation, University of Oregon-Eugene.

Brophy, J. E., & Good, T. L. (1986). Teacher behavior and student achievement. In M. C. Wittrock (Ed.), *Handbook of research on teaching* (3rd ed., pp. 328–375). New York, NY: Macmillan.

Chase, W., & Chi, M. (1980). Cognitive skill: Implications for spatial skill in large-scale environments. In J. Harvey (Ed.), *Cognition, social behavior, and the environment* (pp. 55–71). Potomac, MD: Erlbaum.

Chase, W. G., & Simon, H. A. (1973). The mind's eye in chess. In W. G. Chase (Ed.), *Visual information processing* (pp. 215–281). New York: Academic Press.

Collins, A., Brown, J. S., & Newman, S. E. (1990). Cognitive apprenticeship: Teaching the crafts of reading, writing, and mathematics. In L. Resnick (Ed.), *Knowing, learning, and instruction: Essays in honor of Robert Glaser* (pp. 453–494). Hillsdale, NJ: Erlbaum.

Delpit, L. (1986). Skills and other dilemmas of a progressive Black educator. *Harvard Educational Review, 56,* 379–385.

Dermody, M. M. (1988). *Metacognitive strategies for development of reading comprehension for younger children.* Paper presented at the annual meeting of the American Association of Colleges for Teacher Education, New Orleans, LA (ERIC Document No. ED 292 070).

Education Week, Report of the National Mathematics Advisory Panel. March 19, 2008, p. 12.

Englert, C. S., Raphael, T. E., Anderson, L. M., Anthony, H., & Stevens, D. D. (1991). Making strategies and self-talk visible: Writing instruction in regular and Special Education classrooms. *American Educational Research Journal, 28,* 337–372.

Evertson, C. E., Anderson, C., Anderson, L., & Brophy, J. (1980). Relationship between classroom behaviors and student outcomes in junior high mathematics and English classes. *American Educational Research Journal, 17,* 43–60.

Fisher, C. W., Filby, N. M., Marliave, R., Cohen, L. S., Dishaw, M. M., Moore, J. E., & Berliner, D. C. (1978). *Teaching behaviors, academic learning time, and student achievement* (Final report of Phase III B, Beginning Teacher Evaluation Study). San Francisco, CA: Far West Educational Laboratory for Educational Research and Development.

Frederiksen, N. (1984). Implications of cognitive theory for instruction in problem solving. *Review of Educational Research, 54*(3), 363–407.

Gage, N. L., & Needles, M. C. (1989). Process–product research on teaching: A review of criticisms. *Elementary School Journal, 89,* 253–300.

Good, T. L., & Grouws, D. A. (1977). Teaching effects: A process–product study in fourth grade mathematics classrooms. *Journal of Teacher Education, 28,* 40–54.

Good, T. L., & Grouws, D. A. (1979). The Missouri mathematics effectiveness project. *Journal of Educational Psychology, 71,* 143–155.

Grajia, M. L. (1988). *Direct instruction of a summarization strategy: Effect on text comprehension and recall in learning disabled students.* Doctoral dissertation, Pennsylvania State University, PA.

Greeno, J. G. (1978). Understanding and procedural knowledge in mathematics instruction. *Educational Psychologist, 12,* 262–283.

Guzzetti, B., Snyder, T., Glass, G., & Gamas, W. (1993). Promoting conceptual change in science: A comparative meta-analysis of instructional interventions from reading education and science education. *Reading Research Quarterly, 28,* 117–159.

Hirsch, E. J., Jr. (2006). The case for bringing content into the language arts block and for a knowledge-rich curriculum core for all children. *American Educator, 19,* 4–13.

Katz, L. G. (1994). The project approach. *ERIC Digest. Clearinghouse on elementary and early childhood education.* (ERIC Document No. ED368509). Champaign, IL: ERIC.

King, A. (1991). Effects of training in strategic questioning on children's problem-solving success. *Journal of Educational Psychology, 83*(3), 307–317.

King, A. (1994). Guiding knowledge construction in the classroom: Effects of teaching children how to question and how to explain. *American Educational Research Journal, 30,* 338–368.

Kintsch, W., & Van Dijk, T. A. (1978). Toward a model of text comprehension and production. *Psychological Review, 85*(5), 363–394.

Kirschner, P. A., Sweller, J., & Clark, R. E. (2006). Why minimal guidance during instruction does not work: An analysis of the failure of constructivist, discovery, problem-based, experiential, and inquiry based teaching. *Educational Psychologist, 41,* 75–86.

Kozinn, Allan (2002, March 26). *Dorothy DeLay, teacher of many of the world's leading violinists, dies at 84.* Retrieved from www.nytimes.com/.

Kuhn, D. (2007). Is direct instruction an answer to the right question? *Educational Psychologist, 42*(2), 109–113.

Kulik, J. A., & Kulik, C. C. (1979). College teaching. In P. L. Peterson & H. J. Walberg (Eds.), *Research on teaching: Concepts, findings, and implications* (pp. 70–93). Berkeley, CA: McCutchan.

Laberge, D., & Samuels, S. J. (1974). Toward a theory of automatic information processing in reading. *Cognitive Psychology, 6*, 293–323.

Larkin, J. H., & Reif, F. (1976). Analysis and teaching of a general skill for studying scientific text. *Journal of Educational Psychology, 72*, 348–350.

Linn, M. C. (1977). *Free choice experiences: How do they help children learn? Advancing education through science oriented programs* (Report PSC-20). Lawrence Hall of Science. University of California, Berkeley, CA (ERIC Document Reproduction Service No. ED 139 61).

Lonberger, R. B. (1988). *The effects of training in a self-generated learning strategy on the prose processing abilities of fourth and sixth graders.* Doctoral dissertation, State University of New York at Buffalo.

McDonald, F., & Elias, P. (1976). *The effects of teaching performance on pupil learning, Vol. I: Beginning teacher evaluation study, Phase 2.* Princeton, NJ: Educational Testing Service.

Medley, D. M., & Mitzel, H. E. (1963). Measuring classroom behavior by systematic observation. In N. L. Gage (Ed.), *Handbook of research on teaching* (pp. 247–329). Chicago, IL: Rand-McNally.

Miller, G. A. (1956). The magical number seven, plus or minus two: Some limits on our capacity for processing information. *Psychological Review, 63*, 81–97.

Morrison, H. C. (1926). *The practice of teaching in the secondary school.* Chicago, IL: University of Chicago Press.

National Mathematics Advisory Panel. (2008). *Foundations for success: The Final Report of the National Mathematics.* Washington, DC. Department of Education.

Newell, A., & Simon, H. A. (1972). *Human problem solving.* Englewood Cliffs, NJ: Prentice-Hall.

Norman, D. A., & Brokow, D. G. (1975). On data-limited and resource-limited processes. *Cognitive Psychology, 7*, 44–64.

Palincsar, A. S. (1987, April). *Collaborating for collaborative learning of text comprehension.* Paper presented at the annual meeting of the American Educational Research Association, Washington, DC.

Palincsar, A. S., & Brown, A. L. (1984). Reciprocal teaching of comprehension-fostering and comprehension-monitoring activities. *Cognition and Instruction, 2*, 117–175.

Palincsar, A. S., & Brown, A. L. (1989). Instruction for self-regulated learning. In L. Resnick & L. E. Klopfer (Eds.), *Toward the thinking curriculum: Current cognitive research* (pp. 19–39). Arlington, VA: Association for Supervision and Curriculum.

Pellegrino, J. W., & Glaser, R. (1980). Components of inductive reasoning. In R. E. Snow, P.-A. Federico, & W. E. Montague (Eds.), *Aptitude, learning, and instruction: Vol. 1. Cognitive process analyses of aptitude* (pp. 177–218). Hillsdale, NJ: Erlbaum.

Pressley, M., Burkell, J., Cariglia-Bull, T., Lysynchuk, L., McGoldrick, J. A., Schneider, B., et al. (1995). *Cognitive strategy instruction* (2nd ed.). Cambridge, MA: Brookline Books.

Raphael, T. E., & Pearson, P. D. (1985). Increasing students' awareness of sources of information for answering questions. *American Educational Research Journal, 22*, 217–236.

Rinehart, S. D., Stahl, S. A., & Erickson, L. G. (1986). Some effects of summarization training on reading and studying. *Reading Research Quarterly, 21*, 422–437.

Rosenshine, B. (1976). Classroom instruction. In N. L. Gage (Ed.), *The psychology of teaching methods* (75th NSSE Yearbook) (pp. 335–371). Chicago, IL: University of Chicago Press.

Rosenshine, B., Chapman, S., & Meister, C. (1996). Teaching students to generate questions: A review of the intervention studies. *Review of Educational Research, 66,* 181–221.

Rosenshine, B., & Meister, C. (1992). The use of scaffolds for teaching higher-level cognitive strategies. *Educational Leadership,* April, 26–33.

Rosenshine, B., & Meister, C. (1994). Reciprocal teaching: A review of the research. *Review of Educational Research, 64,* 479–531.

Rosenshine, B., & Stevens, R. (1986). Teaching functions. In M. C. Witrock (Ed.), *Handbook of research on teaching* (3rd ed., pp. 376–391). New York: Macmillan.

Schoenfeld, A. H. (1985). *Mathematical problem solving.* New York: Academic Press.

Singer, H., & Donlan, D. (1982). Active comprehension: Problem-solving schema with question generation of complex short stories. *Reading Research Quarterly, 17,* 166–186.

Stallings, J. A., & Kaskowitz, D. (1974). *Follow through classroom observation.* Menlo Park, CA: SRI International.

Stanovich, K. E. (1980). Toward an interactive-compensatory model of individual differences in the development of reading fluency. *Reading Research Quarterly, 16,* 32–71.

Stein, R. P. (1999). *The effect of direct instruction in moral reasoning on the moral reasoning of high-aptitude pre-adolescents and average ability pre-adolescents.* Doctoral dissertation, Teachers College, Columbia University.

Tobias, S. (1982). When do instructional methods make a difference? *Educational Researcher, 11,* 4–10.

Weiner, C. J. (1978). *The effect of training in questioning and student question generation on reading achievement.* Paper presented at the annual meeting of the American Educational Research Association, Toronto, Canada. (ERIC Document: ED No. 158223).

Part IV

An Examination of Specific Learning and Motivational Issues

12 Learning and Constructivism[*]

Walter Kintsch University of Colorado

In this chapter, I try to make explicit some issues that have been somewhat over-looked in the debate over the "Failure of constructivist, discovery, problem-based, experiential, and inquiry-based teaching" (Kirschner, Sweller, & Clark, 2006). The tendency has been to lump all these methods under the term "constructivist" and hence to identify constructivism with minimal guidance in instruction. This practice is quite general, but it obscures another meaning of the term constructivism: that learning is an active process, that knowledge is constructed. This is a very important point, about which there is considerable agreement in the research literature. In rejecting "constructivism" we do not want to revert to a view of learning as passive knowledge acquisition. The active role that the learner plays in acquiring knowledge must be clearly understood. Learners are not simply receiving information or acquiring knowledge by osmosis, but must be actively engaged in knowledge building. The role of instruction is to constrain and guide their activities. The question of how much guidance is optimal for learning is a separate issue.

This is not to say that Kirschner et al. (2006) advocate a view of learning as passive information reception. They are quite clear and explicit about this: the goal of instruction is to alter long-term memory, and long-term memory is not a passive repository of information; knowledge in long-term memory must be constructed. Thus, what I am discussing here is nothing new. Nevertheless, it is an issue that could use further clarification. Although the terminological confusion in the term constructivism is clearly recognized by Kirschner et al. (2006) as well as the authors who replied to their article, it may easily be misunderstood by some readers. Therefore, I would like to elaborate on how knowledge is constructed, on the differences between novices and experts, and on the role of guidance in instruction. I shall do this from a viewpoint that is a little different. The discussion so far has focused on problem solving, whereas I propose to view the issue of constructivism from the viewpoint of comprehension, specifically text comprehension. There is a rich literature in this area that, as I shall show, complements the literature on problem solving in sometimes illuminating ways. Furthermore, text comprehension is not a well-structured domain such as problem solving in mathematics or physics, and extending the discussion beyond such

[*] I thank Gerhard Fischer and Eileen Kintsch for their helpful comments.

domains would be useful, as Schmidt, Loyens, van Gog, and Paas (2007) have suggested.

My goal here is to distinguish clearly the constructive aspects of learning, the process of knowledge construction, from the question of how much guidance is optimal for learning. Although minimal guidance and discovery learning have frequently been advocated by constructivists, minimal guidance does not necessarily follow from a constructivist view of learning. Instructional methods are most effective when they respect the view of learning as an active (and, indeed, often effortful) process, with the right amount of guidance determined by the characteristics of the learner and the to-be-learned material—which is not necessarily minimal guidance. Again, there is nothing new about this claim: Kirschner et al. (2006), as well as Hmelo-Silver, Duncan, and Chinn (2007) and Schmidt et al. (2007) explicitly agree that the level of guidance for optimal learning must be adapted to the learner and the material they are supposed to master (although they might disagree on what constitutes a minimal and optimal level of guidance). However, considering how this issue plays out in the domain of text comprehension might help us to obtain a better grasp of it.

Learning as an Active Process

What do we mean when we say "Learning is an active process"? We first need to specify the term "learning," as there are many types of learning. Pavlovian conditioning, operant conditioning, associative learning, skill learning, rote memorization, learning by doing, and leaning from text differ in important ways. The focus here is on school learning, that is, the processes whereby students acquire knowledge and skills in school settings. Indeed, for clarity and specificity, I shall limit this discussion to a particular type of school learning—learning from texts.

To see why learning must be regarded as a constructive process, consider the input and end result of that process (see Kintsch, 1998, for more detail). The input is a text, that is, a series of written words, organized into sentences, paragraphs, and higher-order discourse units. The end result is a situation model that faithfully represents the meaning of that text, both at a local and global level, and integrates it with the reader's prior knowledge and learning goals. Turning the written text into a situation model in the reader's mind requires going beyond the written word. Even constructing a decent representation of the text itself—a textbase—requires active processing, for texts are never fully explicit. Inferences of several kinds are required from the reader—referents have to be identified, coherence gaps have to be bridged, the macrostructure of the text must be mentally represented. A well-written text gives the reader all kinds of cues on how to go about textbase construction, but it is up to the reader to infer the discourse entity a pronoun refers to, to come up with the right bridging inference linking two seemingly unrelated sentences, or a suitable high-level generalization to characterize a macro-unit of the text. The passive reader, who does not perform this required activity, will end up with an inadequate textbase. But the activity required for the construction of a textbase is much less of a problem for most readers than that required to construct a good situation model. After all, the text usually cues the reader on how to construct a textbase, but for the construction of the situation model the reader is on his/her own. It is their specific background knowledge that matters, their particular interests and reading goals that have to be integrated with the text, and the text cannot provide detailed guidance for every reader, since knowledge and goals differ widely among readers. Thus, a major problem in school learning is the student's failure to construct a situation model at all, or the inability to construct an adequate one.

What kind of situation model will be constructed depends, inter alia, on the reader's goals. Readers whose goal is to prepare for a test emphasizing fact retrieval will focus on different aspects of the text than readers who try to understand the text in preparation for a class discussion. Similarly, reading for appreciation or reading for doing will give rise to different situation models. Thus, an important aspect of a situation model is how students perceive the learning environment, which depends on how that environment is implemented by the teacher. Hence the kind of expectations the teacher creates in a classroom play a large role in fostering either superficial reading or deep understanding. In our experiments on text recall with college students we regularly find that they faithfully reproduce whatever names and numbers there are in the text, because that is the sort of thing they are often asked about in tests, but fail to generate inferences that would result in a deeper understanding of the text, even when they are able to recall all the premises.

Since situation models link an individual's background knowledge and personal experience, goals and purposes with information from the text, they differ among individuals more than textbases, which generally hew closely to the text. Nevertheless, veridical situation models have much in common, because they must be constrained by the text (van Dijk & Kintsch, 1983; Trabasso & Suh, 1993; Zwaan & Radvansky, 1998; Tapiero, 2007; Therriault & Rinck, 2007). The situation model includes not only verbal or propositional information like the textbase, but may also include sensory imagery (either retrieved from prior knowledge or constructed on the basis of the text itself), emotional markers, and action plans. Importantly, situation models are cumulative: as one reads more and more on a given topic, the situation model changes, not only by accretion, but also by reorganization and error correction. The situation model is the product of the learning process. Bereiter and Scardamalia, in talking about learning in general, not just learning from texts, have used the term knowledge building for this process (Bereiter, 2002; Bereiter & Scardamalia, 2003; Scardamalia & Bereiter, 2003).

The goal of instruction is to make knowledge building possible. Two aspects of knowledge building are critical for instruction. First, in the words of Harel and Papert (1991), "(the building of knowledge structures) happens especially felicitously in a context when the learner is consciously engaged in constructing a public entity, whether it's a sand castle on the beach or a theory of the universe," or, we might add, when the learner summarizes a report or writes a critical essay. Second, knowledge objects do not stand alone but are grounded on a shared, cultural knowledge base (Hirsch, 1987, 2006). Not only is cultural knowledge necessary for understanding objects in a culture (such as texts); common knowledge also assures that different individuals in that culture build situation models that share important features, thereby becoming members of a cultural community. It must be emphasized, however, that the way that knowledge is acquired, and the way it is used in building new knowledge, is an active, constructive process. Cultural objects become building blocks for the construction of knowledge, not something that can be absorbed through passive reading. The question of how much guidance is optimal to facilitate knowledge building will be considered below, but first we need to discuss knowledge building in more detail.

It is important to understand the difference between how experts and novices go about constructing a situation model (Ericsson & Kintsch, 1995; Kintsch, 1998). In both cases, the text is processed in cycles corresponding more or less to sentence units. The information about the sentence currently being read is held in working memory and processed in various ways. For instance, the inferences required to form a coherent textbase are performed, often automatically (as in the case of most bridging inferences), but sometimes they depend on conscious search and reasoning. Novices are undoubtedly not as good as experts at these tasks, but there is really no qualitative difference in what they do. However, processing is not restricted to the level of the textbase, since at the same time a situation model is also being constructed. Here, experts and novices differ qualitatively. Domain experts, reading texts within their domain of expertise, have available retrieval structures that link the information in working memory—the current portion of the text they are working on—automatically with relevant information in their long-term memory. Thus, as they read, a situation model is formed, largely without conscious effort. Reading goals come into play in much the same way, via retrieval structures that favor goal-relevant portions of long-term memory. Thus, their reading results in the automatic generation of a situation model that integrates the textbase with their prior knowledge and that is structured in a way that reflects their interests and goals.

Novices are in a very different situation with regard to text comprehension and learning from texts. By the upper grades in school many students have successfully acquired expert adult reading strategies enabling them to form an adequate textbase more or less automatically and effortlessly. These strategies receive a great deal of practice during the school years, and to some extent there is transfer from general comprehension strategies used in listening, which are practiced even more throughout life. Thus, many young adults are no longer novices in this sense—they are practiced readers, even experts, so long as their reading material concerns everyday matters for which they have adequate background knowledge. However, there are many readers in middle school and high school, and even in college, for whom that is not the case. For these, the formation of a textbase remains a task that involves conscious effort, even when they are reading about familiar topics. They must employ explicit strategies to assure comprehension, strategies that must be directly taught. Thus the novice reader has to learn to consciously search for relevant prior knowledge, since it will not be automatically activated; he must learn to ask himself what the author meant with a particular sentence, or why the author said it, or how it relates to what was said before; and he must learn to discern what is the main argument and what are ancillary points, where the author presents evidence and where she makes claims.

But even if students are expert in reading general, familiar texts (such as stories or newspapers), this is seldom the case with the instructional texts that they read in school. They are lacking the retrieval structures that ensure smooth comprehension for domain experts when they read these texts. Retrieval structures are links between items held in working memory (roughly conscious awareness) and relevant associated knowledge in long-term memory that is thereby activated without overloading the limited-capacity working memory. Knowledge activation with retrieval structures is automatic and effortless, and hence characterizes expert knowledge and reading behavior (Ericsson & Kintsch, 1995). However, expert retrieval structures are the product of extended practice in knowledge building, the kind of deep comprehension that results in a well-grounded situation model. Constructing a situation model for novices requires conscious, effortful memory searches to retrieve relevant background knowledge and the use of explicit comprehension strategies to compensate for their lack of automatic retrieval structures. Novices must problem solve their way through the text by identifying places that call for elaboration and clarification. They must paraphrase and re-explain text passages in their own words to explicate the relation between the new information in the text and what they already know.

Thus, we can distinguish four types of readers: readers with good general comprehension strategies and expert domain knowledge; good readers without domain knowledge; poor readers without domain knowledge; and, finally, poor readers with high domain knowledge (such as the soccer experts studied by Schneider, Körkel, & Weinert, 1989). Most students fall into either one of the two middle categories. For these students, comprehension is an active, effortful, resource-demanding construction process as described above. The role of instruction is to support this process (Brown & Campione, 1994; King, 1997; Palincsar & Brown, 1984; Pearson & Fielding, 1991; Scardamalia, Bereiter, & Lamon, 1994).

A number of instructional implications for readers lacking domain knowledge follow from such an active view of learning. Two examples that we have explored in our work will be briefly discussed here.

Deep comprehension, and hence learning from text, is not possible unless there is at least some background knowledge present. Thus, educators try to assign instructional texts that are attuned to the students' level of prior knowledge. The texts need to be within a "zone of proximal learning" to make knowledge acquisition possible (Kintsch, 1994; Wolfe et al., 1998). Just how much one must know about a topic before one can learn more about it, and what one does not have to know but can learn on demand is by no means a straightforward problem, however.

Another implication of the constructivist view of learning is the role of metacognition. If meaning construction is an effortful, demanding process, readers may try to get by without the effort. The easiest way to do so is by not thoroughly analyzing the level of comprehension that is being achieved. Since a superficial level of understanding is easy enough to attain, students need to learn that this is not sufficient. By superficial, I mean understanding at the textbase level, without forming a reasonable situation model. Such understanding is good enough to reproduce the gist of the text and some of its detail, but it remains inert knowledge, unconnected to a person's store of knowledge and hence it is easily forgotten and unusable in novel situations (Kintsch, 1998, Chapter 9).

One way to make readers aware of their lack of comprehension is to problematize instruction (Reiser, 2004). An experiment that nicely illustrates the possibilities and pitfalls of such an approach was reported by McNamara, Kintsch, Songer, and Kintsch (1996). This study employed readers with good background knowledge and readers with inadequate background knowledge with respect to a particular science text they were asked to learn. Two versions of the text were used: one was well-written, well-structured, explicit, and in general provided the reader with all the support that was possible. The other version was deliberately lesioned: there were gaps in the text requiring bridging inferences, undefined terms, the organization of the text was obscured, and in general the text was made hard to read.

The results of this study were instructive. When only superficial comprehension was required (the ability to recall part of the text), the well-written version was always superior, whether students had high or low background knowledge. However, when the text required deeper understanding, that is, a well-worked-out situation model (as assessed by inference questions and a problem-solving task), students with high background knowledge performed better with the poorly written text than they did with the well-written version. With the well-written text, they easily formed a good textbase, which made them think they understood what there was to understand, but they never did the processing that was required for building a situation model (in spite of their background knowledge, they were far from being domain experts who would have understood this text without further effort). When the text was difficult, they realized they did not understand it well and were forced into processing at a deeper level, with beneficial results for their understanding.

Our high-knowledge students had just enough background knowledge to make it possible for them to draw the required inferences and construct an adequate situation model. For the students with little background knowledge of the domain, the situation was different. When the text was well-written, they could at least come up with a good textbase, and hence were able to reproduce the text. But they could not construct the required situation model, for the text lay outside their zone of proximal learning. When they were given the difficult text to study, they were lost: lacking the knowledge to fill in coherence gaps or identify the referents, they became confused by the lack of a clear organization in the text, and hence they could neither recall it well, nor understand it at a deeper level. Problematizing a text is fine, but you need to make sure that the reader can solve the problem!

The claim so far has been that successful learning from texts requires the construction of a good situation model, which, unless the reader is already a domain expert, is a resource-demanding process involving conscious effort. So what are the conditions that are necessary for the success of this effort?

Cognitive-load theory (Sweller, 1988) provides some useful answers. The reader's resources are finite and they have to be used purposefully. We have seen that increasing the cognitive load under certain circumstances can improve learning (the high-knowledge readers with the poorly written text in the McNamara et al. experiment). In that case the increased cognitive load arose from activities that were directly relevant to the learning process: in overcoming the difficulties of the text, the readers were able to reach a deeper level of understanding. Increases in cognitive load are not beneficial, however, when the activities involved are extrinsic to the learning process. Thus, reading a text in a foreign language may overload working memory because the text has to be translated to be understood, with the result that very little information about that text reaches long-term memory.

Motivating learners to expend the required effort to construct a situation model is just as important as considerations of cognitive load. Project-based learning and related approaches that engage the student in problems that are interesting and relevant to the student offer great possibilities in this respect. As Kuhn (2007) has pointed out, learners make their own choices about how to construct knowledge. They need to have some reason to be interested in what they are doing (Hidi & Renninger, 2006). In our work, we have used a software program in several hundred classrooms in Colorado to teach middle school students how to write summaries. The program was demonstrably successful in doing so, but not in all classrooms. One crucial variable was whether the teacher gave the students a good reason for the activity of summary writing (e.g., preparing for a class discussion or a presentation, or a particular project) or whether the program was introduced as just another decontextualized activity, in which case students typically failed to learn anything (Caccamise et al., in preparation). Learning is an active process, it is the student who must be active, and instruction must provide reasons for the active effort, which can be done by engaging the student's interests and motivation. Problem-based learning, project-based learning, or scientific inquiry appear to be effective means toward that end. It is important, however, that the problem-solving activity does not become a goal in itself when the real goal is to learn the science involved. The project is not the important outcome—science knowledge is.

Learning and Learning-to-Learn

Learning from texts often has two goals that operate simultaneously. Suppose I ask students to study a text on the theory of plate tectonics. I want them to learn about plate tectonics—what are the claims, the data, the controversies, etc. To do so, the students must form a good situation model that integrates the text they have just read with their prior knowledge about geology and geography, as discussed above. But I also have a second goal: I want my students to become not exactly experts in geology, but more expert-like in their ability to read science texts.

Simon's estimate that it takes 10,000 hours or 10 years of deliberate practice to become an expert in any area of science, sport, or the arts is widely accepted today (Simon, 1996). Schools, generally, do not produce real experts, but strive to move students a bit closer to expertise and provide them with the tools to develop further on their own. Therefore, it is worthwhile to look at the literature on expertise for hints about how to become an expert (Ericsson, Charness, Hoffman, & Feltovich, 2006). What strikes one first is the sheer amount of practice necessary for expertise, not just practice but deliberate, guided practice. The important lesson for classroom instruction and learning is the need to provide the opportunity for guided practice of the skill that is to be learned, including the skill of text comprehension.

Guided practice is best illustrated by what a sports coach is doing, say a ski instructor (Fischer, Brown, & Burton, 1984). On the one hand, the instructor provides feedback about the student's current performance, and on the other she selects new, more advanced tasks for the student that are within his proximal zone of learning. This is a tricky business, for too much challenge just scares the skier off the slopes, while without challenge he will be consigned to the groomed slopes forever, and soon get bored with the sport. Csikszentmihalyi (1990) has discussed this dilemma in terms of maintaining the flow experience, which is threatened on the one hand by anxiety when the learner is over-challenged, and tedium when not challenged enough, in reading comprehension as in skiing. But while the pleasure of flow can play an important motivating role, learning is the result of deliberate practice, "in which individuals engage in (typically planned) activity aimed at reaching a level just beyond the currently attainable level of performance by engaging in full concentration, analysis after feedback, and repetitions with refinement" (Ericsson & Ward, 2007, p. 349). Thus the flow is not the goal of instruction, learning is, which is hard work, but the flow may provide motivation to engage in the hard work of deliberate practice.

Instruction, therefore, must provide students with ample opportunity for guided practice. If we want them to acquire expert-like strategies for reading science texts, just making them read (and maybe take a test afterwards) will not suffice. We must provide feedback that allows the student to assess her current level of understanding, hints about what to do when her understanding is inadequate, and we must carefully select new texts to be studied that afford the student opportunities to learn more advanced strategies. If we want to teach students how to summarize, we must give them feedback about what they have written, hints on how to improve it, and the opportunity to work on more and more difficult tasks. Franzke, Kintsch, Caccamise, Johnson, and Dooley (2005) provide an example of such an approach to teaching summarizing, embedded in a computer-based tool, called *Summary Street*. Using the content-based feedback delivered by the system, students not only improved the quality of their summaries, but the benefits persisted over time, even when the students summarized without the support. Especially telling is the fact that students in the control group, who summarized an equivalent number of texts without the guidance from *Summary Street*, did not improve at all. They made the same errors after practice as they did before. Similarly, mere activity in a flight simulator does not improve the performance of pilots, but guided practice does (see the discussion in Ericsson & Ward, 2007).

It is clear that one cannot become an expert without guided practice, a great deal of guided practice, in fact. But what kind of guided practice? Two approaches have been suggested, one involving the teaching of general thinking skills, the other focusing instead on domain-specific strategies. The first modern theories of problem solving emphasized general problem-solving strategies (Newell & Simon, 1972). Instruction, accordingly, should focus on teaching "students to use their minds well,... skills of inquiry and skills of argument" (Kuhn, 2007). However, it soon became apparent that effective problem solving tends to be domain specific: expert problem solving is characterized by the use of domain-specific strategies rather than general problem-solving skills (Chase & Simon, 1973; Schunn & Anderson, 2001). Experts develop retrieval structures that link particular contents in working memory with relevant knowledge in long-term memory. Both the patterns in working memory that trigger the operation of retrieval structures and the contents of long-term memory are highly domain specific. Problem-solving skills are situated and in general do not transfer across situations. Being an expert in one domain does not make one an expert in a different domain.

This domain specificity of expertise poses a serious dilemma for schools. Schools (preceding law school or medical school) are not expected to produce experts, but well-rounded general problem solvers who can function in many different environments and are capable of becoming experts in some environments with further training. Thus, school learning is designed to un-situate, decontextualize knowledge and skills, so as to make it flexible and usable in a variety of situations. As is well known, that is a tricky task, because there is a delicate balance between knowledge that is so situation-bound that it is usable only in that very situation and knowledge that is so decontextualized that it becomes inert knowledge, usable in no situation whatever. School learning is always in danger of producing inert knowledge, but nevertheless its goal remains to provide students with general knowledge that is broadly usable and is not tied to the context of its acquisition (Bereiter, 1997). Schools need to teach students to construct knowledge at the right level of abstraction, knowledge that is neither limited to concrete situations nor completely decontextualized, but rather linked to abstract, generalizable features of situations.

Irrespective of the importance of domain-specific strategies and domain knowledge, general-purpose strategies also play a role in thinking and problem solving. First of all, it has been shown that expert problem solving is not limited to domain-specific strategies but typically employs a mixture of general and specific reasoning methods (e.g., Greeno, 1983; Duncan, 2007). Second, there are at least two genuine skills that are generalizable across domains: metacognitive strategies (Flavell & Wellman, 1977) and reading-comprehension strategies (Perfetti, 1989). By the time we are young adults, most of us are expert comprehenders: we have had many years of practice with spoken-language comprehension, as well as more than a decade of practice (not always deliberate) with reading comprehension. We read fluently and comprehend automatically—but only as long as we read familiar texts (Ericsson & Kintsch, 1995), like true experts who rely upon automatic retrieval structures. But a curious thing happens when we read texts in an unfamiliar domain, say about string theory or meiosis and mitosis, rather than the daily newspaper or an airplane novel. To read such texts we need two kinds of expertise: general reading skills as well as domain expertise.

Students, when they read for learning, may be good readers, but they still do not comprehend because of their lack of domain knowledge. Reading-comprehension strategies can help them deal with this situation. Where the domain expert would rely on automatic retrieval structures to construct a valid situation model, the reader who is not a domain expert must consciously and intentionally go through the many steps required in this process—make inferences to fill gaps in the text, retrieve relevant background knowledge, identify the structure of an argument, and so on. The teacher can model the required behaviors, teaching in effect comprehension strategies that students can use to achieve their goals. There exists a great deal of evidence that such strategies can be very helpful to students, that they smooth the path towards expert comprehension (e.g., Palincsar & Brown, 1984; McNamara, 2007). Thus, reading-comprehension strategies play an important role in instruction in helping the learner to build new knowledge from the instructional texts they read in school.

There are some open questions about how comprehension strategies should be taught. Some computer tutors (such as *Summary Street*, Caccamise et al., in preparation; Franzke et al., 2005) do not teach students specific comprehension strategies, but guide their practice through judicious feedback so that they learn to adopt suitable strategies. In contrast, other successful systems (such as reciprocal teaching, Palincsar & Brown, 1984; questioning the author, Beck & McKeown, 2006; or *iSTART*, McNamara, 2007) explicitly teach relevant comprehension strategies, providing students with a set of consciously available comprehension tools. It is not clear at this point what combination of these approaches is most effective, for which students, and at what stages of learning.

An example of how learning from a text can be combined with training in general comprehension strategies can be found in the teacher and student manuals of Hampton (2007) for Grades 7 and 8. She has students working on strategies for constructing a faithful textbase (such as pronoun identification, sentence connectives, vocabulary, text structure) as well as for building a situation model (think-aloud and teacher modeling, discussion, summarizing, and essay writing). There is nothing new about these strategies; what is different here is how they are embedded within the textbase–situation model framework and, crucially, that this is all done within one specific knowledge domain that is relatively familiar to students to begin with and that is systematically expanded during the course of 30 lessons. Thus, students learn at the same time a set of general reading strategies and build a cumulative situation model about an important concept in biology. For the students, the strategy knowledge remains implicit; for the teachers, a general understanding of how comprehension works provides a meaningful framework for their activities.

Levels of Guidance for Learning

Learning from text is by its very nature a constructive process, guided through feedback. Learning effective comprehension strategies requires a great deal of deliberate practice, which also implies some kind of guidance. The guidance can come from the teacher, the nature and organization of the instructional texts, or it can be self-guidance through metacognitive control. At one extreme we have direct instruction, where the teacher and the learning materials firmly guide the learning process, leaving little to the discretion of the student. At the other extreme would be completely unguided discovery learning, with, of course, numerous shades of gray in between. The eventual goal is to have a self-guided learner, but what is the best road to that goal is not so clear, which is one of the things the "constructivist" controversy is all about. Other chapters in this volume speak to this general issue. Here, I am merely exploring the implications of the literature on text comprehension with respect to that complex question.

One area where the guidance issue has been extensively explored is hypertext. The familiar linear text guides the reader by sequencing the text in the order the author thought would be optimal. Sometimes, however, the way the author has ordered an expository text does not mesh well with a reader's goals. For instance, if a reader is looking for certain pieces of information, these may not be easy to locate in a linear text. A well-organized hypertext with a transparent structure and proper navigation aids can be searched much more efficiently. So, for instance, when students are given a particular problem to solve for which purpose they need to find relevant information from textual sources, hypertext can be very helpful (Dillon & Gabbard, 1998).

A different question is whether hypertext is a good alternative to linear text for promoting learning, when the goal is not to find a specific piece of information needed to solve a problem, but to acquire knowledge about some domain. Originally, the expectation was very much that hypertext would be helpful in this respect, too (McKnight, Dillon, & Richards, 1993). However, the burgeoning literature soon disappointed these expectations (e.g., Unz & Hesse, 1999). Hypertext users tend to use three different strategies for choosing which node to follow (Salmerón, Kintsch, & Cañas, 2006): (a) they choose the node that promises to provide the most coherent continuation of what they have just read; (b) they choose the node that looks like it would be of most interest to them; or (c) they follow some superficial strategy, like selecting the node printed at the top of the screen. If they follow the coherence strategy, they learn quite well (Foltz, 1996), but not otherwise. Specifically, low-knowledge readers do poorly at situation-model-level comprehension unless the text is presented in a coherent order (Salmerón, Cañas, Kintsch, & Fajardo, 2005) or follow a coherence strategy in selecting their own order (Salmerón et al., 2006). High-knowledge readers, on the other hand, can do well even if they follow an interest strategy in selecting nodes.

Giving a hypertext to high-knowledge readers is one of the techniques that can be used to ensure active reading and construction of a proper situation model—they cannot read superficially, because at each choice point they must select a good continuation. Since they have enough knowledge to either find a coherent continuation or, if they follow their own interests, are capable of forming coherence links with other parts of the text, this activity is beneficial for their comprehension, just as the need to fill coherence gaps and identify referents was beneficial for high-knowledge readers in the McNamara et al. (1996) studies with linear texts reported earlier. Increasing the cognitive load for these readers is more than balanced by the benefits of active processing. The situation is different for low-knowledge readers. If they do not follow a coherence strategy, they end up with a disorganized and fragmentary situation model; if they do, the increased cognitive load may not leave them with enough resources for processing other aspects of the text (Sweller, 1988). Thus, using hypertexts for learning problematizes comprehension, which can be beneficial, but carries considerable risk. One cannot claim that the level of guidance provided by linear text is necessarily superior to letting the reader make his own choices in a hypertext, but the conditions under which hypertext is superior for learning are narrowly circumscribed.

It seems not unreasonable to generalize the conclusions about the role of guidance arrived at above in the discussion of learning from hypertext. Minimally guided learning (hypertext is not unguided—you cannot just go anywhere, but must follow a given set of links, and typically you have available overviews and other navigation aids) can be as good as or better than guided instruction, but the potential risks must be carefully thought out and weighed for different kinds of learners.

What I have stressed here is that learning is a constructive activity, an active, intentional process that may demand considerable commitment and effort from the learner. It is difficult to state in general terms what the appropriate level of guidance is for the learning process. As we have seen, the amount of guidance needed differs, depending on the nature of the material, the background of the learner, as well as the stage of learning. The level of guidance should support the goal of keeping the learner actively engaged; it must motivate the learner, by challenging him or by interesting him, to engage in the laborious task of comprehension.

Conclusions

The title of this volume refers to the success or failure of "constructivist instructional theory." In these notes I have tried to forestall a possible terminological confusion about constructivism. At issue here is the effectiveness of minimally guided instructional methods, such as discovery, problem-based, experiential, project-based, and inquiry-based teaching, which are commonly labeled "constructivist." Constructivism, however, is also a theory of comprehension and learning. The central idea of this theory is that meaning must be constructed, that knowledge building is an active process on the part of the learner, not a passive process of information absorption. Just about every current learning theory is constructivist in that sense. Minimal guidance is a separate issue, but if we do not clearly and explicitly distinguish between these two uses of the term "constructivism" we invite confusion.

I have also tried to bring to the discussion a fresh viewpoint and a novel set of evidence. The discussion so far has been framed mostly in terms of problem solving in domains like math and physics. Here I have examined results from the field of text comprehension and learning from text, which nicely complement the literature on problem solving. Text comprehension is an ill-structured domain, unlike problem solving in formal disciplines. I have discussed the ways in which comprehension and learning from text are considered constructive processes. Central to this argument is the need to construct situation models on the basis of texts. The primary instructional problem is to get learners to construct adequate situation models and not be satisfied with a superficial understanding.

The cumulative construction and elaboration of situation models is a form of knowledge building. Since situation models always build on a foundation of prior knowledge, the process of situation-model construction is very different for domain experts and domain novices, smooth and automatic for the former and effortful and intentional for the latter. The crucial role of deliberate practice in becoming an expert was discussed.

As to the central question of the present volume—how much guidance is optimal for learning—the literature on text comprehension suggests a nuanced answer. Minimal guidance, such as in unconstrained discovery learning, is not generally effective, because it makes demands that easily exceed the resources of the learner, especially learners who lack appropriate background knowledge. However, maximal guidance, as in forms of instruction that reduce the learner to a passive information recipient, can also be counterproductive when it prevents the learner from the active, deep processing of the text that is required for the construction of adequate situation models. It is difficult to state in general terms what the optimal level of guidance is for the learning process. As we have seen, optimal levels of guidance differ, depending on the nature of the material, the background of the learner, as well as the stage of learning. The level of guidance should support the goal of keeping the learner focused on the topic of interest and actively engaged.

Question: Spiro and DeSchryver. *One of the great strengths of your chapter is the careful, nuanced demonstration that the answer to the question "How much guidance is optimal for learning?" depends on "the nature of the material, the background of the learner, as well as the stage of learning." Can you extend your conclusions beyond "how much" (levels or amounts of support) to questions of kind of guidance. Part of what we argued in our chapter is that the nature of optimal guidance shifts in more ill-structured domains from the kind that has been shown to be most beneficial in studies of predominantly well-structured domains. If this might be so, it would be useful in the constructivism–direct instruction debate to be able to specify where this shift occurs.*

You present text comprehension and learning from text as ill-structured domains, and point to kinds of guidance that have been shown empirically to be effective (e.g., those used in Reciprocal Teaching and Questioning the Author). To what extent do the kinds of strategies advocated in such approaches fall on the other side of a qualitative divide from the Kirschner et al. criteria? That is, would successful strategies for learning from text be able to be characterized as fully explaining essential proce-dures? Or in domains like learning from text is the support necessarily of a vaguer kind (e.g., "Look for connections to prior knowledge")?

Reply: Kintsch. You raise an important point. How much guidance is needed is only part of the story; what kind of guidance is needed is equally important, and it depends, too. But having agreed with you on this point, I must plead ignorance about how to frame an adequate answer to your question. Research like your own will surely provide more detailed answers, but at present we know little more than the bare outlines of this problem.

For well-formed problems, Kirschner et al.'s emphasis on essential informa-tion and full explanation seems right. An example from the field of text compre-hension would be arithmetic word problems, and the kind of technological support that can guide the construction of situation models for students, as I have discussed in my answer to another question. But, as you suggest in your question, learning from text can make quite different demands. In some domains (you cite biology—not exactly an ill-formed domain, there are correct answers!) the distinction between essential and inessential information is difficult to make, and it is not even clear what would count as a full explanation. Content-free prompts can be as effective as explanation and feedback—but just where the boundaries are must await further research.

Reaction to Kintsch's reply: Spiro and DeSchryver. *We find ourselves happily in agreement with your response to our question, but we do have one point of excep-tion, which we think is worth discussion: you contest our claim that aspects of biology are ill-structured. There are two important points here. First, we don't claim that domains are entirely well- or ill-structured, though some may be predominantly more one than the other. It's clear, for example, that Newtonian mechanics is pre-dominantly well-structured and the concept of "period" in art history is predomi-nantly ill-structured, according to our use of these notions. All domains have both well- and ill-structured aspects. Similarly, we don't claim that biology is predomi-nantly ill-structured, just that some important aspects of it are. For example, the mechanisms of adaptation are both complex in individual instances and, more importantly, evince considerable conceptual irregularity across instances in the way conceptual features are instantiated and configured, making generalizations and abstractive reductions problematic. Further, understanding of adaptation instances often involves interpretive processes that it would be a stretch to refer to as "correct answers."*

The second important point is that we argue that instruction and support are a function of the degree of well-structuredness of a given aspect, not the overall, pre-dominant pattern of the domain, and that the ill-structured aspects require a differ-ent kind of instruction and instructional support than the well-structured aspects. So, for example, we would expect there to be qualitative differences in the nature of instructional support for the more determinate microbiological arena than for some topics in the macrobiological realm (like adaptation). By the way, we take no stand on whether the ill-structured aspects of biology are that way in principle, or, instead, are a reflection of limitations of current knowledge which might be remedied at some future time. The implications for instruction at this time would be the same.

Question: Schwartz et al. *In our read of the chapter, we had a small confusion that we think has important ramifications. The confusion involved a separation between students learning "content knowledge" and students learning "process knowledge." It is an important question whether content knowledge should be taken as separate from the processes and contexts associated with its acquisition. However, our question is simpler. We did not understand why, on the one hand, you stated,*

> *Problem-based learning, project-based learning, or scientific inquiry appear to be effective means towards that end [motivation]; it is important, however, that the problem-solving activity does not become a goal in itself when the real goal is to learn the science involved. The project is not the important outcome—science knowledge is.*

But, on the other hand, in the context of reading instruction, you stated that you wanted "students to become not exactly experts in geology, but more expert-like in their ability to read science texts." Did you mean to imply that people should learn the content of the text and the process of reading well, whereas for science, the goal is learning science content but learning the process of inquiry is irrelevant except for its motivational value?

Reply: Kintsch. I expressed myself badly about the role of general problem-solving strategies, both in science learning and in reading instruction. Let me see whether I can get it straight. I do not think one can separate content and process in science learning. When I said "science knowledge," I meant knowledge both of content and process. In science, the process of inquiry is closely tied to the content: strategies are domain specific, as the problem-solving literature shows; general problem-solving strategies that could be used in all science domains play a minor role. The process of inquiry is sufficiently different in different branches of science, so that an expert in one domain has little advantage in another domain. Thus, science instruction must involve both content and process at the same time. When I objected to the emphasis on projects, I had in mind the fancy packaging and presentation that one sometimes observes in science fairs and class projects. This may have some motivational value, but should not be the primary focus of a science project.

With respect to reading instruction, things are a little different. I cited in my chapter a paper by Perfetti who claims that reading strategies are in fact general problem-solving strategies. Thus, teaching students general reading strategies and giving them plenty of opportunity for guided practice is indeed important. The eventual goal in developing reading expertise is the automatic use of these strategies.

Question: Schwartz. *Your distinction between the text-base and the situation model is powerful, well-supported, and it adds nuance to the otherwise flat claim* *that all knowledge is constructed. For readers who have not read your chapter yet, the distinction might be coarsely characterized as the difference between "parsing" the text and "understanding" the text. Have you or others applied your framework successfully to other domains where the primary input is also symbolic? For instance, when confronted with a mathematics word problem or equation, people might make a "symbol base" of the quantities in the problem and then a mental model of the situation to which the quantities could apply. Alternatively, the mental model may drive the construction of the symbol base. There are other possible applications of your framework, for example, when it comes to parsing graphs and constructing a mental model of their referents. It would be interesting to hear your thoughts on the construction–integration framework when applied to domains other than reading.*

Reply: Kintsch. I enthusiastically agree with your suggestion: there is a great deal that could be done along those lines. In fact, some time ago we worked out a model for understanding and solving word problems that made explicit the distinction between different levels of representations and their interdependence (Kintsch & Greeno, 1985) and designed a software program (Nathan, Kintsch, & Young, 1992) that guided students' efforts to solve algebra word problems by showing them the consequences at the situation-model level of what their equations implied. When they saw the faster plane leave before the slower one in an overtake problem, they immediately realized the mistake they had made! Much has been learned since then that would force us to modify some of the details of this work, but I am convinced that this remains a very promising approach where modern technology could have a direct impact on instruction, not only in mathematics, but in the other areas you mention too.

References

Beck, I. L., & McKeown, M. G. (2006). *Improving comprehension with Questioning the Author: A fresh and expanded view of a powerful approach.* New York: Scholastic.

Bereiter, C. (1997). Situated cognition and how to overcome it. In D. Kirshner & J. A. Whitson (Eds.), *Situated cognition: Social, semiotic, and psychological perspectives* (pp. 281–300). Hillsdale, NJ: Erlbaum.

Bereiter, C. (2002). *Education and mind in the knowledge age.* Mahwah, NJ: Erlbaum.

Bereiter, C., & Scardamalia, M. (2003). Learning to work creatively with knowledge. In E. De Corte, L. Verschaffel, N. Entwistle, & K. van Merriënboer (Eds.), *Powerful learning environments* (pp. 55–68). Amsterdam: Elsevier.

Brown, A. L., & Campione, J. C. (1994). Guided discovery in a community of learners. In K. McGilly (Ed.), *Classroom lessons: Cognitive theory and classroom practice* (pp. 229–272). Cambridge, MA: MIT Press.

Caccamise, D., Snyder, L., Johnson, N., Allen, C., DeHart, M., Kintsch, E., et al. (in preparation). *Summary Street: Scale-up and evaluation.*

Chase, W. G., & Simon, H. A. (1973). The mind's eye in chess. In W. G. Chase (Ed.), *Visual information processing.* New York: Academic Press.

Csikszentmihalyi, M. (1990). *Flow: The psychology of optimal experience.* New York: HarperCollins.

Dillon, A., & Gabbard, R. (1998). Hypermedia as an educational technology: A review of the quantitative research literature on learner comprehension, control and style. *Review of Educational Research, 68*, 322–349.

Duncan, R. G. (2007). The role of domain-specific knowledge in generative reasoning about complicated multileveled phenomena. *Cognition and Instruction, 25*, 271–336.

Ericsson, K. A., Charness, N., Hoffman, R. R., & Feltovich, P. J. (2006). *The Cambridge handbook of expertise and expert performance.* New York: Cambridge University Press.

Ericsson, K. A., & Kintsch, W. (1995). Long-term working memory. *Psychological Review, 102*, 211–245.

Ericsson, K. A., & Ward, P. (2007). Capturing the naturally occurring superior performance of experts in the laboratory. *Current Trends in Psychological Science, 16*, 346–350.

Fischer, G., Brown, J. S., & Burton, R. (1984). Analysis of skiing as a success model of instruction: Manipulating the learning environment to enhance skill acquisition. In B. Rogoff & J. Lave (Eds.), *Everyday cognition: Its development in social context.* Cambridge, MA: Harvard University Press.

Flavell, J. H., & Wellman, H. M. (1977). Metamemory. In R. V. Kail & J. W. Hagen (Eds.), *Perspectives on the development of memory and cognition.* Hillsdale, NJ: Erlbaum.

Foltz, P. W. (1996). Comprehension, coherence, and strategies in hypertext and linear text. In J.-F. Rouet, J. J. Levonen, A. Dillon, & R. J. Spiro (Eds.), *Hypertext and cognition* (pp. 106–136). Mahwah, NJ: Erlbaum.

Franzke, M., Kintsch, E., Caccamise, D., Johnson, N., & Dooley, S. (2005). Summary Street®: Computer support for comprehension and writing. *Journal of Educational Computing Research, 33*, 53–80.

Greeno, J. G. (1983). Conceptual entities. In D. Gentner & A. Stevens (Eds.), *Mental models* (pp. 227–252). Mahwah, NJ: Erlbaum.

Hampton, S. (2007). *Foundations: Comprehending texts.* Washington, DC: America's Choice.

Harel, I., & Papert, S. (Eds.). (1991). *Constructionism.* Norwood, NJ: Ablex Publishing Corporation.

Hidi, S., & Renninger, K. A. (2006). The four-phase model of interest development. *Educational Psychologist, 41*, 111–127.

Hirsch, E. D. (1987). *Cultural literacy: What every American needs to know.* Boston, MA: Houghton Mifflin.

Hirsch, E. D. (2006). *The knowledge deficit.* Boston, MA: Houghton Mifflin.

Hmelo-Silver, C. E., Duncan, R., & Chinn, C. A. (2007). Scaffolding and achievement in problem-based and inquiry learning: A response to Kirschner, Sweller, and Clark (2006). *Educational Psychologist, 42*, 99–107.

King, A. (1997). ASK to THINK-TEL WHY: A model of transactive peer tutoring for scaffolding higher-level complex learning. *Educational Psychologist, 32*, 221–235.

Kintsch, W. (1994). Text comprehension, memory, and learning. *American Psychologist, 49*, 294–303.

Kintsch, W. (1998). *Comprehension: A paradigm for cognition.* New York: Cambridge University Press.

Kintsch, W., & Greeno, J. G. (1985). Understanding and solving word arithmetic problems. *Psychological Review, 92*, 109–129.

Kirschner, P. A., Sweller, J., & Clark, R. E. (2006). Why minimal guidance during instruction does not work: An analysis of the failure of constructivist, discovery, problem-based, experiential, and inquiry-based teaching. *Educational Psychologist, 41*, 75–86.

Kuhn, D. (2007). Is direct instruction an answer to the right question? *Educational Psychologist, 41*, 109–113.

McKnight, C., Dillon, A., & Richards, J. (Eds.). (1993). *Hypertext: A psychological perspective*. Mahwah, NJ: Erlbaum.

McNamara, D. S. (Ed.). (2007). *Reading comprehension strategies*. New York: Erlbaum.

McNamara, D. S., Kintsch, E., Songer, N., & Kintsch, W. (1996). Are good texts always better? Text coherence, background knowledge, and levels of understanding in learning from text. *Cognition and Instruction, 14,* 1–43.

Nathan, M. J., Kintsch, W., & Young, E. (1992). A theory of word algebra problem comprehension and its implications for the design of learning environments. *Cognition and Instruction, 9,* 329–389.

Newell, A., & Simon, H. A. (1972). *Human problem solving*. Englewood Cliffs, NJ: Prentice-Hall.

Palincsar, A. S., & Brown, A. L. (1984). Reciprocal teaching of comprehension-fostering and monitoring strategies. *Cognition and Instruction, 1,* 117–175.

Pearson, P. D., & Fielding, L. (1991). Comprehension instruction. In R. Barr, M. L. Kamil, P. B. Bosenthal, & P. D. Pearson (Eds.), *Handbook of reading research* (Vol. 2, pp. 8115–8860). White Plains, NY: Longman.

Perfetti, C. A. (1989). There are generalized abilities and one of them is reading. In L. B. Resnick (Ed.), *Knowing, learning, and instruction* (pp. 307–336). Hillsdale, NJ: Erlbaum.

Reiser, B. J. (2004). Scaffolding complex learning: The mechanisms of structuring and problematizing student work. *The Journal of the Learning Sciences, 13,* 273–304.

Salmerón, L., Cañas, J. J., Kintsch, W., & Fajardo, L. (2005). Reading strategies and hypertext comprehension. *Discourse Process, 40,* 171–191.

Salmerón, L., Kintsch, W., & Cañas, J. J. (2006). Reading strategies and prior knowledge in learning from hypertext. *Memory & Cognition, 34,* 1157–1171.

Scardamalia, M., & Bereiter, C. (2003). Knowledge building. In *Encyclopedia of education* (2nd ed., pp. 1370–1373). New York: Macmillan.

Scardamalia, M., Bereiter, C., & Lamon, M. (1994). The CSILE Project: Trying to bring the classroom into World 3. In K. McGilly (Ed.), *Classroom lessons* (pp. 201–228). Cambridge, MA: MIT Press.

Schmidt, H. G., Loyens, S. M. M., van Gog, T., & Paas, F. (2007). Problem-based learning is compatible with human cognitive architecture: Commentary on Kirschner, Sweller, and Clark (2006). *Educational Psychologist, 42,* 91–97.

Schneider, W., Körkel, J., & Weinert, F. E. (1989). Domain-specific knowledge and memory performance: A comparison of high- and low-aptitude children. *Journal of Educational Psychology, 81,* 306–312.

Schunn, C. D., & Anderson, J. R. (2001). Acquiring expertise in science: Exploration of what, when, and how. In K. Crowley, C. D. Schunn, & T. Okada (Eds.), *Designing for science: Implications from everyday, classroom, and professional settings* (pp. 83–114). Hillsdale, NJ: Erlbaum.

Simon, H. A. (1996). *The sciences of the artificial* (3rd ed.). Cambridge, MA: MIT Press.

Sweller, J. (1988). Cognitive load during problem solving. *Cognitive Science, 12,* 257–285.

Tapiero, I. (2007). *Situation models and levels of coherence*. Mahwah, NJ: Erlbaum.

Therriault, D. J., & Rinck, M. (2007). Multidimensional situation models. In F. Schmalhofer & C. A. Perfetti (Eds.), *Higher level language processes in the brain*. Mahwah, NJ: Erlbaum.

Trabasso, T., & Suh, S. (1993). Understanding text: Achieving explanatory coherence through on-line inferences and mental operations in working memory. *Discourse Processes, 16,* 3–34.

Unz, D. C., & Hesse, F. W. (1999). The use of hypertext for learning. *Journal of Educational Computing Research, 20,* 279–295.

Van Dijk, T. A., & Kintsch, W. (1983). *Strategies of discourse comprehension.* New York: Academic Press.

Wolfe, M. B., Schreiner, M. E., Rehder, R., Laham, D., Foltz, P. W., Landauer, T. K., et al. (1998). Learning from text: Matching reader and text by Latent Semantic Analysis. *Discourse Processes, 25,* 309–336.

Zwaan, R. A., & Radvansky, G. A. (1998). Situation models in language comprehension and memory. *Psychological Bulletin, 123,* 162–185.

13 From Behaviorism to Constructivism

A Philosophical Journey from Drill and Practice to Situated Learning

J. D. Fletcher Institute for Defense Analyses, Alexandria, VA

Both behaviorism and constructivism stem from centuries of philosophical musing concerning the nature of reality, our perceptions of reality, and even whether reality, as we perceive it, actually exists. The first and third of these issues are perhaps more than we might want to discuss here, but the second seems fair game. It allows us to progress from philosophy to experimental psychology and, finally, to what we might say about one aspect of constructivist thinking, namely, the situation of learning in authentic experiences. This chapter suggests that constructivist prescriptions for situated learning may be derived from our philosophical roots, empirical findings from experimental psychology, and experiences with situated-learning environments that rely on simulations. Much of the empirical support that is reported here derives from the use of simulation in military training, but let's start with some philosophers.

The Philosophers[1]

Like most concepts, including those in psychological science, constructivist ideas have a basis in philosophy. Earlier and other philosophical ruminations could be cited, but for this discussion we might well begin in the 17th century with John Locke's *Essay on Human Understanding*. Locke argued that everything in the mind was first in the senses, the mind being the now-famous *tabula rasa* for recording our perceptions. His notions led to the conclusion that observational evidence alone, received by the senses, produces knowledge of the world.

Reacting to Locke, the 18th-century philosopher, Bishop George Berkeley, issued his *Treatise Concerning the Principles of Human Knowledge*, asserting that nothing exists or has meaning unless it is perceived by some mind.[2] The cat sleeping under my dining-room table exists only because my senses have told my mind that he does.[3] Words and images are essential because they give both existence and meaning to matter. Berkeley went so far as to point out that the words we use for abstracting and labeling what our senses bring to our minds may evoke in other minds different meanings and, as we might say today, different associations. In his terms, the definition of reality is, for each of us, idiosyncratic.

So far, so good, but then David Hume came along to suggest in *A Treatise of Human Nature* that we know the mind itself exists in the same way we know the cat does—through our perceptions, although in the case of the mind the perceptions (e.g., ideas, memories, feelings) are internal rather than external. So we cannot be any more sure of what our internal senses are telling us about the existence of our minds than we can of what our external senses are telling us about the cat. At this point and as Durant (1933/1961) notes, "Hume had as effectively destroyed mind as Berkeley had destroyed matter" (p. 195). This is where Immanuel Kant comes in to rescue, perhaps, the cat and our minds.

Kant's *Critique of Pure Reason* asserted that not all knowledge is derived from the senses and he set out to prove it—at least as far as the notions of 18th-century philosophical proof allowed. He meant to establish the idea (and existence) of "pure reason" that allows us to discover a priori truths that are independent of all sense experience. Kant argued that pure reason is particularly impelled to find these truths. It is as if our reason is anxiously and irrepressibly searching for the reality, the general truths, that the fire reflects as shadows on the back of Plato's cave.

Durant noted that, "[Kant's] truths derive their necessary character from the inherent structure of our minds, from the natural and inevitable manner in which our minds must operate" (1933/1961, p. 202). Kant's idea of pure reason then seems reflected in Chomsky's (1965) notion of innate, deep-structure grammar, which he likened to the basic instruction set that comes with every computer. This notion draws an analogy between, on one hand, the effects of machine microcode on the higher-order functionalities of computers, and, on the other, the effects of very basic cognitive operations on the form and character of human thought, knowledge, and, in Chomsky's case, linguistic universals. If we had evolved from silicon instead of carbon, the pure reason underlying our mathematics, science, and language might be quite different than it is. One wonders how today's rapidly emerging findings on brain functioning would have affected Kant's reflections on the nature of pure reason.

The Psychologists

The intent of this discussion is not to burden the reader with philosophical ruminations but just to suggest that the roots of constructivism are long and honorable, that these ruminations transcend Locke's tabula rasa to posit active, constructive cognitive activity underlying all that we know, and that they lend depth and perspective to our constructivist notions today.[4] They anticipate William James' General Law of Perception, which he described as follows: "Whilst part of what we perceive comes through our senses from the object before us, another part (and it may be the larger part) always comes out of our mind" (1890/1950, p. 747).

Both Locke's positivist empiricism and James' constructivist views remain with us. Neither point of view is without controversy, but both appear to have a place in psychological theory and research, just as they do in the pragmatic business of applying psychological findings to the design and development of instruction.

Psychological researchers have long debated what the fundamental phenomena of their study should be. Those who prevailed roughly from the 1920s to the 1960s followed the early logical positivists and insisted that their research be limited to directly observable and measurable behavior. Consider the views of the quintessential 1930s behaviorist, John Watson. Never one to mince words, Watson asserted that: "consciousness is neither a definite nor a usable concept. The Behaviorist, who has been trained as an experimentalist, holds further, that belief in the existence of consciousness goes back to the ancient days of superstition and magic" (Watson, 1930, p. 2).

By way of contrast, consider the "central assertion" from Ulric Neisser's seminal 1967 text, *Cognitive Psychology*, that "seeing, hearing, and remembering are all acts of *construction*, which may make more or less use of stimulus information depending on circumstances" (p. 10; the italics are Neisser's). This quote raises a point worth emphasizing. Although the foundations of educational constructivism can be found in philosophy, they are also rooted in empirical data from reputable and extensive psychological research. Locke's own empiricism may lead us to reject his tabula rasa. One suspects he would have approved.

The basis for Neisser's assertion was a large body of research showing that the behavior we observe and measure under experimental conditions cannot be satisfactorily explained without postulating some features, characteristics, and activity for the mechanisms underlying it. For instance, he points to the considerable evidence that words in text can be recognized even when all the letters in the words are absent or illegible. He suggests that there must be some internal "analysis by synthesis" or a continuing "silent stream of thought" at work to account for this evidence (Neisser, 1967, p. 186). He makes a similar argument for phonemes, words, and sentences presented aurally. For these cases, he posits a relatively passive, pre-attentive perceptual mechanism supplemented by an active, internal, and ongoing synthesis that we use to make sense of the sparse perceptual cues being provided by our senses.

Neisser concluded that although the physical capabilities of our sensory receptors and the physical information they send to the brain can account for hearing and seeing, they cannot account for such cognitive processes as reading, speech perception, language understanding, analyses of complex visual scenes, or even the recognition of evocative aromas. Locke and the behaviorists can explain seeing, but we need Berkeley, Hume, and Kant along with constructivist psychology to understand perception. Sherlock Holmes understands this as he admonishes an earlier Dr. Watson, "You see, Watson, but you do not observe. The distinction is clear" (Doyle, 1892, p. 162). It appears that if we are to understand behavior, we must understand the constructive, internal workings of cognition.

Cognitive scientists have, then, come around to the view that human cognition, involving all perception, memory, and learning, is an overwhelmingly constructive process—that the world is to a significant extent, and as George Berkeley suggested, the creation of each observer who brings it about through a sensory simulation of his/her own devising. Even straightforward recall is not viewed as the retrieval of items whole cloth from memory, but as their reconstruction from more primitive cues—perhaps substantially aided and shaped by Kant's pure reason.

Neisser is not alone in this point of view. Psychological concepts ranging from Bartlett's (1932) schemata, Lashley's (1950) systems of associations, Tulving's subjective organization in free recall (1962), Craik and Lockhart's (1972) levels of processing, Baddeley and Hitch's (1974) multi-component model of working memory, and Mayer's (2005) model of multimedia learning can all be cited to support an empirically based, constructivist view of memory and cognition. Others could be added. On this basis and as some (e.g., Fletcher, 1982; von Glasersfeld, 1989, 1997) have suggested, we might, then, be advised to view perceivers and learners not as passive recorders of information transmitted to them over channels, but as active participants who use the fragmentary cues permitted them by their limited sensory receptors to construct, verify, and modify their own sensory simulations of the world.

Beyond issues of recall, constructivist views have persisted across many schools of thought in scientific psychology, suppressed as they were by Watson, Skinner, and others. These views can be found in the work of Gestalt psychologists such as Lewin (1951)—whose field theory and group dynamics described behavior in terms of the complex vectors we use to function in our environments—and even in the work of neo-behaviorists such as Tolman (1948)—who was willing to investigate internal phenomena such as goals, purpose, and cognitive maps. In short, a wide spectrum of psychologists saw a need to swing the research pendulum back from the strict logical positivism of behaviorism to consideration of internal, constructivist, cognitive processes.

Both sides of the behaviorist–constructivist issue have merit. Neither point of view is without controversy, but both appear to have a place in psychological theory and research, just as they do in the pragmatic business of instruction. In general, we do not want behavioral science to regress into an armchair study of gedanken phenomena independent of empirical verification. But, with a nod to Locke's empiricism, we would like to go where our data take us and better understand the empirical findings that emerge from experimental psychology, including, perhaps, today's neuro-physiological revelations about the organization of the brain and its functioning. And we would like to draw on them in designing and developing instruction.

Learning and Instruction

For some time and in a number of venues (cf. Duffy & Cunningham, 1996; Fletcher, 1982; Savery & Duffy, 1996; Tobias & Frase, 2000), we have been asking what the above findings of philosophers and experimental psychologists have to say for learning and instruction. The above discussion led us perilously close to the "Radical Constructivism" of Ernst von Glasersfeld, who also starts with George Berkeley but stirs in the philosophical considerations of Berkeley's contemporary, Giambattista Vico (e.g., von Glasersfeld, 1997). Though he follows different paths, von Glasersfeld ends up very close to the conclusions suggested here.

Dissatisfied with the "Radical Behaviorism" of Watson (quoted above) and in keeping with William James (quoted above), von Glasersfeld described Radical Constructivism as a form of pragmatism in which the uncertainty that our knowledge reflects an external, independent, objective reality leads necessarily to a concern with the world each of us constructs through our experience. He suggests that students "share with ... science, the goal of constructing a relatively stable and coherent model of their individual experiential worlds," and that without this fundamental assumption "we cannot lead them to expand their understanding" (von Glasersfeld, 1989, p. 13). So far, so good. However, he goes on to assert that "memorizing facts and training in rote procedures cannot achieve this" (von Glasersfeld, 1989, p. 13). This may swing the pendulum back too far. There may be good reason to consider the value of committing facts, basic concepts, and rote procedures to memory in learning and instruction. If we choose to be radically pragmatic, there may be much to say for drill and practice.

Drill and Practice

Drill and practice has become a popular target for derision among many designers and developers of instruction and especially those developing technology-based instruction. "Drill and kill" evokes images of bored students being driven relentlessly through linear sequences of meaningless instructional items. However, many early drill and practice programs worked very well and were enjoyed by their students (e.g., Fletcher & Atkinson, 1973; Fletcher & Suppes, 1975; Suppes & Morningstar, 1972; Vinsonhaler & Bass, 1972). These drill and practice programs adjusted content, sequence, difficulty, and pace for individual learners—capabilities occasionally listed today as defining characteristics of "intelligent tutoring systems." These programs were effective because they focused on explicit instructional objectives, data-based evidence of progress in achieving the objectives, promoting motivation and learner engagement through frequent interaction, and tailoring those interactions in real time to the needs of individuals.

Drill and practice programs appear to be particularly effective when their objectives require only a few cognitive steps to construct correct responses from stimuli or prompts.[5] For instance, associating the phoneme /at/ with the spelling pattern "at" in beginning reading or the word "gato" with "cat" in learning foreign-language vocabulary does not take many cognitive steps compared to problem solving or decision making. The same might apply to learning that "cat" is a mammal or the procedures to use in operating a can opener. Basically, this material involves simple, if not rote, remembering, understanding, and applying—to use terms adopted from Bloom's (1956) and Anderson and Krathwohl's (2001) hierarchies of learning.

Instructional content of this sort does not draw heavily on Hume's internal perceptions or Kant's pure reason. Learning in these cases resembles the business of plugging in items on Locke's tabula rasa. Drill and practice programs on arithmetic "facts" and spelling patterns and sight vocabulary in beginning reading that involve relatively straightforward associations between the stimulus presented and a correct response have in meta-analyses been quite successful, showing effect sizes of 0.50 and higher (e.g., Fletcher, 1997, 2003, 2004; Kulik, 1994). In these cases there is an unambiguous correct answer to each question, and the student's answer signifies fairly well if it has been learned or not. Students could eventually discover their way through properly constructed situated environments to learn material of this sort, but it seems far more efficient to deal with learning of this sort directly through drill and practice—students' time is after all worth something.

Logical positivism appears to work well in the design of these programs. One very precise measure of the Stanford mathematics program effectiveness was reported in "trajectory theory" evaluations developed by Suppes, Fletcher, and Zanotti (1975, 1976). Rather than employ the usual competitive race for achievement between control and experimental groups, trajectory theory attempted to account for student achievement strictly from the amount of time on task—the amount of time each student spent working with, in this case, computer-assisted instruction in arithmetic. Suppes et al. found that they could predict to the nearest one-tenth the comprehensive mathematics grade placement score on a standard test for 90% of the learners.

One aspect of instructional effectiveness keys on cost. Most administrative decisions about education concern not simply identifying and making improvements in instructional practice, but determining what must be given up in order to put them in place. Cost often turns out to be the most accessible measure of what must be given up, making the cost-effectiveness of instructional practices relative to others that are available a matter of central concern to decision makers.

The cost-effectiveness of computer-based drill and practice was examined by Fletcher, Hawley, and Piele (1990). Using experimental data reported by Jamison, Fletcher, Suppes, and Atkinson (1976), Levin, Glass, and Meister (1987), and a controlled study of their own, Fletcher et al. examined the costs (in constant dollars) to raise comprehensive mathematics scores on a standardized test one standard deviation using different instructional approaches: peer tutors, professional tutors, reduced class size, increased instructional time, and computer-assisted instruction. They found that the most cost-effective approaches among all these alternatives were computer-based instruction and peer tutoring and that, of the two, computer-based instruction was more cost-effective in three of four cases.

This result echoes the findings of Niemiec, Sikorski, and Walberg (1989) who compared studies of the costs and effectiveness of peer tutoring with studies of computer-based instruction. They found the two approaches to be equally effective and both to be more effective by about 0.4 standard deviations than conventional classroom instruction. Niemiec et al. also found a clear cost-effectiveness superiority (by a factor of about three) for computer-based instruction over peer tutoring—although as Fletcher et al. (1990) pointed out, the two are not incompatible and can be used together.

These positivist approaches take little note of learners' internal processing, but they, especially the effective ones, used various means to estimate the current state of the learners' progress toward achieving instructional objectives. For instance, consider a model, adapted from Paulson (1973), for use in tailoring instruction to individual learners. This model attempted to account for what happens when a student is asked a question concerning an item of knowledge— for example an arithmetic fact, an economic concept, or the next step in a standard procedure—and what happens when that item is not addressed but the student is asked to answer a question concerning some other item.

The model assumes that every item to be learned by a student is in one of three states in memory—learned, short-term, or unlearned. An item in the learned state for the student is assumed to stay in that state forever. When a question concerning an item in the unlearned state is presented, the item can advance to the learned state, the short-term state, or stay where it is. Similarly, when a question concerning an item in the short-term state is presented, the item can either advance to the learned state or stay where it is. When any item is presented to a student, other items in the short-term state for that student will either drop back to the unlearned state or stay where they are. All items for every student are assumed to begin in the unlearned state.

The model then attempts to account for transitions of items from one state to another by estimating the probability that they will occur. The model takes form in a transition matrix (Figure 13.1):

In words:

- If a learned item (state L) is presented, then:
  - with probability = *1*, it stays there.
- If an unlearned item (state U) is presented, then:
  - with probability = *a*, it will transition to the learned state;
  - with probability = *b*, it will transition to a short-term state from which it can either be learned or forgotten; and finally,
  - with probability = *1−a−b*, it will remain unlearned.
- If an item is in short-term state (S), then:
  - with probability = *c*, it will transition to the learned state; otherwise,
  - with probability = *1−c*, it will remain in the short-term state.

A key feature of this model is that it accounts for items that are *not* presented on a trial. In Paulson's (1973) formulation—based on Rumelhart's General Forget-

		State on trial n+1			
		L	S	U	P (correct)
State on trial n	L	1	0	0	1
	S	c	1−c	0	1
	U	a	b	1−a−b	g

Figure 13.1 Probability of an item's state transition when it is presented on trial n+1, given its state on trial n.

		State on trial n+1		
		L	S	U
State on trial n	L	1	0	0
	S	0	1–f	f
	U	0	0	1

Figure 13.2 Probability of an item's state transition when it is *not* presented on trial n+1, given its state on trial n.

ting Theory (1967)—when an item is not presented but some other item is, transitions between states are expected to occur in accord with the transition matrix in Figure 13.2:

In words, when an item is not presented:

- if it is in the learned or unlearned state, it stays there with probability = *1*;
- If it is in the short-term state, it may regress to the unlearned state with probability *f* or remain in the short-term state with probability *1–f*.

Formulations such as this, which are based on explicit transition models of memory, tell us what state every problem or item is in for each learner. They focus on discrete items that are to be remembered, understood, or applied and stop there. They lead to very effective instructional strategies that are provably optimal in maximizing the number of items learned by an individual student in the total time allocated for instruction. Although these strategies account for the learner's state, they do not directly support the cognitive processes used by learners to develop, test, and revise their internal representations or models of the subject matter.

Situated, Simulated Environments

At some point, then, learners may need to move up the knowledge hierarchy having first acquired a body of discrete items that can be learned—memorized, understood, and applied—through repetitive, behavioral, positivist approaches like drill and practice. These separate items of knowledge are often gleaned from a detailed analysis of the targeted subject matter and are intended to identify the elemental components it requires for competent performance. Once these items are learned and in order to advance their knowledge and competency, students must assemble, connect, and integrate these items into the analytic, evaluative, and even creative capabilities they need to solve problems, make decisions, and take effective action. In designing and developing learning environments to encourage this synthesis of discrete items into competent performance it seems reasonable, if not imperative, to support learners as much as possible in constructing, assessing, and modifying their internal, cognitive models and representations of the subject matter. One way to do this is to situate learners in "authentic" environments that they can use to develop, test, and hone these representations along with their subject-matter knowledge and skills.

Enter "learning by doing" and John Dewey. In Dewey's words, learning "is a continuous reconstruction, moving from the child's present experience out into that represented by the organized bodies of truth that we call studies" (1947, p. 11). Dewey focused on the learner's experience in such activities as planning, interpreting, problem solving, and decision making rather than the acquisition of discrete elements of "studies" such as facts and concepts. Most probably influenced by his study of philosophy, including his doctoral dissertation on Kant, Dewey emphasized the need for students to learn not just content but also processes of thinking—by becoming, in today's terms, "cognitive apprentices." This focus is echoed by Schuell's (1988) discussion of the learner's role in adding and constructing knowledge not explicitly provided by classroom teachers but that the learner needs in order to organize and make sense of the learning environment teachers provide. These and similar considerations lead us to constructivist, student-centered interests in situated-learning environments, which in turn lead us to the use of simulations in learning.

A claim of this chapter and its author is that constructivist theory in philosophy and experimental psychology leads directly to situated learning and that empirical support for constructivist notions in education may therefore be found in the considerable body of knowledge that has been collected, especially by the military, on the use and value of simulations in training. Before discussing instructional practice in this area we might caution against carrying it too far. Experience derived from situated, authentic environments is an essential element in learning and instruction, but research both early and recent suggests that unguided, free play does not yield the learning being sought (Clark, 2005; Gay, 1986; Kalyuga, Ayres, Chandler, & Sweller, 2003; Kirschner, Sweller, & Clark, 2006; Morrison & Meliza, 1999).

Enthusiasm for providing environments in which students reliably discover their way to the valid, internal representations required for human competence in any area must be tempered by the need for both guidance and explicit feedback. For example, Clark, in taking account of the need for guidance, developed Guided Experiential Learning (GEL) (2005). GEL is a pragmatic, systematically developed approach, based on research findings in information feedback, performance measurement, cognition and memory, and principles of instructional design, which integrates instructionally productive features of guidance and problem solving with situated, authentic environments.

In responding to the need for feedback, the US Army developed after-action reviews (AARs), which are based on similar research findings. Feedback provided by AARs after training exercises is not presented in a didactic manner, but as a facilitated discussion among the participants (Morrison & Meliza, 1999). All participants interact as equals discovering and diagnosing, with the help of exercise instrumentation, what happened during their engagements and how to develop what may be described as a shared mental model of the action. AARs have proven to be an invaluable source of feedback to participants in free-play training exercises that otherwise would remain shrouded in the fog of exigencies that these environments require for authenticity.

On the basis of these considerations, it may be past time to review some processes, analyses, and data extracted from the military's use of simulation-based training. Consider, for instance, the task of training pilots for combat operations. As discussed by Pohlman and Fletcher (1999), combat pilots must learn:

- *Basic Airmanship.* There are four basic dimensions to flight: Altitude (height above a point); Attitude (position in the air); Position (relative to a point in space); and Time (normally a function of airspeed). A pilot must control these four dimensions simultaneously. Doing so allows the aircraft to take off, remain in flight, travel from point A to point B, approach, and land.
- *Aircraft Systems Operation.* Combat pilots must also operate the aircraft systems. These systems include engine controls, navigation, fuel controls, communications, airframe controls, and environmental controls, among others. Some aircraft have on-board systems that can be run by other crew members, but the pilot remains responsible for them and must be aware of the status of each system at all times.
- *Navigation.* Once pilots master basic airmanship and aircraft system operations, they must learn to navigate in four dimensions. Pilots must maintain the aircraft in all types of airspace, in all manner of environmental conditions, at an assigned position, on an assigned course and heading. They must maintain altitude, or modify it at an assigned rate and airspeed while acknowledging and implementing constantly changing instructions.
- *Combat Weapons Systems.* Combat aircraft confront pilots with many additional systems to contend with. Combat pilots must understand how each weapon affects the aircraft when it is aboard and when it is launched. They must understand the launch parameters of the weapons, their flight characteristics, and the additional system controls they require. These controls consist of buttons, switches, rockers, and sliders located on the throttles and stick grip. The pilot must understand, monitor, and operate properly (while wearing flight gloves) all controls belonging to each system.
- *Survival.* All of the above must be attended to while people on the ground, at sea, and/or in the air are trying their best to remove our pilot from the scene—by any means available.

The task of flying fighter aircraft is one of the most complex cognitive tasks imaginable. A fighter pilot must be so versed in flying and operating the aircraft that nearly all of the tasks just described become automatic. Pilots describe this ability as "strapping the aircraft on." Although the temporal distance between stimulus and response must frequently and necessarily be very short for combat pilots, the number of cognitive processes between stimulus and response needed to identify, weigh, prioritize, evaluate, manage, and adjust issues of some urgency is very large. Refining these processes to the point of automaticity helps, but pilots must temper and balance these processes with cognitive judgments required to deal with specific circumstances, missions, and equally competent individuals who are trying to out-guess them.

The instruction we now provide to produce combat pilots uses a bottom-up process, providing drill and practice for the discrete knowledge and skills required. This process is complemented with top-down, simulation-based learning that situates the learner in approximations of the ultimate performance environment. Both instructional approaches are used to produce combat pilots and others who must perform similarly demanding activities. Locke still has his place, but so do Berkeley, Hume, and Kant.

Combat piloting may be an extreme example because of its time pressures, to say nothing of life-and-death issues, but the programs of instruction we provide seem applicable to many non-combat activities, such as emergency-room medical care, first responses to disasters, athletic competition, and so forth. Further, there are cases without similar time and/or survival pressures, such as business and operational planning, equipment troubleshooting and repair, and medical diagnosis, where cognitive steps between stimulus (internally and/or externally generated) and response are equally plentiful and complex and where the internal cognitive processes used to solve problems and make decisions must be optimized at least for correctness, if not, in these cases, for speed.

For all these cases, we may turn to learning environments supported by simulation, which can provide both full-task, highly realistic environments needed for situated practice and partial-task "coached" environments needed for more diagnostic, systematic instruction. Both environments can support development, testing, and modification of the representations that are needed for competent performance and both can compress the time needed to attain levels of expertise that would otherwise require a lifetime of job-site experience to acquire. Evidence of the impact of these simulation environments on development of internal cognitive models has been discussed by Andrews and Bell (2000)—among others—and can be found in research on shared mental models by Cannon-Bowers, Salas, Blickensderfer, and Bowers (1998) and Rouse, Cannon-Bowers, and Salas (1992)—among others.

The benefits of simulation include safety, economy, controlled visibility, and reproducibility (Andrews & Bell, 2000; O'Neil & Robertson, 1992; Orlansky et al., 1994; Raser, 1969). Simulated environments permit the attainment of training objectives that cannot or should not be attempted without simulation. Aircraft can be crashed, expensive equipment ruined, and lives hazarded in simulated environments in ways that otherwise range from the impractical to the unthinkable. Simulated environments can make the invisible visible, compress or expand time required in the real world for events to occur, and repeatedly reproduce events, situations, and decision points. They enable the attainment of instructional objectives that are otherwise inaccessible.

Simulation environments are intended to link instructional intervention directly to performance. In aircrew training the issue keys on transfer to see if the skills and knowledge acquired in simulation are of value in flying actual aircraft. Many attempts to answer this question rely on transfer-effectiveness ratios (TER) (e.g., Roscoe & Williges, 1980). These ratios may be defined for pilot training in the following way:

$$TER = \frac{Ac - As}{S}$$

Where:

TER= Transfer-Effectiveness Ratio;
Ac = Aircraft time required to reach criterion performance, without access to simulation;
As = Aircraft time required to reach criterion performance, with access to simulation;
S   = Simulator time.

Roughly, this TER tells us how much aircraft time is saved for every unit of simulator time invested. Orlansky and String (1977) investigated this issue in an often-cited study. They found (or calculated, as needed) 34 TERs from assessments performed from 1967 to 1977 by military, commercial, and academic organizations. The TERs ranged from −0.4 to 1.9, with a median value of 0.45, suggesting that, overall, an hour in a simulator saves about 27 minutes (0.45 × 60 minutes) in an aircraft. Orlansky, Knapp, and String (1984) also compared the costs to fly actual aircraft with the cost to "fly" simulators. Very generally they found that the cost to operate a flight simulator is about one-tenth the cost to operate representative military aircraft. Assuming that an hour in a simulator saves about one half-hour in an aircraft, the use of flight simulators, overall, is cost-effective if the TER is 0.2 or greater.

At one level, this finding is useful and significant. However, a few caveats may be in order. First, Provenmire and Roscoe (1973) pointed out that not all simulator hours are equal—early hours in the simulator appear to save more aircraft time than later ones. This consideration leads to learning-curve differences between cumulative TERs and incremental TERs, with diminishing returns best captured by the latter.

Second, transfer is not a characteristic of the simulator alone. Estimates of transfer from a simulator or simulated environment must also consider what the training is trying to accomplish—the training objectives. This issue is well illustrated in a study by Holman (1979) who found 24 TERs for a CH-47 helicopter simulator ranging from 2.8 to 0.0, depending on which training objective was under consideration.

Third, there is an interaction between knowledge of the subject matter and the value of simulation alone. Clark and Estes (2002), Gay (1986), Tobias (1989, 2003), and others have emphasized that the less the student knows about the subject matter, the greater the need for tutorial guidance in simulation. Kalyuga et al. (2003) summarized a number of studies demonstrating an "expertise reversal effect" indicating that high levels of instructional support are needed for novice learners but have little effect on experts and may actually interfere with their learning.

Fourth, the operating costs of aircraft differ markedly and will create quite different trade-offs between the cost-effectiveness of training with simulators and without them. In contrast to the military aircraft considered by Orlansky et al.

(1984) where the cost ratio of aircraft to simulator was about 0.1, Provenmire and Roscoe (1973) considered flight simulation for the Piper Cherokee, where the cost ratio was 0.73.

Still, TERs are a significant capability for making instruction accountable in a quantitative fashion across many subject areas beyond pilot training. We have but to generalize their application by substituting actual equipment time (whatever that equipment may be) or real-world experience for aircraft time in the above TER definition and we are on the path to assessing the costs and effectiveness of situated instruction in achieving whatever competencies we wish the learner to achieve.

Given their probable utility, if and how TERs might be relevant to education deserves attention. Their utility may be found across many aspects of instruction—those involving the ability to solve ill-structured problems as well as those keyed to specific tasks and skills. Their use may reduce costs, increase safety, compress the experience needed to achieve both competence and mastery, and ensure that the instruction given is the instruction needed in a wide variety of applications. It suggests that TERs may deserve as much serious attention from educators as they have received from trainers—and from anyone concerned with informing decision makers about situating learning in relevant experience.

Does situated learning/instruction work? How well? These issues have been discussed at length in the area of military training by many commentators (e.g., Orlansky et al., 1994; Gorman, 1990). A prime example of the approach is found in a natural experiment that occurred during the Vietnam War and led to the establishment of the US Navy's now famous Top Gun exercises, the US Army's National Training Center, and other combat training centers across the US military (Fletcher, 1999, in press).

In the air war over North Vietnam, the US Navy and US Air Force flew aircraft of comparable capabilities. In fact, many of the aircraft used were exactly the same, armed with the same weapons. During the first four years of air-to-air combat, both the Navy and the Air Force experienced an identical, and disappointingly low, loss-exchange ratio of North Vietnamese to US aircraft downed—2.2 to 2.4 North Vietnamese aircraft for every US aircraft.

There was a halt in air combat operations over North Vietnam from 1968 to 1970. During this period, the US Navy, but not the Air Force, initiated a training program using simulated, well-instrumented, force-on-force combat engagements to enhance pilot performance in air-to-air combat. The pilots flew aircraft, not simulators, so the flying was real, only the combat was simulated. Navy student pilots were pitted against "enemy" pilots—other, highly proficient Navy pilots trained in enemy tactics and flying MIG-type aircraft. Engagements were played and re-played until the Navy student flyers got them right.

In 1970 when the air war resumed, Navy pilots, still flying the same aircraft as their Air Force counterparts but trained using engagement simulation, performed about six times better than Air Force pilots whose training had remained unchanged. The new loss-exchange ratios were 2.0 for Air Force pilots and 12.5 for Navy pilots. No one calculated a TER for this experience, but the value of the simulated combat experience seems evident.

The success of situated learning in mock-combat environments gave birth to a host of combat training centers used to prepare military personnel for real-world operations (Chatham, in press; Fletcher, in press). These environments provide serious, situated practice with feedback. They are intended to provide training in emergent task environments involving tasks and activities that cannot be pre-specified in any deterministic fashion. The tasks evolve rapidly over time and in response to actions taken in the simulated environment. Communication and coordination between individuals, crews, teams, and units are free and uncontrolled. Outcomes are determined only by the participants' decisions and actions.

It is now commonly said (e.g., Gorman, 1990) that everything short of actual combat is simulation. In the First Gulf War, a cavalry troop commander led his nine tanks into a 23-minute attack that destroyed about 50 opposing tanks, 25 armored personnel carriers, 40 trucks, and a variety of other vehicles with no losses on his part. He was asked how he, who had no prior combat experience, had managed to accomplish this. He countered that was not the first time he had fought a battle. He had fought them in force-on-force engagements at the National Training Center (a mock-combat environment for land forces), in combined-arms live-fire exercises, and other simulations. He stated that he and his crews had simply carried out the correct drills automatically and completed them before realizing fully that they were not in a simulation (Fletcher, in press; McMaster, 1992, 2005).

Combat training centers may appear to be situated learning on steroids and a long way from the philosophical ruminations of Locke, Berkeley, Hume, and Kant on perception, reason, and reality; they may also seem remote from findings of psychological researchers on human cognition and learning, but the connections seem genuine. Designers and developers of these centers focus on the ability of participants to perceive the engagement through an internal cognitive representation they describe as "situation awareness" (e.g., Endsley, 1988). The centers themselves apply applications based on psychological principles of information feedback, performance measurement, cognition and memory, group processes, communication theory, sophisticated principles of instructional design, as well as much that the military has learned about situating training through the use of simulations.

Simulations have been used in much less dramatic training and education performed by the military. For instance, 24 studies of instruction using simulations based on videodiscs in residential military training for subject matter ranging from maintenance of electronic equipment to command and control to leadership found an overall effect size of 0.39 (Fletcher, 1997). Effect sizes for nine similar comparisons in industrial training averaged 0.51, and effect sizes for 14 comparisons in higher education averaged 0.69. Simulation based on videodiscs is, of course, passé today, but follow-on technologies using technology-based simulations in classroom use should show at least equal, if not superior, instructional effectiveness.

In considering learners as active constructors of cognitive models and mental simulations of the external environment, it should be emphasized that simulations and situated learning also help them test and verify these cognitive representations. Instruction using these approaches provides students opportunity to devise and test their own hypotheses concerning the subject matter by allowing them to manipulate and experiment with the simulations and view the results directly for themselves. It may take us back to Dewey's learning by doing, but it is common practice in today's military and elsewhere among today's game players.

Final Thoughts

Let's conclude with a few assertions that the preceding discussion was intended to support.

Constructivism has deep roots in philosophical thought. This foundation has led to a large body of findings in empirical, scientific research suggesting a need to posit internal, cognitive representations and "runnable models" (cognitive simulations) that we use to understand and deal with our environment. These representations are developed, tested, and modified based on the limited evidence provided by our senses. Effective instruction must, to some extent, create environments that support learners in this representation-building activity.

Most learning involves straightforward remembering, understanding, and applying, in fairly rote fashion, facts, concepts, and rudimentary procedures. This activity is most effectively and efficiently accomplished through repetitive, behavioral, positivist approaches such as well-designed drill and practice that promotes motivation and learner engagement through frequent interaction tailored to the individual learner's needs. These approaches should take account of the learner's state of knowledge with respect to the targeted instructional objectives, but it need not go farther to be effective in achieving these necessary, lower-order, objectives.

Much instruction is intended to go beyond these limited learning objectives and is intended to develop analytical, evaluative, and creative capabilities. Such instruction requires richer learning environments to support the learner's representation-building efforts. Prominent among these environments are those that situate the learner in "authentic" experience. These situated learning environments may be produced and provided through the use of simulations.

There exists much empirical evidence in training research literature concerning the design and effectiveness of simulation-based learning. This evidence may be used to support the tenets of constructivism in education.

Empirical evidence on effectiveness matters. It should support progress in developing our capabilities for producing environments in which people learn and decisions concerning our choices among alternative education and training interventions. It should provide systematically derived data on both effectiveness and costs. Perhaps in the spirit of Kant's concern with pure reason and/or Dewey's emphasis on the processes of learning rather than the content of knowledge, constructivists may resort to rhetoric and essays to support their instructional recommendations. It may be time to remember Locke's empirical positivism and attend more to providing data to support the representation-building efforts of skeptics.

Finally, it should be noted that in both philosophy and experimental psychology, behaviorism and constructivism may be driven to extremes. They should be viewed not as competing opposites but as complementary approaches in the pragmatic business of designing, developing, and delivering instruction.

Question: Kintsch. *Is decontextualized drill prior to authentic learning experiences the best way to go? Instead of forcing students to drill something they are not interested in (say, we make them memorize useful arithmetic facts until they thoroughly hate math), could we put them into the simulator first so that they discover what they need to learn? With a personal goal they care about, people are willing to put up with a lot of drill and practice—it is not just the soccer players who practice endlessly, but those few who develop more intellectual interests spend many hours of serious work in their pursuits, too.*

Reply: Fletcher. Merrill used to talk about "rule," "example," "practice" as, generally, the sequence best used in learning. We found through some experiments that "example," "rule," "practice" was more motivating and productive. This is to just to say righto—I agree with your notion of providing some simulator experience first as a way to motivate students to drudge their way through drill and practice on the facts, simple concepts, and straightforward, possibly rote, procedures they need in order to function successfully in whatever simulated or real environment you are preparing them for. It would also help learners solve the abductive problem of figuring out what, in a messy scene, is relevant and what is not. However, we probably don't want to throw students into simulated situations that are so difficult and bewildering that they are discouraged from the very start of instruction. And we probably wouldn't want to condemn students to an environment in which they are solely dependent on discovery to learn whatever they need to learn. For one thing it is inefficient— trainees' time is obviously valuable if we are paying for their training—but even in K-12 education, I claim students' time is, for many reasons, worth something. For another thing, discovery without support can actually be frustrating and de-motivating.

Drill and practice, if individualized and incentivized through competition, M&Ms, or whatever, can be quite motivating. Students in the Suppes and Atkinson K-12 drill and practice programs at Stanford could usually be coerced into good behavior by threatening banishment from the computer. All this is to suggest avoiding instruction that relies solely on simulation, discovery, guidance, or drill but rather seeking some balance among them. Okay, what's the balance? For what students, what instructional objectives, under what conditions? This looks like a job for research.

Question: Kintsch. *You make a good argument for drill and a good argument for simulators; can you elaborate on your claim that to have "acquired a body of discrete items ... through ... drill and practice" is a precondition for constructive learning, such as is involved in a simulator? What discrete items does a pilot have to be drilled in? How are they selected? How much drill? Is there evidence for the effectiveness of such drill in pilots undergoing simulator training?*

Reply: Fletcher. A glance, however cursory, into the cockpit of any airplane reveals the mess of instruments, gauges, dials, displays, and switches that pilots have to understand and apply. Those of us who fly frequently will be interested to know that the location and functionality of all this instrumentation differs markedly among different types of airplanes. This information needs to be well in hand, or in mind, in order to successfully fly an airplane or a simulator. I would cite the literature on individualized drill and practice as evidence for its use as an effective and efficient way for pilots to learn this material. There may be more effective and efficient environments in which to learn discrete matter of this sort, but none leap to mind. What does leap to mind are the problems, such as those discussed by Mayer (2004), that naive learners have with discovery learning. I would be tempted to cite these as evidence that a body of discrete items is a precondition for success in situated, simulator-based learning, and again I would be tempted to cite drill and practice as the most effective and efficient way to acquire them.

Also, there are things we would like pilots, surgeons, firefighters, cooks, and truck drivers to do automatically and correctly. People speak of just-in-time learning as a virtue, but there is much to say in favor of just-in-case learning. If a pilot notes from instruments that an engine is about to catch fire, we would not be encouraged if his first step is to turn to the index of an operator's manual to look up fire, engine, prevention. Again, I would point to drill and practice as the most effective, efficient way of achieving the necessary levels of automatic responding. I'd even go so far as to recommend over-learning through drill and practice as a way to ensure pilots and others will have retained these responses on those rare occasions when they are called for.

You asked, quite correctly, what sorts of things are appropriate for drill, how are they selected, and if drilled does that matter? Well, we might consider two dimensions: what is learned (facts, concepts, procedures, and metacognition) and the criterion for learning (remember, understand, apply, analyze, evaluate, and create). I claim that the closer we are to the fact-remember ends of the dimensions the closer we are to matters that are appropriate for drill. The closer we get to the metacognitive-create end of the dimensions, the closer we may be to items that are appropriate for situated, simulation-based approaches. So where, you might ask, is the point where we should shift from one approach to the other? Wish I knew. Your good question suggests the value of principles for determining the optimal quantitative balance between drill and simulation (for specific students, objectives, and conditions).

Question: Herman and Gomez. *We take your point that the pilot's simulator example is a good example of the blending of factual knowledge in the context of a highly situated practice that is significantly guided. The question for us is what is the relationship of knowledge that is required to be a pilot and the sorts of knowledge necessary for learning in traditional disciplines of schooling?*

Reply: Fletcher. That's a very good question for those of us who spend time bouncing between education and training and sitting on the cusp between. We might start with the notion that training is intended to prepare individuals and teams to perform specific tasks or jobs. In this sense training is strictly a means to an end. Success in terms of the knowledge and skills targeted is measured by success in doing the targeted tasks or job. Despite all the promotion of education as a key to expanded opportunities and income, I'd say that education is, in a very fundamental sense, an end in itself. It is preparation for life. And I'd say that the business of K-16 schools is primarily education and the preparation of people to fly aircraft is primarily training. However, there seem to be few training programs that do not contain elements of education and few education programs that do not prepare people to perform specific tasks. Also, they are both intended to produce learning. We teach penmanship, lab procedures, and arithmetic "facts" in education, and aerodynamics and Ohm's law in training. So I'd put education and training at opposite ends of a single dimension we might, for lack of anything better, call "instruction."

These considerations maybe point to John Dewey's concentration on process in education—generally learning to learn, problem solve, make decisions—rather than the specific things we are supposed to learn in training—specific problems we are supposed to solve or specific decisions we are supposed to make. So in training we might say that content is king and, in education, it's processes—perhaps the more abstract and "higher order" the better. However, I'd venture to say that the core differences between training to be a pilot and mastering the traditional disciplines of schooling do not key on the kinds of knowledge we present. Instead, I'd say, at least for the moment, that the primary difference lies in the intent or purpose of the instruction. We have to get electronic technicians to learn, understand, and apply Ohm's law so that they can repair radar repeaters, and we have to do the same to prepare students to be physicists. And I end up with the notion that situated (but guided!) simulation-based learning is as appropriate for educating K-12 students as it is for training fighter pilots.

Question: Herman and Gomez. *Some scholars argue that children and adolescents, unlike adult pilots, are not capable of carrying out the abstract cognitive transformations that are necessary for true knowledge construction. Presumably, such transformations are required to successfully use simulators for learning. Is this a valid concern when thinking of bringing simulator-like learning to the education of children and early adolescents?*

Reply: Fletcher. The glib response might be that if children and adolescents are incapable of the abstract cognitive transformations that are necessary for true knowledge construction how did they learn to talk? And maybe that's not so bad after all. As Chomsky pointed out ages ago (i.e., 1965), very young children learn (using Kant's pure reason?) to construct and utter sentences that they have never heard and have never themselves produced before. And they do so out of a resolutely situated, constructivist, discovery-learning environment. Could they do that without some capability for the abstract cognitive transformations needed for knowledge construction in simulation-based training? But that's not an entirely rhetorical question. Perhaps language learning is so different from all other kinds of learning that it simply doesn't apply to the use of simulators for learning. Perhaps the capability dies out at age six or so when language learning seems to require quite different cognitive pathways than it did for first-language learning.

That said, it seems likely that, through repetition and practice in a simulated environment, children might well be able to acquire the kinds of near-transfer, domain-specific skills required by a number of training settings. However, children do learn soccer, kite flying, violin playing, and quite complicated computer games. One might guess that they would be less capable of performing tasks requiring far and non-domain transfer. Someone once said that we constantly overestimate the language capabilities of children and underestimate their thinking abilities. A series of experiments with simulated environments involving different degrees of transfer might be called for here. No doubt you have noticed that I've answered your question by calling for more research. But I am tromping around in an area, developmental processes, that I rarely visit. I had better leave these issues to those who know what they are talking about.

Notes

1 Bibliographic note—in reviewing these arguments, I found Will Durant's *Story of Philosophy* (1961) to be most helpful. I quote from his book here and there and therefore feel obliged to cite my 1961 edition, which is out of print.
2 God's mind fortunately included, so that the physical world did not, for Berkeley, depend for its existence on human minds.
3 Let's set the cat's mind and perceptions aside for this discussion.
4 A more extensive discussion of the philosophical roots of constructivism, but following somewhat different paths, is provided by Duffy and Cunningham (1996).
5 The reader may discern an effort here to avoid debate over the distinguishing characteristics of declarative versus procedural knowledge.

References

Anderson, L. W., & Krathwohl, D. R. (Eds.). (2001). *A taxonomy for learning, teaching, and assessing: A taxonomy of educational objectives.* Columbus, OH: Allyn & Bacon.

Andrews, D. H., & Bell, H. H. (2000). Simulation based training. In S. Tobias & J. D. Fletcher (Eds.), *Training and retraining: A handbook for business, industry, government, and the military* (pp. 357–384). New York: Macmillan Gale Group.

Baddeley, A. D., & Hitch, G. J. (1974). Working memory. In G. A. Bower (Ed.), *The psychology of learning and motivation: Advances in research and theory* (Vol. 8, pp. 47–89). New York: Academic Press.

Bartlett, F. C. (1932). *Remembering.* Cambridge: Cambridge University Press.

Bloom, B. S. (1956). *Taxonomy of educational objectives, handbook I: The cognitive domain.* New York: David McKay Co. Inc.

Cannon-Bowers, J. A., Salas, E., Blickensderfer, E. L., & Bowers, C. A. (1998). The impact of cross-training and workload on team functioning: A replication and extension of initial findings. *Human Factors, 40,* 92–101.

Chatham, R. E. (in press). Toward a second training revolution: Promise and pitfalls of digital experiential training. In K. A. Ericcson (Ed.), *Development of professional performance: Approaches to objective measurement and designed learning environments.* New York: Cambridge University Press.

Chomsky, N. (1965). *Aspects of the theory of syntax*. Cambridge, MA: MIT Press.

Clark, R. E. (2005). *Guided experiential learning: Training design and evaluation*. Retrieved from http://projects.ict.usc.edu/itw/gel/.

Clark, R. E., & Estes, F. (2002). *Turning research into results: A guide to selecting the right performance solutions*. Atlanta, GA: CEP Press.

Craik, E. I. M., & Lockhart, R. S. (1972). Levels of processing: A framework for memory research. *Journal of Verbal Learning and Verbal Behavior, 11,* 671–684.

Dewey, J. (1947). *The child and the curriculum and the school and society*. Chicago, IL: University of Chicago Press.

Duffy, T. M., & Cunningham, D. J. (1996). Constructivism: Implications for the design and delivery of instruction. In D. H. Jonassen & P. Harris (Eds.), *Handbook of research on educational communications and technology* (AECT) (pp. 170–198). Mahwah, NJ: Lawrence Erlbaum.

Durant, W. (1933; paperback printing from 1961). *The story of philosophy: The lives and opinions of the great philosophers*. New York: Simon & Schuster.

Endsley, M. R. (1988). Design and evaluation for situation awareness enhancement. In *Proceedings of the 32nd Annual Meeting of the Human Factors Society* (pp. 97–101). Santa Monica, CA: Human Factors Society.

Fletcher, J. D. (1982). Training technology: An ecological point of view. In R. A. Kasschau, R. Lachman, & K. R. Laughery (Eds.), *Psychology and society: Information technology in the 1980s* (pp. 166–191). New York: Holt, Reinhart, and Winston.

Fletcher, J. D. (1997). What have we learned about computer based instruction in military training? In R. J. Seidel & P. R. Chatelier (Eds.), *Virtual reality, training's future?* (pp. 169–177). New York: Plenum Publishing.

Fletcher, J. D. (1999). Using networked simulation to assess problem solving by tactical teams. *Computers in Human Behavior, 15,* 375–402.

Fletcher, J. D. (2003). Evidence for learning from technology-assisted instruction. In H. F. O'Neil, Jr. & R. Perez (Eds.), *Technology applications in education: A learning view* (pp. 79–99). Hillsdale, NJ: Lawrence Erlbaum Associates.

Fletcher, J. D. (2004). Technology, the Columbus effect, and the third revolution in learning. In M. Rabinowitz, F. C. Blumberg, & H. Everson (Eds.), *The design of instruction and evaluation: Affordances of using media and technology* (pp. 139–157). Mahwah, NJ: Lawrence Erlbaum Associates.

Fletcher, J. D. (in press). The value of expertise and expert performance: A review of evidence from the military. In K. A. Ericcson (Ed.), *Development of professional performance: Approaches to objective measurement and designed learning environments*. New York: Cambridge University Press.

Fletcher, J. D., & Atkinson, R. C. (1973). An evaluation of the Stanford CAI program in initial reading (Grades K through 3). *Journal of Educational Psychology, 63,* 597–602.

Fletcher, J. D., Hawley, D. E., & Piele, P. K. (1990). Costs, effects, and utility of microcomputer assisted instruction in the classroom. *American Educational Research Journal, 27,* 783–806.

Fletcher, J. D., & Suppes, P. (1975). The Stanford project on computer-assisted instruction for hearing-impaired students. *Journal of Computer-Based Instruction, 3,* 1–12.

Gay, G. (1986). Interaction of learner control and prior understanding in computer-assisted video instruction. *Journal of Educational Psychology, 78,* 225–227.

Gorman, P. F. (1990). *The military value of training* (IDA Paper P-2515). Alexandria, VA: Institute for Defense Analyses. (DTIC/NTIS No. ADA 232 460.)

Holman, G. J. (1979). *Training effectiveness of the CH-47 flight simulator* (ARI Research Report 1209). Alexandria, VA: US Army Research Institute for the Behavioral and Social Sciences.

James, W. (1890/1950). *Principles of psychology: Volume I.* New York: Dover Press.

Jamison, D. T., Fletcher, J. D., Suppes, P., & Atkinson, R. C. (1976). Cost and performance of computer-assisted instruction for education of disadvantaged children. In J. T. Froomkin, D. T. Jamison, & R. Radner (Eds.), *Education as an industry* (pp. 201–240). Cambridge, MA: Ballinger Publishing Company.

Kalyuga, S., Ayres, P., Chandler, P., & Sweller, J. (2003). The expertise reversal effect. *Educational Psychologist, 38,* 23–31.

Kirschner, P. A., Sweller, J., & Clark, R. E. (2006). Why minimal guidance during instruction does not work: An analysis of the failure of constructivist, discovery, problem-based, experiential, and inquiry-based teaching. *Educational Psychologist, 41,* 75–86.

Kulik, J. A. (1994). Meta-analytic studies of findings on computer-based instruction. In E. L. Baker & H. F. O'Neil, Jr. (Eds.), *Technology assessment in education and training* (pp. 9–33). Hillsdale, NJ: Lawrence Erlbaum Associates.

Lashley, K. S. (1950). In search of the engram. *Proceedings of the Society for Experimental Biology and Medicine, 4,* 454–482.

Levin, H. M., Glass, G. V., & Meister, G. R. (1987). Cost-effectiveness of computer-assisted instruction. *Evaluation Review, 11,* 50–71.

Lewin, K. (1951). *Field theory in social science.* New York: Harper & Brothers.

Mayer, R. E. (2004). Should there be a three-strikes rule against pure discovery learning? *American Psychologist, 59,* 14–19.

Mayer, R. E. (2005). Cognitive theory of multimedia learning. In R. E. Mayer (Ed.), *The Cambridge handbook of multimedia learning* (pp. 31–48). New York: Cambridge University Press.

McMaster, H. R. (1992). *May 21, 1992 testimony before the United States Senate Armed Services Committee.*

McMaster, H. R. (2005). The Battle of 73 Easting. In F. Kagan (Ed.), *Leaders in war: West Point remembers the 1991 Gulf War* (pp. 103–117). London: Frank Cass Publishers.

Morrison, J. E., & Meliza, L. L. (1999). *Foundations of the After Action Review Process* (IDA Document D-2332). Alexandria, VA: Institute for Defense Analyses.

Neisser, U. (1967). *Cognitive psychology.* New York: Appleton, Century, Crofts.

Niemiec, R. P., Sikorski, M., & Walberg, H. J. (1989). Comparing the cost-effectiveness of tutoring and computer-based instruction. *Journal of Educational Computing Research, 5,* 395–407.

O'Neil, H. F., Jr., & Robertson, M. (1992). Simulations: Occupationally oriented. In M. C. Alkin (Ed.), *Encyclopedia of educational research* (6th ed., pp. 1216–1222). New York: Macmillan.

Orlansky, J., Dahlman, C. J., Hammon, C. P., Metzko, J., Taylor, H. L., & Youngblut, C. (1994). *The value of simulation for training* (IDA Paper P-2982). Alexandria, VA: Institute for Defense Analyses. (ADA 289 174.)

Orlanksy, J., Knapp, M. I., & String, J. (1984). *Operating costs of military aircraft and flight simulators* (IDA Paper P-1733). Alexandria, VA: Institute for Defense Analyses. (DTIC/NTIS ADA 144 241.)

Orlansky, J., & String, J. (1977). *Cost-effectiveness of flight simulators for military training* (IDA Paper P-1275). Alexandria, VA: Institute for Defense Analyses. (DTIC/NTIS ADA 052 801.)

Paulson, J. A. (1973). *An evaluation of instructional strategies in a simple learning situation* (Technical Report No. 209). Stanford, CA: Institute for Mathematical Studies in the Social Sciences, Stanford University.

Pohlman, D. L., & Fletcher, J. D. (1999). Aviation personnel selection and training. In

D. J. Garland, J. A. Wise, & V. D. Hopkin (Eds.), *Handbook of aviation human factors* (pp. 277–308). Mahwah, NJ: Lawrence Erlbaum.

Provenmire, H. K., & Roscoe, S. N. (1973). Incremental transfer effectiveness of a ground-based aviation trainer. *Human Factors, 15*, 534–542.

Raser, J. R. (1969). *Simulation and society: An exploration of scientific gaming.* Boston, MA: Allyn and Bacon.

Roscoe, S. N., & Williges, B. H. (1980). Measurement of transfer of training. In S. N. Roscoe (Ed.), *Aviation psychology* (pp. 182–193). Ames, IA: Iowa State University Press.

Rouse, W. B., Cannon-Bowers, J. A., & Salas, E. (1992). The role of mental models in team performance in complex systems. *IEEE Transactions on Systems, Man, and Cybernetics, 22*, 1296–1308.

Rumelhart, D. E. (1967). *The effects of inter-presentation intervals on performance in a continuous paired-associate task* (Technical Report No. 27). Stanford, CA: Institute for Mathematical Studies in the Social Sciences, Stanford University.

Savery, J. R., & Duffy, T. M. (1996). Problem-based learning: An instructional model and its constructivist framework. In B. G. Wilson (Ed.), *Constructivist learning environments: Case studies in instructional design* (pp. 135–148). Englewood Cliffs, NJ: Educational Technology Publications.

Schuell, T. J. (1988). The role of the student in learning from instruction. *Contemporary Educational Psychology, 13*, 276–295.

Suppes, P., Fletcher, J. D., & Zanotti, M. (1975). Performance models of American Indian students on computer-assisted instruction in elementary mathematics. *Instructional Science, 4*, 303–313.

Suppes, P., Fletcher, J. D., & Zanotti, M. (1976). Models of individual trajectories in computer-assisted instruction for deaf students. *Journal of Educational Psychology, 68*, 117–127.

Suppes, P., & Morningstar, M. (1972). *Computer-assisted instruction at Stanford 1966–68: Data, models, and evaluation of the arithmetic programs.* New York: Academic Press.

Tobias, S. (1989). Another look at research on the adaptation of instruction to student characteristics. *Educational Psychologist, 24*, 213–227.

Tobias, S. (2003). Extending Snow's conceptions of aptitudes. *Contemporary Psychology, 48*, 277–279.

Tobias, S., & Frase, L. T. (2000). Educational psychology and training. In S. Tobias & J. D. Fletcher (Eds.), *Training and retraining: A handbook for business, industry, government, and the military* (pp. 3–24). New York: Macmillan Library Reference.

Tolman, E. C. (1948). Cognitive maps in rats and men. *Psychological Review, 55*, 189–208.

Tulving, E. (1962). Subjective organization in free recall of "unrelated" words. *Psychological Bulletin, 69*, 344–354.

Vinsonhaler, J. F., & Bass, R. K. (1972). A summary of ten major studies on CAI drill and practice. *Educational Technology, 12*, 29–32.

Von Glasersfeld, E. (1989). Cognition, construction of knowledge, and teaching. *Synthese, 801*, 121–140.

Von Glasersfeld, E. (1997). Homage to Jean Piaget. *Irish Journal of Psychology, 18*, 293–306.

Watson, J. (1930). *Behaviorism.* New York: Norton Press.

14 What's Worth Knowing in Mathematics?

Melissa Sommerfeld Gresalfi and Frank Lester
Indiana University

This chapter, like the others in this book, was undertaken in response to a paper by Kirschner, Sweller, and Clark (2006) which discussed the apparent failure of "constructivist" and related teaching approaches to support learning. We were invited to write a chapter that addressed the issue from the perspective of mathematics education. Our response does not consider which instructional approaches are most effective. Rather, the purpose of this chapter is to address assumptions about learning and instruction, and to offer an alternative conceptualization of learning and instruction as it relates to mathematics. In so doing, we seek not to champion particular perspectives over others, but rather to consider the usefulness of particular theories for supporting our understanding and designing for learning (Cobb, 2007).

Claims about Learning and Instruction

Kirschner et al. (2006) present an argument against the feasibility of pedagogical approaches which they call "minimally guided." First, they critique minimally guided methods by referring to findings about human cognitive architecture, and explain why such approaches are insensible given our understanding of the function of human memory. Second, they review selected research that contrasts "direct instruction" with minimally guided approaches and illustrate that, in those studies, students in the direct-instruction condition exhibited higher rates of memory and transfer. In so doing, Kirschner et al. make claims about the nature of learning and instruction that are at odds with the ways that many in the mathematics-education community have conceptualized these constructs. More specifically, their characterization of learning and their resulting claims about instruction are general and do not take into consideration the complexities of classroom instruction and human interaction.

In the sections that follow, we begin by reviewing the claims made by Kirschner and his co-authors about learning and instruction, and highlight our challenges to these claims as they relate to mathematics learning. We then present our perspective on learning and instruction, and note the points of divergence from the claims made by Kirschner et al. To illustrate the consequentiality of these differences, we present examples from two classrooms that use different instructional approaches to teach the same material, and present an analysis of these cases in terms of both our own and Kirschner et al.'s claims about learning and instruction. It is important to note that in this chapter we are not representing the entire mathematics-education community, but rather our own perspective, which follows a *situative*[1] approach to learning and instruction in mathematics.

Issue 1: The Definition of Learning

Kirschner et al. (2006) adopt an analytic lens for considering learning that focuses on memory, and define learning as "a change in long term memory" (p. 75). Although few would disagree that this *is* a characteristic of learning, on its own it is insufficient as a guide for instruction. First, there is the question of how to conceive of changes in long-term memory. A change might mean that new information has been added, lost, or re-ordered—making recall more *or* less likely. Because the desired outcome is not specified, focusing solely on a change in long-term memory is inadequate for guiding the development either of instructional strategies or curricula.

Kirschner et al. also review the structure and function of human memory. They note that long-term memory is the site of our ability to act in novel situations, and review findings on expert practice to note that "expert problem solvers derive their skill by drawing on the extensive experience stored in their long-term memory and then quickly select and apply the best procedures for solving problems" (2006, p. 76). Again, this is insufficiently specified to be useful for the purposes of designing instruction. Novice chess players, algebra learners, or art students *also* rely on their long-term memory to attempt to solve problems. The difference between the novice and expert player is not their *use* of long-term memory, as novices and experts alike retrieve memories from long-term storage throughout the course of play. Instead, the difference between experts and novices is the way they understand the same information, and how that relates to their appropriate retrieval of those memories. In other words, the question is about the *structure* of long-term memory, and how it *becomes* structured—not its function.

The question that is relevant to mathematics education is therefore not simply how to make a change to long-term memory, but rather, how to support students to, as quoted above by Kirschner et al., "select and apply the best procedures for solving problems." Indeed, the issue here is one that plagues educators across disciplines, which is not one of memory, but of *transfer*. Work on transfer has demonstrated quite compellingly that people can appear to have made changes to their long-term memories by solving problems in expected ways in one situation, and then fail to transfer the same information in another situation (Dettermann, 1993).

This problem requires a different conceptualization of learning, one that extends beyond a focus on the structure of long-term memory. For example, more recent theories (Cobb & Bowers, 1999; Greeno & MMAP, 1998; Lave, 1997; Rogoff, 1990) suggest that learning is about more than a change in memory, but a change in ability to interact with resources in the environment. To take the example of expert and novice chess players cited above, the difference between performance can be understood to be due to different histories of interactions with the resources of a particular activity system (in this case, involving chess pieces, strategies, more or less expert players, etc.). Individuals' differential activation of these memories can be understood as differences both in their initial experiences of these strategies (Lave, Murtaugh, & de la Rocha, 1984) and in their attunement to the affordances of a new situation for which the use of a particular strategy would be appropriate (Gibson, 1979; Greeno, 1991).

Issue 2: The Definition of Instruction

Kirschner et al. classify a range of pedagogical approaches, including *inquiry*, *problem-based learning*, *discovery learning*, *experiential learning*, and *constructivist learning*, as "minimally guided," which they define as requiring learners to discover or construct essential information for themselves (rather than being "presented with information," 2006, p. 75).[2] They state that these approaches include a commitment to having students solve authentic problems and engage complex information, and to do so in a setting that mimics the methods of the discipline. In addition, according to Kirschner et al., these pedagogical approaches provide instructional guidance in the form of relevant information that is available if learners "choose to use it" (p. 76).[3] In contrast, direct instruction is defined as "information that fully explains the concepts and procedures that students are required to learn as well as learning strategy support that is compatible with human cognitive architecture" (p. 75).

There are two issues that we raise in response to Kirschner et al.'s characterization of instruction. The first involves the relationship between instructional goals and instructional methods. Kirschner et al. do not delineate the relationship between instructional methods and the ends that educators seek. Thus, we believe that the question should not be "which instructional approach is better," but rather, "which instructional approach is best suited to achieving the ends we have in mind?" Indeed, it could reasonably be asked why we would ever NOT create curricula that include activities that involve inquiry. Engaging in inquiry practices involves having opportunities to learn how to inquire. If we care about students being able to initiate and evaluate questions and hypotheses, and offer explanations, then it seems reasonable that they need chances to participate in activities where they can learn to do those things.

The second issue involves the characterization of particular instructional approaches as "minimally guided." Although there are classrooms in which students are asked to engage independently with material without intervention from teachers, it is not clear that this is a characteristic specifically of the approaches they classify as "minimal guidance." The distinction between minimal guidance and direct instructional guidance is not, as Kirschner et al. suggest, seen in the *amount* of assistance given to students by instructors, but rather the *form* of guidance that is provided.

Kirschner et al.'s characterization of inquiry appears to stem from a common misconception that such approaches involve sending children out to a field armed with a trowel and a magnifying glass, in hopes that they will "rediscover" foundational scientific principles. We argue that this is not an example of discovery learning, but rather an example of bad teaching. Bruner (1996) was quite clear in his expectation that discovery learning leads to the understanding of the underlying structure of a discipline, and that experiences for children had to be carefully developed in order that a model of the phenomena under investigation be constructed. This, he claimed, involved careful preparation, guidance, and modeling on the part of the teacher. Thus, to refer to such approaches as "unguided" or even "minimally guided" is a gross mischaracterization (cf. Lampert, 1998, 2001; McClain, 2000; Schifter, 2001). For this reason, in our discussions that follow, we will refer to the minimal guidance approaches characterized by Kirschner et al. as "inquiry approaches," a term that better captures the intention of these pedagogical designs.

In effective discovery-, inquiry-, or problem-based classrooms, teachers are certainly positioned differently with respect to students and information, as Kirschner et al. imply. They question, probe, redirect, and offer explanations when asked. Rather than this being seen as *less* guidance, however, it is simply guidance of a different kind that has been well-established by the professional-development community to be more demanding and requiring a different understanding of the content that is being taught (Schifter, 2001; Ball, 1988, 2000, 2001).

Knowing and Learning in Mathematics

As we have noted, Kirschner et al. (2006) define learning as a change in long-term memory, a definition that we consider to be insufficient both because it is too broad to be informative for designing instruction, and because it ignores the complexities involved in the use and application of knowledge. Thus, in this section we discuss learning, specifically as it relates to mathematics, and propose an alternate conceptualization of the one advanced by Kirschner et al.

Demonstrating that something has been learned requires behaving differently in a situation with respect to a particular idea than how one has behaved before. Different theories of learning attend more or less to the circumstances associated with the observable behavior and to hypotheses about the structure of information that relate to these behavioral outcomes. The approach advocated by Kirschner et al., that is, the study of human cognitive architecture, focuses primarily on conjectures about the ways that information is worked on and stored in memory. We suggest, however, that defining learning as merely a change in long-term memory neglects the understandings that the field has built about the circumstances associated with observable behaviors, contributed by situative and sociocultural theorists[4] (Brown, Collins, & Duguid, 1989; Greeno, 1991; Lave, 1997; Lave & Wenger, 1991; Pea, 1993; Rogoff, 1990).

It has been well documented that what people learn and are able to do cannot be separated from how they learn to do it (Boaler, 1999, 2000; Cobb, Stephan, McClain, & Gravemeijer, 2001; Greeno, 1991; Hiebert et al., 1997; Saxe, 1999). Thus, understanding what someone is able to do at a particular time requires examining the practices with which that person has engaged. For example, Lave and Wenger (1991) outlined a framework on learning that considers trajectories of individuals' participation as they become members of a community of practice. For them, learning occurs as individuals participate in the practices of the community; changes in their participation reflect their increased capabilities. Thus, learning is not considered to be an individual achievement, but an accomplishment of an interactive system (Greeno, 2006; Prawat, 1996). Said differently, learning is achieved through changes in a *system* that includes elements such as people, social norms and expectations, resources such as books or calculators, history, institutional expectations, *and* individual cognitive architecture—all of which work together in ways that cannot be separated.

The shift to considering learning as a social activity reframes the unit of analysis to the kinds of practices that people come to participate in, and the ways people relate to each other within a particular activity setting. This perspective suggests that renewed attention be paid to the nature of students' mathematical engagement—as inseparable from the specific content with which students engage—as a critical aspect of what students actually come to know and who they come to be. In other words, the ways that students participate with mathematical content—for example, by being encouraged to create solutions to problems and to contrast one's own solution with others—shapes the nature of students' mathematical knowing. In this way, knowing in activity can be understood by regarding the classroom as a system of interaction and focusing on both the properties of those systems and the ways they are coordinated (Greeno, 2006). Thus, in order to understand how students become increasingly expert at knowing which mathematical procedures to use in order to solve novel problems, the focus is not on how their long-term memories change, but on how they have engaged with the information initially such that they are able to recognize novel contexts in which the use of that information is relevant. Following Engle (2006), we suggest that this can best be accomplished by investigating students' engagement with both "content" and "context" in order to understand how initial participation frames the opportunities to apply the same content in novel situations.

Conceptualizing learning as an accomplishment of an activity setting means that individual action must be understood as being bound up in the expectations, obligations, and entitlements that are constructed among the participants (cf. Vygotsky, 1978) and therefore requires attending to what students do given what they have opportunities to do. For example, it is unlikely that a student who had a history of having opportunities to express his understanding by explaining the relationships between different methods or ways of thinking about a problem would understand information in the same way as a student who had many opportunities to practice using one particular algorithm with fluency (cf. Boaler, 1999)—although notably, both of these activities result in a change to long-term memory.

We have suggested a different model of learning to account for observed changes in behavior. Notably, this account does not contradict the one advanced by Kirschner et al., but rather specifies the mechanisms by which change might occur. Specifically, rather than focusing only on the internal structure of information, we have advocated an approach that integrates the ways that students participate with information. Key to this perspective therefore is the acknowledgement that the nature of what is known is inextricably linked to how one came to know it (Lampert, 1990; Lave et al., 1984; Saxe, 1991). Given the focus on the role of participation in practices of knowing and learning, it is therefore of paramount importance to consider the instructional practices that are established in mathematics classrooms. We turn to this issue in the following section.

Instruction in Mathematics

It is essential that instruction be built solidly on a theory of learning, and appreciate the implications or suggestions of that theory for how people become increasingly knowledgeable. Thus, we take seriously concerns voiced by Kirschner et al. (2006), who suggest that many instructional approaches appear to ignore established research findings about the structure and function of memory. Instructional approaches that are not consistent with an understanding of how learning happens are likely to fail (or support the development of an entirely new theory). However, designing instruction is not only about building on theories of learning, but also requires specifying the goals of instruction, such that instruction can be planned to meet those goals.

Instructional Goals of Mathematics

With respect to mathematics, discussions about instructional goals have been rife with conflict (Schoenfeld, 2004). At the heart of the matter are conflicting expectations for what students should know and be able to do in mathematics. Notably, mathematics, like every other content area, concept, word, or meaning, is a co-constructed activity. Thus, what it means to know or understand mathematics differs depending on the ways that mathematics is locally defined in interaction (Boaler, 2000; Cobb, 2007; Cobb, Gresalfi, & Hodge, in press; Franke, Kazemi, & Battey, 2007; Hand, 2003; Moschkovich, 2002). Do students need to be able to merely *use* particular mathematical procedures accurately (a "content approach"), or do they need to be able to understand how to inquire into when and why those procedures are useful (a "process approach")? An example of the difference between these two instructional goals can be seen in the standards produced by different groups on the same topic. The *National Council of Teachers of Mathematics*, a group that spearheaded mathematics reform efforts (Schoenfeld, 2004), put forth the following criteria for "understanding numbers" for Grades 3–5:

- Understand the place-value structure of the base-ten number system and be able to represent and compare whole numbers and decimals;
- Recognize equivalent representations for the same number and generate them by decomposing and composing numbers;
- Develop understanding of fractions as parts of unit wholes, as parts of a collection, as locations on number lines, and as divisions of whole numbers;

- Use models, benchmarks, and equivalent forms to judge the size of fractions;
- Recognize and generate equivalent forms of commonly used fractions, decimals, and percents;
- Explore numbers less than 0 by extending the number line and through familiar applications;
- Describe classes of numbers according to characteristics such as the nature of their factors (National Council of Teachers of Mathematics, n.d.).

This standard focuses on the relationships between mathematical ideas. In contrast, *Mathematically Correct*, a group that opposes the process-oriented approach and seeks to "restore basic skills to math education" (Mathematically Correct, n.d.), advocated very different criteria for number sense for third grade:

- Read and write numbers from 0 to 999,999 with digits and words;
- Write numbers in expanded form to 999,999;
- Identify the place value for each digit up to the hundred-thousands;
- Compare two whole numbers between 0 and 999,999, using symbols (>, <, or =) and words ("greater than," "less than," or "equal to");
- Round a whole number, 999 or less, to the nearest ten and hundred;
- Identify ordinal positions from first to one-hundredth;
- Read and write decimals to the hundredths (mathematicallycorrect.com/kprea.htm#G3).

These criteria are focused at the level of procedural manipulations, rather than on relationships between mathematical ideas (cf. Stein, Remillard, & Smith, 2007). The point here is that these standards represent very different assumptions about the nature of number sense (cf. Greeno, 1991), and therefore what students' performance would have to look like in order to be satisfied that students have an "understanding" of number.

The contrast between the instructional goals of the two groups is similar to a distinction made by Thompson, Philipp, Thompson, and Boyd (1994), who introduced characterizations of orientations that one might have toward teaching (and learning) mathematics. A *calculational* orientation refers to a relationship with mathematics characterized by an emphasis on the accuracy of calculations and procedures. In contrast, a *conceptual* orientation refers to a relationship with mathematics characterized by considering the act of meaning-making as the goal for accurate mathematical work. This distinction is consequential in understanding both how teachers support students' reasoning, and students' resulting understanding of their own mathematical work. As we have noted, being able to accurately use procedures does not necessarily translate to knowing *when* to use those procedures, or being able to explain why using procedures is reasonable or meaningful (Peterson & Walberg, 1979; Schoenfeld, 1988).

The issue of instructional goals was not raised by Kirschner et al., but it seems to us to be a crucial component of any critique of instructional design. Discussions about which instructional design is superior are only relevant if both are being compared against the same instructional goals. If the goals for instruction are not the same, then the comparison is meaningless. Take, for example, the two sets of standards outlined above about number sense. As previously stated, these standards represent different goals to be satisfied in order to demonstrate an understanding of number. Putting that issue aside, *meeting* these goals would require two different forms of instruction. If an instructional goal is, as stated by Mathematically Correct, to "identify the place value for each digit up to the hundred-thousands," then the most efficient way to ensure that a student could do so would be to instruct students about the name of each place for each digit, and give them opportunities to practice matching the place value name with the digit. This is aligned with the definition of "direct instruction" outlined by Kirschner et al. In this way, students should be able to associate the names of different place values with the appropriate digit. However, if the goal is instead, as stated by the NCTM, to "understand the place-value structure of the base-ten number system and be able to represent and compare whole numbers and decimals," telling and practicing might not be sufficient, because demonstrating the ability to match names with places does not require *understanding* of place-value structure.

If "understanding" place value means, for example, knowing that the position of a digit communicates something about the value of that digit, students need opportunities to do more than simply associate a name with the position (Hiebert & Wearne, 1992; Varelas & Becker, 1997). Instead, students need chances to explore the structure of our (Western) numeration system. One example of a way that this might be accomplished is to ask students to invent their own numeration system which works by position (or a system that does not work by position), and then engage them in conversations about how different invented numeration systems work, and how they compare with our standard numeration system. This kind of instructional approach might be categorized as "inquiry," in that students are asked to engage creatively with the rules of a discipline in order to uncover underlying structure of the discipline.

Aligning Practice with Instructional Goals

The intention of the mathematics pedagogies and curricula that might be called "inquiry" is to engage students in the practices of a discipline, shifting authority from the teacher or the textbook to the students and the discipline (Brown & Campione, 1994; Hiebert et al., 1996; Lampert, 1990). As Engle (2006) notes,

> being framed as an author—rather than simply as a recipient of others' knowledge—creates social expectations that one will be able to comment intelligently on anything related to the content that one has authored, making one answerable for that content in the future.

(p. 457)

In other words, rather than positioning students as recipients of information, these pedagogies can serve to position students as producers and critical consumers of information, which involves interrogating, developing, and applying ideas to new problems (Gresalfi, Barab, Siyahhan, & Christensen, in press). This is aligned with the theory of learning outlined above, which emphasizes the relationship between practices and knowing.

For example, Lampert (1990) detailed the differences between mathematical practice and school mathematics by noting that in most school mathematics, "*doing* mathematics means following the rules laid down by the teacher, *knowing* mathematics means remembering and applying the correct rule when the teacher asks a question, and mathematical *truth is determined* when the answer is ratified by the teacher" (p. 32). We do not challenge the obvious claim that learners (novices) might engage with information differently than experts. However, we do ask why it seems sensible to organize classroom activity in such a way that school practice is so different from expert practice that it becomes practically unrecognizable as an example of mathematics.

The mathematics reforms discussed above, with their focus on process and conceptual development rather than only content objectives, require that teachers make significant changes on several levels. First, teachers necessarily have to develop a relatively deep understanding of the mathematical ideas that they are asked to teach (Ball & Rowan, 2004; Cochran-Smith & Lytle, 1999; Schifter & Fosnot, 1993). Doing so requires that teachers personally engage in forms of mathematical activity that differ from their own experiences as students, and also requires that they reconceptualize the nature of what it means to do mathematics (Cohen & Ball, 1990; Schifter, 2001). Second, teachers have to develop new teaching practices that support students' engagement with central mathematical ideas (Heaton, 2000; Schifter, 2001; Sherin, 2002).

These new practices are the focus of the Kirschner et al. article, which they characterize as minimally guided. As noted earlier, we take issue with this characterization. It has been well-established that inquiry-oriented teaching practice can fail to meet instructional goals (Henningsen & Stein, 1997; Kazemi & Stipek, 2001). This can be attributed to myriad reasons, such as the novelty of the practice (Stein et al., 2007), the challenges between epistemological commitments between teachers and curricula (Cohen & Ball, 1990), an adherence to surface features of reform (Kazemi & Stipek, 2001), and inadequate professional development (Sowder, 2007). However, this is certainly not a problem limited to inquiry practices, as direct-instruction practices have been demonstrated to have their own shortcomings (Boaler, 2000; Ladson-Billings, 1994, 1998; Schoenfeld, 1988). It is for this reason that when comparing instructional practices, it is imperative that we include information about the ways that these instructional practices are realized, such that it is certain that the practices are truly aligned with the curricula they are said to represent (cf. Kazemi & Stipek, 2001).

Here we are not arguing that *any* inquiry practice, regardless of its execution, is superior to other forms of instruction. Because Kirschner et al. do not discuss the nature of classroom practice in studies they reviewed that compared inquiry and "direct instruction," we cannot be sure about what, precisely, was being compared. In what follows, we discuss inquiry instructional practices as they relate to the envisioned goals of the curriculum (cf. Boaler, 1997; Hiebert et al.,

1997; Silver & Stein, 1996; Wood & Sellers, 1997), and challenge their characterization of such practices as being "minimally guided."

Guidance in Instructional Practice

Kirschner et al. define direct guidance as "providing information that fully explains the concepts and procedures that students are required to learn as well as learning strategy support that is compatible with human cognitive architecture" (2006, p. 75). In contrast, minimal guidance is defined as "guidance ... offered in the form of process- or task-relevant information that is available if learners choose to use it" (p. 76). From these definitions, we surmise that Kirschner et al. consider guidance as verbal or written information that is relevant to the task at hand—either in the form of clearly articulated explanations of concepts (direct guidance), or information about "what to do" (minimal guidance). As previously stated, we challenge the designation of inquiry practices as including guidance that only occurs in this form. In addition, we propose that verbal and written instructional guidance is only one of many forms of guidance that support students' engagement with information. Although the list of factors that have an impact on students' engagement with content is potentially limitless in a complex system such as a classroom, aspects of classroom practice that have received the most attention include: the design of instructional tasks (Stein, Smith, Henningsen, & Silver, 2000); the norms of the classroom that contribute to how mathematical activity is constituted in the classroom (Yackel & Cobb, 1996); and the kinds of questions that teachers pose and the way they support student thinking.

A key form of guidance that teachers provide involves the tasks that they design or select for their classes. Instructional tasks are a key component of the students' developing understanding of mathematics (Doyle, 1988; Hiebert et al., 1997; Schoenfeld, 1988; Stein et al., 2000). Tasks form the basis of the work that students do, and different task designs support the development of different understandings. Stein and her colleagues (Stein & Lane, 1996; Stein et al., 2000) discussed the different levels of cognitive demand afforded by classroom instructional tasks. From their research in classrooms, they catalogued four levels of cognitive demand. The lowest-level tasks required only that students recite something from memory. Second-level tasks required correct performance of a procedure, but without need to relate the procedure to general concepts. The third level, called *procedures with connections*, required students to attend to concepts that made the procedure meaningful, and the fourth level, called *doing mathematics*, required students to consider meanings of concepts and methods explicitly.[5]

One key point that Stein et al. (2000) make is to note that the structure of the task only provides a framework for the ultimate cognitive demand of the task. The implementation of the task, that is, how it is introduced, worked on, supported, and completed in real time, ultimately determines how cognitively demanding the task will actually be. The norms of the classroom, that is, the taken-as-shared expectations and obligations that participating members are expected and entitled to fulfill (cf. Cobb, 1999; Cobb, Jaworski, & Presmeg, 1996; Yackel & Cobb, 1996), affect the ways that instructional tasks are realized in the classroom (cf. Staples, 2008).

The act of *maintaining* cognitive demand in tasks is therefore non-trivial, and requires significant work on the part of teachers (Henningsen & Stein, 1997; Lampert, 2001). Specifically, teachers provide instructional guidance through their orchestration and support of student thinking. The work of teachers who have chronicled their own practice have clearly demonstrated the extreme thoughtfulness that goes into supporting student thinking, both in whole-class discussion (Ball, 1993; Lampert, 2001; Staples, 2007), and in individual work (Schifter, 2001). The form of the guidance comes in questions, probes, orchestrations of turns of talk, and decisions about when to move on. To call this guidance "minimal," therefore, is to miss the work of teaching and the impact of the guidance on student thinking. For example, Fraivillig, Murphy, and Fuson (1999) developed a framework called *Advancing Children's Thinking* to describe teaching practices that supported students' mathematical thinking. They identified three practices: eliciting children's solution methods; supporting children's conceptual understanding; and extending children's mathematical thinking. This framework suggests that teachers are offering significant guidance to students as they engage with information.

How can we account for the characterization of such practices as "minimally guided"? In well-functioning inquiry classrooms, the focus of the activity—the people who are discussing, debating, conjecturing, and inventing—is the students, not the teacher. In such classrooms, students are asked to create solutions, compare their strategies, and resolve differences (Cobb, 1999; Hiebert et al., 1997; Kazemi & Stipek, 2001). In these classrooms, the teacher is rarely at the front of the room, dispensing information. Rather, he or she is moving around between groups, or listening to conversations, intervening to redirect, reframe (O'Connor & Michaels, 1993), and remind students about connections between different ideas. Thus, it is indeed true that in classes which have well-established practices (Goos, 2004; Staples, 2007), teachers might not always be at the center of the activity. But, to claim that they are not centrally *participating* and guiding activity is simply wrong and a gross mis-statement of teaching practice.

Equally misleading is the implication that "direct instruction" is an example of maximal guidance. We submit that the type of guidance provided in many classrooms that use direct instruction, while likely to be clear and unambiguous, is unlikely to lead to deeper conceptual understanding (Boaler, 1997; Hiebert et al., 2005; Stigler, Fernandez, & Yoshida, 1996; Stigler & Perry, 1988). Instead, such instructions position mathematical activity as a passive endeavor that is more about listening than generating (cf. Gresalfi et al., in press; Ladson-Billings, 1998). In the section that follows, we share excerpts from two classroom discussions about the same mathematical ideas. One classroom leverages inquiry practices, while the other used direct instruction. In our presentation of these examples, we discuss differences in the instructional practices, highlight the forms of guidance that teachers offer, and note the relationship between these practices and what students are being given opportunities to learn.

Analysis of Instruction: Representations of Variables

The following examples come from two eighth-grade algebra classes in the California Bay area. These classes were the subject of a larger study of the development of mathematical identities (Gresalfi, 2004). The teachers who were part of the study were chosen because they were well respected by the community (parents, other teachers, and administrators), and because they organized their classrooms very differently. Ms. S's teaching style was consistent with those characterized as inquiry oriented. She often presented students with open-ended, complex problems, and expected students to work together. She usually brought the whole class together *after* they had first worked in their groups, and whole-class discussions generally focused on having students sharing their strategies and solutions. In contrast, Ms. H's teaching style tended more towards direct instruction. On any given day, the class began with Ms. H demonstrating or explaining a new idea, and students were then left to work on problems in pairs or individually.

The focal lessons both occurred at the beginning of September, when students were working with algebra tiles for the first time. Algebra tiles are manipulative materials designed by Cuisenaire™, which can be used to represent unknown quantities (such as x and x^2). Algebra tiles have the potential to give students another point of access into the often difficult topic of abstract representations. By offering another representational form, students have the opportunity to approach ideas from more than one perspective, and, in thinking across representations, might presumably arrive at a deeper understanding of the concept. These kinds of representations can also become yet another procedure that students memorize, however. The inclusion of algebra tiles does not guarantee that students will interact more meaningfully with the material; the tiles simply provide an opportunity for that to happen.

Excerpt 1: Direct Instruction

In this class, Ms. H introduced the algebra tiles as a tool that students could use to help them work through ideas or problems. For example, the students relied on the algebra tiles when introduced to "like terms." The idea that only like terms can be combined is more transparent when looking at three vastly different shapes. This view of algebra tiles was supported through their introduction, as the teacher told the students what each tile represented, and the students were then able to practice with the tiles.

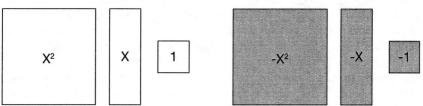

Figure 14.1 Algebra tiles.

1   T: ...OK, now what's the name of this? (*pointing to the small square tile*
2   *displayed on the overhead*) This is a one (*pointing to the rectangular tile*
3   *on the overhead*) This is an *x*.
4   ST1: or an (*x*)
5   T: or an *s*. Could be an *a*. This stands for one unknown number. What-
6   ever it is. G, W, W, pick your favorite letter, OK? What do you think
7   this one is? (*points to the rectangular tile*)
8   ST2: Oh, I know!
9   T: Let's make this one, this is my favorite, let's make this one *a* (*writes* ***a***
10   *next to the rectangle tile*) and make this one opposite *a* (*writes −**a** next*
11   *to the red rectangle*). OK, whatever problem you get, you will have a
12   letter, and this represents for the number that we don't know. What
13   do you think this one is? (*points to the blue square tile*) (*pause*) I'm
14   gonna give you a hint, these pieces are based on area, you see this is *x*
15   by one (*pointing to the rectangle*), so it's *x* long, and one wide, so it has
16   an area of *x* times one, or x^2? This one (*points to the blue square*) has an
17   area of *x* and an *x*, so what do you think this piece is called?
18   ST3: *x* by *x*, or *x* squared
19   T: ...*x* by *x*, or *x* squared, I'll just say *x* squared ... Alright, I'm going to
20   give you some tiles, you and your partners, and I'm going to ask you
21   to show me some expressions (*passes out tiles*). I should give you the
22   problem.... *x* squared, minus three *x*, plus two. I would like you to do
23   *x* squared minus three *x* plus two on your desk. *x* squared minus three
24   *x* plus two is on your desk.

In this excerpt the teacher provided clear guidance about the name of the algebra tiles, and included a rationale for the names. This is an example of direct instruction, in that the students were presented with clearly articulated information which, as Kirschner et al. (2006) stated, "[provide] information that fully explains the concepts and procedures that students are required to learn." The information that the students had to work with—the names of the algebra tiles and how they matched up with traditional variable representations—was presented, interpreted, and explained by the teacher. In this excerpt, the teacher's guidance is quite direct: for example, in lines 10–13, the teacher tells the students that the pieces are named for area, and then reminds the students what the equation for area is. Thus, she is directly instructing them, and guiding them in terms of the naming of the pieces.

However, her guidance, while direct, is also rather minimal, involving reminding students of a (hopefully) previously learned fact, but not supporting them to understand how that previously learned fact is related to the name of the square. Specifically, although students might remember having learned the formula for area, they do not necessarily remember or understand why *x* times *x* is *x* squared. In this way, the connections between algebra tiles and other mathematical ideas, such as the rationale behind the naming of the pieces, were left in the air, so to speak. The information was stated aloud, with the expectation that students would internalize the information and remember it. However, the students' role was not to make the connections between these ideas themselves, but to remember the connections that Ms. H explained.

This presentation afforded opportunities for students to be able to attach names to different shapes of algebra tiles, and to map these names onto traditional written representations of the same information. However, this presentation did not focus on students' *understanding* of the manipulatives as they related to other previously encountered ideas. Rather, the presentation created opportunities for students to *use* the algebra tiles. Indeed, the remainder of the class period was spent practicing the use of algebra tiles to represent traditional algebraic sentences.

Excerpt 2: Inquiry Instruction

Ms. S's approach to the introduction and use of the tiles was quite different. She began with the meaning of the tools, as constructed by the students, and then moved on to name them. Rather than treating the tiles as tools to help the students work through ideas, she treated them as an access point into the idea of representation itself. When Ms. S introduced the algebra tiles, her students had an extended discussion about what each should be named, and why. The excerpt below comes from the part of the class when the students were working on naming the largest (x^2) piece. This occurred approximately 20 minutes into the discussion (as opposed to the very beginning of the discussion, as seen above). This transcript begins in the middle of class, after the teacher gave students time to arrive at names for the pieces themselves, and then write their suggested names on an overhead for the consideration of the entire class.

1	T:	Ok, can I have eyes up here please? First of all, I want to talk about the
2		squared because that's the part that seems must confusing ... so could
3		someone, one of the groups that thought of that, please go ahead and
4		explain how you came up with ... either the z squared or the x squared.
5		(*Hannah raises her hand*) Hannah.
6	H:	Oh. (*goes up to the front*) Well, I got, well we got, this one (*points to*
7		(x^2)) because well we went, we said that since the area equals base
8		times height, then uh, then we did x times x—er (*erasing the tiny x she*
9		*has written as a multiplication sign*). Um, so we did x times x because
10		it's base times height. And it equals x squared. So then um usually we
11		just take that number and put units squared next to it, but then that'd
12		look kind of weird, so then we just went like that (*putting parentheses*
13		*around the* x^2).
14	T:	How did you get the x times x equals x squared?
15	H:	Wait oh oh, cause it's like, cause x squared equals x times x.
16	T:	(*pause*) Everyone agree with that? Does x squared...
17		Well you call like x squared, if you were to do like three squared, that
18		means three times three, then x squared means x times x.
19		(*murmurings from students that sound positive*)
20	T:	OK, so does someone disagree with that, that x squared does not mean

21   x times x, or that three squared does not equal three times three. OK,
22   so, do you all agree with that, that if you had x times x you could also
23   write that as x squared? OK, so then I would like, so that's maybe
24   where someone got the z squared from ... so what I would like to talk
25   about is who, huh, let's go ahead and talk about the z squared next. So
26   that group, could you explain what you were thinking?

Ms. S's presentation of the material located the responsibility for making connections with the students themselves. She began the conversation by building on students' work and students' thinking, based on the task she had set for them (to name the square piece, bearing in mind the names that they had settled on for the "ones" piece and the "x" piece). Based on these practices Ms. S's approach would be characterized as "inquiry," in that the work of generating explanations was done by the students. However, this conversation is hardly an example of minimal guidance. Instead, it is an example of *intentional* guidance. The teacher's utterances were not targeted at supplying information or sharing connections between ideas. Rather, her work was to *problematize* claims or statements made by students, in order to ensure that ideas were accessible to all. Being able to interject in this way requires having a theory of what students know, what they might get confused about, and what is essential to understand in order to productively move ahead. In this very brief exchange, the teacher guided the students in three ways. First, she decided which solutions should be discussed, based on (her interpretation of) what would be mathematically significant. Specifically, she targeted the ideas that x times x is x squared, and that one variable always needs to represent the same information (and the inverse, that the same information can be represented by the same variable). Second, the teacher interjected comments and questions into the student's presentation in order to clarify a contribution that was stated quite quickly and without justification (line 10: How did you get the x times x equals x squared?). This move served to create an opportunity to further elicit information, and to model an expectation of how solutions and ideas should be shared. Third, when the student justified her statement by simply restating the same claim, the teacher interjected again, this time as an act of assessment to see if other students were following (and agreeing with) the claims that the student was making.

This presentation afforded opportunities for students to make connections between manipulatives and other ideas in algebra, and in particular, to develop an *understanding* of how these manipulatives worked. Students can only make connections between ideas when they understand all (or multiple) aspects of the idea. This classroom focused on these connections as the instructional goal, rather than solely on students' ability to use these novel tools.

Discussion and Conclusions

The excerpts briefly illustrate an example of what "direct guidance" and "inquiry approaches" might look like when used in the classroom. In presenting these examples, we seek to illustrate some of the claims that we have made throughout this chapter about the nature of learning and instruction. We proposed that a theory of learning that focuses solely on changes in long-term memory is at once too broad, in that it does not specify the nature of the change that we seek, and too specific, in that it does not include considerations of aspects of learning that go beyond individual representation of information. We proposed that learning might be more usefully conceptualized as a change in participation with particular practices of an activity system. This definition does not challenge the idea of individual knowledge construction, but rather repositions the activity of constructing knowledge as a collective accomplishment, which includes not only the individual in question, but other people and resources of the particular setting in which he or she is interacting.

The classrooms introduced in the excerpts above offered different resources for students' engagement, despite the fact that both classrooms were working on the same mathematical task. In Ms. H's classroom, the resources that were available to support understanding came primarily through the teacher, in this case in the form of providing names for pieces with rationale. In this conversation students were not positioned as resources for each other, nor was their previous mathematical understanding highlighted in such a way that it was likely to become a resource (it might have been for some students, but it was not likely to be for all students). In contrast, in Ms. S's classroom, the resources available to support understanding came from the teacher, other students, and from the mathematical content itself. As Ms. S engaged students with mathematical ideas that were fundamental to her lesson, she positioned the mathematics as a resource for the students' understanding of the labeling of algebra tile pieces. Because she asked them to work collaboratively on this task, students also became resources for each other's understanding. Although we do not doubt that in both classrooms any student who was attending had the potential to make a change to their long-term memory, it seems unlikely that the same changes were made in the two classrooms. Understanding why this might be so can only be accomplished by considering the elements of the activity setting and how they interact.

We also proposed that the question of whether particular theories of instruction are effective can only be considered in light of instructional goals. The two classroom episodes leveraged different instructional practices. In addition, however, they also appeared to be designed with different ends in mind. Although it is likely that both teachers wanted to support their students' understanding of algebra tiles, their notions of what understanding looks like appears to be different (based on their presentations). For Ms. H, successfully communicating the names of the algebra tiles and supporting students to connect those names to written variables appeared to be the goals of her presentation. In contrast, Ms. S appeared to want students to use the mathematical rationale of the development of the piece shapes in order to invent names of pieces. The two teachers leveraged instructional practices that were well-aligned with their instructional goals. The implications of these different instructional goals, in terms of what gets learned, and by whom, has been a topic of great debate in the mathematics-education community, but one that we have not taken on in this chapter (Boaler, 2002; Boaler & Staples, 2007; Gresalfi, Boaler, & Cobb, 2004; Lubienski, 2000).

We also challenged the characterization of inquiry approaches as minimal guidance, noting that guidance comes in forms beyond instruction, and that less direct guidance is not equivalent to less overall guidance. Ms. H provided direct guidance to her students by clearly naming the shapes, telling the rationale for the names, and directing them to practice representing sentences that required connecting written representations of variables with their algebra tile counterpart. Ms. S provided guidance in multiple forms. She presented background information that would enable students to engage in the rationale behind the naming of the shapes, and then set as a task the naming of those shapes based on the underlying mathematical theory. In this way she provided direct guidance in the form of providing all students access to the same mathematical background information, and by designing a task that was open-ended. She also had orchestrated classroom norms that required that students work together, listen to each other, and take responsibility for each other's understanding (Gresalfi, 2004). Thus, although Ms. S provided less direct guidance about the name of the pieces, she provided significant guidance in other forms such that the eventual naming of the pieces had meaning for the students.

Finally, it is important to note that neither of the examples positioned the mathematics content in a "real-world" setting. Kirschner et al. (2006) take issue with the tendency of inquiry approaches to attempt to embed content in real-world contexts and procedures of a discipline. This does not correspond to the use of inquiry approaches as they are often instantiated in mathematics classrooms, where inquiry practices do not have to be real-world. Instead, it is important to consider the nature of the inquiry; many legitimate activities are situated in systems of abstract symbols (Greeno, 1997). For example, mathematicians participate in activities that are situated solely in symbolic representations, but their actions are meaningful and legitimate with respect to those representations. When activity is serving to transform symbolic relationships, even seemingly procedural activities, such as learning to simplify equations, has meaning as they are impacting, and being impacted by, the system. Thus, the students in Ms. S's classroom were engaging in legitimate inquiry, but in this case they were inquiring about the development and use of a representation.

This brings us back full circle to the title of our chapter: what's worth knowing in mathematics? We have sought to position this as a philosophical question, which cannot be addressed simply through alliances with particular theoretical positions. Rather, what is worth knowing in mathematics is the central question that shapes and is shaped by individual instructional goals and outcomes for students, and understandings of how people come to be increasingly knowledgeable. We have purposely not answered this question, but instead focused on the interrelations between the different assumptions that theorists, practitioners, and researchers make about mathematical activity. It is only when these assumptions are made clear that true investigations about improving student mathematics learning can be undertaken.

Question: Kirschner. *You define learning as "a change in ability to interact with resources in the environment." The critique that you give to "a change in LTM" is fully applicable here! One can interact better or worse, at a structural or a surface level, in an appropriate or inappropriate way, et cetera.*

Reply: Gresalfi and Lester. This is a very good point, and worthy of some clarification. Our claim that defining learning as a change in long-term memory is insufficiently specified to be useful for the purposes of instruction would indeed apply to a definition of learning that focused on changes in how an individual participates. However, there is an important distinction between these characterizations and how we discussed learning. Specifically, we did not define learning as merely a change in participation, but rather as a change of participation with resources in the environment. The difference is between a characterization of what a person is doing, and a characterization of what a person is doing in relation to the affordances available in a given context. In some ways, this is an issue of unit of analysis: the perspective that underlies our chapter—a situative perspective—posits that individuals as inseparable from contexts should be taken as the unit of analysis. Thus, when claiming that learning is a change in ability to interact with resources in an environment, there is a focus on both the individual and the practices, how they change and evolve together and impact each other. As a consequence, whether or not a student is deemed to be learning is no longer seen as an accomplishment solely of that student, but rather an interaction between the opportunities that a student has to participate, whether and when an individual takes up those opportunities, and the significance associated with doing so.

This shift in unit of analysis is particularly consequential when turning to the question of effective instructional practice. The definition of a unit of analysis has implications for where different researchers might look for evidence of whether instructional objectives have been accomplished (for example, a clinical interview outside of a classroom versus a conversation among students in a naturally occurring classroom structure, such as group work). In addition, critically considering the practices with which students have opportunities to participate gives insight into the nature of students' engagement with content. Students typically become quite adept at engaging in mathematics as it is defined through their particular classroom practices. The question is whether these classroom practices are better or worse in their alignment with the outcomes we have in mind.

Question: Kirschner. *You assume that elementary school teachers have the necessary deep understanding of mathematics to "guide" in a deep, meaningful, conceptual way. Unfortunately a plethora of literature on the level of mathematical skills of elementary school teachers refutes this. Teacher preparation programs usually do not include many mathematics or science courses, and it is well-known that many elementary school teachers lack strong math skills. Simply stated: Teachers can't teach what they don't know. What do you propose?*

Question: Kirschner. *Most expert–novice research has shown that novices cannot recognize what is relevant to a problem or problem solution and also what is novel to a specific situation (in other words: What you know determines what you see). Recent research has shown that left to their own devices novices concentrate on surface features and not structural features of problems when solving problems and choosing further problems for study and solution. And guidance by teachers who are not competent in mathematics really cannot help this!*

Reply to both questions: Gresalfi and Lester. The above questions seem to be focusing on the same issue, and so we will address them together. It seems that the objection that is being raised is that effectively using inquiry-teaching methods requires significant mathematical understanding on the part of teachers, which many teachers lack. This pragmatic challenge is quite significant, and appropriately, has been the focus of significant attention. Indeed, the challenges go beyond a concern merely with teachers' content knowledge, although, as Kirschner states, this is a key issue. Two additional constraints that have been identified involve the extent to which teachers' beliefs about the nature of teaching and learning have changed, and the alignment of these practices with constraints of institutional contexts. Thus, the challenges for changing the nature of classroom practice are significant.

The question is if it is worth the effort. If it were the case that any instructional method was equally likely to lead to the same learning outcomes for students, then it would be foolish to invest time, resources, and effort to support teachers in teaching using inquiry methods. However, research has suggested that the nature of students' engagement with content is indeed closely linked to the kinds of instructional practices with which they have had an opportunity to participate. This does not necessarily mean that these differences are captured on gross measures such as state standardized tests, however. This raises the question of what our goals are for student learning, and what we think it means to know and be able to do mathematics. If our goals are to improve performance on particular exams, then it is sensible to go with the easiest and most efficient teaching method. If our goals are to support a different kind of engagement—one that involves mathematical problem solving and posing, investigating, and answering questions—then a different kind of instructional approach is required. To put it simply, engaging in inquiry methods creates opportunities to learn how to inquire—students don't have chances to inquire if they are always told the right answer. If this is an important goal, then we propose that efforts to involve students in inquiry practices will be worthwhile.

Question: Mayer. *Educational research is often criticized as being low in quality, such as not having testable theories, not using scientifically rigorous research methods, and not basing arguments on valid research evidence. Do you think it is appropriate to ask, "What works in mathematics instruction?" If so, please provide three examples of research studies showing that inquiry methods are more effective than direct instruction in promoting learning for mathematical problem solving. I could not find any such evidence in your chapter.*

Reply: Gresalfi and Lester. We agree that it is appropriate, and indeed essential, to ask about "what works" in mathematics education. Without asking such questions, it would be difficult to undertake the process of preparing future teachers, or working with practicing teachers to enhance their own practice. We didn't address this question, intentionally, because of our perception that by not sufficiently defining terms and categories, conversations were not drawing from, or building on, common assumptions and evidence. Thus, this chapter began by addressing the assumptions underlying the questions that we ask in the field of mathematics education, and how they shape the ways that we attempt to collect evidence about relative effectiveness. Indeed, we argue that there are two essential components that have to be made clear in research in order to address, with empirical evidence, the question of what works. The first is defining our desired outcomes: what does "competent mathematical performance" look like? The second is to specify our instructional methods, to ensure that the categorizations we use ("inquiry" or "direct instruction," or whatever else), are being universally defined and applied.

Building on the discussion in our chapter, we would pose a slightly different question than the one you posed, and ask: "What works for whom to learn what?". This seems to us to be a question that is likely to lead to testable theories, and to the accumulation of valid research evidence. Based on the extensive writings that address different components of knowledgeable mathematical performance and unpack different aspects of instructional practice, our guess is that there isn't "one best" instructional practice. Instead, it seems likely that particular instructional practices are better or worse aligned with particular instructional goals, and the best solution is to support teachers to use a range of strategies with their students in order to support their understanding.

Question: Mayer. *An important starting point for selecting an appropriate instructional method is to clearly specify the instructional objective. In your chapter, you appear to reject the idea that instructional objectives should be stated in terms of a desired change in the learner's knowledge. However, I am unable to determine how you would characterize what is learned. At one point you say that learning is a "change in ability to interact with resources in the environment." However, I do not see how that statement is incompatible with specifying the desired changes in the learner's knowledge, such as changes in the learner's cognitive strategies and meta-strategies. If mathematical competence is not based on the learner's knowledge (e.g., facts, concepts, procedures, strategies, and beliefs), then what is the desired change you seek as a result of mathematics instruction?*

Reply: Gresalfi and Lester. In short, you're right. This is a great question, and one that, we believe, speaks primarily to the semantics of different theoretical perspectives. We do not at all reject the idea that instructional objectives should be defined—as clarified above. However, we define those objectives in terms of changes in what a student is able to do (knowing), rather than in changes in a learner's cognitive strategies (knowledge). There are theoretical reasons for this semantic decision. The perspective that underlies our chapter—a situative or sociocultural perspective—posits that individuals as inseparable from contexts should be taken as the unit of analysis. This different definition of a unit of analysis has implications for where different researchers might look for evidence of whether instructional objectives have been met. However, this difference in evidence does not mean that there is an incompatibility between perspectives—just a different way of defining the boundaries around evidentiary claims. These differences may lead to different conclusions, but as long as the boundaries of the unit of analysis are defined, this should lead to more, not fewer, interesting discussions.

A second point is whether a focus on change in cognitive structures is a sufficient consideration when discussing learning. One of the advantages of considering changes in participation in an activity setting is that involves both demonstrations of knowledge and ways of approaching and relating to particular practices. Do we care if we have children who are knowledgeable but don't enjoy what they are doing? What is the relationship between the way we teach and the kinds of affiliations that students develop with a particular discipline? Drawing on the work of Lave and Wenger, who have brought the notion of participation so centrally into the field, learning is a transformation of the role that one has in a particular community of practice, and the simultaneous crafting of a new identity with respect to that community. This is consequential, because it relates not only to the nature of students' engagement (an important end in itself), but also to notions of affiliation and enjoyment of a discipline. Specifically, it has been documented that students' experiences in particular disciplines have an impact on their willingness to continue to engage, and that those experiences aren't solely about success, but rather are related to value of the discipline.

Question: Mayer. *If I understand your chapter correctly, you reject the idea that the outcome of learning is a long-lasting change in the learner's knowledge. As an alternative, you characterize mathematics learning as a "social activity," "a co-constructed activity," and "an accomplishment of an activity setting." This kind of rhetoric is sometimes interpreted by teachers to mean that the only acceptable instructional methods in mathematics are to ask students to learn in groups with minimal teacher intervention. What would you say to a teacher who draws this conclusion? Do you have any evidence—other than carefully selected portions of transcripts—to support the claim that socially based activity is more effective in promoting mathematics learning than individually based instruction?*

Reply: Gresalfi and Lester. It sounds like there are two different issues being addressed here: one that has to do with the notion of where "learning" is located (in the head versus in practice), and the second is the way that such discussions about learning translate to instruction. For the record, considering learning to be an interaction is a statement simply about the unit of analysis—not a statement about the kind of instructional method that should be used. Of course, our understanding of how learning happens does, and should, have implications for instruction (one of the main points of the Kirschner et al. (2006) article), and herein lies the quandary.

Surely no one would claim that students' experience in the classroom should be entirely individualized; likewise it doesn't make much sense to think that the only way to learn is to talk to other people constantly. This is a misinterpretation of the notion of practice, which involves not just conversations, but also, for example, normative expectations of acceptable ways of engaging. The point here is that the kinds of practices with which one engages shapes the very nature of the content that is learned. Thus, the question isn't whether individual instruction is superior to collaborative group activity, but rather, what the different practices are useful for. If our goals are to support engagement that involves mathematical problem solving and posing, investigating, and answering questions, then an instructional approach that supports these kinds of practices is required. Specifically, engaging in collaborative activities creates opportunities to learn how to collaborate.

Reaction to Gresalfi and Lester's reply: Mayer. *I am glad that we are all in agreement that we should base instructional practice on solid research evidence. In particular, we all agree on the importance of conducting research on "what works for whom to learn what," including finding out which instructional practices best achieve which instructional goals. This point is consistent with my very first published article with Jim Greeno, in which we showed that inductive methods for teaching a mathematical concept worked best for transfer problems and a deductive method worked best for conventional problems.*

Overall, I think we also agree that promoting student understanding of mathematics is an important goal. Thus, it appears that we should look to the published research evidence to inform decisions about how best to achieve the goal of promoting mathematical understanding. In my assessment, the preponderance of evidence shows the ineffectiveness of minimally guided methods for promoting mathematical understanding.

Notes

1 Following Greeno (1997), we refer to a *situative* perspective on learning, rather than using a more common term, *situated cognition*. Our purpose in doing so is to highlight that *all* cognition is always situated, and thus referring to cognition as situated is redundant and also misleading, in that the term implies that there might be times when cognition is "unsituated."

2 Kirschner et al. (2006) do not make distinctions between these different instructional approaches, nor do they acknowledge the wealth of scholarship on the variations among the different instantiations of these theories. For example, they refer to "unguided discovery" as an example of discovery learning, when few researchers who advocate for inquiry approaches would support such a model. It is important to note the distinctions between different instantiations of these pedagogical approaches, lest an argument be constructed against a confirmed straw man.

3 Of course, each of these "characteristics" could be challenged; at the very least, they don't adequately describe the core pedagogical goals of all of these disparate approaches.

4 Situativity theory and sociocultural theory are not identical theories, chiefly because of their different histories of development. For an example of the differences between the two theories, see Gee (2008) and Greeno and Gresalfi (2008), who address the same

topic (assessment of opportunities to learn) from a sociocultural (Gee) and situative (Greeno & Gresalfi) perspective. However, many of the central assumptions of the two perspectives are similar; of particular importance to the discussion here is the shared assumption that all activity is an interaction between people, histories, social tools, and norms and expectations that are inextricable from what one can be said to "know."

5 Students' histories of completing particular types of instructional tasks are also related to their problem-solving behaviors (Boaler, 1998, 1999; Hodge, McClain, & Cobb, 2003; Schoenfeld, 1988). For example, Schoenfeld (1988) discussed the relationship between the types of problems that students were routinely asked to solve and the resulting ideas about mathematics they formed. As an example, he noted that the prevalent emphasis in math classrooms on solving many problems in a short amount of time leads to a perception of mathematics as a domain that is either immediately understandable, or can never be understood (some characterize this as "black and white"). Schoenfeld noted that this belief has consequences for students' performance, in that they persist at solving problems for a short time only: "If you can't work the exercises within a reasonable amount of time, then you don't know the material" (pp. 159–160).

References

Ball, D. L. (1988). I haven't done these since high school: Prospective teachers' understandings of mathematics. In M. Behr, C. Lacampagne, & M. Wheeler (Eds.), *Proceedings of the Conference of the Psychology of Mathematics Education – North America* (pp. 268–274). Dekalb, IL: Northern Illinois University.

Ball, D. L. (1993). Halves, pieces, and twoths: Constructing and using representational contexts in teaching fractions. In T. A. Romberg, E. Fennema, & T. P. Carpenter (Eds.), *Rational numbers: An integration of research* (pp. 157–198). Hillside, NJ: Erlbaum.

Ball, D. L. (2000). Bridging practices: Intertwining content and pedagogy in teaching and learning to teach. *Journal of Teacher Education, 51*, 241–247.

Ball, D. L. (2001). Teaching, with respect to mathematics and students. In T. Wood, B. Nelson, & J. Warfield (Eds.), *Beyond classical pedagogy: Teaching elementary school mathematics* (pp. 11–22). Mahwah, NJ: Erlbaum.

Ball, D. L., & Rowan, B. (2004). Introduction: Measuring instruction. *The Elementary School Journal, 105*(1), 3–10.

Boaler, J. (1997). *Experiencing school mathematics: Teaching styles, sex, and setting.* Philadelphia, PA: Open University Press.

Boaler, J. (1998). Open and closed mathematics: Student experiences and understandings. *Journal for Research in Mathematics Education, 29*, 41–62.

Boaler, J. (1999). Participation, knowledge, and beliefs: A community perspective on mathematics learning. *Educational Studies in Mathematics, 40*, 258–281.

Boaler, J. (2000). Exploring situated insights into research and learning. *Journal for Research in Mathematics Education, 31*, 113–119.

Boaler, J. (2002). Learning from teaching: Exploring the relationship between reform curriculum and equity. *Journal for Research in Mathematics Education, 33*, 239–258.

Boaler, J., & Staples, M. (2007). Creating mathematical futures through an equitable teaching approach: The case of Railside school. *Teachers College Record, 110*(3), 608–645.

Brown, A. L., & Campione, J. C. (1994). Guided discovery in a community of learners. In K. McGilly (Ed.), *Classroom lessons: Integrating cognitive theory and classroom practice* (pp. 229–272). Cambridge, MA: MIT Press.

Brown, J. S., Collins, A., & Duguid, P. (1989). Situated cognition and the culture of learning. *Educational Researcher, 18*, 32–42.

Bruner, J. S. (1966). *Towards a theory of instruction.* Cambridge, MA: Belknap Press.

Cobb, P. (1999). Individual and collective mathematical learning: The case of statistical data analysis. *Mathematical Thinking and Learning, 1*, 5–44.

Cobb, P. (2007). Putting philosophy to work: Coping with multiple theoretical perspectives. In F. K. Lester (Ed.), *Second handbook of research on mathematics teaching and learning* (Vol. 1, pp. 3–38). Charlotte, NC: Information Age Publishing.

Cobb, P., & Bowers, J. S. (1999). Cognitive and situated learning perspectives in theory and practice. *Educational Researcher, 28*(2), 4–15.

Cobb, P., Gresalfi, M. S., & Hodge, L. (in press). An interpretive scheme for analyzing the identities that students develop in mathematics classrooms. *Journal for Research in Mathematics Education.*

Cobb, P., Jaworski, B., & Presmeg, N. C. (1996). Emergent and sociocultural views of mathematical activity. In L. P. Steffe, P. Nesher, P. Cobb, G. A. Goldin, & B. Greer (Eds.), *Theories of mathematical learning* (pp. 3–20). Mahwah, NJ: Erlbaum.

Cobb, P., Stephan, M., McClain, K., & Gravemeijer, K. (2001). Participating in classroom mathematical practices. *Journal of the Learning Sciences, 10*, 113–164.

Cochran-Smith, M., & Lytle, S. L. (1999). Relationships of knowledge and practice: Teacher learning in communities. *Review of Research in Education, 24*, 249–305.

Cohen, D. K., & Ball, D. L. (1990). Relations between policy and practice: A commentary. *Educational Evaluation and Policy Analysis, 12*, 331–338.

Dettermann, D. K. (1993). The case for the prosecution: Transfer as an epiphenomenon. In D. K. Detterman & R. J. Sternberg (Eds.), *Transfer on trial: Intelligence, cognition, and instruction* (pp. 1–24). Norwood, NJ: Ablex.

Doyle, W. (1988). Work in mathematics classes: The context of students' thinking during instruction. *Educational Psychologist, 23*(2), 167–180.

Engle, R. A. (2006). Framing interactions to foster generative learning: A situative explanation of transfer in a community of learners classroom. *Journal of the Learning Sciences, 14*(4), 451–498.

Fraivillig, J. L., Murphy, L. A., & Fuson, K. C. (1999). Advancing children's mathematical thinking in *Everyday Mathematics* classrooms. *Journal for Research in Mathematics Education, 30*, 148–170.

Franke, M. L., Kazemi, E., & Battey, D. (2007). Understanding teaching and classroom practice. In F. K. Lester (Ed.), *Second handbook of research on mathematics teaching and learning* (Vol. 1, pp. 225–256). Charlotte, NC: Information Age Publishing.

Gee, J. P. (2008). A sociocultural perspective on Opportunity to Learn. In P. A. Moss, D. C. Mullin, J. P. Gee, E. H. Haertel, & L. J. Young (Eds.), *Assessment, equity, and opportunity to learn* (pp. 76–108). New York: Cambridge University Press.

Gibson, J. J. (1979). *The ecological approach to visual perception.* Boston, MA: Houghton Mifflin.

Goos, M. (2004). Learning mathematics in a classroom community of inquiry. *Journal for Research in Mathematics Education, 35*(4), 258–291.

Greeno, J. G. (1991). Number sense as situated knowing in a conceptual domain. *Journal for Research in Mathematics Education, 22*, 170–218.

Greeno, J. G. (1997). On claims that answer the wrong questions. *Educational Researcher, 26*(1), 5–17.

Greeno, J. G. (2006). Learning in activity. In R. K. Sawyer (Ed.), *The Cambridge handbook of the learning sciences* (pp. 79–96). Cambridge: Cambridge University Press.

Greeno, J. G., & Gresalfi, M. S. (2008). Opportunities to learn in practice and identity. In

P. A. Moss, D. C. Mullin, J. P. Gee, E. H. Haertel, & L. J. Young (Eds.), *Assessment, equity, and opportunity to learn* (pp. 170–199). New York: Cambridge University Press.

Greeno, J. G., & MMAP. (1998). The situativity of knowing, learning, and research. *American Psychologist, 53,* 5–26.

Gresalfi, M. S. (2004). *Taking up opportunities to learn: Examining the construction of participatory mathematical identities in middle school students.* Unpublished dissertation, Stanford University, CA.

Gresalfi, M. S., Barab, S., Siyahhan, S., & Christensen, T. (in press). Virtual worlds, conceptual understanding, and me: Designing for critical engagement. *Horizons.*

Gresalfi, M. S., Boaler, J., & Cobb, P. (2004). *Exploring an elusive link between knowledge and practice: Students' disciplinary orientations.* Paper presented at the North American Chapter of the International group for the Psychology of Mathematics Toronto.

Hand, V. (2003). *Reframing participation: How mathematics classrooms afford opportunities for mathematical activity that is meaningful to students from diverse social and cultural backgrounds.* Unpublished dissertation, Stanford University, CA.

Heaton, R. M. (2000). *Teaching mathematics to the new standards: Relearning the dance.* New York: Teachers College Press.

Henningsen, M. A., & Stein, M. K. (1997). Mathematical tasks and student cognition: Classroom-based factors that support and inhibit high-level mathematical thinking and reasoning. *Journal for Research in Mathematics Education, 28*(5), 524–549.

Hiebert, J., Carpenter, T. P., Fennema, E., Fuson, K. C., Human, P., Murray, H., et al. (1996). Problem solving as a basis for reform in curriculum and instruction: The case of mathematics. *Educational Researcher, 25*(4), 12–22.

Hiebert, J., Carpenter, T. P., Fennema, E., Fuson, K. C., Wearne, D., & Murray, H. (1997). *Making sense: Teaching and learning mathematics with understanding.* Portsmouth, NH: Heinemann.

Hiebert, J., Stigler, J. W., Jacobs, J. K., Givvin, K. B., Garnier, H., Smith, M. S., et al. (2005). Mathematics teaching in the United States today (and tomorrow): Results from the TIMSS 1999 Video Study. *Educational Evaluation and Policy Analysis, 27,* 111–132.

Hiebert, J., & Wearne, D. (1992). Links between teaching and learning place value with understanding in first grade. *Journal for Research in Mathematics Education, 23*(2), 98–122.

Hodge, L. L., McClain, K., & Cobb, P. (2003, April). *Classrooms as design spaces for supporting students' identities as doers of mathematics.* Paper presented at the annual meeting of the American Educational Research Association, Chicago.

Kazemi, E., & Stipek, D. (2001). Promoting conceptual thinking in four upper-elementary mathematics classrooms. *The Elementary School Journal, 102*(1), 59–80.

Kirschner, P. A., Sweller, J., & Clark, R. E. (2006). Why minimal guidance during instruction does not work: An analysis of the failure of constructivist, discovery, problem-based, experiential, and inquiry-based teaching. *Educational Psychologist, 41,* 75–86.

Ladson-Billings, G. (1994). *The dreamkeepers: Successful teachers of African American children.* San Francisco, CA: Jossey-Bass.

Ladson-Billings, G. (1998). It doesn't add up: African American students' mathematics achievement. *Journal for Research in Mathematics Education, 28,* 697–708.

Lampert, M. (1990). When the problem is not the question and the solution is not the answer: Mathematical knowing and teaching. *American Educational Research Journal, 27,* 29–63.

Lampert, M. (1998). Studying teaching as a thinking practice. In J. G. Greeno & S. G. Goldman (Eds.), *Thinking practices in mathematics and science learning* (pp. 53–78). Mahwah, NJ: Erlbaum.

Lampert, M. (2001). *Teaching problems and the problems of teaching*. New Haven, CT: Yale University Press.

Lave, J. (1997). The culture of acquisition and the practice of understanding. In D. Kirschner & J. A. Whitson (Eds.), *Situated cognition: Social, semiotic, and psychological perspectives* (pp. 17–35). Mahwah, NJ: Erlbaum.

Lave, J., Murtaugh, M., & de la Rocha, O. (1984). The dialectic of arithmatic in grocery shopping. In B. Rogoff & J. Lave (Eds.), *Everyday cognition: Its development in social context* (pp. 67–94). Cambridge, MA: Harvard University Press.

Lave, J., & Wenger, E. (1991). *Situated learning: Legitimate peripheral participation*. New York: Cambridge University Press.

Lubienski, S. T. (2000). Problem solving as a means towards mathematics for all: An exploratory look through a glass lens. *Journal for Research in Mathematics Education, 31*, 454–482.

Mathematically Correct (n.d.). *Number Sense in California*. Retrieved December 20, 2007, from www.mathematicallycorrect.com/ns.htm#part01.

McClain, K. (2000). The teacher's role in supporting the emergence of ways of symbolizing. *The Journal of Mathematical Behavior, 19*, 189–226.

Moschkovich, J. (2002). A situated and sociocultural perspective on bilingual mathematics learners. *Mathematical Thinking and Learning, 4*, 189–212.

National Council of Teachers of Mathematics (n.d.) *Number Sense, Grades 3–5*. Retrieved December 20, 2007 from http://standardstrial.nctm.org/document/chapter5/numb.htm.

O'Connor, M. C., & Michaels, S. (1993). Aligning academic task and participation status through revoicing: Analysis of a classroom discourse strategy. *Anthropology and Education Quarterly, 24*(4), 318–335.

Pea, R. D. (1993). Practices of distributed intelligence and designs for education. In G. Salomon (Ed.), *Distributed cognitions* (pp. 47–87). New York: Cambridge University Press.

Peterson, P., & Walberg, H. J. (1979). *Research in teaching*. Berkeley, CA: McCutchan.

Prawat, R. S. (1996). Constructivisms, modern and postmodern. *Educational Psychologist, 31*(3/4), 215–225.

Rogoff, B. (1990). *Apprenticeship in thinking: Cognitive development in social context*. Oxford: Oxford University Press.

Saxe, G. B. (1991). *Culture and cognitive development: Studies in mathematical understanding*. Hillsdale, NJ: Erlbaum.

Saxe, G. B. (1999). Cognition, development, and cultural practices. In E. Turiel (Ed.), *Development and cultural change: Reciprocal processes* (pp. 19–35). San Francisco, CA: Jossey-Bass.

Schifter, D. (2001). Learning to see the invisible: What skills and knowledge are needed to engage with students' mathematical ideas? In T. Wood, B. S. Nelson, & J. Warfield (Eds.), *Beyond classical pedagogy: Teaching elementary school mathematics* (pp. 109–134). Mahwah, NJ: Lawrence Erlbaum.

Schifter, D., & Fosnot, C. T. (1993). *Reconsidering mathematics education: Stories of teachers meeting the challenge of reform*. New York: Teachers College Press.

Schoenfeld, A. H. (1988). When good teaching leads to bad results: The disasters of "well-taught" mathematics courses. *Educational Psychologist, 23*(2), 145–166.

Schoenfeld, A. H. (2004). The math wars. *Educational Policy, 18*(1), 253–286.

Sherin, M. G. (2002). When teaching becomes learning. *Cognition and Instruction, 20*(2), 119–150.

Silver, E. A., & Stein, M. K. (1996). The QUASAR Project: The "revolution of the possible" in mathematics instruction in urban middle schools. *Urban Education, 30,* 476–521.

Sowder, J. T. (2007). The mathematical education and development of teachers. In F. K. Lester (Ed.), *Second handbook of research on mathematics teaching and learning* (Vol. 1, pp. 157–223). Charlotte, NC: Information Age Publishing.

Staples, M. (2007). Supporting whole-class collaborative inquiry in a secondary mathematics classroom. *Cognition and Instruction, 25*(2/3), 161–217.

Staples, M. (2008). Promoting student collaboration in a detracked, heterogeneous secondary mathematics classroom. *Journal of Mathematics Teacher Education, 11*(5), 349–371.

Stein, M. K., & Lane, S. (1996). Instructional tasks and the development of student capacity to think and reason: An analysis of the relationship between teaching and learning in a reform mathematics project. *Educational Research and Evaluation, 2,* 50–80.

Stein, M. K., Remillard, J., & Smith, M. (2007). How curriculum influences student learning. In F. K. Lester (Ed.), *Second handbook of research on mathematics teaching and learning* (Vol. 1, pp. 319–369). Charlotte, NC: Information Age Publishing.

Stein, M. K., Smith, M. S., Henningsen, M. A., & Silver, E. A. (2000). *Implementing standards-based mathematics instruction: A casebook for professional development.* New York: Teachers College Press.

Stigler, J. W., Fernandez, C., & Yoshida, M. (1996). Traditions of school mathematics in Japanese and American elementary classrooms. In L. P. Steffe, P. Nesher, P. Cobb, G. A. Goldin, & B. Greer (Eds.), *Theories of mathematical learning* (pp. 149–175). Mahwah, NJ: Erlbaum.

Stigler, J. W., & Perry, M. (1988). Mathematics learning in Japanese, Chinese, and American classrooms. In G. Saxe & M. Gearhart (Eds.), *Children's mathematics* (pp. 27–54). San Francisco, CA: Jossey-Bass.

Thompson, A. G., Philipp, R. A., Thompson, P. W., & Boyd, B. A. (1994). Calculational and conceptual orientations in teaching mathematics. In *1994 Yearbook of the National Council of Teachers of Mathematics* (pp. 79–92). Reston, VA: National Council of Teachers of Mathematics.

Varelas, M., & Becker, J. (1997). Children's developing understanding of place value: Semiotic aspects. *Cognition and Instruction, 15*(2), 265–286.

Vygotsky, L. S. (1978). *Mind and society: The development of higher psychological processes.* Cambridge, MA: Harvard University Press.

Wood, T., & Sellers, P. (1997). Deepening the analysis: Longitudinal assessment of a problem-centered mathematics program. *Journal for Research in Mathematics Education, 28*(2), 163–186.

Yackel, E., & Cobb, P. (1996). Sociomathematical norms, argumentation, and autonomy in mathematics. *Journal for Research in Mathematics Education, 27,* 458–477.

15 "To Every Thing There is a Season, and a Time to Every Purpose Under the Heavens"

What about Direct Instruction?*

David Klahr Carnegie Mellon University

In this chapter, I address three questions that recur through this volume: (a) How does direct instruction differ from discovery learning? (b) When should direct instruction be used? and (c) What aspects of disciplinary practice should be included in early science education?

The first issue focuses on the features that distinguish direct instruction from discovery learning. Over the past 20 years or so, and culminating in the critique (Kirschner, Sweller, & Clark, 2006) and debate at the 2007 AERA meeting that motivated this volume, there have been extensive and heated exchanges among education researchers, learning scientists, and science educators about "discovery learning," "direct instruction," "authentic inquiry," and "hands-on science" (Adelson, 2004; Begley, 2004; EDC, 2006; Hmelo-Silver, Duncan, & Chinn, 2007; Janulaw, 2004; Klahr, Triona, & Williams, 2007; Kuhn, 2007; Ruby, 2001; Strauss, 2004; Tweed, 2004; Schmidt, Loyens, van Gog, & Paas, 2007). However, these arguments typically fail to establish a common vocabulary to define the essential aspects of the types of instruction being compared. I believe that in order to advance our ability to create effective instructional procedures, our field needs to become much more precise in the terminology it uses to describe instructional contexts and procedures, before moving on to advocacy about curriculum design. In the area of science education, more than others, it is particularly troubling—and ironic—that these debates often abandon one of the foundations of science: the operational definition. But a scientific field cannot advance without clear, unambiguous, and replicable procedures.

The second issue is about the place of direct instruction in the context of a constructivist perspective. Simply put: "When is it appropriate to use direct instruction?". The answer to the question is certainly not "never." Even the most zealous constructivist would acknowledge that there exist combinations of time, place, topic, learner, and context, when it is optimal to simply tell students something, or to show them something, or to give them explicit instruction about something. But how can we identify and characterize such instances?

* Thanks to my colleagues Sharon Carver, Jodi Davenport, Ido Roll, and Mari Strand-Cary for comments and suggestions. The work described here has been supported in part by grants from NICHD (HD25211), the James S. McDonnell Foundation (CSEP 96-37), the National Science Foundation, BCS-0132315 and IES award R305H060034.

The third issue is about content. Should early science education include instruction—at any location on the direct to discovery dimension—about disciplinary practices? Advocates of constructivism believe that the answer is "yes." For example, Hmelo-Silver et al. (2007) claim that "In the case of science education in particular, a large body of research supports the importance of understanding the nature of scientific research and the practices involved as a critical part of scientific literacy" (p. 105). Although there are several aspects of constructivist approaches to science of which I am critical, on this point I tend to agree. However, my emphasis differs in two respects from what constructivist advocates usually mean by "disciplinary practice." One point of difference is about content: I propose that the aspect of disciplinary practice that should be included in the science curriculum is our knowledge about basic cognitive processes. More specifically, I will argue that students should be taught something about what the learning sciences have discovered regarding how people think, and how those thinking processes lead to scientific discovery. The other point of difference is that I believe that this topic should be taught as explicitly and directly as possible.

What is Direct Instruction in Science?

Because instructional methods are inextricably bound to specific learning goals, I will start by describing the context in which my colleagues and I have contrasted the different types of instruction described in this chapter. Our focal domain— the Control of Variables Strategy (CVS)—is a small but essential part of the middle school science instruction. Procedurally, CVS is a domain-general method for creating experiments in which a single contrast is made between experimental conditions so that the causal status of the contrasted variable on the outcome can be unambiguously determined. Mastery of CVS includes the ability to create unconfounded experiments, to make appropriate inferences from their outcomes, and to understand and articulate the indeterminacy of confounded experiments.

The experimental set up depicted in Figure 15.1 provides a referent for the following example. The aim of our initial instruction is to teach a set of conditional rules that enable students to (a) identify the focal variable in a simple experiment (e.g., ramp height); (b) establish two different, contrasting values for that variable (a high ramp and a low ramp); (c) ensure that all the other variables are the same in both conditions (e.g., ball type, ramp surface, length of run); (d) understand that if the two ramps produce different outcomes (distance the ball travels), then they can make the inference that height is a causal factor, but that this inference is only possible because the other potentially causal variables have identical values on each ramp. The specific experimental set up depicted in Figure 15.1 is, of course, completely confounded because each of the potentially causal variables is set at a different level.

The aim of the Chen and Klahr (1999) study was to determine the relative effectiveness of three levels of "directness" in teaching CVS. The three types of instruction are described in the next section. Before turning to that, it is impor-

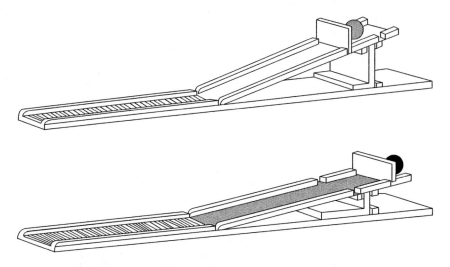

Figure 15.1 Ramps. One of several types of physical materials used in our CVS training studies. On each of the two ramps, children could vary the steepness, surface, and length of the ramp, as well as the type of ball. The confounded experiment depicted here contrasts (a) a golf ball on a steep, smooth, short ramp with (b) a rubber ball on a shallow, rough, long ramp.

tant to note that, in order to minimize potential effects of physical context, the study also used—as another between-subjects variable—three different sets of materials with the same underlying factorial structure: (a) slopes, as shown in Figure 15.1; (b) springs of varying length, width, wire size, and weight; and (c) sinking objects of different size, material, shape, and height above water. (See

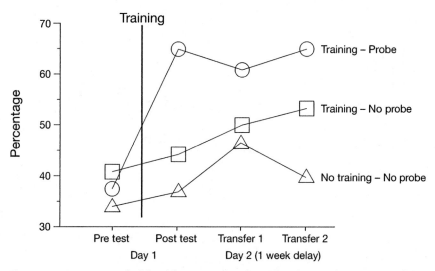

Figure 15.2 Percentage of trials with correct use of CVS by phase and training condition (source: adapted from Chen & Klahr, 1999, Figure 3).

Table 15.1 Materials Used in Chen and Klahr (1999)

	Domain		
	Springs	Slopes	Sinking
Primary materials	Eight springs that vary on three variables	Two ramps each with adjustable angle and "starting gate" location	Two water-filled cylinders, with two drop heights indicated
	A frame for hanging two springs	Two sets of two balls, golf and rubber (squash)	Eight objects that vary on three variables
	Two sets of weights, a heavy pair and a light pair	Two two-sided surface inserts (for ramps) with different coefficients of friction	Scooper and magnet for retrieving sunken objects
To be determined	What factors determine how far a spring will stretch?	What factors determine how far a ball will roll down a ramp?	What factors determine how fast an object will sink in water?
Variable two independent values for each of four variables	• length long, short • coil diameter wide, narrow • wire diameter thick, thin • weight size heavy, light	• angle high, low • starting gate short, long • surface smooth, rough • ball golf, rubber	• shape cube, sphere • material steel, Teflon • size large, small • height high, low
Dependent measure	Length of extension (for distance from base of rack when weight is added)	Distance ball rolls at end of ramp	Speed of sinking in water (for which reaches bottom first)
Subject activity Experimental design	From set of eight springs: • Select two springs • Hang spring on rack hooks • Select weights to go with each spring	For each of two ramps: • Select one or two angles • One of two surfaces • One of two starting positions • Select one of two balls to run	From set of eight objects: • Select two objects • For each object select one of two heights from which to drop object

Experiment execution	Hang weights on springs	Release gates (not necessarily simultaneously), allowing balls to roll	Simultaneously drop each object into water-filled cylinder
	Observe amount of stretching (for distance from base)	Observe distance balls roll after leaving ramp	Observe relative sink rates for arrival times at bottom of cylinder
Notable aspects of domain and procedure	All variables investigated are integral to selected spring	Variables are independent, object is constructed from choice of values for each variable	All variables investigated are integral to selected object
	Choice is from among pre-existing springs having a "cluster" of variable values	Comparison objects are constructed; variable values are not clustered	Choice is among pre-existing objects having a "cluster" of variable values
	Experiment is easy to set up and execute (no timing issues)	Outcome is evanescent (if based on speed), or stable (if based on final distance)	Easy to set up (simply choose two objects and heights)
	Measurement is easy (stable outcome)		Simultaneity necessary at start of drop
			Outcome must be observed instantly, otherwise it is lost

Table 15.1 for details.) These three domains were also used to assess transfer of CVS knowledge elements beyond the physical domain in which they were acquired. Thus, children whose initial instruction occurred in the ramps domain were assessed on the transfer trials using springs and sinking objects. Children who had worked with springs during instruction were assessed with ramps and sinking objects on the transfer trials, and so on. This counterbalancing allowed Chen and Klahr (1999) to assess the extent to which the deep structure of CVS procedures and concepts had been generalized beyond the specific physical context in which they had been acquired.

Terminology Used to Describe Different Types of Instruction

Chen and Klahr (1999) did not use the terms "direct instruction" or "discovery learning" in describing their three contrasting instructional conditions. They called them "Training-Probe," "No-Training Probe," and "No-Training, No-Probe," and defined them as follows:

> In the *Training–Probe* condition, children were given explicit instruction regarding CVS. Training ... included an explanation of the rationale behind controlling variables as well as examples of how to make unconfounded comparisons. ... A probe question before the test was executed asked children to explain why they designed the particular test they did. After the test was executed, children were asked if they could "tell for sure" from the test whether the variable they were testing made a difference and also why they were sure or not sure. In the *No-Training Probe* condition, children received no explicit training, but they did receive the same series of probe questions surrounding each comparison as were used in the *Training–Probe* condition. Children in the *No Training–No Probe* condition received neither training nor probes.
>
> (Chen & Klahr, 1999, p. 1101)

The results of the study were unambiguous. As shown in Figure 15.2, the Training-Probe condition, in which students received explicit instruction and were prompted to explain their reasoning, was by far the most effective, both immediately following training and after a one-week delay.

However, since I am arguing here that unambiguous definitions are essential to the advance of a science and the resolution of its controversies, it is embarrassing to admit that we used more conventional (and controversial) usage in other sections of that paper by discussing the contrast between "direct instruction" and "discovery learning." In a subsequent paper on teaching CVS to third- and fourth-graders (Klahr & Nigam, 2004), we abandoned all caution and called the contrasting instructional procedures—in this study, only two types of instruction, rather than three as in Chen and Klahr (1999)—"Direct Instruction" (previously called "Training-Probe") and "Discovery Learning" (previously called "No-Training, No-Probe"). We did attempt to clarify the way in which we defined these two types of instruction:

The ... difference between Direct Instruction and Discovery Learning does not involve a difference between "active" and "passive" learning. In both conditions, students were actively engaged in the design of their experiments and the physical manipulation of the apparatus. The main distinction is that in Direct Instruction, the instructor provided good and bad examples of CVS, explained what the differences were between them, and told the students how and why CVS worked; whereas, in the discovery condition, there were no examples and no explanations, even though there was an equivalent amount of design and manipulation of materials.

(Klahr & Nigam, 2004, p. 663)

Interpretations of Our Procedures

Responses to our studies reveal the lack of a widely shared understanding of what a constructivist science curriculum entails, even among its advocates. The first type of critique was that our discovery-learning condition is not representative of what really transpires in discovery-oriented instruction because it provides so little guidance, motivation, and interactive engagement. Hake (2004) wrote that:

Of course, neither "inquiry" nor "interactive engagement" methods should be confused with the extreme "discovery learning" mode, researched by Klahr and Nigam (2004). Their research suggests that, not surprisingly, an *extreme* mode of "discovery learning," in which there is almost no teacher guidance, is inferior to "direct instruction" for increasing third and fourth grade children's effective use of the control of variables strategy, a so-called "process skill".

But our discovery condition included hands-on instruction in which the teacher described the experimental apparatus and suggested a goal ("see if you can set up the ramps to see if the height of the ramp makes a difference"), and then the child was free to explore various kinds of arrangements, run the experiments, observe the results, and finally, under teacher suggestion, move on to another goal, such as "see if you can set up the ramps to see if the surface of the ramp makes a difference in how far the ball rolls." Rather than being a parody of the lack of structure in discovery learning, our discovery condition actually included more scaffolding than discovery learning as typically practiced.

The second type of critique took a diametrically opposite position to the first in its interpretation of the relation between our conditions and "authentic" discovery learning. It argued that our more effective procedure—our "Direct Instruction"—was, in fact, very close to what good constructivist pedagogy would recommend. In a personal letter that I received from a world-class scientist and ardent advocate of discovery learning, I was cautioned that:

In California, and in many other places, the term "direct instruction" ... basically means telling, without any doing.... Your ... studies were of course all about guided inquiry.... The fact that you used the bare term "direct instruction" for your favored option must have delighted those who want to teach with no inquiry at all.

Note that, under this interpretation, our direct-instruction condition, criticized as being unfairly compared to a parody of discovery learning by the first type of critique, has become an instance of guided inquiry!

The third type of critique was that our findings might be used to "return to a traditional, fact-oriented, teacher-centered model" (Kohn & Janulaw, 2004, p. 41). Such a critique suggests that more attention was paid to our terminology than to our actual instructional procedures because our instructional objective was neither traditional nor fact-oriented. (Although it is hard to understand why, in science of all areas, "fact oriented" is used pejoratively.) Instead, the instructional goal was that children know how to design and interpret unconfounded experiments, that is, how to vary only one factor at a time, how to avoid varying multiple factors simultaneously, and why it is possible to make an unambiguous causal inference from the former type of experiment but not the latter. It is true that the teacher followed a very careful script, directed the child's attention to features of confounded and unconfounded experiments, asked questions, and corrected faulty causal reasoning. Is this being teacher-centered, or is it "scaffolding"?

In all of these studies, the immediate effect of the contrasting instructional methods consistently favored direct instruction. For example Klahr and Nigam (2004) found that 77% of the children in the direct-instruction condition, but only 23% of those in the "discovery" condition, reached the mastery criterion on CVS immediate post-tests. This finding is typical of our series of studies in three respects. First, many more children reach high levels of performance in our direct-instruction condition. Second, so do a non-trivial proportion of children in the "discovery" condition (see also Chen & Klahr, 1999; Triona & Klahr, 2003; Toth, Klahr, & Chen, 2000). Third, even in our direct-instruction condition another non-trivial proportion of children did not reach high performance levels, so direct instruction is certainly not perfect.

However, the primary goal of the Klahr and Nigam paper was not to compare the relative effectiveness of one form of instruction over another on an immediate, near-transfer assessment. Instead, the goal was to show that once students have mastered a procedure (such as how to design a simple, unconfounded experiment), then the *way* that they achieved that mastery—via one instructional method or another—does not matter on a "far-transfer task." Klahr and Nigam (2004) called this the "path independence hypothesis." More specifically, their assessment included a more "authentic" activity than simply designing unconfounded experiments: they asked children to judge the quality of other children's science fair posters and they found that "the many children who learned about experimental design from direct instruction performed as well as those few children who discovered the method on their own" (Klahr & Nigam, 2004, p. 661).

Another important finding from our first study (Chen & Klahr, 1999)—and one that should be viewed favorably by discovery-learning advocates—is that children showed increases in their knowledge about different factors, even though they had not been taught anything directly about them (that is, they learned that the ball rolls further on a smooth ramp than on a rough ramp, even though there was no explicit instruction about the effect of different factors levels on the outcome of an experiment). As Chen and Klahr (1999) put it, "direct instruction about a process skill facilitated discovery learning about domain knowledge" (p. 1116). Although we did not emphasize this aspect of our study, it is directly relevant to Kuhn's (2007) response to the initial Kirschner et al. (2006) paper.

> But note the anomaly that confronts us at this point. If we agree that devel-opment of inquiry skills is a worthwhile educational goal,... and we also accept Kirschner et al.'s claims regarding the desirability of direct over inquiry methods of instruction, the following conclusion is unavoidable: Students should learn inquiry skills but they should not be involved in inquiry as an instructional method for mastering these skills.
>
> (Kuhn, 2007, p. 112)

But, as our results demonstrate, there is no paradox; by using direct instruction to teach children how to construct and interpret unconfounded experiments, we enabled them to use CVS to discover—via the very inquiry skill that we taught them—the effects of different levels of each causal variable.

Replication, Extension, and Improved Operational Definitions of Contrasting Instructional Methods

Given the extensive controversy about the benefits and costs of instruction located at different points along the "discovery to direct spectrum" (e.g., Adelson, 2004; Begley, 2004; Cavanagh, 2004; Kirschner et al., 2006; Tweed, 2004), and the idea that results can change drastically with different operationalizations of both instruction and assessment procedures, Strand-Cary and Klahr (in press) repli-cated and extended several features of the Klahr and Nigam (2004) study using the ramps apparatus described above, the same contrasting training conditions (here called "Explicit Instruction" and "Exploration"), and several assessments of near and far transfer, as well as delays of 3 and 36 months between instruction and assessment.

As noted above, the controversy about the defining properties of instructional procedures such as "hands-on science," "direct instruction," "discovery learn-ing," and "inquiry based science instruction" makes it important to articulate both the common and the distinct features of the contrasting instructional pro-cedures. Table 15.2 (taken from Strand-Cary and Klahr, 2008) shows how the two types of instruction differed along several dimensions. Several of the typical direct/discovery dichotomies do not map cleanly onto the contrasts used here. Consider first the common features of both types of instruction. Children in *both* conditions were engaged in physical manipulation of the apparatus involving "hands-on" experiences. During the ramps pre- and post-tests children in both

Table 15.2 Common and Distinct Features of Explicit Instruction Condition and Exploration Condition in Phase 1b

	Aspect	Training condition	
		Explicit Instruction	Exploration
Common features	Materials	Pair of ramps and balls apparatus	Pair of ramps and balls apparatus
	Goal setting	By Experimenter: "can you find out whether X makes a difference in how far the ball rolls?"	By Experimenter: "can you find out whether X makes a difference in how far the ball rolls?"
Distinct features	Physical manipulation of materials by child	Child assisted in taking down ramps after each set up by experimenter	Child set up ramps, rolled ball, and took down ramps from self-designed experiments
	Number of experiments designed	Four	Eight
	Focal dimensions	Steepness (two experiments) Run length (two experiments)	Steepness (two experiments) Run length (four experiments) Surface (two experiments)
	Design of each experiment	By Experimenter: one "good" (unconfounded) and one "bad" (confounded) experiment for each variable under consideration	By child: child designed experiment to determine effect of focal variable chosen by experimenter
	Probe questions	Experimenter asked about whether experiment was "smart" or not, and whether (hypothetical) outcome of experiment would "let you know for sure" about causal variable	No probe questions
	Explanations	Experimenter explained why an experiment was good or bad and how it could be corrected	No explanation
	Summary	Experimenter summarized CVS logic	No summary
	Execution of experiments	None: child only observed and discussed set up and a possible outcome	By child
	Observation of outcomes		Child observed outcome of each experiment
	Exposure to good and bad experiments	One good and one bad experiment (identified as such by Experimenter) for each focal variable	Varied according to child (because there was no feedback from Experimenter as to good or bad design)

conditions set up the ramps, rolled the balls, and took apart the ramps. Also, in both conditions the experimenter challenged the children with an explicit goal and children participated in goal-directed investigations in which the aim—to find out about the effect of a single causal variable—was generated by the experimenter, not the child. In *neither* condition were children unguided with respect to the purpose of the activity.

The many differences between the two types of instruction are also listed in Table 15.2. Some of these were motivated by the underlying theoretical issue being investigated: who designed each experiment, whether or not there were probe questions and explanations, systematic exposure to good and bad experiments. Others were engineering compromises imposed by pragmatic concerns: number of experiments designed (varied to compensate for extra time taken by explanations and probes), number of different factors used as focal dimensions for an experiment.

Knowing *which* one(s) of these differences between the Explicit and Exploration conditions are responsible for differences in children's learning about CVS is not possible in this particular study. Given that the goal was to compare two educationally realistic instructional strategies, it is necessary to take the conditions in their entirety as the experimental contrast. However, by carefully describing these differences, we are able to provide a reasonably detailed operational definition of what we mean, in this study, by Explicit Instruction and Exploration, and this operational definition facilitates future analysis of the effects of any of the specific features that differ between the two types of instruction.

When to Use Direct Instruction?

Decisions about instructional methods, procedures, and sequences—aka "curricula"—are acts of engineering. They involve theoretically motivated, but ultimately pragmatic, tradeoffs among a complex mixture of potentially causal factors. Suggestions about when to use direct instruction must therefore consider many characteristics of the overall curriculum. In this section, I will describe four particularly important features that argue in favor of direct instruction in the science curriculum: duration, feedback, sequencing, and consistency of implementation.

Duration of Instruction

Direct instruction is efficient. In our experimental studies, the training condition took about 25 minutes, and consistently produced significant increases in the proportion of children who master CVS. In our classroom studies in middle class schools, in which regular science teachers adapted our experiment "script" into a lesson plan, we achieved similarly high levels of mastery over the course of three or four 45-minute science classes (Toth et al., 2000). In contrast, discovery approaches to teaching CVS have been proven to take substantially more time to reach much lower levels of performance. For example, Kuhn and Dean (2005), employed a microgenetic approach in which they provided no explicit instruction at all as children attempted to isolate causal factors in a simple context employing five binary variables, very similar, structurally, to our materials. They found that even after a dozen 45-minute "discovery" sessions, spread over 8 weeks, only 75% of the children in their discovery condition met their lenient criterion of "mostly or exclusively" making valid inferences.

Feedback

Instructional contexts vary widely in the extent to which they provide feedback that is inherently self-correcting. For example, in the classic balance-scale tasks studied by Siegler (1976), trial-to-trial performance of the balance scale provides clear feedback about whether or not the child's prediction is correct. "Minimally guided instruction" with these materials could be quite effective, because the materials, in effect, provide the instruction. In contrast, the CVS context provides no such consistent, self-correcting feedback about a confounded experimental set up. In our studies, only explicit training focusing on the confound was effective in enabling children to master CVS.

Sequencing

In our most recent study (Strand-Cary & Klahr, 2008), we assessed CVS performance immediately following the training condition, and 3 months later. Figure 15.3 shows that, as in our other studies, the immediate effect of the two types of instruction was that children in the Explicit-Instruction condition produced significantly higher CVS scores than children in the Exploration condition. However, after a 3-month interval, and without any further instruction, the

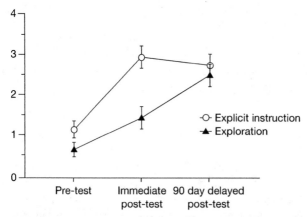

Figure 15.3 Mean CVS score showing the mean number of unconfounded experiments (out of 4) for children in Exploration condition and Explicit condition at three different points: (i) at pre-test, (ii) on an immediate post-test following training on the same day as pretest and training, and (iii) after a 90 day delay (source: from Strand-Cary & Klahr, 2008).

Exploration group performance rose to the same level as the Explicit group. The possible explanations for this "spontaneous" improvement are addressed in Strand-Cary and Klahr, but here I will focus only on the sequencing implications of this finding. If two different instructional methods are equally effective in the long run, but one of them gets students to a high performance level very quickly, then the method containing the "fast acting ingredient" should be preferred. Thus, the argument for Explicit Instruction is that it allows curriculum designers to teach CVS early rather than waiting for it to appear 3 months down the road. Given its position at the core of experimental science, CVS is clearly a prerequisite for much of the science curriculum, and the method of instruction should be one that maximizes the level of student performance in the minimum amount of time. One common critique of Explicit Instruction is that it provides only a temporary and somewhat narrow learning context. However, if CVS is taught early in the science curriculum, then there will be many opportunities for students to apply it to different contexts, later in the curriculum, thereby solidifying that knowledge.

Implementation Fidelity

Discovery-learning approaches are inherently vague about the sorts of learning events that should or might occur during the child's exploration and inquiry about the domain to be learned. While our particular implementation of the exploration condition in Strand-Cary and Klahr (2008), or the discovery-learning condition in Klahr and Nigam (2004), included a pre-specified number of trials and explicit goal-setting by the experimenter (see Table 15.2), this is rarely the way that discovery learning is implemented in the classroom. Instead, discovery-learning episodes in real classrooms are delimited more by inputs (time and effort) than by outputs (specific activities of the learner) because the method is inherently unstructured and minimally constrained. As the recent National Research Council volume on early science instruction notes:

> While ... intervention studies suggest that students can learn science ... through highly scaffolded and carefully structured experiences designing and conducting investigations, we also note that having students design and conduct investigations may be particularly difficult and *require a very high level of teacher knowledge and skill* in order for students to master content across the strands.
>
> (Duschl, Schweingruber, & Shouse, 2007, p. 257; emphasis added)

Put more boldly, the absence of an "instructional cook book" leads to extremely wide variability in what actually transpires in a constructivist curriculum. Thus, such an approach depends much more heavily on the skill, knowledge, and pedagogical acumen of the teacher than does direct instruction. While one can point to a handful of exquisitely sensitive and skilled examples of constructivist-based science instruction (Hennessey, 2002; Lehrer & Schauble,

2004; Smith, Maclin, Houghton, & Hennessey, 2000), there is no evidence that the majority of science teachers have the pedagogical skills, the time needed for preparation and analysis, or the deep science content knowledge to emulate these exemplary cases. Even if there were evidence that the best forms of discovery learning are more effective than pedestrian implementations of direct instruction, the best is too rare to provide a sound basis for curriculum policy.

Adding Cognitive Psychology to the Science Curriculum

One consistent theme in constructivist approaches to science education is that in addition to learning a rich and varied sample of the *content* of scientific knowledge, students need to understand and experience the *processes* that produced that knowledge. "In a word, students need to learn what it is scientists do and why they bother to do it. Students can develop that understanding only by engaging, in however rudimentary a way, in the practice of science" (Kuhn, 2007, p. 114). This is usually taken to mean that science instruction should include many features of scientific practice, including group projects, participation in appropriate modes of argumentation and communication, processes of notation and representation, and so on. Kirschner et al. (2006) challenge this perspective by noting that

> The major fallacy of this rationale is that it makes no distinction between the behaviors and methods of a researcher who is an expert practicing a profession and those students who are new to the discipline and who are, thus, essentially novices.
>
> (p. 79)

But there is a grain of truth to the constructivist claim that we should teach budding scientists about how scientists think. In particular, we should teach them that they think like everyone else: that they have at their disposal the same cognitive processes that have been discovered, studied, and refined by cognitive scientists for the past 50 years.

Although the "science as problem solving" perspective has been useful for those of us who study the psychology of scientific reasoning (Klahr, 2000; Kuhn, Garcia-Mila, Zohar, & Andersen, 1995; Mynatt, Doherty, & Tweney, 1977, 1978; Schauble, 1990; Klahr, Fay, & Dunbar, 1993), it has never been explicitly conveyed to children. For example, consider just one of the methods that are part of every working scientist's portfolio of problem-solving methods: analogy. Analogy-based instruction in science and mathematics has been proven to enhance learning (Clement & Steinberg, 2002; Dagher, 1995; Else, Clement, & Ramirez, 2003; Glynn, Britton, Semrud-Clikeman, & Muth, 1989; Paris & Glynn, 2004; Richland, Holyoak, & Stigler, 2004; Stephens & Clement, 2006) and such studies use the theoretical constructs associated with analogical reasoning to design different types of analogies, to identify different ways that teachers use them, and to assess the impact of different types of analogical reasoning on student (and teacher) performance. However, those constructs are, in effect, reserved for the analyst. But students are never explicitly instructed about what cognitive science knows about analogical reasoning: its forms, types, and associated processes.

In effect, the very knowledge that psychologists use to design studies of analogy or problem solving has been kept as a kind of "secret" from the children involved in those studies. That is, in none of the cited work were children explicitly instructed about the fact that they—or the scientists they were learning about—were working in multiple spaces, solving problems, using means–ends analysis, or pattern detection or analogy. They were not informed that the challenge of coming up with a discriminating experiment or an informative and consistent way to represent the results of a series of experiments was itself a problem to be solved, or that analogies have both surface similarity, structural similarity, and a set of mappings between the source and the target. I am suggesting that we make these ideas an integral part of the science curriculum—that we "let students in" on what is known about analogical reasoning—both as an account of fundamental disciplinary practice and as a set of heuristics that children can use in their own scientific endeavors. The goal here is to ensure that rather than just acting like scientists, students are thinking like scientists.

Direct Instruction on a Constructivist Knowledge Element?

I view this suggestion as a partial rapprochement between the two "warring" perspectives on science education that motivated this book: (a) the constructivist approach emphasizing discovery learning about the nature of disciplinary practice in science, and (b) the information-processing approach focusing on direct instruction about higher-order problem solving. In summary, although many of the constructivist methods aim to teach science by embedding young children in the methods and processes of scientists, none of them yet adequately address an essential feature of the scientific method: utilization of a powerful set of general problem-solving heuristics.

Kuhn (2001) and her colleagues have made a convincing case for the importance of metacognition—thinking about thinking—in the development of children's scientific-reasoning capacity. Most of the focus in that work is on having children understand the difference between theory and evidence and, in some studies, children have been encouraged to use a specific type of metacognitive knowledge, by being trained in methods of argumentation (Kuhn & Udell, 2003; Kuhn & Pearsall, 1998). As Kuhn and Dean (2004) note: "studies of people reasoning scientifically have something to tell us about thinking in the less rarefied contexts of everyday life outside of science" (p. 286). My suggestion turns that argument around: by instructing children in the range of everyday thinking processes that have been identified by cognitive psychology, we can enhance their ability to understand and to do science.

Conclusion

Like all of the venerable "isms" in education, constructivism has many faces and facets. In this essay, I have attempted to address only a few: what distinguishes direct instruction from discovery learning; when should we use direct instruction; and which aspects of scientific practice might be both teachable and useful for young science students? My answer to the first question is that there is no universally agreed upon definition of something as broad as an "approach," so we need to be as explicit as possible about our instructional procedures, striving for operational definitions that will facilitate unambiguous comparisons. My answer to the second question is that direct instruction should be used whenever we have evidence that it is both efficient and effective in the short and long term. This is most likely to occur in situations where corrective feedback on misconceptions and errors is unlikely to be systematically generated by the instructional context. My answer to the third question is that an important part of scientific practice is the use of general "weak methods" (Newell & Simon, 1972), and that we should begin to integrate such cognitive psychology topics into the early science curriculum. That is, students should not just be asked to *use* analogies that they or others have generated in approaching a scientific problem. Nor should they be told simply to "look for patterns" in their data. Instead, they should receive explicit instruction about the nature of human problem-solving processes, and how scientists have used them in the past and will inevitably use them in the future.

Question: Schwartz et al. *This was a useful and clarifying review of your work on children's learning "the control of variable" strategy. With respect to the "constructivism debate," you highlighted the critical role of operationalization in science. Do you have any thoughts on the role of circumscribing generalizations based on a singular operationalization? The claims in this chapter mostly arise from studies that operationalize instructional terms in the context of young children learning one particular scientific strategy. There are many other aspects of inquiry, for example generating important and tractable questions, deciding what and how to measure, consulting relevant prior research, deploying representational tools, postulating models, and knowing the assumptions that warrant generalization. It would be nice to have your explicit thoughts, given the possibility that your findings have been over-generalized by the greater education community.*

Reply: Klahr. Good question. First, let me disavow any personal responsibility for anything attributed to the "greater education community," because I don't know exactly who that includes, and I can't grapple with a bag of feathers. Let me respond to your more fundamental point about "circumscribing generalizations based on a singular operationalization" (which, I duly acknowledge, is the most eloquently phrased critique of my claims for direct instruction (DI) that I have yet encountered!). With respect to the universality of DI, I tried to be careful in my chapter about delineating some of the considerations that might favor DI: constraints on available instructional time, lack of explicit feedback from the instructional context, early location of the to-be-learned material in a sequence of topics, and likelihood that teachers could consistently and competently use direct vs. discovery instructional methods. It turns out that the particular domain that I have studied for several years—the control-of-variables strategy (CVS), favors DI on all of these, but I would be quite surprised if DI was ever the only game in town. In fact, my extensive work on scientific reasoning (Klahr, 2000) was derived from some earlier research on what we called "instructionless learning," in which we identified some of the processes that people use when they have absolutely no instruction whatsoever. Indeed, they can learn. But the fact that they can learn doesn't mean that they wouldn't have learned even more in less time if they had received some instruction.

Question: Schwartz et al. *You suggest that students should learn principles of human learning, because this will improve their own learning. We are very sympathetic to this point. When we have similar thoughts, which we do, we fear that we may be falling into a common trap. The trap is thinking that everybody needs to know what we know, and that the most effective way to learn is to do what we do. It is pretty obvious that just because we study cognition we are not any better at learning than the sociologists down the hall. Do you think the literature on metacognition, as it stands, justifies teaching scientific knowledge about cognition as a way to improve learning in general? Maybe just telling people what to do and having them practice with variable reinforcement would be more effective.*

Reply: Klahr. This is speculative at this point. We do know that young children can be instructed in how to use rehearsal and other processes—discovered by lab psychologists—to improve their short-term memory, so there is at least an existence of proof that the stuff that we know is worth disseminating. I am not proposing that we add a course in general problem-solving methods to early science instruction, just because my colleagues and I think it's cool stuff. Indeed, the evidence thus far is that attempts to teach general problem-solving skills, applicable over a wide range of domains, have not been very successful. The proposal in my chapter is that we teach a much more focused set of problem-solving skills related to science. Rather than teach about, say, pattern detection or analogical problem solving in general, I am suggesting teaching how those cognitive processes have worked in the sciences. And I would then have students apply that to the science content they are learning in a variety of substantive domains. I would not expect students to automatically generalize such skills to pattern detection or analogical problem solving in the economy, personal development, or historical trends.

Question: Gresalfi and Lester. *What is direct instruction, anyway? The discussion of the series of studies that you conducted contrasts two different instructional practices, one which you call direct instruction, and the other which you call discovery. What I began to wonder was why you chose to call your "instruction-first" method "direct instruction." Indeed, with respect to the history and particular definitions of direct instruction (see in particular Rosenshine, Chapter 11, this volume), the* *instructional method outlined in this chapter is not well-aligned. What is your ratio-nale for continuing to refer to this method as direct instruction?*

Reply: Klahr. Questions about labels miss the point of my chapter. It matters not what one calls the instructional method that I devote at least one-third of my chapter to: "direct instruction," "explicit instruction," "training with probes," etc. etc. What does matter is the effectiveness of the combination of features associated with type of instruction when contrasted with methods that lack some or all of those features described. This kind of instruction is clearly distinct from the broad family of instructional methods associated with constructivist views of learning, so the scientific question is what the evidential base is for the relative effectiveness of each type of teaching in different contexts.

References

Adelson, R. (2004). Instruction versus exploration in science learning. *Monitor on Psychology, 35,* 34–36.

Begley, S. (2004, December 10). The best ways to make schoolchildren learn? We just don't know. *The Wall Street Journal Online,* p. B1. Retrieved December 10, 2004 from http://online. wsj.com/article/0,,SB110263537231796249,00.html.

Cavanagh, S. (2004, November 10). NCLB could alter science teaching. *Education Week, 24*(11), 1; 12–13.

Chen, Z., & Klahr, D. (1999). All other things being equal: Children's acquisition of the control of variables strategy. *Child Development. 70,* 1098–1120.

Clement, J., & Steinberg, M. (2002). Step-wise evolution of models of electric circuits: A "learning-aloud" case study. *Journal of the Learning Sciences, 11*(4), 389–452.

Dagher, Z. R. (1995). Analysis of analogies used by science teachers. *Journal of Research in Science Teaching, 32,* 259–270.

Duschl, R. A., Schweingruber, H. A., & Shouse, A. W. (Eds.). (2007). *Taking science to school: Learning and teaching science in grades K-9.* Washington, DC: National Research Council.

EDC. (2006). The Inquiry Synthesis Project, Center for Science Education, Education Development Center, Inc. (EDC) (2006, April). *Technical report 2: Conceptualizing Inquiry Science Instruction.* Retrieved February 14, 2008 from http://cse.edc.org/work/research/inquirysynth/technicalreport2.pdf.

Else, M., Clement, J., & Ramirez, M. (2003). Should different types of analogies be treated differently in instruction? Observations from a middle-school life science curriculum. *Proceedings of the National Association for Research in Science Teaching,* Philadelphia, PA.

Glynn, S. M., Britton, B. K., Semrud-Clikeman, M., & Muth, D. K. (1989). Analogical reasoning and problem solving in science textbooks. In J. A. Glover, R. A. Ronning, & C. R. Reynolds (Eds.), *Handbook of creativity* (pp. 383–398). New York: Plenum Press.

Hake, R. R. (2004). Direct instruction suffers a setback in California – Or does it? Paper presented at the 129th National AAPT meeting in Sacramento, CA, August 1–5, 2004. Retrieved February 5, 2008 from www.physics.indiana.edu/~hake/DirInstSetback-041104f.pdf

Hennessey, M. G. (2002). Metacognitive aspects of students' reflective discourse: Implications for intentional conceptual change teaching and learning. In G. M. Sinatra & P. R. Pintrich (Eds.), *Intentional conceptual change* (pp. 103–132). Mahwah, NJ: Lawrence Erlbaum Associates.

Hmelo-Silver, C. E., Duncan, R. G., & Chinn, C. A. (2007). Scaffolding and achievement in problem-based and inquiry learning: A response to Kirschner, Sweller, and Clark (2006). *Educational Psychologist, 42,* 99–107.

Janulaw, S. (2004, January 9). *Letter to California Curriculum Commission from California Science Teachers Association.* Retrieved on April 7, 2004 from http://science.nsta.org/nstaexpress/ltr to commission.htm.

Kirschner, P. A., Sweller, J., & Clark, R. E. (2006). Why minimal guidance during instruction does not work: An analysis of the failure of constructivist, discovery, problem-based, experiential, and inquiry-based teaching. *Educational Psychologist, 41,* 75–86.

Klahr, D. (2000). *Exploring science: The cognition and development of discovery processes.* Cambridge, MA: MIT Press.

Klahr, D., Fay, A. L., & Dunbar, K. (1993). Heuristics for scientific experimentation: A developmental study. *Cognitive Psychology, 24,* 111–146.

Klahr, D., & Nigam, M. (2004). The equivalence of learning paths in early science instruction: Effects of direct instruction and discovery learning. *Psychological Science, 15,* 661–667.

Klahr, D., Triona, L. M., & Williams, C. (2007). Hands on what? The relative effectiveness of physical vs. virtual materials in an engineering design project by middle school children. *Journal of Research in Science Teaching, 44,* 183–203.

Kohn, A., & Janulaw, S. (2004, December 1). Standardized science. Mandatory testing's impact on teaching and learning [Letter to the Editor]. *Education Week,* p. 41.

Kuhn, D. (2001). Why development does (and does not) occur: Evidence from the domain of inductive reasoning. In J. L. McClelland & R. S. Siegler (Eds.), *Mechanisms of cognitive development: Behavioral and neural perspectives* (221–249). Mahwah, NJ: Lawrence Erlbaum Associates Publishers.

Kuhn, D. (2007). Is direct instruction an answer to the right question? *Educational Psychologist, 42*(2), 109–113.

Kuhn, D., & Dean, D. (2004). Connecting scientific reasoning and causal inference. *Journal of Cognition and Development, 5*(2), 261–288.

Kuhn, D., & Dean, D. (2005). Is developing scientific thinking all about learning to control variables? *Psychological Science, 16,* 866–870.

Kuhn, D., Garcia-Mila, M., Zohar, A., & Andersen, C. (1995). *Strategies of knowledge acquisition. Monographs of the Society for Research in Child Development, 60*(4), Serial No. 245.

Kuhn, D., & Pearsall, S. (1998). Relations between metastrategic knowledge and strategic performance. *Cognitive Development, 13,* 227–247.

Kuhn, D., & Udell, W. (2003). The development of argument skills. *Child Development, 74*(5), 1245–1260.

Lehrer, R., & Schauble, L. (2004). Modeling natural variation through distribution. *American Educational Research Journal, 41,* 635–679.

Mynatt, C. R., Doherty, M. E., & Tweney, R. D. (1977). Confirmation bias in a simulated research environment: An experimental study of scientific inference. *Quarterly Journal of Experimental Psychology, 29,* 85–95.

Mynatt, C. R., Doherty, M. E., & Tweney, R. D. (1978). Consequences of confirmation and disconfirmation in a simulated research environment. *Quarterly Journal of Experimental Psychology, 30,* 395–406.

Newell, A., & Simon, H. (1972). *Human problem solving.* Englewood Cliffs, NJ: Prentice-Hall.

Paris, N. A., & Glynn, S. M. (2004). Elaborate analogies in science text: Tools for enhancing preservice teachers' knowledge and attitudes. *Contemporary Educational Psychology,* *29*(3), 230–247.

Richland, L. E., Holyoak, K. J., & Stigler, J. W. (2004). Analogy use in eighth-grade mathematics classrooms. *Cognition and Instruction, 22*(1), 37–60.

Ruby, A. (2001). *Hands-on science and student achievement,* RAND, Santa Monica, CA, Retrieved December 1, 2004 from www.rand.org/publications/RGSD/RGSD159/.

Schauble, L. (1990). Belief revision in children: The role of prior knowledge and strategies for generating evidence. *Journal of Experimental Child Psychology, 49,* 31–57.

Schmidt, H. G., Loyens, S. M. M., van Gog, T., & Paas, F. (2007). Problem-based learning *is* compatible with human cognitive architecture: Commentary on Kirschner, Sweller, and Clark (2006). *Educational Psychologist, 42*(2), 91–97.

Siegler, R. S. (1976). Three aspects of cognitive development. *Cognitive Psychology, 8,* 481–520.

Smith, C., Maclin, D., Houghton, C., & Hennessey, M. G. (2000). Sixth-grade students' epistemologies of science: The impact of school science experiences on epistemological development. *Cognition and Instruction, 18*(3), 349–422.

Stephens, L., & Clement, J. (2006). Designing classroom thought experiments: What we can learn from imagery indicators and expert protocols. *Proceedings of the NARST 2006 Annual Meeting,* San Francisco, CA.

Strand-Cary, M., & Klahr, D. (2008). Developing elementary science skills: Instructional effectiveness and path independence. *Cognitive Development, 23,* 488–511.

Strauss, V. (2004, February 3). Back to basics vs. hands-on instruction: California rethinks science labs. *The Washington Post,* p. A12.

Toth, E., Klahr, D., & Chen, Z. (2000). Bridging research and practice: A cognitively-based classroom intervention for teaching experimentation skills to elementary school children. *Cognition and Instruction, 18,* 423–459.

Triona, L. M., & Klahr, D. (2003). Point and click or grab and heft: Comparing the influence of physical and virtual instructional materials on elementary school students' ability to design experiments. *Cognition and Instruction, 21,* 149–173.

Tweed, A. (2004, December 15). Direct instruction: Is it the most effective science teaching strategy? *NSTA WebNews Digest.* Retreived January 3, 2005 from www.nsta.org/main/news/stories/education story.php?news story ID=50045.

16 Beyond the Fringe

Building and Evaluating Scientific Knowledge Systems

Richard A. Duschl Penn State University

Ravit Golan Duncan Rutgers, The State University of New Jersey

The fundamental aspect of "doing science" is using evidence to build theories, models, and mechanisms that explain the natural world. Use of evidence and explanations are the basis of scientific understanding and of scientific inquiry. However, as Laudan (1981) points out, some initial scientific theories have been misguided or outright wrong (for example catastrophic geology, caloric theory of heat, and vital force theory of physiology). In spite of these "scientific failures," societies still persist in lauding scientific knowledge and scientific inquiry as the gold standard for understanding nature and solving problems. Thagard (2007) posits that truth and explanatory coherence are achieved through complementary processes in which theories broaden and deepen over time by accounting for new facts and providing explanations of why the theory works.

We argue that the general features of theory articulation and refinement, as well as theory broadening and deepening, are the basis for both "doing science" and "learning science." As specified in the National Research Council's research summary report *Taking Science to School (TSTS)* (NRC, 2007) the basis for a sound science education is dependent on learners' progress across four interwoven strands of proficiency:

1. Know, use, and interpret scientific explanation of the natural world.
2. Generate and evaluate scientific evidence and explanations.
3. Understand the nature and development of scientific knowledge.
4. Participate productively in scientific practices and discourse.

The message is that science education is more than teaching "what we know," as Kirschner, Sweller, and Clark (2006) and Sweller, Kirschner, and Clark (2007) suggest when recommending the elimination of inquiry, problem-based, and experiential models of science education. Science education is importantly about "how we know" and "why we believe what we know over alternatives." Our response to Kirschner et al. (2006) and Sweller et al. (2007) is directed at Kirschner's interpretation of school science and science inquiry in his 1992 article "Epistemology, practical work and academic skills in science education." These positions continue to frame the current debate. Specifically, our discussion is centered on the role of epistemic and scientific practices in both science and science education. The flaws in Kirschner's continued arguments for a strict dichotomy between epistemology and pedagogy are that he has (1) chosen the wrong scientific and epistemic practices as a focus for scientific inquiry, (2) misrepresented the cognitive abilities of young learners, and (3) mischaracterized science learning as mere knowledge accumulation rather than acknowledging the importance of refining and restructuring knowledge.

The scientific and epistemic practices issue is the focus of the first section. We provide an overview of developments in the interdisciplinary fields "learning sciences" and "science studies" to make the case that an exclusive focus on experimentation and discovery is an incomplete representation of contemporary scientific practices. In the second section, we argue against a "deficit model" view of young learners and for the importance of knowledge restructuring as a core element of science learning. We draw on the research contained in the *TSTS* synthesis report chaired by this chapter's first author (NRC, 2007). In particular, we highlight new images of learners and learning, and new frameworks for the design of science curriculum, instruction, and assessment that promote scientific practices, scientific understanding, and scientific reasoning.

Epistemic Goals and Scientific Practices in Science Education

The agenda for science education has broadened in ways that demand a rethinking of approaches to curriculum, instruction, and assessment. We live in a time when there is rapid growth of scientific knowledge. Like the first science-education reformers in the 1950s and 1960s, we are faced today with the challenge of making important decisions about what and how to teach. But unlike the 1960s reform effort we now have a deeper understanding of how and under what conditions learning occurs (NRC, 2007; Sawyer, 2006; NRC, 1999). We have learned about science learning through advancements in two scholarly domains: "*Learning Sciences*" and "*Science Studies.*"

Learning Sciences and Science Education

The learning sciences emerged from research in the cognitive sciences. Our deeper understanding of how children's thinking is fundamentally different from that of adults, coupled with richer understandings of expertise, representation, reflection, problem solving and thinking, provided a foundation for a major tenet of the learning sciences: "students learn deeper knowledge when they engage in activities that are similar to the everyday activities of professionals who work in a discipline" (Sawyer, 2006, p. 4). Subsequent research on informal learning reveals the importance of participatory structures (Rogoff, 1990) and the development of practices in culturally valued activities (Cole, 1996).

Science takes place in complex settings of cognitive, epistemic, and social practices (Giere, 1988; Kuhn, 1962/1996; Knorr-Cetina, 1999; Longino, 1990, 2002; Nersessian, 2008). The advancement of the learning sciences (Sawyer, 2006) and our deeper understanding of children's cognitive development (NRC, 2007) has led us to recognize and seek coordination of the same triad of practices—cognitive, epistemic, and social—in the learning of science. The epistemological commitment by Kirschner (1992) to experimentation is a necessary but not a sufficient condition for science learning. We recognize and appreciate today the need to see science as a set of dialogical engagements that involve (1) reasoning about data and evidence, (2) building and evaluating theories, and (3) participation in a wide array of communicative scientific practices. Kirschner (1992) accepts hypothesis testing as the central epistemology of science curriculum. He writes, "The epistemology of science is essentially experimental, and since this is so, then experimentation could and probably should be an important part of the science curriculum" (p. 277). However, such experimental practices are conducted in service of other important dynamic elements of what it means to be doing science:

- building theories and models;
- constructing arguments;
- using specialized ways of talking, writing, and representing phenomena.

The recommendation of the *TSTS* committee is that science instruction should be coordinated around "doing science" practices that go well beyond investigations or practicals. Kirschner (1992) takes up the issue of practicals and strongly questions whether this is a good way to teach science. His argument is that science educators have confused epistemology (inductive experiments) and pedagogy (conducting investigations). In Kirschner et al. (2006) we find that many of Kirschner's (1992) arguments about confounding epistemology and pedagogy persist:

> [T]hey appear to assume that knowledge can best be acquired through experience based on the procedures of the discipline (i.e., seeing the pedagogic content of the learning experience as identical to the methods and processes or epistemology of the discipline being studied).
>
> (Kirschner et al., 2006, p. 76)

> Yet it may be a fundamental error to assume that the pedagogic content of the learning experience is identical to the methods and processes (i.e., the epistemology) of the discipline being studied and a mistake to assume that instruction should exclusively focus on methods and processes.
>
> (Kirschner et al., 2006, p. 78)

Kirschner (1992) refers to the commitment to discovery learning based on practicals as the "abstractness of science" problem. He quotes Woolnough and Allsop (1985) to support his Piagetian stage-development position:

> [S]cience deals with theoretical concepts and their interrelationships. They are abstract and have to be considered and manipulated in the abstract. It is essential that these concepts are separated from their concrete reality if the maturing scientific mind is to gain mastery of them. We mislead and restrict

the thinking of students when we give the appearance of relating everything to the lab experience.

(p. 281)

Kirschner (1992) grounds his deficit-model-of-learners argument by stating that learning from practicals

would only be true if the student has already achieved this cognitive level of reasoning (the formal operational level) as defined by Piaget ... For those who have not, these "trumped-up" experiments ... tend to lead to misconceptions and misrepresentations of actual phenomena.

(p. 281)

A focus on what children cannot do is a deficit model of learning. In Kirschner et al. (2006) the "abstractness of science" problem and deficit model of learners shifts from Piagetian stages to cognitive architecture and cognitive-load theory as an explanation for what children cannot do in inquiry and problem-based learning environments.

Chapter 3 of the *TSTS* report (NRC, 2007) presents a research review on infant and young children's cognitive capacities. The research results are very clear that the deficit models of young learners are no longer tenable. Development takes place but the research clearly shows that there are no age-related stages and at any given age variability in scientific knowledge and reasoning is large. When development or learning is stalled because of cognitive complexity or the need for abstract reasoning, thoughtful and informed curriculum designs and effective mediation on the part of teachers and peers can move learners forward.

We know from the *TSTS* research report that young children are capable of abstract reasoning within select domains (e.g., actions and organization of living things, makeup and substance of materials). However, many of the extant K-8 science curriculum programs have been found wanting in terms of the lean reasoning demands required of students (cf. Hapgood, Magnusson & Palincsar, 2004; Ford, 2005; Metz, 1995; NRC, 2007). What the research shows is that curricula addressing domain-general reasoning skills and surface-level knowledge dominate over curricula addressing core knowledge and domain-specific reasoning opportunities that meaningfully integrate knowledge. If learning begins or is linked to these select domains, then the Kirschner et al. (2006) problem of novel knowledge and need to engage in direct teaching is diminished.

The reasoning-lean curriculum approaches found in use today (1) tend to separate reasoning and learning into discrete lessons thus blurring and glossing over the salient themes and big ideas of science, thus making curricula "a mile wide and an inch deep" (Schmidt, McKnight, & Raizen, 1997), and (2) in the case of middle school textbooks, tends to present science topics as unrelated items with little or no regard to relations among them (Kesidou & Roseman, 2002). Such conditions that dismantle learning sequences contribute to the novel-knowledge problem. The *TSTS* recommendation is that science learning be connected through longer sequences of instruction (e.g., learning progressions) that function vertically across and horizontally within years of instruction. Learning progressions represent a shift in emphasis from teaching that focuses on what we know (e.g., facts and skills) to teaching that focuses on core ideas central to the disciplines of science, accessible to students in kindergarten, and have potential for sustained exploration across grades K-8. Such sequencing and linking of learning stands in stark opposition to the recommendations from Kirschner et al. (2006) and Sweller et al. (2007).

Science Studies and Science Education

In very broad brushstrokes, 20th-century developments in science studies can be divided into three periods. The first, logical positivism, with its emphasis on mathematical logic and the hypothetico-deductive method, reflects Kirschner's (1992) commitment to experimentation and discovery.

The second period is defined by Thomas Kuhn's (1962/1996) conception of paradigm shifts occurring within a disciplinary matrix. In his disciplinary-matrix view of science, theories play a central role, but they share the stage with other elements of science, including modeling and a social dimension of values and judgments. Although Kuhn saw the scientific communities as essential elements in the cognitive functioning of science, his early work did not present a detailed analysis.

The third and most recent period is grounded in naturalized philosophy (Godfrey-Smith, 2003). It fills in the gaps left by Kuhn's undoing of the basic tenets of logical positivism. This movement (Duschl & Grandy, 2008):

- emphasizes the role of models and data construction in the scientific practices of theory development;
- sees the scientific community, and not the individual scientist alone, as an essential part of the scientific process;
- sees the cognitive scientific processes as a distributed system that includes instruments, forms of representation, and agreed-upon systems for communication and argument.

The contemporary understanding of the nature of science is the recognition that most of the theory change that occurs in science is not final theory acceptance, but improvement and refinement of a theory (Duschl & Grandy, 2008). What occurs in science is not predominantly the context of discovery or the context of justification as the logical positivists proposed, but the context of theory development, of conceptual modification.

Kirschner (1992) and Kirschner et al. (2006), by choosing to frame inquiry as experimentation and discovery, are playing the wrong epistemic game. The preferred epistemic game is the refinement of knowledge systems to enhance explanatory coherence (Duschl & Grandy, 2008; NRC, 2007; Thagard, 2007). Traditionally, science curriculum has focused on what one needs to *know* to do science. Schwab (1962) called this the "rhetoric of conclusions" approach to science education. Some 30 years later Duschl (1990) commented on the problem of "final form science" instruction. The argument now is for the importance of conversation, critique, cooperation and collaboration among teachers and students in classroom learning (Ford, 2008; Ford & Forman, 2006; NRC, 2007). Unfortunately, Kirschner, Sweller, and Clark invoke the cognitive-load argument to dismiss these important learning dimensions when they write:

> Cooperation or collaboration, however, imposes costs in terms of cognitive load in that the coordination and execution of communication and interaction in groups is, in itself, often a cognitively taxing experience. If the communication and coordination of the problem-solving process in the group (i.e., the interaction processes) proceeds effectively and efficiently, this will only add new germane load to the already existent intrinsic, germane, and extraneous load caused by PBL.
>
> (Sweller et al., 2007, p. 117)

The learning sciences and science-studies research over the past 20 years speaks to the importance of using knowledge, evidence, and explanations in the service of building scientific knowledge—learning by any other name. The *TSTS* recommendations are to center science learning on theory building and argumentation coordinated around scientific practices and discourse. To do so *TSTS* recommends that new curriculum sequences—learning progressions—need to be developed, grounded in research on children's domain-specific learning. The *TSTS* recommendations are based on the assumption that in the right domain-specific contexts with support and guidance from teachers, complex learning and reasoning can occur. Kirschner, Sweller, and Clark, we believe, who are working within the frameworks of extant curriculum and pedagogical practices, think otherwise. While the focus on scientific practices and discourse in *TSTS* is seen as a foundation for reforming science learning in classrooms, they dismiss it outright as increasing the cognitive load of learners and thus see it as an obstacle to learning.

We share with Kirschner, Sweller, and Clark the idea that providing guidance for learning is important for effective instructional conditions; worked examples should certainly have a prominent place in effective learning environments. The question is when and where to employ worked examples. Where we part company is how that guidance is provided and to what ends. The previous section has addressed the epistemological orientation for science and science education. Another fundamental dividing point is our conflicting images of what students can and cannot do in classroom learning. Some aspects of this argument have already been introduced. The next section takes up in more detail the issue and consequences of embracing deficit models of learning.

Deficit Models of Learners

Statements about learners that claim that "what they know determines what they see; an empty minds sees little and understands even less" (Sweller et al., 2007,

p. 118), make explicit the deficit model of learners espoused by cognitive-load advocates. While Sweller and colleagues are right to say that discovery favors the prepared mind (Bruner, 1961); the notion of learners as blank slates flies in the face of research on conceptual change and developmental psychology. Research on children's development and conceptual change (Carey, 1985) suggests that even young children possess impressive cognitive capabilities and are able to reason in complex ways and about abstract concepts (NRC, 2007). In a classroom, with carefully designed sequenced curricula and with targeted teacher mediation, young learners are able to learn how to reason effectively about abstract scientific concepts, represent data patterns, develop and revise explanations, and argue about their conceptual constructions (cf. Schauble, Glaser, Duschl, Schulze, & John, 1995; Herrenkohl & Guerra, 1998; Metz, 2004).

The Cognitive Abilities of Young Children

By the time young children enter school, they already possess substantial knowledge about the natural and social world. *Ready Set, Science!* lists the following examples of core domains or knowledge systems that research establishes as accessible to young learners (NRC, 2007, 2008):

- simple mechanics of solid bounded objects;
- behaviors of psychological agents;
- actions and organization of living things;
- makeup and substance of materials.

Several studies suggest that even preverbal infants have a sense of mechanism and causality (Baillargeon, 2004). This early sense of cause and effect develops further during the preschool years. Gopnik and colleagues (Gopnik & Sobel, 2000; Gopnik, Sobel, Schulz, & Glymour, 2001) found that even 2-year-olds could draw appropriate conclusions about causality and covariation by observing contingency patterns. Preschoolers in these studies were able to infer causality in complex situations involving multiple causes and probabilistic causality. Thus, young children can reason about causal mechanisms even before formal schooling begins. Carefully planned and mediated instruction at the kindergarten and early grades can capitalize on these abilities and continue to develop them further.

The Preschool Pathways to Science (PrePS©), an NSF-funded science and math program for pre-K children developed by Rochel Gelman and her colleagues (Gelman & Brenneman, 2004), is an example of a theory-based curriculum that builds on young learners' emerging scientific understanding. In this program the teachers introduce the language and ideas of *observe, predict,* and *check,* early on in the year (during separate circle-time sessions). Children then use their five senses to observe phenomena and objects such as an apple while the teacher records these observations on a publicly displayed chart. The interplay between engaging in science practice and developing understandings of science content allows the learning to spiral as skills and practices are applied to familiar content supporting the development of new knowledge. It is important to note that the PrePS curriculum takes place over multiple months and is centered on core concepts, or big ideas, in domains that young children already have some substantive experience with and thus already possess some relevant knowledge about (such as insides and outsides of objects, form and function, systems and interactions).

Along with an emergent understanding of physical mechanism and causal interactions, infants and young children have knowledge of social interactions (Spelke & Kinzler, 2007) that develops into a theory of mind later in childhood (Perner, Leekam & Wimmer, 1987; Wellman, 1990; Wimmer & Perner, 1983). Before the age of three most preschoolers assume that others have the same thoughts and knowledge as they do, at this stage they are unaware that other individuals possess minds that are different than their own. A theory of mind, the idea that others may think and believe differently, emerges around the age of three and at this point preschoolers are able to understand that others may have false beliefs, that is, believe something that is at odds with reality (or at least the child's perception of reality). An individual's theory of mind is a critical precursor to several aspects of their scientific reasoning.

A theory of mind affords the understanding that knowledge can be subjective and people may have different interpretations of natural phenomena. This is relevant in grasping the revisionary nature of scientific knowledge and the existence of alternative models for explaining a phenomenon. It follows that in order to engage in scientific argumentation (a core practice we would like students to master), children need to have a theory of mind and notion of false belief that allows them to assume that explanations vary and that explanations may be more or less accurate depictions of the phenomenon in question. Herein lies the foundation for engaging young science learners in modeling phenomena and arguing about alternative models and theories (NRC, 2008). It also follows that if learning environments do not present science as a theory-building or model-building enterprise with a specialized way of talking, writing, and representing ideas, then these innate abilities may fade away (Gopnik, 1996).

Let us now turn to children's capacities for representation and the ways in which this practice can also serve as a foundation for model building in science. Engagement with measurement and data representation can be introduced early on as the PrePS curriculum demonstrates. Preschool children can sort objects based on size, color, shape, or other features and then be guided to display this information in the form of lists, tables, and simple graphs. Children can compare measurements, for example shoe size and height of children in different classes (and ages), as well as chart growth in these quantities over time (Gelman & Brenneman, 2004). Understandings about counting, measuring, and illustrating patterns provide an anchor for the design of learning progressions that develop more sophisticated notions of descriptive statistics and data modeling introduced in formal schooling.

Research on elementary students' ability to measure and represent data suggests that young children can engage in productive discussions about what aspects of an object to measure (for example, how one would measure plant growth) and how these data should be graphically represented (Lehrer & Schauble, 2000, 2002, 2006; Lehrer, Jaslow, & Curtis, 2003). Children's invented and teacher-guided representations of data can serve as a focus for discussions about simple statistical qualities of data, as well as the values of different forms of representations for illustrating different features of data patterns (Lehrer & Schauble, 2004). The extensive research on infants' and young children's cognitive development underscores the multitude of knowledge resources and reasoning capabilities children bring to formal schooling.

Young learners are anything but empty minds. They are, within effective instructional conditions (Lehrer & Schauble, 2002), capable of noticing patterns and attributes in the natural world, linking the patterns and attributes to science concepts, developing explanations of natural phenomena, and reasoning about abstract ideas in meaningful and productive ways. Whether or not we chose to capitalize on children's emerging scientific-reasoning abilities and further develop them depends on how we construe the goals of science learning and how such learning outcomes can be achieved. A focus on understanding the doing of science and how scientific knowledge is developed and evaluated will entail building on students' emerging capacities for representation, model-building, casual reasoning, etc. If the focus of science education is on the accumulation of scientific facts, or final-form science, then it is not clear how one might capitalize on the emerging understandings we describe in this section. We, of course, argue for a science-education focus on the practices and discourse of scientific theory building; and with such a perspective it is clear that students bring significant conceptual resources that can, and should be, used as leverages for developing more sophisticated understandings of the scientific enterprise throughout schooling.

Deepening students' ideas over time, as suggested in the learning-progressions approach discussed earlier, is not developmentally inevitable. Learning has to be mediated carefully by teachers and through designed curriculum, instruction, and assessments. Students do bring useful understandings to the classroom, and with targeted instruction, like worked examples and reciprocal teaching, among others, these ideas can be developed into more sophisticated understandings. However, without guided instruction and carefully planned instructional sequences, such developments are unlikely to occur on their own. To our minds, careful instruction should not be exclusively direct instruction, nor should it be devoid of direct instruction. Rather, the choice of instructional strategy and sequence should be informed by instructional goals and a theory of learning. We next discuss the differences between recent research on theories of learning as conceptual change and the theory of learning espoused by Kirschner and colleagues.

Science Learning as Conceptual Change

Sweller et al. (2007) argue that the "aim of learning is to increase knowledge in long term memory" (Sweller et al., 2007, p. 118). This construal of learning is one of knowledge accumulation, and this process is constrained by rigid capacity limitations of working memory. While this may be the case for certain aspects of science content, research on science learning suggests that, often, learning in science entails conceptual change rather than mere knowledge accumulation (Chi, in press; Limón & Mason, 2002; Posner, Strike, Hewson, & Gertzog, 1982). The instructional proposals from Kirschner et al. (2006) do not align with what research tells us about children's learning in science.

Conceptual change involves changes to knowledge structures in long-term memory (Carey, 1988) and such changes in knowledge organization are a significant aspect of developing expertise (Chi, 1992). Such changes take time and usually require targeted guided instruction and designed curriculum (Posner et al., 1982; Smith, Maclin, Grosslight, & Davis, 1997; White & Gunstone, 1989). It is also important that students' prior knowledge be actively engaged and that they be encouraged to share their ideas and argue about them (Niaz, Aguilera, Maza, & Liendo, 2002; Osborne & Freyberg, 1985; White & Gunstone, 1989; White & Frederiksen, 2000).

Differences in the organizational structure of knowledge in experts versus novices have been documented extensively (e.g., DeGroot, 1965; Chase & Simon, 1973; Chi, Feltovich, & Glaser, 1981; Chi, 1988; Glaser, 1992; Wineburg, 1991). Experts' knowledge tends to be organized around core concepts or big ideas that guide their thinking and problem solving in the domain (NRC, 2001). When asked to solve physics problems, experts represent them in terms of underlying physics laws and principles that can be applied, rather than the specific context or equations they use, as novices tend to do (Chi et al., 1981). When experts do evoke equations to be used in the solution process, they seem to evoke sets of related equations, which suggest that their knowledge is organized in a way that facilitates retrieval of relevant equations grouped under deeper organizing principles (Larkin, 1979). Thus, learning and the development of expertise in a domain entail much more than mere knowledge accumulation.

Changes in the structure and organization of knowledge in long-term memory are not only signature characteristics of expertise; they also have important implications regarding the capacity of working memory in handling novel information. Chi (1978) tested 10-year-old expert and novice adult chess players' memory recall of chess positions. The children's memory of chess positions was far superior to the adults' memory of chess positions. This was not due to simple differences in memory capacities, as the children scored lower than adults on digit memorization tasks.

These findings reflect the influence of knowledge organization on the processing capacity of working memory. In a report on the role of knowledge in education and thinking, Glaser (1983) concludes that "the problem solving difficulty of novices can be attributed, to a large extent, to the inadequacies of their knowledge bases, and not to limitations in their processing capabilities" (p. 18). A deeply principled knowledge structure can minimize the cognitive load associated with problem solving. Even young children show remarkable processing capabilities in domains for which they have deeply principled knowledge structures (Chi, 1978; Chi & Koeske, 1983).

Thus far we have shown that a notion of learning that is synonymous with knowledge accumulation is far too simplistic to account for learning of big ideas in science, and that a better description of such learning involves conceptual change and reorganization of knowledge. A different view of learning implies different instructional pedagogies. Sweller et al. (2007) advocate for a pedagogy of "telling" whereby learners are provided with problem solutions that explicate all the knowledge and steps necessary for solving the problem, and this way learners can accrue the necessary knowledge. A conceptual-change perspective entails a very different pedagogical approach as learning goes beyond mere knowledge accretion. A key instructional implication of conceptual-change theories for learning is that any form of instruction must take into account learners' existing knowledge structure, as new knowledge is interpreted in light of existing understandings. If the theory to be learned is very different than the child's existing understandings, merely telling the new ideas (as an expert would understand them) will not result in conceptual change (Posner et al., 1982).

In the next, and final, section we summarize our arguments and present a model of learning as participation in scientific practice, in which theory construction and argumentation are prominent activities that can foster meaningful science learning and conceptual change.

Science Learning as Participation in Practice

The ongoing reform efforts in the USA and UK have called for a shift in focus from a sole emphasis on disciplinary content to shared focus on both disciplinary content and disciplinary practices. Policy documents (AAAS, 1993; NRC, 1996, Millar & Osborne, 1998) place an emphasis on the learning of how scientific knowledge is developed and evaluated in the scientific community. The *TSTS* report, in particular, advocates for students to participate productively in scientific practices and dialogue pertaining to the creation, evaluation, and revision of scientific explanations and models. As discussed earlier, science is no longer viewed (nor should it be taught) as an endeavor of discovery and experimentation, but rather as an endeavor of theory building (where experimentation is a means to an end).

The new view of science education focuses on what students need *to do* to learn science. The notion of "to do" in science education has traditionally been associated with the manipulation of objects and materials to engage learners with phenomena to teach conceptual "what we know," or final-form knowledge through experiments and demonstrations. Kirschner (1992) is right to criticize this model of science-education instruction. Conceptual knowledge, scientific reasoning, understanding how scientific knowledge is produced, and participating in science represent elements that are intimately intertwined in the doing of science. Conceptual, epistemic, and social goals all need to be components of science instruction along with the engagement with phenomena.

The four strands of scientific proficiency discussed in the *TSTS* report reflect an important change in focus for science education. One important change is recognizing that very young children are more competent than we think and are able to reason about concepts and claims. They can think abstractly early on and do NOT go through universal, well-defined stages of development. Another important change is a shift in emphasis from teaching that focuses on what we know (e.g., facts and skills) to teaching that focuses on how we come to know and develop scientific knowledge and on why we believe what we know over alternative competing perspectives (e.g., model-based science). While the emphasis on facts and skills goals may be grounds for the separation of epistemology and pedagogy, an emphasis on the restructuring and growth of scientific knowledge necessitates a fusion (Duschl & Grandy, 2008; NRC, 2007).

The emphasis on how and why reflects the *TSTS* research review recommendation that science learning needs to be strongly grounded in the use and consideration of evidence. This, in turn, leads to the recommendation that science learning be coordinated through "learning progressions" that function across modules, units, and years of instruction. The rationale, once again, is to facilitate the learning of core science knowledge and practices that are critical for development of scientific knowledge and of the reasoning inherent in the four strands of proficiency. Again, Kirschner's depiction of experimentation and discovery as the epistemic cornerstone of science and the exclusion of these same science practices from instructional models leaves out important cognitive, epistemic, and social scientific practices that research demonstrates (NRC, 2007, see chapters 6 and 7) promote learning, understanding, and reasoning.

Given the focus on learning of scientific practices as educational goals, what are the implications for instruction and the development of learning environments? To address this question we need to consider the nature of the practices we wish students to learn. First, these practices occur in the context of epistemic communities of practice; scientists have norms of knowledge representation and communication, norms of argumentation, norms for what counts as evidence, and norms for how experiments are done and data are collected. These norms are consensually developed within the community and as such change over time (as new knowledge is developed and new tools are built). Science learning also occurs within a community of practice—the classroom—however, the two communities operate under entirely distinct sets of norms, epistemologies, and activities (Collins, Brown, & Newman, 1989; Reif & Larkin, 1991). If we want students to be scientifically literate in the ways we described, then the science classroom needs to include the social and cognitive norms and practices of the scientific community. This argument is at the core of the contention between our inquiry-based view of science learning and the teacher-directed view of learning that Kirschner et al. (2006) espouse.

The argument that classroom practice and norms need to reflect the practices and norms of scientific communities is grounded in a sociocultural theory of learning, which conceptualizes learning as increased participation in communities of practice and teaching as guided practice (Lave & Wenger, 1991). This theoretical perspective emphasizes the roles and activities of learners in the context of communities of practice, and learning is described as movement from peripheral to more central participation patterns. Accordingly, teaching students about a practice, in this case scientific practice, requires that the students themselves engage in the activities necessary for a practice to achieve its goals. In scientific communities the goal of practice is to build knowledge and to decide what claims "count" as knowledge in that discipline. It follows that students should be able to engage in activities (such as modeling, experimentation, and argumentation) that result in the development and evaluation of knowledge claims.

We join Ford and Forman (2006) in believing that learners need to become familiar with and able to carry out two interrelated roles that are at the core of scientific practice. The roles of "critiquer" and "constructor" reflect both the social and material nature of science. Engagement with these roles help develop a "grasp of practice" that reflects the essence of how the scientific discipline enterprise works and what are truthful scientific claims. We would stress that the roles of critiquer and constructor also promote the learning of concepts and conceptual networks.

We share with Kirschner et al. (2006) the commitment to improve science learning in classroom settings. Many of their ideas about conceptual learning (e.g., worked examples and guided support from teachers) would fit within our understanding of effective instructional environments. Our aims for learners, though, are more comprehensive, seeking not only conceptual goals but epistemic and social goals, too. Where they see the epistemic and social dimensions as extraneous cognitive load, we see the important rudiments of effective instructional environments.

Question: Klahr. *You say that when development or learning is stalled because of cognitive complexity or the need for abstract reasoning, thoughtful and informed curriculum designs and effective mediation on the part of teachers and peers can move learners forward. While I fully agree with the TSTS position (having been a member of the committee that produced it under your able chairmanship!) that Piagetian stage theory is mistaken in its claims about a set sequence of stages, I think your claim is too strong. It seems that the statement quoted above is a slightly disguised version of Bruner's now roundly refuted claim that "any subject can be taught to any child at any age in some form that is honest" (Bruner, 1977). Can you give an example of a situation where a child is "stalled" and a "thoughtful and informed curriculum" can "move learners forward"? Wouldn't such a curriculum have a large dose of direct instruction embedded in it?*

Question: Klahr. *The Glaser citation you use strikes me as entirely consistent with, rather than opposed to, the Sweller et al. position on the interplay between working memory (WM) and long-term memory (LTM) and the novice–expert distinction. For example, the reason that chess experts—whether adults or children—can recall many more chess positions than novices is not because they have larger WM capacity, but because they have a vast amount of well-organized, and easily retrievable, chess information in LTM. When Sweller says "an empty mind sees little and understands even less," he is simply restating the well-known expertise-encoding effect a bit dramatically. Thus, would you agree that, in order for children to acquire efficient and rich encodings of complex situations, quite a lot of explicit, heavily scaffolded, and (perish the thought) direct instruction would be an intrinsic part of your proposed "carefully designed sequenced curricula and ... targeted teacher mediation" (p. 11)?*

Reply to both questions: Duschl and Duncan. There is a "Time for Telling" as Schwartz and Bransford (1998) have argued. The role of direct teaching does have an important place in the design of effective learning environments. The issue is when, at what time, and toward what goals, so that the maximum benefits of learning accrue. The field has long recognized the impact prior knowledge has on learning, and probing students' understandings is a cornerstone of science education. We understand that alternative perspectives can interfere with learning and unless these "misconceptions" are made the target of instruction, they can be pernicious and endure into adulthood (e.g., the causes of the seasons being the Earth's distance from the Sun). Telling the learner the correct answer does not always work, as many knowledge systems based on naive beliefs often persist. We know from evidence like that reported in the *A Private Universe* video (Harvard-Smithsonian Center for Astrophysics, 1987) that new or subsequent learning often perturbs bright learners' knowledge systems, causing them to retrograde to or reorganize prior beliefs without grasping new concepts. This has implications for how we conceive of the sequence of curriculum, the ways we engage learners with phenomena, and when and how we invoke direct teaching.

Teachers can use students' prior knowledge to help children make sense of the world. For example, we have learned that students' competing alternative conceptions can be used effectively as contrast cases to engender the discussions about which knowledge systems are preferred and why. We have also come to an understanding that students' incomplete and intuitive knowledge can be resources for conceptual change. Research on science learning recognizes three types of conceptual change: (1) elaborating on a pre-existing concept; (2) restructuring a network of concepts; and (3) achieving new levels of explanation. Conceptual change requires understanding and integrating the information through scaffolded and guided instruction, not direct instruction of what's right and what's wrong.

Attention to evidence and to the comprehension and coordination of evidence is needed to combat "folk" commonsense-type knowledge systems. The development of reasoning practices for recognizing evidentiary patterns, reorganizing knowledge and refining explanatory models are needed. This evidence comes in two forms: empirical evidence (e.g., the measured changing position and height of the Sun's skyward path during the Earth's annual orbit) and evidence for conceptual coherence (e.g., changing position and height of the Moon's path over monthly orbits around the Earth). Explanatory coherence and conceptual understanding requires both empirical and conceptual alliance. Chi (2005) has shown how ontological shifts are often needed to progress stalled learning. Clement (1998) has demonstrated the power that analogical bridges have when learning about abstract concepts has stalled. Adey, Shayer, and Yates (2001) have demonstrated the effectiveness that designed thinking activities and group-learning sessions can have on advancing stalled domain-general reasoning skills. Schwartz and Bransford (1998) report positive results for the use of contrast cases when prior knowledge stalls the learning of relevant attributes and concepts for meaning making.

When learning goals are targeted to the development of knowledge systems, to the development of cognitive and epistemic scientific practices and to the integration of meaningful learning of facts and concepts, then reasoning and reasoning opportunities are paramount. There is an important role for guided instruction based on modeling the practices and scaffolding learning. However, deep reorganizations of knowledge for productive conceptual change needs (1) to be grounded in prolonged engagement with phenomena; (2) supported by dialogic exchanges that produce thoughtful representations of students' understandings; and (3) guided by mediation/feedback from teachers and peers. Thus, the recommendations from research to incorporate formative assessment practices and learning progressions in science education.

Reaction to Duschl and Duncan's reply: Klahr. *You state, "Conceptual change is not achieved by exposure to new knowledge. It requires understanding and integrating the information through scaffolded and guided instruction, not direct instruction of what's right and what's wrong." Does this assertion apply to all of the enumerated types of conceptual change? If so, then how could anyone learn anything from reading, or listening to a lecture, or running an experiment? How did conceptual change take place in the minds of the great scientists of the 18th and 19th century when they examined the outcomes of their experiments? And how will the readers of this book learn anything at all from just reading and thinking about what they read? I can only conclude that you don't expect such conceptual change to occur unless the readers are also engaged in an extended "scaffolded and guided" type of instruction. However, when Crick and Watson discovered the structure of DNA 55 years ago, most people who read their revolutionary paper ... and nothing else ... sure did experience profound conceptual change, from the simple "direct instruction" it provided.*

Response to Klahr: Duschl and Duncan. The sentence from Watson and Crick[1] is indeed a turning point in our understanding of biological systems. We are left wondering, though, how many individuals outside the then small community of molecular thinking biologists understood upon first reading the *Nature* article and the implications it would have for forging a new discipline of molecular biology. Only with hindsight judgment can we claim a single sentence as revolutionary.

There are two important distinctions to be made regarding conceptual change. One is the difference in growth of knowledge processes between the K-12 classroom learners and the various communities of scientists. The other is the current understanding that conceptual change involves both shifts and restructuring in knowledge systems as well as in the methodological practices that establish scientific evidence. Concepts and the evidentiary bases for conceptual systems matter in science learning.

Question: Kirschner. *How can support and guidance be given if it "depends upon teachers having adequate knowledge of science ... [and] sustained science-specific professional development in preparation and while in service" (NRC, 2007, Chapter 10, p. 1) if teachers do not possess this knowledge or do not have sufficient opportunities for this development? Evidence for the lack of knowledge can be seen in the* statement by Patricia O'Connell Ross, Team Leader for the Mathematics and Science Partnership Program, US Department of Education:

> *While primary education in math and sciences is highly variable, depending on each teacher's comfort zone, by middle school it gets worse, with less than 50% of math and science teachers holding a major or minor degree in those subject areas. In some districts, up to 25% of high school math and science teachers do not have major or minor degrees in these subjects; however, this varies widely.*

The preceding suggests that guidance and support is vital in the preparation of science teachers. This is not only the case in the US. In senior secondary schools in Australia, more than one-quarter of chemistry teachers, 43% of physics teachers, and well over half of geology teachers had not studied the subject beyond second year at university (Harris, Jensz, & Baldwin, 2005).

Reply: Duschl and Duncan. The problem of teacher knowledge is fully noted, particularly at the elementary level where teachers have a very limited exposure to science courses and science-methods courses. Thus, we have the current agenda to emphasize in-service teacher education along with research showing that it takes approximately 100 hours of professional development over 2 to 3 years to get elementary teachers competent and comfortable in the delivery of inquiry-based science education. Competence involves knowledge of the science in the lessons and use of effective formative assessment strategies to monitor student learning. Practice coupled with coaching makes the difference.

For example, the new "immersion unit" approach to science education, 4–6-week-long units of instruction on a limited set of science concepts and practices, is having a positive effect on teachers' science knowledge. Teaching the units and discussing experiences with colleagues about the teaching and learning proves to be a very powerful professional-development strategy. After several implementations of the units, the teachers' knowledge of the science and understanding of how students learn the science improves. In contrast to the short, lesson-driven sequences that stress teachers teaching definitions and facts, the longer immersion units that emphasize using knowledge stress knowledge integration and meaningful learning.

The research recommendations for practice are to focus on the most important concepts, to achieve rigorous understandings and, importantly, to build coherence into the curriculum sequence in order to facilitate the deepening and broadening of understanding for both students and teachers. Educative curriculum materials, professional learning communities, and in-service education that focuses on teachers' specific classroom needs and includes coaching are some of the strategies that make a difference. In the end we must ask, do we fit the research on learning into the instructional culture of schools or do we change the culture of schools to accommodate the learning research? There are significant policy and practice issues that come to the table. Investing in ongoing teacher professional development that helps change the culture of schools is a policy issue.

Reaction to Duschl and Duncan's reply: Kirschner. *Though it is nice that "highly successful teacher professional development programs in science shows that it takes approximately 100 hours of professional development over 2 to 3 years to get elementary teachers competent and comfortable in the delivery of inquiry-based science education," this is not an answer to my question. I referred specifically to teachers' lack of domain-based knowledge. Good pedagogy without knowledge of the area will not lead to any learning, regardless of the pedagogy. And that the "new 'immersion unit' approach to science education, 4–6-week-long units of instruction on a limited set of science concepts and practices, is having a positive effect on teachers science knowledge, as well" means that teachers knowing very little now know something. This is a far cry from "teachers having adequate knowledge of science ... [and] sustained science-specific professional development in preparation and while in service."*

Question: Kirschner. *To paraphrase Leibniz, in this "best of all possible worlds" how, if constructivism is such a good pedagogy and if unbridled inquiry and discovery can lead to such impressive results for learners and society, do we account for the rampant scientific illiteracy and poor results? For example, one-half of the American public does not know the Earth goes around the Sun once a year and believes that the earliest humans lived at the same time as the dinosaurs. Finally, the 2006 Program for Student Assessment conducted by the Organization of Economic Cooperation and Development (OECD) results show the average combined science literacy-scale score for US students to be lower than the average. US students scored lower on science literacy than their peers in 16 of the other 29 countries. US students also had lower scores than the average score for two of the three content area subscales (explaining phenomena scientifically and using scientific evidence).*

Reply to Kirschner: Duschl and Duncan. Perhaps, just perhaps, scientific literacy is defined and taught in schools as knowing facts and concepts. If so, then why are we surprised that literacy rates are low and attitudes among students in OECD countries for learning science are lower than in developing countries as indicated in the results of the ROSE studies—an international survey of students' attitudes about the Relevance of Science Education (Jenkins & Pell, 2006). The unacceptable state of affairs regarding the attraction and retention of students and qualified teachers into STEM disciplines in the USA and UK are quite similar, as evidenced, respectively, by the NRC (2006) report *Rising above the Gathering Storm* (RAGS) and by the Robert's Report (2002). Three of the recommendations from the Osborne and Dillon (2007) report point the finger at the curriculum and the school experiences of the students, noting the following needed changes:

- The primary goal of science education across the EU should be to educate students both about the major explanations of the material world that science offers and about the way science works. Science courses whose basic aim is to provide a foundational education for future scientists and engineers should be optional.
- More attempts at innovative curricula and ways of organizing the teaching of science that address the issue of low student motivation are required.

These innovations need to be evaluated. In particular, a physical science curriculum that specifically focuses on developing an understanding of science
in contexts that are known to interest girls should be developed and trialed
within the EU.

•   EU countries need to invest in improving the human and physical resources
available to schools for informing students, both about careers in science—
where the emphasis should be on why working in science is an important
cultural and humanitarian activity—and careers from science—where the
emphasis should be on the extensive range of potential careers that the study
of science affords.

The evidence is quite strong that science taught to obtain facts and
concept-learning outcomes for purposes of turning out the next generation of
scientists just doesn't appeal to the majority of students. Context matters.

Reaction to Duschl and Duncan's reply: Kirschner. *Though the answer given
begs the question I will first deal with motivation. I am willing to wager that changing the curriculum will not cause landslide changes in learners' love of STEM nor
cause massive numbers of students to enter the field as scientists or as teachers. PSSC,
BSCS, Chem Study and other such curriculum changes have left us in the situation
we are today, namely too few well-educated citizens in the fields of STEM. Getting
back to learning, if the "primary goal of science education across the EU should be to
educate students both about the major explanations of the material world that
science offers and about the way science works," then I think knowing that the earth
is round belongs in this category.*

Note

1 It is humbling to consider what may be the most understated sentence ever written in a
scientific paper: "It has not escaped our notice that the specific pairing we have postu-
lated immediately suggests a possible copying mechanism for the genetic material."
Crick & Watson, *Nature,* April 25, 1953.

References

Adey, P., Shayer, M., & Yates, C. (2001). *Thinking science: The curriculum materials of the
CASE project* (3rd ed.). London: Routledge.
American Association for the Advancement of Science. (1993). *Benchmarks for science lit-
eracy.* New York: Oxford University Press.
Baillargeon, R. (2004). Infants' physical world. *Current Directions in Psychological Science,
13*(3), 89–94.
Bruner, J. (1961). The act of discovery. *Harvard Educational Review, 31,* 21–32.
Bruner, J. (1977). *The process of education.* Cambridge, MA: Harvard University Press.
Carey, S. (1985). *Conceptual change in childhood.* Cambridge, MA: MIT Press.
Carey, S. (1988). Conceptual differences between children and adults. *Mind and Language,
3,* 167–181.
Chase, W. G., & Simon, H. A. (1973). Perceptions in chess. *Cognitive Psychology, 4,* 55–81.
Chi, M. T. H. (1978). Knowledge structures and memory development. In R. Siegler (Ed.),

Children's thinking: What develops? (pp. 73–96). Hillsdale, NJ: Erlbaum. [Reprinted in: Wozniak, R. H. (1993). *Worlds of childhood* (pp. 232–240). New York: HarperCollins College Publishers.]

Chi, M. T. H. (1988). Children's lack of access and knowledge reorganization: An example from the concept of animism. In F. Weinert & M. Perlmutter (Eds.), *Memory development: Universal changes and individual differences* (pp. 169–194). Hillsdale, NJ: Erlbaum.

Chi, M. T. H. (1992). Conceptual change within and across ontological categories: Examples from learning and discovery in science. In R. Giere (Ed.), *Cognitive models of science: Minnesota Studies in the Philosophy of Science* (pp. 129–186). Minneapolis, MN: University of Minnesota Press.

Chi, M. T. H. (2005). Commonsense conceptions of emergent processes. Why some misconceptions are robust. *The Journal of the Learning Sciences, 14,* 161–199.

Chi, M. T. H. (2008). Three types of conceptual change: Belief revision, mental model transformation, and categorical shift. In S. Vosniadou (Ed.), *Handbook of research on conceptual change* (pp. 61–82). Hillsdale, NJ: Erlbaum.

Chi, M. T. H., Feltovich, P., & Glaser, R. (1981). Categorization and representation of physics problems by experts and novices. *Cognitive Science, 5,* 121–152.

Chi, M. T. H., & Koeske, R. (1983). Network representation of a child's dinosaur knowledge. *Developmental Psychology, 19,* 29–39.

Clements, J. (1998). Expert novice similarities and instruction using analogies. *International Journal of Science Education, 20*(10), 1271–1286.

Cole, M. (1996). *Cultural psychology: A once and future discipline.* Cambridge, MA: Belknap Press.

Collins, A., Brown, J. S., & Newman, S. E. (1989). Cognitive apprenticeship: Teaching the crafts of reading, writing and mathematics. In L. B. Resnick (Ed.), *Knowing, learning and instruction: Essays in honor of Robert Glaser* (pp. 453–494). Hillsdale, NJ: Erlbaum.

de Groot, A. D. (1965). *Thought and choice in chess.* The Hague: Mouton.

Duschl, R. A. (1990). *Restructuring science education. The importance of theories and their development.* New York: Teachers' College Press.

Duschl, R., & Grandy, R. (Eds.). (2008). *Teaching scientific inquiry: Recommendations for research and implementation.* Rotterdam, Netherlands: Sense Publishers.

Ford, D. (2005). The challenges of observing geologically: Third grades descriptions of rock and mineral properties. *Science Education, 89,* 276–295.

Ford, M. J. (2008). Disciplinary authority and accountability in scientific practice and learning. *Science Education, 92*(3), 404–423.

Ford, M. J., & Forman, E. A. (2006). Redefining disciplinary learning in classroom contexts. *Review of Research in Education, 30,* 1–32.

Gelman, R., & Brenneman, K. (2004). Science pathways for young children. *Early Childhood Research Quarterly, 19*(1), 150–158.

Giere, R. (1988). *Explaining science: A cognitive approach.* Chicago, IL: University of Chicago Press.

Glaser, R. (1983). *Education and thinking: The role of knowledge* (technical report), Learning Research and Development Center, University of Pittsburgh, Pittsburgh, PA.

Glaser, R. (1992). Expert knowledge and processes of thinking. In D. F. Halpern (Ed.), *Enhancing thinking skills in the sciences and mathematics.* Hillsdale, NJ: Lawrence Erlbaum Associates.

Godfrey-Smith, P. (2003). *Theory and reality.* Chicago, IL: University of Chicago Press.

Gopnik, A. (1996). The scientist as child. *Philosophy of Science, 63,* 485–514.

Gopnik, A., & Sobel, D. M. (2000). Detecting blickets: How young children use information about causal properties in categorization and induction. *Child Development, 71,* 1205–1222.

Gopnik, A., Sobel, D. M., Schulz, L., & Glymour, C. (2001). Causal learning mechanisms in very young children: Two, three, and four-year-olds infer causal relations from patterns of variation and co-variation. *Developmental Psychology, 37,* 620–629.

Hapgood, S., Magnusson, S. J., & Palincsar, A. S. (2004). Teacher, text, and experience: A case of young children's scientific inquiry. *Journal of the Learning Sciences, 13,* 455–505.

Harris, K.-L., Jensz, F., & Baldwin, G. (2005). *Who's teaching science? Meeting the demand for qualified science teachers in Australian secondary schools.* Report prepared for the Australian Council of Deans of Science, Australian Council of Deans of Science. Centre for the Study of Higher Education, University of Melbourne, Australia.

Harvard-Smithsonian Center for Astrophysics. (1987). A Private Universe. Annenberg Media Learner. Retrieved from www.learner.org/resources/series28.html.

Herrenkohl, L., & Guerra, M. (1998). Participant structures, scientific discourse, and student engagement in fourth grade. *Cognition and Instruction, 16*(4), 431–473.

Jenkins, E. W., & Pell, R. G. (2006). *The Relevance of Science Education project (ROSE) in England: A summary of findings.* Leeds, UK: Centre for Studies in Science and Mathematics Education.

Kesidou, S., & Roseman, J. (2002). How well do middle school science programs measure up? Findings from Project 2061's curriculum review. *Journal of Research in Science Teaching, 39*(6), 522–549.

Kirschner, P. (1992). Epistemology, practical work and academic skills in science education. *Science & Education, 1*(3), 273–299.

Kirschner, P., Sweller, J., & Clark, R. E. (2006). Why minimal guidance during instruction does not work: An analysis of the failure of constructivist, discovery, problem-based, experiential and inquiry-based teaching. *Educational Psychologist, 41,* 75–86.

Knorr-Cetina, K. (1999). *Epistemic cultures: How science makes knowledge.* Cambridge, MA: Harvard University Press.

Kuhn, T. (1962/1996). *The structure of scientific revolutions* (4th ed.). Chicago, IL: University of Chicago Press.

Larkin, J. H. (1979). Processing information for effective problems solving. *Engineering Education, 70*(3), 285–288.

Laudan, L. (1981). A confutation of convergent realism. *Philosophy of Science, 48,* 19–49.

Lave, J., & Wenger, E. (1991). *Situated learning: Legitimate peripheral participation.* Cambridge: Cambridge University Press.

Lehrer, R., Jaslow, L., & Curtis, C. (2003). Developing understanding of measurement in the elementary grades. In D. H. Clements & G. Bright (Eds.), *Learning and teaching measurement. 2003 Yearbook* (pp. 100–121). Reston, VA: National Council of Teachers of Mathematics.

Lehrer, R., & Schauble, L. (2000). Inventing data structures for representational purposes: Elementary grade students' classification models. *Mathematical Thinking and Learning, 2,* 49–72.

Lehrer, R., & Schauble, L. (Eds.). (2002). *Investigating real data in the classroom: Expanding children's understanding of math and science.* New York: Teachers College Press.

Lehrer, R., & Schauble, L. (2004). Modeling natural variation through distribution. *American Educational Research Journal, 41*(3), 635–679.

Lehrer, R., & Schauble, L. (2006). Cultivating model-based reasoning in science education. In K. Sawyer (Ed.), *The Cambridge handbook of the learning sciences* (pp. 371–388). New York: Cambridge University Press.

Limón, M., & Mason, L. (Eds.). (2002). *Reconsidering conceptual change: Issues in theory and practice.* Dordrecht, Netherlands: Kluwer.

Longino, H. (1990). *Science as social knowledge.* Princeton, NJ: Princeton University Press.

Longino, H. (2002). *The fate of knowledge.* Princeton, NJ: Princeton University Press.

Metz, K. (1995). Reassessment of developmental constraints on children's science instruction. *Review of Educational Research, 65,* 93–127.

Metz, K. (2004). Children's understanding of scientific inquiry: Their conceptualization of uncertainty in investigations of their own design. *Cognition and Instruction, 22,* 219–290.

Millar, R., & Osborne, J. (Eds.). (1998). *Beyond 2000: Science education for the future.* London: King's College, London.

National Research Council. (1996). *National science education standards.* Washington, DC: National Academy Press.

National Research Council. (1999). *How people learn.* J. Bransford, A. Brown &. R. Cocking (Eds.). Center for Education, Division of Behavioral and Social Sciences. Washington, DC: The National Academy Press.

National Research Council. (2001). *Knowing what students know: The science and design of educational assessment.* J. Pellegrino, N. Chudowsky, & R. Glaser (Eds.). Center for Education, Division of Behavioral and Social Sciences. Washington, DC: The National Academy Press.

National Research Council. (2007). *Taking science to school: Learning and teaching science kindergarten to eight grade.* R. A. Duschl, H. A. Schweingruber, & A. W. Shouse (Eds.). Center for Education, Division of Behavioral and Social Sciences. Washington, DC: The National Academy Press.

National Research Council. (2008). *Ready, set, science!: Putting research to work in K-8 science classrooms.* S. Michaels, A. W. Shouse, & H. A. Schweingruber (Eds.). Center for Education, Division of Behavioral and Social Sciences. Washington, DC: The National Academy Press.

Nersessian, N. (2008). Model-based reasoning in scientific practice. In R. Duschl & R. Grandy (Eds.), *Teaching scientific inquiry: Recommendations for research and implementation* (pp. 57–79). Rotterdam, Netherlands: Sense Publishers.

Niaz, M., Aguilera, D., Maza, A., & Liendo, G. (2002). Arguments, contradictions, resistances, and conceptual change in students' understanding of atomic structure. *Science Education, 86,* 505–525.

Osborne, J. F., & Dillon, J. (2008). *Science education in Europe: Report to the Nuffield Foundation.* London: King's College London.

Osborne, R., & Freyberg, P. (1985). *Learning in science: The implications of children's science.* Auckland, NZ: Heinemann.

Perner, J., Leekam, S. R., & Wimmer, H. (1987). Three-year-olds' difficulty with false belief: The case for a conceptual deficit. *British Journal of Developmental Psychology, 5,* 125–137.

Posner, G. J., Strike, K. A., Hewson, P. W., & Gertzog, W. A. (1982). Accommodation of a scientific conception: Towards a theory of conceptual change. *Science Education, 66*(2), 211–227.

Reif, F., & Larkin, J. H. (1991). Cognition in scientific and everyday domains: Comparison and learning implications. *Journal of Research in Science Teaching, 28*(9), 733–760.

Roberts, G. (2002). *SET for Success: The supply of people with science, technology, engineering and mathematic skills.* www.hm-treasury.gov.uk/roberts.

Rogoff, B. (1990). *Apprenticeship in thinking: Cognitive development in a social context.* New York: Oxford University Press.

Sawyer, R. K. (Ed.). (2006). *The Cambridge handbook of the learning sciences*. New York: Cambridge University Press.

Schauble, L., Glaser, R., Duschl, R., Schulze, S., & John, J. (1995). Students' understanding of the objectives and procedures of experimentation in the science classroom. *The Journal of the Learning Sciences, 4*(2) 131–166.

Schmidt, W. H., McKnight, C. C., & Raizen, S. A. (1997). *A splintered vision: An investigation of US science and mathematics education*. Boston, MA: Kluwer Academic Publishers.

Schwab, J. (1962). The teaching of science as inquiry. In J. Schwab & P. Brandwein (Eds.), *The teaching of science* (pp. 1–104). Cambridge, MA: Harvard University Press.

Schwartz, D., & Bransford, J. (1998). A time for telling. *Cognition and Instruction, 16*, 475–522.

Smith, C., Maclin, D., Grosslight, L., & Davis, H. (1997). Teaching for understanding: A comparison of two approaches to teaching students about matter and density. *Cognition and Instruction, 15*(3), 317–393.

Spelke, E. S., & Kinzler, K. D. (2007). Core knowledge. *Developmental Science, 10*, 89–96.

Sweller, J., Kirschner, P., & Clark, R. (2007). Why minimally guided teaching techniques do not work: A reply to commentaries. *Educational Psychologist, 42*(2), 115–121.

Thagard, P. (2007). Coherence, truth, and the development of scientific knowledge. *Philosophy of Science, 74*(1), 28–47.

Wellman, H. (1990). *The child's theory of mind*. Cambridge, MA: MIT Press.

White, B., & Frederiksen, J. (2000). Metacognitive facilitation: An approach to making scientific inquiry accessible to all. In J. Minstrell & E. van Zee (Eds.), *Inquiring into inquiry learning and teaching in science* (pp. 331–370). Washington, DC: American Association for the Advancement of Science.

White, R., & Gunstone, R. (1989). *Probing understanding*. London: Falmer Press.

Wimmer, H., & Perner, J. (1983). Beliefs about beliefs: Representation and constraining function of wrong beliefs in young children's understanding of deception. *Cognition, 13*, 41–68.

Wineburg, S. S. (1991). Historical problem solving: A study of cognitive processes used in the evaluation of documentary and pictorial evidence. *Journal of Educational Psychology, 83*, 73–87.

Woolnough, B. E., & Allsop, T. (1985). *Practical work in science*. Cambridge: Cambridge University Press.

Part V

Summing Up

17 An Eclectic Appraisal of the Success or Failure of Constructivist Instruction

Sigmund Tobias Institute for Urban and Minority Education,
Teachers College, Columbia University

This volume was started to discuss the present status of constructivism, one of the prominent contemporary approaches to instruction. Controversy about the value of the constructivist paradigm has existed for some time, and the most recent developments were summarized both in the introductory chapter of this volume and in Klahr's chapter. Of course, such controversies are common in active fields of research and hopefully lead to a better understanding of the phenomena being studied. The purpose of this chapter is to comment on some of the themes sounded in the volume from an eclectic perspective, that is, rather than being either a critic or a supporter of constructivist approaches, I want to endorse, whenever possible, practices supported by research results. As suggested while commenting on a similar controversy between constructivists and advocates of instructional systems design (Tobias, 1992), it is important that controversies generate research so that data, rather than stirring rhetoric, may be brought to bear to clarify issues that are in dispute. A further purpose of this chapter was to evaluate the different positions from the perspective of a number of issues of importance to the controversy. Finally, specific suggestions for further research are made throughout the chapter.

Our hope in developing this volume was to identify some of the cognitive processes engaged by different types of instruction. Some authors suggest that different approaches lead to varying instructional outcomes, presumably engaging different cognitive processes; however, few authors specify which cognitive processes are engaged by their recommended approach. That issue will be discussed further below. It was also expected that some narrowing of differences might be perceived beneath the spirited debates between supporters and critics of constructivist instruction. Some common ground did emerge in the chapters, for example constructivists and critics of that position agree that some form of guidance is needed for effective instruction, although—as expected—they disagree on the types of guidance. Finally, it was hoped that this volume would identify areas needing research. To some extent that did occur, and this chapter attempts to expand on these to suggest specific researchable questions that could clarify some issues between constructivists and their critics.

Researchers, both in this volume and in the field generally, refer to non-constructivist approaches by a variety of names such as *direct instruction, instructionism, and cognitive instruction,* among others. These labels seem to share a preference for *explicit instruction*, rather than encouraging students to fend for themselves, and that term will be used to describe these approaches in this chapter.

Paradigms and Paradigm Shifts

All areas of research experience changes in the paradigms stimulating their work (Kuhn, 1970), and human learning from instruction is no exception. When a new paradigm becomes prominent it captures most of the attention, though some supporters continue to endorse the prior view and conduct research and development activities on the prior paradigm. An associationist orientation was the predominant paradigm in psychology from the 1950s through the early 1960s and sought to reduce even complex learning to its simplest components: stimulus and response connections. Even though this set of theories is often referred to as *behavioral*, it is more accurate to call it *associationist* because it sought not only to identify the relationships between external stimuli and students' responses, but also to propose constructs accounting for their connections. Associationists like Thorndike (1932) and Hull (1951), whose theories were largely devoted to understanding the reasons for stimulus–response connections, can certainly not be called behaviorists. The behaviorist label is probably a reaction to Skinner (1953), one of the few associationists who was actually a behaviorist. Skinner sought to apply the principles of operant conditioning—where learning was assumed to occur only as a result of reinforcement—to instruction and was the prime advocate for the use of teaching machines (Skinner, 1954) and behavior modification in education.

The associationist paradigm waned in the 1960s and early 1970s and a cognitive orientation became prominent, stimulated by such scholars as Bruner (1960), Ausubel (1963, 1968) and Neisser (1967), among others. In contrast to the associationists, the cognitive paradigm emphasized the internal representation of external events and their organization. Of course, another paradigm, constructivism, influenced by the work of Vygotsky (1962, 1978), then came into prominence. Interestingly, Vygotsky's work was published in the Soviet Union during the 1930s, actually preceding much of the associationist orientation, but it did not influence Western thinking until the 1960s when his work was translated into English. As noted in Chapter 1 and many others, constructivists argue that all learning is constructed by the person, rather than merely being a simple reflection of external events. It should be noted, as Kintsch, Mayer, Jonassen, and Fletcher (this volume), among others, point out, that this assumption is widely shared even by those not advocating constructivist instruction, and by all the authors represented in this book.

An overview of the constructivist paradigm and its situative extension is provided in other chapters (Tobias & Duffy, Gresalfi & Lester, and Duschl & Duncan, this volume). Fletcher (this volume) adds an interesting note by indicating that simulations, whose development was motivated by practical training concerns that were entirely independent of the situativity movement, are excellent implementations of situated cognition.

Many of the instructional arrangements favored by situativity theorists were actually not new to either the education or training communities. In education, many of the activities recommended by constructivists are quite similar to those advocated by Dewey (1938). In a handbook devoted to training (Tobias & Fletcher, 2000) apprenticeships were discussed in several chapters (Shute, Lajoie, & Gluck, 2000; Semb, Ellis, Fitch, & Kuti, 2000; Allen, Otto, & Hoffman, 2000). Interestingly, constructivists' insistence that learning should be structured to solve real, or *authentic*, problems was also recommended in many of the chapters of that training handbook, and Fletcher (this volume) notes that simulations, also widely used in training (Andrews & Bell, 2000), are a popular implementation of that idea. Even though widely adopted, the social-constructivist paradigm stimulated quite a bit of controversy (Klahr, this volume; Duffy & Jonassen, 1992; Anderson, Reder, & Simon, 1996, 1998) even before the current challenge by advocates of explicit instruction.

The soundness of a paradigm can rarely be established, since scientific research is not well-suited to answering questions about the validity of an entire theory (see Duschl & Duncan, this volume). For example, Hilgard (1964) saw signs of the demise of Gestalt psychology (Bower & Hilgard, 1981), a precursor of cognitive psychology, even though he acknowledged that *none* of its basic hypotheses had been refuted. Hilgard (1964) claimed that the "decline and fall" of Gestalt psychology was attributable to its having stimulated very little research during the 1950s and early 1960s compared to the vast number of studies stimulated by the associationist paradigm then in vogue. Thus, it appears that paradigms tend to fade away when they fail to stimulate research and generate new knowledge, a concern I will return to later.

In retrospect it is amusing to note that Hilgard's (1964) claim of Gestalt psychology's demise was perhaps too general, since the Gestalt theorists were important precursors and sources of stimulation to major cognitive theorists (Ausubel, 1963, 1968; Bruner, 1960; Neisser, 1967). Hilgard's assumption of Gestalt psychology's decline was published in 1964, but it was probably written a year or two earlier, at about the time the paradigm shift from an associationist to a cognitive orientation was beginning. Clearly, it is always dangerous to predict the demise of a paradigm, for just as it seems to be passing into obscurity it may stimulate the birth or rebirth of a closely related orientation.

Perhaps the only development that can be predicted with certainty is that paradigms will shift (Tobias, 1988). Whatever the present paradigm may be, it too shall pass, perhaps to be reborn in a slightly different form. Ideally, of course, new paradigms should make it possible to deal more effectively with research and practical problems that were difficult to accommodate under the preceding paradigm.

Even though theories and research concerning human learning and instruction are presently dominated by the constructivist paradigm and instruction is heavily influenced by it, an interesting change in the overall goals of learning theory has occurred during the last 30 years. Previously, associationist theorists such as Thorndike (1932), Hull (1951), and Skinner (1953) and cognitive theorists such as those in the Gestalt school aimed to develop all-embracing theories that would describe all behavior, both human and animal. Anderson (1983) has proposed a fairly general theory dealing explicitly with human learning, but generally, contemporary research has concentrated less on testing all-embracing theories of learning and more on understanding major processes such as those underlying metacognition, the analysis of misconceptions, and expert–novice differences, to name only a few (Shuell, 1986, 1996). It remains to be seen whether concentrating on specific important processes rather than more general paradigms leads to greater clarification of the issues involved.

For the remainder of this chapter, major issues in the controversy about constructivist instruction will be discussed and research suggested that may help to clarify these issues.

Motivation

An assumption underlying the constructivist approaches is that such instruction will be more motivating to students than other approaches (Herman & Gomez, this volume). It seems reasonable to assume that learning to deal with problems that are important in daily life would be more motivating to students than more academic materials, or than the process–product teaching procedures described by Rosenshine (this volume). Therefore, as Herman and Gomez also noted, it was surprising to find little specific discussion of motivation other than in their chapter. Furthermore, it was also surprising that chapters, again excepting Herman and Gomez, on either side of the controversy do not cite a body of research on the motivational effects of their instructional approaches. These assumptions should be studied, especially since they are one of the key elements of constructivist instruction.

Similarly, those advocating the procedures described by Rosenshine (this volume) need to determine their effects on students' motivation. As Fletcher (this volume) noted, many of these procedures have been ridiculed as boring "drill and kill" exercises but, as he also suggested, evidence demonstrated that such drills worked well and were enjoyed by the students. Clearly then, research is needed comparing students' motivation while working on instructional materials prepared according to a constructivist or an explicit instructional orientation.

The motivational impact of any instruction can be studied by comparing students' attitudes to materials covering the same subject matter prepared according to the procedures of any instructional approach. Research on motivational issues is often conducted by administering self-report questionnaires assessing students' motivational goal orientation. There is reason to be cautious about the four-fold division of motivational goals into mastery and performance, each with an approach and avoidance valence (Pintrich, 2000). As suggested elsewhere (Tobias & Everson, in press), there is research suggesting that while the 2×2 conceptualization of motivational goals receives support from research using self-report inventories, little evidence for this conception appears when students talk freely about their motivation (Pressley, Van Etten, Yokoi, Freebern, & Van Meter, 1998; Light, 2001; Nathan, 2006).

It may be more fruitful to use different indices of motivation than the motivational goal orientation questionnaires. One such measure is persistence (Tobias & Everson, in press), that is observing how long students continue to work on a task or activity. Of course, the greater the persistence the higher motivation can be assumed to be. Since obtaining performance measures of persistence is time consuming, getting students to express a specific behavioral intention, such as asking them to select a specific task they wish to work on, is less difficult. One educational example of behavioral intentions was in a study of students' evaluations of instructors (Tobias & Hanlon, 1975). It was reasoned that a useful measure of students' feelings about an instructor was whether they intended to take another course in the same domain with that instructor. A spurious pre-registration procedure was implemented so that students could express their intention to register for the next course in the sequence with that instructor or any one of a number of others.

A meta-analysis of the behavioral-intention literature (Webb & Sheeran, 2006) showed that a medium-to-large change in intention leads to a small-to-medium change in behavior. Research on motivation for constructivist or explicit instruction could ask students to declare specific intentions, perhaps by choosing among alternative instructional materials, methods, or types of instruction covering the same subject matter. Half of the choices should be clearly identified as constructivist while the other half should be recognized as being explicit instruction.

Another suggestion is to use computer games to induce motivation during instruction. Games have usually been found to induce high motivation (Tobias & Fletcher, 2007, 2008) among participants. It should be possible to study learning from a game developed in either a constructivist or an explicit-instruction format, or to offer games as incentives either for completion of an instructional sequence or for attaining a specified criterion.

Cognitive Processing and Domain Structure

The question of whether constructivist or explicit instruction leads to improved student learning ultimately depends on whether either approach engages more effective, "deeper" cognitive processes, or more frequent processing. As suggested previously (Tobias, 1982), alternate instructional methods can lead to different outcomes only if they lead to more frequent processing, or by engaging different and presumably more effective cognitive strategies. Unfortunately, with some exceptions (Sweller, Schwartz et al., this volume), the controversy discussed in this book has not generated much research on that question. Therefore, studies identifying the cognitive processes invoked by either instructional approach or examining the frequency or intensity of processing are urgently needed. Such research can do more to clarify the differences between constructivist and explicit instruction than even the most persuasive rhetoric surrounding this issue.

Kirschner, Sweller, and Clark (2006) asserted that constructivist instruction imposes a greater load on working memory than explicit instruction. Constructivists in this volume or elsewhere apparently do not challenge that assumption.

Jonassen (this volume) specifically agreed with that assertion and no disagreement appears in any of the chapters by other constructivists, or in the literature in this area. Nevertheless, it is interesting to note that Kirschner et al.'s argument relies on research in related domains and has apparently not been tested directly by comparing instruction developed according to constructivist or explicit instructional recommendations. Hopefully this volume will stimulate scholars in both camps to investigate that problem. Such research will be a major contribution to clarifying the differences between the approaches.

Research on the cognitive load on working memory posed by different instructional approaches could use the self-report assessments described by Paas, Tuovinen, Tabbers, and Van Gerven (2003). Alternatively, Brünken, Plass, and Leutner (2003) suggest that reaction times to easy tasks could be used for such assessments. Finally, Kyllonen (1996) describes a comprehensive test battery to assess working memory.

Mayer's (this volume) distinction between behavioral and cognitive activity and processing of instruction is also useful for this discussion. He suggests that it is important to clarify the confusion between students' behavioral activity stimulated in some instruction, which does not necessarily lead to learning, and cognitive activity which does. Of course, Mayer's distinction presupposes that the cognitive processes engaged by different instructional approaches have been identified, further emphasizing the importance of conducting such research.

Schwartz et al., Grisalfi and Lester, Spiro and DeSchryver, and Fletcher (all in this volume), among others, suggest that constructivist and explicit approaches to instruction may be useful for different purposes. The intentions of instructors or developers are *not* the critical factor in determining which types of outcomes are most effectively attained, it is the cognitive processes engaged that determine outcomes. Therefore, the need to identify the processes engaged is emphasized yet again.

Gresalfi and Lester (this volume) discuss the importance of aligning classroom practice with instructional goals in the teaching of mathematics, and provide illustrations of constructivist and direct instructional classroom practices. While such alignments would be useful, identification of the cognitive processes engaged by the alignments is even more important. Observations of classrooms indicating that different instructional practices are used do not demonstrate that they engage different cognitive processes. If the processes engaged do not differ, neither will the outcomes.

Domain Structure

Constructivist authors, both in this volume and more generally (Kuhn, 2007), seem to agree that explicit instruction is appropriate for well-structured domains, like typing, for example (Savery & Duffy, 1996). Spiro, this volume, specifically indicates that constructivist instruction is ideal for ill-structured domains, but not for those that are well-structured. It would be useful to investigate this hypothesis experimentally by preparing materials in constructivist and explicit instructional formats using a well-structured domain, and then intentionally degrading the structure. This could be accomplished by eliminating some of the content, as done by McNamara, Kintsch, Songer, and Kintsch (1996; see also Kintsch, this volume), or by changing the sequence of the materials to one that is less logically organized, and perhaps even by including randomly organized instructional sequences (Tobias, 1973a).

It should be noted that Kyllonen (1996) reported such high correlations between measures of working memory and intelligence that he concluded that they might well be the same construct. If that conclusion is verified by succeeding research, an interesting hypothesis is suggested that constructivist instruction may be more effective for intellectually capable students, while explicit instruction may be more beneficial for their less able peers. As also noted by Clark (this volume), that hypothesis also emerged both from reviews of the literature on aptitude treatment interactions (ATIs) by Cronbach and Snow (1977) and by Gustaffson and Undheim (1996).

A similar hypothesis was stated in terms of students' prior domain knowledge and supported in a program of research (Tobias, 1973b, 1976, 1989) using programmed instructional materials to examine questions dealing with human learning and instruction, including ATIs. The hypothesis predicted that students with lower levels of prior domain knowledge profited from more carefully organized materials and more instructional support generally; such organization and support was expected to be less necessary for knowledgeable students. In one study (Tobias, 1973a), both familiar and novel content was sequenced either logically or randomly. As expected, there were no learning differences between the sequences on familiar content, but huge differences emerged (accounting for 31% of the post-test variance, and yielding a large effect of 1.25) on unfamiliar, technical materials, confirming that instructional support was needed on such content.

Measures of intelligence and achievement usually correlate between 0.40 and 0.70 (Deary, Strand, Smith, & Fernandes, 2007). Thus very little difference may be expected between the hypothesized superiority of constructivist materials for either more intellectually capable or more knowledgeable students. However, there are several advantages to formulating the interaction in terms of prior domain knowledge. First, prior knowledge can easily be varied experimentally, while intelligence cannot. Students can be randomly assigned to materials of varying familiarity, or some students could be pre-familiarized with the research materials. Second, when students' knowledge is assessed, the evaluation samples knowledge from the domain in which instruction is to occur. Therefore, the pretest is likely to engage some of the same cognitive processes important in studying that domain, somewhat reducing the problems of identifying these processes. Furthermore, as suggested previously (Tobias, 2003), assessments of prior knowledge can be obtained either in contexts similar to, or markedly different from, those in which the prior learning occurred, making it possible to examine constructivist claims of the importance attached to the situation. Finally, intriguing research questions about the effects of knowledge and interest can be investigated, such as whether interest can compensate for limited prior knowledge. Even though it has been estimated (Tobias, 1994) that interest and prior knowledge have a common variance of about 20%, that overlap should still make it possible to identify participants for research who are high on one of the variables and low on the other.

The sequence findings (Tobias, 1973a) were similar to those reported by McNamara et al. (1996; also see Kintsch's chapter, this volume), in a study comparing a coherent, well-written text and one deliberately made less coherent by eliminating some material. Students always learned more from the well-organized text when recall was required, but when deeper understanding was needed, those with high background knowledge performed better with the poorly prepared than with the well-written version. Apparently, in poorly prepared instructional materials students' prior knowledge is most important in determining what is learned.

Thus, converging evidence from different fields such as text processing, ATI research, work using programmed instructional materials, and cognitive-flexibility theory (Spiro, this volume) suggest a general hypothesis that constructivist materials may be differentially effective for knowledgeable students, whereas explicit instruction may be more beneficial for their less knowledgeable counterparts. That hypothesis is also supported by the unchallenged assumption that constructivist instruction requires more working memory from those with little domain knowledge than it does for more knowledgeable students.

Guidance, Instructional Support, and Prior Knowledge

There was general agreement in the chapters that some guidance is needed for learning to occur, though there is continuing disagreement about the types of guidance needed, and how much of it should be provided. Rosenshine (this volume) reviewed both correlational and experimental evidence in the process–product literature documenting the importance of guidance. Presumably, the emphasis on guidance springs from the contention by advocates of explicit instruction (see chapters by Sweller, Clark, and Kirschner, this volume), and confirmed by constructivists such as Swaak and de Jong (2001), that students tend to flounder when little guidance is offered in discovery learning, and in constructivist instruction more generally.

My preference (Tobias, 1982) has been to think more broadly than guidance and consider additional forms of *instructional support*, i.e., any types of assistance to help students learn. Clark (this volume) also refers to instructional support, though he also uses the term as a synonym for instructional method. Wise and O'Neill (this volume) indicate that the term guidance seems to include such forms of instructional support as explanations, feedback, help, modeling, scaffolding, procedural direction, and others. Clark (this volume) also indicates that the operational and lexical definitions of guidance vary widely. Herman and Gomez (this volume) also seem to be thinking in these terms. Therefore, rather than limiting the discussion to guidance, these additional forms of instructional support need to be discussed and investigated.

The questions raised in Wise and O'Neill's chapter about what constitutes more or less guidance emphasize the importance of developing a hierarchy of various forms of instructional support instantiated with specific examples. Clark (this volume) also agrees that such a hierarchy is essential and may do much to answer questions and clarify disagreements. Klahr (this volume) notes that comments on the research procedures in some of his studies described the same study as being constructivist and as an example of direct instruction. Obviously, if a hierarchy of the types of instructional support were available, such ambiguous interpretations of the same study would be reduced. Developing such a hierarchy would be an important theoretical and research contribution.

Offering help to students is a major concern in this volume, and in the discussion regarding the efficacy of constructivist instruction generally. Aleven, Stahl, Schworm, Fischer, and Wallace (2003) reviewed research dealing with interactive learning environments. That review suggested that "an increasing number of studies provide evidence that learners often do not use help functions very effectively or even ignore them totally" (p. 278). Similarly, in a review of the effectiveness of explanations, Wittwer and Renkl (2008) suggest that "the vast majority of empirical research has demonstrated that the provision of instructional explanations does not necessarily foster learning outcomes" (p. 52). On the other hand, results indicated that help was used extensively, 56% of the time, in metacognitive knowledge monitoring research (Tobias & Everson, in press). Of course, further research is needed to clarify the conditions in which assistance is used either extensively or rarely. If future research finds that help is used extensively only in rare situations, and the findings of both Wittwer and Renkl and Aleven et al. are upheld in most instructional contexts, there is little reason to have a major controversy over a feature that is barely used.

Student choice may be a confounding variable in the discussion of instructional support and other forms of assistance. Aleven et al. (2003) concluded that students "with low prior knowledge—those who need help the most—are least likely to use help appropriately when help is under student control" (p. 298). Clark (1982; Sugrue & Clark, 2000) has also shown that students select options in order to make things easier for themselves rather than because they are most beneficial, indicating that they are poor judges of when to select assistance. In addition, it has been shown (Tobias, 1989) that optional instructional support, such as making reviews of previously read material available, was beneficial for students with high prior domain knowledge whereas requiring review was beneficial for those with lower prior knowledge. Therefore, research needs to cross use of instructional support with student choice, i.e., have support available either as an option or require it depending on students' progress through the content. Such investigations may clarify whether students' selection of different forms of instructional support interact with prior domain knowledge so that knowledgeable students profit most from the option to select support whenever they wish, whereas mandating support may be more beneficial for less-knowledgeable students.

It may be somewhat difficult to conduct such research from a constructivist perspective, since constructivists usually recommend giving students free choice and generally avoid mandating what students need to do. Nonetheless, it ought to be possible to study this problem by developing constructivist instructional sequences that require use of options depending upon indications that students are lost in the instructional sequence. The chapters by Clark and Wise and O'Neill (this volume) describe different types of instructional support that could be used in such investigations.

All approaches to instruction will agree (see also Clark's chapter, this volume) that offering students support when it is *not* needed is at best a waste of time, and at worst leads to student boredom and ineffective learning. This idea is supported by research on the expert reversal effect reported by Kalyuga, Ayres, Chandler, and Sweller (2003), and also discussed in the chapters by Sweller, Mayer, and Fletcher (this volume). At present it is more of an art than it should be to offer only the support that students need to learn, and withdraw or withhold support when they can determine for themselves what they need in order to succeed. Of course, it is important to support this maxim by research so that the art of making such assignments becomes a research-based prescription.

Miscellaneous Issues in the Constructivist Instruction Controversy

Research on a number of variables such as time, teaching ability, and varying outcomes is needed to clarify issues dealing with instruction generally and the differences between constructivist and explicit instruction specifically. These will be discussed below.

Time

In his chapter, Klahr (this volume), after comparing his instructional conditions to those of a constructivist researcher, indicates that the latter took considerably more time and suggests that constructivist instruction is substantially more time consuming than explicit instruction. The examples in Schwartz et al.'s chapter (this volume) also suggest that such instruction is more time consuming for both students and researchers. It is important to attend to time needed to complete instruction in research comparisons between constructivist and explicit instruction, another aspect of the cost–benefit issue referred to in Fletcher's chapter (this volume).

Fisher and Berliner (1985) demonstrated that the amount of engaged time students spent on curricular materials was a major contributor to learning—a conclusion also reached by Suppes, Fletcher, and Zanotti (1975, 1976), and discussed in Fletcher's chapter (this volume). It is important to ascertain whether any benefits of different instructional approaches may in fact be attributable to the amount of time students spend on the task. Minimizing time to attain desired instructional outcomes is a major concern in the training community (Tobias & Fletcher, 2000) because trainees are usually paid during training. Educational researchers tend to be less concerned about the time students take to learn because it is usually free. On the other hand, students may get bored with instruction that is very time consuming, ultimately reducing learning. Therefore, it would be useful for educational researchers to attend to time issues, as their colleagues in the training community have, and on the effect of time spent on learning.

Furthermore, if markedly different amounts of time are needed by alternate instructional approaches, it underlines the importance of examining the cost–benefits issue (Fletcher, 1999; Fletcher & Chatelier, 2000), i.e., to evaluate whether any claimed benefits for one approach are worth the additional time required. Schwartz et al. (this volume) suggested that the greater amount of time needed for constructivist instruction is worth it because transfer was higher for students taught by constructivist procedures. Schwartz et al.'s findings, if replicated, suggest that instructional designers need to consider the importance of both immediate and longer-term outcomes in deciding on instructional approaches. Ultimately, decisions regarding choice of instructional method and student time are a values question that cannot be decided by research comparing different instructional methods, but such research can provide the data needed to reach a reasonable decision.

Teacher Ability

In his chapter, Klahr suggests that discovery approaches, for example, require a higher level of teacher knowledge and ability than is usually found in most classrooms, a view also endorsed by Kirschner (this volume). The issue of teacher knowledge and ability also deserves further research. If an instructional method requires unusually able and/or knowledgeable teachers, questions can be raised about how effective it may be in schools where most of the teachers are likely to cluster around the mean in terms of teaching ability, or knowledge of different content domains. Any instructional method requiring abilities that occur infrequently in the population is bound to be ineffective when applied generally in situations where individuals cannot be selected for that ability. Perhaps in response to these concerns, Herman and Gomez (this volume) indicate that teacher professional development was an essential component of their program, though it remains to be seen whether any such development activities succeed in turning the majority of individuals with average teaching abilities into superior teachers.

Outcomes

As indicated above, many of the chapters (see especially Schwartz et al., Spiro, and Fletcher, this volume), suggest that constructivist and explicit instruction may be useful for different purposes. That creates some difficulties in studying instructional outcomes, since different criteria of success have to be employed to examine the results of instruction. In general, constructivist researchers maintain that such instruction is ideal for more cognitively complex outcomes. For example, Schwartz et al. (this volume) suggest that constructivist instruction may be ideal for preparing people for future learning that becomes evident long after instruction has ended, whereas explicit instruction may be optimal for sequestered problem solving. Therefore, researchers should assess learning both shortly after the completion of instruction and also some time later. Research may also need to use a number of instructional samples of varying complexity to test hypotheses that alternative instructional approaches are optimal for content that differs in complexity. Finally, motivational and attitudinal outcomes should also be assessed in such studies because motivational differences may ultimately lead to different cognitive and behavioral outcomes.

Final Thoughts

When the AERA 2007 debate was organized, I described myself as an eclectic with respect to whether constructivist instruction was a success or failure, a position I also took in print earlier (Tobias, 1992). The constructivist approach of immersing students in real problems and having them figure out solutions was intuitively appealing. It seemed reasonable that students would feel more motivated to engage in such activities than in those occurring in traditional classrooms. It was, therefore, disappointing to find so little research documenting increased motivation for constructivist activities.

A personal note may be useful here. My Ph.D. was in clinical psychology at the time when projective diagnostic techniques in general, and the Rorschach in particular, were receiving a good deal of criticism. The logic for these techniques was compelling and it seemed reasonable that people's personality would have a major impact on their interpretation of ambiguous stimuli. Unfortunately, the empirical evidence in support of the validity of projective techniques was largely negative. They are now a minor element in the training of clinical psychologists, except for a few hamlets here or there that still specialize in teaching about projective techniques.

The example of projective techniques seems similar to the issues raised about constructivist instruction. A careful reading and re-reading of all the chapters in this book, and the related literature, has indicated to me that there is stimulating rhetoric for the constructivist position, but relatively little research supporting it. For example, it is encouraging to see that Schwartz et al. (this volume) are conducting research on their hypothesis that constructivist instruction is better for preparing individuals for future learning. Unfortunately, as they acknowledge, there is too little research documenting that hypothesis. As suggested above, such research requires more complex procedures and is more time consuming, for both the researcher and the participants, than procedures advocated by supporters of explicit instruction. However, without supporting research these remain merely a set of interesting hypotheses.

In comparison to constructivists, advocates for explicit instruction seem to justify their recommendations more by references to research than rhetoric. Constructivist approaches have been advocated vigorously for almost two decades now, and it is surprising to find how little research they have stimulated during that time. If constructivist instruction were evaluated by the same criterion that Hilgard (1964) applied to Gestalt psychology, the paucity of research stimulated by that paradigm should be a cause for concern for supporters of constructivist views.

Chall (2000) reviewed the literature comparing student-centered instruction, roughly similar to constructivist approaches, and teacher-centered instruction, generally comparable to explicit instruction. She found that teacher-centered approaches usually resulted in higher achievement, especially for children from lower socio-economic backgrounds, a finding similar to the hypothesized superiority of explicit instruction for such students suggested above. Chall was especially impressed by how frequently research findings were ignored by those advocating student-centered approaches. One purpose of this volume was to remind researchers and practitioners to carefully examine the research base for their positions. Chall's discussion, many of the chapters in this book and the ensuing dialog, and the slim research base supporting constructivist instruction underline the importance for advocates of that position to conduct research to support their positions or, if necessary, to modify them.

This chapter and the whole book have identified areas where research support is urgently needed. It is hoped that researchers of all persuasions will be stimulated to investigate these questions to support their assertions. Ultimately, the findings of such research, rather than the forcefulness of rhetoric, should determine the viability of both constructivist and explicit approaches to instruction. Our late colleague Dick Snow once described research on educational innovations as being little more than a random walk through the panacea garden. The research recommended here should help to provide a firm research foundation for instructional approaches, hopefully making it less likely that today's panacea becomes tomorrow's failure. Theoretical paradigms come and go, but the problems of providing effective instruction to learners in school and training contexts remain.

References

Aleven, V., Stahl, E., Schworm, S., Fischer, F., & Wallace, R. (2003). Help seeking and help design in interactive learning environments. *Review of Educational Research, 73*, 277–320.

Allen, B. J., Otto, R. G., & Hoffman, B. (2000). Case based learning: Context and communities of practice. In S. Tobias & J. D. Fletcher (Eds.), *Training and retraining: A handbook for business, industry, government, and the military* (pp. 443–471). New York: Macmillan Reference.

Anderson, J. R. (1983). *The architecture of cognition.* Cambridge, MA: Harvard University Press.

Anderson, J. R., Reder, L. M., & Simon, H. A. (1996). Situated learning and education. *Educational Researcher, 25*(4), 5–11.

Anderson, J. R., Reder, L. M., & Simon, H. A. (1998). Radical constructivism and cognitive psychology. In D. Ravitch (Ed.), *Brookings papers on education policy* (pp. 227–278). Washington, DC: Brookings Institution Press.

Andrews, D. H., & Bell, H. H. (2000). Simulation based training. In S. Tobias & J. D. Fletcher (Eds.), *Training and retraining: A handbook for business, industry, government, and the military* (pp. 357–384). New York: Macmillan Gale Group.

Ausubel, D. P. (1963). *The psychology of meaningful verbal learning.* New York: Grune & Stratton.

Ausubel, D. P. (1968). *Educational psychology: A cognitive view*. New York: Holt, Rinehardt, & Winston.

Bower, G. H., & Hilgard, E. R. (1981). *Theories of learning* (5th ed.). Englewood Cliffs, NJ: Prentice Hall.

Bruner, J. (1960). *The process of education*. Cambridge, MA: Harvard University Press.

Brünken, R., Plass, J. L., & Leutner, D. (2003). Direct measurement of cognitive load in multimedia learning. *Educational Psychologist, 38*, 53–61.

Chall, J. (2000). *The academic achievement challenge: What really works in the classroom*. New York: Guilford.

Clark, R. E. (1982). Antagonism between achievement and enjoyment in ATI studies. *Educational Psychologist, 17*, 92–101.

Cronbach, L. J., & Snow, R. E. (1977). *Aptitudes and instructional methods: A handbook for research on interactions*. New York: Irvington.

Deary, I. J., Strand, S., Smith, P., & Fernandes, C. (2007). Intelligence and educational achievement. *Intelligence, 35*, 13–21.

Dewey, J. (1938). *Experience and education*. New York: Macmillan.

Duffy, T. M., & Jonasssen, D. (1992). *Constructivism and the technology of instruction: A conversation*. Hillsdale, NJ: Erlbaum.

Fisher, C. W., & Berliner, D. C. (Eds.). (1985). *Perspectives on instructional time*. New York: Longman.

Fletcher, J. D. (1999). Using networked simulation to assess problem solving by tactical teams. *Computers in Human Behavior, 15*, 375–402.

Fletcher, J. D., & Chatelier, P. R. (2000). Military training. In S. Tobias and J. D. Fletcher (Eds.), *Training and retraining: A handbook for business, industry, government, and the military* (pp. 267–288). New York: Macmillan.

Gustaffson, J., & Undheim, J. O. (1996). Individual differences in cognitive functions. In D. C. Berliner & R. C. Calfee (Eds.), *Handbook of educational psychology* (pp. 186–242). New York: Macmillan Reference.

Hilgard, E. R. (1964). The place of Gestalt psychology and field theories in contemporary learning theory. In E. R. Hilgard (Ed.), *Theories of learning and instruction. 63rd Yearbook of the National Society for the Study of Education* (Part 1, pp. 54–77). Chicago, IL: University of Chicago Press.

Hull, C. L. (1951). *Essentials of behavior*. New Haven, CT: Yale University Press.

Kalyuga, S., Ayres, P., Chandler, P., & Sweller, J. (2003). The expertise reversal effect. *Educational Psychologist, 38*, 23–31.

Kirschner, P. A., Sweller, J., & Clark, R. (2006). Why minimal guidance during instruction does not work: An analysis of the failure of constructivist, discovery, problem-based, experiential and inquiry-based teaching. *Educational Psychologist, 41*, 75–86.

Kuhn, D. (2007). Is direct instruction the answer to the right question? *Educational Psychologist, 42*, 109–113.

Kuhn, T. S. (1970). *The structure of scientific revolutions* (2nd. ed.). Chicago, IL: University of Chicago Press.

Kyllonen, P. C. (1996). Is working-memory capacity Spearman's g? In I. Dennis & P. Tapsfield (Eds.), *Human abilities: Their nature and measurement* (pp. 49–76). Mahwah, NJ: Lawrence Erlbaum Associates.

Light, R. J. (2001). *Making the most of college: Students speak their minds*. Cambridge, MA: Harvard University Press.

McNamara, D. S., Kintsch, E., Songer, N., & Kintsch, W. (1996). Are good texts always better? Interactions of text coherence, background knowledge, and levels of understanding in learning from text. *Cognition and Instruction, 14*, 1–43.

Nathan, R. (2006). *My freshman year: What a professor learned by becoming a student.* London: Penguin Books.

Neisser, U. (1967). *Cognitive psychology.* New York: Appleton, Century, Crofts.

Paas, F., Tuovinen, J. E., Tabbers, H., & Van Gerven, P. W. M. (2003). Cognitive load measurement as a means to advance cognitive load theory. *Educational Psychologist, 38,* 63–71.

Pintrich, P. R. (2000). The role of goal orientation in self-regulated learning. In M. Boekarts, P. R. Pintrich, & M. Zeidner (Eds.), *Handbook of self-regulation* (pp. 451–502). San Diego, CA: Academic Press.

Pressley, M., Van Etten, S., Yokoi, L., Freebern, G., & Van Meter, P. (1998). The metacognition of college studentship: A grounded theory approach. In D. Hacker, J. Dunlosky, & A. G. Grasses (Eds.), *Metacognition in educational theory and practice* (pp. 347–366). Mahwah, NJ: Erlbaum.

Savery, J. R., & Duffy, T. M. (1996). Problem-based learning: An instructional model and its constructivist framework. In B. G. Wilson (Ed.), *Constructivist learning environments: Case studies in instructional design* (pp. 135–148). Englewood Cliffs, NJ: Educational Technology Publications.

Semb, G. H., Ellis, J. A. Fitch, M. A., & Kuti, M. B. (2000). On the job training (OJT): Theory, research, and practice. In S. Tobias & J. D. Fletcher (Eds.), *Training and retraining: A handbook for business, industry, government, and the military* (pp. 289–311). New York: Macmillan Reference.

Shuell, T. J. (1986). Cognitive conceptions of learning. *Review of Educational Research, 56,* 411–436.

Shuell, T. J. (1996). Teaching and learning in a classroom context. In D. C. Berliner & R. C. Calfee (Eds.), *Handbook of educational psychology* (pp. 726–764). New York: Macmillan Reference.

Shute, V. J., Lajoie, S. P., & Gluck, K. (2000). Individualized and group approaches to training. In S. Tobias & J. D. Fletcher (Eds.), *Training and retraining: A handbook for business, industry, government, and the military* (pp. 171–207). New York: Macmillan Reference.

Skinner, B. F. (1953). *Science and human behavior.* New York: Macmillan.

Skinner, B. F. (1954). The science of learning and the art of teaching. *Harvard Educational Review, 24,* 86–97.

Sugrue, B., & Clark, R. (2000). Media selection for training. In S. Tobias & J. D. Fletcher (Eds.), *Training and retraining: A handbook for business, industry, government, and the military* (pp. 208–234). New York: Macmillan Gale Group.

Suppes, P., Fletcher, J. D., & Zanotti, M. (1975). Performance models of American Indian students on computer-assisted instruction in elementary mathematics. *Instructional Science, 4,* 303–313.

Suppes, P., Fletcher, J. D., & Zanotti, M. (1976). Models of individual trajectories in computer-assisted instruction for deaf students. *Journal of Educational Psychology, 68,* 117–127.

Swaak, J., & de Jong, T. (2001). Discovery simulations and the assessment of intuitive knowledge. *Journal of Computer Assisted Learning, 17,* 284–294.

Thorndike, E. L. (1932). *The fundamentals of learning.* New York: Teachers College Press.

Tobias, S. (1973a). Sequence, familiarity, and attribute by treatment interactions in programmed instruction. *Journal of Educational Psychology, 64,* 133–141.

Tobias, S. (1973b). Review of the response mode issue. *Review of Educational Research, 43,* 193–204.

Tobias, S. (1976). Achievement treatment interactions. *Review of Educational Research, 46,* 61–74.

Tobias, S. (1982). When do instructional methods make a difference? *Educational Researcher, 11*(4), 4–9.

Tobias, S. (1988). Paradox in educational psychology. *Theoretical and Philosophical Psychology, 8,* 42–44.

Tobias, S. (1989). Another look at research on the adaptation of instruction to student characteristics. *Educational Psychologist, 24,* 213–227.

Tobias, S. (1992). An examination of some issues in the constructivist-ISD controversy from an eclectic perspective. In T. M. Duffy & D. H. Jonassen (Eds.), *Constructivism and the technology of instruction* (pp 205–209). Hillsdale, NJ: Lawrence Erlbaum.

Tobias, S. (1994). Interest, prior knowledge, and learning. *Review of Educational Research, 64,* 37–54.

Tobias, S. (2003). Extending Snow's conceptions of aptitudes. *Contemporary Psychology, 48,* 277–279.

Tobias, S., & Everson, H. T. (in press). The importance of knowing what you know: A knowledge monitoring framework for studying metacognition in education. In D. L. Hacker, J. Dunlosky, & A. Graesser (Eds.), *Handbook of metacognition in education.* New York: Routledge.

Tobias, S., & Fletcher, J. D. (2000). *Training and retraining: A handbook for business, industry, government, and the military.* New York: Macmillan Gale Group.

Tobias, S., & Fletcher, J. D. (2007). What research has to say about designing computer games for learning. *Educational Technology, 47*(5), 20–29.

Tobias, S., & Fletcher, J. D. (2008). *What do we know about the learning effectiveness of computer games?* Paper presented at the annual convention of the American Educational Research Association, New York, NY, March.

Tobias, S., & Hanlon, R. (1975). Attitudes towards instructors, social desirability and behavioral intentions. *Journal of Educational Psychology, 67,* 405–408.

Vygotsky, L. S. (1962). *Thought and language.* Cambridge, MA: MIT Press.

Vygotsky, L. S. (1978). *Mind in society.* Cambridge, MA: Harvard University Press.

Webb, T. L., & Sheeran, P. (2006). Does changing behavioral intentions engender behavior change? A meta-analysis of the experimental evidence. *Psychological Bulletin, 132,* 249–268.

Wittwer, J., & Renkl, A. (2008). Why instructional explanations often do not work: A framework for understanding the effectiveness of instructional explanations. *Educational Psychologist, 43,* 49–64.

18 Building Lines of Communication and a Research Agenda[*]

Thomas M. Duffy School of Education, Indiana University

"Constructivism and the Design of Instruction: Success or Failure?" That was the question underlying this volume. The not-so-surprising answer seems to be that success—or failure—is in the eye of the beholder. It has been valuable to see the various perspectives expressed in these chapters. I am particularly pleased with the efforts of Kintsch (this volume) and Fletcher (this volume) to find a middle ground, and of Clark (this volume) and Wise and O'Neill (this volume) for their call for a collaborative research agenda to understand the dimensions of guidance and the interaction with different contextual variables. I am also pleased with the quality of the discussion that arose from the chapters—it has helped to spotlight many of the issues and clarify the underlying rationale for the different perspectives. Indeed, several authors commented in conversation with me that after reading the other chapters they were more in agreement with authors of the alternative view than they had ever expected to be.

In this chapter I want to focus primarily on the very stark disagreements that were clear in the chapters and discuss the possible factors that underlie the failure to communicate that is reflected in those disagreements. I will then discuss guidance or scaffolding—a major focus in the chapters and generally considered a primary distinguishing variable between the two perspectives. I will argue that it does not distinguish between the views. Rather, the fundamental disagreement, and the factor that distinguishes the views seems to be the view of learner goals—the need for sense making—as the stimulus for learning. Other issues follow from that. Finally, I want to briefly address a question that has gone unanswered—the ability of teachers to adopt an inquiry curriculum.

A Failure to Communicate

Kirschner, Sweller, and Clark (2006), in their article preceding this volume, characterized instruction based on constructivist views as "minimally guided." That view persisted in this volume in the chapters by Sweller and Kirschner, the first two authors of that article, and is also reflected in the chapters by Klahr and Mayer. Indeed, Klahr describes his discovery-learning comparison condition as,

[*] The preparation of this chapter was supported in part by funding through an Inter Personnel Agreement with the US Army Research Institute – Fort Benning.

"Rather than being a parody of the lack of structure in discovery learning, our discovery condition actually included more scaffolding than discovery learning as typically practiced" (this volume, p. 297). And Mayer proposes to "view constructivism as a prescription for instruction in which learners must be behaviorally active during learning" (this volume, p. 184). He goes on to contrast constructivism with his perspective, a perspective that emphasizes cognitive rather than behavioral activity. Typically, these views persisted into the discussions—after these authors had read chapters by constructivists.

Yet, the constructivist authors have argued consistently that guidance is essential; that it is simply a matter of the context of the guidance. And in an examination of the research described in the chapters and in the key journals, e.g., *The Journal of the Learning Sciences*, we find numerous studies where there is considerable guidance, even direct instruction (Schwartz, Lindgren, & Lewis, this volume), and an emphasis on the need for a consistent structure (guidance) not only in the immediate instructional context but in the larger schooling context in which the instruction occurs (Herman & Gomez, this volume; Duschl & Duncan, this volume; Kolodner et al., 2003). Indeed, there are no studies described in this volume where guidance is absent.

The constructivists have their own myopic view, seemingly adverse to talking about mechanisms, in particular, information-processing mechanisms, that may underlie the effectiveness of guidance or scaffolding. As a consequence, the rationale for guidance and prescription for guidance remains ill-defined. Klahr (this volume), quite reasonably, calls for an operational definition of the various constructivist instructional models—definitions that would identify the key variables. I can understand the frustration of Klahr and the misinterpretations of Kirschner (this volume), Sweller (this volume), and Mayer (this volume) when the constructivist instructional approach is so ill-defined. Indeed, perhaps the constructivists should design a learning environment to support learning about the instructional implications of constructivism—certainly an ill-structured problem.

These differences make communication difficult at best. I will address three factors that I think underlie this disconnect between the two theoretical perspectives: a theoretical myopia, a focus on process vs. product, and the cognitive load faced by the researchers.

Theoretical Myopia

Much of the difficulty in this discussion arises from authors working from competing theories of how we come to know. The traditional model is the information-processing model based on a computing metaphor that sees learning as a process of acquisition. In this framework, the framework underlying the direct instruction discussed in this volume, knowledge is an object that is acquired and then applied. For example, the emphasis in the direct instruction chapters is on reducing cognitive load so that concepts and procedures can be acquired.

The constructivist view reflects a sociocultural perspective where the participation metaphor for learning dominates. The constructivist view emphasizes that learning is in the doing (Brown, Collins, & Duguid, 1989; Barab & Duffy, 2000). Thus, with the participation metaphor, learning is in the participation in the various aspects of society. One is always learning to be: learning to be a student; a mathematician; a football player; a parent; a member of the community. And as a person learns, she develops her sense of identity as a member of that group. Rather than concepts that are acquired and stored in the head, the constructivist view focuses on the concepts as part of the social practice, i.e., the participation.

These metaphors have been widely discussed over the last decade with continuing calls for an integration of the metaphors (Sfard, 1998; Cobb, 1994; Mason, 2007). At a fundamental level, this seems to be a difficult task. How can we view learning as the acquisition of concepts stored in the head and also as discourse practices where they are societally constructed and situated? However, if we start at a more practice-oriented approach and leave the epistemology for a moment, there would seem to be reasonable overlap. Certainly, the individual processes information—memory, attention, perception are important to determining what we learn. Similarly, learning is certainly in the doing and part of identity development. We judge our status as researchers, parents, and community members based on our ability to engage in discourse and activities—our ability to participate and act—in the particular community.

The consequence of the failure to seek an integration of the metaphors is reflected in the authors in this volume too often talking past each other in the design and interpretation of their research—and in what they consider to be evidence. Those critiquing the constructivists focus on narrowly conceived learning tasks and criteria for success, not considering the larger context of that understanding in schooling or membership in society. While learning may be efficient, it is certainly likely to result in inert knowledge (Whitehead, 1929), knowledge not used beyond the classroom. And this is not even taking into consideration the probable lack of success of integrating the instructional approach into classroom and schooling practices (see Herman & Gomez, this volume; and Fishman, Marx, Blumenfeld, Krajcik, & Soloway, 2004).

The constructivists similarly ignore the information processing of the learner, at least in terms of direct reference. Indeed, the constructivists seem to suffer from denial with regard to information processing. They talk about forming routines, noting that an instructional approach only works if it is embedded in the routines of the school. And they talk about a variety of tools to support learning, but these tools for the most part serve to reduce memory load, to direct attention, to aid visualization (perception), and to build linkages between concepts. All of these reflect supporting information processing, yet there is little if any reference to information-processing concepts.

It might be argued that a call for constructivists (socio-historical and situative perspectives) to include information processing is simply a call for reductionism. The constructivist approaches are focused on the dialogue and the social context. Indeed, there is an emphasis on distributed cognition (a concept that truly puzzles many of the uninitiated), not just cognition in the head. However, I would argue that it is not a reductionist perspective. Certainly the focus on scaffolding is a focus on managing information—and thus it is quite reasonable to consider that information-processing theory (including cognitive load) may have something to contribute to the understanding of scaffolding. Further, the constructivists have yet to develop any strong theoretical framing for discussing scaffolding (Pea, 2004).

In addition to the obvious (to me) place for information processing as a part of constructivist theory, there also should be some acknowledgement of how constructivism has grown from information-processing theory. We need to be looking at the evolution rather than the revolution. As Sinatra and Mason (2007) note, it is as if the constructivists are attempting to replace information processing rather than building on it. Indeed, consideration of information processing may help identify shortcomings of that model, as Jonassen (this volume) suggests, in the more complex and situated learning environments. It may also help to better understand what aspects of the learning environment and task really are part of the authentic context and which create extraneous cognitive load (Sweller, this volume).

Conflicting Research Methods

The direct-instruction researchers have focused on research in which variables are manipulated in tightly controlled experiments. The argument is that this approach is the only method that will permit us to draw casual inferences as to what works (Slavin, 2002). The result has been a focus on a clear set of variables that they believe are central to effective instruction. When we go to that literature we expect to find research on practice strategies, the use of examples, the use of media in presentation, etc. They ask for the same specificity from the constructivists: again, the appeal by Klahr for some specification as to how constructivist instruction differs from direct instruction.

The constructivists, in turn, argue that the experimental method is too limiting. There has been extensive discussion of the shortcomings of the experimental approach (cf. *Educational Researcher*, 2003 (1); *Journal of the Learning Sciences*, 2004 (1)) and I will not rehash them here. The basic argument, however, is that context matters in understanding the effects of variables. As Engle (2008, p. 2) notes, "it is not just the content of what students learn that matters for whether they are likely to transfer what they have learned, but also how the contexts in which students learn that content are defined interactionally." This situativity of learning is reflected throughout the present volume. Herman and Gomez discuss the importance of instructional regimes, arguing that the success of a particular instructional routine, e.g., teaching factoring, will depend on the larger instructional and social context of the school. Similarly, Duschl and Duncan (this volume) argue for the importance of learning progressions, integrating domain learning across years. Gresalfi and Lester (this volume, p. 268) present the broadest view of situativity, based on Lave and Wenger's (1990) work, stating that

> learning is achieved through changes in a *system* that includes elements such as people, social norms and expectations, resources such as books or calculators, history, institutional expectations, *and* individual cognitive architecture—all of which work together in ways that cannot be separated.

Thus, the constructivist approach is to study rich learning environments, examining the variables in the context of those environments. A design-based research (DBR) methodology is evolving to support drawing casual inferences from the mixed methods used in this situated or field-research approach. Basically the DBR approach focuses on developing a theory of practice, i.e., the (learning) practices of the individuals in that environment. The strategy is to use a sequence of design and redesign cycles increasingly refining our understanding of the key variables in the learning environment. Variables are manipulated and there are design contrasts in the context, but they typically reflect quasi-experimental designs at best. The DBR strategy is very much in keeping with a theoretical model-building strategy. Variables are identified and refined as we attempt to understand and eventually predict behavior in that situation. Experimental studies may be used to isolate variables, but the real tests are when the variables are integrated into the full model.

I strongly support the DBR approach as a strategy for overcoming the limitations of the experimental paradigm and meeting the needs of understanding learning as a participatory process. However, I feel an uneasiness in the status of the research underlying the approach. Truth be told, I have a very hard time understanding what the important variables are that span the various learning environments. I come back to Klahr's appeal for defining characteristics frequently because I have the same uneasiness about the lack of clarity. What are the parameters of a good problem? If a teacher is developing an instructional plan, what do we tell him about the type of inquiry to be promoted? Bereiter (2002) talks about this extensively and Engle (2008) has investigated it in her research but overall, research on this issue is scarce. Similarly, while scaffolding or guiding learning is critical, the recent set of papers on scaffolding (*Journal of the Learning Sciences*, 2004) shows little agreement as to what the key variables are or how to categorize them. Indeed, Pea (2004) notes that there was some failure to even distinguish between scaffolding, where the guidance is gradually removed, and performance support, where the guidance is a permanent aid to performance (e.g., a calculator). This is a far cry from the clear set of variables, limited though they might be, that we find in the chapters on direct instruction.

Perhaps it is the DBR research strategy in practice rather than in principle that results in this lack of specificity. For example, the practical factors in managing a field-research site are enormous and the practical issues in instruction blend with the theoretical variables. Indeed, the field sites are as committed to understanding the school culture, capabilities, and policy/management as well as the instructional variables in the success of the instructional effort (see, for example, Blumenfeld, Fishman, Krajcik, Marx, & Soloway, 2000). While our understanding of the interplay of theoretical and practical is incredibly important to understanding the learning processes, and it in fact clearly reflects the situative perspective of constructivists, there is also the potential for a lack of clarity of the theoretical variables, e.g., the parameters or dimensions of tutoring, reflection, etc. that may be relevant to other learning situations and should be tested more widely.

The second potential impact of DBR approach is a silo effect, with each research team focusing on their own field environment. There certainly are variables in common (Orrill, Hannafin, & Glazer, 2004; Kolodner et al., 2003) but that commonality tends to be at a very surface level. Seldom do we see collaboration across field sites attempting to be specific as to the parameters of an instructionally relevant variable and how it impacts learning/participation in those different environments.

Cognitive Overload

Finally, the failure to communicate between the two theoretical camps may be a function of cognitive overload. In the process of working with the authors, several (from both "camps") noted the difficulty of tracking the literature outside their particular perspective and hence confessed to some level of unfamiliarity with the other view. Of course, this is a problem most, if not all, of us have faced. The profitability of journals for publishers and the publish-or-perish requirements of academia have created such a volume of "peer-reviewed" research that it is certainly impossible for most of us to maintain currency in the variety of relevant domains of research—boundary crossing is difficult. However, we do know from research on communities of practice (e.g., Wellman, 1971) that real advances occur when we cross boundaries—when we get outside our niche and seriously engage with alternative perspectives. This includes not only competing perspectives, as in the current context, but perspectives that may take a whole different disciplinary approach to the problem or issue.

Overcoming the narrowness of contact is difficult and perhaps impossible to achieve under the publishing demands and opportunities. However, there are several possible strategies for addressing the issue. First, as Clark (this volume) and Wise and O'Neill (this volume) propose, we could establish collaborative research efforts. The collaboration would establish test beds for instruction, i.e., well-defined learning outcomes and demographic specification that the members of the collaboration would use to test, compare, and refine their instructional theories. Each theorist could then test his or her theory in a common context that permits comparison to findings from the alternative views as well as collaborative and progressive development of their own theory. Of course, the trick will be to gain agreement as to these common environments—in particular the learning outcomes we seek. However, the lack of any common reference points in the current discussion—and the willingness to create strawman (or ill-informed) control conditions—makes meaningful dialogue very difficult, if not impossible.

The publishing industry could also facilitate the process. More journals could adopt a discussion format for each article published; not an online discussion where anyone can participate, but a systematic attempt to engage the diversity of perspectives of leaders in the research field. We, of course, have excellent examples of this in *Behavioral and Brain Sciences* and *Cultural Studies in Science Education.*

Finally, the funding agencies may also facilitate the process, not just in funding collaborative efforts but also in building discourse across perspectives into the grant requirements (groans are heard). Indeed, the review panel in most

NSF efforts provides that diversity and it is not uncommon to invoke a groan from the proposers as they read comments that certainly reflect a lack of understanding of their work—at least as they read the review. But that is exactly the point. The only concern is that there is only feedback to the proposer rather than a dialogue that would promote deeper understanding on both sides.

Instructional Implications of the Metaphors

I want now to focus more directly on instructional issues that arise from the acquisition and participatory metaphors underlying the work of the direct-instruction and constructivist perspectives, respectively. I will first discuss what I think is the key distinguishing feature of the two perspectives—which is different from the emphasis found in the chapters in this volume. I will then discuss some of the research variables I think we need to be addressing systematically in contrasting the two perspectives and in developing guidance for teachers and instructional designers.

Many of the authors in this volume suggest that the key issue distinguishing the two groups is the nature of the guidance provided. While the initial emphasis was on the amount of guidance (Kirschner et al., 2006), Wise and O'Neill (this volume) noted the multiple dimensions of guidance that must be addressed and Clark (this volume) agreed that a collaborative research project focused on guidance is an important goal. Fletcher (this volume) focuses on the kind of guidance: when to use drill and practice instruction and when to use simulations.

I would like to argue that guidance is not the driving issue that distinguishes the two perspectives. Both simulation and drill and practice are consistent with both the participatory and the acquisition metaphors. I think we all agree that we learn from lectures and reading books as well as through active, situated participation, and that, at times, drill and practice is necessary. As noted earlier, many of the constructivist environments described in this volume provided considerable guidance. For example, Spiro and DeSchryver (this volume) engage the learners in a variety of micro-learning environments, supporting them in criss-crossing the conceptual landscape. And Herman and Gomez (this volume) describe school-level support systems (regimes) for more localized routines. Indeed, Schwartz et al. (this volume) and Schwartz and Bransford (1998) provide lectures, examples, and practice in their "constructivist" instructional designs. Thus it is neither the amount nor the type of guidance that is distinguishing.

The distinguishing variable that should be the driving force for research is the stimulus for learning. The stimulus for learning from the perspective of direct instruction is seldom discussed. Of course, students must be motivated to learn but that is generally seen as a general activator rather than impacting what is learned or how we teach. Most generally, students are told why something is important to learn, how it will be used (including, at times, that it will be necessary for the next phase of learning), and what their learning objectives should be. Thus, instruction is designed, learning expectations set, and transfer assumptions made regardless of the learner's purpose for learning. This is in keeping with an acquisition metaphor that objectifies the concepts that are acquired.

In contrast, the stimulus for learning is central to the constructivist perspective. Fundamental to the participatory metaphor is that the individual is engaged in sense making: learning is stimulated by the desire to make sense of the world or to be able to participate/"do" (Brown et al., 1989; Brown & Duguid, 1991). Sense making is similar to Kintsch's (this volume) situation model. Kintsch argues that for learners to understand text beyond the literal text, i.e., literal comprehension of the textbase, they must be able to put the topic in a larger, rich context and make sense of it from that context. Kintsch describes the role of culture and goals as well as background knowledge in determining the situation model that will be used to "make sense" of the text.

We know from earlier research that if the learner does not have a situation model, there will be little understanding. For example, Bransford and Johnson (1972) found little comprehension of a text passage until they provided the label "washerwoman." With that label, and the ability to envision the situation of a washerwoman, the text made sense to virtually all participants. Similarly, one's goals or purpose for learning influences what is acquired—how information is understood. Anderson, Reynolds, Schallert, and Goetz (1977) demonstrated this in the comprehension of an ambiguous text passage. When participants were told it was about a wrestler, they easily understood the text as referring to a wrestling match; the prompt of a prisoner led to that interpretation. The paragraph made sense from both perspectives, but the interests of the participants or the title provided impacted not only how they interpreted the passage, but what they learned.

One might suspect that the above results suggest we simply have to provide the background knowledge (the label in the cases above) to support learning—thus suggesting a direct-instruction model. However, the series of studies discussed by Schwartz et al. (this volume) indicates that the learner must have a need for the learning—the direct instruction must be relevant to the need for sense making. This is also demonstrated by another classic study (Perfetto, Bransford, & Franks, 1983) in which learners were given the background knowledge before they had a need. Half of the participants looked at 12 statements for 20 seconds each and rated the degree of truthfulness of each, e.g., "A minister marries several couples each week." They were then told that their next task was to provide the solution for jokes, for example,

> A man who lived in a small town in the US married 20 different women of the same town. All are still living and he has never divorced one of them. Yet, he has broken no law. Can you explain?

Those students who learned the answers did no better at this task than students who did not engage in that learning. Thus, as Schwartz and Bransford (1998) suggest, there is a time for telling: but if there is not a need (it is not the time), little will be learned from that telling. The process of learning is one of creating a situation model that allows the individual to interpret the situation in a way consistent with their larger world view—or to modify that larger world view as, for example, when there is conceptual change. The role of instruction is to support, not direct, that sense making.

The Individual's Goals

These classic studies and considerable research since then (see, for example, Bereiter, 2002) suggests that the learner's goals will determine what is learned from a given experience. Thus, students may learn to pass a test or to better understand how the concepts function or can be applied in the world. Each outcome will lead to different learning, much as the wrestling and prison prompts led to different learning from the paragraph in the Anderson et al. (1977) study. Hence, from an instructional design perspective, it is essential that we engage the learner in problems of the domain rather than problems of schooling. That is, we want the student to learn about physics in such a way that she sees the world differently—that she has new tools for navigating the world—rather than learning to pass the test or get by (a different goal leading to a different understanding of the material). How do we foster ownership of the domain-relevant goal, i.e., how do we foster participation in the domain of physics (a world-view situation model) rather than participation in the domain of schooling?

Certainly, allowing instruction to derive from the learners' own interests is the most direct way of having them take ownership. In life-long learning, the inquiry is typically not initiated by the instructor in the course, but rather the student arrives with the sense of inquiry. Thus, the learning environment is simply a resource to support the student's already-established inquiry (although the instructor may not understand it that way).

This is an important consideration in analyzing learning environments. For example, Klahr, in the discussion of the Duschl and Duncan chapter, refers to the number of people who learned from the classic paper of Crick and Watson on their discovery of the structure of DNA. He proposes that many people experienced profound conceptual change (learning) from that direct instruction. While it is learning from direct instruction, I can point to many, many more college students in genetics courses who have learned little from that paper, even with additional direct instruction by a teacher. The difference is that those Klahr is talking about are people already immersed in the genetics issues—they are already involved in inquiry in the domain—and that paper helped them in their sense making about genetics. The college students, in contrast, most likely are approaching the information with a task of passing the test and are not really engaged in inquiry into genetic theory and its application. Thus, understanding the learner's goal—the situation model they are trying to construct—is important in understanding the impact of instructional methods.

It may be argued that Klahr's learners were professionals while my college students are novices and thus the difference is simply one of expert–novice differences. Certainly the college students would not be expected to gain the level of insight that the experts gained from that experience. However, the study of genetics and understanding DNA even at the college level (or high school level) can certainly lead to profound conceptual change, i.e., a change in the individual's interpretation of the world. It would be disappointing from a teaching and instructional design perspective if students fully engaged in the sense making regarding genetic theory were not stimulated by and did not learn from that classic paper. Yet we seldom see such engagement in college classes—rather the focus is on the schooling goal: what must be reproduced or done to get a grade.

As another example of the role of the learner's sense-making goal as the interpretive focus for instructional effects, let me briefly consider Rosenshine's (this volume) discussion of learning chess. He notes that there are numerous books on chess, and uses this to argue that direct instruction is appropriate for ill-structured problems like chess. But just imagine if this really were direct instruction offered in the typical fashion of assigned reading, examples, and pre-specified practice contexts in a month-long course. I do not think that is how anyone would choose to learn to play chess. I would certainly expect novices and experts alike to use books (different books to be sure) to improve their game. The books serve as guidance. But note that that guidance comes in support of the learners' goals as they are engaged in playing chess. For the more novice individual, those chess books will serve as reference guides to reflect on what they did or need to do to solve an immediate problem.

Projects and Problems as the Stimulus for Sense Making

The discussion thus far has focused on student-generated goals for learning, which is relevant to informal and life-long learning. However, in the context of traditional schooling it is generally not politically feasible to rely on student goals for directing learning, though the efforts with the Knowledge Forum (Scardamalia & Bereiter, 1999; Bereiter, 2002) and Aalborg University (Kjersdam & Enemark, 1994) indicate it could be feasible given the political will. Thus, most of the instructional work from the constructivist perspective focuses on engaging students in projects and problems designed for use in instruction. Of course, simply giving the students a problem does not do—it can easily be translated into a school problem with the learning requirement being to complete the task and pass whatever assessment is posed. Thus, a critical component in problem- and project-based learning is engaging the students in the problem and giving them ownership (Barrows, 1986, 1992; Savery & Duffy, 1995; Bereiter, 2002). While proposed to be critical, there is little research on the effect of the learner's goal and sense of ownership on what is learned.

Most inquiry-learning problems tend to be situated in very specific contexts, e.g., diagnosing a patient, determining the pollutants in a lake, predicting the weather, designing an animal habitat, maintaining a garden. Many of the problems are artificial, e.g., games and simulations, role-play scenarios, or pretend problems like how much crème will fit on an Oreo cookie without spilling over when compressed. Many of these problems have building components, e.g., building a diorama, that have questionable associated learning outcomes. Finally, many problems are integrative across disciplines or across concepts within a discipline, while others are very narrowly focused. I know of little if any research that examines the effects of manipulating these problem dimensions on what is learned.

We know that specific problems can be very motivating to learners, they are solving a hands-on problem, but what are the consequences for learning?

Bereiter (2002) has argued, and I think that practical experience bears out, that these problems have two shortcomings. First, students tend to spend far too much time and too much attention on the practical stuff, e.g., creating a poster, getting to the lake to get water samples. Learning of the concepts is often bypassed for the practicality of "doing" the project. This is especially true when time is limited, as it always is. Indeed, when I was interviewing graduate students participating in a problem-based learning curriculum where a problem lasted for a month, the students' only complaint was they needed time at the end to go back and develop a better understanding of some of the concepts they had to skip over because of time constraints. The practical stuff *must* be done because it is the basis of the grade (if I did not do my poster, no one will know what I learned; if I do not go to the lake for water samples, I will not have the data to do the intellectual work). The understanding of the concepts will be truncated to meet the time constraints—leading to a focus on schooling and what must be done to get a grade rather than understanding. The distraction of the project work is similar to the concern expressed by Sweller (this volume) for extraneous cognitive load. The constructivists seldom focus on issues of extraneous learning requirements. Perhaps this is an area where the theories might find some common interests (see also Whitney, Ritchie, & Clark, 1991 and the effect of individual differences in span on forming a situation model).

Second, and more seriously, Bereiter (2002) argues that these practical problems tend to focus the learners' attention too narrowly on solving the problem. That is, they seek to understand the concepts just enough to do the problem, which is the focus of their interests (again, the issue of the learner's goal). However, they are not interested in understanding the concepts in a deeper fashion, i.e., they are not engaged in deeper inquiry into the issues as they apply outside that context. In some sense, learning in order to complete the project is very similar to learning in order to pass the test—both lead to a narrow understanding of the concepts. We might think of this as analogous to Kintsch's (this volume) comprehension of the textbase (literal understanding of that text) but without the development of a situation model (integration of that text into a broader understanding and use). Thus, for example, one might learn about motion and force as it is relevant and applies to a particular project, or motion may be an issue of inquiry as it is manifested in everyday experience—with many examples, generated by students and the instructor, to explain (Bereiter, 2002).

Complexity of the Problem

Thus far we have focused on what tended to be a single concept or a set of concepts constrained by the curriculum. But of course, outside school, problems and issues do not come so neatly packaged. Indeed, Jonassen (this volume) argues the focus of inquiry-based learning environments should be on the use of ill-structured problems that typically include multi-domains or disciplines. Lesh, Yoon, and Zawojewski (2007) make a similar cross-disciplinary argument for the desired quality of problems.

I do not know of any research that evaluates this issue but it is certainly of practical relevance since it has curriculum implications. Herman and Gomez (this volume) focus on larger, integrative problems in which the students cross disciplines. As they describe it, teachers were more accepting of the classroom time investment when they saw not only learning of many science concepts and relationships but also the development of literacy skills. Stinson (2004) similarly argues for larger integrative problems in his problem-centered MBA and undergraduate curricula at Ohio University. Stinson uses whole business problems that integrate finance, personnel, marketing, etc. A problem that students may work on for a month may be framed simply as, "Will Yahoo survive?". This contrasts to the frequent strategy of giving students a narrow problem in each discipline, e.g., a marketing problem (Duffy & Kirkley, 2004). Stinson argues, as does Lesh et al. (2007), that with this cross-disciplinary approach students develop the skill of looking at issues from different perspectives. In addition to this flexibility in perspective taking, we also would expect that this integrative experience would lead to a richer and more discriminating understanding of the individual concepts. In my interviews with students in the Stinson program, however, there continues to be the time pressure where students push ahead to get the problem done even when they realize they do not have a deep enough understanding (for their broader use) of key concepts.

This issue of problem complexity falls, at least in part, in the domain of whole vs. part learning. There is considerable research on whole–part vs. part–whole learning but most has been done in the context of a traditional direct-instruction perspective. A review of this research needs to be undertaken and new research requirements identified that examine the issue from an inquiry-learning, whole-to-part strategy in comparison to a directed-learning, part-to-whole strategy, where the strategies take into consideration not only the scope or ill-structuredness of the problem, but also the support for inquiry and the outcome measures.

A Practical Consideration

I conclude this chapter with a brief discussion of two practical issues that arose in the discussions: the amount of effort and the level of skill required to teach in a constructivist-inspired learning environment. The issue is the feasibility of implementing the constructivist instruction in the schools, beyond the research initiative where teachers are funded and experts are near at hand to lend support. We often hear concerns that the constructivist environments are very complex and hence take a lot of time and effort—are the teachers up to that much work and can the school curriculum accommodate those lengthy learning engagements? Certainly these are issues in the scaling up and sustainability of these innovative learning environments. Both Fletcher and Kintsch asked Herman and Gomez about this time-and-effort issue. Fletcher asked: "There seems to be a lot more 'work' on the part of teachers in preparing the routines and tools and implementing the guidance you suggest ... what would you say about the overall practicability of your approach?" (this volume, p. 77). Kintsch expressed excitement for the Herman and Gomez instructional approach but wondered how timely feedback is provided to students when they are working individually.

Herman and Gomez offer two responses to these questions, responses that I think will apply to many of the problem-centered learning environments. First, they noted that the teachers had the same concerns over amount of effort—but when they realized other curriculum goals, for example reading, were being achieved in the work on the science problem they were assuaged. Second, Herman and Gomez noted the importance of technology to support the teachers' efforts. Technology interfaces can provide shareable data, thus, for example, allowing teachers to monitor and give feedback on student work. Further, they argue, efforts to provide a dashboard that permits easy monitoring would make the feedback effort even more efficient.

I think the technology solution is typical of the constructivist approach. There is typically a lot of weight placed on the use of technology tools to support the management and facilitation of the learning process. However, experience with schools suggests the technology is as often a time sink as it is a tool for facilitation. I think there are important tools and from a research perspective we certainly want to continue the work. But what of the actual classroom implementation—those teachers who do not have the university support, who have a computer system with all sorts of restrictions on data uploading, and who still do not feel comfortable with technology? In 2000, only 27% of teachers felt very well-prepared to use technology in the classroom. While 74% of teachers had technology-related professional development in 2000, only 23% of them (31% just focusing on high school teachers) felt well-prepared to use technology in the classroom (Parsad, Lewis, & Ferris, 2001). Thus the scaling up would require a considerable increase in the amount and the quality of professional development simply focused on the use of technology.

The second practical issue raised in the discussions is the ability of the teachers—their science knowledge in particular but also their pedagogical content knowledge. Kirschner raised this issue quite forcefully in the discussion of the Duschl and Duncan paper: "How can support and guidance be given if it 'depends upon teachers having adequate knowledge of science … [and] sustained science-specific professional development in preparation and while in service' (NRC, 2007, Chapter 10, p. 1)?" (this volume, p. 325).

Kirschner goes on to present data on the lack of preparation of teachers in the US and Australia to teach science or math. Duschl and Duncan point to research suggesting that it takes 100 hours of professional development over 2–3 years to develop a teacher who is competent and confident in inquiry-based instruction. I think that is overly optimistic. For example, Parsad et al. (2001) found that of those teachers who received more than eight hours of professional development in the year, only 37% felt their teaching improved a lot as a function of that experience.

Parsad et al. (2001) also found that 72% of teachers reported they participated in professional development related to their subject matter. However, only 23% spent more than 32 hours, roughly the amount of time proposed that teachers would require per year. Thus there would need to be a fourfold increase in professional development in the content area just to meet the requirements proposed by Duschl and Duncan. And this would be added to the professional development in technology discussed above.

Duschl and Duncan go on to ask whether we "fit the research on learning into the instructional culture of schools or do we change the culture of schools to accommodate the learning research?" (this volume, p. 326). But of course we know the difficulty of culture change and so the question is similar to the question related to technology: what do we do in the interim—while teachers are developing the skills!

I think scaling up and sustainability are critical issues for the constructivist debate that have not been adequately addressed (see Blumenfeld et al., 2000 and Fishman et al., 2004 for a similar concern and some examples of potentially effective scaling). The constructivist move to field-based research was to better understand the situation variables impacting learning. However, the impact of payment of teachers to participate and the ready at hand guidance provided by the researchers do not seem very often to be the focus of that research. Are we simply designing an ideal but unrealistic approach to instruction? An approach that can be demonstrated as long as the researcher is there working with volunteer teachers, but that falls apart once the funding ends or when there is an attempt to scale can lead to very misleading advice to administrators and teachers. Of course, a related critique can be made of the work with direct instruction. That work is most often conducted in an experimental context and it is unclear, as Herman and Gomez in particular suggest, if the instruction would be effective in the full schooling context. In each case, we need to question whether the prescriptions are great in principle but a failure in general practice.

Summary and Conclusions

This chapter is a reflection on what I considered to be some of the key issues raised in this book. I did not try to comment on all of the chapters and there were certainly other issues, for example the many discussions of experts and novices, that I would have liked to comment on. The three issues that were the focus of this chapter were the degree to which the authors talked past one another, the key instructional research issues, and the practical concern as to whether the research described, even that done in the field, will be scalable and sustainable outside a research context.

Certainly we need to recognize the impact of our instructional design on the information-processing demands. The constructivists and direct-instruction authors each address the processing demands in different ways, but, because the constructivists seem to be in denial as to the role of information processing, those differences are not subject to comparison in research. Similarly, with the acquisition metaphor and the objectification of the concepts to be learned, the direct-instruction researchers seem to view the larger context in which we learn and why we learn as irrelevant—or rather "extraneous" to learning. While collaborative efforts across paradigms are critical to success of this learning enterprise (Sfard, 1998), and I offer three suggestions of promoting that collaboration, I hold little hope given the entrenchment that seems to exist.

While the focus of most of the chapters were on different approaches to guidance, I argue that the two positions differ in their views on the stimulus for learning and it is these differences that dictate differences in guidance as well as assessment. For the constructivist (in my construal), but not for the direct-instruction researchers, learning is a process of the learners' sense making. Learning is driven by the learner's need to make sense of (to understand). Thus, for the constructivists, the stimulus for learning—the problem or project or student interest—and the students' ownership of that stimulus are critical determiners of the learning process. Since learning is in the student's inquiry, guidance for the constructivists is in response to the inquiry—not directed before there is a perceived need for specific information. The direct-instruction researchers, with the acquisition metaphor, simply seek to help the student acquire the knowledge. Very different framings of the learning process!

Moving forward it is certainly essential that a mixed-methods research strategy become more prominent for both groups. A greater use of naturalistic studies in the classroom would help the direct-instruction researchers better understand the range of relevant variables that interact with their key variables and, of course, provide a situated rather than simply a theoretical test of their perspective. This broader view would greatly aid in defining relevant experimental research requirements and in understanding and communicating with the constructivists. Inclusion of some experimental studies by the constructivists, on the other hand, might help in better identifying and understanding key variables and lead to some greater specificity and clarity of the underlying mechanisms. While the theoretical development from a situative and participatory perspective is considerably more difficult, there is a clear need for some greater specificity of variables, relationships, and mechanisms if there is to be progress.

References

Anderson, R. C., Reynolds, R. E., Schallert, D. L., & Goetz, E. T. (1977). Frameworks for comprehending discourse. *American Educational Research Journal, 14*, 367–381.

Barab, Sasha & Duffy, Thomas (2000). From practice fields to communities of practice. In D. Jonassen & S. Land (Eds.), *Theoretical foundations of learning environments* (pp. 25–56). Mahwah, NJ: Lawrence Erlbaum Associates.

Barrows, H. S. (1986). A taxonomy of problem based learning methods. *Medical Education, 20*, 481–486.

Barrows, H. S. (1992). *The tutorial process.* Springfield, IL: Southern Illinois University School of Medicine.

Bereiter, C. (2002). *Education and mind in the knowledge age.* Mahwah, NJ: Lawrence Erlbaum Associates.

Blumenfeld, P., Fishman, B., Krajcik, J. S., Marx, R. W., & Soloway, E. (2000). Creating usable innovations in systemic reform: Scaling-up technology-embedded project-based science in urban schools. *Educational Psychologist, 35*(3), 149–164.

Bransford, J. D., & Johnson, M. K. (1972). Contextual prerequisites for understanding: Some investigations of comprehension and recall. *Journal of Verbal Learning and Verbal Behavior, 11*, 717–726.

Brown, J. S., Collins, A., & Duguid, P. (1989). Situated cognition and the culture of learning. *Educational Researcher, 18,* 32–42.

Brown, J. S., & Duguid, P. (1991). Organizational learning and communities-of-practice: toward a unified view of working, learning, and innovation. *Organization Science, 2*(1), 40–57.

Cobb, P. (1994). Where is the mind? Constructivist and sociocultural perspectives on mathematical development. *Educational Researcher, 23,* 13–20.

Duffy, Thomas M., & Kirkley, Jamie R. (2004). Learning theory and pedagogy applied in distance learning: The case of Cardean University. In T. Duffy & J. Kirkley (Eds.), *Learner centered theory and practice in distance education: Cases from higher education.* Mahwah, NJ: Lawrence Erlbaum and Associates.

Engle, Randi (2008). *Framing interactions to foster generative learning: A situative explanation of transfer in a community of learners classroom.* Paper presented at the International Conference of the Learning Sciences, Utrecht, Netherlands.

Fishman, B., Marx, R., Blumenfeld, P., Krajcik, J. S., & Soloway, E. (2004). Creating a framework for research on systemic technology innovations. *The Journal of the Learning Sciences, 13*(1), 43–76.

Kirschner, P. A., Sweller, J., & Clark, R. (2006). Why minimal guidance during instruction does not work: An analysis of the failure of constructivist, discovery, problem-based, experiential and inquiry-based teaching. *Educational Psychologist, 41,* 75–86.

Kjersdam, F., & Enemark, S. (1994). The Aalborg experiment: Project innovation in university education. Aalborg, Denmark: Aalborg University.

Kolodner, J., Camp, P., Crismond, D., Fasse, B., Gray, J. Holbrook, J., et al. (2003). Problem-based learning meets case-based reasoning in the middle-school science classroom: Putting learning by design(tm) into practice. *Journal of the Learning Sciences, 12,* 495–548.

Lave, J., & Wenger, E. (1990). *Situated learning: Legitimate peripheral participation.* Cambridge: Cambridge University Press.

Lesh, R., Yoon, C., & Zawojewski, C. (2007). John Dewey revisited: Making mathematics practical versus making practice mathematical. In R. Lesh, E. Hamilton, & J. Kaput (Eds.), *Models & modeling as foundations for the future in mathematics education* (pp. 315–348). Hillsdale, NJ: Erlbaum.

Mason, Lucia (2007). Introduction: Bridging the cognitive and sociocultural approaches in research on conceptual change: Is it feasible? *Educational Researcher, 42,* 1–7.

Orrill, C. H., Hannafin, M. J., & Glazer, E. M. (2004). Disciplined inquiry and the study of emerging technology. In D. H. Jonassen (Ed.), *Handbook of research for educational communications and technologies* (2nd ed., pp. 335–354). Mahwah, NJ: Lawrence Earlbaum Associates.

Parsad, B., Lewis, L., & Ferris, E. (2001). *Teacher preparation and professional development.* Washington, DC: National Center for Education Statistics.

Pea, R. (2004). The social and technological dimensions of scaffolding and related theoretical concepts for learning, education, and human activity. *Journal of the Learning Sciences, 13,* 423–451.

Perfetto, G. A., Bransford, J. D., & Franks, J. (1983). Constraints on access in a problem solving context. *Memory & Cognition, 11*(1), 24–31.

Savery, J., & Duffy, Thomas M. (1995). Problem based learning: An instructional model and its constructivist framework. *Educational Technology, 35,* 31–38.

Scardamalia, M., & Bereiter, C. (1999). Schools as knowledge building organizations. In D. Keating & C. Hertzman (Eds.), *Today's children, tomorrow's society: The developmental health and wealth of nations* (pp. 274–289). New York: Guilford.

Schwartz, Daniel L., & Bransford, John D. (1998). A time for telling. *Cognition and Instruction, 16*, 475–522.

Sfard, A. (1998). On two metaphors for learning and the danger of choosing just one. *Educational Researcher, 27*(2), 4–13.

Sinatra, G. M., & Mason, L. (2007). Beyond knowledge: Learner characteristics influencing conceptual change. In S. Vosniadou (Ed.), *Handbook on conceptual change* (pp. 560–582). Mahwah, NJ: Lawrence Erlbaum Associates.

Slavin, R. E. (2002). Evidence-based education policies: Transforming educational practice and research. *Educational Researcher, 31*(7), 15–21.

Stinson, John (2004). A continuing learning community for graduates of an MBA program: The experiment at Ohio University. In T. Duffy & J. Kirkley (Eds.), *Learner centered theory and practice in distance education: Cases from higher education* (pp. 167–182). Mahwah, NJ: Lawrence Erlbaum and Associates.

Wellman, B. (1971). Crossing social boundaries. *Social Science Quarterly, 52*, 602–624.

Whitehead, A. N. (1929). *The aims of education and other essays.* New York: Macmillan.

Whitney, P., Ritchie, B., & Clark, M. (1991). Working memory capacity and the use of elaborative inferences in text comprehension. *Discourse Processes, 13*, 133–146.

Index

achievement 66, 78, 169–70, 173, 210; high 67, 76, 347; low 65; measures 341
acquisition 42, 129, 352; metaphor 364–5
activity 73, 113; analyzing 40, 53, 72; decontextualized 229; theorists 17, 24
adaptability 115, 167–8, 170
Adaptive Control of Thought-Revised 162–3, 165, 168; flow-of-information 169; model 177
Air Traffic Controller Task 177
algebra tiles 275, 276, 277, 280
American Educational Research Association 201, 291; debate 51, 346
analysis-plus-lecture activities 40, 42
Anderson's power law of practice 177
annotation 70, 73, 77, 79
application 165, 268; limits 178; practice 162; situation-specific 108
aptitude-treatment interactions 172–3, 341–2
argumentation 304–5, 316, 321–3
assessment 34, 40, 45, 65, 73; change of 55; learning 345
assimilation 145; of culture 132, 139
associationist 336–7
authentic learning 85, 150, 250, 257, 291; problems 65, 160–1, 337
automaticity 207, 251

background knowledge 214–15, 225–8, 232, 358
Bartlett, F.C. 187, 198–9n1
behavior 267–8; change 15, 131, 339; intentions 339; patterns 15; reinforceable 44; rigidity 46; task analysis 165
behavioral activity 8, 185, 186, 340
behaviorism 244–5, 257, 336; radical 246
Berkeley, Bishop George 242, 245
biological factors 15, 136, 145

borrowing and reorganizing principle 132–3, 139
bridging inferences 226, 228

causal factors 302, 317; interactions 318
changing people's beliefs 36
chess grand masters 130, 131, 146
children 7, 145, 298–9, 302, 314, 320, 324, 347; cognitive development 187, 312, 317, 319
Chomsky, Noam 243, 259
classroom 28, 51, 75, 101, 148, 273, 325; attention level 202; environments 145; experiences 66; implementations 78, 363; instruction 153, 201, 208, 230; practices 212, 281, 322, 340; social context 7, 65, 67, 268; teacher-led 101, 206; time investment 362
cognitive activity 8, 13–17, 20, 145–6, 164, 186, 197, 243–4, 340, 352; capabilities 251, 317; capacity 192–3, 245; experimentation 53; instruction 335; low 185; processes 28, 159, 188, 194, 244–5, 292, 304, 307, 312–13; schemas 148, 153; skills 98, 177; stages 16, 252; strategies 208, 210, 214; task analysis 165–6, 176–8; theories 36, 337; transformations 259
Cognitive Flexibility Theory 7, 114–15, 119, 342
cognitive load 16–17, 25–7, 55, 62, 84, 109, 128, 132, 136–8, 141, 163, 167, 189, 229, 234, 314–17, 320, 340, 352–4, 361; extraneous 193; germane 194; overload 160, 168, 173–4, 356
cognitive processing 28, 112, 163, 184, 188–9, 192, 194–5, 339; extraneous 193; routine 178
cognitive structure 18–20, 146, 207, 273–4, 284; complex 115, 251, 314, 323, 336
coherence 193; links 234; strategy 233–4

collaboration 28, 170, 285, 316, 351, 356–7, 364

communication 22, 291, 365; failure 356

communities of practice 4, 17, 164, 268, 284; cultural 226; epistemic 322

complexity 18, 83, 108, 111, 168, 176

component attention 177

comprehension 24, 44, 228, 234; strategies 210, 227, 233; of text passage 358

computer-based systems 192, 232; instruction 247; problem-solving 92; software program 238

concept 107, 111, 169; abstract 313; games 107, 109; narrow understanding 361; network 324; objectification of 364; relationships 19–20, 24

conceptual level 147, 319, 321, 323; change 16, 20, 317, 320, 324–5, 359; framework 150, 152; knowledge 20; mastery 111; models 20, 25

conceptualization 154, 268

connections 116, 205, 277, 278

construction 169, 197; theory 316, 321

construction–integration framework 238

constructivism 3–6, 34–6, 57–8, 100, 118, 159, 166, 174–5, 198–9, 223, 234, 256–7, 306, 352; educational 244; radical 245; varieties of 198n1

constructivist 59, 78, 82–3, 86–9, 92–101, 144, 158, 177, 242, 364–5; approach 109, 113–14, 120, 160, 197, 347; assessments 35, 49, 86, 93; curriculum 303; educators 149; goals 35; hypermedia projects 172; materials for novices 57; paradigm 335–6; pedagogies 34, 38, 145, 297; perspective 171, 197, 357–8, 360; science curriculum 292, 297; social 17; support 120; theory 3, 250, 354

constructivist instruction 6–9, 35, 44, 50, 54–7, 99, 121, 340–6; design 197; sequences 343

constructivist learning 51, 117, 184–8, 195, 308; environment 362

constructivist teaching 27, 86–7, 129, 134, 184, 198; fallacy 185, 188–9, 195; techniques 128, 131–2, 139–40

content 259, 282, 292, 364; elimination 341; embedded 280; instructional 246; novel 341

content-free prompts 236

content knowledge 7, 48, 52, 140, 145, 237; accessible 147; scientific 304

context 3, 82, 85, 88, 90–1, 94–9, 110, 170, 197–8, 296, 302, 320, 328; of applicability 115, 147; different 303;

effects 293; institutional 282; instructional 307; novel 84; social 62–3, 75, 99

contextual features 85; interacting 109

control of variables strategy 9, 35, 100, 292, 302, 306–7; knowledge 296; training *293–5*

correct answers 206, 247; percentage 205

corrective feedback 44, 162, 174, 206, 306; cost-effective 247, 253–4; cost–benefits 344–5

criteria for number sense 269–70

cross-disciplinary approach 361–2

curriculum 362; design 9, 303; goals 363; organization 151; reform 148

dead-ends 133–4

declarative knowledge 8, 19, 25, 41, 161–3, 168–71, 177; integration 20; teaching 174

deep understanding 193, 225, 227–8, 342; conceptual 274; of mathematics 281

demonstration 161–2, 171

dependence on support 46, 111, 114

Dewey, John 250, 256, 259, 337

direct instruction 9, 13–15, 25, 29–30, 34–9, 42–4, 48–9, 54–9, 62–5, 68, 100, 119, 139–40, 151, 159, 167, 175, 191–2, 203, 211–16, 233, 264–6, 271–6, 283, 291, 296–9, 304–8, 335, 352, 357, 360–4; duration 301; guidance 11, 106–18, 201; learning 51; limitations 152; researchers 365

disciplinary practice 291–2, 321; matrix 315

discourse 353; units 224

discovery 151–2, 158, 196, 257, 312, 315; activities 44; ineffective 150

discovery learning 5, 8, 112, 119, 128, 131, 149–50, 166, 185, 189–92, 224, 233–5, 258, 267, 291, 285n2, 296–9, 305–6, 313, 342, 351; environment 259; failure 184

discussions 356; whole-class 275

domain *294–5*, 296, 320; complex 107, 109, 177; structure 165, 339, 340

domain experts 176–8, 195, 226, 232, 235

domain knowledge 129, 227, 299; lack 232, 327

double-entry journals 70, 73, 77, 79

drill and practice 8, 35, 249, 252, 256–8, 338, 357; computer-based 247; repetitive practice 38; rote procedures 246

education 129, 259; reformers 66

educators 37, 254, 266

empirical positivism 256

encoding concepts 40–1, 150
engagement 229, 267–8, 271–2, 285, 297, 318, 323, 357, 359; learners 235; simulation 254
environmental affordances 17
epigenetic system 135–6
epistemology 7, 144–9, 151, 153, 272, 311–13, 322; generic 16; obsolete 151
errors 214, 306; correction 225; learners 93, 95
European Union countries 328
evidence 89, 324; evidence-based principles 193
evolution by natural selection 128, 130, 133, 138
experience 41, 108, 115, 192–3; compressed 254
experimental studies 7, 201–2; design 108, 153–4, *294*, 298; method 95, 313, 354
experimentation 53, 153, 312–15, 321–3
experiments 54–5, 305; natural 254; unconfounded 298–9, *302*
expert 7, 18, 56–7, 93, 112, 130–1, 138, 146–50, 153, 163, 165, 177, 226, 229–31, 253, 265, 268, 272, 304, 360; 70% principle 164; cognitive strategies 208; flexible 168; knowledge, 176; overconfident 178; procedures 209; solution 94
expert–novice differences 146–7, 151, 320, 323, 338, 359; chess players 265; research 282
expertise 138, 163–8, 230–1, 252, 320; 10-year rule 109; acquired 207; development 204; encoding effect 323; measurement 172; reading 237; reversal effect 193, 253
explanation 83, 93, 111–13, 119, 204, 342; instructional 343; in isolation 90
explicit guidance 108, 113
explicit instruction 7, 9, 34, 53, 128, 130, 137–9, 141, 212–13, 296, 299–303, 336–41, 344–7
exploration 29, 44, 49, 53, 107, *300*, 303; activities 41, 49; group performance 303
extraneous processing 189, 194

fading 160, 172, 174–5, 344
false belief 318
far-transfer 86, 298; measures 99–100; test 151
feedback 49, 70, 79, 83, 92–3, 98, 166, 171–2, 174, 179, 191, 206–7, 216, 230–2, 255, 301–2, 342, 357, 363; content-based 230; immediate 161; misleading 150

flexibility 52, 115, 168, 362
flow experience 230
fluency 206, 208
formal education 24–5, 37, 318; contexts 19; processes 150
forward chaining 176

games 119–20; epistemic 315; as incentives 339
General Law of Perception 243
generative processing 189, 194
Glaserfeld, Ernst von 245–6
goals 25, 74, 96, 100, 140, 145, 148, 153, 176, 245, 257, 282, 305, 321, 358–9; of education 167, 322; epistemic 312; explicit 107, 301, 303; instructional 37, 56–7, 89, 92–3, 185, 195, 225, 266, 269–72, 278, 280, 283, 298, 340; learner 3, 10, 64, 169, 197, 351, 360; learning 58, 66, 73, 88, 171, 213, 224, 256, 292, 325; learning to learn 51, 259; meaningful 91; motivational 338; of presentation 279; of school instruction 50
granularity 89–90, 97
guidance 5–9, 15, 63–4, 68, 72–5, 77, 82–4, 90, 92–8, 114, 117, 162, 165–7, 171–5, 178, 191, 193, 196, 233, 274–6, 287, 335, 342, 351–2, 357, 360; additional 89; advocates 160; direct 278; effective 256; instructional 86–8, 96, 158, 161, 173, 179, 273–4; intentional 278; just-in-time 101; less direct 280; level 87–90, 224, 234–5; maximum 67; in specific situations 37, 89; and support 107, 115–18, 326
guided discovery 185–6, 190, 192–3
Guided Experiential Learning (GEL) 250
guided practice 79, 171, 206–9, 211, 213–14, 230–1, 237; student 204–5, 215–16

hands-on activities 36, 178, 196
Heisenberg's uncertainty principle 27
hierarchy of instructional support 342–3
high school dropouts 65
homework 202; correction 203
how learning happens 14, 185, *187*, 198–9, 285
human cognition 113, 130–1, 136–7, 255
human cognitive architecture 5–8, 13–14, 16–23, 25–6, 34, 51–4, 63, 128–9, 130, 133–8, 166, 174, 187, 204, 211, 264, 267–8, 314, 354
human learning 307, 336–8, 341

Hume, David 243, 246
hypertexts 233–4
hypotheses 192, 266–7, 298, 341, 346

ill-structured domains 107–17, 118–20, 140, 165, 176, 216, 235–6; in science 110
ill-structured problem 7, 26–7, 82, 94–5, 141, 175, 215, 217, 254, 352, 362
ill-structured tasks 208–9, 214
imitation 132, 139
immersion approach 129, 346
implementation fidelity 303
inferences 226, 232; causal 354; valid 302
information 4, 129, 132, 135–9, 146, 153, 162, 266, 271, 276–8, 280; abstraction 170; available 133; essential 110–13, 119–20, 128, 140, 236; feedback 250; incomplete 164; internal structure 268; propositional 225; store 130–1
information processing 9, 14, 18, 128, 197, 305, 353–4; cognitive theory 162, 201; mechanisms 352; natural systems 130, 135, 138
inquiry 49–50, 57, 65, 75–6, 267, 271, 274, 278, 280; curriculum 351; guided 69, 82, 87, 139, 298; instruction 29, 62–3, 68–9, 73, 136, 277, 363; learning 362; methods 30, 283; practices 266; skills 39, 299; systematic programs 177
inquiry-based learning 72, 130, 134, 151, 216; curricula 191; environments 361; problems 360; procedures 137; techniques 135, 138, 140
in-service teachers 39; education 326
instruction 8, 36–9, 41–3, 44–5, 66, 73, 87–9, 106, 113, 163–4, 167–9, 171, 174, 188, 193, 205, 236, 245, 248, 252–6, 259, 264–6, 269, 335, 340; ambitious 71; analysis 38, 275; anchored 198; effective 48, 53, 347; guided 58–9, 67–8, 177, 319; hands-on 297; initial 292; meaningful 18; motivational impact 338; passive 184–6, 194–6; problem-based 167; purpose 131; starting point 119; structure 172; styles 144; telling or showing 84, 91; teacher-provided 207; test beds 356; theories 279
instructional approaches 25–6, 36, 48, 56, 83, 252, 271, 346, 355–7; benefits 344; conditions 344; different 285n2; goals 246–8, 283, 298; techniques 35, 98–9; theories 6, 51, 167, 172
instructional design 3–4, 35, 54, 76, 83–4, 90, 93–5, 129–30, 151, 165, 176, 187–9,

195–8, 243, 257, 267–9, 270–1, 351, 359; systems 162
instructional designers 57–8, 88, 149, 151, 167–9, 195, 246, 357
instructional materials 57, 338; programmed 342
instructional methods 29, 72–5, 96, 172, 185, *186*, 188–9, 196, 210, 285, 301, 308, 345; active 185–6, 190–2, 194; contrasting 299; impact 359; regimes 62, 64–5, 77; routines 63, 67, 70
instructional practice 213, 250, 279, 283, 307; effective 281; improvements 247
instructional procedures 98, 128, 137, 166, 201, 209, 211–15, 298; effective 291; programs 177, 208; treatments 40, 159, 161, 164
instructional research 55, 364; and practice 178
instructionists 82–4, 87–9, 92, 96, 98–9
instructivist 158; support 58, 97
integrating 188, 194; domain learning 354; new experiences 23; problems 362
intelligent-tutoring systems 92, 99, 178–9, 246
interest 35–6, 66, 341–2; of participants 358
inventions 42, 44, 46–8, 50, 59, 129

James, William 243, 246
Jasper Woodbury series 197–8
Journal of the Learning Sciences, The 5, 352, 355

Kant, Immanuel 243, 245–6, 256
knowledge 18–25, 29, 34, 129–34, 148, 152, 225, 253, 259; accumulation 319–20; acquired 133, 139, 144, 150, 226; activation 115, 227; application 45, 108, 113, 119–20; automated 165–6; decontextualization 231; inert 231, 353; lack of 325; multiple measures 28; ontological 147; passive acquisition 223; problem 56; resources 319; types 162; use 99, 267
knowledge domain 175, 232; specific 129
knowledge structures 19–20, 148, 320; construction 7–8, 16, 22, 25, 28, 35–9, 42, 46–8, 101, 129, 146, 152, 223–7, 235, 238, 259, 279; reorganization 321, 325; restructuring 312

language learning 25, 259; first language 129; spoken-language comprehension 231 learners 63, 68, 74, 84–5, 89–91, 92, 95, 111, 116–20, 129, 133, 138, 140–1, 145–9, 151–2, 160–1, 168–9, 174, 192–3, 197, 224, 247–9, 255, 266, 311, 323, 358; deficit model 314–17; experience 250; guidance to 71; internal knowledge 256, 283; misdirected 114; prior knowledge 195; progress 248

learning 9, 11–14, 16–18, 22, 24, 26–9, 36, 42–5, 51–2, 66–7, 90, 98, 106–7, 113, 116–17, 128, 131, 158, 186, 188, 190, 192, 229–30, 242, 256, 264–5, 268, 279, 282, 284, 314, 320–1, 352–4, 356, 360; active 185, 193, 195, 224; complex 109, 115, 162, 177; concepts 361; constructive 234, 257, 336; definition 6, 265, 281; difficulties 129, 164; direct 217; effective 41, 44, 74; events 303; in everyday activities 3–4; experience 313; external control 172; gains 89, 99; guided 62, 233, 316; hierarchies 246; of incorrect knowledge 179; ineffective 344; informal 312; innovation 88; lifelong 359; mechanism 55; media 117; participatory 355; passive 189; practical 250; progressions 160, 315, 318–19, 322; project-based 100; research 326, 364; tasks 153, 161; theories 8, 267, 269; trajectories 65; from verbal materials 49

learning environments 3, 114, 148, 153, 225, 249, 316–18, 322–4, 357–9; design 115, 151; interactive 343; variability 49

lecture 40–1, 90–1

limits of change principle 137

literacy 77; skills 362

Locke, John 242–4, 246

logical positivism 247, 315

long-term memory 6, 14–19, 23–5, 40, 42, 113, 130, 134–8, 187, 205–6, 223, 226–7, 319, 323; changes 8, 13, 136, 267, 279, 281; connections 204; contents 231; function 131; information store 132–3; pre-packaged prescriptions 107, 112–14; structure 265, 320; systems 162

loss–exchange ratios 254

manipulations 189, 270, 278

mastery 298, 338; high levels 301

mathematics 264, 272–3, 284; reforms 269

means–ends analysis 129, 305

measurement 53, 318, 341; of knowledge 172

mechanisms 177, 352; causal 5, 317; pre-attentive perceptual 244

memory 20, 85, 130, 187, 248–9, 264–5; of

chess positions 320; differential activation 266; dynamic form 23; experiments 40, *41*; limitations 9; sequence search 148; structure 269

mental processes 163; models 146–7; theory 318

metacognition 21, 196, 227, 305–7, 338; control 233; development 74; student capacities 48

minimally guided 6, 71, 76, 167, 190, 196, 201, 223–4, 234–5, 264–7, 272–4, 280, 284–5, 351; instruction 13, 63–7, 74, 128, 191, 302

mirror neurons 132, 139

modeling 83, 93–7, 100, 154, 160, 211, 319, 323, 342; cognitive 255; guidance 101; instruction 54, 111; and practice strategy 166

models 4–5; and data construction 315; fact-oriented 298; of learning 158, 268

Montessori education 34

motivation 7, 36, 57, 62–7, 75, 78, 160, 164, 170, 193, 230, 234, 257, 297, 301, 328, 338–9, 346, 360; for learning 196; low 327; strategy 91

multimedia 193–4; learning 188, 197, 245; presentations 184; simulations 178

National Research Council 311

National Training Center 255

near-transfer 260; assessment 298

Neisser, Ulric 244–5, 336

New Gutenberg Revolution 116, 118

non-constructivist 335; assessment 35, 38

novice 56–7, 83, 86, 112–13, 146–50, 165, 176–7, 185, 226–7, 235, 265, 272, 282, 304, 359–60; achievement 209; learners 111, 137, 153, 176, 195, 253, 258; problem-solvers 141, 320; progress to expert 153; support 96

operational definition 291, 299, 306

outcomes 35–6, 39, 41, 51, 265, 340, 345, 359; attitudinal 346; constructivist 38, 42, 44, 46, 48, 55; of high efficiency 45; instructional 280, 335; learning 18, 26, 29–30, 35, 37, 49, 58, 63, 65, 82, 95, 190, 282, 284, 343; measures 38, 160, 174–5, 209, 362; motivational 346

overlearning 204, 216, 258

paradigm 336; shifts 9, 315, 337

participation 269, 284, 321, 352–3, 356; change in 279, 281; metaphors 357;

social matrix 36; structures 312; trajectories 268
patterns 318; family resemblance 109
pedagogies 7, 97, 144–53, 266, 312–13, 322; constructivist 48, 50; evaluated 34; goals 286n3; instructional 321; learner-centered 150; problem-based 129, 145
perceptions 17, 21, 242–4; individual 22
performance 16, 47, 110, 158–9, 163, 166, 174, 230, 249, 266, 286n5, 305, 338–9; adaptable 170; competent 252; defeated 168; goals 213; improvement 165, 282; investigative 150; levels 298, 301, 303; outperforming peers 66; skilled 137, 207–8, 214; whole-task 177
Piaget, Jean 16, 18, 145, 187, 198; theory 128
pilot training 251, 252, 254, 259
practice 45, 171–3, 207, 275, 277, 285, 312–13; deliberate 235; independent 206, 213, 216; of science 75, 304; theory 355
prediction 40–1, 302
premature efficiency 46
preparation for future learning 7, 41–2, 51–2, 55–6, 95, 98, 345, 346; assessment 38–9, 43–4, 47–9
preparing future teachers 283, 326
Preschool Pathways to Science program 317–18
presentation 204–7, 213, 278, 354; principled 185, *186,* 193
prior knowledge 39, 56, 68, 164, 172, 205–7, 224–7, 229, 235, 324, 341–3; benefits 174; determining 203; limited 341; low 56, 192
problem 87, 91, 338, 362; complex 275, 361; domain 86, 96, 98; domain-specific 171; non-routine 112–13; non-specific goal 153; solvers 129, 131, 133; well-defined 141
problem solving 2, 13, 16–18, 21–3, 28, 92–3, 97, 112, 135–6, 138, 153, 162–3, 165, 191, 204, 210–11, 216, 223, 235, 305, 361; analogical 134; behaviors 286n5; complex 85, 95; domain 141; methods 113, 134, 265, 304, 316; rules 190; skills 131, 231, 307; transfer 194
problematization 228, 278
problem-based learning 82, 87, 94, 128, 131, 150, 158, 160, 166–7, 215, 217, 229, 360–1
procedural knowledge 20–1, 161–3, 165, 167, 177; automated 164; empirical research 26; prompts 215–16; solutions 46; task-related 20

procedures 48, 50, 111–12, 168, 174, 269, *295,* 301; with connections 273; domain-specific 176; embedded 43; forced 170–1, 174; mastered 298; ridiculed 338; standard 47
process 23, 205–6, 237, 259, 269–70, 304, 338, 358; creative 113; feedback 206; inquiry 237; learning 36–7, 95, 97, 256, 365; thinking 250
process–product 211, 216, 352; research 100–1, 201–3, 206–8, 214–15; teaching procedures 338
processing 174, 189, 205, 340; active 224, 234
professional 108, 110, 118, 144–6, 312, 359
professional development 69, 71–2, 77, 267, 326, 363–4; inadequate 272
projective diagnostic techniques 346
psychologists 244–5, 255, 346; behavioral 15; ecological 17; educational 109; Gestalt 337
psychology 245, 304–6, 337; developmental 145; evolutionary 129–30; experimental 250, 256; research 13
pure discovery 87, *186,* 190–2, 196
pure reason 243, 245, 256
purpose 73, 82, 131, 245; for learning 357–8

questions 205, 210, 216, 248, 266, 273–4, 296; Clark 57–8, 96–7; Duschl and Duncan 139–40, 152–3, 195–6; Fletcher 55–6, 77–8; Gresalfi and Lester 212–13, 307; Herman and Gomez 153, 258–9; Jonassen 175–6, 215; Kintsch 78, 257; Kirschner 281–2, 325–7; Klahr 119, 323; Mayer 29, 282–4; Rosenshine 98, 100, 118; Schwartz et al. 237, 306–7; Spiro and DeSchryver 140, 235; Sweller 25–6, 51, 53; Wise and O'Neill 177–8, 196–8

readers 227, 233–4; goals 225; passive 224; practiced 226; struggling 71
reading 70–3, 111; advanced level 71; development 106; expert strategies 226; instruction 237; and listening 132; proficiency 69; superficial 225; strategies 77, 232
reading comprehension 77, 113, 118, 209–10, 214–15; strategies 79, 119, 211, 232; tasks 141
reading support 68; tools 69–70, 73
reasoning 226, 314; abstract 323; analogical 23, 24, 304; causal 23–4, 319; psychological 167; scientific 211; skills 324

reciprocal teaching 208, 210, 214, 232, 319
redundancy principle 138, 193
relationships 66; concept 152; cause-and-effect 170; family resemblance 112; part–whole 83–5
representation 50, 113, 304, 319; abstract 275; access point 277; building activity 256; capacities for 318; of information 279, 319; internal 18, 184, 250, 255; knowledge 322; multiple 115; symbolic 280
research 100, 138, 140, 165, 197, 339–40, 347, 355–6, 364–5; agenda 96; causal 54; efficacy 54; evidence 6, 283, 285; experiences 34; eye-movement 147; instructional 165; integrity compromised 27; methods conflicting 354; observational 94; procedures 343; protocols 167; questions 335, 341
research studies 29, 39, 46, 65, 87; discovery learning 190; educational 29, 38, 158, 282, 344; guidance 167, 292; science learning 320, 324
retrieval 38, 85, 148, 231, 320; automatic 204, 232, 258; from memory 244; structures 225–7
review 203, 213; after-action 250; daily 204; panel 356; weekly and monthly 207

scaffolding 4–5, 68, 74, 83–7, 98, 108, 118, 130, 154, 159–60, 167, 172, 178, 209–17, 297–8, 303, 323, 325, 342, 352–5; soft scaffolding 86
schema 24; theories 18, 40, 114–16
school 64–7, 129, 327; contexts 360; disciplines 258; goals 62–3, 65, 71, 75, 360; learning 224–5, 231; practice 272; reform efforts 68; task 84
science 77, 303, 315–16; careers 328; cognitive 312; concepts 362; content knowledge 71; hands-on 291, 299; inquiry-based 68, 151, 299, 326; instruction 69, 75, 237, 313; learning and doing 149–52, 311–13, 319, 327; literacy-scale score 327; model-based 318, 322; reading strategies 69–70; studies 315; teachers 149, 304; theory building 321; vocation 76
science education 9, 62, 140, 305, 311–12, 316, 319; curriculum 301, 303, 313–14; early 291–2; immersion unit approach 326–7; instruction 321; new approaches 75; primary goal 327–8; reform efforts 74; reformers 312

science learning 237, 313–14, 321; in classroom settings 323; goals 72, 78
Science Technology Engineering and Math education 75–6, 327–8
scientific argumentation 75, 101, 318
scientific knowledge 311, 317–19; building 316; domains 108; proficiency 321
scientific procedures 168; inquiry 150, 229, 311–12; practice 306, 322, 325; problem solving 161
scientific reasoning 196, 307, 318–19; capacity 305; skills 191–2, 196
scientists 76, 149, 304; cognitive neuroscientists 15; communities 325; natural 153; norms 322
Secondary Teacher Education Project (STEP) 94
self-determination 51, 66, 164, 233
self-report protocols 164, 338
sensory receptors 244–5
sequence 301–2, 307; curriculum 324; design cycles 355; findings 342; implications 303; of instruction 46, 50, 315, 319, 341
sequestered problem solving 38, 41, 44, 55, 84; assessments 48–9; questions 47
short-term memory 14, 92, 248, 307
simulation 171, 252, 255–6, 258–9, 337, 357; environments 253, 260; sensory 244; training 242, 250–1, 257
simulator 259–60; time 253
situated learning 250, 254–5; environment 256, 354; practice 252, 258
situation model 224–6, 228, 232–8, 358, 361
situational knowledge 20–1, 115–16, 148
situativity theory 3–4, 8, 285n1, 286n4, 337
skills 259, 362; complex 168; domain-specific 260; improvement 191
social interactions 198, 318
sociocultural theory 22, 284, 286n4
socioeconomic background 212–13
solution paths 92, 160, 175–6; multiple 165, 217
solutions 176–7; advanced 160, 174; efficient 46–7; inventing 43, 43–4, 47, 91, 165, 176; standard 50
standardized scores 42, 43, 91
stimulus 251–2; for learning 351, 358, 365; for sense making 360
stories 22–3; problems 45
strategies 231–2, 237, 249; cognitive 284; domain-specific 100; high-guidance 90; instructional 88; learners 21; practice 354; problem-solving 129, 135, 140, 176;

random generate and test 133–6; successful 235

structure 59, 173, 296; and variance 45

student errors 101, 212; error rates 207

students 29, 50, 64–7, 79, 149, 150, 191, 206, 341–3, 359; achievement 75, 201–3, 209, 212–15; classroom experience 284–5; discovery activities 50; discussion 101, 205; engagement 36, 207, 272, 279, 282; goal orientation 78, 360; interaction 95; interest 36–7, 66; learning 48, 354; low-performing 164, 192; performance 68; support 344; understanding 73, 204

sub-goals 90, 94–5, 141

summarization 40, 53, 70, 72, 77, 79, 91, 205, 211; Summary Street 229–30, 232

support 88, 115, 118, 152, 154, 236, 274, 325, 358; additional 208; fading 160, 174, 344; instructional 8–9, 97, 158–9, 174–5, 178, 236, 341–2, 344; for learning 159, 161, 176, 273; in science reading 70–1, 74, 78; for struggling readers 69; transfer 45

tabula rasa 242–4, 246, 317

Taking Science to School 311; committee 313; recommendations 316; research report 314, 321

task analysis 164, 204, 216

teacher 39, 63–4, 67–9, 71–4, 77–9, 88, 101, 110, 145, 164, 168, 188, 202, 272, 274–6, 326, 345, 362–3; ability 95, 303; authority 271; effective 203–7, 345; elementary school 282; guidance 357; instruction 211, 270, 297–8, 347; intervention 196; modeling 208; preparation programs 281; professional development 70, 327; role 174

teaching 83, 108, 213, 274, 282, 362; complex knowledge 164; corrective 203; in different contexts 308; effective 206; explicit 129, 203; ill-structured tasks 215; manual 202; orientation 270–2, 275, 282; science 148–9, 152

teaching strategies 159, 211, 285, 324; inappropriate 114, 129

technology 4, 173–5, 246, 363; developments 113; environments 49; in school 66

template 154; retrieval 112

tests 38, 202; experimenter-developed 209–16; post-tests 46, 205, 299; pre-tests 299; standardized 39, 48, 201, 208–10, 212–16, 247, 282; transfer performance 189

textbase 228, 232, 237; construction 224–6

texts 70–3, 232–6, 342, 358; comprehension 223, 230; instructional 227; learning from 224, 228; linear 234; narratives 101; processing 226; recall 225; words recognized 244

thinking 292, 305; aloud 211; engaged 50; general 231; non-linear 116; skills 52

time 344; constraints 361; spent working 247, 306; temporal contiguity principle 193

timing 88, 94; of feedback 179; of guidance 82, 92–3, 95–6, 98

tools 64, 69–75, 96, 138, 359, 363; computer-based 70, 79, 230; for literacy 72; and routines 68, 72, 77–8

training 252–3, 259, 296, 301–2; military 254–5

transfer 8, 45, 52–3, 85–6, 90, 95–100, 114, 152, 158, 168–70, 179, 192, 252, 264, 265, 296, 345, 354, 357; adaptive 161; benefits 175; cross-contextual 96; environment 171; failed 56, 59; intellectual 93; knowledge 41, 58; learning 83–4, 93, 172; long-term 24; problem 43–4, 91, 285; studies 59, 84; task 55; tests 190, 193

Transfer-Effectiveness Ratios 252–4

tutorial 253; peer tutoring 247

under-served schools 75–6

unguided discovery 139, 285n2

United States forces 250; training program 254

unprincipled presentations 185, *186*, 194

up-front instruction 82, 84, 86–7, 94–5

variability 52, 133, 159; background 45; of learning space 44; of problems 59

variables 53, 63, 355–6, 365; between-subjects 293; causal 299, 301; confounding 27, 343; contextual 44, 108; distinguishing 357; independent 29; representation 275–6, 280

varied practice 98, 170–2, 174

Watson, John 244, 264

web 107, 115–17; use of Google 113

well-structured domains 106, 108–9, 110–15, 121, 211, 235–6, 340

well-structured problems 94, 140, 212

what works 282–3, 354

withholding information 7–8, 34, 128–9, 132, 134, 138, 140

worked-examples 44, 64–8, 89, 92, 94–7, 141, 152, 167, 171, 184–5, 319; effect 137–9, 191; embedded 47; studies 82–4, 87, 90–1, 93, 136

working memory 13, 15–16, 18, 130, 135, 137–8, 163, 187, 226–7, 231, 323, 341–2; automatic 206; burden on 64; capacity 137, 212, 320; cognitive load 339–40; limitations 8, 26, 62, 86, 136, 174, 205; overload 55; role in problem solving 27

zone of proximal learning 227–8, 230